STANDARD LOAN

Early Category and Concept Development

Early Category and Concept Development

Making Sense of the Blooming, Buzzing Confusion

Edited by
David H. Rakison and Lisa M. Oakes

OXFORD

UNIVERSITY PRESS

2003

OXFORD
UNIVERSITY PRESS

Oxford   New York
Auckland   Bangkok   Buenos Aires   Cape Town   Chennai
Dar es Salaam   Delhi   Hong Kong   Istanbul   Karachi   Kolkata
Kuala Lumpur   Madrid   Melbourne   Mexico City   Mumbai   Nairobi
São Paulo   Shanghai   Taipei   Tokyo   Toronto

Copyright © 2003 by Oxford University Press, Inc.

Published by Oxford University Press, Inc.
198 Madison Avenue, New York, New York 10016

www.oup.com

Oxford is a registered trademark of Oxford University Press

Library of Congress Cataloging-in-Publication Data
Early category and concept development : making sense of the blooming,
buzzing confusion / edited by David H. Rakison and Lisa M. Oakes.
p. cm.
Includes bibliographical references and index.
ISBN 0-19-514293-4
1. Cognition in infants.   2. Perception in infants.   I. Rakison, David
H., 1969–   II. Oakes, Lisa M., 1963–.
BF720.C63 E27 2003
155.42'2323—dc21   2002000772

2 4 6 8 9 7 5 3 1

Printed in the United States of America
on acid-free paper

Foreword

Categories, Cognitive Development, and Cognitive Science

Frank C. Keil

Because we are linguistic creatures, it is immediately obvious that we constantly think in terms of categories. We cannot utter more than a few words without categorizing objects, events, or even abstract relations. The youngest members of our linguistic community use labels in ways that show the ability both to discriminate among members of a category and to treat them as an equivalence class. This much is self-evident. Language also makes clear that we do not always agree. Different adults occasionally disagree on labels, and children can disagree with adults more dramatically, sometimes in predictable ways. Language therefore reveals both the ubiquity of categorization and its potential to change over time and different contexts. The utter salience of categorization in language use, however, is also a liability, for it may bias one to see all categorization, and the mental representations that aid categorization, as of the sort that we see in language use. A developmental approach, however, especially one that goes from early infancy on, weans us from this linguacentric perspective. By considering categorization and the potential mental representations that must subserve categorization from a time well before the onset of language to well after, we are forced to consider a much wider range of senses of categorization and perhaps of concepts as well.

The collection of chapters in the book that follows illustrates the great value of considering categorization in all its diversity and glory. In doing so, a much wider range of cognitive science issues also naturally emerge. This collection is especially valuable because it includes insightful and integrative commentaries that help the reader draw connections across the various chapters. Indeed, the commentaries and the introductory chapter illustrate the extraordinary creativity of categorization through the ways in which they cluster together chapters and themes within these chapters. I leave to those discussions more detailed analyses of themes that cut across the book. Here, as a way of whetting the reader's appetite, I point to a few broader themes that go far beyond concepts and categorization but which are made salient by this collection.

Levels of Processing

It becomes evident that there are many ways that organisms can treat discriminable stimuli as equivalent. This point was made eloquently many years ago in an essay by Herrnstein (1990), and one is powerfully reminded of it in this book. It also raises the question, alluded to by many contributors, of what is to really count as categorization. Even instances of categorical perception of speech and color, for example, can be shown to also include the ability to discriminate instances within the categories. Countless organisms are able to recognize conspecifics as well as individuals within those categories. At what point does categorization cease to be considered true categorization? This issue reminds one of Fodor's question as to whether "paramecium have mental representations," a set of slippery-slope arguments that can lead the reader unwillingly to the potential conclusion that there is no clear line to draw about when mental representations end and something more primitive takes over (Fodor, 1986). Similarly for categorization, the immune system can be seen as a set of hierarchically organized "recognizers," with a cascade of responses for families of compounds. A form of categorization is therefore observed in which a set of similar compounds is responded to similarly but is also discriminated on further exposure and with more subtle reactions.

If a system is able to treat a class of entities as equivalent but in other contexts responds to them differently, is that enough to count as categorization, and are the internal structures responsible for those responses concepts? Intuition rebels at that being sufficient for categorization, but there remains a clear need to sharpen ways these contrasts are viewed. In a manner quite similar to debates on what constitute true mental representations, debates on what constitute true instances of categorization are still very much with us. The hope is that, as we learn more detail about what information is used to form categories and about how that information is mentally represented, classes of genuine categorization will fall out as distinct from those that are not. This book helps us considerably to move in that direction.

Implicit versus Explicit Performance

All organisms engage in behaviors without awareness of the behaviors as such. Indeed, implicit cognition is the norm for less cognitively complex species. Humans, however, also do many things in highly systematic ways that normally occur outside of awareness, whether it be a particular way one sits in a familiar sports car, the use of certain strategies in reading, or the adoption of various stereotypes in thinking about others. This obvious fact also extends to categorization. Much of the categorization we do happens outside of awareness, whether it be in categorical perception of speech and color or of a syntactic category in the flow of speech. Yet we tend to think of categories in more explicit awareness terms. To what extent are the implicit and explicit forms of categorization of the same sort and subject to the same principles?

It is sometimes argued that implicit cognition involves associative principles and explicit cognition more rulelike and prepositional forms; yet some implicit forms may occur within classic Fodorian modules and be both rulelike and cognitively impenetrable. Does that make them different from those that are constructed explicitly? How are the implicit primitive categories emerging from modules different from those that emerge in implicit learning paradigms (e.g., Brooks, 1978; Brooks, LeBlanc, & Norman, 2000)? A related question asks about the role of awareness of the properties and relations that are associated with categories. One may categorize and be aware of the categories in an explicit sense but normally not be aware at all of the informational properties used to construct the category. This has been known for many years but keeps reappearing as a relevant issue. For example, some argue that concepts and categorization can only be understood in terms of the ways concepts are embedded in theories, yet less clear is whether those theories themselves must be explicit. Often researchers point out the inability of participants to explain a relation as the lack of an awareness of theoretical relations, yet their behavior often reveals a clear tracking of such relations.

I doubt that there will be an easy dichotomy between implicit and explicit cognition in any domain or task and certainly not in the case of categorization. As has been noted in memory research, there seem to be several distinct forms of implicit cognition and perhaps several distinct forms of explicit cognition as well. It is tempting to look for a clear dichotomy and to then try to map that dichotomy onto the developmental differences between preverbal and verbal thought, but the story is likely to be a great deal more complex for categorization just as it is appearing to be in other areas of cognition. A careful look at these chapters as a whole starts to suggest such a more intricate view.

Information versus Representation

Much has been written about the nature of those mental representations that are responsible for categorization, usually referred to as concepts. Should they be understood as lists of features, as probabilistic weights on summary features, as sets of exemplars, as large nets of subsymbolic relations, or as nodes in webs of belief (Murphy, 2002)? These debates are important and central to cognitive science; but they also can be greatly frustrating to resolve. The power of many of the computational models developed to simulate cognition in one of these representational formats very often allows for simulation of an enormous of range of behaviors, many of them which are most decidedly outside the realm of normal cognition. Ideally, a model will generate all and only the behaviors that are within the normal repertoire of an organism, neatly excluding those that are cognitively non-natural from the cognitively natural without the use of ad hoc constraints on the models of learning and representation. At present, however, the models are much less constrained and hence are difficult to choose among, especially since further modifications of them seem quite unconstrained so that refutations of one particular model are invariably answered with modifications that are rarely prohibited by any sorts of principles.

Slowly, debates about the nature of representation will advance and start to narrow down the options; but these debates need not be the only way for scientific inquiry about categorization to proceed. A related endeavor, that can often proceed without such a strong dependence on particular models of representation, is to ask what sorts of information people seem to use to execute a given behavior. Consider, for example, how much of the classic research on depth perception has proceeded. Researchers specified a typology of variables that could specify the depth of objects in layout, such as dynamic cues (e.g., motion parallax), binocular cues (e.g., binocular disparity), and pictorial cues (e.g., interposition). Independent of theories of how depth is internally represented or computed, it has been possible to ask what information is used and under what circumstances. From a developmental point of view, this approach has been particularly fruitful, leading to the discovery that first the infant seems to use dynamic cues and then a gradually increasing proficiency with binocular cues occurs, followed by use of pictorial cues (e.g., Kellman & Banks, 1998). This developmental sequence has led to more refined views about the nature of representation and computation, but it was discovered first and without dependence on those views.

The suggestion that a focus on the invariants in the world that specify information that can guide action has been a fruitful one in the study of perception and owes much to the visionary ideas of James Gibson in a general approach to perception and Eleanor Gibson in an approach to perceptual development. It has been less obviously used in cognition and categorization, yet there too it can be a very useful way to ask questions that may ultimately constrain models of representation and computation without depending on them. With respect to categorization, one can ask about the kinds of information that infants, children, and adults seem to rely on to learn and use categories. Traditionally this has been approached as questions about features types, such as the relative roles of shape versus color in driving categorization; but that is just the tip of the iceberg. Many other types of information might play differing roles. Moreover, as is the case with many instances in perception, a developmental approach can often provide better information on the differential roles of each type than can solely adult studies where several types all work together in a complex interactive fashion.

The challenge, of course, is coming up with a systematic way of characterizing the kinds of information that might be relevant to categorization and that can be described an objective manner. For example, one contrast that has been frequently mentioned in the literature is that between perceptual and functional features (e.g., Kemler-Nelson et al., 2000). The contrast makes intuitive sense but can lead to difficult debates on whether a particular feature is understood as functional or perceptual. Is the handle on a hammer merely a perceptual feature or does it have an additional status as a functional one? Despite these difficulties, there is much to be gained by attempting to develop typologies of property types and their relations and their relative roles in categorization across different kinds of tasks and across development and increasing expertise. Moreover, consistent with the theme of this essay, these issues are much broader and extend far beyond those merely of categorization.

Consider a few other contrasts that help illustrate the point. One can ask about the relative contributions of one- versus n-place predicates, that is, verbs and adjectives that take one versus many arguments. It has been argued that younger children have considerably more difficulty with two-or-greater place predicates, such as "give" or "put," than one-place ones (e.g., Gentner & Loewenstein, 2001). If so, how does that developmental pattern influence the kind of information that might be used to guide inferences? Move up another level and now consider more abstract causal relational patterns. For example, is this first element in a causal chain given extra weighting relative to others (Aim, Kim, Lassaline, & Dennis, 2000) and is this a bias seen throughout development (Ahn, Gelman, Amsterlaw, Hohenstein, & Kalish, 2000)? There is evidence that infants as well do give greater weight to the first element in a causal chain (Cohen, Rundell, Spellman, & Cashon, 1999). Are linear causal chains with clear beginning and end states easier to grasp than feedback loops and cycles? My own sense of the trajectory of research on kinds of causal information is that something quite dramatic and surprising is emerging. Young children are often very good at picking up on the most abstract relations and patterns before more concrete ones; but a great deal more work needs to be done here to clarify that account. It also leads to questions about implicit versus explicit ways of knowing and using causal structure.

Necessary Hybrids?

There is a powerful tension between attempts to explain many aspects of cognition in terms of a model that has only one form and one that is a hybrid consisting of sharply contrasting components. On the one hand, there is an elegance and appealing simplicity to a model that works in the same way throughout, say through principles of association or deductive inference. On the other hand, it seems very difficult to fit most phenomena into the perspectives adopted by one of those models. The alternative is to try to build theories that incorporate multiple aspects, such as a model of categorization that brings together both mechanisms for tabulating up feature frequencies and mechanisms for propositional interpretation of features and relations. Such hybrids can appear to be post hoc compromises that bring every possible trick into a motley and incoherent collection; but they also raise central questions of how mechanisms such as those involving associations and propositions might interact in lawful and predictive manners. Categorization may be an especially good case where a true hybrid is needed, not just to explain the categorization seen in older children and adults but potentially at all points of development. Not just preverbal children but even very young infants may never be stripped completely of the components of the hybrid that seem so prominent in adults. Whether this conjecture is correct or not, the chapters in this book raise a clear need to more carefully consider hybrid models not just as post hoc fixes but as principled ways of modeling the development and use of categories.

Development as Insight into the Mature State

It may be preaching to the converted to say to readers of a book on the development of categorization that a developmental perspective is important; but the case of categorization is an especially strong demonstration of a much more general point that development often affords unique insights into the nature of adult cognition. It seems that this perspective is much more common in cognitive science approaches to problems than the more traditional "cognitive psychology" ones, perhaps because of the ways linguistic theory and language acquisition have been so closely intertwined in recent years. A powerful theme that emerges again and again in this book is that a reader who cares little about children per se will learn much from these chapters that will enable a better understanding of adult cognition. If, for example, one is convinced that some aspects of categorization are intrinsically dependent on one's also having a natural language, then the presence of those aspects in preverbal infants constitutes a profound challenge to those claims. If one believes that "real categorization" is the province of one form of cognition, say a connectionist net, and that the rest of categorization is a slow deliberative process only found when one has the rare luxury of carefully reflecting on the task, it matters greatly whether those other forms are seen early on in development. There is a notion that the developmentally earliest emerging patterns of cognition are the most basic and important in adult real time cognition. This notion may sometimes lead one astray, but it is a powerful heuristic to use in evaluating the relative importance of components in adult models.

Many other arguments could be made for how developmental studies can inform models of adult cognition both in terms of patterns of computation and representation. The chapters collected in this book show just how valuable such insights can be, just as they also show how important it is for current researchers in cognitive development to be fully versed on the most up-to-date adult models of cognition. Take, for example, an approach that seeks to model some aspect of cognitive development in terms of changing weights in a connectionist net. That approach would be foolhardy without full expertise in the most current models of learning in connectionism, regardless of the age of the learner involved. One great virtue of work on connectionism is that it has generally recognized this point all along, perhaps just because of its notion that learning is learning regardless of the age of the organism. It now seems that researchers from a much wider variety of perspectives are embracing the same general point. Issues of learning, representation, and computation are not best addressed by limiting one's expertise to a particular age group.

The chapters of this book represent a major step forward in the study of categories and concepts not just because of the detailed insights offered throughout but also because of the more general approaches taken to asking questions about how we think and make sense of the world around us. Moreover, they illustrate how extremely diverse views by authors who in many cases strongly disagree with each other can nonetheless come together in a manner that greatly enriches our understanding of concepts and categorization. I was struck by how much I learned from each and every chapter and commentary and at the value of having such contrasting views in the same collection, integrated in a manner that does not have the authors talking past each other but talking to each other in a common effort to better understand the remarkable phenomena that they have collectively uncovered in recent years. This collection is an illustration of cognitive science at its best.

References

Ahn, W., Gelman, S. A., Amsterlaw, J. A., Hohenstein, J., & Kalish, C. W. (2000). Causal status effect in children's categorization. *Cognition, 76*, 35–43.

Aim, W., Kim, N. S., Lassaline, M. E., & Dennis, M. J. (2000). Causal status as a determinant of feature centrality. *Cognitive Psychology, 41*, 1–55.

Brooks, L. R. (1978). Nonanalytic concept formation and memory for instances. In E. Rosch & B. B. Lloyd (Eds.), *Cognition and categorization*. Hillsdale, NJ: Lawrence Eribaum.

Brooks, L. R., LeBlanc, V. R., & Norman, G. R. (2000). On the difficulty of noticing obvious features in patient appearance. *Psychological Science 11*, 112–117.

Cohen, L. B., Rundell, L. J., Spellman, B. A., & Cashon, C. H. (1999). Infants' perception of causal chains. *Psychological Science, 10*, 412–418.

Fodor, J. (1986). Why paramecia don't have mental representations. *Midwest Studies in Philosophy, 10*, 3–23.

Gentner, D., & Loewenstein, J. (2001). Relational language and relational thought. In J. Byrnes & E. Amsel (Eds.), *Language, literacy, and cognitive development* (pp. 87–120). Mahwah, NJ: Erlbaum.

Herrnstein, R. J. (1990). Levels of stimulus control: A functional approach. *Cognition 37*, 133–166.

Kellman, P. J., & Banks, M. S. (1998). Infant visual perception. In R. Siegler and D. Kuhn (Eds.), *Handbook of child psychology: Vol. 2. Cognition, perception, and language* (5th ed., pp. 103–146). New York: Wiley.

Kemler Nelson, D. G., Frankenfield, A., Morris, C., & Blair, E. (2000). Young children's use of functional information to categorize artifacts: Three factors that matter. *Cognition, 77*, 133–168.

Murphy, G. L. (2002). *The big book of concepts.* Cambridge, MA: MIT Press.

Preface

This book emerged out of our discussions about the need for a volume focusing on categories and concepts in early development. Our conversations began at a poster session at a meeting of the Society for Research in Child Development and continued the next year over coffee at the meeting of the International Society for Infant Studies. These conversations were an extension of our many discussions of the exciting research findings and theories in the study of the early development of categorization and concepts.

Our decision to put together this volume at this time was motivated by a clear increase in interest in this topic in the field. In recent years, a number of symposia focusing on these findings and theories have been presented at society meetings. In addition, recent editions of new and well-established journals have devoted entire sections to discussions of issues in this area of research. Despite this increased interest, we know of no book dedicated to this stimulating and important aspect of child development. Many previous books have included a chapter or a section on this general area of cognitive development, but we thought the time was right for a book devoted entirely to the topic. As researchers and instructors, we have been frustrated by the lack of a single source for different perspectives and research programs that have been emerging in the last 10 years or so. This book is intended to fill this need. Thus, this book was inspired by the perceived need to bring together researchers and theorists who focus on the origins and early development of categories and concepts.

Whether or not infants' earliest perception of the world is a "blooming, buzzing, confusion," it is not long before they come to perceive structure and order among the objects and events around them. Researchers agreed some time ago that infants can and do form categories from a very early age. The questions then became focused on more specific issues: How do infants and young children form categories? Are the categories and concepts formed early in life similar to those formed later in life? And do these early categories and concepts act as the foundation of those formed in childhood and beyond? Are the same processes and information employed in form-ing categories at different points during development? These and other questions have been the motivating force behind a large and growing body of literature. The goal of this book is to show how far research and theory have gone in answering these questions and to illustrate some of the diverse approaches that have been taken to address these questions.

The contributors to this book represent the foremost researchers and theorists in this field. A variety of different (and often conflicting) theoretical perspectives are represented, and therefore this book captures the spirit of debate in the field. We believe that we have met our goal of providing for the reader a set of chapters that exemplify the main questions that are being asked and the different kinds of answers that have been proposed, and that the chapters represent a wide range of topics and theoretical positions within the field of categorization and conceptual development. The first chapters show how we can study infants' perception of speech (Jusczyk), spatial relations (Quinn), and objects (Younger, Rakison) from the per-spective of categorization. Other chapters are focused on how children come to understand important categorical distinctions, such as that between animates (e.g., people and animals) and inanimates (e.g., plants, furniture, and vehicles) (Mandler, Rakison, Gelman, & Koenig). Several chapters evaluate the role that language plays in children's developing understanding of categories and concepts (Mervis, Pani, & Pani; Waxman; Smith, Colunga, & Yoshida). There is also discussion of the way that computational models can shed light on early category and concept formation (Smith et al.; Mareschal). In addition, a number of chapters examine controversies such as what is the role of conceptual knowledge or theories in children's developing cat-egories and concepts (Mandler; Mareschal; Oakes & Madole; Rakison; Gopnik & Nazzi; Gelman & Koenig). In sum, this book provides examples of the many ways that theorists think (and have thought) about the origins and early development of categories and concepts.

Our main goal, however, was not to simply bring together a set of loosely related chapters but to create a coherent book that would provide a reader with a sense of the field as a whole. Thus, we have organized the chapters somewhat chronologi-cally—by the age of the children discussed in the chapter, that is—and we have placed chapters adjacent to one another when we felt the content benefited from a com-parison. Students learning about these issues for the first time could therefore read the book from start to finish and gain an understanding of how categorization and conceptual understanding develops over the first several years of life. At the same time, each of the chapters stands alone, so researchers familiar with the field can find up-to-date discussions of the issues in whichever of the chapters they choose to read. Our goal was that this book would benefit both readers relatively new to and read-ers quite familiar with this general area of inquiry.

One unusual feature of this book is that we have included three commentaries, with the goal of putting the ideas and conclusions from the individual chapters in a broader context. Leslie Cohen has provided a commentary on the first set of chap-ters, and Ellen Markman and Vikram Jaswal have provided a commentary on the second set. These two commentaries summarize many of the issues relevant to the chapters in each part and provide a broad overview of how those chapters address the questions that have been posed in the area. Robert Goldstone and Mark Johansen have provided a final commentary on the entire book. This commentary shows how we can interpret this developmental work from the viewpoint of researchers studying categories and concepts in adults. These three commentaries are important because they show the connections between chapters and they illustrate points of disagreement as well as agreement between the particular authors. Moreover, the commentaries are written by researchers who themselves are experts in the field, and, as the reader will observe, they bring their own perspective to bear on the important issues.

Another feature of this book is that we have highlighted current issues and future directions in this area. Substantial advances have been made in our understanding of early category and concept development; however, from these advances have emerged additional, perhaps more complex issues that need to be addressed. Not only are the contributors the major researchers who have provided the most important theoretical and empirical advances in the study of early categorization but their current work is also among the most "cutting edge" in this area. It is our hope that this book will provide the reader with insight about the future of the field and as such may help to guide future research endeavors. More specifically, the recent advances described here may lead to a new theoretical framework in the field. The contributors have contributed significantly to these theoretical advances.

The book is organized into two parts. The first is devoted to the processes of categorization before and during the emergence of language (roughly birth through 18 months). The second is devoted to the processes of categorization after and during the emergence of language (roughly the second and third years of life). Our hope is that this format will provide a comprehensive picture of the course of category and concept development in the first three years of life, and the three commentaries will help emphasize the coherence (and divergence) of the contributed chapters.

Acknowledgments

This book was made possible by the support we received from our many outstanding colleagues at several different institutions, as well as the financial support from several sources. First, our mentors, George Butterworth and Les Cohen, provided us with a strong foundation in thinking about developmental science. Their guidance allowed us to develop to a point where we could undertake a project like this one. We are forever grateful for the excellent training we received from them and the stimulating and enjoyable time we spent with them. George passed away in the spring of 1999, and his loss is a huge blow to those in the field; he will continue to be sorely missed.

Both of us are fortunate to be affiliated with outstanding psychology departments and to have exceptional colleagues. We extend our thanks to our colleagues in the departments of psychology at Carnegie Mellon University and the University of Iowa for their encouragement of this project, and for stimulating and exciting discussions about issues related to categorization and cognitive development. This book would not have been possible without the enthusiastic response from our excellent contributing authors. As a group, the contributors provided us with outstanding chapters and were responsive to our feedback. We are grateful for their contributions. Catharine Carlin at Oxford University Press was nothing but supportive of this venture from the outset. Throughout the process, Catharine was encouraging and enthusiastic. We appreciate all her guidance and help. Many thanks also to Bob Milks for his attention to detail in all aspects of the production of the book.

We also must acknowledge the financial support we received during the time we worked on this book. The psychology departments at Carnegie Mellon University and the University of Iowa generously supported this endeavor. Additional support came from grant HD36060 awarded to Lisa Oakes by the National Institutes of Health.

Finally, this book would not have been possible without the support of our friends and families. Lisa expresses her appreciation to Steve and Alison Luck for their support; they also provided an important diversion at times when such a diversion was most needed. Lisa also thanks Jeannie Oakes and Marty Lipton for their advice and enthusiasm, and Rod and Krystyna Oakes for generally being encouraging. David would like to extend a special thanks to Caro Simard for her constant encouragement, passion, and support. He would also like to thank Michael Rakison and Jon and Nick Crossick for their friendship and humor prior to and during, and hopefully after, the period in which this book was completed. David would also like to offer thanks to Nick Bell, Alex Campbell, Andy Goodman, Belinda Heywood, Rohit Lehki, James Reekie, and Mitchell Wolf for their great comradeship over many years, and Annika Fasnacht for her help in the preparation of this book

Contents

Foreword: Categories, Cognitive Development, and Cognitive Science   v
    Frank C. Keil
Preface   xiii
Acknowledgments   xvii
Contributors   xxi

1.   Issues in the Early Development of Concepts and Categories:
     An Introduction   3
     Lisa M. Oakes and David H. Rakison

PART I. CONCEPTS AND CATEGORIES BEFORE
THE EMERGENCE OF LANGUAGE

2.   Chunking Language Input to Find Patterns   27
     Peter W. Jusczyk
3.   Concepts Are Not Just for Objects: Categorization of
     Spatial Relation Information by Infants   50
     Paul C. Quinn
4.   Parsing Objects into Categories: Infants' Perception and
     Use of Correlated Attributes   77
     Barbara A. Younger
5.   Conceptual Categorization   103
     Jean M. Mandler
6.   Principles of Developmental Change in Infants'
     Category Formation   132
     Lisa M. Oakes and Kelly L. Madole
7.   Parts, Motion, and the Development of the Animate-Inanimate
     Distinction in Infancy   159
     David H. Rakison

8. Commentary on Part I: Unresolved Issues in
    Infant Categorization   193
    Leslie B. Cohen

PART II: CONCEPTS AND CATEGORIES DURING EARLY
LANGUAGE DEVELOPMENT

9. Links between Object Categorization and Naming: Origins and
    Emergence in Human Infants   213
    Sandra R. Waxman
10. Transaction of Child Cognitive-Linguistic Abilities
    and Adult Input in the Acquisition of Lexical Categories at
    the Basic and Subordinate Levels   242
    Carolyn B. Mervis, John R. Pani, and Ariel M. Pani
11. Making an Ontology: Cross-linguistic Evidence   275
    Linda B. Smith, Eliana Colunga, and Hanako Yoshida
12. Words, Kinds, and Causal Powers: A Theory Theory Perspective
    on Early Naming and Categorization   303
    Alison Gopnik and Thierry Nazzi
13. Theory-Based Categorization in Early Childhood   330
    Susan A. Gelman and Melissa A. Koenig
14. The Acquisition and Use of Implicit Categories
    in Early Development   360
    Denis Mareschal
15. Commentary on Part II: Abilities and Assumptions Underlying
    Conceptual Development   384
    Ellen M. Markman and Vikram K. Jaswal

16. Final Commentary: Conceptual Development from
    Origins to Asymptotes   403
    Robert L. Goldstone and Mark K. Johansen

Author Index   419
Subject Index   427

Contributors

Eliana Colunga, Indiana University

Susan A. Gelman, University of Michigan

Robert L. Goldstone, Indiana University

Alison Gopnik, University of California at Berkeley

Vikram K. Jaswal, Stanford University

Mark K. Johansen, Indiana University

Peter W. Jusczyk, Johns Hopkins University

Melissa A. Koenig, University of Texas at Austin

Kelly L. Madole, Western Kentucky University

Jean M. Mandler, University of California, San Diego

Denis Mareschal, Berkbeck College, University of London

Ellen M. Markman, Stanford University

Thierry Nazzi, Université Paris 5

Lisa M. Oakes, University of Iowa

Paul C. Quinn, Washington & Jefferson College

David H. Rakison, Carnegie Mellon University

Linda B. Smith, Indiana University

Sandra R. Waxman, Northwestern University

Hanako Yoshida, Indiana University

Barbara A. Younger, Purdue University

Early Category and Concept Development

CHAPTER ONE

Issues in the Early Development of Concepts and Categories
An Introduction

Lisa M. Oakes and David H. Rakison

Concepts and Categories Defined

William James once described infants' earliest perceptions of the world as a "blooming, buzzing, confusion," speculating that infants perceive the visual world as an unrelated, disorganized series of images rather than, as is the case for adults, a structured world composed of discrete objects and events. More than 40 years of research has shown that in contrast to James's view, from the very first months of life infants develop the ability to perceive and conceptualize in ways akin to that of adults. At the core of this process, and of cognitive development in general, is the ability to *categorize* or *classify* or, more specifically, the ability to group discriminable properties, objects, or events into classes by means of some principle or rule. Thus, to categorize is to "render discriminably different things equivalent, to group objects and events and people around us into classes, and to respond to them in terms of their class membership rather than their uniqueness" (Bruner, Goodnow, & Austin, 1956, p. 231). Or, more informally, to categorize is "to treat a set of things as somehow equivalent: to put them in the same pile, or call them by the same name, or respond to them in the same way" (Neisser, 1987, p. 1).

This ability differs from *discrimination* or *differentiation* in that more than two distinctive properties, objects, or events are involved. For example, to categorize is to consider a number of animals as similar to each other but different from various vehicles, whereas to discriminate is to treat a single dog as different from a single cat (or from another dog). The mental representation that encapsulates the commonalities and structure that exist among items within categories is generally referred to as a *concept*. Thus, in some sense categories are collections of things in the world and concepts are the internal mental depiction of those collections (Margolis, 1994; Smith, 1995).

The importance of categorization and concept formation to cognitive development, and to cognition in adults, should not be underestimated. Forming categories reduces demands on our inherently limited memory storage and perceptual processes, and without it we would have to remember independently the same or similar information about each individual member of a category. For example, we would have to remember that a particular Rottweiler has four legs, and so does a particular poodle, Chihuahua, Labrador, and so on. Categorizing an object also allows us to make inductive inferences about that object; for instance, once we have categorized a particular object as a *dog*, we can make inferences about whether that object is alive, what its offspring might be, and if it likes to chase squirrels. Categorization is also inextricably linked to language in that words often refer to categories of objects and events, or properties of those things, and as a consequence the question concerning the causal direction between language and thought has been long debated.

Over the last 25 years, a proliferation of research on the development of category and concept formation—largely due to the introduction of new methodological techniques and radical theoretical propositions—has advanced our understanding of the origins and early development of classification abilities and the processes behind those abilities. Despite these advancements, a number of key issues at the center of thinking about categorization are still very much under debate. Many of these issues concern age-related changes in concept development, the external and internal structure of early categories, and the mechanisms involved in concept and category development. For example, theorists have asked what mechanisms for categorization are available at birth, what mechanisms emerge later in development, and whether conceptual development involves continual enrichment or stagelike advances. One debate central to the study of categorization is the relative roles of perceptual similarity (e.g., overall shape or color) and nonobservable properties (e.g., whether something has blood and is alive or has silicon chips and is not alive) in early classification. Others have asked more methodologically oriented questions. For example, what is the role of contextual variation on categorization by infants and children? Do different experimental procedures tap the same kind of knowledge? Can computational models simulate infant and child categorization, and if so, how do these models inform behavioral research? Finally, questions have been posed about the causal direction between language and categorization. Specifically, what is the impact of language on category development? How does language partition the world? And do cross-linguistic differences in describing the world lead us to parse the world differently? These questions are of immense interest not only to developmentalists but also to investigators in fields as far-ranging as philosophy, adult cognition, computational modeling, and linguistics. Nonetheless, there has been little opportunity for crosstalk between these fields and, perhaps more important, there has been little in the way of a comprehensive portrayal of the development of categorization in the first years of life.

One of the goals of this volume is to bring together different perspectives on the emergence and early development of categorization. The chapters presented here address many, if not all, of the questions posed here, and a number of others besides.

Current Issues in Early Concept and Categorization

As will become evident from the chapters in this book, although there is agreement on the questions that need to be asked in relation to early category and concept formation (although see Cohen's commentary, chap. 8, for what he considers to be the neglected questions), there is also great divergence in the theoretical positions and empirical findings of researchers who address those questions. In this sense, the field is perhaps no different from any other within cognitive science. To make matters worse, the field has had to come to terms with a rapidly growing set of techniques for assessing concepts and categories in young children and a collection of often apparently conflicting results.

The issues in addressed in this book focus to a large extent on these controversial themes, including: (1) Are there differences between perceptual and conceptual categorization? (2) At what level are children's first categories? (3) What is the role of language in children's concept formation? (4) What is the role of theories in children's concept formation? (5) Is categorization just for objects, or is it a general purpose ability that can be applied broadly? We outline these issues in what follows, providing an overview of the topics that will be addressed and described in much more detail in the chapters included.

The Distinction between Perceptual and Conceptual Categorization

One highly contentious topic that concerns classification throughout the lifespan relates to the distinction between *perceptual* and *conceptual* categorization. In general, the notion of perceptual categorization refers to the grouping of properties, objects, and events on the basis of their observable features (e.g., has four legs and a flat surface, for tables) whereas conceptual categorization refers to grouping things by more abstract, nonobservable properties (e.g., "can provide support" or "decorative," for tables). Some argue that there is a clear distinction between these two types of categorization. For example, Mandler (1992, 2000, chap. 5) has argued that within the first year of life infants start to develop concepts of object that are based on shared *meaning*. According to Mandler, infants have two distinct systems for categorizing: one for forming categories based on perceptual similarity and another for forming conceptual categories based on similarity in kind. Thus, infants may identify an object as a dog on the basis of its perceptual features but choose to group it with other animals because it is, for instance, a self-propelled entity that acts as an agent in a causal event. Importantly, these two modes of representation operate simultaneously, so infants can have both perceptual representations and somewhat independent conceptual representations.

A variation on this view is that infants and children form categories based on perceptual or conceptual information at different points in development (chap. 3). According to this view, nonobvious properties are not available until the second year of life or later (Carey, 1985; Gelman & Koenig, chap. 13; Keil, 1991). This does not mean, however, that the acquisition of knowledge about the deeper, nonobvious properties of objects does not start earlier in infancy. Indeed, attention to motion-related and psychologically-related characteristics presumably emerges in infancy (e.g., chaps. 5, 7, 12). However, some have argued that children do not incorporate such information into their concepts of objects until between 2 and 4 years of age (e.g., chap. 13).

Central to this perspective is the idea that humans infer that objects have an *essence*—a kind of abstract theory that provides a mental "explanation" of causal relations (Medin & Ortony, 1989; Murphy & Medin, 1985). Thus, people's theory of these essences not only forms the cornerstone for knowledge of things in the world but also organizes the structure of that knowledge. According to this view, attribute matching and similarity are inherently insufficient to explain category coherence because they are too unconstrained; that is, they do not explain which attributes should be important in category membership decisions (Keil, 1991; Gelman & Koenig, chap. 13; Gopnik & Nazzi, chap. 12). This *theory theory*, as it is often called, emphasizes that concepts are rooted in knowledge that embodies a theory of the world, and the features that are diagnostic for category membership are those that are less perceptible, or even nonobservable (see the section later on the role of theories in categorization). For instance, theoretical knowledge about the nature of air speed and uplift connects "has flies" to "wings" as part of the concept of airplane, and a lay theory of genetic structure and the reproductive system allow us to determine to which species a particular animal exemplar belongs.

Other researchers have argued, however, that the distinction between perceptual and conceptual information is fuzzy or even nonexistent (Eimas, 1994; Madole & Oakes, 1999; Oakes & Madole, chap. 6; Quinn, chap. 3; Quinn & Eimas, 1997; Rakison, chap. 7; Rakison & Poulin-Dubois, 2001). A number of studies have revealed that, whether one is talking about geometric forms (Ricciuti, 1965), faces (Cohen & Strauss, 1979), or a host of real-world objects such as cats, dogs, mammals, or furniture (Behl-Chadha, 1996; Eimas & Quinn, 1994), infants' earliest categories are grounded in perceptual information. These perceptual categories, which are formed on the basis of the surface appearance of things, are most likely represented in terms of a perceptual prototype or schema (Mandler, 1997; Quinn & Eimas, 1997). For these researchers, the question becomes how these early perceptual representations related to later conceptual ones. As described earlier, some have argued for separate systems or processes for different types of representations—with either operating simultaneously or with the system for forming perceptual representations giving way to a system for forming conceptual representations. Others have argued for more continuity in the system for dealing with perceptual and conceptual bases of categorization (e.g., Eimas, 1994; Jones & Smith, 1993; chaps. 3, 6, 7).

Several different arguments have been made in support of this second approach. First, it has been pointed out that perceptual and conceptual cues are often confounded—mammals are alive but also possess legs, eyes, and so on—so it is difficult to know which kind of information is used as the basis for categorization. Second, some researchers claim that both perceptual and conceptual categorization rely on the same basic processes and are therefore inherently related. For example, Oakes and Madole (chap. 6) argue that the basic processes by which infants and young children form categories changes little during development, though the categories themselves change as children gain access to new types of information. Younger (chap. 4) similarly argues that infants develop the ability to use invariant attribute relations in the environment to form categories. Third, several researchers claim that, in principle, there is no fundamental representational difference between perceptual and nonobvious cues, as both kinds of information enter through the sensory systems. Quinn (chap. 3), for example, claims that representations become increasingly enriched in detail throughout development and it is this enrichment that provides gradual conceptual change. Rakison (Rakison & Poulin-Dubois, 2001; chap. 7) suggests that infants start to learn about the nonobvious properties or actions of objects—such as whether they are self-propelled or not—through the association between those properties and the causal attributes inherently involved with them (e.g., the legs of an animal). For Rakison, however, these associations are conceptually no different from, for example, the association between static features like wings and beaks or wheels and a windshield. Such perspectives are not unique to the study of the early development of categorization. Researchers studying adult categorization, for example, have argued similarly that there may not be a clear distinction between perceptual and conceptual categorization (e.g., Goldstone & Barsalou, 1998).

Whether the distinction between perceptual and conceptual categories is useful or real is one of the most central arguments in the study of the early development of categorization. Many of the chapters in this book discuss this debate in detail and argue forcefully for one position or the other (for summaries see chaps. 8, 15, 16). As is made clear in these chapters, this is an important and timely issue in the study of category and concept development, and considerable progress has been made, though the matter is far from resolved.

At What Level of Exclusivity Do Children First Categorize?

A second major issue in the study of categorization is the level of exclusivity of children's first categories. Do children first form categories that are relatively exclusive, such as dog and chair, or are their first categories broader, including a more diverse set of objects into a single category, such as animal or furniture? This issue is important because although infants' first words often refer to the more exclusive categories (Anglin, 1977; Clark, 1973) they extend those words to items that an adult would not; for example, calling a cow a doggie or an orange a ball (Clark, 1973; Mervis, 1984; Mervis, Pani, & Pani, chap. 10). The observation of such overextensions has lead researchers to debate about the nature of children's first categories.

Eleanor Rosch's work on category taxonomies was the first systematic statement about the level of children's first categories (e.g., Rosch, 1978; Rosch, Mervis, Gray, Johnson, & Boyes-Braem, 1976). According to Rosch, there are three hierarchical levels of categories: basic, superordinate, and subordinate. The basic level, which Rosch claimed was the first conceptual—that is, mentally represented—category to develop, maximizes within-category similarity and between-category dissimilarity (e.g., car, boat, bed, table, dog). Thus, instances from a single basic-level category are alike in many ways (e.g., form, function, structure) and are very different from other basic-level category types. In contrast, at the superordinate level, which Rosch thought emerged later in development, objects within a category are relatively diverse and therefore perceptually dissimilar (e.g., cars, planes, and boats within the superordinate category of vehicles) and are quite different from members of other superordinate categories. Hence the superordinate level is minimally dependent on perceptual similarity and maximizes between-category differences. Finally, at the subordinate level (armchair, rocking chair) the category is more specific than at the basic level. Objects within a given subordinate category are quite similar (e.g., armchairs are more similar to each other than to chairs generally), but this means that subordinate-level exemplars do not contrast with each other and are consequently hard to differentiate from objects of the same basic level (e.g., an armchair could be confused with a rocking chair or dining chair).

According to Rosch and others, the basic level is "psychologically privileged" and developmentally primary (e.g., Markman, 1989; Mervis, 1987; Mervis & Rosch, 1981; Mervis et al., chap. 10; Rosch et al., 1976). Rosch assumed that the basic level is special because objects at this level tend to share many features with each other while sharing few features with other category members. In addition, basic-level categories are most likely to reflect the correlational structure of objects. For example, animals with beaks and claws are also likely to have feathers (e.g., birds), while those with mouths and fur are more likely to have hands or paws (Markman, 1989; Younger, chap. 4). And indeed, early work on this issue supported Rosch's hypothesis that the basic level is "psychologically privileged" as well as developmentally primary (for an extensive review see Mervis & Rosch, 1981). Evidence that the basic level is psychologically privileged comes from a number of studies showing that children and adults more easily categorize at the basic level than at the other levels. In sorting and match-to-sample studies in which children were asked to put objects that are alike together, 3-, 5-, and 6-year-old children sorted poorly at the superordinate level but performed almost perfectly at the basic level (Rosch et al., 1976). Finally, in studies where adults were asked to list attributes of categories, they tended to provide most of what they know at the basic level (dog, bed, car) and very little at the superordinate (furniture, vehicles) or subordinate level (waterbed, station wagon) (Rosch et al., 1976; Tversky & Hemenway, 1984). There are also a couple of different sources for the conclusion that the basic level is developmentally primary. Vocabulary acquisition studies, for example, revealed that basic-level terms are highly represented in the first 50 or so words that infants learn (Anglin, 1977; Clark, 1973) and that 3-year-olds use basic-level labels when asked to name pictures of objects (Rosch et al., 1976). Furthermore, Mervis and Crisafi (1982) found that children between 2 and 4 years of age who were taught artificial categories at different hierarchical levels more easily learned terms at the basic level than any other level. In response to these findings, however, it should be pointed out that adults' labeling of objects for children is also often at the basic level; for instance, adults will more likely use the label "dog" than "animal" to refer to a canine.

Recently, Mandler has argued forcefully for an alternative developmental trajectory. Specifically, Mandler claimed that infants' first conceptual categories are not at the basic level but instead are at what she labeled the global-level. These categories resemble superordinate domains—such as animals and vehicles—but differ from them in that there are no basic-level classes nested within them. This claim was based largely on evidence that infants attended to global distinctions before they attended to basic-level ones. In one study by Mandler and Bauer (1988), for example, 16- and 20-month-old infants responded to basic-level categories from different superordinate domains (e.g., dogs and cars) but not basic-level categories drawn from the same superordinate domain (e.g., dogs and horses). Similarly, Mandler, Bauer, and McDonough (1991) found that 18-month-old infants responded to the superordinate-level categorical distinction between animals and vehicles but not to basic-level contrasts within these domains such as dogs versus horses. Mandler et al. took these findings as confirmation that basic-level categories are not the first to develop.

There continues to be much debate about whether infants first form relatively global categories or more exclusive basic-level categories, as is clear from the chapters in the book. Mandler (chap. 5) shows that in her studies infants consistently respond to global categories before they respond to basic-level ones, and likewise Quinn (chap. 3) and Rakison (chap. 7) have suggested a similar developmental trend, though they posit a different basis for this behavior. In contrast, Waxman (chap. 9) presents evidence from categorization studies with novel labels that reveal that infants respond first to basic-level categories and only later respond to superordinate or global-level ones. At this point, it is not yet clear which depiction of early category taxonomies is more accurate, but it is becoming increasingly clear that contextual factors—such as how the stimuli are presented—have a powerful influence on the particular category to which infants respond (chaps. 4, 6).

What Is the Role of Language in Children's Concept Formation?

The connection between language and thought has long been debated (e.g., Whorf, 1956). At least two different kinds of issues have been raised. First, researchers have asked whether language is necessary for the formation of categories and for conceptual understanding. For example, Choi and Bowerman (1991) have argued that the particular language children learn shapes the concepts they eventually posses. Clearly, infants are able to form categories before they learn language, however. A number of chapters in the first part of this book reveal putatively sophisticated categorization abilities by prelinguistic infants. These chapters show that infants can form categories that correspond to adult labels such as dog and vehicle (see chaps. 3, 5, 7). Thus, language does not seem to be necessary for the formation of categories. However, language might be necessary for the development of some types of concepts and categories. Choi and Bowerman (1991), for example, suggest that children's categorization of motion events is a function of the way the language they are learning lexicalizes the components of those events. Indeed Markman and Jaswal (chap. 15) argue that language "plays a critical role in the . . . conceptual system" and that concepts can not be acquired through associationist mechanisms alone (p. 385).

The second question is: What exactly is the relationship between conceptual development and language? That is, regardless of whether or not language is necessary for conceptual development, language and concepts are clearly related. Thus, the question, simply put, can be formalized as this: Does children's language development reflect their underlying conceptual development, or is children's conceptual development shaped by their language? As pointed out by Goldstone and Johansen (chap. 16), developing concepts both provide a basis for development language and are transformed as children acquire language. The chapters in this book provide some level of support for both perspectives. For example, infants' first words may map directly onto existing concepts that, at least in part, are akin to those of adults. Evaluating children's early vocabulary development, therefore, would provide understanding of the underlying conceptual development. For example, Mervis's description of child-basic categories (1987; chap. 10) emerged from the observation that although children's first words correspond to adults' basic-level categories (e.g., dog, ball), those words are often extended to items that adults would not consider as belonging to the same category. In some cases the categories to which words are extended are more broad (e.g., calling the moon a ball), and in other cases they are more narrow (e.g., referring only to the family dog as a pet). The point is that conclusions about the kinds of categories infants have formed, and how those categories are extended, are drawn from how infants use words. Mervis, Pani, and Pani (chap. 10) have provided a powerful demonstration of this approach by following the developmental trajectory of one child's vocabulary acquisition and showing how this illustrates changes in the child's conceptual understanding within a domain.

However, it is also becoming increasingly clear that the acquisition of language itself shapes the kinds of categories that children form and attend to. For example, children attend to different properties of labeled objects than of nonlabeled objects, suggesting that the act of labeling an object causes different features of that object to be salient (chaps. 9, 11). Waxman (chap. 9) argues that children begin the process of word learning with the broad expectation that words refer to commonalities among items, and to this end she presents evidence that language cues highlight commonalities among items such as color or texture for infants as young as 11 months. Language experience, according to Waxman, helps children learn that different kinds of words refer to different kinds of commonalities. For example, Waxman shows that in the second year of life infants learn that nouns refer to object categories, adjectives refer to object properties, and verbs refer to object actions.

Smith, Colunga, and Yoshida (chap. 11) argue that language can have an even more profound effect on children's categorization. Specifically, they argue that there are regularities that distinguish different kinds of categories, for example, solid things tend to be complexly shaped, nonsolid things tend to be simply shaped, and animate things tend to possess bundles of correlated properties. They claim that the nominal categories of languages honor these regularities and language-specific properties bend psychological ontologies in language-specific ways. This gives rise to the implication that there are culturally distinct ways of knowing: linguistic regularities across cultures create specific ontologies. Thus, not only does language reflect children's underlying conceptual development but the acquisition of language also seems to play a key role in shaping the kinds of concepts children form and the kinds of information or features that are salient. It is important to point out, however, that there is disagreement about whether these effects of language on conceptual development reflect language-specific processes (i.e., language-specific expectations about conceptual relations) or are the result of general purpose cognitive mechanisms (see chaps. 9, 11). Despite these differences in perspective, there is clear evidence that the kinds of categorical relations to which children respond change as they acquire language.

What Is the Role of Theories in Children's Concept Formation?

An additional issue that has received a good deal of attention in the literature relates to whether children's concepts are based in theories. As in the perceptual–conceptual debate described earlier, the main issue concerns the role of nonobvious properties in children's concepts. When children acquire new concepts, are those concepts derived from, or binded by, a naïve theory about the world?

In some senses, this issue boils down to the question of whether we can construct categories without theories. Some have argued that theories are necessary for the formation of categories (see chap. 12). As described earlier, the theory theory emphasizes that concepts are derived from the child's theories of the world. According to this view, the features that are most diagnostic of category membership are not necessarily observable. Specifically, the claim is there are no a priori constraints on how we parse the perceptual world (Keil, 1981; Murphy & Medin, 1985), and it is therefore difficult to explain how theory-based categories can arise from the sensory primitives available to infants. Moreover, theorists have argued that perceptual features can be misleading or inaccurate, but core features are causal and stable (Murphy & Medin, 1985; Wellman & Gelman, 1988). Therefore, because in the perceptual world it is difficult to find the kind of stability needed for coherent concepts, the most important features of concepts must be based on deep, nonobvious features (Wellman & Gelman, 1988). According to this perspective, then, the categories revealed using habituation procedures with young infants are based on perceptual similarity among the items and may not, therefore, be the same kinds of categories as those possessed by adults. As pointed out by Markman and Jaswal (chap. 15), it is clear that such perceptual processes are important in children's developing conceptual system—without such processes it would be impossible to identify new members of a category. Rather, the argument is that such processes are not sufficient for the development of the rich conceptual system putatively held by young children (see chap. 13).

For this view, theories are particularly important in the development of categories and concepts. As suggested by Gelman and Koenig (chap. 13), the acquisition of concepts may proceed more smoothly with the help of theories. Gelman and Koenig review evidence that children's categories do include information about nonobservable properties such as ontology, causation, function, and intentions. Armed with such information, children can make inferences about aspects of the object that are not immediately available, such as whether they are likely to have some internal part or possess some causal property. Although the theories themselves change with development (chaps. 12, 13), over time children acquire concepts of kinds with the help of those changing theories.

There is no question that theories or background information influence categorization by children and adults. Adults form categories more easily when the features cohere according to the adults' background knowledge than when the same features do not cohere according to their background knowledge (e.g., Spalding & Murphy, 1996). Children's inferences about novel objects reflect theory-based understanding and reasoning (chaps. 12, 13). Even in infancy, not all perceptual information is treated equivalently. For example, infants attend to legs versus wheels to differentiate animals from vehicles (Rakison & Butterworth, 1998b), attend to some correlations among features and ignore others (Rakison & Poulin-Dubois, in press), or focus on features of the head and face for differentiating different types of animals (Quinn & Eimas, 1996). Madole and Cohen (1995) showed that with development infants constrained their attention to the kinds of form/function correlations that adults would consider to be sensible (e.g., the form of the wheels of an object was correlated with whether or not they rolled) but younger infants attended both to sensible and arbitrary correlations (e.g., the form of a top protrusion predicted whether or not the wheels rolled). The kinds of features and correlations to which infants will attend, therefore, appear to be shaped by their increasing understanding of the world.

· The question is: Where do such biases come from? Do they arise from the child's creation of core theories about objects and having categories that are based on ontological, causal, and functional information (chaps. 12, 13)? Or are there other kinds of mechanisms for explaining how children acquire such understanding and for how children's categories come to be constrained in these ways (see Jones & Smith, 1993; chaps. 6, 7, 14, 16). Mareschal (chap. 14) has provided intriguing evidence that children's conceptual categorization need not be theory based. Specifically, Mareschal discusses evidence that connectionist models behave in the same way as do preschool children. These data are important for the discussion on the role of theories in children's categorization.

How Does Categorization of Objects Relate
to Categorization of Other Entities More Broadly?

The discussion in the preceding pages is focused primarily on the development of object categories. That is, theorizing and research in this area have focused mainly on studying the development of categorization of entities such as animals, vehicles, dogs, chairs, airplanes, and so on. There are important reasons for this bias. As described earlier, object labels (e.g., dog, car, ball) tend heavily to be represented in children's early vocabularies. However, these early object labels are often overextended, raising questions about whether children's first object categories are the same or different from those of adults.

Categorization can be applied more broadly, however, and it is clear that humans, and other animals, categorize entities other than physical objects. There is a long history of studying the categorization of speech sounds by infants and adults (e.g., Eimas, Siqueland, Jusczyk, & Vigorito, 1971; Kuhl, 1991; and see chap. 2). Many researchers have explicitly used categorization models to understand speech perception. Kuhl (1991), for example, has used the notion of prototypes to explain the processes of categorizing speech sounds. Lalonde and Werker (1995) have shown that infants' perception of speech sounds is related to infants' object categorization abilities. Jusczyk (chap. 2) has provided several examples of how infants' perception of speech and language can be seen as involving categorization processes. Moreover, he shows how the infants' categorizations of speech sounds are similar to and different from those of adults. Thus, categorization is a general ability that can be used in the auditory modality. Even within the visual modality, however, we form categories other than object categories. Quinn (chap. 3) provides a fine illustration of how the principles of categorization can be applied to the study of spatial relations in infancy. He shows how the development of infants' ability to form categories of spatial relations such as above and below is similar to infants' ability to form object categories.

Thus, categorization is, at one level, a general purpose cognitive ability that can be applied broadly in a variety of domains and modalities. Although there is some indication that the ability to categorize in different modalities is related, additional work needs to be undertaken to establish how categorization of different kinds of entities is related.

Methodological Issues

One of the primary challenges for researchers studying the development of categories and concepts in early development is to devise tasks that assess those cognitive skills. How do you get babies, who cannot communicate with language, to "tell you" how they perceive a certain stimulus? Or how do you get infants with a small productive vocabulary to "tell you" which part of a stimulus they interpret a new label as referring to? The chapters in this book provide many excellent examples of the ingenious solutions that researchers have devised to overcome this problem of assessing the development of categories and concepts in prelinguistic or newly linguistic children. One serious consideration for these researchers is whether behaviors across various tasks can be compared; for example, do different tasks tap fundamentally different processes? Or do the tasks tap the same underlying processes of categorization, and differences in results reflect other disparities? An additional consideration of import is how to interpret performance—often measured in terms of looking or playing time with a stimulus—in terms of mental "stuff"; for instance, if an infant puts model vehicles in one spatially distinct group and model animals in a separate group, at what level does the infant understand that the objects in each pile are the "same kind of thing"?

Given the inherent nature of these problems on research with infants and young children, it is hardly surprising that investigators using different tasks often obtain different (and conflicting) results and that diverging conclusions and theoretical views arise from quite similar data sets. This issue is not resolved and has been the topic of much recent discussion in the literature (Mandler, 2000; Oakes & Madole, 1999, 2000). These discussions are important and show how advances in the field in terms of the methods we use to assess a cognitive ability provide insight into the development of that skill. The challenge now is to try to understand what window to the young mind we are looking through when we use these different tasks, and how we can relate the findings from one task to the findings from other tasks. In the following paragraphs, we will briefly describe many of the major tasks used to assess categorization in infancy and early childhood. This brief introduction will provide a foundation for the more elaborate discussions of methods described in the individual chapters.

Methods Used in Infancy

A primary method used to examine infants' categorization has been the familiarization-test procedure. In this general procedure, infants first are shown a number of items from the same category and then their response to novel items is assessed. Many versions of the familiarization procedure have been developed and used to study categorization. Often infants are presented with pictures of category items and the duration of their looking at those items is recorded. For example, infants might be shown 12 pictures of different dogs for 10 seconds each, and then their looking at a novel dog and a novel cat is assessed; if infants look longer at the novel cat than at the novel dog, it is inferred that they have formed a category of dogs that excludes cats (see chap. 8 for a discussion of what habituation tasks tell us about categorization). Versions of this procedure have been employed presenting infants with photographs of category exemplars (e.g., Quinn, Eimas, & Rosenkrantz, 1993), schematic drawings of artificially constructed categories (e.g., Younger, 1985), or realistic plastic replicas of category instances (e.g., Mandler & McDonough, 1993; Oakes, Madole, & Cohen, 1991).

A large number of studies have used such procedures and have yielded an impressive body of research about infants' abilities to form and respond to categorical contrasts. Quinn, Eimas, and Rosenkrantz (1993), for example, used a familiarization procedure to show that 3- to 4-month-old infants will form categorical representations for basic-level classes that exclude other basic-level classes from the same superordinate domain (e.g., a category of dogs that excludes cats). Quinn (chap. 3) has also used this procedure to evaluate infants' spatial categorization. Younger (chap. 4; Younger & Cohen, 1986) has used variations of this procedure to assess older infants' use of correlated attributes to form categories of schematic animals. Thus, these types of paradigms have been quite successful at revealing infants' early categorization abilities.

Familiarization procedures also have been adapted to study other kinds of categorization. Jusczyk and Aslin (1995), for example, adapted the head-turn preference procedure to study how infants segment fluent speech. Infants first are familiarized with a stimulus for a fixed amount of time (e.g., 2 minutes of continuous speech) and then their preference for hearing a familiar aspect of that speech versus a novel aspect of that speech is observed. This procedure has been used to assess infants' attention to a variety of speech related distinctions (see chap. 2). The point is that familiarization procedures have yielded many important results related to our understanding of categorization in infancy.

Some have questioned whether familiarization procedures reveal the same kinds of categorization or conceptual process as the responding of older children and adults in labeling or sorting tasks (e.g., Gopnik & Nazzi, chap. 12; Mandler, 1988). In response to this criticism, a number of researchers have used the object manipulation or sequential-touching task (Mandler, 1988; Mandler et al., 1991; Rakison & Butterworth, 1998a, 1998b; Ricciuti, 1965) to assess categorization in infants. In this task, infants are presented with a number of objects—usually scale models—from two different categories and are allowed to play with them in any way they wish. The order of infants' touching to those items is recorded. Sequential touching to items from the same category is taken as indicative of systematic, category-driven behavior. This task has become increasingly popular for assessing categorization in the second year of life. Investigators have used variations of this procedure to assess, for example, the development of infants' attention to categories at different levels of exclusivity (Mandler, 1988; Mandler et al., 1991), infants' attention to object attributes during categorization (Rakison & Butterworth, 1998a, 1998b; Rakison & Cohen, 1999; chap. 7), and the relation of categorizing behavior to infants' other cognitive developments (Gopnik & Meltzoff, 1987, 1992). Although Mandler and colleagues (Mandler, 1988; Mandler et al., 1991) argued that the sequential touching task taps more conceptual processes than familiarization (because infants can actively handle, manipulate, and compare the items), others have argued that this task may involve the same general categorization processes as do familiarization tasks but require different information-processing demands (Oakes, Plumert, Lansink, & Merryman, 1996). Regardless of whether procedures like this tap into the same or different processes as familiarization and the precise nature of the category distinctions observed, this task has revealed important insight into developmental changes in how infants respond to categorical contrasts.

Other researchers have used operant conditioning to study categorization in infancy. Rovee-Collier and her colleagues, for example, have uncovered developmental changes between 3 and 7 months of life in the kinds of information infants use in forming categories by training infants to kick in response to the movement of a mobile (see Hayne, 1996, for a summary). In these studies, infants receive training when their leg is attached to a mobile: each time the infant kicks, the mobile moves. To study categorization, infants are trained with several different mobiles, and the rate of their kicking is measured. By evaluating to which mobiles infants generalize their kicking response, Rovee-Collier and her colleagues have gained insight into what kinds of information infants use when forming a category of those mobiles. For example, infants seem to include perceptually similar mobiles in a category.

Finally, Mandler and McDonough (1996, 1998; chap. 5) have recently developed the generalized imitation task to assess infants' understanding of categories. This task goes beyond asking which objects infants group into categories and evaluates the kinds of inferences they make about category exemplars. An experimenter uses props to show the infant a sequence of actions—for example, a dog taking a drink from a cup—and then the child is provided with a set of props to imitate the actions (e.g., the cup, a cat, and a truck). If infants infer that the cat will also drink from a cup (because it is an animal) but that the truck will not (because it is a vehicle), then they should more often make the cat drink from the cup. Indeed, this is exactly the kind of result Mandler and McDonough report (see chap. 5 for a review), and they have used such results to describe the kinds of conceptual categories apparently possessed by infants of different ages. Again, the basis of infants' responding in this task is not uncontroversial. Rakison (chap. 7), for example, argues that infants generalize the action to the exemplar that is most perceptually similar to the model (see also Oakes & Madole, 1999). Despite this controversy, this task is another tool that researchers can use to uncover the processes involved in category formation in infancy, and systematic evaluations of the basis of infants' generalizations in this task will add to our understanding of the development of classification in the first years of life.

There are, then, many different methods that have been developed to study categorization and conceptual development in infancy. As is clear from the chapters in the first part of this book, these inventive methods have yielded many interesting results and have added to our understanding of how categories and concepts develop in the first months of life. However, the chapters also make it clear that there is much disagreement about which methods are the best for assessing infants' category and concept development and about what exactly those methods assess. Questions have been posed about whether different methods assess the same underlying processes or different ones (Mandler, 2000; Oakes & Madole, 2000). Until these issues are resolved, the debates about how best to evaluate infants' categorization and conceptual development will continue.

Methods Used with Preschoolers

Once children acquire some level of language, either in terms of productive or comprehensive vocabulary, assessing their categorization and conceptual development can become a linguistic task. As is clear from the chapters in the second half of this book, most of the research on the kinds of categories and concepts young children form or possess depends on evaluating the kinds of objects to which they will extend novel labels. Despite this general approach, there are few standard tasks in the study of categorization and conceptual development in the preschool years.

One approach is to systematically evaluate the language children learn naturally and observe the kinds of extensions and overextensions they make. Mervis and her colleagues (chap. 10) provide an excellent example of this approach with a case-study design. Similarly, Smith and her colleagues (see chap. 11) have explored the kinds of words in children's early lexicons for insights into the kinds of categorical relations that children learn. For example, Samuelson and Smith (1999) found that solid objects that are organized by shape are overrepresented in the first nouns that children learn. Studies taking this approach have yielded important insight into conceptual development in the preschool years, and much of our understanding of categorization during this time has its foundation in this kind of work.

A more experimental approach is to teach children a new word or fact about an item, and then investigate how children will extend that word or fact to other items. For example, many studies have used some version of the task Susan Gelman developed in her now classic work on children's use of perceptual and conceptual cues in preschoolers' inferences about novel objects (e.g., Gelman & Markman, 1986). In this task, children are taught properties about exemplars and then they are shown one or more novel exemplars. The novel exemplars are designed to pit perceptual information against deeper-level conceptual information. So some of the novel exemplars look like the target item and some do not, some of the novel exemplars are given the same label as the target item and some are not. The question is: Do children use a common label or perceptual similarity to determine whether novel exemplars have a particular property? In the original study, for example, Gelman and Markman (1986) taught 4-year-old children facts about two different items (e.g., a tropical fish and a dolphin). Children were then asked which of those facts was true of a third object that looked like one of the original items (e.g., a shark) but that had the same label as the other item (e.g., "fish"). In other studies, children were taught a fact or label for only a single exemplar and then were asked to make inferences about multiple novel items that either did or did not look like the original item (Gelman & Markman, 1987). This procedure has been widely used to evaluate children's inferences about natural kinds and artifacts (Gelman & Markman, 1987), as well as social categories such as gender (Gelman, Collman, & Maccoby, 1986).

Variations of essentially this task have been used to assess different aspects of children's conceptual understanding. Keil (1989), for example, showed children and adults pictures of a category exemplar (e.g., a picture of a horse) and told them something about the nonobvious properties of that exemplar (e.g., that although it looked like a horse it had been born from cow parents and had the blood, bones, brains, and so on, of a cow). Five-year-olds attended to perceptual information and maintained that the animal was a horse, whereas adults attended to the internal features and maintained that the animal was a cow. The 9- and 11-year-olds' judgments fell in between the adults and the 5-year-olds. Gopnik and Nazzi (chap. 12) have used a different adaptation of the same basic procedure in which young children are taught that an object with a novel label also has some novel property (i.e., it makes a machine light up). Importantly, children in these studies are shown actual objects and the nonobvious property is demonstrated to the children (i.e., the object is placed on the machine, which then lights up). The main question is what other objects will children assume have the same label and thus presumably belong to the same category. Using this procedure, Gopnik and Nazzi pit perceptual cues against nonobvious ones, and they evaluate the conditions under which children make inferences about the nonobvious property.

As with the tasks used in infancy, questions have been raised about this general task (Jones & Smith, 1993). Investigators have shown that the kinds of inferences children make depend on a number of factors, such as how the stimuli are presented and how questions are asked (Deak & Bauer, 1996; Florian, 1994). Deak and Bauer (1996), for example, observed that presenting children with realistic 3-dimensional objects induced them to make more conceptual choices in this task. Thus, the kind of stimuli seems to affect young children's categorizing behavior, although further research is needed to fully understand the relation between the stimulus format and the kinds of inferences children make. Obviously, children can make conceptual inferences about pictures of objects, as has been shown in a number of studies by Gelman and her colleagues (Gelman & Markman, 1986, 1987). Massey and R. Gelman (1988) demonstrated that preschoolers who were shown pictures of objects understood that they were representations of real-world objects and did not respond to them as if they were merely 2-dimensional figures. Though this issue has been raised by a number of infancy researchers (e.g., Mandler, chap. 5; Oakes & Madole, 1999;

Rakison & Butterworth, 1998b), the implications of stimuli choice on preschooler's behavior remains an empirical question and needs to be addressed.

A different task used to test young children's extension of categories is the novel noun generalization task described in detail by Smith, Colunga, and Yoshida (chap. 11). In this task children are shown a novel item and this item is labeled using a novel name. Then, children are shown other new items and they are asked to indicate which of those new objects also have the same name as the original item. As Smith et al. (chap. 11) point out, children's responses in this task "provide insights into children's expectations about how nouns map to categories" (p. 276). This kind of procedure has been used to assess children's extensions of nouns to novel objects on the basis of shape and function (e.g., Gentner, 1978; Kemler Nelson, Russell, Duke, & Jones, 2000) and, because of the ease with which it can be administered, has been extensively used in cross-cultural studies (e.g., Imai, Gentner, & Uchida, 1994). Thus, this task is an extremely useful tool for understanding the relation between language and categorization. Indeed, based on the kinds of generalizations children make in the task, Smith and her colleagues (Landau, Smith, & Jones, 1992) have concluded that children organize kinds into animates, inanimate objects, and substances and that overall shape is a powerful cue for novel word generalization.

Despite this apparent uniformity in the methods researchers use, there are questions about how best to understand and assess children's responding in such tasks. As pointed out by Gopnik and Nazzi (chap. 12), the methodological and theoretical question of importance is how to determine whether children's categories include members that share a common, abstract ontological property. Often researchers interpret children's extension of a novel name to a novel object to mean that they infer that those novel objects have the same conceptual core as the original object (see chap. 13). However, because it is in many cases hard to unconfound perceptual and nonobvious cues, the basis for children's label extension is often not as clearcut as it may first appear. Thus, although the vast majority of the studies conducted with preschool-aged children have used some variation of a task in which researchers observe the extensions of children's object labels, the basis of such extension is debated and is often the focus of empirical investigation.

Connectionist Models

Researchers have begun to develop other methods for understanding the development of categories and concepts in infancy and early childhood. Computational modeling, for example, allows researchers to generate and test hypotheses about the underlying mechanisms of category and concept development. Recently, there has been an increase in the use of computational models to study the development of categorization in infancy and early childhood. Two excellent examples of this approach are provided by Mareschal (chap. 14) and Smith et al. (chap. 11).

Computational models provide a different kind of information about the developmental process underlying categorization, or more generally, underlying cognition. As pointed out by Mareschal (chap. 14), using computational models it is possible explicitly to formulate the information processing mechanisms that drive performance on a task. Specifically, computational models can provide an explanation of how information is processed to produce the observed behavior. Mareschal, French, and Quinn (2000), for example, showed that infants' ability to differentiate the categories of *dog* and *cat* was related to the distribution of particular features of the exemplars. By manipulating the kinds of information about those features available to a connectionist network, Mareschal et al. were able to model infants' responding in a standard familiarization task. Likewise, in line with Mandler's claims concerning the trajectory of category emergence, Quinn and Johnson (1997, 2000) showed that a simple connectionist simulation forms global categories such as animals, vehicles, and furniture before basic-level categories such as dog, cat, and car.

The chapters by Mareschal and Smith et al. provide evidence that connectionist models can account for the patterns of data obtained from children. Because connectionist models are simple associative learners, the categories formed by these networks are based solely on the statistical properties of experienced feature distributions. Thus, connectionist models can provide powerful demonstrations that developmental change can be modeled using a system that recognizes only statistical regularities. Such modeling is important, therefore, for showing that the kinds of developmental change observed in children can, in principle, be accomplished by applying relatively unsophisticated mechanisms for detecting regularities in the environment. Importantly, both Mareschal and Smith et al. also use these models to generate hypotheses for how children will perform in new circumstances. Thus, connectionist models are important not only for providing a possible mechanism for observed developmental changes but also for providing a means for generating new hypotheses for the development of categorization.

It must be borne in mind, however, that although connectionist models can be created that show that the patterns of results obtained from children can be accounted for by simple associative networks, these models do not demonstrate that these are *the* mechanisms actually responsible for developmental change in categorization and conceptual abilities (see chap. 15, for a discussion of the limitations of connectionist models for explaining conceptual development). Indeed, some theorists (e.g., Mandler, 2000) have argued against such models as providing explanations for developmental changes in children's behavior. However, connectionist models are useful as demonstrations of the minimum that is required to obtain specific patterns of behavior. Thus these methods are an important addition to our set of tools for understanding the early development of categories and concepts.

Conclusions

The chapters in this book provide insight into the state of our knowledge about the early development of categories and concepts. Several diverse theoretical positions are represented here, and thus many of the conclusions drawn will seem contradictory. However, it will become increasingly clear that the infants' world is not a "blooming, buzzing, confusion." Rather, from an early age infants are capable of organizing the information they acquire. These early organizations provide the foundation for children's ability to make inferences about the nonobvious properties of objects as well as the creation of increasingly complex systems of organization. Regardless of the particular theoretical perspective adopted by the authors in this book, each would agree that from an early age children have the ability to form categories and use those categories to organize and make sense of the world around them.

Despite the fact that we have been studying categorization in infancy and early childhood for over 20 years, there is little consensus about many aspects of the processes and representations involved. Questions continue to be debated about whether categorization early in life is related to, or is the foundation of, categorization later in life. Researchers disagree about the role of perceptual and nonobvious information in categorization at different points in development, have different opinions about the role of language in the process of categorization, and even disagree on what a methodological procedure can tell us about the behavior of infants and children. These issues are among the key themes of this book, and as each reader will find out for herself or himself, the chapters present often radically different points of view. The chapters in this book, therefore, also reveal that the field itself could be well described by James's classic phrase.

Acknowledgments

Preparation of this manuscript was supported, in part, by grant HD36060 awarded to Lisa Oakes by the National Institutes of Health. We thank Laura Namy and Larissa Samuelson for extremely helpful comments on drafts of this manuscript. Correspondence should be addressed to Lisa M. Oakes, Department of Psychology, University of Iowa, Iowa City, IA, 52240 (lisa-oakes@uiowa.edu), or David H. Rakison, Department of Psychology, Carnegie Mellon University, Pittsburgh, PA 15213 (rakison@andrew.cmu.edu).

References

Anglin, J. M. (1977). *Word, objects, and conceptual development.* New York: Norton.

Behl-Chadha, G. (1996). Basic-level and superordinate-like categorical representations early in infancy. *Cognition, 60,* 105–141.

Bruner, J. S., Goodnow, J. J., & Austin, G. A. (1956). *A study of thinking.* New York: Wiley.

Carey, S. (1985). *Conceptual change in childhood.* Cambridge, MA: MIT Press.

Choi, S., & Bowerman, M. (1991). Learning to express motion events in English and Korean: The influence of language-specific lexicalization patterns. *Cognition, 41,* 83–121.

Clark, E. V. (1973). What's in a word? On the child's acquisition of semantics in his first language. In T. E. Moore (Ed.), *Cognitive development and the acquisition of language* (pp. 65–110). New York: Academic Press.

Cohen, L. B., & Strauss, M. S. (1979). Concept acquisition in the human infant. *Child Development, 50,* 419–424.

Deak, G. O., & Bauer, P. J. (1996). The dynamics of preschoolers' categorization choices. *Child Development, 67,* 740–767.

Eimas, P. (1994). Categorization in early infancy and the continuity of development. *Cognition, 50,* 83–93.

Eimas, P. D., & Quinn, P. C. (1994). Studies on the formation of perceptually based basic-level categories in young infants. *Child Development, 65,* 903–917.

Eimas, P. D., Siqueland, E. R., Jusczyk, P., & Vigorito, J. (1971). Speech perception in infants. *Science, 171,* 303–306.

Florian, J. E. (1994). Stripes do not a zebra make, or do they? Conceptual and perceptual information in inductive inference. *Developmental Psychology, 30,* 88–101.

Gelman, S. A., Collman, P., & Maccoby, E. E. (1986). Inferring properties from categories versus inferring categories from properties: The case of gender. *Child Development, 57*, 396–404.

Gelman, S. A., & Markman, E. M. (1986). Categories and induction in young children. *Cognition, 23*, 183–209.

Gelman, S. A., & Markman, E. M. (1987). Young children's inductions from natural kinds: The role of categories and appearances. *Child Development, 58*, 1532–1541.

Gentner, D. (1978). What looks like a jiggy but acts like a zimbo: A study of early word meaning using artificial objects. *Papers and Reports on Language Development, 15*, 1–6.

Goldstone, R. L., & Barsalou, L. W. (1998). Reuniting perception and conception. *Cognition, 65*, 231–262.

Gopnik, A., & Meltzoff, A. (1987). The development of categorization in the second year and its relation to other cognitive and linguistic developments. *Child Development, 58*, 1523–1531.

Gopnik, A., & Meltzoff, A. N. (1992). Categorization and naming: Basic-level sorting in 18-month-olds and its relation to language. *Child Development, 63*, 1091–1103.

Hayne, H. (1996). Categorization in infancy. In C. Rovee-Collier & L. P. Lipsitt (Eds.), *Advances in infancy* (Vol. 10, pp. 79–120). Norwood, NJ: Ablex.

Imai, M., Gentner, D., & Uchida, N. (1994). Children's theories of word meaning: The role of shape similarity in early acquisition. *Cognitive Development, 9*, 45–75.

Jones, S. S., & Smith, L. B. (1993). The place of perception in children's concepts. *Cognitive Development, 8*, 113–139.

Jusczyk, P. W., & Aslin, R. N. (1995). Infants' detection of the sound patterns of words in fluent speech. *Cognitive Psychology, 29*, 1–23.

Keil, F. C. (1981). Constraints on knowledge and cognitive development. *Psychological Review, 88*, 197–227.

Keil, F. C. (1989). *Concepts, kinds, and cognitive development.* Cambridge, MA: MIT Press.

Keil, F. C. (1991). The emergence of theoretical beliefs as constraints on concepts. In S. Carey & R. Gelman (Eds.), *The epigenesis of mind* (pp. 133–169). Hillsdale, NJ: Erlbaum.

Kemler Nelson, D. G., Russell, R., Duke, N., & Jones, K. (2000). Two-year-olds will name artifacts by their functions. *Child Development, 71*, 1271–1288.

Kuhl, P. K. (1991). Human adults and human infants show a "perceptual magnet effect" for the prototypes of speech categories, monkeys do not. *Perception and Psychophysics, 50*, 93–107.

Lalonde, C. E., & Werker, J. F. (1995). Cognitive influences on cross-language speech perception in infancy. *Infant Behavior and Development, 18*, 459–475.

Landau, B., Smith, L. B., & Jones, S. S. (1992). Syntactic context and the shape bias in children's and adults' lexical learning. *Journal of Memory and Language, 51*, 807–825.

Madole, K. L., & Cohen, L. B. (1995). The role of object parts in infants' attention to form-function correlations. *Developmental Psychology, 31*, 317–332.

Madole, K. L., & Oakes, L. M. (1999). Making sense of infant categorization: Stable processes and changing representations. *Developmental Review, 19*, 263–296.

Mandler, J. M. (1988). How to build a baby: On the development of an accessible representational system. *Cognitive Development, 3*, 113–136.

Mandler, J. M. (1992). How to build a baby: II. Conceptual primitives. *Psychological Review, 99*, 587–604.

Mandler, J. M. (1997). Development of categorisation: Perceptual and conceptual categories. In G. E. S. Bremner, A. Slater, & G. Butterworth (Eds.), *Infant development: Recent advances* (pp. 163–189). Hove, UK: Psychology Press.

Mandler, J. M. (2000). Perceptual and conceptual processes in infancy. *Journal of Cognition and Development, 1,* 3–36.

Mandler, J. M., & Bauer, P. J. (1988). The cradle of categorization: Is the basic level basic? *Cognitive Development, 3,* 247–264.

Mandler, J. M., Bauer, P. J., & McDonough, L. (1991). Separating the sheep from the goats: Differentiating global categories. *Cognitive Psychology, 23,* 263–298.

Mandler, J. M., & McDonough, L. (1993). Concept formation in infancy. *Cognitive Development, 8,* 281–318.

Mandler, J. M., & McDonough, L. (1996). Drinking and driving don't mix: Inductive generalization in infancy. *Cognition, 59,* 307–335.

Mandler, J. M., & McDonough, L. (1998). Studies in inductive inference in infancy. *Cognitive Psychology, 23,* 60–96.

Mareschal, D., French, R. M., & Quinn, P. C. (2000). A connectionist account of asymmetric category learning in early infancy. *Developmental Psychology, 36,* 635–645.

Margolis, E. (1994). A reassessment of the shift from classical theory of concepts to prototype theory. *Cognition, 51,* 73–89.

Markman, E. M. (1989). *Categorization and naming in children: Problems of induction.* Cambridge, MA: MIT Press.

Massey, C. M., & Gelman, R. (1988). Preschoolers' ability to decide whether a photographed unfamiliar object can move itself. *Developmental Psychology, 24,* 307–317.

Medin, D. L., & Ortony, A. (1989). Psychological essentialism. In S. Vosniadou & A. Ortony (Eds.), *Similarity and analogical reasoning* (pp. 179–195). New York: Cambridge University Press.

Mervis, C. B. (1984). Early lexical development: The contributions of mother and child. In C. Sophian (Ed.), *Origins of cognitive skills* (pp. 339–370). Hillsdale, NJ: Erlbaum.

Mervis, C. B. (1987). Child-basic object categories and early lexical development. In U. Neisser (Ed.), *Concepts and conceptual development: Ecological and intellectual factors in categorization* [Emory Symposia in Cognition], (pp. 201–233). New York: Cambridge University Press.

Mervis, C. B., & Crisafi, M. A. (1982). Order of acquisition of subordinate-, basic, and superordinate-level categories. *Child Development, 53,* 258–266.

Mervis, C. B., & Rosch, E. (1981). Categorization of natural objects. *Annual Review of Psychology, 32,* 89–115.

Murphy, G. L., & Medin, D. L. (1985). The role of theories in conceptual coherence. *Psychological Review, 92,* 289–316.

Neisser, U. (1987). From direct perception to conceptual structure. In U. Neisser (Ed.), *Concepts and conceptual development: Ecological and intellectual factors in categorization* [Emory Symposia in Cognition], (pp. 11–24). New York: Cambridge University Press.

Oakes, L. M., & Madole, K. L. (1999). From seeing to thinking: Reply to Mandler. *Developmental Review, 19,* 307–318.

Oakes, L. M., & Madole, K. L. (2000). The future of infant categorization research: A process-oriented approach. *Child Development, 71,* 119–126.

Oakes, L. M., Madole, K. L., & Cohen, L. B. (1991). Infant habituation and categorization of real objects. *Cognitive Development, 6,* 337–392.

Oakes, L. M., Plumert, J. M., Lansink, J. M., & Merryman, J. D. (1996). Evidence for task-dependent categorization in infancy. *Infant Behavior and Development, 19,* 425–440.

Quinn, P. C., & Eimas, P. D. (1996). Young infants' use of facial information in the categorical differentiation of natural animal species: The effect of inversion. *Infant Behavior and Development, 19,* 381–384.

Quinn, P. C., & Eimas, P. D. (1997). A reexamination of the perceptual-to-conceptual shift in mental representations. *Review of General Psychology, 1,* 171–187.

Quinn, P. C., Eimas, P. D., & Rosenkrantz, S. L. (1993). Evidence for repesentations of perceptually similar categoires by 3-month-old and 4-month-old infants. *Perception, 22,* 463–475.

Quinn, P. C., & Johnson, M. H. (1997). The emergence of perceptual categorization in young infants: A connectionist analysis. *Journal of Experimental Child Psychology, 66,* 236–263.

Quinn, P. C., & Johnson, M. H. (2000). Global-before-basic object categorization in connectionist networks and 2-month-old infants. *Infancy, 1,* 31–46.

Rakison, D. H., & Butterworth, G. E. (1998a). Infants' attention to object structure in early categorization. *Developmental Psychology, 34,* 1310–1325.

Rakison, D. H., & Butterworth, G. E. (1998b). Infants' use of object parts in early categorization. *Developmental Psychology, 34,* 49–62.

Rakison, D. H., & Cohen, L. B., (1999). Infants' use of functional parts in basic-like categorization. *Developmental Science, 2,* 423–432.

Rakison, D. H., & Poulin-Dubois, D. (2001). Developmental origin of the animate-inanimate distinction. *Psychological Bulletin, 127,* 209–228.

Rakison, D. H., & Poulin-Dubois, D. (in press). You go this way and I'll go that way: Developmental changes in infants' attention to correlations among dynamic features in motion events. *Child Development.*

Ricciuti, H. N. (1965). Object grouping and selective ordering behavior in infants 12 to 24 months old. *Merrill Palmer Quarterly, 11,* 129–148.

Rosch, E. (1978). Principles of categorization. In E. Rosch & B. Lloyd (Eds.), *Cognition and categorization* (pp. 27–48). Hillsdale, NJ: Erlbaum.

Rosch, E., Mervis, C. B., Gray, W. D., Johnson, D. M., & Boyes-Braem, P. (1976). Basic objects in natural categories. *Cognitive Psychology, 8,* 382–439.

Samuelson, L. K., & Smith, L. B. (1999). Early noun vocabularies: Do ontology, category structure and syntax correspond? *Cognition, 73,* 1–33.

Smith, E. E. (1995). Concepts and categorization. In E. E. Smith & D. N. Osherson (Eds.), *Thinking: An invitation to cognitive science,* (2nd ed., Vol. 3, pp. 3–33). Cambridge, MA: MIT Press.

Spalding, T. L., & Murphy, G. L. (1996). Effects of background knowledge on category construction. *Journal of Experimental Psychology: Learning, Memory, and Cognition, 22,* 525–538.

Tversky, B., & Hemenway, K. (1984). Objects, parts, and categories. *Journal of Experimental Psychology: General, 113,* 169–191.

Wellman, H. M., & Gelman, S. A. (1988). Children's understanding of the non-obvious. In R. Sternberg (Ed.), *Advances in the psychology of human intelligence* (Vol. 4, pp. 99–135). Hillsdale, NJ: Erlbaum.

Whorf, B. L. (1956). *Language, thought, and reality: Selected writings of Benjamin Lee Whorf* [Edited by John B. Carroll]. Cambridge, MA: MIT Press.

Younger, B. A. (1985). The segregation of items into categories by 10-month-old infants. *Child Development, 56,* 1574–1583.

Younger, B. A., & Cohen, L. B. (1986). Developmental changes in infants' perception of correlations among attributes. *Child Development, 57,* 803–815.

PART ONE

Concepts and Categories before the Emergence of Language

CHAPTER TWO

Chunking Language Input to Find Patterns

Peter W. Jusczyk

Prior to the first studies of infant speech perception, the primary question for researchers was: How do infants come to perceive differences between speech sounds? Knowledge of infants' perceptual abilities, in general, was extremely limited; knowledge of their speech perception capacities was nonexistent. In a little more than 30 years, a great deal has been learned about infants' capacities for perceiving speech. Indeed, it is fair to say that today most investigators are not so interested in the nature of infants' perceptual capacities as they are in understanding how these capacities are used in acquiring language. Yet, although the focus in infant speech research has shifted from trying to identify perceptual capacities to understanding the use of these capacities in language acquisition, the primary goal is still to determine how infants make sense of their linguistic input. How do they discover the regularities that underlie the language spoken in their environment? Necessarily, categorization abilities are critical to infants' efforts to apprehend the structural organization of their native language. Detecting regularities requires some means of recognizing when different instances of the same pattern occur in the input. Similarly, determining the frequency with which certain patterns appear in the input depends on a prior ability to recognize and remember these patterns.

In this chapter, I focus on the nature of infants' speech perception capacities and how these capacities are used in acquiring different aspects of native language structure. Although speech perception capacities are clearly important for acquiring the sound structure of one's native language, they also seem to play a significant supporting role in discovering the grammatical organization of the language. Moreover, in each of these domains, a similar developmental process appears. Infants' first categorizations of the input only approximate those used by fluent users of the language. Still, they provide a starting point for making sense of the input, and for noting the frequency with which certain patterns appear. The grounding that these initial categories provide, together with further experience with the input, eventually enables learners to discover more subtle regularities and to refine their categories to conform to those of fluent users of the language. The similarities manifested in the nature of the initial categorization schemes used by infants acquiring different languages are consistent with the view that these starting points are innately given, and that developing the correct categorization of one's native language input is a form of innately guided learning (Gould & Marler, 1987; Jusczyk, 1997; Jusczyk & Bertoncini, 1988; Marler, 1990; Rauschecker & Marler, 1987).

Categorizing Speech Sounds

The issue that was at the heart of many of the first studies of speech perception by infants concerned their ability to perceive contrasts in speech sounds that belong to different phonemic categories, such as /b/ and /p/ in English. Prior research had revealed an interesting phenomenon in the way that adults perceive differences between certain phonemes. Perception of certain contrasts, such as /b/ versus /p/, is said to be categorical, in that sounds belonging to different phonemic categories are easily distinguished, whereas sounds belonging to the same phonemic category are poorly discriminated (Abramson & Lisker, 1967; Liberman, Cooper, Shankweiler, & Studdert-Kennedy, 1967; Liberman, Harris, Kinney, & Lane, 1961; Studdert-Kennedy, Liberman, Harris, & Cooper, 1970). This tendency for speech sound differences to be discriminable only when they belong to different phonemic categories stood in contrast to distinctions on many other acoustic dimensions where the ability to discriminate differences far exceeds listeners' abilities to assign these sounds to separate categories (Miller, 1956; Miller, Heise, & Lichten, 1951). Thus, when Eimas and his colleagues began to study infant speech perception abilities, they were interested in not only whether infants as young as 1 month could discriminate a contrast between /ba/ and /pa/ but also whether discrimination of this contrast was categorical or not (Eimas, Siqueland, Jusczyk, & Vigorito, 1971). In fact, Eimas et al. found that while 1-month-olds discriminated the subtle voicing contrast that distinguishes /ba/ from /pa/, they showed no ability to distinguish comparable voicing differences between different instances of /pa/ (or /ba/). Consequently, Eimas et al. argued that the origins of categorical perception of speech contrasts were innately determined.

Subsequent investigations revealed that young infants are capable of discriminating a wide range of speech sound contrasts along phonemic dimensions other than voicing. For example, studies confirmed that infants could discriminate place-of-articulation contrasts such as /b/ versus /d/ (Eimas, 1974; Morse, 1972) and manner-of-articulation contrasts such as /r/ and /l/ (Eimas, 1975) and /w/ and /y/ (Hillenbrand, Minifie, & Edwards, 1979). Moreover, the findings suggested that, like adults, infants' discrimination of contrasts involving consonants is categorical. By comparison, adults' and infants' discrimination of contrasts involving vowels, such as the ones in "beet" and "bit," is *continuous*, in that differences between different instances of the same vowel are discriminated (Fry, Abramson, Eimas, & Liberman, 1962; Swoboda, Morse, & Leavitt, 1976).

These early investigations produced much evidence of young infants' abilities to discriminate a wide range of speech contrasts. However, they also demonstrated that infants' discrimination abilities are limited in an interesting way. Namely, they discriminate some types of contrasts along a phonemic dimension such as voicing but not others. Consider the case of the infants that Eimas et al. tested. Their greatest sensitivity to voicing differences occurred in the vicinity of where English-speaking adults locate the phonemic boundary between /b/ and /p/. Given only these facts, it is tempting to conclude that infants are born with phonemic categories. However, a consideration of findings from other studies indicates that the situation is much more complicated than this.

The notion that categorical perception is unique to speech processing came under attack from two different directions: animal research and studies of nonspeech processing (Harnad, 1987). Kuhl and Miller (1975; Kuhl, 1981) demonstrated that chinchillas exposed to a continuum of speech sounds appear to display categorical perception of these sounds. This finding suggested that the neurological underpinnings of categorical perception may be a general property of how mammalian auditory systems process these types of signals rather than an outcome of a specialized adaptation for speech processing. Additional support for this view came from further studies with adult humans in which categorical perception was shown to occur for a variety of different types of nonspeech stimuli (Miller, Weir, Pastore, Kelly, & Dooling, 1976; Pastore et al., 1977; Pisoni, 1977). For example, Pisoni asked listeners to categorize a series of two-component tones in which the onset of one tone was varied in relation to the other. Listeners displayed abrupt changes in their labeling of these stimuli and showed peaks in their discrimination functions at these category boundaries, suggesting categorical perception of these stimuli. Moreover, infants, too, exhibited categorical perception for certain types of nonspeech sounds, suggesting that this type of processing is present from the outset (Jusczyk, Pisoni, Reed, Fernald, & Myers, 1983; Jusczyk, Pisoni, Walley, & Murray, 1980; Jusczyk, Rosner, Reed, & Kennedy, 1989). Jusczyk et al. (1980) tested infants on the two-component tone stimuli used by Pisoni (1977) and found that infants discriminated these stimuli categorically.

Thus, by now, it is a generally accepted fact that categorical perception is not unique to speech processing by humans. However, although categorical perception may not be confined to speech processing, the mechanisms responsible for the categorical perception of speech sounds in humans need not be the same as those responsible for categorical perception of nonspeech sounds or for the categorical perception of speech by nonhumans. Not all phenomena that occur in the processing of speech sounds have been shown to have an analog in nonspeech processing. One such example is "duplex perception," whereby listeners, presented with an isolated third formant transition from a syllable in one ear and the remainder of the syllable in the other ear, report hearing both a complete syllable and a tone (Liberman & Whalen, 2000). In other words, the third formant transition appears to be processed simultaneously as a speech sound and a nonspeech. Infants, too, appear to show duplex perception for these types of stimuli (Eimas & Miller, 1992). In any case, the issue of whether the underlying basis for categorical perception is specific to speech processing or not is orthogonal to the issue of whether infants' phonemic categories are equivalent to those of adults. Infants clearly begin with some ability to categorize different speech sounds, regardless of whether the underlying mechanisms for this are specific to speech processing or to auditory processing in general.

In fact, there is considerable evidence to suggest that infants' categorization of speech sounds does differ substantially from that of mature speakers of the same language. First of all, early studies of adult speech processing revealed clear and significant differences in the location of phonemic category boundaries for speakers of different languages (Lisker & Abramson, 1970). By comparison, studies with infants under 6 months of age indicate that infants exposed to different languages appear to have very similar category boundaries for speech sound contrasts, even when their native languages have very different phonemic category boundary locations (Lasky, Syrdal-Lasky, & Klein, 1975; Streeter, 1976). Thus, Lasky et al. found that Spanish-learning infants seemed to observe a category boundary for voicing contrasts that corresponds to that of English learners, even though the category boundary for Spanish-speaking adults is at another location. Clearly, then, the category boundary for voicing contrasts that Spanish-learning infants begin with differs from the one that they will end up with as Spanish-speaking adults. What accounts for the shift in the voicing boundary location during development? As Lisker (1986) has elegantly shown, many different acoustic features can be used in specifying voicing contrasts. It seems likely that experience with input from their particular native language leads infants to give greater weight to some features over others (Jusczyk, 1993, 1997). In effect, experience works to tune infants' initial categories to those of adult speakers of their native language (Aslin, 1981).

How might such tuning occur? One necessary component of this process is the ability to store information about the instances of speech sounds that one has encountered. An ability to remember details about speech sounds that one has heard is a prerequisite for learning about the distribution of particular speech sounds in the input. There are indications that even 2-month-olds can retain information about the speech sounds that they hear, at least for brief intervals (Jusczyk, Jusczyk, Kennedy, Schomberg, & Koenig, 1995; Jusczyk, Kennedy, & Jusczyk, 1995; Jusczyk, Pisoni, & Mullennix, 1992). By 8 to 9 months, infants display evidence of learning about distributional patterns that are present in speech input (Jusczyk, Cutler, & Redanz, 1993; Jusczyk, Friederici, Wessels, Svenkerud, & Jusczyk, 1993; Jusczyk, Luce, & Charles Luce, 1994; Saffran, Aslin, & Newport, 1996), as well as retention of particular words that they hear frequently (Jusczyk & Hohne, 1997). Thus, these findings indicate that infants are able to store and remember the kind of information that is needed to reorganize their speech sound categories. Recently, Maye and Gerken (2000) have shown that sensitivity to the frequency distribution of speech tokens can play a role in how adult learners impute phonemic category boundaries.

Experience with native language input begins to exert its influence on infants' categorization of speech sounds during the second half of the first year. During this period, as infants show gains in their knowledge of their native language's sound organization (Friederici & Wessels, 1993; Jusczyk, Cutler, et al., 1993; Jusczyk, Friederici, et al., 1993), their ability to discriminate certain nonnative speech contrasts declines (Best, Lafleur, & McRoberts, 1995; Tsushima et al., 1994; Werker & Lalonde, 1988; Werker & Tees, 1984). In addition, some findings suggest that by

6 months, infants have begun to develop representations of prototypical instances of native language vowel categories (Grieser & Kuhl, 1989; Kuhl, 1991; Kuhl, Williams, Lacerda, Stevens, & Lindblom, 1992) and that experience with maternal input plays a critical role in developing these representations (Kuhl et al., 1997). The bases for the latter claims are asymmetries that are observed in the perception of certain vowel contrasts (i.e., "perceptual magnet effects"). Specifically, listeners are less likely to discriminate contrasts between a prototypical instance and another exemplar of the category than they are to discriminate the same exemplar from a more peripheral instance of the category (Kuhl, 1991). However, the source and robustness of these perceptual asymmetries in adult studies have been seriously questioned (Iverson & Kuhl, 1995; Lively & Pisoni, 1997; Sussman & Lauckner-Morano, 1995; Thyer, Hickson, & Dodd, 2000). Moreover, there are some reports that infants display these asymmetries for vowel contrasts that are not present in their native language (Polka & Bohn, 1996). Consequently, it is not clear whether these perceptual asymmetries are the result of experience with language input or attributable to the basic structure of the human auditory processing system.

Whether the experience with native language input during the first year is sufficient to tune infants' categories fully to the phonemic categories used by adult speakers of the language is not clear at this point. Critical information is lacking about a number of aspects of infants' categories for speech sounds. For instance, despite the efforts of many speech researchers, we still lack evidence regarding infants' identification of different speech sounds from a speech continuum, such as voicing. As opposed to studies with adults in which data are gathered on both the identification and discrimination of speech sounds, inferences about categorical perception by infants have been based exclusively on data about the discrimination of speech sound contrasts. The absence of reliable data from infants about the identification of speech sounds is attributable to the lack of suitable testing procedures. Burnham, Earnshaw, and Clark (1991) attempted to provide identification data for infants, but their results are uninterpretable because infants' performance on the endpoints of their voicing continuum were at chance. Thus, we still do not know whether infants' categorical discrimination of speech sound contrasts is matched by sharp changes in their identification of these speech sounds.

Another critical aspect of phonemic perception for which we lack important information concerns infants' responses to different acoustic manifestations of the same phoneme. Although there is evidence that infants cope with the acoustic variability in utterances of the same phoneme spoken by different talkers (Jusczyk, Pisoni, et al., 1992; Kuhl, 1979, 1983) or at different speaking rates (Miller & Eimas, 1983), not much is known about how they respond to the different variants of the same phoneme (i.e. allophones) spoken in different phonetic contexts. For instance, the English phoneme /t/ is marked by different acoustic variants depending on its immediate surrounding environment in a word. At the beginning of a word, the English /t/ is represented by an aspirated sound [tʰ], but when it occurs before an /r/ it is a retroflexed sound [t8]. When /t/ occurs at the end of a word or after a syllable-initial /s/, it is represented by an unaspirated sound [t]. When do infants begin to treat these different allophones as instances of the same English phoneme, /t/? Pegg and Werker (1997) have attempted to address this issue in a study that examined infants' ability to discriminate two different allophones of the same phoneme. They found that younger infants (6–8 months) discriminated this contrast but older infants (10–12 months) did not. They interpreted this finding as an indication that the older infants had categorized the two allophones as variants of the same phoneme. Other data indicate that 10.5-month-olds are able to use information about differences between allophones of the same phoneme as a cue to the location of word boundaries in fluent speech (Jusczyk, Hohne, & Bauman, 1999). Although the data from these two studies are suggestive, a clearer indication that infants are beginning to form adultlike phonemic categories would be to show that they treat all the various allophones of some phoneme as belonging to the same category. A task requiring infants to make the same response to each occurrence of a phoneme would be one way to demonstrate that they have developed the phonemic category of their native language.

Therefore, the available data indicate that while infants are born with the ability to begin categorizing different speech sounds, their categories are not identical to those of the native language. Still, infants' initial categorization of speech sounds allows them to begin learning about the particular speech sound categories that are represented in their native language (which ones occur often in the input and which ones do not). Furthermore, their capacity to retain sufficiently detailed information about speech sounds present in the input provides them with the means to begin to align their categories more precisely to the particular categories used in their native language.

Finding the Right Rhythm

The initial studies of infant speech perception capacities focused on how infants processed rather fine-grained features of the speech signal (i.e., information about phonemic contrasts). The demonstration of infants' excellent capacities for discriminating such minimal differences in speech sounds might lead to the view that infants are focused on fine-grained differences to the exclusion of larger units of organization that are present in fluent speech. However, were infants focused only on elementary speech sounds to the exclusion of larger units of organization, then it is difficult to see how they could succeed in distinguishing utterances in one language from those of another without a great deal of prior experience. An infant focused on which phonetic segments are present in the input would eventually come to recognize the familiar set of elements that occur in the native language, and consequently treat utterances with phonetic segments outside this set as belonging to a different language. But there is evidence that even newborn infants show some ability to discriminate utterances in one language from those of another (Mehler et al., 1988). Thus infants appear to be sensitive to patterns that occur among larger units of linguistic organization and to have some ability to categorize the input in this way. In particular, even newborns appear to be sensitive to broad categories in the rhythmic organization of languages. Once again, the categorization that infants begin with is less than a fully developed categorization of the rhythmic properties of their native language. However, this initial categorization of the input is the foundation for learning about the specific properties of the rhythmic organization of their native language.

Many infants in the world are raised in environments where they are likely to hear more than one language spoken frequently. On the surface, this situation presents a difficult problem for language learners, namely, how are they able to keep utterances spoken in one of these languages separate from those of another language? A failure to do so would likely be disastrous for extracting the right set of generalizations about the underlying organization of a particular language. Infants growing up in such multilingual environments do not appear to have any special difficulty in acquiring language, so they must have some way of correctly separating utterances from different languages.

Mehler and his colleagues began to explore this issue in an investigation with French newborns and American 2-month-olds (Mehler et al., 1988). They made recordings of two fluent bilingual speakers, one of whom spoke French and Russian, the other of whom spoke Italian and English. Then they examined whether infants exposed to excerpts of narratives produced by a given speaker in each of her languages would notice a change from one language to the other. Because the samples changed from trial to trial and the speaker always remained the same, the only way that infants could detect a change in the languages was if they extracted out the common properties shared by utterances in a particular language. The French and American infants did discriminate utterances in their native language from those in the other language. Potentially the infants could have been using a number of different properties to discriminate the utterances of one language from the other (e.g., differences in the inventories of phonetic elements, the sequences of segments that are permissible, and prosodic properties such as rhythm, pitch contours, and intonation patterns). To narrow down the possible sources of information that infants might use, Mehler et al. also tested infants on low-pass filtered versions of these samples. Low-pass filtering serves to eliminate most of the information about phonetic segments, while leaving intact prosodic properties. The infants were still able to discriminate the utterances from the two languages, suggesting that prosodic properties of the utterances contain sufficient information to distinguish them.

To determine how widespread infants' abilities are to distinguish utterances from different languages, Mehler et al. also tested the French newborns on the English and Italian samples and the American 2-month-olds on the French and Russian samples. Neither group appeared to discriminate the contrasts involving two nonnative languages. However, a subsequent reanalysis of the data indicated that the French newborns did give some evidence of discriminating the English and Italian samples, although the American infants did not discriminate the French and Russian utterances (Mehler & Christophe, 1995). Mehler and Christophe suggested that the newborns may have been using rhythmic differences between English and Italian to discriminate the utterances but, by 2 months, English learners may have already been tuned in more closely to the rhythmic patterns of their native language.

Although other studies further documented infants' abilities to discriminate utterances from different languages (Bahrick & Pickens, 1988; Dehaene-Lambertz & Houston, 1998; Moon, Cooper, & Fifer, 1993), the issue of infants' use of rhythmic properties to discriminate utterances from different languages was not directly addressed until an investigation by Nazzi, Bertoncini, and Mehler (1998). The starting point for their study was linguists' classification of linguistic rhythms into three general categories: stress-timed, syllable-timed, and mora-timed. Languages such as English and Dutch, which alternate strong syllables (ones containing full vowels) and weak syllables (ones with reduced vowels), are considered to be stress-timed, whereas languages such as Spanish and Italian, in which each syllable receives equal stress, are said to be syllable-timed. Languages such as Japanese and Tamil are considered to be mora-timed. The mora is a rhythmic unit that can either be syllabic or subsyllabic. In English, a mora roughly corresponds to a CV syllable with a short vowel (e.g. "the" as opposed to "thee," which has a long vowel, or to "them," which ends with a consonant. Consequently, even though they are both monosyllabic words, "thee" and "them" have two moras). Nazzi et al. hypothesized that infants might begin with an ability to distinguish two languages when they belong to different rhythmic classes, even when neither language is the native language that they are learning. Consistent with their hypothesis, they found that French newborns discriminated two languages from different rhythmic classes (e.g., English from Japanese) but not two languages from the same rhythmic class (e.g., English from Dutch). As a further check on their hypothesis, they conducted an additional experiment in which they mixed utterances from two different languages and tested whether infants discriminated these from a mixture of utterances from two other languages. For one group of infants, the utterances were chosen from languages within the same rhythmic class (i.e., English and Dutch vs. Italian and Spanish); for the other group, the mixed utterances were chosen from languages that did not belong to the same rhythmic class (i.e., English and Italian vs. Dutch and Spanish). Only the former group gave evidence of discriminating the utterances. Thus, when there was a rhythmic basis for discriminating the utterances, the newborns were successful; otherwise they were not.

Not only are newborns able to discriminate utterances from two languages belonging to different rhythmic classes, but their ability for discriminating utterances from different languages is also limited to this particular situation. For example, Christophe and Morton (1998) found that 2-month-olds displayed no ability to discriminate two languages from the same rhythmic class, even when one of these was the native language. Hence, British infants did not distinguish English from Dutch utterances. Thus, with respect to their ability to categorize utterances from different languages, newborns appear to begin with a broad categorization that allows them to distinguish the major rhythmic classes but not to make distinctions among languages belonging to the same class.

How might infants' abilities to discriminate different languages develop? One possibility is that infants simply get better at discriminating languages from within the same rhythmic class, even ones outside the one that the native language belongs to. A second possibility is that infants become sensitive to the rhythmic features of languages within the native language rhythmic class. That is, they learn something about the possible range of variation of languages from within that rhythmic class that permits them to distinguish any two languages within this class. A third possibility is that they learn something much more specific about the particular rhythmic properties and organization of their native language, which then allows them to distinguish utterances in it from utterances in other languages within this rhythmic class. What is learned in this case is similar to what one learns about the phonemic categories in one's native language. In particular, one learns about the specific organization of the language. In fact, recent findings suggest that the developmental pattern most resembles this third possibility.

Infants first display some ability to distinguish between languages belonging to the same rhythmic class between 4 and 5 months of age. Bosch and Sebastián-Gallés (1997) tested the abilities of infants from Barcelona to discriminate a number of different language pairs. As in earlier investigations, the infants had no difficulty in discriminating two languages from different rhythmic classes. However, in contrast to the British 2-month-olds tested by Christophe and Morton (1998), these older infants were also able to discriminate between their native language and another language from the same rhythmic class. Specifically, the infants discriminated Spanish and Catalan, both of which are syllable-timed languages.

More information about older infants' abilities to discriminate languages from within the same rhythmic class comes from an investigation by Nazzi, Jusczyk, and Johnson (2000). In particular, Nazzi et al. found that American 5-month-olds' abilities to discriminate two languages from within the same rhythmic class were limited to the class that included the native language. Thus, these English learners did not discriminate Spanish from Italian, although they did discriminate English from Dutch. Perhaps even more surprising, these infants displayed an ability to distinguish their own native dialect of English (i.e., American English) from another dialect (British English). Next, Nazzi et al. sought to determine whether these infants' abilities were a reflection of the specific knowledge that they had acquired about the rhythmic properties of their native language or a more general knowledge of the range of variation of languages in the stress-timed rhythmic class. Therefore, they tested infants on a pair of unfamiliar languages from this rhythmic class, German and Dutch. This time the infants showed no evidence of discriminating the languages. Thus, the ability to discriminate utterances from languages within a rhythmic class appears to be tied to infants' knowledge of their native language. Infants appear to learn about the specific rhythmic structure and organization of the native language that they are acquiring. Indeed, what they do learn about these rhythmic features is sufficiently specific to allow them to distinguish their own native dialect from that of another dialect of the same language.

Consequently, infants observed in a variety of different language learning environments seem to begin with the same general ability to discriminate among the major rhythmic classes of languages. Nevertheless, these initial abilities to categorize languages according to their rhythmic class is not sufficiently precise for distinguishing among languages within the same class. However, as experience with native language input increases, infants begin to learn about the specific rhythmic properties and organization of their native language, which then allows them to distinguish it from other languages within the same rhythmic class. That experience with specific language input is a critical factor in refining this ability is shown by the fact that infants display little ability to distinguish between two unfamiliar languages belonging to the same rhythmic class, even when these are from the same rhythmic class as the native language.

Solving the Word Segmentation Problem

Languages differ considerably in the nature of the forms that their words take. In a language like Sesotho, a word must have at least two syllables. By comparison, English has words that are only a single syllable long, such as *long*. In English, the syntactic role that a content word plays in a sentence does not affect the form of the word; *cat* remains *cat* regardless of whether it is the subject, the direct object, indirect object, or object of a preposition in a sentence. In a Semitic language, such as Hebrew, the consonants in the root of the word remain more or less the same, but the vowels change. Other languages, such as Polish, add different endings to words as they change their syntactic roles. A natural implication of the differences that exist in word forms in different languages is that learners have to discover what the appropriate word forms are for their language. In processing native language input, learners have to determine what the elementary forms are that convey meanings in that language. This, too, is a categorization problem; one that involves not only deciding what the right-sized unit is but also determining whether there are alternative forms (i.e., allomorphs) that are tied to the same meaning. In this case, learners must detect the structural regularities in the input that correspond to the word forms, a problem that is complicated by the fact that words usually occur in multiword utterances.

When reading written language, it is easy to forget about the difficulties that fluent speech presents for identifying what the individual words are that make up an utterance. Words arrayed on a page have convenient spaces between them, making it easy to determine where one word ends and another begins. However, in fluent speech, there are rarely pauses between successive words. We are not often aware of this when listening to our native language because we have learned to use information in the speech signal to tell us where the word boundaries are. However, when we listen to speech in an unfamiliar language, it is difficult to locate the boundaries between successive words. Our difficulty in the latter case is attributable to the fact that the reliable markers of word boundaries in one language are not necessarily the same as those in another language. Consequently, acquiring a language necessarily involves learning what the appropriate word boundary markers are for that language.

Most words that infants hear are produced not in isolation but in the context of other words in multiword utterances (van de Weijer, 1998; Woodward & Aslin, 1990). Hence, in order to learn the vocabulary of their native language, infants must develop some ability to correctly segment words from fluent speech. By now, there is considerable evidence that this process begins at the point at which infants are learning about the specific organization of the sound structure of their native language. Moreover, as in the other cases of categorization discussed in the preceding two sections, infants' first attempts to segment the speech stream and categorize the word forms are rather crude approximations of those used by fluent perceivers of the language. Nevertheless, these initial attempts at deriving the appropriate word form categories allow infants to acquire the additional information needed to become efficient at recovering words from the speech stream. The categorization problem in this context is to correctly determine which types of sound patterns in the speech stream correspond to the words of the language.

For many years, little was known about how or when infants begin to segment words from fluent speech. Research on this issue was hampered by the lack of suitable test procedures to study how infants segment fluent speech. Most of the early test procedures were designed to present only brief stimuli, consisting of several syllables. However, when the headturn preference procedure was developed, investigators were able to present long passages of speech on a given test trial. Jusczyk and Aslin (1995) then adapted the procedure to investigate infants' word segmentation abilities. In one experiment, they familiarized English-learning 7.5-month-olds with repetitions of a pair of isolated words (*cup* and *dog* or *feet* and *bike*) on alternating trials. Then they presented infants with four different test passages, two of which contained one of the words that they had been familiarized with and two of which did not. The 7.5-month-olds listened significantly longer to the passages that contained the familiarized words, suggesting that they were able to recognize these words in the passages. Furthermore, even when infants were first familiarized with a pair of passages and then tested on four isolated words, they listened longer to the two words that had appeared in the passages. Thus, 7.5-month-olds were able to segment the words from fluent speech. By comparison, a group of 6-month-olds tested with the same materials gave no evidence of segmenting the words from the passages.

Although Jusczyk and Aslin's study demonstrated that English-learning 7.5-month-olds segment some words from fluent speech, it did not address how infants accomplish this. Subsequent studies have attempted to determine what kind of information infants use in segmenting potential words from the speech stream. There are several potential cues that infants could use to begin segmenting words from the speech signal and discovering the underlying word forms of the language. One potential source has to do with the typical prosodic patterns of words in the language. For instance, some languages such as Czech have very regular accent patterns. The first syllable of Czech words carries the primary stress. Knowledge of these basic patterns could help locate the likely beginnings and endings of words. Another potential source of word boundary information is inherent in the phonotactic properties of the language. Phonotactics refers to constraints on the possible orderings of phonetic segments within morphemes, syllables, and words in a language (Trask, 1996). In English, certain sequences of segments, such as [mg] are not permitted within a syllable. The English listener encountering such sequences in fluent speech can be reasonably sure that these mark syllable boundaries. Similarly, different phonetic variants (i.e., allophones) of the same phoneme are often restricted in terms of the positions where they can appear within a word. Consider some of the allophones of the English phoneme /t/. The aspirated allophone [tʰ] occurs at the beginning of English words, whereas the unaspirated allophone [t] is found at the ends of English words. Knowledge of the contexts in which such allophones typically appear could inform listeners about the locations of possible word boundaries. Finally, statistical and distributional properties can be exploited to segment words from fluent speech. In "funny sign," the cooccurrence relation between the two syllables "fun" and "ny" is greater than the one between "ny" and "sign" since "funny" can be followed by many other words (e.g. "funny man," "funny story," etc). Thus, matching known lexical items to utterances could help in segmenting other words.

Which of the four different types of cues, just described, provides the most effective information for locating boundaries between words and correctly categorizing the word forms depends very much on the particular sound organization of a language. For example, relying on prosodic stress cues would be ineffective in a language with no consistent word stress patterns because it would divide the speech stream into units that do not correspond closely to that language's word form categories. In contrast, reliance on prosodic stress cues could be useful for a language with a predominant word stress pattern such as English. Cutler and Carter (1987) have observed that a very high proportion of content words in English conversational speech begin with an initial stressed syllable followed by one or more unstressed syllables. Given the predominance of this stress pattern, Cutler and Norris (1988) proposed that a reasonable first pass strategy for segmenting words in English is to posit that each stressed syllable marks the onset of a new word in an utterance. Moreover, it has been demonstrated that English-learning infants first display sensitivity to the predominant stress pattern of words at between 6 and 9 months (Jusczyk, Cutler, et al., 1993). For this reason, Jusczyk, Houston, and Newsome (1999) decided to investigate whether English learners might initially rely on the location of stressed syllables to segment words from fluent speech. If so, then infants should have an easier time segmenting words that begin with stressed syllables than ones that begin with unstressed syllables. This is exactly the result that they found. English-learning 7.5-month-olds had no difficulty segmenting words with initial stressed syllables (e.g., *hamlet* and *kingdom*) but were unable to segment words beginning with unstressed syllables (e.g., *guitar* and *device*). In fact, 7.5-month-olds tended to missegment the latter words at the onset of their stressed syllables (i.e., as *tar* and *vice*). This pattern of behavior is consistent with the view that infants identify the beginnings of words with the occurrence of stressed syllables. Because the predominant pattern in English is stressed initial syllables, infants will more often correctly segment words than incorrectly segment them. However, if they are going to be successful in segmenting words without the predominant stress pattern, they need to modify their initial word segmentation procedure.

Once again, the word form category that infants derive by segmenting speech at strong syllables is only a first approximation of what they need to deal effectively with the sound structure of the native language. How might such an imperfect segmentation of the speech stream evolve into the one that will recover the correct words in the utterance? Simply segmenting longer utterances into smaller chunks may help infants to recover additional information that is useful in determining the true location of word boundaries. For instance, attention to the nature of the phonetic information at the edges of these chunks could inform infants about phonotactic and allophonic cues to word boundaries. Thus, attention to which sequences of phonetic segments do or do not occur at the edges of these chunks reveals something about the range of permissible phonotactic sequences at the beginnings and ends of words. Similarly, focusing on whether certain allophones occur exclusively at the beginnings or ends of such chunks would help infants to learn about the distributional contexts of these allophones and their potential as predictors of word boundaries. Once infants have detected these sorts of regularities, they may use these as additional checks on possible word boundaries in utterances. An indication that phonotactic and allophonic cues conflict with stress cues on some occasions could lead infants to produce an alternative parse of the speech stream.

In fact, there are indications that English learners carve the speech signal up differently after they become sensitive to phonotactic and allophonic cues. Mattys, Jusczyk, Luce, and Morgan (1999) found that, at 9 months, English learners are sensitive to the way that phonotactic cues typically align with prosodic stress cues at word boundaries. In another investigation, Mattys and Jusczyk (2001) found that English-learning 9-month-olds segmented words that were marked by good phonotactic cues but not ones that were marked by poor phonotactic cues. For example, a phonotactic sequence such as [vt] is very rare within English words but more likely to occur across a word boundary, as in *five toes*. By comparison, the phonotactic sequences [ft] is much more likely to occur within English words such as in *lift*. Consequently, when listeners encounter a sequence such as [vt], they have good reason to suspect that a word boundary occurs between [v] and [t]. English-learning 9-month-olds responded in this way. They were more likely to segment a word like *tove* when it was preceded by a word like *brave* than when it was preceded by one like *gruff*.

Sensitivity to allophonic cues to word boundaries appears to develop a little more slowly in English learners. Jusczyk, Hohne, and Bauman (1999) investigated infants' abilities to use allophonic differences to correctly segment items such as *night rates* and *nitrates* from fluent speech. The critical allophonic differences that distinguish these items have to do with the initial /t/ and the /r/ in each of these items. Nine-month-olds did not appear to use the allophonic information to segment the familiarized word from the fluent speech passages. Infants who were familiarized with *nitrates* were just as likely to listen to a passage containing *night rates* as they were to one containing *nitrates*. However, by 10.5 months, the infants were able to use the allophonic differences to correctly segment the familiarized words.

Thus in terms of the sources of information used to locate the boundaries of potential word forms in fluent speech, English learners are able to use prosodic stress cues at 7.5 months, phonotactic cues at 9 months, and allophonic cues at 10.5 months. Interestingly enough, it is at 10.5 months that they are able to identify word forms in the language (i.e., ones with initial unstressed syllables, such as *guitar* and *device*) that do not conform to the predominant pattern. These findings are consistent with the view that the use of prosodic stress cues to segment the input initially into potential word form categories may facilitate the discovery of other potential cues that enable them to arrive correct word forms in an utterance.

Using the Speech Signal to Discover Grammatical Organization

The words of any utterance are related by structures at a higher level of organization. The way that words are grouped together into units at this higher level of organization, the one that governs the construction of sentences, is critical for understanding the meaning of the utterance. To be successful at speaking and understanding the language, learners must recover this organization, which is inherent in the speech signal. Again, this is a matter of perceiving the appropriate structural units of organization. The learner's task is to determine the higher-level units of organization of sentences that govern the particular meaning that the utterance conveys. Because the surface features of constituents vary considerably across languages, one critical task for learners is to detect the major constituents and their ordering in the utterances that they are exposed to. In order to accomplish this, learners need to categorize the higher-level units appropriately. In other words, they must break the signal up into the right-sized units (i.e., the ones that correspond to the constituents that govern the relations among particular words). Thus, to derive the meaning of sentences, one needs to identify its clausal constituents, and for clauses, one must identify the correct phrasal constituents. Misparsing the signal into units that do not correspond to the appropriate constituents (e.g., fragments of one phrase combined with fragments of an adjacent phrase) not only would lead to misunderstanding the utterance but also could hinder the learner in discovering the grammatical organization of the language.

The issue of how the learner correctly locates the boundaries of higher-level units of organization such as clauses and phrases is not one that received a great deal of attention until the 1980s. Most discussions of how learners acquire syntax simply assumed that learners have categorized the input appropriately into the correct units needed to determine the syntactic organization of an utterance. The issue of how learners locate the correct units was first seriously addressed by Gleitman and Wanner (1982) and by Peters (1983), who independently suggested that information in the speech signal might help to identify such units.[1] The plausibility of this view, termed "prosodic bootstrapping," depends on the satisfaction of several conditions. First, there must be information in the speech signal that marks the structural boundaries of important grammatical units. Second, learners must be capable of detecting the markers of such units in speech. Third, learners must make use of the units specified by these markers when they process the linguistic input.

In fact, all of these conditions appear to be fully met in the way that learners categorize clausal units in the input. Thus, there is considerable evidence that boundaries of clausal units are acoustically marked in both adult-directed (Lehiste, 1973; Nakatani & Dukes, 1977; Price, Ostendorf, Shattuck-Hufnagel, & Fong, 1991) and child-directed speech (Bernstein Ratner, 1986; Fisher & Tokura, 1996). Moreover, infants are sensitive to the occurrence of such cues in the input. For example, Hirsh-Pasek et al. (1987) found that English-learning 7- and 10-month-olds preferred listening to speech passages in which pauses were inserted at clause boundaries, as opposed to in the middle of clauses (see also Morgan, 1994). Finally, there is evidence that infants use the cues in speech about clausal units to encode and remember the information in these units. For instance, Nazzi, Kemler Nelson, Jusczyk, and Jusczyk (2000) found that 6-month-olds are better able to detect clausal units embedded in continuous speech than comparable nonclausal units. Furthermore, even 2-month-olds display better memory for speech information when it is packaged in clausal units, as opposed to comparable, but nonclausal, word sequences (Mandel, Jusczyk, & Kemler-Nelson, 1994; Mandel, Kemler-Nelson, & Jusczyk, 1996). Thus, infants begin with some means of dividing continuous speech into units that correspond to the appropriate constituent clauses of a sentence.

The case for infants using speech cues to locate syntactic phrases is less straight-forward. In fact, the situation here very much resembles those considered in the previous sections. Infants' initial attempts to categorize units corresponding to syntactic phrases only approximate the actual phrasal units. Still, these initial attempts at recovering phrasal units provide learners with a foothold from which they can access additional cues to the correct phrasal units of their native language.

That locating phrasal units of syntactic organization should be more difficult than locating clausal units is understandable because languages differ considerably in how they organize phrases within clauses. Languages that rely heavily on word order to convey syntactic information are likely to group words from the same phrase together. However, the same does not necessarily hold for languages that allow for freer word orders, which might separate elements from the same phrase. Still, for a language such as English, there are indications that phrasal units are often marked by acoustic cues (Beach, 1991; Price et al., 1991; Scott, 1982; Scott & Cutler, 1984). When such information is available in child-directed speech, English-learning 9-month-olds not only detect it (Jusczyk, Hirsh-Pasek, et al., 1992) but also appear to use it in encoding and remembering information contained in such units (Soderstrom, Jusczyk, & Kemler Nelson, 2000). Nevertheless, even within languages that rely on word order, such as English, syntactic phrases are not consistently marked in the input that the child receives (Fisher & Tokura, 1996). The problem arises because the markers present in the speech signal tend to relate to prosodic phrases, which do not correspond consistently to particular types of syntactic phrases. To understand this point, consider the following sentences:

1. Billy / mowed the lawn.
2. He mowed / the lawn.

In (1) the prosodic phrase boundary (indicated by "/") coincides with the syntactic boundary between the subject phrase and the predicate phrase. However, in (2), the prosodic phrase boundary occurs within the predicate phrase between the verb and its object. Note that in both cases a syntactic boundary is marked by the prosodic phrase boundary, but it is not the same one in each sentence. When faced with such a conflict between prosodic phrase marking and syntactic phrase marking as in (2), English-learning 9-month-olds have been shown to display listening preferences that accord with the prosodic, rather than with the syntactic, organization of the utterances (Gerken, Jusczyk, & Mandel, 1994).

At first glance, the inconsistency that exists between how words are grouped into constituents corresponding to prosodic phrases as opposed to ones corresponding to syntactic phrases would seem to rule out the notion that speech information could be useful in discovering syntactic phrases. However, might the division of utterances into units corresponding to prosodic phrases still be helpful in learning to extract the categories corresponding to syntactic phrases? One potentially useful source of information within prosodic phrases that could aid in the recovery of the appropriate syntactic units is the occurrence of grammatical morphemes (Morgan, Meier, & Newport, 1987, 1989). In English, certain function words typically occur only at certain locations inside phrasal units. For instance, "the" marks the beginning of a noun phrase and is extremely unlikely to occur as the last word of a phrasal unit. Hence grouping the input into prosodic phrases and noting regularities in how certain morphemes are distributed within such phrases may help in delineating their syntactic roles. (Note the parallel here to the situation with word segmentation in which the initial parse according to prosodic stress allows learners to reference phonotactic and allophonic cues with respect to the beginnings and endings of the chunks.)

Of course, tracking the occurrence and positioning of function words in utterances demands some ability to detect such words in the speech stream. However, despite the well-known fact that children often leave function words out of their earliest utterances (Brown, 1973), infants do not seem to have any difficulty in perceiving the occurrence of function words. In fact, Shi, Werker, and Morgan (1999) report that newborns detect and discriminate the acoustic and phonological differences between function words and content words. Moreover, there is evidence that English-learning infants begin to track the occurrence of function words in utterances at least as early as 10.5 months. For example, Shafer, Shucard, Gerken, and Shucard (1998) used an evoked potential measure and found that 11-month-olds displayed different responses to sentences that contained real English function words as opposed to ones in which nonsense words were substituted for the function words. These findings were replicated and extended in studies using behavioral measures. In one investigation, English-learning 10.5-month-olds were shown to respond differentially to passages with or without real English function words, although they did not appear to detect misorderings of function words until 16 months of age (Shady, Jusczyk, & Gerken, 1998). German learners even show some ability to segment some function words from fluent speech by 7.5 months (Höhle & Weissenborn, 1998). Hence the notion that infants could advance their knowledge of syntactic organization by referencing the positioning of particular function words to prosodic phrase boundaries, and the particular content words that they frequently co-occur with, seems plausible. This is not to say that sensitivity to information in the speech signal is sufficient to ensure the acquisition of grammatical structure. However, an initial categorization of the speech signal that serves to group words into prosodic phrases may be an important step in determining how to uncover the organization that specifies the syntactic phrases of the native language.

Summary and Conclusions

The speech signal conveys many different levels of linguistic organization, from phonemes to sentences. To become successful users of their native language, learners need to be able to find the relevant units at each level of organization. It appears that when infants first display some ability to process language at each of these levels, they begin more or less in the same way in categorizing the input. The initial categories that learners use do not seem to vary much across individuals. The categories are broad and yield a less-than-perfect fit with the categories used by fluent communicators of the language. Nevertheless, the infants' initial categories provide a foundation for them to begin to acquire the additional information required to arrive at the appropriate set of units for the native language. In at least three of the four cases considered here (phonemic categorization, rhythmic organization, and prosodic units), the initial categorization scheme appears to be innately given. The fourth case, word segmentation, is less certain. It is certainly possible that all infants might begin with a bias to treat stressed syllables as markers of word onsets, but this would seem to be an obstacle when learning a language whose words do not have initial stressed syllables (such as French or Polish). Another potential starting point for word segmentation may be the presence of some recurring properties in the isolated words that a child hears frequently, such as names and diminutives. The features extracted from such items could then form a bias for using such information to locate the onset of words in fluent speech contexts.

In any case, the presence of common starting points in categorizing the levels of organization carried by speech suggests a process of innately guided learning whereby learners are preprogrammed to learn certain things and to learn them in a particular way. This process need not involve any set of specialized processing mechanisms. Instead, what may be central to the process is a bias to attend selectively to signals of a particular form. These signals, then, would be more apt to undergo further processing and to be included in memory. The initial categories, then, provide a way to divide or partition the input that then allows the infant to detect the regularities that mark that particular native language (what I have referred to elsewhere [Jusczyk, 1998] as a "divide and conquer" strategy). By this process, infants' initial categories are tuned to those of adult language users.

Acknowledgments

Preparation of this chapter was facilitated by a Research Grant from NICHD (HD 15795) and a Senior Scientist Award from NIMH (MH 01490). I wish to thank Delia Hom, Ann Marie Jusczyk, and Elizabeth Johnson for helpful comments on earlier versions of the chapter.

Note

1. It should be noted that the idea that the speech signal could help learners to discover the grammatical organization of sentences had been considered earlier (McNeill, 1966). However, this idea was abandoned as an unworkable solution because of observations suggesting that one's knowledge of syntax often influences judgments about which prosodic contours are present, suggesting that one could not directly read the syntactic organization from the prosody (Lieberman, 1965).

References

Abramson, A. S., & Lisker, L. (1967, September). *Discriminability along the voice continuum: Cross-language tests.* Paper presented at the Sixth International Congress of Phonetic Sciences, Prague.

Aslin, R. N. (1981). Experiential differences and sensitive periods in perceptual development: A unified model. In R. N. Aslin, J. R. Alberts, & M. R. Petersen (Eds.), *Development of perception: Psychobiological perspectives* (Vol. 2, pp. 219–255). New York: Academic Press.

Bahrick, L. E., & Pickens, J. N. (1988). Classification of bimodal English and Spanish language passages by infants. *Infant Behavior and Development, 11,* 277–296.

Beach, C. M. (1991). The interpretation of prosodic patterns at points of syntactic structure ambiguity: Evidence for cue-trading relations. *Journal of Memory and Language, 30,*
644–663.

Bernstein Ratner, N. (1986). Durational cues which mark clause boundaries in mother-child
speech. *Phonetics, 14,* 303–309.

Best, C. T., Lafleur, R., & McRoberts, G. W. (1995). Divergent developmental patterns for
infants' perception of two non-native contrasts. *Infant Behavior and Development, 18,*
339–350.

Bosch, L., & Sebastián-Gallés, N. (1997). Native-language recognition abilities in 4-month-
old infants from monolingual and bilingual environments. *Cogniton, 65,* 33–69.

Brown, R. (1973). *A first language.* Cambridge, MA: Harvard University Press.

Burnham, D. K., Earnshaw, L. J., & Clark, J. E. (1991). Development of categorical identification of native and non-native bilabial stops: Infants, children, and adults. *Journal of
Child Language, 18,* 231–260.

Christophe, A., & Morton, J. (1998). Is Dutch native English? Linguistic analysis by 2-month-
olds. *Developmental Science, 1,* 215–219.

Cutler, A., & Carter, D. M. (1987). The predominance of strong initial syllables in the English
vocabulary. *Computer Speech and Language, 2,* 133–142.

Cutler, A., & Norris, D. G. (1988). The role of strong syllables in segmentation for lexical access.
Journal of Experimental Psychology: Human Perception and Performance, 14, 113–121.

Dehaene-Lambertz, G., & Houston, D. M. (1998). Faster orientation latencies toward native
language in two-month-olds. *Language and Speech, 41,* 21–43.

Eimas, P. D. (1974). Auditory and linguistic processing of cues for place of articulation by
infants. *Perception and Psychophysics, 16,* 513–521.

Eimas, P. D. (1975). Auditory and phonetic coding of the cues for speech: Discrimination of
the [r-l] distinction by young infants. *Perception and Psychophysics, 18,* 341–347.

Eimas, P. D., & Miller, J. L. (1992). Organization in the perception of speech by young infants. *Psychological Science, 3,* 340–345.

Eimas, P. D., Siqueland, E. R., Jusczyk, P. W., & Vigorito, J. (1971). Speech perception in
infants. *Science, 171,* 303–306.

Fisher, C. L., & Tokura, H. (1996). Acoustic cues to grammatical structure in infant-directed
speech: Cross-linguistic evidence. *Child Development, 67,* 3192–3218.

Friederici, A. D., & Wessels, J. M. I. (1993). Phonotactic knowledge and its use in infant speech
perception. *Perception and Psychophysics, 54,* 287–295.

Fry, D. B., Abramson, A. S., Eimas, P. D., & Liberman, A. M. (1962). The identification and
discrimination of synthetic vowels. *Language and Speech, 5,* 171–189.

Gerken, L. A., Jusczyk, P. W., & Mandel, D. R. (1994). When prosody fails to cue syntactic
structure: Nine-month-olds' sensitivity to phonological vs. syntactic phrases. *Cognition, 51,* 237–265.

Gleitman, L., & Wanner, E. (1982). The state of the state of the art. In E. Wanner & L. Gleitman
(Eds.), *Language acquisition: The state of the art* (pp. 3–48). Cambridge: Cambridge
University Press.

Gould, J. L., & Marler, P. (1987). Learning by instinct. *Scientific American, 256,* 62–73.

Grieser, D., & Kuhl, P. K. (1989). The categorization of speech by infants: Support for speech-
sound prototypes. *Developmental Psychology, 25,* 577–588.

Harnad, S. (Ed.). (1987). *Categorical perception: The groundwork of cognition.* Cambridge:
Cambridge University Press.

Hillenbrand, J. M., Minifie, F. D., & Edwards, T. J. (1979). Tempo of spectrum change as a
cue in speech sound discrimination by infants. *Journal of Speech and Hearing Research,
22,* 147–165.

Hirsh-Pasek, K., Kemler Nelson, D. G., Jusczyk, P. W., Wright Cassidy, K., Druss, B., & Kennedy, L. (1987). Clauses are perceptual units for young infants. *Cognition, 26*, 269–286.

Höhle, B., & Weissenborn, J. (1998). Sensitivity to closed-class elements in preverbal children. In A. Greenhill, M. Hughes, H. Littlefield, & H. Walsh (Eds.), *Proceedings of the twenty-second Annual Boston University Conference on Language Development* (Vol. 1, pp. 348–359). Somerville, MA: Cascadilla Press.

Iverson, P., & Kuhl, P. K. (1995). Mapping the perceptual magnet effect for speech using signal detection theory and multidimensional scaling. *Journal of the Acoustical Society of America, 97*, 553–562.

Jusczyk, P. W. (1993). From general to language specific capacities: The WRAPSA Model of how speech perception develops. *Journal of Phonetics, 21*, 3–28.

Jusczyk, P. W. (1997). *The discovery of spoken language.* Cambridge, MA: MIT Press.

Jusczyk, P. W. (1998). Dividing and conquering the linguistic input. In M.C. Gruber, D. Higgins, K. S. Olson, & T. Wysocki (Eds.), *CLS 34: The panels* (Vol. 2, pp. 293–310). Chicago: University of Chicago.

Jusczyk, P. W., & Aslin, R. N. (1995). Infants' detection of sound patterns of words in fluent speech. *Cognitive Psychology, 29*, 1–23.

Jusczyk, P. W., & Bertoncini, J. (1988). Viewing the development of speech perception as an innately guided learning process. *Language and Speech, 31*, 217–238.

Jusczyk, P. W., Cutler, A., & Redanz, N. (1993). Preference for the predominant stress patterns of English words. *Child Development, 64*, 675–687.

Jusczyk, P. W., Friederici, A. D., Wessels, J., Svenkerud, V. Y., & Jusczyk, A. M. (1993). Infants' sensitivity to the sound patterns of native language words. *Journal of Memory and Language, 32*, 402–420.

Jusczyk, P. W., Hirsh-Pasek, K., Kemler Nelson, D. G., Kennedy, L., Woodward, A., & Piwoz, J. (1992). Perception of acoustic correlates of major phrasal units by young infants. *Cognitive Psychology, 24*, 252–293.

Jusczyk, P. W., & Hohne, E. A. (1997). Infants' memory for spoken words. *Science, 277*, 1984–1986.

Jusczyk, P. W., Hohne, E. A., & Bauman, A. (1999). Infants' sensitivity to allophonic cues for word segmentation. *Perception & Psychophysics, 61*, 1465–1476.

Jusczyk, P. W., Houston, D., & Newsome, M. (1999). The beginnings of word segmentation in English-learning infants. *Cognitive Psychology, 39*, 159–207.

Jusczyk, P. W., Jusczyk, A. M., Kennedy, L. J., Schomberg, T., & Koenig, N. (1995). Young infants' retention of information about bisyllabic utterances. *Journal of Experimental Psychology: Human Perception and Performance, 21*, 822–836.

Jusczyk, P. W., Kennedy, L. J., & Jusczyk, A. M. (1995). Young infants' retention of information about syllables. *Infant Behavior and Development, 18*, 27–42.

Jusczyk, P. W., Luce, P. A., & Charles Luce, J. (1994). Infants' sensitivity to phonotactic patterns in the native language. *Journal of Memory and Language, 33*, 630–645.

Jusczyk, P. W., Pisoni, D. B., & Mullennix, J. (1992). Some consequences of stimulus variability on speech processing by 2-month old infants. *Cognition, 43*, 253–291.

Jusczyk, P. W., Pisoni, D. B., Reed, M., Fernald, A., & Myers, M. (1983). Infants' discrimination of the duration of a rapid spectrum change in nonspeech signals. *Science, 222*, 175–177.

Jusczyk, P. W., Pisoni, D. B., Walley, A. C., & Murray, J. (1980). Discrimination of the relative onset of two-component tones by infants. *Journal of the Acoustical Society of America, 67*, 262–270.

Jusczyk, P. W., Rosner, B. S., Reed, M., & Kennedy, L. J. (1989). Could temporal order differences underlie 2-month-olds' discrimination of English voicing contrasts? *Journal of the Acoustical Society of America, 85*, 1741–1749.

Kuhl, P. K. (1979). Speech perception in early infancy: Perceptual constancy for spectrally dissimilar vowel categories. *Journal of the Acoustical Society of America, 66*, 1668–1679.

Kuhl, P. K. (1981). Discrimination of speech by nonhuman animals: Basic auditory sensitivities conducive to the perception of speech-sound categories. *Journal of the Acoustical Society of America, 70*, 340–349.

Kuhl, P. K. (1983). Perception of auditory equivalence classes for speech in early infancy. *Infant Behavior and Development, 6*, 263–285.

Kuhl, P. K. (1991). Human adults and human infants show a "perceptual magnet effect" for the prototypes of speech categories, monkeys do not. *Perception and Psychophysics, 50*, 93–107.

Kuhl, P. K., Andruski, J. E., Chistovich, L. A., Kozhevnikova, E. V., Ryskina, V. L., Stolyarova, E. I., Sundberg, U., & Lacerda, F. (1997). Cross-language analysis of phonetic units addressed to infants. *Science, 277*, 684–686.

Kuhl, P. K., & Miller, J. D. (1975). Speech perception by the chinchilla: Voiced-voiceless distinction in alveolar plosive consonants. *Science, 190*, 69–72.

Kuhl, P. K., Williams, K. A., Lacerda, F., Stevens, K. N., & Lindblom, B. (1992). Linguistic experiences alter phonetic perception in infants by 6 months of age. *Science, 255*, 606–608.

Lasky, R. E., Syrdal-Lasky, A., & Klein, R. E. (1975). VOT discrimination by four to six and a half month old infants from Spanish environments. *Journal of Experimental Child Psychology, 20*, 215–225.

Lehiste, I. (1973). Phonetic disambiguation of syntactic ambiguity. *Glossa, 7*, 107–122.

Liberman, A. M., Cooper, F. S., Shankweiler, D. P., & Studdert-Kennedy, M. G. (1967). Perception of the speech code. *Psychological Review, 74*, 431–461.

Liberman, A. M., Harris, K. S., Kinney, J. A., & Lane, H. L. (1961). The discrimination of relative-onset time of the components of certain speech and non-speech patterns. *Journal of Experimental Psychology, 61*, 379–388.

Liberman, A. M., & Whalen, D. H. (2000). On the relation of speech to language. *Trends in Cognitive Science, 4*, 187–196.

Lieberman, P. (1965). On the acoustic basis of the perception of intonation by linguists. *Word, 21*, 40–54.

Lisker, L. (1986). "Voicing" in English: A catalog of acoustic features signalling /b/ versus /p/ in trochees. *Language and Speech, 29*, 3–11.

Lisker, L., & Abramson, A. S. (1970). The voicing dimension: Some experiments in comparative phonetics. In *Proceedings of the Sixth International Congress of Phonetic Sciences* (pp. 563–567). Prague: Academia.

Lively, S. E., & Pisoni, D. B. (1997). On prototypes and phonetic categories: A critical magnet effect in speech perception. *Journal of Experimental Psychology: Human Perception and Performance, 23*, 1665–1679.

Mandel, D. R., Jusczyk, P. W., & Kemler Nelson, D. G. (1994). Does sentential prosody help infants to organize and remember speech information? *Cognition, 53*, 155–180.

Mandel, D. R., Kemler Nelson, D. G., & Jusczyk, P. W. (1996). Infants remember the order of words in a spoken sentence. *Cognitive Development, 11*, 181–196.

Marler, P. (1990). Innate learning preferences: Signals for communication. *Developmental Psychobiology, 23*, 557–569.

Mattys, S. L., & Jusczyk, P. W. (2001). Phonotactic cues for segmentation of fluent speech by infants. *Cognition, 78*, 91–121.

Mattys, S. L., Jusczyk, P. W., Luce, P. A., & Morgan, J. L. (1999). Word segmentation in infants: How phonotactics and prosody combine. *Cognitive Psychology, 38*, 465–494.

Maye, J., & Gerken, L. A. (2000, November 5). *Learning phonemes: How far can the input take us?* Paper presented at the 25th Annual Boston University Conference on Language Development, Boston.

McNeill, D. (1966). Developmental psycholinguistics. In F. Smith & G. A. Miller (Eds.), *The genesis of language* (pp. 15–84). Cambridge, MA: MIT Press.

Mehler, J., & Christophe, A. (1995). Maturation and learning of language in the first year of life. In M. S. Gazzaniga (Ed.), *The cognitive neurosciences* (pp. 943–954). Cambridge, MA: Bradford Books.

Mehler, J., Jusczyk, P. W., Lambertz, G., Halsted, N., Bertoncini, J., & Amiel-Tison, C. (1988). A precursor of language acquisition in young infants. *Cognition, 29,* 144–178.

Miller, G. A. (1956). The magical number seven, plus or minus two: Some limits on our capacity for processing information. *Psychological Review, 63,* 81–96.

Miller, G. A., Heise, G. A., & Lichten, W. (1951). The intelligibility of speech as a function of the context of the test materials. *Journal of Experimental Psychology, 41,* 329–335.

Miller, J. D., Weir, C. C., Pastore, L., Kelly, W. J., & Dooling, R. J. (1976). Discrimination and labeling of noise-buzz sequences with varying noise-lead times: An example of categorical perception. *Journal of the Acoustical Society of America, 60,* 410–417.

Miller, J. L., & Eimas, P. D. (1983). Studies on the categorization of speech by infants. *Cognition, 13,* 135–165.

Moon, C., Cooper, R. P., & Fifer, W. P. (1993). Two-day old infants prefer their native language. *Infant Behavior and Development, 16,* 495–500.

Morgan, J. L. (1994). Converging measures of speech segmentation in prelingual infants. *Infant Behavior & Development, 17,* 387–400.

Morgan, J. L., Meier, R. P., & Newport, E. L. (1987). Structural packaging in the input to language learning: Contributions of prosodic and morphological marking of phrases to the acquisition of language? *Cognitive Psychology, 19,* 498–550.

Morgan, J. L., Meier, R. P., & Newport, E. L. (1989). Facilitating the acquisition of syntax with transformational cues to phrase structure. *Journal of Memory and Language, 28,* 360–374.

Morse, P. A. (1972). The discrimination of speech and nonspeech stimuli in early infancy. *Journal of Experimental Child Psychology, 13,* 477–492.

Nakatani, L., & Dukes, K. (1977). Locus of segmental cues for word juncture. *Journal of the Acoustical Society of America, 62,* 714–719.

Nazzi, T., Bertoncini, J., & Mehler, J. (1998). Language discrimination by newborns: Towards an understanding of the role of rhythm. *Journal of Experimental Psychology: Human Perception and Performance, 24,* 756–766.

Nazzi, T., Jusczyk, P. W., & Johnson, E. K. (2000). Language discrimination by English-learning 5-month-olds: Effects of rhythm and familiarity. *Journal of Memory and Language, 43,* 1–19.

Nazzi, T., Kemler Nelson, D. G., Jusczyk, P. W., & Jusczyk, A. M. (2000). Six-month-olds' detection of clauses embedded in continuous speech: Effects of prosodic well-formedness. *Infancy, 1,* 123–147.

Pastore, R. E., Ahroon, W. A., Buffuto, K. A., Friedman, C. J., Puleo, J. S., & Fink, E. A. (1977). Common factor model of categorical perception. *Journal of Experimental Psychology: Human Perception and Performance, 4,* 686–696.

Pegg, J. E., & Werker, J. F. (1997). Adult and infant perception of two English phones. *Journal of the Acoustical Society of America, 102,* 3742–3753.

Peters, A. (1983). *The units of language acquisition.* Cambridge: Cambridge University Press.

Pisoni, D. B. (1977). Identification and discrimination of the relative onset of two component tones: Implications for voicing perception in stops. *Journal of the Acoustical Society of America*, 61, 1352–1361.

Polka, L., & Bohn, O.-S. (1996). Cross-language comparison of vowel perception in English-learning and German-learning infants. *Journal of the Acoustical Society of America*, 100, 577–592.

Price, P. J., Ostendorf, M., Shattuck-Hufnagel, S., & Fong, C. (1991). The use of prosody in syntactic disambiguation. *Journal of the Acoustical Society of America*, 90, 2956–2970.

Rauschecker, J. P., & Marler, P. (1987). Cortical plasticity and imprinting: Behaviorial and physiological contrasts and parallels. In J. P. Rauschecker & P. Marler (Eds.), *Imprinting and cortical plasticity* (pp. 349–366). New York: Wiley.

Saffran, J. R., Aslin, R. N., & Newport, E. L. (1996). Statistical learning by 8-month-old infants. *Science*, 274, 1926–1928.

Scott, D. R. (1982). Duration as a cue to the perception of a phrase boundary. *Journal of the Acoustical Society of America*, 71, 996–1007.

Scott, D. R., & Cutler, A. (1984). Segmental phonology and the perception of syntactic structure. *Journal of Verbal Learning and Verbal Behavior*, 23, 450–466.

Shady, M., Jusczyk, P. W., & Gerken, L. A. (1998, November). *Infants' sensitivity to function morphemes.* Paper presented at the 23rd Annual Boston University Conference on Language Development, Boston, MA.

Shafer, V. L., Shucard, J. L., Gerken, L. A., & Shucard, D. W. (1998). "The" and the brain: An electrophysiological examination of infants' responses to familiar and unfamiliar function morphemes. *Journal of Speech, Language and Hearing Research*, 41, 874–886.

Shi, R., Werker, J. F., & Morgan, J. L. (1999). Newborn infants sensitivity to perceptual cues to lexical and grammatical words. *Cognition*, 72, B11–B21.

Soderstrom, M., Jusczyk, P. W., & Kemler Nelson, D. G. (2000). Evidence for the use of phrasal packaging by English-learning 9-month-olds. In S. C. Howell, S. A. Fish, & T. Keith-Lucas (Eds.), *Proceedings of the 24th Annual Boston University Conference on Language Development* (Vol. 2, pp. 708–718). Somerville, MA: Cascadilla Press.

Streeter, L. A. (1976). Language perception of 2-month old infants shows effects of both innate mechanisms and experience. *Nature*, 259, 39–41.

Studdert-Kennedy, M. G., Liberman, A. M., Harris, K. S., & Cooper, F. S. (1970). Motor theory of speech perception: A reply to Lane's critical review. *Psychological review*, 77, 234–249.

Sussman, J. E., & Lauckner-Morano, V. J. (1995). Further tests of the "perceptual magnet effect" in the perception of [i]: Identification and change/no change discrimination. *Journal of the Acoustical Society of America*, 97, 539–552.

Swoboda, P., Morse, P. A., & Leavitt, L. A. (1976). Continuous vowel discrimination in normal and at-risk infants. *Child Development*, 47, 459–465.

Thyer, N., Hickson, L., & Dodd, B. (2000). The perceptual magnet effect in Australian English vowels. *Perception & Psychophysics*, 62, 1–20.

Trask, R. L. (1996). *A dictionary of phonetics and phonology.* London: Routledge.

Tsushima, T., Takizawa, O., Sasaki, M., Siraki, S., Nishi, K., Kohno, M., Menyuk, P., & Best, C. (1994 September). Discrimination of English /r-l/ and /w-y/ by Japanese infants at 6–12 months: Language specific developmental changes in speech perception abilities. Paper presented at the International Conference on Spoken Language Processing, Yokohama, Japan.

van de Weijer, J. (1998). *Language input for word discovery.* Unpublished doctoral dissertation, University of Nijmegen, Nijmegen, The Netherlands.

Werker, J. F., & Lalonde, C. E. (1988). Cross-language speech perception: Initial capabilities and developmental change. *Developmental Psychology, 24,* 672–683.

Werker, J. F., & Tees, R. C. (1984). Cross-language speech perception: Evidence for perceptual reorganization during the first year of life. *Infant Behavior and Development, 7,* 49–63.

Woodward, J. Z., & Aslin, R. N. (1990, April). *Segmentation cues in maternal speech to infants.* Paper presented at the Seventh Biennial Meeting of the International Conference on Infant Studies, Montreal.

CHAPTER THREE

Concepts Are Not Just for Objects
Categorization of Spatial Relation Information by Infants

Paul C. Quinn

Recent research indicates that young infants possess abilities to organize objects into perceptually based category groupings that come to have conceptual significance for adults (Quinn & Eimas, 1996b). This work challenges views that language, formal tuition, or specialized processes are necessary for the initial construction of category representations (Quinn, 2002). But categorization is not just for objects, and a question of interest is whether young infants can also form categorical representations of physical space that are defined by the positional relations of objects (Quinn, 1998, 1999). That is, can young infants form categorical representations for the spatial relations among objects, such as above versus below, between, left versus right, and inside versus outside? The ability to form categorical representations for spatial relations early in development should make it possible for infants to experience objects in organized spatial arrangements rather than as spatially disconnected entities located in unrelated positions.

After briefly describing data on the early development of perceptually based object categorization, this chapter will review evidence that infants less than one year of age can form categorical representations of small-scale spatial relation information. Also discussed will be evidence for two developmental changes. First, categorical representations for different spatial relations may emerge at different points during development. Infants may at first encode the location of a target relative to a single landmark and subsequently encode the location of a target in relation to multiple landmarks that define a local spatial framework. Second, categorical representations of spatial relations may initially be limited to the objects depicting the relations but later become more abstract so that various objects can be presented in the same relation and the equivalence of the relation is maintained despite this variation. The chapter will conclude with (1) a comparison of developmental trends in object and spatial categorization, (2) a discussion of the significance of spatial categorization by infants, and (3) a description of possible next steps for further investigation of the development of spatial categorization.

Perceptual Categorization of Objects: Early Development

Perceptual categorization refers to the recognition of discriminably different entities as members of the same category based on some internal representation of the category (Bruner, Goodnow, & Austin, 1956; Edelman, 1987). A system of mental representation lacking in categorical representation would be dominated by unrelated instance information and would have to learn to respond anew to each novel object encountered. The ability to categorize one's experiences is thus believed to be a critical cognitive skill, with some scholars describing it as "the primitive in all behavior and mental functioning" (Thelen & Smith, 1994, p. 143).

Since the writings of Rosch (1978), cognitive psychologists have argued that many object categories may be marked by bundles of correlated attributes (Malt, 1995; Younger, 1990). By the Rosch view, an organism that can detect such correlated bundles and compile them into separate representations is capable of categorization. For this reason, developmental psychologists have looked into the period of early infancy for evidence of categorization. The formation of categorical representations by young infants is something that developmentalists would want to know about inasmuch as it may be from these representations that the complex categories of the adult are constructed (Eimas, 1994; Madole & Oakes, 1999; Quinn & Eimas, 1997).

With the use of novelty-preference procedures, investigators have determined that 3- to 4-month-old infants can form basic-level category representations, for example, a representation for cats that includes novel cats but excludes birds, dogs, horses, and tigers, and a representation for horses that includes novel horses but excludes cats, giraffes, and zebras (Eimas & Quinn, 1994; Quinn, Eimas, & Rosenkrantz, 1993). With additional probing, it became clear that these early representations were more like child-basic representations (Mervis, 1987), in that they were more broadly inclusive than corresponding adult-basic representations. For example, the representation for cats was found to include female lions (Eimas & Quinn, 1994); only with maturation or experience did the representation attain a more adult-basic level of exclusivity (Eimas & Quinn, 1994; Eimas, Quinn, & Cowan, 1994).

Infants in the age range from 3 to 4 months can also form more global representations, for example, a representation for mammals that includes instances from novel mammal categories but excludes birds, fish, and furniture, and a representation for furniture that includes novel furniture items but excludes mammals (Behl-Chadha, 1996; Behl-Chadha, Eimas, & Quinn, 1995). Consistent with the developmental trend from child-basic to adult-basic representations, it has further been observed that global representations can be evidenced more readily than basic-level representations in newborn through 10-month-old infants and in connectionist networks (Quinn & Eimas, 1998; Quinn & Johnson, 1997, 2000; Quinn, Johnson, Mareschal, Rakison, & Younger, 2000; Quinn, Slater, Brown, & Hayes, 2001; Younger & Fear-

ing, 1999, 2000). Notably, the connectionist networks learned the categorical representations from input features that were measured directly from the surfaces of the stimuli that had been presented to the infants.

Before proceeding, it is important to note just what it is in the responding of infants performing in the familiarization/novelty-preference procedure that permits the inference that categorization has occurred. Categorization is assumed to occur when observers respond in an equivalent manner to discriminably different stimuli. Consider, for example, infants who are familiarized with a wide variety of discriminably different cats that vary in breed, color, posture, hair length, and presence of stripes. If the infants generalize this familiarization to a novel, discriminably different cat but not to an equally discriminable dog, and this pattern of responding cannot be attributed to an a priori preference, then it can be concluded that a categorical representation of the cats has been formed. That is, one can infer that the familiar cats have in some manner been grouped together or categorized and that this cluster representation excludes the dog. The novel cat is responded to as being more similar to the representation of the set of familiar cats than is the novel dog. This is all that is implied by the term "categorical representation," and it is this basic logic that underlies much of the literature on infant categorization.

Of interest is the information that enables infants to form category representations at basic, child-basic, and global levels in these studies. The age of the participants and nature of the stimuli (i.e., static photographic instances of the categories) make it improbable that infants are relying on conceptual knowledge about the "kind of thing" something is in order to perform successfully in these tasks (see Mandler & McDonough, 1993). For example, it seems unlikely that young infants' organization of visual patterns is guided by word cues (i.e., verbal labels), as may be the case in older infants (Balaban & Waxman, 1997; Waxman & Markow, 1995; Xu & Carey, 1996) or more conceptual attributes like self-initiated motion (e.g., Mandler & McDonough, 1993; Poulin-Dubois, Lepage, & Ferland, 1996) or even less obvious information regarding the biological or cognitive status of the animals (Carey, 1985; Keil, 1989; Wellman, 1990). It is more likely that young infants' categorical representations are based on perceptual characteristics (i.e., surface qualities) of the objects that populate our environments. Thus, infants might categorically separate cats from birds on the basis of the number of legs, cats from horses on the basis of overall body shape, and cats from dogs on the basis of information extracted from the head and face region (Quinn & Eimas, 1996a; Quinn, Eimas, & Tarr, 2001; Spencer, Quinn, Johnson, & Karmiloff-Smith, 1997). In addition, mammals and furniture might be categorically partitioned because of the presence versus absence of faces, fur, and tails (Quinn & Johnson, 1997; see also Rakison & Butterworth, 1998).

A perceptual learning account has been advanced to describe the overall pattern of findings on the early development of object categorization (Quinn, 2002; Quinn & Eimas, 1997, 2000; Quinn & Johnson, 1997, 2000). Both infants and neural networks may first learn to represent global categories like mammals and furniture on the basis of presence versus absence of salient features and only subsequently learn to represent basic-level categories like cats and dogs on the basis of specific values of shared features. Such parsing would presumably be controlled by relatively general mechanisms, including a complex learning system plus sufficiently sensitive perceptual systems. Certain very basic processes may exist independently of knowledge domains and make development in any knowledge domain possible. Mechanisms of this nature call little on innate structures, unlike Fodor's (1981) position, and that such mechanisms appear to build a veridical representation of the world would appear to nicely serve child and adult cognition. Questions regarding this proposed startup of categorization include: What is the potential for parsing? How finely tuned are the representations that can result from the initial parses? And how can the initial parses of young infants lead to the complex knowledge structures of children and adults?

The representation of perceptually based category information by young infants has become more central in recent discussions of mechanisms of conceptual representation in general. Although it can be argued that the formation of perceptual category representations by infants is only loosely related to the formation of certain goal-directed categories formed by adults, for example, things to do on the weekend (Barsalou, 1983), it is also the case that infant performance is consistent with Malt's (1995) suggestion that many object categories are "strongly influenced by regularities in the input that are recognized by the categorizer" (p. 130). Moreover, Millikan (1998) has suggested that much of the conceptual constancy of adulthood is built up from a foundation of perceptual constancy in infancy. Even Xu, Tenenbaum, and Sorrentino (1998), writing from a different theoretical perspective, have acknowledged that "infants have a perceptual system that is similar to that of adults, so that infants carve up the world in more or less the same way adults do" (p. 89).

While the role that early perceptually based categorical representations play in support of higher-level cognitive structures (i.e., inferences, beliefs, and theories) remains controversial (Mandler & McDonough, 1996, 1998; Xu & Carey, 1996), it is possible that some of the conceptual representations found later in life are informational enrichments of the original perceptually based categorical representations of young infants (Jones & Smith, 1993; Madole & Oakes, 1999; Quinn & Eimas, 1996b, 1997, 2000). That is, the early parsing of the world should permit the formation of perceptually based categorical representations into which subsequently acquired knowledge can be incorporated. Although the process of further conceptual knowledge acquisition by children and adults is far from agreed-on—ranging from more empirical to more classical developmental approaches, that is, those in which new forms of representation are created with maturation and experience (Piaget, 1954), it is significant that the infant has the correct parse to start the process of further knowledge acquisition whatever that process turns out to be. By this view, young infants' representation of within-category perceptual similarity and between-category perceptual dissimilarity may form the "primitive base" or "bottom layer" from which adult conceptions of objects develop (Markman, 1989; Millikan, 1998).

Categorical Representations Are Not Just for Objects: The Case of Above versus Below

It may be instructive to begin a discussion of development of categorization in the spatial domain by considering some of the tasks that appear to require the representation of spatial relation information. Because many human experiences take place in environmental space, our memories are likely to include information about the relative arrangement of objects, buildings, and physical landmarks (McNamara, Hardy, & Hirtle, 1989). Our locomotion through environmental space is presumably guided by such spatial memories, as well as by our immediate perception of spatial layout, inclusive of obstacles that lie along our planned route (Bertenthal & Campos, 1990; Campos et al., 2000). In addition, when we form a cognitive map of an environmental space, we are likely to construct an "overview" of the spatial relations of the objects within that space (Hirtle & Jonides, 1985; Kosslyn, Pick, & Fariello, 1974). Moreover, when we comprehend the information from a geographic or travel map, we process the spatial relations among point locations and regions (Landau, 1986).

In some models of object recognition, an object is believed to be represented as a set of parts in particular spatial relations (Biederman, 1987). Word recognition and reading are additional cognitive skills that may require maintenance of spatial relations of individual features of letters, left-right relations of individual letters of words, left-right relations of words on the same line of text, and above-below relations of words on different lines of text (Caramazza & Hillis, 1990). Reasoning about dynamic physical relations and events such as support, collision, and containment may also rely on the ability to represent spatial relations such as above versus below, left versus right, and inside versus outside (Baillargeon, 1995). Finally, acquiring a lexicon of spatial terms would appear to require at least some level of parsing of spatial relation information (Bowerman, 1996; Bowerman & Choi, 2001).

The remainder of the chapter will center on the beginnings of the ability to represent spatial relation information, a focus shared by other cognitive developmentalists. As Sandberg, Huttenlocher, and Newcombe (1996) have written, "tracing the development of spatial representations is . . . a central task for the study of cognitive development" (p. 721). What is known about the development of the ability to represent spatial relation information? In childhood, there is evidence that 4- to 6-year-olds can organize objects located in an experimental space about the size of a large room into categorical-like clusters or regions with internal boundaries determined by physical landmarks or barriers (Kosslyn, Pick, & Fariello, 1974; Newcombe & Liben, 1982). In addition, younger participants, 16-month-olds, remember the location of a toy in a rectangular sandbox by forming a categorical space with a prototype at the center (Huttenlocher, Newcombe, & Sandberg, 1994). Furthermore, 16- to 20-month-olds from different linguistic backgrounds are beginning to acquire a lexicon of spatial terms (Choi & Bowerman, 1991).

When considering starting points for the development of representations for spatial relation information, it may be observed that even young infants encounter numerous objects in various locations and in different spatial arrangements. It is therefore possible that categorical organization in spatial memory may exist quite early, perhaps during the first few months of life. The question is whether infants can parse physical space into categories defined by the positional arrangements of objects. That is, can infants make categorical distinctions between spatial relations?

To study the representation of spatial relation information by young infants, a methodology was adopted that was originally used to study infant perceptual discrimination and memory abilities. This methodology, called the familiarization/ novelty-preference procedure, is based on the established preference that infants have for novel stimulation (Fagan, 1970; Fantz, 1964; Slater, 1995). To determine if two stimuli are discriminable, infants are repeatedly presented with two copies of one stimulus and subsequently presented with the familiar stimulus paired with a novel stimulus. A preference for the novel stimulus (that can be measured in looking time) implies both memory for the familiar stimulus and the ability to discriminate between it and the novel stimulus.

To study categorization of spatial relation information by the infant, two modifications of the basic familiarization/novelty-preference procedure are required. First, a number of stimuli, all of which belong to the same category, are presented during familiarization. Second, two new stimuli are presented during what is called a novel category preference test—one is from the familiar category, the other from a novel category. Generalization of familiarization to a novel discriminably different exemplar from the familiar category and a preference for an equally discriminable exemplar from a novel category are taken as evidence that the familiar exemplars have been grouped together or categorized and that the representation of this category excludes the noninstance—the novel category exemplar.

With the familiarization/novelty-preference procedure adapted to study spatial categorization, the first question asked was whether 3-month-olds could categorize the above and below spatial relations between a dot and a horizontal bar (Quinn, 1994). Figure 3.1 illustrates the temporal aspects of the experiment. In the top panel, infants in an "above" familiarization group were presented with four exemplars, each depicting a single dot in a different position above a horizontal bar. The infants were then administered a novel category preference test that paired two novel exemplars; in one, the dot was located in a novel position above the bar; in the other, the dot was below the bar. The rationale of this test is as follows. If infants form a categorical representation of "dot above bar," then the novel above exemplar should be recognized as familiar, whereas the novel below exemplar should be perceived as novel and therefore be preferred. If, however, infants do not form a categorical representation of "dot above bar" and represent only information about the dot or the bar, or represent information about the dot and the bar independently of each other, then neither test exemplar should be preferred. The bottom panel displays how the same procedure was used to test whether infants could also form a categorical representation of "dot below bar."

Figure 3.2 displays the spatial design of the experiment. For half of the infants in the *above* group, shown in panel A, the dot appeared in each of the four corner positions in the upper left quadrant of the stimulus. For the other half of the infants in the *above* group, shown in panel B, the dot appeared in the four corner locations of the upper right quadrant of the stimulus. In both groups, the order of presentation of the four dot positions was randomized for each infant. All of the infants were administered a novel category preference test that paired two novel exemplars, one in which the dot was shifted to the right (in panel A) or left (in Panel B) of the familiar exemplars, and one in which the dot was shifted below the familiar exemplars and the reference bar. Panels C and D display how the same spatial design was used to test whether infants could also form a categorical representation of "dot below bar."

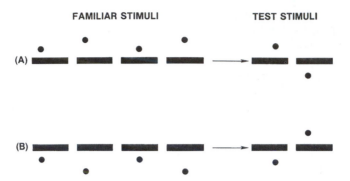

Figure 3.1. *Familiarization and test exemplars used in the above (panel A) versus below (panel B) categorization experiment of Quinn (1994).*

To measure categorization performance in the preference test for each infant, the looking time to the novel category instance was computed as a percentage of the total looking time to both test stimuli. The mean novel category preference scores for infants in the "dot above bar" and "dot below bar" conditions were found to be reliably above chance (i.e., 50 percent). Both groups displayed a preference for the novel spatial category—a result consistent with the idea that they had formed categorical representations for the above and below relations between the dot and the horizontal bar.

In the spirit of determining the most parsimonious explanation for infant performance (Haith, 1998), one may ask whether there might be a simpler way to account for the novelty preferences displayed by the infants. For example, might the infant looking patterns have been the result of simple generalization based on distance information? This explanation is unlikely, because the dot in the novel category exemplar was moved the same distance from the familiar dot locations (either down or up) as the dot in the novel exemplar of the familiar category (which was moved either to the right or to the left). One might observe further that the dot in the novel category exemplar was slightly closer to the bar than was the dot in the novel exemplar of the familiar category. This placement was the result of the test stimuli depicting the dot an equivalent distance away from the familiar dot locations. The question thus arises as to whether the infant looking patterns might reflect a spontaneous preference for a stimulus in which the dot was located closer to the bar. However, this was not the case, because when the original categorization experiment was repeated, but without the familiarization stimuli, the infants divided their attention between the test stimuli and displayed no preference for the stimulus in which the dot was located closer to the bar. In short, the preference for the novel spatial relation could not be attributed to an a priori preference.

Another question that might be raised about the preference for the novel spatial relation in the initial categorization study is whether this result can be taken as evidence of categorization or whether it reflects a more basic discrimination result. It is possible that the infants were not even sensitive to the position changes of the dot

Familiar Stimuli   Test Stimuli

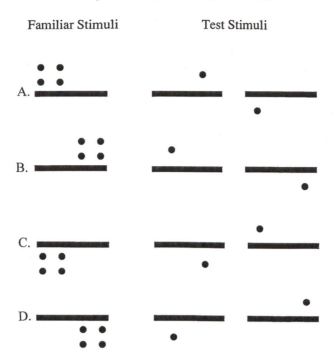

Figure 3.2. Familiarization exemplars (a composite of the four exemplars) and test exemplars used to investigate formation of the categorical representation "dot above bar" (panels A and B) and "dot below bar"(panels C and D) in Quinn (1994).

that occurred within the familiar category. If this was the case, then the categorization experiment involved mere discrimination of a dot above the bar versus a dot below the bar. As a response to this concern, a within-category discrimination experiment was conducted in which each infant was familiarized with a single member of the "dot above bar" or "dot below bar" categories, and then preference tested with the familiar stimulus paired with a novel stimulus from the same category. The two within-category exemplars for each discrimination pairing were randomly chosen for each infant. The resulting mean novelty preferences indicated that infants were able to discriminate exemplars of the above category and also able to discriminate instances from the below category. The preferences obtained in the categorization experiment were thus not attributable to a failure to discriminate among members of the familiar category.

Before reaching a definitive conclusion regarding infant performance in the above versus below categorization task, one still needs to consider two additional alternative interpretations. First, it could simply have been that infants responded preferentially to vertical (up-down) as opposed to horizontal (left-right) changes in dot location. That is, during the test trials, the dot in the novel category exemplar was positioned below or above the familiar dot locations, whereas the dot in the novel exemplar of the familiar category was positioned to the right or left of the familiar dot locations. Infants might have spontaneously preferred vertical over horizontal changes in dot location. Second, one also needs to consider the possibility that infants might have encoded the dot locations categorically, but relative to an *internal* horizontal midline rather than the external horizontal bar (Huttenlocher et al., 1994). That is, infants might have spontaneously bisected the stimulus into top and bottom halves and encoded the dot locations in relation to the mental line of bisection.

To assess the validity of the location change and internal bisection accounts, the initial categorization experiment was repeated, but in this case with stimuli that contained only the dot and not the horizontal bar. If infants performed in this control experiment as they did in the initial categorization experiment, then both the location change and internal bisection explanations would receive support. Alternatively, if infants divided their attention between the two test stimuli in this experiment, then the interpretation that infants had categorically represented the above and below relations of the dot relative to the bar in the initial experiment would be upheld. Infants in the no-bar control did not prefer either test stimulus, thereby supporting the conclusion that infants had formed categorical representations of the dot's above and below relations with the horizontal bar.

After obtaining these initial findings regarding spatial categorization in young infants, the next step was to extend them to a slightly different set of stimuli—just to make sure that the data were not a fluke and obtainable with only one stimulus set (Quinn, Cummins, Kase, Martin, & Weissman, 1996). Figure 3.3 reveals that each new stimulus consisted of a diamond in an above or below relation with a more complex horizontal bar that was composed of a row of small square elements. The result was that 3- to 4-month-olds familiarized with above or below preferred the novel spatial relation, thereby replicating the major outcome of Quinn (1994).

A Representation for the Spatial Relation Between

The replication result made it possible for the investigations to proceed in two different directions. The objectives of the new round of studies were to (1) examine the formation of categorical representations for spatial relations other than above versus below, and (2) determine the degree of "abstraction" of the representations.

The first question asked was whether infants could form a categorical representation of between, that is, of a diamond between two bars. There were a couple of reasons to believe that between might be a more difficult representation for infants to form than above versus below. First, Huttenlocher and Newcombe (1984) reviewed the literature on the encoding of spatial location by children and distinguished between location coding in relation to a single landmark and location coding in relation to a set of landmarks that constitute a local spatial framework (see also Weist & Uzunov, 1990). The specific proposal was that "children progress from coding in terms of a . . . landmark, to coding in terms of local spatial frameworks" (Huttenlocher & Newcombe, 1984, p. 109). It is possible that the categorical distinction that young infants make between above and below is analogous to location coding in relation to a single landmark—the diamond's location is coded relative to the horizontal bar, whereas the categorical representation of between may be more akin to

Familiar Stimuli   Test Stimuli

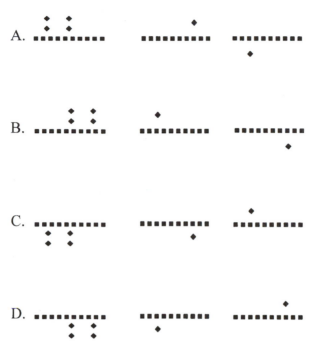

Figure 3.3. Familiarization exemplars (a composite of the four exemplars) and test exemplars used to determine whether infants could form a categorical representation for "diamond above bar" (panels A and B) and "diamond below bar" (panels C and D) in Quinn, Cummins, Kase, Martin, and Weissman (1996).

location coding in relation to two bars, one on each side of the diamond, and in this respect more like framework coding. If this analogy is reasonable, and the Hutten-locher and Newcombe proposal is correct, then one might expect between to be a more difficult representation to form than above versus below.

Second, Choi and Bowerman's (1991) work on vocabulary acquisition of spatial terms indicates that "up" and "down" are among the words that appear in the age range of 16 to 20 months. The early appearance of these terms is consistent with the early emergence of representations for above and below. However, one cannot find the word "between" in Bowerman and Choi's description of the child's developing spatial lexicon. In addition, Weist, Lyytinen, Wysocka, and Atanassova (1997) have reported that the terms "above" and "below" are comprehended by 2- to 3-year-olds, whereas "between" is not comprehended until 3 to 4.5 years (see also Johnston, 1988). These lexical acquisition data provide further reason to question whether a categorical representation for between would be in evidence as early as the categorical representations for above versus below.

To investigate whether young infants can categorize "between," two groups of 3- to 4-month-olds were familiarized with four instances of a diamond appearing between two bars (Quinn, Norris, Pasko, Schmader, & Mash, 1999). One group was exposed to stimuli in which the bars were horizontal rows. As is shown in the top two panels of figure 3.4, for half of the infants in this group, the diamond appeared in each of the four corners in the left half of the space between the rows, whereas for the other half, the diamond appeared in each of the four corners in the right half of the space between the rows. During the novel category preference test, the infants were presented with the diamond appearing in a novel position between the rows paired with a diamond appearing either above or below the rows.

The other group was shown stimuli with vertical columns. As is shown in C and D panels of figure 3.4, for infants in this group, the diamond appeared during familiarization in the corner locations of the top or bottom halves of the area between the columns. During the novel category preference test, the infants were presented with the diamond appearing in a novel position between the columns, paired with a diamond appearing either to the left or to the right of the columns. For both the row and column groups, the prediction is that if infants form a categorical representation for "diamond between bars," then they should display a preference for the novel category exemplar depicting the diamond outside the bars. However, if infants do not form a categorical representation for "diamond between bars," then one would not expect a consistent preference for either test exemplar, since both are novel.

Neither group displayed a preference for the novel category exemplar depicting the diamond outside the bars, indicating that the infants had not formed a categorical representation for between. One might first ask whether this result could be attributed to the fact that there was just more information for the infants to encode. By this reasoning, if provided with more familiarization time, the infants might form a categorical representation for between. To this end, infants in a follow-up study were provided with double the familiarization time, and the same results were obtained.

An alternative interpretation of performance is that the 3- to 4-month-olds were not capable of forming a representation for between on the grounds that it is a cognitively more complex spatial representation than above versus below. Consistent with the proposal made by Huttenlocher and Newcombe (1984), it may be that between requires infants to represent a local spatial framework, as opposed to just encoding the spatial relation of an object and a single landmark. If this is the case, then it can be argued that with maturation or experience or both, infants will at some later point during development come to represent between. The next experiment was therefore designed to determine whether older infants would form a categorical representation for between. The between categorization experiment was thus repeated, but with a group of 6- to 7-month-olds. The older infants were found to categorize between. The mean novel category preference scores for both the row and column groups were reliably above chance. The findings are consistent with the idea that the 6- to 7-month-olds could form a categorical representation for between.

To support our interpretation of infant performance, two control experiments were conducted. In the first, the test stimuli were presented without the familiarization stimuli to a separate group of 6- to 7-month-olds. The infants did not show a

Familiar Stimuli   **Test Stimuli**

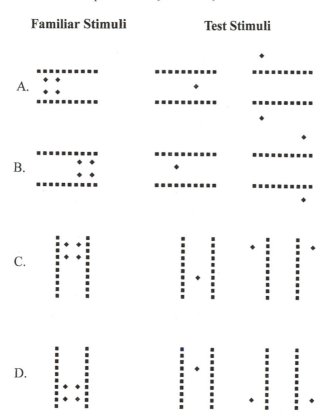

Figure 3.4. Panels A and B display familiarization stimuli (a composite of the four diamond-between-rows exemplars) and test stimuli used to determine whether infants could form a categorical representation for diamond-between-rows. The test stimulus depicted on the right of each panel is a composite of the two diamond-outside-rows exemplars. Panels C and D display familiarization stimuli (a composite of the four diamond-between-columns exemplars) and test stimuli used to determine whether infants could form a categorical representation for diamond-between-columns. The test stimulus depicted on the right of each panel is a composite of the two diamond-outside-columns exemplars. Adapted from Quinn, Norris, Pasko, Schmader, & Mash (1999).

preference for the stimuli in which the diamond was depicted outside the bars. This result indicates that the preference for the novel spatial relation that was observed in the categorization experiment was not the outcome of a spontaneous preference for stimuli depicting the diamond outside the bars.

A second control experiment examined infants' abilities to discriminate the location changes of the diamond within the familiar category. Infants were familiarized with one exemplar from the familiar category and preference tested with that exemplar and a novel exemplar from the familiar category. Discrimination performance was above chance. The combined results from the discrimination and categorization experiments suggest that even though the infants observed the diamond appear in distinct locations between the bars, they also perceived the equivalence of the exemplars and responded preferentially to the novel exemplar depicting the diamond outside the bars.

The overall pattern of findings indicates that the older infants had categorically represented between. Together with the investigations of above versus below (Quinn, 1994; Quinn et al., 1996), the between studies suggest that representations for different spatial relations emerge at different points during development. The evidence is consistent with the idea that there may be a developmental trend from first encoding the spatial relation of a target and a single landmark to later encoding the spatial relation of a target and multiple landmarks that form a local spatial framework (Huttenlocher & Newcombe, 1984).

Development of Abstract Categorical Representations for Spatial Relations

There is a question that arises regarding the spatial categorization performance of infants that centers on the degree of abstraction of the representations. The question is whether infants are able to form abstract representations for spatial relations that can be maintained independently of the particular objects depicting the relations. For example, children and adults in cognitive activities such as object recognition, word recognition, and map learning experience various objects, object parts, symbols, and features in different spatial relations and are presumably able to maintain their spatial concepts despite variation of the entities in the relations. In other words, children and adults appear to encode the equivalence of a spatial relation across contexts (Deloache, Kolstad, & Anderson, 1991; Uttal, Schreiber, & Deloache, 1995).

To determine whether the abilities of young infants to categorize spatial relation information are functionally equivalent to those presumably possessed by children and adults, an experiment was conducted to determine whether 3- to 4-month-olds could form categorical representations for above and below that were independent of the objects used to signal these relations (Quinn et al., 1996). As depicted in figure 3.5, the above versus below experiment was repeated, but in this instance with four distinct shapes appearing above or below the bar. The shapes were randomly selected for each infant from among seven shapes shown to be discriminably different from each other in a control experiment (i.e., arrow, diamond, dollar sign, dot, letter E, plus sign, triangle). Infants were then preference tested as they were in the original above versus below study, but with the change that a novel shape in the familiar spatial relation was paired with the same shape in the novel spatial relation.

If the infants form categorical representations for above and below, despite changes in the objects depicting these relations, then they should perform as they did in the original above versus below experiment conducted without object variation. That is, they should prefer the novel spatial relation. Alternatively, if infants do not form categorical representations for above and below with object variation, then one would not expect a preference for either test stimulus. Similar experimental protocols have been used previously to investigate whether infants form abstract representations of causality and number irrespective of the particular objects displayed (Cohen & Oakes, 1993; Starkey, Spelke, & Gelman, 1990; Strauss & Curtis, 1981).

Familiar Stimuli   **Test Stimuli**

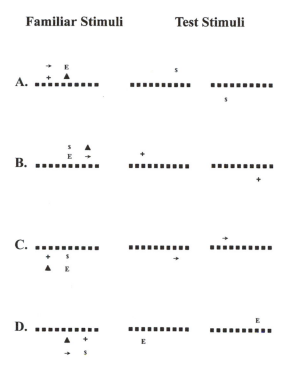

Figure 3.5. Panels A, B, C, and D display familiarization exemplars (a composite of the four exemplars) and test stimuli used on the object variation version of the above versus below categorization task in Quinn, Cummins, Kase, Martin, and Weissman (1996).

The results were that the 3- and 4-month-olds tested in the object variation version of the spatial categorization task did not show a preference for the novel category test stimulus, dividing their attention instead across both test stimuli. The findings indicated that the 3- and 4-month-olds did not form more abstract categorical representations for above and below that existed independently of the particular objects signaling these relations, and this result held true even when the infants were provided with extra familiarization time (Quinn, Polly, Dobson, & Narter, 1998).

The next experiment was conducted to determine when during development infants would display an ability to categorically represent abstract spatial relations that were independent of the objects portraying these relations (Quinn et al., 1996). The object-variation version of the above–below categorization task was thus repeated, but this time with a group of 6- to 7-month-olds. The older infants responded by preferring the novel spatial relation in the preference test, indicating that they were able to maintain their categorical representations for above and below despite changes in the objects during familiarization and preference test.

The findings from the 3- to 4-month-olds and 6- to 7-month-olds support the idea that categorical representations of spatial relations may initially be limited to objects depicting the relations but later become more abstract so that various objects can be presented in the same relation and the equivalence of the relation is maintained despite this variation. In this respect, the spatial categorization abilities of the 6- to 7-month-olds may be more like those of children and adults, although it is possible that even the abilities of the older infants might have broken down had the identity of the reference bar also changed from trial to trial.

Given the specific-to-abstract developmental trend observed for representation of above versus below, it became important to determine whether this trend would also hold true for representation of between. Based on the between data reported by Quinn et al. (1999) and the abstract above versus below findings obtained by Quinn et al. (1996), the 6- to 7-month-olds constituted a critical age group for investigating an abstract representation of between. The Quinn et al. (1999) results indicate that this group can form a specific spatial representation for "diamond between bars," and the Quinn et al. (1996) investigation reveals that these infants can form a more abstract representation for "object above or below bar." But how will the 6- to 7-month-olds perform on an object variation version of the between categorization task? Will these infants form an abstract representation for "object between bars," or will this ability not appear until later in development (e.g., 9 to 10 months)? More broadly, does a generalized abstraction ability become functional at 6 to 7 months of age, one that would apply to all spatial relation concepts formed by that age? Or is there a specific-to-abstract developmental trend observed for representation of each spatial relation such that each representation undergoes its own period of development from specific to abstract?

To answer these questions, Quinn (2000) examined the development of an abstract representation for the spatial relation between by infants in the age range from 6 to 10 months. In the first experiment, a group of 6- to 7-month-olds was familiarized with four exemplars, each depicting a different object in a distinct location between two bars. The objects were shown to be discriminably different in a control experiment. For half of the infants, the bars were horizontal rows (as shown in the top two panels of fig. 3.6), and for the other half, the bars were vertical columns (as shown in the bottom two panels of fig. 3.6). Both groups were then preference tested with a stimulus depicting a novel object in a novel location between the bars paired with a stimulus in which a novel object was located outside the bars. The infants did not display a preference for the stimulus depicting the object outside the bars that was reliably different from chance. In a second experiment, a separate group of 6- to 7-month-olds was tested on the abstract version of the between spatial categorization task, but in this instance with double the familiarization time, and the results were the same.

The third experiment was a replication of the first but conducted with 9- to 10-month-olds. This age group seemed reasonable to test because the developmental change from concrete to abstract observed for above and below was measured over a time span of three months (Quinn et al., 1996). The older infants responded with a reliable preference for the object-outside-bars stimulus. The overall findings indicated that 9- to 10-month-olds formed an abstract category representation for between, whereas 6- to 7-month-olds did not. Taken together with the findings from the above versus below studies (Quinn et al., 1996), the evidence from the between studies confirms that representations for different spatial relations emerge at dif-

Familiar Stimuli   **Test Stimuli**

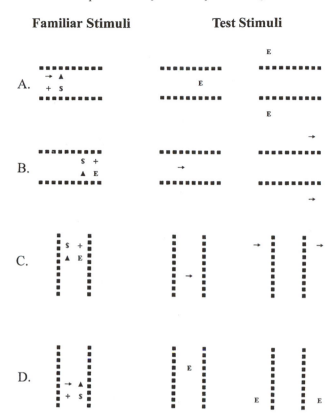

Figure 3.6. Panels A and B display familiarization stimuli (a composite of the four object-between-rows exemplars) and test stimuli used in the object variation version of the between categorization task. The novel category test stimulus (depicted on the far right of each panel) is a composite of the two object-outside-rows exemplars. Panels C and D display additional familiarization stimuli (a composite of the four object-between-columns exemplars) and test stimuli used in the object variation version of the between categorization task. The novel category test stimulus (depicted on the far right of each panel) is a composite of the two object-outside-columns exemplars.

ferent points during development, and moreover suggests that each representation undergoes its own period of development from concrete to abstract.

Object Variation and Its Effect on Spatial Categorization: A Further Inquiry

A lingering issue in the development of spatial categorization by infants is why the object variation manipulation disrupted the spatial categorization performance of the 3- to 4-month-olds in the Quinn et al. (1996) study. One way to think about infant performance in the object variation version of the spatial categorization task is in terms of perceptual or attentional distraction. For example, during familiarization, trial-to-trial changes in the objects appearing above or below the bar might recruit infant attention away from the spatial nature of the task. That is, the object variation may prompt the infant to focus attention on the target object, at the expense of processing the spatial relation between the target object and landmark bar. Likewise, during the test trials, the novel object that appeared in both the familiar and novel category exemplars may cause the infant to divide attention between the two stimuli.

The perceptual-attentional distraction explanation is also consistent with what is known about the cognitive neuroscience of the systems that are believed to process "what" and "where" information (Mishkin, Ungerleider, & Macko, 1983; Ungerleider & Haxby, 1994). In particular, a "what" processing stream may be formed by the ventral pathway from primary visual cortex to inferior temporal cortex and may be responsible for processing object properties like shape and surface markings. A complementary "where" processing stream may be formed by the dorsal pathway out of primary visual cortex to posterior parietal cortex and may be responsible for processing spatial relations among objects. Vecera and Farah (1994) have furthermore suggested that these independent neural systems for processing "what" and "where" information may compete for general attentional capacity.

If the perceptual-attentional distraction explanation of infant performance in the object variation version of the above versus below categorization task is correct, then it should be possible to improve performance by reducing (1) object variation during the familiarization trials or (2) object novelty during the test trials. To this end, Quinn, Polly, Furer, Dobson, and Narter (2002) presented 3- to 4-month-olds with an above versus below spatial categorization task in which a novel object was depicted in both the novel and familiar spatial relations during the preference test trials, but with no object variation during familiarization. As shown in figure 3.7, this task matched the original object variation version of the above versus below categorization task on the preference test trials but differed in the familiarization trials, with the presentation of a consistent object from trial to trial. If infants in the original object variation version of the spatial categorization task were distracted because of the changes in the object during familiarization trials, then one would expect infants in the Quinn et al. (2002) task to display a preference for the novel spatial relation during the preference test trials. However, this preference was not observed: the infants again divided their attention between the two test stimuli.

Although the perceptual-attentional distraction explanation did not receive support from the first Quinn et al. (2002) experiment, it is possible that the object novelty during the preference test trials, rather than the object variation during the familiarization trials, was the source of distraction for the young infants in the object variation version of the above versus below categorization task. Quinn et al. (2002) therefore conducted a second experiment that matched the original object variation version of the above versus below categorization task, except that the 3- to 4-month-olds were initially administered a single prefamiliarization trial depicting the object to be presented on the test trials. This prefamiliarization trial occurred immediately before the standard familiarization trials, and showed the object in the center of the stimulus display, without the horizontal bar. The rationale was that if the novelty of

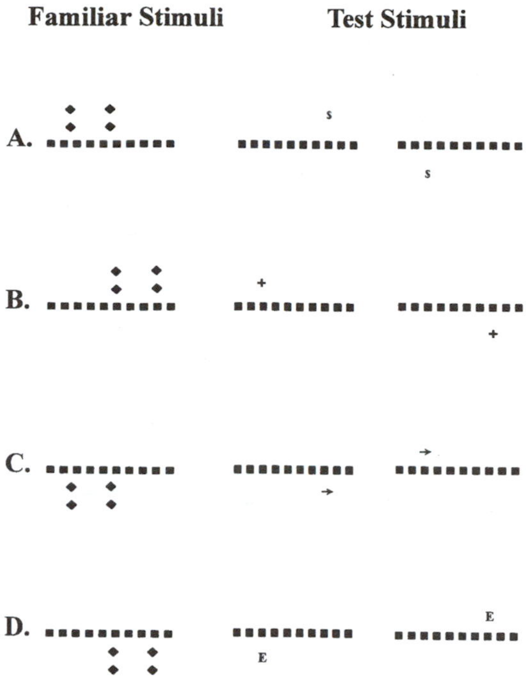

Familiar Stimuli   **Test Stimuli**

Figure 3.7. Panels A, B, C, and D display familiarization exemplars (a composite of the four exemplars) and test exemplars used in the modification of the object variation version of the spatial categorization task in Quinn, Polly, Furer, Dobson, and Narter (2002). Object variation did not occur during the familiarization trials; however, a novel object was presented on the preference test trials. Reprinted with permission of Lawrence Erlbaum Associates from Quinn, P. C., Polly, J. L., Furer, M. J., Dobson, V., & Narter, D. B. (2002). Young infants' performance in the object-variation version of the above–below categorization task: A result of perceptual distraction or conceptual limitation? Infancy, 3, 323–347.

the object is distracting the infants on the preference test trials, then prior experience with the object should reduce this distraction, thereby allowing infants to display a preference for the novel spatial relation. Once more, however, the infants divided their attention between the two test stimuli.

Given the failure of the two experiments to provide support for the perceptual-attentional distraction account of young infant performance in the Quinn et al. (1996) study, Quinn et al. (2002) hypothesized that the difficulty in the object variation version of the above versus below categorization task may arise because of a limitation in conceptually based generalization. The term "conceptually based" refers to a categorical representation that is "freed" from the perceptual particulars of the category instances. Interestingly, the conceptual limitation hypothesis implies that young infants in the object variation spatial categorization task are representing spatial relation information, but not in an abstract format. That is, the infants may be mapping specific objects into individual spatial representations. On each trial, when a new pair of objects is encountered, a new spatial representation is constructed. Thus, infants presented with the familiarization sequence depicted in figure 3.5A may form separate representations for "arrow above bar," "plus sign above bar," "E above bar," and "triangle above bar" but not join these representations together in a more abstract representation of "object above bar" or "above." During the test trials, "dollar sign above bar" would be represented as a novel stimulus, as would "dollar sign below bar." One would thus not expect generalization to the novel exemplar from the familiar category and a preference for the novel exemplar from the novel category. Both of these stimuli would be assimilated into the young infant's spatial representation system as individuated units.

If infant performance can be explained in terms of a limit on conceptually based generalization, then young infants should perform successfully (with a preference for the novel spatial relation) in a modified version of the object variation version of the above versus below categorization task—one in which the object–bar relation shown during the preference test trials matches an object–bar relation that appeared during familiarization. The design for this task is shown in figure 3.8. For infants shown the familiarization sequence in figure 3.8A, the "triangle above bar" stimulus should match the representation of the "triangle above bar" stimulus shown during familiarization, whereas the "triangle below bar" stimulus should not match any of the representations constructed during familiarization and should thus be preferred. This was in fact the result obtained by Quinn et al. (2002).

The positive and negative findings of Quinn et al. (2002), when considered together, suggest that young infants encode the spatial relations between specific pairs of objects (e.g., triangle above bar) but do not encode the spatial relations abstracted across a number of different pairs of objects. Although this encoding format is deficient in terms of abstraction, it may be adaptively sufficient for the primary problem that a young infant's spatial memory system must confront, namely, remembering the location of one specific object relative to another particular object. In this respect, the process of spatial categorization may be secondary to the formation of spatial memories during early infancy. That is, the ability to form a specific representation for object A above object Z may have developmental primacy over the ability to maintain a more abstract categorical representation for objects A, B, C, and D above object Z that can be generalized to object E above object Z.

Development of Object and Spatial Categorization: A Common Framework?

It is interesting to question whether the development of spatial categorization can be accommodated by the same kind of theoretical framework that was described for the development of object categorization. On the one hand, it has been argued that object and spatial processing are accomplished by two different neural systems in adults (Mishkin et al., 1983; Ungerleider & Haxby, 1994). In addition, on the basis of comparing fullterm and preterm infants on object versus spatial categorization tasks, Mash, Quinn, Dobson, and Narter (1998) have argued that the development

Familiar Stimuli **Test Stimuli**

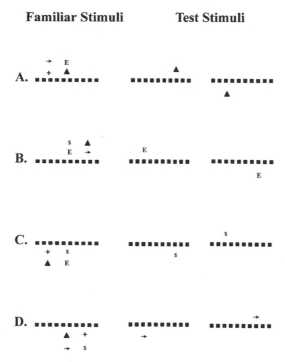

Figure 3.8. Panels A, B, C, and D display familiarization exemplars (a composite of the four exemplars) and test exemplars used to investigate formation of specific categorical representations for above and below in the object variation version of the spatial categorization task used by Quinn et al. (2002). Reprinted with permission of Lawrence Erlbaum Associates from Quinn, P. C., Polly, J. L., Furer, M. J., Dobson, V., & Narter, D. B. (2002). Young infants' performance in the object-variation version of the above-below categorization task: A result of perceptual distraction or conceptual limitation? Infancy, 3, 323–347.

of object and spatial categorization may have different determinants. The object system may be influenced more by environmental experience, and the spatial system may be governed more by biological maturation. Moreover, the broad-to-narrow, differentiation-driven trend in the development of object categorization seems rather different from the specific-percept to general-concept trajectory in the development of spatial categorization. These constrasts are suggestive of "specificities" in the domains of object and spatial categorization.

On the other hand, additional comparisons imply "generalities" in the what and where categorization domains. For example, it was suggested in the object part of the chapter that the more readily formed global representations might be based on single-attribute comparisons (e.g., legs versus wheels or curvilinear versus rectilinear contours, in the case of animals versus vehicles), whereas the less readily formed basic-level representations might be based on specific values of a number of shared attributes (e.g., comparison of input vectors comprised of values of the common features of cats versus dogs). This difference in structural complexity and ease of formation of global and basic representations in the object domain might have a correspondence with the difference observed for above-below and between in the spatial domain. The readily formed representation of above versus below may be achieved by comparing the location of a target object to just one other object (a landmark representation), whereas the less readily formed representation of between appears to require comparison of a target object to multiple objects that define a spatial framework (a framework representation). Like global- and basic-level representations in the object domain, landmark and framework representations in the spatial domain may also differ in terms of structural complexity in ways that affect ease of acquisition. Structural complexity may thus be a domain-general principle affecting the development of object and spatial categorization.

Another developmental trend that appears to occur in both the object and spatial categorization systems is that of increasing abstraction. In the object domain, it was noted that early categorical representations that are constructed from surface attributes may serve as perceptual placeholders for the accumulation of more abstract knowledge acquired beyond infancy. In the spatial domain, representations for spatial relations are tied to the perceptual particulars of the objects depicting these relations during early infancy but become more abstract as the representations come to incorporate a variety of objects that uphold the relation. In these respects, the category representations formed by infants for objects and spatial relations may be viewed as functional: they serve to organize experience in ways that facilitate the growth of cognitive structure and content. Although increasing abstraction can be observed in both the object and spatial domains, a task for future research will be to determine whether this trend is the result of common or different underlying mechanisms functioning in the two domains.

Concluding Remarks

The findings reviewed on the development of spatial categorization indicate that infants younger than one year of age can form categorical representations for spatial relations such as above, below, and between. In addition, there may be a developmental trend from infants first encoding the spatial location of a target relative to a single landmark (i.e., a diamond above vs. below a bar) to later encoding the location of a target in relation to multiple landmarks that define a local spatial framework (i.e., diamond between bars). Moreover, categorical representations of spatial relations may initially be limited to the objects depicting the relations but subsequently become more abstract so that various objects can be presented in the same relation and the equivalence of the relation is maintained despite the variation. Casasola and Cohen (2002) have recently reported experimental results on spatial categorization by infants that are consistent with these developmental trends and also extend them to dynamic events depicted with complex objects.

Substantive questions remain for future research. First, it will be informative to investigate the formation of categorical representations for spatial relations other than above versus below and between. For example, how will infants perform on spatial categorization tasks that require the representation of left versus right or inside versus outside? Based on the Huttenlocher and Newcombe (1984) distinction between landmark and framework representations, it is expected that left versus right would behave like above versus below and be available to younger infants (see Behl-Chadha & Eimas, 1995, for evidence consistent with this suggestion) whereas inside versus outside would behave like between and be formed later in development. Second, it will be important to study spatial categorization with more natural stimuli. As can be seen in figure 3.9, the demands on the spatial representation system become more complex with such stimuli. How will infants perform if asked to represent "dog above or below the surface of the table" or "dog between the legs of the table"? It will be interesting to determine if the above versus below relation of the dog and table surface is represented developmentally earlier than the between relation of the dog and table legs.

Regardless of how these questions are resolved, the general significance of the work already conducted is that the categorical representation of spatial relation information should allow infants to experience objects in coherent spatial layouts rather than as spatially unrelated entities residing in disconnected locations. The categorical representation of spatial relation information by young infants may also yield the functional units (e.g., primitives) necessary for (1) the construction of more complex representations of larger scale spaces and (2) successful performance in the variety of cognitive tasks mentioned at the beginning of the chapter.

Figure 3.9. Representation of spatial relation information becomes more complex with natural stimuli. Will infants represent "dog above or below table surface" and "dog between table legs"?

Acknowledgments

Preparation of this chapter was supported by National Science Foundation Research Grant BCS-0096300. I thank Lisa Oakes and David Rakison for their helpful comments on an earlier version of the manuscript. I also thank Jason Parkhill and Jason Pergola from the Instructional Technology Center at Washington and Jefferson College and Ramesh Bhatt for their assistance in creating the figures.

Correspondence concerning this chapter should be addressed to Paul C. Quinn, Department of Psychology, Washington and Jefferson College, 60 South Lincoln Street, Washington, PA, 15301. Electronic mail may be sent via the internet to (pquinn@washjeff.edu).

References

Baillargeon, R. (1995). A model of physical reasoning in infancy. In C. Rovee-Collier & L. P. Lipsitt (Eds.), *Advances infancy research* (Vol. 9, pp. 305–371). Norwood, NJ: Ablex.

Balaban, M. T., & Waxman, S. R. (1997). Do words facilitate object categorization in 9-month-old infants? *Journal of Experimental Child Psychology, 64,* 3–26.

Barsalou, L. W. (1983). Ad hoc categories. *Memory and Cognition, 10,* 82–93.

Behl-Chadha, G. (1996). Basic-level and superordinate-like categorical representations in early infancy. *Cognition, 60,* 105–141.

Behl-Chadha, G., & Eimas, P. D. (1995). Infant categorization of left-right spatial relations. *British Journal of Developmental Psychology, 13,* 69–79.

Behl-Chadha, G., Eimas, P. D., & Quinn, P. C. (1995, March). *Perceptually driven superordinate categorization by young infants.* Paper presented at the meeting of the Society for Research in Child Development, Indianapolis, IN.

Bertenthal, B. I., & Campos, J. J. (1990). A systems approach to the organizing effects of self-produced locomotion during infancy. In C. Rovee-Collier & L. P. Lipsitt (Eds.), *Advances in infancy research* (Vol. 6, pp. 1–60). Norwood, NJ: Ablex.

Biederman, I. (1987). Recognition-by-components: A theory of human image understanding. *Psychological Review, 94,* 115–147.

Bowerman, M. (1996). Learning how to structure space for language: A cross-linguistic perspective. In P. Bloom, M. A. Peterson, L. Nadel, & M. F. Garrett (Eds.), *Language and space* (pp. 385–436). Cambridge, MA: MIT Press.

Bowerman, M., & Choi, S. (2001). Shaping meanings for language: universal and language specific in the acquisition of spatial semantic categories. In M. Bowerman & S. C. Levinson (Eds.), *Language acquisition and conceptual development* (pp. 475–511). Cambridge: Cambridge University Press:.

Bruner, J. S., Goodnow, J. J., & Austin, G. A. (1956). *A study of thinking.* New York: Wiley.

Campos, J. J., Anderson, D. I., Barbu-Roth, M. A., Hubbard, E. M., Hertenstein, M. J., & Witherington, D. (2000). Travel broadens the mind. *Infancy, 1,* 149–219.

Caramazza, A., & Hillis, A. E. (1990). Levels of representation, coordinate frames, and unilateral neglect. *Cognitive Neuropsychology, 7,* 391–445.

Carey, S. (1985). *Conceptual change in childhood.* Cambridge, MA: MIT Press.

Casasola, M., & Cohen, L. B. (2002). Infant categorization of containment, support and tight-fit spatial relationships. *Developmental Science, 5,* 247–264.

Choi, S., & Bowerman, M. (1991). Learning to express motion events in English and Korean: The influence of language-specific lexicalization patterns. *Cognition, 41,* 83–121.

Cohen, L. B., & Oakes, L. M. (1993). How infants perceive a simple causal event. *Developmental Psychology, 29,* 421–433.

Deloache, J. S., Kolstad, V., & Anderson, K. (1991). Physical similarity and young children's understanding of scale models. *Child Development, 62,* 111–126.

Edelman, G. M. (1987). *Neural Darwinism.* New York: Basic Books.

Eimas, P. D. (1994). Categorization in early infancy and the continuity of development. *Cognition, 50,* 83–93.

Eimas, P. D., & Quinn, P. C. (1994). Studies on the formation of perceptually based basic-level categories in young infants. *Child Development, 65,* 903–917.

Eimas, P. D., Quinn, P. C., & Cowan, P. (1994). Development of exclusivity in perceptually based categories of young infants. *Journal of Experimental Child Psychology, 58,* 418–431.

Fagan, J. F. (1970). Memory in the infant. *Journal of Experimental Child Psychology, 9,* 217–226.

Fantz, R. L. (1964). Visual experience in infants: Decreased attention to familiar patterns relative to novel ones. *Science, 164,* 668–670.

Fodor, J. A. (1981). *Representations.* Cambridge, MA: MIT Press.

Haith, M. M. (1998). Who put the cog in infant cognition? Is rich interpretation too costly? *Infant Behavior and Development, 21,* 167–179.

Hirtle, S. C., & Jonides, J. (1985). Evidence of hierarchies in cognitive maps. *Memory and Cognition, 13,* 208–217.

Huttenlocher, J., & Newcombe, N. (1984). The child's representation of information about location. In C. Sophian (Ed.), *Origins of cognitive skills* (pp. 81–111). Hillsdale, NJ: Erlbaum.

Huttenlocher, J., Newcombe, N., & Sandberg, E. H. (1994). The coding of spatial location in young children. *Cognitive Psychology, 27,* 115–147.

Johnston, J. R. (1988). Children's verbal representation of spatial location. In J. Stiles-Davis, M. Kritchevsky, & U. Bellugi (Eds.), *Spatial cognition* (pp. 195–206). Hillsdale, NJ: Erlbaum.

Jones, S. S., & Smith, L. B. (1993). The place of perception in children's concepts. *Cognitive Development, 8,* 113–139.

Keil, F. C. (1989). *Concepts, kinds, and cognitive development.* Cambridge, MA: MIT Press.

Kosslyn, S. M., Pick, H. L., & Fariello, G. R. (1974). Cognitive maps in children and men. *Child Development, 45,* 707–716.

Landau, B. (1986). Early map use as an unlearned ability. *Cognition, 22,* 201–223.

Madole, K., & Oakes, L. (1999). Making sense of infant categorization: Stable processes and changing representations. *Developmental Review, 19,* 263–296.

Malt, B. C. (1995). Category coherence in cross cultural perspective. *Cognitive Psychology, 29,* 85–148.

Mandler, J. M., & McDonough, L. (1993). Concept formation in infancy. *Cognitive Development, 8,* 291–318.

Mandler, J. M., & McDonough, L. (1996). Drinking and driving don't mix: Inductive generalization in infancy. *Cognition, 59,* 307–335.

Mandler, J. M., & McDonough, L. (1998). Studies in inductive inference in infancy. *Cognitive Psychology, 37,* 60–96.

Markman, E. M. (1989). *Categorization and naming in children: Problems of induction.* Cambridge, MA: MIT Press.

Mash, C., Quinn, P. C., Dobson, V., & Narter, D. B. (1998). Global influences on the development of spatial and object perceptual categorization abilities: Evidence from preterm infants. *Developmental Science, 1,* 85–102.

McNamara, T. P., Hardy, J. K., & Hirtle, S. C. (1989). Subjective hierarchies in spatial memory. *Journal of Experimental Psychology: Learning, Memory and Cognition, 15,* 211–227.

Mervis, C. B. (1987). Child-basic object categories and early development. In U. Neisser (Ed.), *Concepts and conceptual development* (pp. 201–233). Cambridge: Cambridge University Press.

Millikan, R. G. (1998). A common structure for concepts of individuals, stuffs, and real kinds: More mama, more milk, and more mouse. *Behavioral and Brain Sciences, 21,* 55–100.

Mishkin, M., Ungerleider, L. G., & Macko, K. A. (1983). Object vision and spatial vision: Two cortical pathways. *Trends in Neuroscience, 6,* 414–417.

Newcombe, N., & Liben, L. S. (1982). Barrier effects in the cognitive maps of children and adults. *Journal of Experimental Child Psychology, 34,* 46–58.

Piaget, J. (1954). *The construction of reality in the child.* New York: Basic Books.

Poulin-Dubois, D., Lepage, A., & Ferland, D. (1996). Infants' concept of animacy. *Cognitive Development, 11,* 19–36.

Quinn, P. C. (1994). The categorization of above and below spatial relations by young infants. *Child Development, 65,* 58–69.

Quinn, P. C. (1998). Object and spatial categorization in young infants: "What" and "where" in early visual perception. In A. M. Slater (Ed.), *Perceptual development: Visual, auditory, and speech perception in infancy* (pp. 131–165). Hove, UK: Psychology Press.

Quinn, P. C. (1999). Development of recognition and categorization of objects and their spatial relations in young infants. In C. Tamis-LeMonda & L. Balter (Eds.), *Child psychology: A handbook of contemporary issues* (pp. 85–115). Philadelphia: Psychology Press.

Quinn, P. C. (2000, July). Development of spatial categorization in young infants. In R. Gilmore (Organizer), *Do they know where they're going? Development of spatial processing in infancy,* Symposium conducted at the International Conference on Infant Studies, Brighton, UK.

Quinn, P. C. (2002). Early categorization: A new synthesis. In U. Goswami (Ed.), *Blackwell handbook of childhood cognitive development* (pp. 84–101). Oxford, UK: Blackwell.

Quinn, P. C., Cummins, M., Kase, J., Martin, E., & Weissman, S. (1996). Development of categorical representations for above and below spatial relations in 3- to 7-month-old infants. *Developmental Psychology, 32,* 942–950.

Quinn, P. C., & Eimas, P. D. (1996a). Perceptual cues that permit categorical differentiation of animal species by infants. *Journal of Experimental Child Psychology, 63,* 189–211.

Quinn, P. C., & Eimas, P. D. (1996b). Perceptual organization and categorization in young infants. In C. Rovee-Collier & L. P. Lipsitt (Eds.), *Advances in infancy research* (Vol. 10, pp. 1–36). Norwood, NJ: Ablex.

Quinn, P. C., & Eimas, P. D. (1997). A reexamination of the perceptual-to-conceptual shift in mental representations. *Review of General Psychology, 1,* 271–287.

Quinn, P. C., & Eimas, P. D. (1998). Evidence for a global categorical representation for humans by young infants. *Journal of Experimental Child Psychology, 69,* 151–174.

Quinn, P. C., & Eimas, P. D. (2000). The emergence of category representations during infancy: Are separate perceptual and conceptual processes required? *Journal of Cognition and Development, 1,* 55–61.

Quinn, P. C., Eimas, P. D., & Rosenkrantz, S. L. (1993). Evidence for representations of perceptually similar natural categories by 3-month-old and 4-month-old infants. *Perception, 22,* 463–475.

Quinn, P. C., Eimas, P. D., & Tarr, M. J. (2001). Perceptual categorization of cat and dog silhouettes by 3- to 4-month-old infants. *Journal of Experimental Child Psychology, 79,* 78–94.

Quinn, P. C., & Johnson, M. H. (1997). The emergence of perceptual category representations in young infants: A connectionist analysis. *Journal of Experimental Child Psychology, 66,* 236–263.

Quinn, P. C., & Johnson, M. H. (2000). Global-before-basic object categorization in connectionist networks and 2-month-old infants. *Infancy*, 1, 31–46.

Quinn, P. C., Johnson, M. H., Mareschal, D., Rakison, D. H., & Younger, B. A. (2000). Understanding early categorization: One process or two? *Infancy*, 1, 111–122.

Quinn, P. C., Norris, C. M., Pasko, R. N., Schmader, T. M., & Mash, C. (1999). Formation of a categorical representation for the spatial relation between by 6- to 7-month-old infants. *Visual Cognition*, 6, 569–585.

Quinn, P. C., Polly, J. L., Dobson, V., & Narter, D. B. (1998, April). *Categorical representation of specific versus abstract above and below spatial relations in 3- to 4-month-old infants.* Paper presented at the International Conference on Infant Studies, Atlanta, GA.

Quinn, P. C., Polly, J. L., Furer, M. J., Dobson, V., & Narter, D. B. (2002). Young infants' performance in the object-variation version of the above-below categorization task: A result of perceptual distraction or conceptual limitation? *Infancy*, 3, 323–347.

Quinn, P. C., Slater, A. M., Brown, E., & Hayes, R. A. (2001). Developmental change in form categorization in early infancy. *British Journal of Developmental Psychology*, 19, 207–218.

Rakison, D. H., & Butterworth, G. E. (1998). Infants' use of object parts in early categorization. *Developmental Psychology*, 34, 49–62.

Rosch, E. (1978). Principles of categorization. In E. Rosch & B. B. Lloyd (Eds.), *Cognition and categorization* (pp. 27–48). Hillsdale, NJ: Erlbaum.

Sandberg, E. H., Huttenlocher, J., & Newcombe, N. (1996). The development of hierarchical representation of two-dimensional space. *Child Development*, 67, 721–739.

Slater, A. M. (1995). Visual perception and memory at birth. In C. Rovee-Collier & L. P. Lipsitt (Eds.), *Advances in infancy research* (Vol. 9, pp. 107–162). Norwood, NJ: Ablex.

Spencer, J., Quinn, P. C., Johnson, M. H., & Karmiloff-Smith, A. (1997). Heads you win, tails you lose: Evidence for young infants categorizing mammals by head and facial attributes. *Early Development and Parenting*, 6, 113–126.

Starkey, P., Spelke, E. S., & Gelman, R. (1990). Numerical abstraction by human infants. *Cognition*, 36, 97–127.

Strauss, M. S., & Curtis, L. E. (1981). Infant perception of numerosity. *Child Development*, 52, 1146–1152.

Thelen, E., & Smith, L. B. (1994). *A dynamic systems approach to the development of cognition and action.* Cambridge, MA: MIT Press.

Ungerleider, L. G., & Haxby, J. V. (1994). "What" and "where" in the human brain. *Current Opinion in Neurobiology*, 4, 157–165.

Uttal, D. H., Schreiber, J. C., & Deloache, J. S. (1995). Waiting to use a symbol: The effects of delay on children's use of models. *Child Development*, 66, 1875–1889.

Vecera, S. P., & Farah, M. J. (1994). Does visual attention select objects or locations? *Journal of Experimental Psychology: General*, 123, 146–160.

Waxman, S. R., & Markow, D. B. (1995). Words as invitations to form categories: Evidence from 12- to 13-month-old infants. *Cognitive Psychology*, 29, 257–302.

Weist, R. M., Lyytinen, P., Wysocka, J., & Atanassova, M. (1997). The interaction of language and thought in children's language acquisition: A cross-linguistic study. *Journal of Child Language*, 24, 81–121.

Weist, R. M., & Uzunov, K. (1990). Spatial location in children's English: On the mono-/bireferential distinction. *Perceptual and Motor Skills*, 71, 1267–1274.

Wellman, H. M. (1990). *The child's theory of mind.* Cambridge, MA: MIT Press.

Xu, F., & Carey, S. (1996). Infants' metaphysics: The case of numerical identity. *Cognitive Psychology*, 30, 111–153.

Xu, F., Tenenbaum, J. B., & Sorrentino, C. M. (1998). Concepts are not beliefs, but having concepts is having beliefs. *Behavioral and Brain Sciences*, 21, 89.

Younger, B. A. (1990). Infants' detection of correlations among feature categories. *Child Development, 61*, 614–620.

Younger, B. A., & Fearing, D. D. (1999). Parsing items into separate categories: Developmental change in infant categorization. *Child Development, 70*, 291–303.

Younger, B. A., & Fearing, D. D. (2000). A global-to-basic trend in early categorization: Evidence from a dual-category habituation task. *Infancy, 1*, 47–58.

CHAPTER FOUR

Parsing Objects into Categories
Infants' Perception and Use of Correlated Attributes

Barbara A. Younger

How do infants form categories? Some time ago, Rosch and her colleagues (e.g., Rosch, 1978; Rosch, Mervis, Gray, Johnson, & Boyes-Braem, 1976) noted that natural object categories reflect the correlational structure of the environment. They pointed out that attributes are not randomly distributed across objects but that clusters of attributes occur with regularity. Thus, a category learner programmed in some sense to detect and utilize correlational information would tend to form distinctive categories (Medin, 1983). In this chapter, I summarize research focused on the infant as such a category learner. In contrast to the top-down or theory-driven approach to the use of correlated attributes typically presented for child and adult category learners (e.g., Barrett, Abdi, Murphy, & Gallagher, 1993; Medin, Altom, Edelson, & Freko, 1982), the view presented in this chapter is of an infant who is attuned to statistical regularities in the input (see Saffran, Aslin, & Newport, 1996). Evidence is presented indicating that infants (and preschool-aged children) are able to detect and utilize correlations among attributes in forming novel categories.

Attention is also given to the mechanisms that underlie the infant's and young child's formation of correlation-based categories. Researchers have debated whether young children are holistic or analytic in their approach to categorization. According to Kemler Nelson (1984, 1990), the advantage young children show in learning categories with a family-resemblance structure over categories having criterial or defining features derives from their holistic mode of processing. Based on the holistic responses that young children make in simple classification tasks (e.g., Smith & Kemler, 1977), Kemler Nelson argued that young children classify on the basis of overall similarity relations and not on the basis of specific dimensional relations or shared features. In contrast, Ward and his colleagues (Ward & Scott, 1987; Ward,

Vela, & Hass, 1990) argued that young children, like adults, are analytic in their approach to category learning and demonstrated that children as young as 4 to 5 years of age learn family-resemblance categories by focusing attention on one or two attributes that are characteristic of a category.

The debate over holistic versus analytic modes of processing in early categorization has been extended to the formation of correlation-based categories (Younger & Mekos, 1992). From a holistic processing perspective, sensitivity to correlated attributes could occur as a byproduct of the child's attention to global or unanalyzed similarity relations. From an analytic processing perspective, categorization by correlated attributes might imply a selective weighting of attributes that are correlated. Evidence presented in this chapter generally favors an analytic processing mechanism of some kind. Preliminary evidence, however, also suggests that individual infants may differ in their approach to categorization.

Substantial evidence also indicates that attention to correlated attributes develops over the child's first year of life. A major focus of this chapter is the nature of the change that occurs over the first year of life in infants' attention to and use of correlated attributes in categorization. The major conclusions and evidence cited in support of those conclusions are summarized in table 4.1. First, it appears that the ability to detect feature relations is present from early infancy but that the types of features and feature relations that infants perceive changes with age (see also chap. 6 for a discussion of developmental change in the features to which infants have access). Evidence is also presented indicating a developmental progression from processing features independently to processing feature relations within objects to processing feature relations within categories.

Finally, I explore the notion that the ability to explicitly categorize objects on the basis of correlated attributes underlies the emergence of a *recategorization* ability late in the first year of life (Lalonde & Werker, 1995). Some researchers have made a distinction between what they believe to be an implicit recognition of categories by infants under a year of age, and the ability of the year-and-a-half-old child to explicitly equate different members of a category (e.g., Gopnik & Meltzoff, 1997; Sugarman, 1982). Evidence is presented indicating that 10-month-old infants exhibit an explicit form of categorization. Evidence from studies of visual categorization and speech perception also converge to suggest that late in the first year, infants impose new category boundaries on earlier perceptual categories and that they do so based on an integration of multiple sources of information.

Infants' Sensitivity to Correlations among Attributes

In essence, the argument put forth by Rosch and her colleagues 20 years ago was that there are statistical regularities in the environment—correlations among what we consider to be attributes of objects—and that the categories of objects that we commonly form and label reflect those regularities. In work that I began with Les Cohen, we were interested in determining whether infants, as young category learners, were capable of detecting regularities in the input that could potentially form the basis for their early categories. Our approach was to create artificial cate-

TABLE 4.1. Key Evidence Cited in Support of Conclusions concerning Developmental Change in Infant Categorization

Investigator	Age (months)	Finding
The ability to detect feature relations is present from early infancy.		
Bhatt & Rovee Collier (1994, 1996)	3	Color-form feature relations were encoded and retained for up to 3 days.
There are age-related changes in the types of feature relations infant detect.		
Younger (1993a)	7–10	Infants detected color-form correlations at 7 months of age but did not detect correlations among body parts in categories of schematic animals until 10 months.
There is a dissociation in memory between features and feature relations and a developmental progression from processing features independently to processing feature relations within objects to processing feature relations embedded within a category.		
Bhatt & Rovee-Collier (1996)	3	Color-form feature relations were forgotten earlier than the individual features constituting the relations.
Younger & Cohen (1983, 1986)	4–10	4-month-olds failed to detect feature relations, responding only to novel vs. familiar features of schematic animals; 7-month-olds processed feature relations only when all attributes were correlated; 10-month-olds processed feature relations when a subset of the varying attributes were correlated.
Wilk, Bhatt, & Rovee-Collier (1995)	6	Infants detected color-form correlations when only 2 of 3 varying attributes were correlated. (Younger infants were not tested in this study.)
The ability to explicitly categorize on the basis of correlated attributes may underlie the emergence of a recategorization ability around 9 to 10 months of age.		
Younger (1985)	10	Infants partition exemplars into categories based on correlations among attributes.
Morgan & Saffran (1995)	6–9	9-month-olds (but not 6-month-olds) segment multisyllabic speech based on an integration of segmental and supra-segmental cues.
Lalonde & Werker (1995)	9	Mature patterns of behavior appeared to emerge in synchrony for a complex speech perception task and for the perception of correlated attributes in visual categorization.
Younger (1993b)	10	Infants were able to disregard discrepant items (noncategory members) presented in a habituation task to form correlation-based categories.
Younger & Fearing (1999, 2000)	4–10	10-month-olds (but not younger infants) spontaneously formed separate categories when familiarized with members of two related categories.

gories in which combinations of features or attributes could be manipulated, and to ask whether infants were able to detect the cooccurrence or correlation among attributes.

In the initial studies (Younger & Cohen, 1983, 1986), we used line drawings of imaginary animals. For example, in the Younger and Cohen (1983) study, the stimuli varied on five attributes, as illustrated in figure 4.1. The kind of body, tail, and feet were perfectly correlated within two sets of four habituation stimuli. A description of one set of stimuli will suffice to illustrate the basic design of the study. Half of the infants were habituated to two animals with giraffe-shaped bodies, fluffy tails, and club-shaped feet, as well as two animals with cow-shaped bodies, feathered tails, and webbed feet. Two additional attributes varied independently within and between categories. Thus, animals within each of the correlation-based categories described earlier could have either ears or antlers and two or four legs. By 10 months of age, infants were able to detect the pattern of correlation evident within the set of familiarization stimuli. Infants generalized habituated levels of looking to a novel stimulus that maintained one of the familiarized attribute clusters and increased their looking to a stimulus that had the same features but in a novel combination (i.e., an animal with a giraffe-shaped body, feathered tail, and webbed feet).

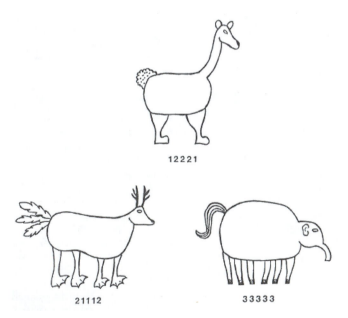

12221

21112   33333

Figure 4.1. Examples of the stimuli used in the Younger and Cohen (1983) experiments. The stimulus figures varied on five attributes—body, tail, feet, ears, and legs. The habituation stimuli and the "correlated" and "uncorrelated" test stimuli were constructed using different combinations of values 1 and 2 on each of the five attributes. Value 3 was used in constructing a totally novel stimulus for the test.

This initial finding has been replicated, using different types of stimuli and different experimental procedures. Younger (1990) used more realistic stimuli—color photographs of real animals in which feature combinations were manipulated by cutting apart and reconstructing animals. As would often be the case within natural object categories, the appearance of each "feature" varied across exemplars. For example, for animals with furry tails and antlers, the instantiation of each feature varied within the category (e.g., the furry tails varied in length, color, and fullness). Again, 10-month-old infants demonstrated their sensitivity to the attribute clusters by increasing their looking to a stimulus that violated the previous pattern of correlation. Similarly, using 3-dimensional objects (i.e., specially designed wooden animals similar in feature composition to the line drawings used by Younger and Cohen, 1986) and a habituation procedure that allowed infants to actively examine the objects presented (i.e., object-examining habituation; Oakes, Madole, & Cohen, 1991), Younger and Fearing (1998) demonstrated that year-old infants were sensitive to correlations among the body parts of animals. Finally, using line drawings of male faces as stimuli, Younger (1992b) demonstrated that 10-month-old infants are able to detect correlations among such properties as the shape of the nose and the distance between the eyes. It should be noted that, in most of the studies just cited, the specific combinations of features varied across the infant participants. In all cases, it did not matter which specific combinations were used. Ten-month-old infants were able to detect whatever correlations were present within the sets of exemplars shown, suggesting that they are highly sensitive to the statistical properties of the input.

Formation of Correlation-Based Categories

The studies discussed here were designed to determine whether infants are able to *detect* the cooccurrence among particular features or attributes of objects (or two-dimensional representations). An equally important question is whether infants are able to *utilize* correlations among attributes to partition a set of stimuli into categories. In other words, can it be shown that infants will structure categories around clusters of correlated attributes? At least by 10 months of age, the answer appears to be yes. Younger (1985) used drawings of novel, imaginary animals in order to manipulate combinations of stimulus features; in this case, combinations of five discrete values along each of four dimensions (i.e., the length of the legs and neck, the thickness of the tail, and the degree of separation between the ears). In the first experiment, infants were shown one of two sets of stimuli that differed in the combinations of dimensional values represented within the set of exemplars. One group of infants was familiarized with a set of eight exemplars in which combinations of values across dimensions were largely unconstrained. For example, animals with long legs had either long or short necks and thick or thin tails (see fig. 4.2A). On the basis of a previous demonstration that infants formed an average representation for a similarly structured category of schematic faces (Strauss, 1979), it was predicted that infants in this condition would form a single category. Infants were expected to treat a stimulus containing the previously unseen average value on each of the four stimulus dimensions (fig. 4.2C) as more familiar than a novel category member containing previously seen values (fig. 4.2D). This prediction was confirmed.

A second group of infants was shown a set of eight exemplars containing the same dimensional values, but with combinations of values across dimensions highly constrained. As can be seen in figure 4.2B, half of the animals had the shorter legs, longer necks, thicker tails, and more closely spaced ears (i.e., values 1 and 2 on each of the four dimensions); half had the longer legs, shorter necks, thinner tails, and more widely spaced ears (i.e., values 4 and 5 on each of the four dimensions). In essence, infants were familiarized with four exemplars from each of two correlation-based categories. If infants formed separate categories (or subcategories) that were structured around the correlated attributes, they were expected to treat the average stimulus as the more novel one in the test. My reasoning was that the average stimulus fell at the boundary between the two correlation-based categories. The comparison

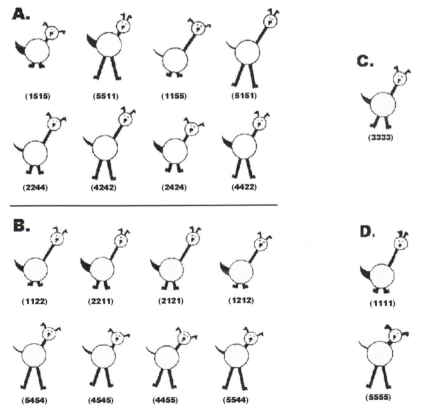

Figure 4.2. Familiarization and test stimuli from Younger (1985; exp. 1). Stimuli had one of 5 discrete values on each of 4 dimensions of variation. (A) Combinations of values across dimensions were largely unconstrained in one set of eight familiarization stimuli. (B) Combinations of values across dimensions were highly constrained in a second set of familiarization stimuli. (C) The "average" test stimulus. (D) The nonaverage test stimuli.

stimulus (containing a novel combination of previously seen values) was consistent with one of the two attribute clusters just described. Thus, if infants had utilized the correlational information to partition the set of exemplars into two categories, the "choice" in the novelty preference test was between two novel exemplars, one that fit into one of the two familiarized categories and one that fell at the boundary between the two categories. As predicted, infants in this condition treated the average stimulus as the more novel one, suggesting that they had formed two categories.

A second experiment provided a stronger test of infants' ability to form distinct correlation-based categories. In the second experiment, value 3 on each of the four dimensions was used both as the modal and average value within the set of familiarization stimuli (i.e., values 1 and 3 were used in constructing exemplars with the shorter legs, longer necks, thicker tails, and more closely spaced ears; values 5 and 3 were used in constructing exemplars with the longer legs, shorter necks, thinner tails, and more widely spaced ears). As in the previous experiment, infants treated the average stimulus as the more novel one in the test, indicating that they had formed two categories reflecting the different clusters of correlated attributes.

Underlying Mechanisms: Analytic or Holistic Processing?

The Younger (1985) findings indicated that 10-month-old infants are able to form novel correlation-based categories. It was unclear, however, what the underlying mechanism might be. Two possibilities were considered in subsequent investigations. From a holistic processing perspective (Kemler Nelson, 1984), correlation-based categories could occur as a byproduct of attention to global or unanalyzed similarity relations. Alternatively, from an analytic processing perspective, categorization by correlated attributes might imply a bias to attend to individual attributes that are correlated and a grouping together of those items that have the same attribute cluster (Younger & Mekos, 1992).

There was some indication in the Younger and Cohen studies that infants' responses were based on their attention to the correlated attributes per se and did not occur as a byproduct of a more global process. In our initial experiments, the "correlated" test stimulus was either highly similar to one or more of the habituation stimuli (differing, for example, in only one of five attributes) or identical to one of the stimuli that infants had been shown during habituation. As a result, maintenance of the familiarized pattern of correlation was confounded with the overall similarity of the test items to the set of habituation stimuli. Beginning with Experiment 3 of the Younger and Cohen (1986) study, however, the stimulus to be used as the "correlated" stimulus in the test was omitted from the set of habituation stimuli. Consequently, by at least two methods of computing similarity, the "uncorrelated" test stimulus (i.e., the stimulus that violated the previously experienced pattern of correlation) was more similar overall to the set of habituation stimuli than was the "correlated" test stimulus.[1] The fact that infants still treated the "uncorrelated" stimulus as the novel one in the test suggests that infants were attending to the correlated attributes per se.

TABLE 4.2. Attribute Values Used in Constructing the Stimulus Sets

| Stimulus set | Attribute | | | |
	A	B	C	D
#1 (wugs/goks)				
Value 1	Feathered tail	Antlers	Webbed feet	Long neck
Value 2	Horse tail	Ears	Club feet	Short neck
#2 (yeeks/nuks)				
Value 1	Long legs	Upright ears	Feathered body	Fluffy tail
Value 2	Short legs	Floppy ears	Furry body	Pointed tail
#3 (geebers/igums)				
Value 1	Straight tail	Long neck	Short antennae	4 feet
Value 2	Curled tail	Short neck	Long antennae	8 feet

Note. From "Category construction in preschool-age children: The use of correlated attributes," by B. Younger and D. Mekos, 1992, *Cognitive Development, 7*, pp. 445–466. Copyright 1992 by Elsevier Science. Reprinted with permission.

Younger and Mekos (1992) also addressed the mechanism by which correlated-attribute categories are formed. In their study, 3- and 4-year-old children were presented with exemplars of artificial animal categories that were similar to those used by Younger and Cohen (1983, 1986). For each of three stimulus sets, four attributes varied as described in table 4.2. As shown in table 4.3, sets of six exemplars were designed in such a way that equal-sized categories could be constructed based on a

TABLE 4.3. Description of the Six Exemplars for Each Stimulus Set

| Exemplar | Attribute | | | |
	A	B	C	D
1	1	1	1	2
2	1	1	2	1
3	1	1	2	2
4	2	2	1	1
5	2	2	1	2
6	2	2	2	1

Note. Values 1 and 2 for attributes A–D are described in table 4.2. Values for two of the four attributes were perfectly correlated within the set of six exemplars. Although attributes A and B are correlated in the table, in practice, all possible combinations of correlated attributes were used. From "Category Construction in Preschool-Age Children: The Use of Correlated Attributes," by B. Younger and D. Mekos, 1992, *Cognitive Development, 7*, pp. 445–466, Copyright (1992), by Elsevier Science. Reprinted with permission.

pair of correlated attributes or based on either of two independently varying attributes (or, as considered in subsequent analyses, based on an assessment of global or unweighted similarity relations).

As in the infant experiments, children were first given a familiarization period in which each of the six exemplars for a particular stimulus set was presented individually. During this time, children were told that there were two kinds. To emphasize this point, contrasting labels (see table 4.2) were provided, though not identified with individual stimuli. Following familiarization, children were told that a puppet liked one kind best, and a prototype or standard (stimulus 1111 or 2222) was presented and placed within the child's view. In the first experiment, children were then presented with an array of the six familiarization stimuli and asked to select one that was the same kind as the labeled standard (e.g., "pick one like this one . . . another *yeek*"). The selected item was removed, and the request was repeated two more times. Thus, in the first experiment, children were asked to pick three items that were judged to be "the same kind" from the original array of six items. In a second experiment, a "yes/no" response was elicited for each of the six exemplars. Following familiarization, each exemplar was presented individually, and children were asked whether each was the same kind as the standard.

In both experiments, children showed a strong tendency to base their categories on attributes that were correlated as opposed to attributes that varied independently. In addition, comparisons of alternative similarity-based response patterns suggested that the correlation-based responses reflected children's selective attention to (or weighting of) attributes that are correlated and did not occur as a byproduct of a global similarity-based process. When children were allowed to select only three items in the first experiment, not only was the frequency of the correlation-based grouping (i.e., the selection of exemplars 1, 2, and 3 in table 4.3) much higher than an alternative similarity-based grouping (exemplars 1, 2, and 4), but order of selection did not differ among the three exemplars. Although one of the three stimuli that matched the standard on the pair of correlated attributes differed from the standard on two of four attributes (exemplar 3), children were as likely to select it as their first choice as either of the two items that differed from the standard on a single attribute (exemplar 1 or 2). In addition, when children were not constrained by the procedure in the number of items they could include in the category—when asked for a series of yes/no responses in the second experiment—children exhibited a strong tendency to include as members of the category all and only those exemplars that shared values of the correlated attributes with the standard. A more graded response pattern might have been expected if overall similarity relations guided children's responses. Finally, although it was relatively rare for children to select one of the independently varying attributes as the basis for inclusion in a category, those children showing this pattern were among the more consistent (i.e., nonrandom) performers across the three experimental trials. The same children who produced independent-attribute groupings on some trials produced correlated-attribute groupings on other trials. The most parsimonious explanation for this finding is that these children were analytic in their approach to categorization. Overall, the greater frequency of the correlated attribute grouping, across children and tasks, suggests that attributes that are correlated have some privileged status for young children. That is, children appear to be biased to attend to and select attributes that are correlated as the basis for their categories.

The question of whether infants were engaged in correlation-based processing per se or some more global similarity-based process is perhaps particularly relevant to the Younger (1985) study. As discussed previously in this chapter, 10-month-old infants in the Younger (1985) experiments formed correlation-based categories when combinations of attributes were highly constrained. For these categories as well, infants could have attended to the individual attributes, grouping together those items that share the same attribute cluster. Alternatively, the categorization response could have been based on a computation of the overall similarity among the stimulus items presented. The latter was demonstrated using an equal-weights adaptation of Medin and Schaffer's (1978) exemplar-based classification model to derive hypothetical estimates of the similarity of each test item to the set of familiarization stimuli (Younger, 1992a). Other methods of computing similarity certainly exist. This particular one was chosen in part because of Kemler Nelson's (1984) claim that Medin and Schaffer's model, without its provision for selective attention (i.e., with equal weights assigned to the various attributes), yields a computation of similarity akin to what she has described as holistic processing.

Within Medin and Schaffer's model, a target or test stimulus that is of high similarity to one or more category instances and of low similarity to other instances will be categorized or recognized more efficiently than a stimulus that is of moderate similarity to all instances. Hypothetical similarity estimates derived from this model— using several different sets of weight—confirmed what seemed intuitive in looking at the sets of stimuli (see fig. 4.2). Whereas the average test stimulus was moderately similar to all exemplars within the set of familiarization stimuli (fig. 4.2B), the nonaverage comparison stimuli were highly similar to half of the exemplars. Thus, the use of the model illustrated that the nonaverage test stimuli were more similar overall to the set of familiarization stimuli than was the average stimulus. As such, the preference for the average stimulus in the Younger (1985) study could have occurred as a byproduct of similarity-based processing, or, following my original argument, infants' preference for the average stimulus could have reflected a grouping-together of those items having the same attribute cluster and a judgment that the average stimulus did not fall within either of the correlation-based categories.

Stylistic Variation in Perceptual Processing

In a preliminary effort to examine individual variation in perceptual processing, Younger and Goffman (1996) redesigned the Younger (1985) task in an attempt to differentiate what we had conceptualized as analytic and holistic approaches to visual categorization. Our interest was in potential biases in perceptual processing (e.g., the relative dominance of analytic or holistic processes within individual infants) as they may relate to individual stylistic variation in early lexical development. For this discussion of mechanisms underlying categorization, the point is that we obtained preliminary support for the idea that *multiple mechanisms* may underlie the formation of correlation-based categories, and that individual infants may differ in their approach to these tasks.

As already discussed, in the original Younger (1985) design, the average test stimulus was less similar overall to the set of familiarization stimuli than were the comparison test stimuli. This was the case both for the "correlated" condition in experiment 1 (shown in fig. 4.2B) and for experiment 2 of the Younger (1985) study. In large part, this was because (in exp. 2) the nonaverage comparison stimuli each represented an average of one of the correlation-based categories and thus was highly similar to each of the four stimuli within that category. In the redesigned task, one exemplar from each correlated attribute grouping in the original familiarization set was replaced by an exemplar that was inconsistent with the general pattern of correlation. The replacement of these stimuli had little bearing on the similarity-based computation. The nonaverage comparison stimulus was still more similar overall to the set of familiarization stimuli than was the average stimulus, by virtue of being highly similar to three of the eight familiarization stimuli. Thus, infants exhibiting a bias toward holistic processing were expected to treat the average stimulus as the more novel one in the test. In contrast, from an analytic (or correlation-based) processing perspective, the inclusion of two exemplars within the familiarization set that were inconsistent with the general pattern of correlation was expected to lessen the tendency for infants to form two distinct categories. Thus, as was the case when combinations of values across dimensions were not highly constrained in the Younger (1985) study, infants relying on analytic processes were expected to recognize all exemplars as members of a single category and to treat the average stimulus as the more familiar one in the test.

Indeed, the majority of infants in the Younger and Goffman study did exhibit the analytic pattern, looking longer at the nonaverage stimulus in the test. However, consistent with the equal-weight similarity-based prediction, some infants did show the opposite pattern, looking longer at the average stimulus. Importantly, the pattern of looking in the categorization task (i.e., percent-looking to the average stimulus) was correlated with a stylistic measure derived from a receptive vocabulary inventory (CDI; Fenson et al., 1993). Although performance on the categorization task did not relate systematically to the size of the receptive vocabulary (i.e., to the total number of words comprehended), it did relate to the *composition* of the infant's vocabulary. Specifically, infants showing the analytic pattern in the categorization task were reported by their parents to have higher proportions of nouns in their receptive vocabularies than infants whose categorization responses seemed to be guided by overall similarity relations ($r = -.51$; $n = 25$). Although the findings are preliminary (it is not clear that infants whose receptive vocabularies include many nouns will exhibit a referential style in production), they are suggestive of a link between perceptual processing biases in categorization and stylistic variation in early lexical development. For the purposes of this discussion, the link between infants' performance on the categorization task and the language measure also strengthens the case for multiple mechanisms underlying the formation of correlation-based categories.

All of the studies discussed in this section converge on the idea that correlated attributes have a privileged status in the categorization of many infants and young children. In the Younger and Mekos (1992) study, I had suggested that a bias to attend to attributes that are correlated may represent a general property of the human cognitive system. Furthermore, I had speculated that the underlying mechanism may be similar to one proposed by Billman and Heit (1988) in relation to untutored observational rule learning. Billman and Heit had proposed an attentional learning mechanism, which they called focused sampling, that is capable of learning contingencies between features based on simple observation. "In effect, focused sampling is a bias to assume that regularities in the input will not be distributed uniformly among features; rather, focused sampling assumes that if a feature is predictive in one (contingency) rule, then the feature is likely to participate in other successful rules" (p. 593). When covariation among features is detected, the salience of those features is increased, thereby increasing the likelihood that the same features will be sampled again. Smith and Heise (1992) make a similar suggestion. In their view, experience with correlations in the environment moves an initially unstructured "similarity space" toward a distorted or structured space that is weighted toward particular features and feature combinations. Experience with correlations in the environment thus leads the infant to pay greater attention to attributes that are part of those correlations.

Whatever the specific computational mechanism, the body of evidence presented here suggests that infants and young children are sensitive to the co-occurrence or correlation among features or attributes of objects, and that categories can be formed on the basis of these co-occurrence relations. A number of important questions remain about constraints that may operate in the computation of co-occurrence relations, both in terms of what may constitute a feature and which feature relations may be used by infants. I will return to the issue of constraints on which correlations are used in the postscript to this chapter.

Development of Attention to Correlated Attributes

Much of the discussion thus far concerning infants' attention to correlations among attributes and the formation of novel correlation-based categories has been in reference to 10-month-old infants. There is also strong evidence for development in attention to correlated attributes during the first year of life. Younger and Cohen (1983, 1986) examined 4-, 7-, and 10-month-old infants' attention to correlations among body parts of schematic animals. In general, 4-month-olds showed an increase in looking only to animals with novel features. These infants provided no evidence of detecting the correlation.

The pattern of performance across experiments was somewhat more complex for the 7-month-olds. At this age, attention to correlated attributes depended on features of the stimuli and task. When the animals varied on five attributes (three of which were correlated), 7-month-olds failed to detect the correlation (Younger & Cohen, 1983). However, when only the body, tail, and feet varied, and all three attributes were correlated, 7-month-olds did attend to the correlation. Note that when all three attributes are correlated, the question is reduced to one of perceiving the stimuli as "wholes" (i.e., processing parts relationally) or as collections of independent parts. In a simplified categorization context (i.e., when two of the three attributes were correlated and the third attribute varied independently across categories), two separate groups of 7-month-olds failed to habituate or to respond differentially to the test stimuli. In light of the previous demonstration that 7-month-olds did process feature relations when only two exemplars were presented during habituation (i.e., when all three attributes were correlated), we interpreted the latter finding as evidence that 7-month-olds had processed each of the stimuli as wholes, though not as members of correlation-based categories. Finally, when habituated to a criterion with the same set of stimuli (rather than for a fixed number of trials, as had been done in previous experiments), 7-month-olds responded like the 4-month-olds, presumably on the basis of the novelty or familiarity of individual features.

This pattern of age-related change was replicated in the Younger (1992b) study, using schematic drawings of faces as stimuli. Whereas 10-month-old infants in this study processed correlations among features of schematic faces (i.e., a correlation between the shape of the nose and the distance between the eyes, or between either of these features and the hairline), 7-month-old infants did not. The 7-month-olds did, however, respond differentially to a face that had a single novel feature (a novel hairstyle). The interpretation given to the general pattern of findings across studies was that younger infants respond more to the presence of novel versus familiar featural information (i.e., to independent features) than to feature relations, as the basis for categorization. Thus, we might think of the "glue" that binds instances of a category together as being one or more salient features for younger infants, and shared feature relations for somewhat older infants.

Stimulus and Task Dependencies

These developmental findings are consistent with evidence that has been accumulating in recent years that there are both stimulus (e.g., Quinn, Eimas, & Rosenkrantz, 1993; Younger & Gotlieb, 1988) and task-related (e.g., Oakes, Plumert, Lansink, & Merryman, 1996) dependencies in infant categorization. A number of investigators have argued that an understanding of task dependencies will contribute to our understanding of the way categorization interacts with or is influenced by other cognitive processes, as well as a more complete understanding of the process of categorization itself (Oakes & Madole, 2000; Thelen & Smith, 1994; see also chap. 6). In this section, I will review additional evidence of stimulus and task differences related to infants' perception of correlations among attributes. Looking ahead, it should become clear that further investigations into the conditions under which infants do or do not process feature relations have the potential to contribute greatly to our understanding of the development of early categorization skills.

Using a different procedure (mobile conjugate reinforcement), Bhatt and Rovee-Collier (1994, 1996) examined both the perception and long-term retention of feature relations in 3-month-old infants. In the mobile task (Rovee & Rovee, 1969), infants are trained to kick to move a mobile. In general, if infants are trained over two daily sessions and then tested 24 hours later with the same mobile, they show no memory deficit and continue to kick. If tested with a novel mobile, however, infants fail to kick (at operant levels), indicating that they discriminate the change in the mobile. In the Bhatt and Rovee-Collier studies, the color of the mobile blocks was correlated with the figure displayed on them and with the color of the figures. Note that this was not a categorization task in the sense that all three features that varied were correlated; the six-block training mobile thus consisted of two sets of three identical objects. The color-form feature relations were encoded and retained for up to 3 days (Bhatt & Rovee-Collier, 1994). Features and feature relations also appeared to be dissociated in memory, in that feature relations were forgotten earlier than the individual features constituting the relations (Bhatt & Rovee-Collier, 1996).

Other investigators have also examined the perception of color-form correlations in young infants. Johnson and Schroeder (1991) reported that 4-month-old infants could detect categories based on correlated attributes if they were allowed to compare instances of different categories during encoding. Using a visual preference paradigm, infants, for example, might have been shown both a green ball and red star on each familiarization trial. Under these conditions, infants demonstrated a novelty preference for a recombined stimulus (e.g., a red ball) over a familiar category member.

The relevance of these findings to categorization has been questioned, however. Instances of Johnson and Schroeder's color-form categories differed from one another only in having either horizontal or vertical stripes. This orientation difference could signal a transformation of a single object rather than the presence of distinctive category members (e.g., two different green balls). Younger (1993a) presented infants with similar color-form categories—red circles and blue diamonds—except that different members of each category had more distinctive markings (i.e., large dots or vertical stripes). Infants were familiarized with two stimuli per trial, one from each color-form category. Following familiarization, 7-month-old infants (but not 4-month-olds) demonstrated their attention to the color-form correlation by looking longer at a recombined stimulus than to a novel member of one of the familiarized categories.

Wilk, Bhatt, and Rovee-Collier (1995, as cited in Bhatt, 1997) reported a similar finding with 6-month-old infants using the mobile task. Infants were trained with a six-block mobile comprising equal numbers of two categories of blocks. As in the earlier Bhatt and Rovee-Collier studies, the blocks varied in color, in the figures displayed on the blocks, and in the color of the figures. In this case, however, only two of the attributes were correlated; the third attribute varied independently across the two categories. In a 24-hour retention test, infants failed to respond to a new mobile in which familiar attributes were recombined. Thus, as was the case for 7- month-olds in the Younger (1993a) study, infants treated as novel a stimulus with familiar features in a novel configuration.

Across two different testing paradigms, then, infants as young as 6 to 7 months have demonstrated sensitivity to color-form correlations in a categorization context (meaning that the correlations involved only a subset of the attributes that varied across instances; thus, there were multiple instances of each color-form category). In both the mobile task and a paired comparison variant of a looking task, infants had the opportunity to directly compare instances of the different correlation-based categories during familiarization. To determine whether this type of comparison would facilitate the perception of correlations among body parts of schematic animals for infants younger than 10 months, Younger (1993a) used a paired stimulus presentation with the stimuli from the Younger and Cohen (1983) study. Infants received eight familiarization trials depicting one member of each correlation-based category. As in the original Younger and Cohen experiments, however, 7-month-olds failed to detect the pattern of correlation using the more complex animal categories, distributing their looking equally between the "correlated" and "uncorrelated" test stimuli.

Finally, to determine whether the direct comparison of instances from the different correlation-based categories was critical or if the different findings could be attributed to the stimulus difference alone, Younger (1993a) reexamined the perception of color-form categories in 7-month-old infants using a successive presentation format in a habituation task. In an experiment using infant-controlled trials and a criterion procedure (i.e., exemplars from the two correlation-based categories were presented one at a time for as long as infants would look on each trial and until they exhibited a 50 percent decline in looking across trials), infants failed to detect the color-form categories.

To summarize, there is evidence of stimulus, context, and procedural dependencies governing infants' perception of feature relations. First, there is evidence that infants as young as 3 months of age are able to encode and retain relatively simple color-form feature relations defining individual objects (Bhatt & Rovee-Collier, 1994). There is also evidence indicating that feature relations defining individual objects are perceived at an earlier age than are the same relations defining groups or categories of objects (Younger & Cohen, 1986).[2] In addition, both stimulus and procedural variations have been shown to affect the perception of correlation-based categories (Younger, 1993a). By at least 7 months of age (though apparently not at 4 months), infants are able to detect simple categories based on color-form correlations, but only if they're allowed to make direct comparisons of contrasting category members. Even with the opportunity to make such comparisons, however, 7-month-olds were not able to perceive more complex categories based on correlations among body parts of animals.

Emergence of a Recategorization Ability Late in the First Year of Life

In the previous sections, I reviewed evidence indicating that the ability to detect feature relations is present from early infancy but that there are developmental changes in the types of feature relations infants detect. The evidence also supports a developmental progression from processing features independently to processing feature relations within objects to processing feature relations within categories. The stimulus and task dependencies make it clear, however, that such progressions cannot be tied to particular ages. In fact, similar progressions have been reported at somewhat older ages by Werker, Cohen, Lloyd, Casasola, and Stager (1998) and by Madole and colleagues (Madole, Oakes, & Cohen, 1993; Madole & Cohen, 1995). In the following section, I review evidence of what does appear to be an age-dependent change in categorization—evidence that changes in the formation of correlation-based categories appear in synchrony with changes in complex speech perception tasks. I then draw on evidence that 10-month-old infants exhibit signs of an explicit form of categorization to explore the notion that a *recategorization* ability emerges around 9 to 10 months of age (Lalonde & Werker, 1995).

In an attempt to examine potential linkages between cognitive development and speech perception, Lalonde and Werker (1995) tested 9-month-old infants on three tasks: discrimination of a nonnative speech contrast (Werker, 1989), the Younger and Cohen (1983) correlated attribute categorization task, and a delayed-response object search task (Diamond, 1985). Their findings suggest that the more mature forms of behavior across the three tasks tend to appear in synchrony. At 9 months of age, the expectation was that about half of the infants would have lost the ability shown by young infants to discriminate the nonnative speech contrast. In the Lalonde and Werker study, infants who succeeded in discriminating the nonnative contrast (as would be expected of younger infants) tended to fail in the visual categorization task and in the object search task. In contrast, infants who failed to discriminate the nonnative speech contrast tended to succeed in both the visual categorization and object search tasks.

Although Lalonde and Werker's findings suggest that developmental changes in infants' performance in the three tasks tend to appear in synchrony, it was not clear what the underlying mechanism might be. A study by Morgan and Saffran (1995) offers some insight in this regard. They examined infants' ability to coordinate multiple sources of information (multiple cues) in a complex speech perception task. Specifically, they asked whether infants integrate distributional information and rhythmic patterning in a task involving segmentation of strings of syllables into wordlike units. What they found fits nicely with the Younger and Cohen (1983, 1986) and Lalonde and Werker (1995) findings. Morgan and Saffran (1995) demonstrated that it is not until 9 months of age that infants detect and make use of correlations between distributional and rhythmic information present in multisyllabic speech stimuli. Although infants as young as 6 to 7 months of age are able to make use of both rhythmic (Morgan & Saffran, 1995) and sequential (Goodsitt, Morgan, & Kuhl, 1993) regularities, 6-month-olds in the Morgan and Saffran (1995) study were not able to integrate the sequential and suprasegmental cues. Together with the Younger and Cohen (1983, 1986) and LaLonde and Werker (1995) findings, Morgan and Saffran's results suggest that changes in integrative abilities at around 9 to 10 months of age operate across domains to influence the formation of complex visual categories as well as changes in complex speech perception tasks.

What might be the nature of these integrative abilities? As indicated earlier, infants as young as 3 months do encode and retain at least some feature relations (color and form) characterizing individual objects. At least by 6 to 7 months, infants are able to detect invariant relations involving color and form information while ignoring features that vary freely across a set of objects (across categories). What is different about what 9- to 10-month-old infants are doing in the Younger and Cohen (1983, 1986) tasks that might mediate the synchrony observed between changes in visual categorization and changes in other perceptual and cognitive domains?

In addition to evidence that 9- to 10-month-old infants *detect* correlations among stimulus features in complex animal categories (Younger & Cohen, 1983, 1986; Younger, 1990), there is independent evidence that infants of this age are able to *utilize* this information in complex parsing tasks. In the Younger (1985) visual categorization study, 10-month-old infants were able to categorize a set of complex stimuli on the basis of correlations among stimulus features. More specifically, infants were able to parse a set of exemplars into multiple categories based on correlations that existed among stimulus features. Similarly, in the Morgan and Saffran (1995) study, 9-month-old infants were able to impose word boundaries on multisyllabic speech based on correlations among disparate sources of information in the speech signal (i.e., the sequencing of syllables and metrical patterning across syllables).

Lalonde and Werker (1995) characterized the difference in performance of the younger versus older infants in the Younger and Cohen (1983) task (as well as concurrent changes in the perception of nonnative speech contrasts) as reflecting the emergence of some kind of recategorization ability whereby new category boundaries are superimposed on earlier perceptual categories. They speculated that both the reorganization in speech perception and developmental changes in visual categorization await the emergence of an ability to explicitly categorize complex stimuli on the basis of correlations among stimulus features. As discussed hereafter, the findings from a recent series of experiments in my laboratory are consistent with this notion of a recategorization occurring around 10 months of age.

Explicit Categorization

The studies that I review hereafter were motivated by a concern with the implicit versus explicit nature of categorization abilities in infancy. Although infants under a year of age are able to form a variety of perceptual categories when members of a single category are presented in direct succession in habituation or familiarization tasks (e.g., Behl-Chadha, 1996; Oakes et al., 1996; Quinn et al., 1993), it is not until the second year that infants begin to actively sort objects into multiple categories. In sorting studies, children are given mixed arrays of objects from two classes, and their spontaneous sorting or sequential-touching behavior is observed. By about 1 year of age, infants begin to sequentially touch objects from a single category (Starkey, 1981; Sugarman, 1982). By 15 to 16 months, they may touch all of the objects in one category followed by objects in the other category (Mandler & Bauer, 1988; Oakes et al., 1996). By 18 to 24 months, children begin to sort objects from two categories into spatially distinct groups (Gopnik & Meltzoff, 1992; Sugarman, 1982).

Although some investigators (e.g., Oakes et al., 1996) have focused on the information-processing demands of the tasks (in relation to the skills of the infant) in an attempt to explain age differences in different categorization tasks, others (e.g., Gopnik & Meltzoff, 1997; Sugarman, 1981, 1982) have suggested that the age difference reflects more of a conceptual change in the infant. Sugarman, for example, argued that the ability to sort objects into spatially distinct categories reflects explicit knowledge that some things are alike, knowledge that she believed to be lacking in younger infants. Young infants, as they habituate to members of a single category (or as they engage in sequential touching of members of a single category), need only recognize implicitly that each stimulus or object presented "is or is not X." By 18 to 24 months, children are thought instead to explicitly equate different members of a category—to make active comparisons across objects and an explicit judgment that two or more objects share something in common.

A similar view has been expressed more recently by Gopnik and Meltzoff (1997). They argue, for example, that within the first year, infants are able to represent only one category at a time or to recognize "that a particular object belongs or doesn't belong with others" (p. 168). In contrast, by midway through the second year, the child is said to be able to hold multiple categories in mind at the same time and to differentiate between them. Gopnik and Meltzoff argue that this is seen most clearly as the 18-month-old exhaustively groups objects into spatially distinct categories, and perhaps as the 15- to 16-month-old engages in exhaustive serial touching (i.e., touching all objects from one category in succession followed by all objects from a second category). They further note that categorization in older children tends to be spontaneous, whereas the categorization responses of younger infants often appear to be "trained" in the context of the task.

Two sets of studies begin to determine whether infants under a year of age are limited to an implicit recognition of categories, or if it is possible to demonstrate aspects of their behavior that are more consistent with characterizations of a more explicit form of categorization. In the first study, Younger (1993b) tried to ascertain, using a familiarization-novelty preference paradigm, whether 10-month-old infants make comparisons among items presented during familiarization, and whether their categorization responses reflect a judgment about what the different exemplars have in common. The approach taken in the study was to insert noncategory members into the familiarization sequence. The aim was to ascertain whether infants' categorization responses are influenced equally by all of the exemplars they are shown, or if infants are able to disregard the discrepant items to base their categorization response on items that are judged to be "the same kind of thing."

The task was based on the Younger (1985) correlated attribute task. Infants were familiarized with exemplars of two correlation-based categories (i.e., three members of each of the two schematic animal categories). In addition, two "nonmembers" were inserted into the sequence of familiarization trials. Importantly, the nonmembers were related in a systematic fashion to the set of six "core" exemplars, making it possible to determine whether or not these stimuli had an impact on infants' categorization responses. As in the Younger (1985) study, the category exemplars varied on four dimensions—the length of the legs and neck, the thickness of the tail, and the degree of separation between the ears. It should be emphasized in this context that the shapes of the tails, ears, and so on were identical across the two correlation-based categories, as illustrated in figure 4.2. As discussed in the early part of this chapter, infants in the Younger (1985) study formed two categories reflecting the different clusters of correlated attributes as indicated by a novelty preference for a stimulus containing the average value on each of the four dimensions.

In the Younger (1993b) study, the two nonmembers differed from the other familiarization stimuli on two of the four dimensions of variation (i.e., the ears and tail differed qualitatively from those of the other exemplars). Like the other stimuli, however, the nonmembers varied in the length of the legs and neck. Importantly, the relation between leg and neck length in the nonmembers was inconsistent with the pattern of correlation evident within the remaining set of exemplars (i.e., one nonmember had short legs and a short neck; the other had long legs and a long neck). If infants judged the nonmembers to be different from the remaining set of exemplars (e.g., by noting the different kind of tail and ears) and excluded them in constructing correlation-based categories, they were expected to treat the average test stimulus as novel. In contrast, if each stimulus in the familiarization sequence was to influence the categorization response equally, infants would be expected to treat the average stimulus in the test as familiar, as infants had done in the Younger (1985) study when attribute values occurred in all combinations.[3] The results indicated that 10-month-old infants did treat the average stimulus as novel, indicating that they had disregarded the nonmembers in the familiarization sequence to form categories based on the pattern of correlation evident within the remaining set of exemplars. Thus, in contrast to the characterization of infants as engaging only in an implicit form of categorization, the Younger (1993b) findings suggest that infants do exhibit at least some characteristics of explicit categorization. Specifically, they appear to make comparisons of the items to be categorized and to disregard items that are discrepant from the others as a basis for their categorization response. By 10 months of age, then, it appears that infants have at least a rudimentary understanding that members of a category are the same kind of thing (an understanding that I would argue might apply even to perceptually based categories where there may be no understanding of "the kind of thing" it is).

In a more recent series of experiments, Younger and Fearing (1999, 2000) sought additional evidence that infants under a year of age are able to represent more than one category at a time, as well as evidence that infants can be spontaneous in their categorization. Our aim was to present infants with an opportunity to form multiple categories, using a task that has fewer demands on the infant's information-processing resources than the sequential-touching or object-sorting tasks used with older infants. We asked whether infants would form a category broad enough to include all of the exemplars presented to them, or if they would spontaneously parse exemplars into multiple categories.

We used a habituation procedure. As is typical in habituation studies of categorization, exemplars were presented one at a time (or in pairs from the same category). Across trials, however, members of two categories were intermixed. For example, in the Younger and Fearing (1999) studies, infants were presented with photographs of cats and horses during the habituation phase (in exp. 1) or with photographs of male and female faces (in exp. 2). Note that in either case, it would be perfectly reasonable to respond to a single inclusive category (e.g., four-legged mammals or human faces) or to partition the exemplars into separate categories (i.e., cats and horses, or male and female faces). Our aim was to try to determine what category or categories had been formed by infants of different ages.

In both experiments, 10-month-old infants appeared to have spontaneously formed two categories. Following familiarization with both cats and horses, for example, 10-month-olds showed significant novelty preferences for dogs over new members of both of the familiarized categories. In the face study, we used a habituation-dishabituation test format. Following familiarization with "good" or prototypical examples of male and female faces (as determined by typicality ratings provided by adults), 10-month-olds generalized habituated levels of looking to novel members of both categories but dishabituated to faces that had been judged by adults to be ambiguous with respect to gender.

In contrast to the older infants, 4- and 7-month-olds formed a single category to include the range of exemplars presented during familiarization. When familiarized with cats and horses, both of the younger age groups distributed their looking equally between members of the familiarized categories and pictures of dogs, indicating that they had formed a category that included at least cats, horses, and dogs. When familiarized with male and female faces, 7-month-old infants generalized habituation to both the gender-typical and gender-ambiguous test faces, indicating that they had formed a category akin to "faces-in-general" or "adult faces" rather than forming distinct categories of male and female faces. It is important to note that, for all of these categories, the younger infants were able to form the more exclusive categories (i.e., categories of male faces, female faces, cats, horses) when familiarized with members of one category at a time. They did not, however, spontaneously form the more exclusive categories when familiarized with members of two related categories.

In demonstrating a tendency to partition exemplars into multiple categories in these studies, I would argue that 10-month-old infants exhibited categorization abilities comparable in some respects to those observed in older infants in the context of sequential-touching or object-sorting tasks. They appeared to be able to form and represent two categories at once, and categorization was spontaneous. Cats and horses (and male and female faces) have many shared properties and could quite reasonably have been treated as members of a single broad category. However, rather than attending only to commonalities across the sets of exemplars, 10-month-old infants apparently were able to attend both to the similarities and differences and to impose their own structure on the set of exemplars presented. In contrast, the performance of the younger infants in these studies is consistent with Sugarman's and Gopnik and Meltzoff's characterizations of early categorization. The 4- and 7-month-olds did appear to represent only one category at a time. Their categories could also be characterized as having been trained in the context of the task, in that infants responded to a category defined by whatever features or properties were common across the range of exemplars presented.

More recently, we have been able to demonstrate that 7-month-olds will form two categories at once using the same procedure, but only when members of highly discrepant categories are presented during familiarization. In a second series of studies (see Younger & Fearing, 2000), we familiarized infants either with cats and birds, or cats and cars. In both cases, 10-month-old infants again appeared to have formed separate categories, as indicated by preferences for members of novel (but perceptually similar) categories over members of both of the familiarized categories. In the cat/bird study, 10-month-olds preferred both a dog over a novel cat, and a bat over a novel bird. In contrast, the 7-month-olds distributed their looking equally between the novel and familiar category exemplars in both comparisons. In the cat/car study, both 7- and 10-month-old infants (but not 4-month-olds) exhibited a preference for a dog over a novel cat, and a truck over a novel car, suggesting that they had been able to form two separate categories.[4]

Redrawing Category Boundaries on the Basis of Correlated Attributes

I began this section with the idea that the performance of the 10-month-old infants in the Younger and Cohen (1983, 1986) correlated attribute tasks may reflect the emergence of some kind of recategorization ability by which new category boundaries are superimposed on earlier perceptual categories. The developmental pattern observed in the Younger and Fearing (1999, 2000) studies could be construed as such a recategorization. For the 10-month-old infants, category boundaries were imposed where none had existed in this context for the younger infants. More specifically, I had suggested earlier that the ability to impose category or word boundaries on the basis of an integration of multiple sources of information (or the perception of correlated stimulus features) may emerge around 9 to 10 months of age. Although the basis for the formation of multiple categories (e.g., male and female faces, cats and horses) was not investigated in the Younger and Fearing studies, it is certainly plausible given the Younger (1985) findings that infants were able to make use of correlations among stimulus features in partitioning items into multiple categories. Although cats and horses have many of the same parts in the same basic configuration, there are subtle differences in their features. Cats, for example, tend to have short noses, narrowly spaced eyes, short necks, and short legs. Horses have long noses, widely spaced eyes, long necks, and long legs. This description of potential stimulus features intentionally parallels the description of the features made to vary in the Younger (1985) study to make the point that infants may well have been sensitive to clusters of correlated attributes as a basis for their categorization.

The demonstration that 7-month-olds formed multiple categories in one of the Younger and Fearing experiments may appear to at odds with the argument presented earlier. Recall, however, that infants as young as 6 months of age in the Morgan and Saffran (1995) study were able to use individual cues (i.e., stress patterns) to segment multidimensional speech into wordlike units. When shown members of highly discrepant categories (e.g., members of different global-level categories like cats and cars) in the Younger and Fearing study, 7-month-old infants may well have partitioned exemplars into categories on the basis of one or more independent stimulus properties (e.g., by attending to salient part differences, visually specified texture differences, or curvilinear versus angular contours).

Summary and Conclusions

I began the chapter by reviewing evidence that 10-month-old infants are able to detect and utilize correlations among static structural features of objects to form distinctive categories. Potential mechanisms underlying the formation of correlation-based categories were also discussed. I pointed out that correlation-based categories could be derived either through "analytic" or "holistic" processes. The bulk of the evidence from studies of infants and preschool-aged children favored some kind of analytic process. That is, young children appear to be biased to attend to attributes that are correlated and to group together those items having the same attribute cluster.

However, support for the idea of multiple mechanisms was found in the form of individual variation in infants' approach to categorization and in correlations between infants' approach to categorization and stylistic variation in a measure of early word comprehension.

The latter part of the chapter dealt with developmental change in processes related to categorization. Although the picture is complicated by a number of task-related dependencies, it appears that infants are able to detect feature relations from a young age, though in all likelihood there are changes with age in what constitutes a feature and thus in the types of feature relations that infants are able to detect. Evidence was presented indicating that infants as young as 3 to 7 months are able to detect simple color-form correlations. It was not until a few months later, however, that infants were sensitive to feature correlations existing within more complex stimuli (e.g., correlations among the body parts of animals or correlations among facial features). Evidence was also presented indicating that there is a dissociation in memory between features and feature relations and a developmental progression from processing features independently to processing feature relations that exist within a single pattern or object to processing feature relations embedded within a category.

Finally, I reviewed evidence indicating that there is a common transition around 9 to 10 months of age in tasks that appear to require an integration of multiple cues. I explored the notion that reorganizations in speech perception (e.g., in the discrimination of nonnative phonetic contrasts), as well as changes in the formation of correlation-based categories, reflect the emergence of an ability to explicitly categorize complex stimuli on the basis of correlations among stimulus features. I presented evidence indicating that 10-month-old infants have at least a rudimentary understanding that members of a category are "the same sort of thing." In addition, I presented evidence indicating that, when shown members of two related categories in a habituation task, 10-month-old infants spontaneously parse objects into multiple categories. In contrast, younger infants in these studies tended to form a single category broad enough to include the range of exemplars presented to them. I argued that this developmental pattern could be construed as an example of recategorization, in that the older infants tended to impose category boundaries where none existed for the younger infants. I offered further speculation that this recategorization involves the infant's attention to correlations among attributes.

Postscript

Given that the scope of this book extends beyond categorization in preverbal infants, it is perhaps fitting to close with a brief note concerning the relation between the infant correlated attribute research and work on the same topic with older children and adults. A general theme in the adult and child literatures has been that the perception and use of correlated attributes in categorization is "theory driven" (Murphy & Medin, 1985). The concern has been that so many correlations exist that it is necessary to posit some kind of constraints on which of the many available correlations will be used. The constraint offered most frequently is in the form of "theories" held by the category learner. In relation to the use of correlated attributes in categorization, the specific argument has been that adults and children form categories based on correlations for which their theories provide causal explanations (e.g., Barrett et al., 1993; Medin et al., 1982).

As an alternative to the view that such conceptual or theoretical biases must be present from very early in life (Keil, 1991), I suggest that it might be worthwhile to look to the immature perceptual or cognitive status of the infant for constraints on which correlations infants will notice and use. The idea of "less is more" was initially presented by Elissa Newport (1990) in relation to language learning. In brief, her hypothesis was that language learning declines with age (or maturation) because cognitive abilities increase. In Newport's view, limitations on the young child's information-processing abilities provide the basis on which successful language acquisition occurs. My suggestion is that this kind of notion may be applied fruitfully to categorization as well. Investigations that focus, for example, on the perceptual biases of the infant in relation to the correlational structure thought to be inherent to basic-level object categories (Rosch, 1978) may contribute greatly to our understanding of the early development of categorization.

Acknowledgments

Thanks are extended to Stephanie Furrer, Lisa Goffman, Kathy Johnson, Lisa Oakes, and David Rakison for their helpful comments on a previous version of this chapter. Correspondence should be addressed to Barbara Younger, Department of Psychological Sciences, Purdue University, West Lafayette, IN 47907-1364 (younger@psych.purdue.edu).

Notes

1. In the set of three habituation stimuli in experiment 3 of the Younger and Cohen (1986) study, one value for each attribute (i.e., one kind of body, tail, and feet) occurred twice as often as the other value. On the basis of a simple count of the more frequently occurring features, the "uncorrelated" test stimulus was more similar overall to the set of habituation stimuli than was the novel "correlated" stimulus. The same rank ordering of the overall similarities of the test items to the set of habituation stimuli was obtained using Medin and Schaffer's (1978) exemplar-based classification model and assuming equal weights for the various attributes.

2. A test of 3-month-old infants' ability to perceive color-form feature relations in a categorization context using the mobile task is needed to determine whether this pattern holds across testing paradigms. Though Wilk et al. (1995) demonstrated that 6-month-olds are able to perceive color-form feature relations in a categorization task, they did not test younger infants.

3. It had previously been demonstrated in the Younger (1993b) study that the inclusion in the familiarization sequence of only two exemplars that violated the pattern of correlation between leg and neck length was sufficient to produce an effect comparable to that obtained in the Younger (1985) study when dimensional values occurred in all combinations.

4. In these experiments, we did not include a direct comparison between members of the two familiarized categories in the test. Such a comparison could provide a more conclusive demonstration that infants had formed separate categories during familiarization. On the basis of recent evidence that infants are sensitive to the frequency of exposure to particular exemplars (Oakes & Spalding, 1997), we are currently attempting to use differences in the frequency

with which infants are exposed to members of the two categories in an attempt to demonstrate conclusively not only that infants distinguish members of the familiarized categories from members of other perceptually similar categories but also that members of the familiarized categories are distinguished from one another.

References

Barrett, S., Abdi, H., Murphy, G., & Gallagher, J. (1993). Theory-based correlations and their role in children's concepts. *Child Development, 64*, 1595–1616.

Behl-Chadha, G. (1996). Basic-level and superordinate-like categorical representations in early infancy. *Cognition, 60*, 105–141.

Bhatt, R. S. (1997). The interface between perception and cognition: Feature detection, visual pop-out effects, feature integration, and long-term memory in infancy. In C. Rovee-Collier & L. Lipsitt (Eds.), *Advances in infancy research* (Vol. 11, pp. 143–191). Norwood, NJ: Ablex.

Bhatt, R. S., & Rovee-Collier, C. (1994). Perception and 24–hour retention of feature relations in infancy. *Developmental Psychology, 30*, 142–150.

Bhatt, R. S., & Rovee-Collier, C. (1996). Infants' forgetting of correlated attributes and object recognition. *Child Development, 67*, 172–187.

Billman, D., & Heit, E. (1988). Observational learning from internal feedback: A simulation of an adaptive learning method. *Cognitive Science, 12*, 587–625.

Diamond, A. (1985). Development of the ability to use recall to guide action, as indicated by infants' performance on A-not-B. *Child Development, 56*, 868–883.

Fenson, L., Dale, P., Reznick, S., Thal, D., Bates, E., Hartung, J., Pethick, S., & Reilly, J. (1993). *Communicative development inventories*. San Diego: Singular.

Goodsitt, J., Morgan, J. L., & Kuhl, P. K. (1993). Perceptual strategies in prelingual speech segmentation. *Journal of Child Language, 20*, 229–252.

Gopnik, A., & Meltzoff, A. (1992). Categorization and naming: Basic-level sorting in 18-month-olds and its relation to language. *Child Development, 63*, 1091–1103.

Gopnik, A., & Meltzoff, A. (1997). *Words, thoughts, and theories*. Cambridge, MA: MIT Press.

Johnson, N. S., & Schroeder, K. E. (1991, April). *Young infants' formation of categories based on co-occurring attributes*. Paper presented at the meeting of the Society for Research in Child Development, Seattle.

Keil, F. (1991). The emergence of theoretical beliefs as constraints on concepts. In S. Carey & R. Gelman (Eds.), *The epigenesis of mind: Essays on biology and cognition* (pp. 237–256). Hillsdale, NJ: Erlbaum.

Kemler Nelson, D. G. (1984). The effect of intention on what concepts are acquired. *Journal of Verbal Learning and Verbal Behavior, 23*, 734–759.

Kemler Nelson, D. G. (1990). When experimental findings conflict with everyday observations: Reflections on children's category learning. *Child Development, 61*, 606–610.

Lalonde, C. E., & Werker, J. F. (1995). Cognitive influences on cross-language speech perception in infancy. *Infant Behavior and Development, 18*, 459–475.

Madole, K. L., & Cohen, L. B. (1995). The role of object parts in infants' attention to form-function correlations. *Developmental Psychology, 31*, 317–332.

Madole, K. L., Oakes, L. M., & Cohen, L. B. (1993). Developmental changes in infants' attention to function and form-function correlations. *Cognitive Development, 8*, 189–209.

Mandler, J. M., & Bauer, P. (1988). The cradle of categorization: Is the basic level basic? *Cognitive Development, 3*, 247–264.

Medin, D. L. (1983). Structural principles in categorization. In T. Tighe & B. Shepp (Eds.), *Perception, cognition, and development* (pp. 203–230). Hillsdale, NJ: Erlbaum.

Medin, D. L., & Schaffer, M. (1978). Context theory of classification learning. *Psychological Review, 85*, 207–238.

Medin, D., Altom, M., Edelson, S., & Freko, D. (1982). Correlated symptoms and simulated medical classification. *Journal of Experimental Psychology: Learning, Memory, and Cognition, 8*, 37–50.

Morgan, J. L., & Saffran, J. R. (1995). Emerging integration of sequential and suprasegmental information in preverbal speech segmentation. *Child Development, 66*, 911–936.

Murphy, G. L. & Medin, D. L. (1985). The role of theories in conceptual coherence. *Psychological Review, 92*, 289–316.

Newport, E. L. (1990). Maturational constraints on language learning. *Cognitive Science, 14*, 11–28.

Oakes, L. M., & Madole, K. L. (2000). The future of infant categorization research: A process-oriented approach. *Child Development, 71*, 119–126.

Oakes, L. M., Madole, K. L., & Cohen, L. B. (1991). Object examining: Habituation and categorization. *Cognitive Development, 6*, 377–392.

Oakes, L. M., Plumert, J. M., Lansink, J. M., & Merryman, J. D. (1996). Evidence for task-dependent categorization in infancy. *Infant Behavior and Development, 19*, 425–440.

Oakes, L. M., & Spalding, T. L. (1997). The role of exemplar distribution in infants' differentiation of categories. *Infant Behavior and Development, 20*, 457–475.

Quinn, P. C., Eimas, P. D., & Rosenkranz, S. L. (1993). Evidence for representations of perceptually similar natural categories by 3-month-old and 4-month-old infants. *Perception, 22*, 463–475.

Rosch, E. (1978). Principles of categorization. In E. Rosch & B. Lloyd (Eds.), *Cognition and categorization* (pp. 27–48). Hillsdale, NJ: Erlbaum.

Rosch, E., Mervis, C. B., Gray, W. D., Johnson, D. M., & Boyes-Braem, P. (1976). Basic objects in natural categories. *Cognitive Psychology, 8*, 382–439.

Rovee, C. K., & Rovee, D. (1969). Conjugate reinforcement of infant exploratory behavior. *Journal of Experimental Child Psychology, 8*, 33–39.

Saffran, J. R., Aslin, R. N., & Newport, E. L. (1996). Statistical learning by 8-month-old infants. *Science, 274*, 1926–1928.

Smith, L. B., & Heise, D. (1992). Perceptual similarity and conceptual structure. In B. Burns (Ed.), *Percepts, concepts, and categories* (pp. 233–272). Amsterdam: Elsevier.

Smith, L. B., & Kemler, D. G. (1977). Developmental trends in free classification: Evidence for a new comceptualization of perceptual development. *Journal of Experimental Child Psychology, 24*, 279–298.

Starkey, D. (1981). The origins of concept formation: Object sorting and object preference in early infancy. *Child Development, 52*, 489–497.

Strauss, M. S. (1979). Abstraction of prototypical information in adults and 10-month-old infants. *Journal of Experimental Psychology: Human Learning and Memory, 5*, 618–632.

Sugarman, S. (1981). The cognitive basis of classification in very young children: An analysis of object-ordering trends. *Child Development, 52*, 1172–1178.

Sugarman, S. (1982). Developmental change in early representational intelligence: Evidence from spatial classification strategies and related verbal expressions. *Cognitive Psychology, 14*, 410–449.

Thelen, E., & Smith, L. B. (1994). *A dynamic systems approach to the development of cognition and action.* Cambridge, MA: MIT Press.

Ward, T. B., & Scott, J. (1987). Analytic and holistic models of learning family-resemblance concepts. *Memory and Cognition, 15*, 42–54.

Ward, T. B., Vela, E., & Hass, S. D. (1990). Children and adults learn family-resemblance categories analytically. *Child Development, 61*, 593–605.

Werker, J. F. (1989). Becoming a native listener. *American Scientist, 77*, 54–59.

Werker, J. F., Cohen, L. B., Lloyd, V. L., Casasola, M., & Stager, C. L. (1998). Acquisition of word-object associations by 14-month-old infants. *Developmental Psychology, 34*, 1289–1309.

Wilk, A. C., Bhatt, R. S., & Rovee-Collier, C. (1995, March–April). *Correlated attributes and categorization in infancy.* Paper presented at the meeting of the Society for Research in Child Development, Indianapolis, IN.

Younger, B. A. (1985). The segregation of items into categories by 10-month-old infants. *Child Development, 56*, 1574–1583.

Younger, B. A. (1990). Infants' detection of correlations among feature categories. *Child Development, 61*, 614–620.

Younger, B. A. (1992b). Developmental change in infant categorization: The perception of correlations among facial features. *Child Development, 63*, 1526–1535.

Younger, B. A. (1992a, April). *Categorization in infants: Sensitivity to overall similarity or correlations among attributes?* Paper presented at the Conference on Human Development, Atlanta, GA.

Younger, B. A. (1993a, March). *Perception of correlated attribute categories by young infants.* Paper presented at the meeting of the Society for Research in Child Development, New Orleans.

Younger, B. A. (1993b). Understanding category members as 'the same sort of thing': Explicit categorization in 10-month-old infants. *Child Development, 64*, 309–320.

Younger, B. A., & Cohen, L. B. (1983). Infant perception of correlations among attributes. *Child Development, 54*, 858–867.

Younger, B. A., & Cohen, L. B. (1986). Developmental change in infants' perception of correlations among attributes. *Child Development, 57*, 803–815.

Younger, B. A., & Fearing, D. (1998). Detecting correlations among form attributes: An object-examining test with infants. *Infant Behavior and Development, 21*, 289–297.

Younger, B. A., & Fearing, D. (1999). Parsing items into separate categories: Developmental change in infant categorization. *Child Development, 70*, 291–303.

Younger, B. A., & Fearing, D. (2000). A global to basic trend in early categorization: Evidence from a dual-category habituation task. *Infancy, 1*, 47–58.

Younger, B. A., & Goffman, L. (1996, April). *Stylistic differences in early language acquisition: Influences from cognitive and social domains.* Paper presented at the International Conference on Infant Studies, Providence, RI.

Younger, B. A., & Gotlieb, S. (1988). Development of categorization skills: Changes in the nature or structure of infant form categories? *Developmental Psychology, 24*, 611–619.

Younger, B. A., & Mekos, D. (1992). Category construction in preschool-age children: The use of correlated attributes. *Cognitive Development, 7*, 445–466.

CHAPTER FIVE

Conceptual Categorization

Jean M. Mandler

FOR THE PAST 15 years my research has concentrated on how infants form their first concepts. Because forming a concept usually involves forming a category, I often call concepts conceptual categories. This is a cumbersome expression, but I believe it is important to distinguish two different kinds of mental structures: conceptual and perceptual categories. Some researchers find this distinction unnecessary, but the view of categorization as a uniform process faces difficulty in accounting for many facets of mental life. As the chapters in this book testify, categorization itself is ubiquitous in mental functioning. But even though some basis of similarity is involved in all kinds of categories, content differs radically. We can categorize on the basis of single or multiple dimensions (square, loud, red), the behavior of things (animate and inanimate), abstract meaning (good and evil), and even ad hoc bases (things to take if the house catches on fire; Barsalou, 1973). This range of content from perceptual dimensions to abstract ideas, combined with the fact that some categorization is deliberate and requires effortful retrieval, whereas other categorization occurs automatically without effort, makes it highly unlikely that all categorization rests on a single process. I refer the reader to a summary of both psychological and neurological evidence showing that adults engage in more than one kind of categorization (Smith, Patalano, & Jonides, 1998).[1] Later in this chapter I summarize some developmental evidence that also militates against the view that all categorization is of the same form. The most obvious example is that we all form perceptual categories as a natural part of perceiving, but on deliberate categorization tasks both children and adults do many different things, such as categorize on the basis of overall appearance, single dimensions, or meaning. This range of variation in the kind of processing that is taking place means that whenever one talks about categorization it is crucial to specify the kind of categories one has in mind. The widespread failure to do so accounts for many of the controversies in this area of research.

From the outset, or at least as young as we have been able to make such comparisons, infants form categories of objects based on their perceptual appearance and also form concepts of objects based on the kinds of events in which objects take part. These do not necessarily match, and one goal of this chapter is to explain why. A good many psychologists have been tempted to call object categories concrete and conceptualizations abstract and, along with this temptation, to assume that development consists of moving from one form of categorization to the other. But these are temptations firmly to be resisted, since there is ample evidence that infants form both perceptual and conceptual categories from a very early age and that both kinds of categories can be quite abstract. If anything, development proceeds from the abstract to the concrete, rather than the other way around (see also Keil, 1998). Although that is undoubtedly something of an oversimplification, at least it redresses the balance a bit by scotching the old notion that there is a shift from concrete perceptual to abstract conceptual categorization as development proceeds.

The plan of this chapter is first to discuss briefly where concepts about objects come from and then to summarize some data on object concepts formed in the first year of life. These concepts are a far cry from those of adults, in that they tend to be global in nature and, from the adult point of view, ill defined and overly general. At the same time they are like adult concepts in that they form the basis for inductive generalizations. Next I briefly summarize the ways these concepts differ from perceptual categories. Then I discuss how these early concepts, crude though they may be, form the foundation of adult object concepts. Finally, I consider how these early concepts become mapped into language, and I allude briefly to the way language helps turn them into something more closely approximating adult notions.

The Origins of the Earliest Concepts

The meaningfulness we ascribe to objects and events is due to our conceptual interpretation of them. One finds in some of the literature on infant categorization a curious lack of attention to meaning or interpretation. Quinn and Eimas (2000), for example, say that to posit conceptual representations in addition to perceptual ones is cumbersome and poses a heavy biological burden. In particular, they object to the notion that there might be two representations, one perceptual and the other conceptual, for each category of objects and events. But, of course, that is not the implication of having a conceptual representational system in addition to the ability to form perceptual schemas. Infants do not just lie in their cribs and form perceptual categories; from a very early age they interpret what they see. To say that a 6-month-old has a concept (conceptual category) of animals along with a perceptual category of dogs does not imply two dissociated sets of categories, as Quinn and Eimas imply. On the contrary, the concept of animal just is the infant's *interpretation* of the dog it is observing (Mandler, 2000). As I will discuss later, however, the same concept of animal (or land animal) is also aroused when observing cats and a good many other mammals as well. This is what is meant by saying that early concepts are more global than many early perceptual categories. Infants see the differences between dogs and cats from an early age, but when interpreting either one they think "animal." (Obviously, they do not think in any natural language, and we do not know exactly what the concept of animal consists of for the infant—this is part of what my research program has been attempting to specify.)

The interpretative system is not an undue biological burden; indeed, it is essential for human functioning. The interpretations infants give to the events they observe in the world around them, and the inferences they draw from them, set down the foundations around which the adult conceptual system is organized (Mandler, 1998b, 2002). Furthermore, as I will discuss later, the global, often overly general nature of early concepts avoids pitfalls that await when learning is too specific.

We have known for some time that infants distinguish the kinds of behaviors in which animate and inanimate objects engage. From birth they are attracted to moving objects and often stare intently at them. I have suggested that from an early age (perhaps beginning with those periods of intense staring) infants begin to engage in a process called perceptual analysis, by which they analyze aspects of the way that objects move (Mandler, 1988). When they stare attentively at moving objects they not only perceive the characteristics of the objects and their motion but also begin to interpret what they see. I suggested that interpretation comes in the form of abstract descriptions (perhaps in the form of image-schemas) of the kinds of paths that objects take, the interactions of these paths, and some other basic spatial information, such as support and containment (Mandler, 1992). These descriptions, which ignore most of the details that are being perceived, form the basis for the ability to interpret (i.e., conceptualize) what objects are doing.

This is a theoretical, not an empirical, account. We can observe and even measure contemplation in infants, but we can only infer the kind of processes that go on during these periods of concentration. A currently popular view is that concepts are merely elaborated perceptions—something like the old empiricist notion of complex ideas being built out of simple ones. On such a view, one perception becomes associated with another, and the resultant percept A plus percept B equals a concept or meaning (Quinn & Eimas, 1997; Rakison & Poulin-Dubois, 2001). However, it seems difficult to understand how merely associating percepts with each other can result in concept formation. Researchers taking this view, which is a kind of perceptual reductionism (percept A + percept B = concept C), have not specified how these perceptual complexes are represented. Since concepts are used to think in the absence of perception, there must be some accessible knowledge store (i.e., what is usually called a conceptual or semantic system). Even though associated perceptual sights can lead to expectations of what will happen next in an event, that is sensorimotor, not conceptual, knowledge. Sensorimotor knowledge is expressed only in action and ongoing perception and does not allow for thought or recall. Piaget (1952) understood this well, although his stage theory failed to solve the resulting problem of how a sensorimotor organism becomes a conceptual one.

Some mechanism is required to get an accessible conceptual store started. Perceptual analysis is an attractive candidate for a number of reasons. First, and most important, it grounds conceptual thought in perception. The earliest concepts arise directly from analysis of perceptual displays. Second, it obviates the need for a developmental shift from one form of representation to another, because it enables concept formation to develop in tandem with perceptual learning. Although we have no direct evidence, it seems likely that conceptual interpretation of perceptual arrays begins either at birth or as soon as stable perceptual schemas are formed in the first month or two. Third, it does not require language and so can account for conceptual thought prior to or in the absence of language. Fourth, it accounts for the simplicity of concepts in comparison to perceptual knowledge, because it is formed by simplifying perceptual information. Fifth, by storing conceptual information separately from perceptual information, it accounts for the otherwise odd fact that conceptual information is accessible, whereas a great deal of perceptual information is inaccessible. (The perceptual information that is accessible has been conceptualized.) Sixth, it avoids positing a host of innate ideas. Of course, there must be some innate biases in the tendency of infants to analyze spatial displays, to concentrate on paths and spatial relations such as containment, and to recast this information into a particular format (whether image-schemas or other). But these are general constraints, not particular ideas, such as a concept of animal or agent. Perceptual analysis allows these ideas to be formed through analysis of the information available in the perceptual world. When perceptual information undergoes analysis in this way, primitive concepts such as animal or goal-directedness result. (This is a bare-boned description of perceptual analysis; for more detail, see Mandler, 1992, 1998a.)

Infants react differently to people and objects almost from birth (Legerstee, 1992). By 3 months they categorize objects that interact contingently with them as different from objects that do not (Frye, Rawling, Moore, & Myers, 1983). By 6 months they expect people to behave differently toward persons and inanimate objects (Legerstee, Barna, & DiAdamo, 2000). At the same age they tend to attend to the "goal" (end of path) of a reaching hand rather than the trajectory itself (Woodward, 1998), and they differentiate caused and uncaused (self-starting) motion (Leslie, 1988). By 9 months they have learned that mechanical objects do not start themselves (Poulin-Dubois, Lepage, & Ferland, 1996). These studies, along with a host of other work along the same lines, show that infants use contingent interaction and self-starting motion to differentiate animate and inanimate things. These are the characteristics, along with "biological" paths,[2] that form the foundation of concepts of animals and inanimate "things" and are the kinds of descriptions that I have suggested arise from perceptual analysis (Mandler, 1992).

These conceptual descriptions depend less on what objects look like than on what they do. Of course, infants see the differences in the appearance of objects and gradually learn to associate what they look like with what they do. But the physical appearance of an object is a predictor of its behavior, not an essential component of the meaning of animate or inanimate things, and infants interpret anything that moves in a goal-directed way as animate. For example, Johnson and Sockaci (2000) found that 14-month-olds treat purple blobs as agents if they engage in goal-directed activity. Similarly, 9-month-olds treat computer-generated circles as animate when they interact contingently and in goal-directed ways (Csibra, Gergely, Bíró, Koós, & Brockbank, 1999). Circles and purple blobs have none of the features of animals. So these data, along with data in this chapter, show that what objects do is more important in interpreting their significance than what they look like.

Could one not merely say instead that infants are categorizing objects on the basis of how they move without positing conceptual representation in addition? It does

seem highly likely that the perceptual categorization of motion by very young infants (Bertenthal, 1993) is one of the starting points for creating a conceptual category of animates, along with the sensitivity to contingencies between events that is
demonstrated by expectancy conditioning. These are perceptual accomplishments.
However, categorizing an object as animate is more than categorizing movement
per se or responding to an environmental contingency. It is an *interpretation* of what
the object is doing. Goal-directedness is not a perceptual attribute but a way the
human mind interprets certain kinds of object paths. For example, even though goal-
directed behavior typically forms a continuous stream of activity, 10- to 11-month-
olds have been shown to parse it into units based on the initiation and completion
of the goal involved (Saylor, Baird, & Baldwin, 2000). A purely perceptual description of what a conceptual mind calls goal-directedness would not mention goals (and
certainly not intentionality) but would give, for example, a vector description.

In spite of their ability to make fine perceptual discriminations, infants are doing
something broader and less dependent on detail when they categorize an object as
an animate. They are assigning a conceptual role to it, on the basis of the paths it
takes and the way it interacts with other objects on paths of their own. These assigned roles predict more than does biological motion alone. For example, how
a person interacts from a distance with an object hidden behind a screen leads
6-month-olds to predict whether an animate or inanimate object will be there
(Legerstee et al., 2000). As shown in the data discussed in the next section, infants
as young as 9 months already know a good deal about the roles played by animates—
the sorts of things that animals do, as opposed to what inanimate things do. These
conceptualizations have moved beyond the perception of how objects move to more
specific characterizations, such as "Animals drink."

The conceptualization of an object as animate or inanimate is likely at first to be
a very general one. Needless to say, it becomes more specific with experience, as
infants learn to associate the physical appearance of objects with animate or inanimate behavior. So, for example, the ability to start motion on one's own or the contingent nature of interactions with other objects eventually become associated with
limbs (and wings). What I am emphasizing here is that it is the conceptualization of
something as animate that controls the association of self-motion with limbs, not
the other way around. This may seem an unduly subtle point, but I believe it is an
underappreciated aspect of associative learning. Even pigeons, when they associate
completely different stimuli with a common event, develop a common meaning or
representation for those stimuli, one that is used to create new untrained associations (Zentall, 2000). So we should not be surprised that infants can use common
motion events to form conceptual categories such as animals, which then control
learning of new associations.

Traditionally, associativity has been discussed in more concrete terms, as does
Rakison in chapter 7. For example, he suggests that legs become associated with
walking and mouths with eating, and that these associations of features with actions
are what create a concept of animal. Furthermore, because he believes that association of parts with their actions is a late-developing capacity, he goes on to claim that
infants do not have any conceptualizations of animacy and inanimacy until quite
late in the infancy period (18 months or so). It actually seems quite implausible that

infants would analyze the role that *parts* of an object play in an event before analyzing the role the object itself plays in an event, but this is an empirical matter. I have
summarized here some of the research indicating that some general conceptions of
animacy and inanimacy affect infants' interpretations of events at least by 6 or 7
months and probably earlier. The Frye et al. (1983) data seem particularly compelling in this regard, because the 3-month-olds in that study responded to objects as
animate mainly on the basis of whether the objects interacted contingently with them
and not on the basis of what the objects looked like. Furthermore, the research that
Laraine McDonough and I have been carrying out in the past few years indicates
that it is the animate (or inanimate) conceptualization that controls what becomes
associated with an object, not the object's parts or features, many of which infants
appear not to notice. I will document this point by summarizing our research on
inductive generalization.

Concepts as Generative Devices

One of the main functions of conceptualization is to provide a basis for generalization. We can only experience a small fraction of the world's activities and must
depend on inductive inference to set limits on how far to generalize a particular observation. It is generally agreed that adults use concepts about objects and events to
limit their inductions. However, the traditional view of the developmental origins
of induction was that the earliest inferences must be based on perceptual similarity
rather than on concepts. The reason for this view was the concomitant belief that
infants have no concepts and therefore do not have anything like an adult basis for
inference (e.g., Quine, 1977). This is the doctrine that Keil (1991) called the doctrine
of original sim: before children develop theories about the world, they can only be
influenced by similarity of appearance. This view is part of the reason for the traditional belief that development proceeds from categorizing by raw physical similarity to categorizing by more abstract similarity that is based on conceptual theories
about the world (and therefore shows qualitative change with age). It was said that
the more two things look alike, the more likely it will be for infants to generalize the
properties of one to the other. In this view, upon seeing the family dog eat, the infant comes to expect that other dogs will eat too. This generalization happens because a category of dogs is formed on the basis of physical similarity. As the infant
observes the family cat and pet goldfish eat as well, it can eventually make the more
difficult and sophisticated inferential leap that all animals eat.

As I have written elsewhere (Mandler, 2000) there are a number of difficulties
with this view of how inductive generalization begins. For one thing, it means that
the infant must already have formed a concept of animal, even though Quine's theory
was devised to allow for induction in a conceptless organism. Without such a concept, there would be no stop rule on the induction, and the child might as well infer
that plants and furniture eat as well. Of course, the infant hasn't observed any of
those things eat, but it hasn't observed most animals eat either. (That is the point of
induction: to overcome the sparsity of human observations.) Perhaps the infant
makes use of a similarity gradient around the objects that have been seen to eat. But

without any conceptualization this would surely be a grossly imperfect procedure. If done solely on the basis of perceptual similarity, then would legged tables be included but legless fish not? How could infants induce that a purple blob is an agent (Johnson & Sockaci, 2000), if they are dependent solely on similarity of appearance? Notice that the motion itself cannot be the basis of similarity here. It is the motion of eating that is to be generalized and the question is how to determine what kinds of objects engage in this action.

Perhaps instead of a similarity gradient the infant has perceptual categories of different levels of generality, such as dogs and animals (but no concepts). Then the dilemma becomes why, as this chapter describes, is one kind of perceptual category used for induction and another not? This, of course, raises the empirical question of exactly what kinds of categories infants do use for purposes of induction. When they observe a dog eat, how far do they generalize this behavior? To this dog alone? To all dogs? To all similar animals? To all animals? To everything?

It was to answer these questions that Laraine McDonough and I began to study the generalizations that infants make. We have been using a technique we call generalized imitation. We model a simple event using little replicas of real-world objects and encourage infants to imitate what they have observed. For example, we might show a dog being given a drink from a cup. Then we give the infants the cup, but instead of the dog used for modeling we give them two other objects instead. We might give them an elephant and a car along with the cup, or a different dog and a cat with the cup, to see which object they choose for their imitations. By varying the selections available to the infants, we can test what they have understood from the event they have observed. In a sense this is a way to get preverbal infants to talk to us.

Infants' imitations are based on what they have understood from their observations. They do try to match what they have seen, but they don't blindly mimic whatever the modeler does. Instead they reproduce what they have understood the modeler to do. Therefore if we give the infants a choice of objects they can tell us how they have interpreted the event they watched. For example, when we model a dog drinking from a cup and then give the infant the cup along with any other animal and a car, they use the other animal. This tells us that at the least they interpreted the event as an animal being given a drink. But we can uncover their interpretation more precisely by narrowing the choices. For example, we can offer them another dog and a bird or another dog and a cat. If they choose randomly they are telling us they have seen an animal drink, without further specification. But if they now choose the dog over the bird but choose the cat as often as the dog, they are telling us they saw a land animal (or some similar description) being given a drink.

Using this technique we found that 14-month-olds generalize very broadly (Mandler & McDonough, 1996a). When we modeled drinking or sleeping with a dog, they generalized it to all animals from fish to birds to aardvarks but rarely demonstrated these behaviors with vehicles. When we modeled keying a car or giving a child a ride, they generalized it to all vehicles, including forklifts and airplanes, but rarely carried out the behavior with animals. Furthermore, when we modeled these behaviors with both the appropriate and inappropriate objects, such as giving both a dog and a car a drink or keying both a dog and a car, the infants typically did not use the inappropriate object even when the experimenter had just modeled it. These experiments gave us the first answer to our question about breadth of generalization: infants generalize from familiar instances such as dogs to the entire domain of animals, and from cars to the entire domain of vehicles. This result means that physical similarity between the observed exemplar and the generalized exemplar did not play an important role; infants generalized from dogs to cats, rabbits, fish, birds, and aardvarks (but not to vehicles) and from cars to trucks, buses, motorcycles, airplanes, and forklifts (but not to animals). Some of their responses were quite suggestive as to what controls associativity. The infants keyed airplanes, although this is something they surely had never observed. They also gave fish a drink and made them sleep in beds. These are examples of overgeneralization that eventually will have to be corrected, but equally they are examples of meaning, rather than exemplars, controlling associations.

We extended this work to 9- and 11-month-olds (McDonough & Mandler, 1998). We had to simplify the technique for these younger subjects, because not until about 9 months do infants begin to imitate complex events in which one object acts on another. To make the task possible at these younger ages, we modeled the same events used in the first two experiments of Mandler and McDonough (1996a) but included an opportunity for direct imitation and also eliminated the choice aspects of the procedure. After modeling, we first encouraged the infants to imitate what they had just observed, using the very same objects (e.g., if we modeled giving a dog a drink from a cup, we gave the infants the dog and cup). Then, we provided a single generalization object along with the prop and measured whether or not the infant imitated using this new object. On half the trials, each infant received an appropriate object to go with the prop (e.g., a bird and the cup) and on the other half they received an inappropriate object (e.g., an airplane and the cup). For both 9- and 11-month-olds the results were very similar to those obtained with 14-month-olds; they broadly generalized appropriate behaviors but infrequently performed the modeled behaviors with inappropriate objects. However, although the simplified procedure worked well with the 11-month-olds, 9-month-olds only produced about 30 percent of the events with direct imitation, and even less than that when they had to generalize their imitative response to a new object. These data suggest that 9 months is about the lower limit on the age at which the generalized imitation technique can be usefully applied.

The results from these two sets of studies showed that 11- to 14-month-old infants categorize animals and vehicles as different kinds but did not examine whether they are making subdivisions within these domains. Offering infants a choice from the same "basic-level" category[3] and a different category might be the most likely situation in which to find an effect of perceptual similarity. Since infants try to match what they have observed, if we modeled giving a dog a drink and then gave the infants a choice between another dog or a cat, any similarity-based explanation should predict they would choose the dog. Therefore, in another series of experiments with 14-month-olds (Mandler & McDonough, 1998b) we used a dog to model drinking and sleeping and for their imitations gave them a choice between another dog and a cat, another dog and a rabbit, and another dog and an anteater or a musk ox. In addition to using contrasts among land animals we also used another dog with a bird. Similarly, we showed a car being keyed and giving a person a ride, and for the imitations we provided another car and a truck, another car and a motorcycle, and another car with either a shoveler or a forklift. In addition to these contrasts among road vehicles, we also used a contrast of another car and an airplane.

For animals, there was no preference for using the same "basic-level" category as observed in the modeled event. Infants' first choice of object to use for their imitation was the cat or the rabbit just as frequently as the other dog, and they even made first choices of the unfamiliar mammals about as often. They did show a preference for another dog, however, when faced with a choice between another dog and a bird. These data tell us that the 14-month-olds were interpreting the dog used for the modeling not as a dog as a distinct kind or at the most global level of animal but as something in between—as a land animal or perhaps a four-legged animal.

These data are especially useful because the first choice tells us infants' interpretation of the observed event—in this case, that they saw a land animal being given a drink. But in addition to providing information about how infants construe various animals, analysis of the second choices showed that infants often went on to imitate the activity using the other category example, thus providing information about the breadth of their generalizations. So, for example, in the case of the dog–bird contrast, the infants seemed to be saying something like "I saw you give a land animal a drink, but birds drink too."

These data demonstrate quite compellingly that the behavior of 14-month-olds in the inductive generalization studies is not carried out merely on the basis of perceptual matching and imitation, as suggested by Rakison and Poulin-Dubois (2001) and by Rakison (chap. 7). There is no doubt that infants this age see the differences in appearance between dogs, cats, and rabbits. If they were engaged in perceptual matching rather than conceptually interpreted matching they would, as Rakison (chap. 7) points out, choose the most similar available stimulus to that exemplar during the test. They do not, choosing a cat or rabbit as often as a dog when having observed a dog acting, and therefore we must discard the perceptual matching explanation for these data.

The infants were more selective with vehicles in this set of experiments. They were much more likely to choose the same subcategory for their first choice of object to use for their imitations. Again, they sometimes used the other category for a second imitation, although quite rarely in the case of the car–airplane contrast.[4] However, when this experiment was recently replicated using atypical exemplars for modeling and testing (for example, modeling with as alligator and testing with another alligator and a camel, or modeling with a fire truck and testing with another fire truck and a shoveler), 14-month-olds again chose the different objects as often as the same "basic-level" kind, and this occurred for both animals and vehicles (McDonough & Marsh, 2002). We are not sure exactly why this difference in results occurred, although in several of our experiments, differentiation of vehicles has preceded differentiation of animals. As discussed later in this section, this tendency may be related to amount of daily experience with the items in question.

That the imitation technique calls on conceptual representations of the world is convincingly shown by two phenomena. First, as discussed earlier, infants typically refuse to imitate inappropriate modeling, which they would not do if they were merely imitating whatever the modeler does. Second, they also behave in a different fashion when the modeled behavior is domain-general (appropriate for more than one domain) instead of domain-specific (appropriate for only one domain). In Mandler and McDonough (1998b) we modeled washing a dog or a car, and we also made a dog or a car go into a building. Now 14-month-olds broadly generalized across domains. If we modeled a dog going into a building and then provided them with another animal and a vehicle, they would first make the other animal go into the building (they do know the difference between animals and vehicles and do try to reproduce what they have observed) but then would typically make the vehicle go into the building too. The same infants, however, restricted their imitations to the modeled domain in the case of domain-specific properties such as drinking. Thus, with the same objects, infants generalized across domains or stayed within the same domain, depending on the real-world status of what was modeled.

The data reported so far show that infants have some very broad concepts of animals and vehicles that they use for purposes of making inferences about these domains. The question arises whether they also use narrower categories for making inferences. One way to study this question is to use properties that are appropriate for only one subcategory within a larger domain. With this in mind, we recently completed a series of experiments investigating whether there are any generalizations that are restricted to the "basic" level. In the first experiment of this series (Mandler & McDonough, 1998b) we used the same generalized imitation technique to investigate 14- and 20-month-olds' knowledge of two artifact properties (beds are used for sleeping, and cups are used for drinking) and two natural kind properties (dogs chew on bones, and flowers are to be smelled). We found that the 14-month-olds overgeneralized all these properties, making many inappropriate responses: for example, when we demonstrated giving a little model of a person a drink from a teacup and then gave the person to the infants along with a coffee mug and a frying pan, they chose the frying pan almost as often as the mug to imitate drinking. It is as if they were conceptualizing these utensils as containers and had not yet encoded enough detail to narrow them down to their common social uses. Similarly, they were as likely to put a little person to sleep in a bathtub as in a bed, to smell a tree as a flower, and to feed a bone to a bird as to a dog. Even at 20 months, infants were still making some of the same overgeneralizations. By this age they had begun to narrow the artifact characteristics appropriately but were still overgeneralizing the natural kind characteristics (presumably because of fewer interactions with animals and plants than with artifacts).

We have since replicated these findings with other properties (Mandler & McDonough, 2000). In one experiment we used animal activities (birds go in nests, but rabbits do not, and rabbits eat carrots, but birds do not) and vehicle activities (cars get gasoline but wagons do not, and you wear a helmet riding on a motorcycle but not in a car). Again 14-month-olds generalized all these properties indiscriminately, for example, making both rabbits and birds go into nests and putting gasoline into both cars and wagons. By 19 months their responses were largely appropriate for the vehicle activities but not the animal ones. Not until 24 months were the children successful at responding appropriately on the animal events.

We also investigated other artifacts to assess the generality of these findings (Mandler & McDonough, 2000). We modeled washing a dinner plate in a kitchen sink and tested generalization with another sink and a bathtub. We modeled sitting on a chair at the dining table and tested generalization with a different chair and a toilet. We brushed hair with a hairbrush and tested with another hairbrush and a toothbrush. We pounded pipes together with a hammer and tested with another hammer and a wrench. Again, at 14 months infants were just as likely to use the inappropriate object for their generalizations as the appropriate one. They seem not yet to have identified specific "basic-level" properties for many artifacts. Rather they seem to understand the characteristics of objects in rather general ways: small containers are "drinkable-from," larger containers are places to sleep or immerse objects, any flat-surfaced furniture is a place to sit, any kind of tool is suitable for hammering, and any kind of brush is suitable for making hair look nice. However, by 19 months, the infants were mostly correct on the artifacts, just as in the previous experiment.

One might propose that the youngest infants were just imitating the actions on any old object. We know from our previous work that this is not the case. Infants typically do not use just any object. If they are not provided with an object they consider appropriate, they often don't imitate at all. However, it is possible that 14-month-olds might have learned some of the properties we tested in a less meaningful way than the gloss of "being drinkable-from" or "making hair look nice" suggests. They might have learned more neutral physical descriptions of the activities. For example, hair grooming might mean no more than running any elongated object over the hair; sitting in a chair at table might be understood only as sitting on any flat surface, not a piece of furniture, and so on. So we conducted a control experiment with 14-month-olds to show that although their understanding of the modeled activities was not yet at the "basic" level, it was nevertheless in the larger conceptual ballpark and not merely at the level of purely physical description, such as a movement of the hand to the hair or putting one object inside another.

We tested 14-month-olds on the same properties again, using physically similar exemplars from unrelated categories as the distracters (Mandler & McDonough, 2000). For washing dishes the inappropriate object was a bed with headboard, footboard, and low sides instead of a bathtub. For sitting at the dining table the inappropriate object was a car with a flat top that was smaller than the table instead of a toilet. For brushing hair the inappropriate object was a spoon instead of a toothbrush. And for hammering, the inappropriate object was a cup instead of a wrench. Each of these inappropriate objects afforded the modeled activity but came from a conceptually unrelated domain. Now 14-month-olds were successful; very few of them chose the inappropriate objects. So 14-month-olds understand something about the nature of the tested objects, but their knowledge is overly general and not yet at the "basic" level.

These experiments suggest that 14-month-olds haven't encoded much information about the parts of animals, plants, or household artifacts and therefore tend to generalize too broadly about subclasses in those domains. This does not mean that infants this age don't know anything about the functions of household artifacts. So, although the infants used a toothbrush to groom hair, they did not use a spoon for this purpose, and although they washed dishes in a bathtub, they did not wash dishes in a bed. At the same time, infants this age do not seem to distinguish between beds and tubs as acceptable places to sleep. This kind of finding suggests that differentiation of the functions of various household objects may be learned in a piecemeal fashion, so that anomalous associations can exist along with correct ones. Acquiring true "basic-level" understanding appears to be a gradual process. Children might first learn that certain kinds of objects are containers (on the basis of overall shape), then that small containers, whether cups or frying pans, are used for drinking, and large containers are used for washing and sleeping, then that some large containers are used for sleeping and others only for washing, and finally the specific parts and functions that differentiate tubs from sinks. This progression bears some affinity to that described by Aguiar and Baillargeon (1998) in their studies of containment. They note that infants begin with crude qualitative concepts and only gradually identify the variables that enrich and define the original concept.

This work is consistent in showing that the refinement in understanding that is taking place is faster for artifacts than for natural kinds. Of course, we have no reason to think that this is special sensitivity to understanding artifact functions. In the southern California urban culture under study, children have much more daily exposure to a wide variety of artifacts than to animals. And although they are surrounded by plants, the culture for the most part does not emphasize these. It seems likely that in a more rural community the details of the progression might differ. A greater variety of animal behaviors might be encountered, as well as greater variety in people's activities with different kinds of plants.

We also should not conclude that young children *cannot* restrict inductions to subcategories in either natural kind or artifact domains. One of the functions of the names that parents use with children is to teach them that there are smaller categories than the domain level that are important and that constrain some kinds of properties (Waxman & Markow, 1995). Nevertheless, before infants begin to understand language, and in many cases for some time afterward, inductive inferences tend to be quite broad. As discussed later, it appears that one of the important results of mastering language is to differentiate the world into finer categories and therefore to make inductive inferences more precise. By age 2½ (and in some cases somewhat younger) this differentiation leads to "basic-level" inductions (Gelman and Coley, 1990), and at least by age 4, as more detail is learned, inferences begin to be more likely in smaller than in larger classes (Gelman & O'Reilley, 1988). This is the age range in which physical similarity begins to be especially useful. Because exemplars of subclasses tend to look more like each other than do exemplars of global classes, as global concepts become refined, exemplar similarity becomes particularly helpful in distinguishing one subcategory from another.

Overall, the data discussed here indicate that what objects do, whether natural kinds or artifacts, is first understood in a global fashion. Infants presumably learn that hands are used to manipulate objects many months before they understand precisely what the hands are doing. Infants see pans put on stoves, watches looked at, and telephones lifted to the ear, but presumably none of these events carries functional significance in the first instance. A few functions may be obvious early on, such as food being something to be eaten. In most cases, however, the specific function or behavior that differentiates one artifact or animal from another must be obscure. Furthermore, when functions do begin to be conceptualized they are apt to be too broad, as we have seen in the case of cups and pans. At first, it appears that infants *see* a cup or a pan but *think* container, hence the overgeneralization. They see a dog eat a bone but think animal and food, with a similar result.

These induction data are consistent with our previous categorization findings (Mandler, Bauer, & McDonough, 1991; Mandler & McDonough, 1993, 1998a). Results from the two categorization tasks we have used (object-examination and sequential-touching) and the generalized imitation task, as well, converge on the conclusion that infants initially form broad, relatively undifferentiated concepts of animals, vehicles, furniture, and plants (with some evidence that vehicles become differentiated earlier than the other domains). Furthermore, these tasks all indicate that these domain-level concepts are in the first instance organized not around individual features or parts or around overall perceptual appearance but rather around some (possibly quite primitive) notion of kind. They also illustrate that the traditional view of the first inductions was exactly backward: rather than beginning with concrete narrow generalizations, infants generalize broadly on the basis of abstract conceptualizations at first and only with experience learn to pay attention to perceptual detail and thus narrow the scope of their inferences.

Equally important, the induction data tell us something very important about the way infants form associations. They indicate that property association and generalization are controlled not by the common features of objects or by the perceptual appearance of the objects that infants have actually observed but instead are organized by the concepts they have formed. In the initial stages the boundaries of these concepts are broad. The world has been divided into a few global domains of different kinds of things. The meaning of these broad classes, such as animals or vehicles, does not arise from commonality of physical features. Babies do learn at least some of these features; indeed, they must learn them to identify an object as a member of a given category. But in terms of *meaning*, it appears that infants observe the events in which animals and vehicles take part and use their interpretation of the events to conceptualize the sort of thing an animal or a vehicle is. Animals are things that move themselves and act on other things; vehicles are things that give rides, and so forth. An important aspect of this meaning creation is that it is the meaning of the class as a whole that determines what gets associated with what, not just the individual objects actually experienced. So, for example, drinking is associated with "self-movers" and with containers, not just with the dogs one has seen drink or the cups one has drunk from. Note that this position does not claim that no associations between dogs and drinking or cups and drinking are formed, only that the associations are broader than that.

Thus, even though infants must use various physical features to tell animals such as dogs and cats apart, they do not rely on them when they are construing the meaning of an event and generalizing from it. The examples given earlier are clear. When we model an event with a dog, and give year-old infants a choice between another dog and a cat or another dog and a rabbit to use for their imitations, they are as apt to choose the cat or the rabbit as the dog. They give a drink to models of animals that have the barest indication of a mouth, but they do not give a drink to a Flying Tiger airplane in spite of its highly prominent mouth. They use a key on forklifts and airplanes, associations that they have never observed. And infants presumably have not seen people sleeping in bathtubs or drinking from frying pans, yet they generalize these behaviors to them. All of these phenomena provide evidence that associations are not controlled by individual parts or objects but instead by object kind.

Conceptual Categories Contrasted with Perceptual Categories

As adults we are accustomed to think of perceptual and conceptual categories as more or less the same thing. We have a concept of dogs that is different from our concept of cats, and each contains information about perceptual appearance. But the situation does not appear to be quite the same for infants. As I have shown, infants do not clearly distinguish between cats and dogs in terms of conceptual knowledge. At the same time there is ample evidence that as early as 3 months of age they can categorize them perceptually (Quinn, Eimas, & Rosenkrantz, 1993). This kind of perceptual categorization takes place merely through exposure to visual stimuli. Given a series of pictures (as is commonly done in the laboratory), or other stimuli that bear some resemblance to each other, the perceptual system abstracts the principal components of the presented information (Posner & Keele, 1968; McClelland & Rumelhart, 1985). It might be called learning a perceptual prototype or a perceptual schema. This kind of categorization is part of the visual input system, and a good deal of evidence suggests that in its basic form it is impenetrable by the conceptual system (Pylyshyn, 1999) and that the information it computes is inaccessible to consciousness (Moscovitch, Goshen-Gottstein, & Vrietzen, 1994). This process enables even very young organisms to recognize visual and auditory patterns they have seen or heard before and to categorize them. However, the ability to respond to a previously seen pattern as familiar is silent about the meaning of the pattern—hence the equal necessity of formulating concepts about what those patterns do, how they interact with each other and with the infant.

In Mandler (2000) I discussed several ways in which perceptual categories of objects differ from concepts, the gist of which I reproduce here. First, the two kinds of categories operate on different kinds of information. Perceptual categories compute what objects look like and in many cases how they move. Conceptual categories compute class membership or kinds, doing so on the basis of the roles objects take in events, that is, the functions they serve (Nelson, 1985) or the way they behave. These are not perceptual data but rather interpretations of perceptual data. Perceptual categorization can take place in the absence of interpretation. For example, this seems likely to occur when 3-month-olds categorize a series of static pictures of dogs or horses, none (or at most one) of which they would have seen before.

Second, infants' perceptual categories appear to contain more detailed information than do their concepts. A perceptual procedure that learns to discriminate pictures of dogs from cats must be making use of fairly extensive information, even if confined to facial regions (Quinn & Eimas, 1996). Infant concepts seem poverty stricken in comparison. They are global and appear to be relatively crude, as illustrated by infants not distinguishing between dogs and cats, something that they do perceptually in great detail.

Third, a good deal of the information that is used to form perceptual categories is inaccessible to conscious awareness. Needless to say, there is no evidence about this in infancy, but it seems reasonable to generalize from adults. There is good evidence that adults' perceptual categories are impenetrable. For example, we have no access to the information that enables us to categorize a face as male or female. Therefore, whatever this information is, it cannot be considered to be part of our conceptual knowledge, even though we have been dividing faces into male and female from at least 6 months of age (Fagan & Singer, 1979). Concepts, on the other hand, are used for conscious thought, problem solving, recall of the past, and so forth. Here we have some positive evidence for accessibility in infancy. From around 9 months of age, infants can imitate events they have observed in the past (Mandler & McDonough, 1996b; Meltzoff, 1988). This capacity requires not only conceptualization but also accessibility, as shown by the inability of amnesic adults to do such imitation (McDonough, Mandler, McKee, & Squire, 1995).

Fourth, there appears to be a different course of acquisition for the two kinds of categories. As I have shown, many of the first object concepts are global and, to the extent that they are not yet divided into subcategories, necessarily lack detail. Development in this area consists in large part of making finer differentiations within these broad categories. There has been only a small amount of research on acquisition of perceptual categories at different levels of generality. However, we do know that some detailed perceptual categories can be formed early, such as 3-month-olds discriminating pictures of cats from tigers or horses from zebras (Eimas & Quinn, 1994). Somewhat more variable perceptual categories, such as pictures of mammals, can also be learned as early as 3 months, although more trials may be required (Behl-Chadha, 1996). In general, variability makes perceptual categorization more difficult. For example, Younger and Fearing (1999) found that when pictures of cats and horses were presented together, categorization did not occur until 10 months of age. Overall, then, although still fairly scanty, the evidence suggests that perceptually similar items (not surprisingly) are easier to categorize perceptually than are more variable ones. At the same time, within a given level of similarity, the process of perceptual learning proceeds from global to more specific representations (Gibson, 1967). For example, the learning that newborns do about speech sounds proceeds in this fashion (Bertoncini, Bijeljac-Babic, Jusczyk, Kennedy, & Mehler, 1988), and there is some suggestion that 2-month-olds learning to categorize complex pictures may also form global representations first (Quinn & Johnson, 2000). As discussed earlier, this is what one would expect if learning complex perceptual patterns involves first extracting the principal components of the patterns. This progression, however, refers to the details of the learning process itself, not to the kinds of perceptual categories that are the easiest for infants to master. Infants have no trouble forming quite detailed perceptual categories and appear to have somewhat more difficulty forming global perceptual categories. There are to date no data on whether 3-month-olds can form a perceptual category of a wider class of animals than mammals, that is, one that includes birds and fish. In contrast, infants often form global concepts first (including this wider class of animals) and only more slowly refine them into smaller (typi-cally more perceptually similar) groups.

The final and most important difference has to do with the function that cate-gories serve. Perceptual categories are used to recognize objects and to identify them. This function provides stability and the sense of familiarity but in itself does not provide the meaning of what is being categorized. People can learn to recognize and categorize randomly generated dot patterns without the patterns having any signifi-cance (Posner & Keele, 1968). It is concepts that give patterns meaning, and it is concepts that infants use (just like adults) for purposes of making inductive gener-alizations. Both adults and infants are influenced by perceptual appearance, of course, but they use it to help determine the kind something represents and not as a basis of induction in its own right. No matter how much something may look like an ani-mal, if we think, for whatever reason, that it is not an animal, we will not ascribe animal properties to it.

Infant Concepts as the Foundation of the Adult Conceptual System

Our data indicate that concept development in infancy proceeds by a process of differentiation from very broad notions to a more precise level of conceptualization. This direction of development may occur because it is easier to notice the relevant characteristics of events that define global categories than it is to notice and remem-ber the details of the objects taking part in them. It may also be advantageous. For example, it has been speculated that limited information-processing skills make it easier to learn language (Elman, 1991; Newport, 1990). The notion behind this "less is more" hypothesis is that mastering language requires structuring a huge database; a restricted capacity that limits the amount of information being considered can make learning possible without overloading the system. The same argument can be ap-plied to the conceptual system. Infants can begin to interpret what is happening around them and gain thereby a degree of predictability about the world without having to process all of the huge amount of information with which they are con-fronted. A lack of attention to detail, accompanied by attention to a few salient char-acteristics of events, also gives infants a better chance of not getting trapped into mistaken hypotheses—hypotheses that are driven by local detail rather than being broadly true (Carey & Markman, 1999). On some occasions, narrow concepts might maximize the accuracy of predictions, but their use would also mean that many things would go unconceptualized. It is probably more efficient in the long run to make overly general predictions (all animals drink) and learn some exceptions (. . . ex-cept for fish) than not to have any idea at all how a new animal exemplar might act. Indeed Medin, Wattenmaker, and Michalski (1987) found that this is what adults often do when learning new categories and making inferences. They found that people often develop overly general rules and then restrict them by adding clauses that eliminate counterexamples.

If children first learned a concept of a dog but did not see any relationship be-tween it and a rabbit or a cow, or if they learned a concept of a chair but did not see any relationship between it and a table or a bed, learning categories such as animals and furniture would not only be uncertain and lack generalizability but the organization of the conceptual system would be wide open, without any principled basis for its development. What we find instead, namely, the formation of broad divisions of the world first, guarantees a stable, hierarchically organized conceptual system. Every time an infant or young child learns a new distinction within a conceptual realm, as part of the very learning process the object is understood as a member of a superordinate class. Insofar as the meaning system is concerned, the infant looking at dogs and cats does not at first conceptualize them as two different kinds but only as, for example, two different-looking, "self-moving, goal-directed interactors." When dogs and cats do become conceptually distinct, it is as two animals that vary in their names, the sounds they make, behaviors, and so forth, but their animal membership is never in question.

This view of early concept learning is diametrically opposed to the view proposed by Rakison and Butterworth (1998a) that 14- to 18-month-olds may not yet have a "knowledge-based understanding of category relations" but instead merely attend to parts such as legs and wheels, which "to some extent define category membership for infants at this age" (Rakison & Cohen, 1999). As I have shown, 14-month-olds don't pay all that much attention to parts in the generalized imitation task. If they consider a pan as good an exemplar of a drinking utensil as a cup, that suggests some indifference to details. They must see the utensil as a container on the basis of its overall shape, but beyond that they seem not to have noticed handles and the like. They don't make an airplane with a mouth drink, and they do put birds with no visible eyes to bed. Similarly, if a cat is considered as good as a dog for imitating feeding a dog, then the differences in features, which we know are used for purposes of perceptual categorization, are not being attended to by the infant and thus are not playing a role in the way an observed event is conceived. The data are clear enough, but at this point they might be interpreted in one of two ways: either 14-month-olds haven't attended to the parts in question sufficiently thoroughly to use them in matching what they have observed, or they have encoded the differences but consider them unimportant. The less-is-more hypothesis would tend to suggest the former view, but either one poses a difficult problem for a position that says that at this age parts of objects play a primary role in conceptual development.

One can imagine circumstances in which infants might pay more attention than usual to parts. For example, Rakison and Butterworth (1998b) gave 14- to 22-month-olds a series of categorization tasks in a single session, some of which consisted of stimuli that were missing parts or mixed up the two categories under study (e.g., a truck top on cow's legs). The unusual stimuli may have led the infants to concentrate on parts such as the moving wheels, which must have been attractive (and would lead to categorization of vehicles as different from objects without moving parts). In other studies (Rakison & Butterworth, 1998a), the changes in parts drastically violated the overall structure of the objects under study. In most of these cases infants did not categorize at all, but in any case, it would not be surprising that when an expected overall shape is badly distorted, infants concentrate on the perceptual appearance of the object rather than make use of their conceptual knowledge.

Such data make plain that it is not always easy to determine what can be concluded from categorization tasks. Both object-examination and sequential-touching tasks are instructionless, on-line tasks, and infants can do a variety of things, depending on what attracts their attention at the time. As just discussed, if stimuli are unusual in appearance or have parts recently attended to for the first time (as might be the case with movable wheels on toy cars), this may well attract infants' attention. However, being interested in making wheels move does not mean that wheels define cars for infants, even if it affects their performance on the sequential-touching task. As another example, McDonough and I found that whenever we used object-examination tasks in a within-subjects design, data on second tasks were noisier; the first task tended to influence the second task in ways that could not be removed merely by counterbalancing. Even the inductive generalization technique must be handled with care. Rakison (chap. 7) describes an experiment in which 14-month-olds' knowledge of animate versus inanimate motion was tested by the inductive generalization technique. The children tended to reproduce whatever motion the experimenter performed, whether it was realistic or not (e.g., making a car go upstairs or act as an agent). However, this technique may not be appropriate to test conceptual knowledge about animate motion, because the experimenter makes all the objects move. Because the objects are caused to move, one of the major components of animate motion is violated. Hence it seems risky to use the data from this kind of experiment to claim that 14-month-olds have not yet associated motion characteristics with different object kinds. Performance on any given categorization task is situation dependent, as Madole and Oakes (1999) have noted, and influenced by both perceptual and conceptual factors (Oakes, Coppage, & Dingel, 1997), so one needs multiple tasks to disambiguate the implications of performance on any one.

When we look across a number of different kinds of tasks, however, there is considerable evidence that infants divide the world into animals and inanimate things from an early age and begin to form a stable and enduring conceptual system. This means not only that every time a new concept is learned within these global domains it is necessarily learned as a subdivision of this larger grouping but also that the features that describe conceptual categories will occur at more than one level of generality—from the abstract roles that characterize the larger categories to the physical features such as legs and wings that distinguish subclasses from each other. We see a hierarchy being formed especially clearly in the case of the division of animals into subcategories (although the data on vehicles and furniture are similar). Our data suggest that animals are first conceptually subdivided into land animals and birds, with fish being perhaps a later division.[5] This means that abstract role information is being supplemented by physical features and perhaps by the typical locations where these creatures are found. Over the first year or two, children are gradually exposed to a variety of mammals. With some, such as dogs and cats, they may have daily experience. As discussed earlier, they can see differences between these two animal kinds from a few months of age, but on our object-examination tests they do not categorize them as different until 11 months (Mandler & McDonough, 1998a), and in terms of generalizing from one to the other, they still treat them as equivalent at 14 months (Mandler & McDonough, 1998b). This means that for a very long period dogs and cats are considered as either the same or as minor variants on each other, which means that their animal (or land animal) status is firmly established before infants learn how to differentiate them conceptually.

This process of differentiation does not necessarily conform to scientific taxonomies. For example, it seems unlikely that infants see any relationship between animals and plants. The first division does not appear to be an animacy-inanimacy distinction, insofar as animacy is meant to include all living things. Rather it appears to be an animal-nonanimal distinction. The animate-inanimate distinction is an adult theoretical construction rather than a species-characteristic way of viewing the world. If my characterization of the basis for the first concept of animal is correct, self-starting movement, biological movement, and contingent interactions from a distance are crucial (Mandler, 1992). These do not characterize plants. We do not have data comparing the animal and plant domains earlier than 11 months, but at that time infants clearly distinguish them. So it seems likely that there is a more fundamental distinction than the animate-inanimate one, namely the distinction between animals and other things. The contrast between self-moving, unpredictable interactors and objects that either don't move at all or do so in a mechanical way, are caused to move, and do not engage in interaction from a distance may be the most fundamental object distinction of all (Mandler, 1992).

Similar comments can be made about the infant categories of furniture and vehicles (Mandler & McDonough, 1998a). Although this is a clear enough distinction, it is probably an overly adult characterization. It may be more accurate to say that infants divide artifacts into indoor and outdoor things. Some years ago when we were exploring the sequential-touching task, Pat Bauer and I found a category of manipulable household items that infants differentiated from vehicles (unpublished data). We discovered this category when we tried to assess responding on the sequential-touching test when there was only one taxonomic category available. We contrasted vehicles with what we considered to be an unrelated set of things. The items in the sets we used (a lamp, hairbrush, teacup, and wristwatch, or a chair, guitar, spoon, and shoe) seemed to us to come from different semantic categories. To our surprise, 17- and 20-month-olds showed clear categorization of these items when they were contrasted with vehicles. In retrospect, what we considered to be a noncategorized group could all be considered household items (or perhaps manipulable things typically found indoors). This kind of category can persist into adulthood even though it would not be found in a "scientific" taxonomy of artifacts. (See, for example, Warrington and McCarthy's 1987 case study of a semantic dementia patient who lost categorical knowledge at different rates and who seemed to have a category of indoor things.) My hunch is that there will be lots of these—categories that do not fit neatly into our accustomed taxonomic sets of categories but that make sense from the point of view of what matters to the 1- or 2-year-old. Other examples are the categories of kitchen things and bathroom things, which children as young as 14 months differentiate on the basis either of the context in which different activities take place or on the nature of the activities themselves (Mandler, Fivush, & Reznick, 1987).

A plausible foundational set of conceptual categories consists of animals, nonanimal things, and food (Mandler, 2002). Within the domain of animals, the small amount of evidence available indicates that humans and other animals may not be at first well differentiated (Quinn & Eimas, 1998) but become so by about 7 months

(Pauen, 2000).[6] I would also expect a conceptual category of buildings to be learned during the first year, although infants are on the whole uninterested in large immovable objects. We do have data showing that 14-month-olds understand that both animals and vehicles go into buildings (Mandler & McDonough, 1998b), which is the kind of abstract relational characterization one expects from the first conceptualizations of a domain. In addition, infants should have enough experience to differentiate between homes and supermarkets from a fairly early age. We have relatively little data on food, but because of the special status food has in an infant's life, I assume it is categorized separately from other nonanimal things from an early age.

In this proposal (see also Santos and Caramazza, 2002), there is at the beginning no overarching animate-inanimate or living-nonliving distinction but only a small number of conceptual divisions of the world, each separate from the others. Until more data are obtained, these foundational divisions remain speculative. It is possible that food might be considered just another nonanimal thing, in which case the initial division I just suggested above reduces to an animal-nonanimal distinction. What we do know is that the categories of humans, other animals, furniture, and vehicles are differentiated from each other at least by 7 to 9 months of age and plants by 11 months. At 9 months kitchen utensils are not yet differentiated from furniture but are by 11 months (Mandler & McDonough, 1998a), giving some support to the grouping of both of them under a category of indoor things that initially is undifferentiated but soon begins to be subdivided.

These data also have implications for the loss of conceptual knowledge under brain damage, in that one would expect a common pattern of lower-level distinctions to be lost before higher-level ones. Because of the nature of the learning process, in which each new distinction is learned as a subdivision of a superordinate category, the superordinate distinctions should be the most firmly established, and therefore one might expect a pattern of "first in, last out" (Mandler, 1998b, in press). The available literature suggests exactly that pattern (Patterson & Hodges, 1995; Warrington, 1975). For example, in their systematic study of the loss of knowledge in a patient with semantic dementia, Hodges, Graham, and Patterson (1995) found that at first low-level distinctions were lost, then higher levels, such as the division of animals into land and air creatures, and only very late in the course of degeneration was the unique beginner level itself sometimes misattributed. One can lose details about tigers (for example, whether they are African or Indian animals) while still retaining enough information to differentiate tigers from other animals, but if one no longer knows what an animal is, it would seem virtually impossible to retrieve the fact that tigers are Indian animals. Thus, the breakdown data are consistent with the acquisition data, and the latter are consistent with a model in which the conceptual system is learned and organized from the top down.

Early Concepts and Language Acquisition

Even though the adult conceptual system has its roots in preverbal concepts and seems to maintain the structure laid down in the preverbal period throughout life, nevertheless language must greatly influence many aspects of this system. There is not space here to do justice to this topic, although happily several other chapters in this book address this issue. I only make a few remarks, primarily about the way in which the earliest concepts become refined under the influence of language. Obviously there is at first quite a mismatch between the precision of adult language and the globality of the preverbal concepts onto which it is being mapped. Language learning must encourage the expansion of the early conceptual system so that it gradually attains the nuances that adult language conveys. Insofar as object concepts are concerned, this frequently involves narrowing the meanings children ascribe to nouns.

Overextension of early nouns is a common phenomenon. Children go through a period in the second year when many of their first-learned nouns are given too broad a meaning. Some of this overextension appears to be the result of having to make do with a limited vocabulary when trying to communicate with others, and some of it appears to be due to making comments on the relationship of one thing to another (Rescorla, 1980). However, much of it also seems to be due to an uncertain assignment of the meaning of the word. That is, when a young child uses the word "dog" to label a cow, it may be due to a lack of clarity as to what the difference is between them. As discussed earlier, such lack of clarity does not have to do with perceptual confusion: an 18-month-old can easily categorize dogs as perceptually different from cows. But we call Chihuahuas and St. Bernards by the same name, so the fact of differing appearance is not always sufficient to predict how things will be labeled. It would not be surprising if 18-month-olds thought that the word "dog" could be applied to different-looking animals, especially to the extent they do not know anything else about how they differ.

Production data alone make it difficult to determine whether a given overextension results from conceptual confusion, making an analogical comparison, or an inability to remember the correct word. Comprehension data are needed to clarify the error. There are fewer comprehension than production studies of this phenomenon, but several that have been conducted show comparable rates of overextension (e.g., Rescorla, 1980; McDonough, 2002). If almost as many words are understood too broadly as are used too broadly, this suggests that a great deal of overextension is actually due to confusion about the boundaries of the concepts to which the words refer. McDonough studied comprehension in a paradigm in which distractor items were drawn from the same superordinate category as well as from different superordinate categories, thus allowing a finer comparison of mistakes in comprehension than in some previous studies. Her data indicate that even at 2 years of age, children are still unclear about the extension of many words in the animal, vehicle, and food categories; overextension rates in comprehension and production tasks were both about 30 percent. For example, when asked to point to a dog among several pictures, they tended first to point to a dog but then included a fox. They hardly ever pointed to an item from another global category—that is, overextension was confined to the same superordinate class. This result is not a question of earlier versus later acquired names ("dog" being earlier than "fox"), because the same thing happened when asked to point to a fox. It seems that 2-year-olds know what a typical dog looks like and what a typical fox looks like and tend to pick a prototypical example first. What they are uncertain about is the extension of the names. A likely reason for this is because of lack of conceptual differentiation between dogs and foxes (or between cakes and pies). Interestingly, this finding suggests that children this age have no compunction about using more than one "basic-level" label for an item.

At this relatively late age, uncertainty about a word's extension may occur only for similar-appearing items. By age 2, children are beginning to acquire a shape bias in noun learning (Jones & Smith, 1993), as they learn that new nouns are apt to be associated with different shapes. So they may no longer extend the word "dog" to cow, but the overall similarity between a dog and fox is enough to make them uncertain as to whether or not the same word should apply. It appears that differentiated meaning is required to limit such words correctly—a set of facts that clearly differentiates dogs from foxes or cakes from pies. Waxman, Shipley, and Shepperson (1991) made a similar point in their study of 3-year-olds learning subordinate categories of dogs, grapes, and fish. When the labels for these categories were accompanied by identifying information, the subcategories were learned much faster. Three-year-olds (presumably) already know the proper extension of "basic-level" words such as dog and grapes, having learned a good deal about the relevant categories. McDonough's data come from 2-year-olds, who know much less about the differences between dogs and other mammals or between grapes and other kinds of food. As the inductive generalization data described earlier show, up until about age 2 infants are often unclear about the differences among various animal and plant kinds (Mandler & McDonough, 2000), and they may need help in delimiting "basic-level" concepts such as dog or fox. Parents do this kind of teaching in many ways, not only by using different labels for the items but also by using a superordinate term to classify the new labels, saying things like "This is a fox. It's a kind of animal" (Callanan, 1985; Shipley, Kuhn, & Madden, 1983).

Even though parents use superordinate terms to clarify new "basic-level" ones, such labels are still infrequent in speech, and so superordinate terms tend to be later in acquisition. The fact that mothers say to their 2-year-olds "This is a fox. It's an animal" suggests some comprehension of the word "animal." Nevertheless, the word is uncommon in daily usage, and in particular there will be limited occasions for its production in the child's own discourse. Some superordinate names occur so rarely in daily language (e.g., "vehicle") that one would expect them to be very late acquisitions indeed. Others, such as "food," should be learned quite early, but to my knowledge the order of acquisition of various superordinate terms has not been studied systematically in 1- to 2-year-olds.

It has been suggested that young children do not understand "true" superordinate categories until after language is learned. For example, Nelson (2000) hypothesizes that preverbal global categories must become reorganized at a higher level that reflects the uses of the linguistic community. I am somewhat dubious about this hypothesis of reorganization (although not in the role of language as an organizer). The tasks that Nelson cites that have been used to demonstrate children's difficulties with understanding the relations among hierarchical levels of concepts (such as class inclusion) have little to do with whether global categories become reorganized in any fundamental way. The process of differentiation, in which global categories become subdivided, goes on continuously with experience, and in itself guarantees that global categories become superordinate ones. Indeed, the data on breakdown of the conceptual system under brain damage discussed earlier suggest that the basic organization of the system laid down in infancy remains, barring damage, throughout life.

None of this has to do with scientific knowledge, of course. Scientific taxonomies may differ from folk taxonomies and require reorganization of "known" relationships. (You mean to say that whales are mammals?) But that is something that happens with schooling and is not a necessary part of development. It is not obvious that even relatively small changes, such as moving whales from the fish to the mammal class, are more than superficially made. I wager that many people still think of whales as fish with mammalian characteristics. I agree with the view that slot-filler categories are the first subdivisions of some global categories (e.g., Lucariello, Kyratzis, & Nelson, 1992). But even though we later learn more formal taxonomies, we retain the early slot-filling organization throughout adulthood, for example, thinking of food in terms of breakfast, lunch, and dinner, as shown by the order in which adults generate exemplars from superordinate categories. Acquiring new organizations seems to me not the same as reorganizing existing knowledge, since the latter implies supplanting an old organization with a new one.

One thing that might contribute to any conceptual shifts that take place in the newly verbal child is that in everyday language the emphasis is different when a superordinate term is used rather than the exemplar being more discretely named. The child may have heard the family dog talked about in many different ways but always being named by the term "dog." But a phrase such as "Get that dirty animal out of the house!" conveys aspects of the global category that the 2-year-old may not have contemplated before. Furthermore, when parents deliberately label objects for children, they tend to mention abstract functions when using superordinate terms, as opposed to mentioning perceptual features and parts when using "basic-level" and subordinate terms (Callanan, 1990). However, the different emphases that are provided by different vocabulary items are more apt to result in knowledge accretion than in a reorganization of the basic relations between animals and inanimate things.

Overall, I see little revealing change in categorization behavior from the preverbal to newly verbal periods. One- to 2-year-old children have occasionally been reported to have trouble with superordinate categorization, which might seem surprising, given that they are already very familiar with the global domains in question. For example, Waxman and Markow (1995), using the same object-examination test we used in Mandler and McDonough (1993), found that 12-month-old infants categorized cows as different from dinosaurs but were not responsive to the differences between animals and vehicles. However, they gave only half the number of familiarization trials we used. Since other investigators have confirmed our finding of global categorization of animals on the object-examination task before 12 months of age (Oakes et al., 1997) it seems likely that the different performance of the infants in Waxman and Markow (1995) was due to this change in technique. Providing only a few familiarization trials may be sufficient to notice the perceptual similarity of cows but insufficient to notice that the highly varied items being presented are all members of a global category; that may simply take more time.

Once children are old enough for verbal instructions to be given, different problems arise. Categorization as a task is a complex activity, involving many assumptions by both the task setter and the task taker. Performance varies as a function of the instructions, how children understand the instructions, and even the pretraining procedure. For example, pretraining on perceptually identical items is apt to arouse a set that makes superordinate categorization more difficult (e.g., Daehler, Lonardo, & Bukatko, 1979). Bauer and Mandler (1989) used a match-to-sample task and a reinforcement procedure to ensure that children understood the game, and found almost no differences in categorization at the "basic" and superordinate levels in 16- to 31-month-old children. In addition, sometimes very basic conceptual information simply does not come to mind in a task, either because language is being used in an atypical way (for example, using the word "animal" to refer to nonmammals) or because of the fundamental "ur" nature of the information itself. Something like the latter may be happening when a 2-year-old who fails a superordinate task immediately succeeds when the items are given a superordinate label (Waxman & Gelman, 1986). This is reminiscent of the phenomenon found among adults when asked to generate characteristics of a class. If asked to list the characteristics of a schoolteacher, almost no one mentions personhood or the ability to move. It seems quite possible that young language learners, who are continually having to learn new contrastive distinctions, are not reminded of the underlying substrate of their conceptual system when asked to decide why two items are alike.

These and other studies suggest that the onset of language is not reorganizing the underlying conceptual system so much as it is increasing the number of detailed categories, the richness of knowledge associated with them, and interconnections among them. It seems to me that, in spite of the changes that language brings and the new kinds of organization that will be learned in school, evidence for continuity from the earliest conceptual base in infancy to later years is stronger than evidence for discontinuity. The relative lack of difference between the way that infants and preschoolers categorize is one more example of the blurring of boundaries between "stages" that we have seen in recent years in research on early cognitive development. Insofar as language provides nuances more than reorganization, then even the labels "verbal" and "preverbal" may be only weakly predictive of categorization behavior in the early years. Becoming more detailed is not becoming different.

Ultimately, language will have a profound effect on mental life. It provides concepts with culturally agreed-on packaging that becomes a shorthand for use in both thinking and talking. It helps precision and stability in thought, and of course its communicative and memory benefits are vast. Still, the tendency most of us have to equate words with concepts must, like the assumption that infants are concrete thinkers, be resisted, especially in the case of young children. Newly learned labels are imperfectly correlated with their referents, as shown in the McDonough (2002) study discussed earlier. At the same time, 1- to 2-year-olds have concepts for which they have no names, such as vehicles and furniture. As this chapter testifies, the foundations of conceptual organization are laid down prior to language and continue as the basis of the conceptual system, whether verbalized or not.

Notes

1. I do not discuss categorical perception, which is a different type of categorization resulting from differential sensitivity of perceptual transducers at various places on certain sensory dimensions.

2. The perception of a "biological" path appears to occur when a moving object oscillates smoothly around a center of gravity, and also moves along a somewhat unpredictable trajectory (e.g., changes direction without contact from another object).

3. I try to avoid the term "basic-level" because of its lack of a precise definition. However, because the term is still in popular use, it is not always easy to avoid, without adding lengthy descriptive material or using euphemisms such as "basic-like." I put the term in quotation marks to alert the reader to the lack of precise meaning.

4. When infants had a choice between an airplane and an animal, after seeing a car being keyed or giving a ride, they quite readily keyed the airplane and used it to give a ride (Mandler & McDonough, 1996a). Clearly, context matters (as it does in adult research as well). When there wasn't any other vehicle available, then a plane could substitute for a car, but when another car was available, the plane was not chosen.

5. In the urban society of San Diego, even though the city is on an ocean, fish as living creatures do not usually figure in the daily lives of infants.

6. There is also some indication that humans are categorized in a different way than are other animals (Quinn & Eimas, 1998). It would not be surprising if the course of learning about people differs from all other categories, and whatever human bias exists might affect the way in which other animal categories are learned as well. This possibility is somewhat unsettling, in that many accounts of infant categorization rely heavily on how infants categorize animals. A comprehensive theory needs to take into account categorization of inanimate objects as much as animate ones.

References

Aguiar, A., & Baillargeon, R. (1998). Eight-and-a-half-month-old infants' reasoning about containment events. *Child Development*, 69, 636–653.

Bauer, P. J. & Mandler, J. M. (1989). Taxonomies and triads: Conceptual organization in one- to two-year olds. *Cognitive Psychology*, 21, 156–184.

Barsalou, L. W. (1973). Ad hoc categories. *Memory and Cognition*, 11, 211–217.

Behl-Chadha, G. (1996). Superordinate-like categorical representations in early infancy. *Cognition*, 60, 104–141.

Bertenthal, B. (1993). Infants' perception of biomechanical motions: Intrinsic image and knowledge-based constraints. In C. Granrud (Ed.), *Visual perception and cognition in infancy* (pp. 175–214). Hillsdale, NJ: Erlbaum.

Bertoncini, J., Bijeljac-Babic, R., Jusczyk, P. W., Kennedy, L. J., & Mehler, J. (1988). An investigation of young infants' perceptual representations of speech sounds. *Journal of Experimental Psychology: General*, 117, 21–33.

Callanan, M. A. (1985). How parents label objects for young children: The role of input in the acquisition of category hierarchies. *Child Development*, 56, 508–523.

Callanan, M. A. (1990). Parents' descriptions of objects: Potential data for children's inferences about category principles. *Cognitive Development*, 5, 101–122.

Carey, S., & Markman, E. M. (1999). Cognitive development. In B. M. Bly & D. E. Rumelhart (Eds.), *Cognitive science* (pp. 201–254). San Diego: Academic Press.

Csibra, G., Gergely, G., Bíró, S., & Koós, O., & Brockbank, M. (1999). Goal attribution without agency cues: The perception of pure reason in infancy. *Cognition*, 72, 237–267.

Daehler, M. W., Lonardo, R., & Bukatko, D. (1979). Matching and equivalence judgments in very young children. *Child Development, 50,* 170–179.

Eimas, P. D., & Quinn, P. C. (1994). Studies on the formation of perceptually based basic-level categories in young infants. *Child Development, 65,* 903–917.

Elman, J. L. (1991). Learning and development in neural networks: The importance of starting small. *Cognition, 48,* 71–99.

Fagan, J. F., III., & Singer, L. T. (1979). The role of simple feature differences in infant recognition of faces. *Infant Behavior and Development, 2,* 39–46.

Frye, D., Rawling, P., Moore, C., & Myers, I. (1983). Object-person discrimination and communication at 3 and 10 months. *Developmental Psychology, 19,* 303–309.

Gelman, S. A., & Coley, J. D. (1990). The importance of knowing a dodo is a bird: Categories and inferences in 2-year-old children. *Developmental Psychology, 26,* 796–804.

Gelman, S. A., & O'Reilley, A. W. (1988). Children's inductive inferences within superordinate categories: The role of language and category structure. *Child Development, 59,* 876–887.

Gibson, E. J. (1967). *Principles of perceptual learning and development.* New York: Appleton Century Crofts.

Hodges, J. R., Graham, N. & Patterson, K. (1995). Charting the progression of semantic dementia: Implications for the organisation of semantic memory. *Memory, 3,* 463–495.

Johnson, S. C., & Sockaci, E. (2000, July). *The categorization of agents from actions.* Poster presented at the International Conference on Infant Studies. Brighton, UK.

Jones, S. S., & Smith, L. B. (1993). The place of perception in children's concepts. *Cognitive Development, 8,* 113–139.

Keil, F. C. (1991). The emergence of theoretical beliefs as constraints on concepts. In S. Carey & R. Gelman (Eds.), *The epigenesis of mind* (pp. 237–256). Hillsdale, NJ: Erlbaum.

Keil, F. C. (1998). Cognitive science and the origins of thought and knowledge. In W. Damon (Series Ed.), R. M. Lerner (Vol. Ed.), *The handbook of child psychology: Vol. 1. Theoretical models of human development.* New York: Wiley.

Legerstee, M. (1992). A review of the animate-inanimate distinction in infancy: Implications for models of social and cognitive knowing. *Early Development and Parenting, 1,* 59–67.

Legerstee, M., Barna, J., & DiAdamo, C. (2000). Precursors to the development of intention. *Developmental Psychology, 36,* 627–634.

Leslie, A. M. (1988). The necessity of illusion: Perception and thought in infancy. In L. Weiskrantz (Ed.), *Thought without language* (pp. 185–210). Oxford: Oxford Science.

Lucariello, J., Kyratzis, A., & Nelson, K. (1992). Taxonomic knowledge: What kind and when. *Child Development, 63,* 978–998.

Madole, K. L., & Oakes, L. M. (1999). Making sense of infant categorization: Stable processes and changing representations. *Developmental Review, 19,* 263–296.

Mandler, J. M. (1988). How to build a baby: On the development of an accessible representational system. *Cognitive Development, 3,* 113–136.

Mandler, J. M. (1992). How to build a baby: II. Conceptual primitives. *Psychological Review, 99,* 587–604.

Mandler, J. M. (1998a). Representation. In W. Damon (Series Ed.) & D. Kuhn & R. Siegler (Vol. Eds.), *Handbook of child psychology: Vol. 2 Cognition, perception, and language* (pp. 255–308). New York: Wiley.

Mandler, J. M. (1998b). The rise and fall of semantic memory. In M. Conway, S. Gathercole, & C. Cornoldi (Eds.), *Theories of memory II* (pp. 147–169). Hove, UK: Psychology Press.

Mandler, J. M. (2000). Perceptual and conceptual processes in infancy. *Journal of Cognition and Development, 1,* 3–36.

Mandler, J. M. (2002). On the foundations of the semantic system. In E. Forde & G. Humphreys (Eds.), *Category-specificity in brain and mind.* Hove, UK: Psychology Press.

Mandler, J. M., Bauer, P. J., & McDonough, L. (1991). Separating the sheep from the goats: Differentiating global categories. *Cognitive Psychology, 23,* 263–298.

Mandler, J. M., Fivush, R., & Reznick, J. S. (1987). The development of contextual categories. *Cognitive Development, 2,* 339–354.

Mandler, J. M., & McDonough, L. (1993). Concept formation in infancy. *Cognitive Development, 8,* 291–318.

Mandler, J. M., & McDonough, L. (1996a). Drinking and driving don't mix: Inductive generalization in infancy. *Cognition, 59,* 307–335.

Mandler, J. M., & McDonough, L. (1996b). Nonverbal recall. In N. L. Stein, P. O. Ornstein, B. Tversky, & C. Brainerd (Eds.), *Memory for everyday and emotional events* (pp. 9–29). Hillsdale, NJ: Erlbaum.

Mandler, J. M., & McDonough, L. (1998a). On developing a knowledge base in infancy. *Developmental Psychology, 34,* 1274–1288.

Mandler, J. M., & McDonough, L. (1998b). Studies in inductive inference in infancy. *Cognitive Psychology, 37,* 60–96.

Mandler, J. M., & McDonough, L. (2000). Advancing downward to the basic level. *Journal of Cognition and Development, 1,* 379–403.

McClelland, J. L., & Rumelhart, D. E. (1985). Distributed memory and the representation of general and specific information. *Journal of Experimental Psychology: General, 114,* 159–188.

McDonough, L. (2002). Early concepts and early language acquisition: What does similarity have to do with either? In N. L. Stein, P. Bauer, & M. Rabinowitz (Eds.), *Representation, memory, and development: Essays in honor of Jean Mandler.* Mahwah, NJ: Erlbaum.

McDonough, L., & Mandler, J. M. (1998). Inductive generalization in 9- and 11-month-olds. *Developmental Science, 1,* 227–232.

McDonough, L., Mandler, J. M., McKee, R. D., & Squire, L. (1995). The deferred imitation task as a nonverbal measure of declarative memory. *Proceedings of the National Academy of Sciences, 92,* 7580–7584.

McDonough, L., & Marsh, R. (2002, April). *Infants' inductive generalizations of novel words and events: Language specific versus domain-general processes.* Paper presented at the Biennial Meeting of the International Conference on Infant Studies. Toronto, Canada.

Medin, D. L., Wattenmaker, W. D., & Michalski, R. S. (1987). Constraints and preferences in inductive learning: An experimental study of human and machine performance. *Cognitive Science, 11,* 299–339.

Meltzoff, A. N. (1988). Infant imitation and memory: Nine-month-olds in immediate and deferred tests. *Child Development, 59,* 217–225.

Moscovitch, M., Goshen-Gottstein, Y., & Vriezen, E. (1994). Memory without conscious recollection: A tutorial review from a neuropsychological perspective. In C. Umiltá & M. Moscovitch (Eds.), *Attention and performance XV: Conscious and nonconscious information processing* (pp. 619–660). Cambridge, MA: MIT Press.

Nelson, K. (1985). *Making sense: The acquisition of shared meaning.* San Diego: Academic Press.

Nelson, K. (2000). Global and functional: Mandler's perceptual and conceptual processes in infancy. *Journal of Cognition and Development, 1,* 49–54.

Newport, E. L. (1990). Maturational constraints on language learning. *Cognitive Science, 14,* 11–28.

Oakes, L. M., Coppage, D. J., & Dingel, A. (1997). By land or by sea: The role of perceptual similarity in infants' categorization of animals. *Developmental Psychology, 33,* 396–407.

Patterson, K., & Hodges, J. R. (1995). Disorders of semantic memory. In A. D. Baddeley, B. A. Wilson, & F. N. Watts (Eds.), *Handbook of memory disorders* (pp. 167–186). London: Wiley.

Pauen, S. (2000). Early differentiation within the animate domain: Are humans something special? *Journal of Experimental Child Psychology, 75,* 134–151.

Piaget, J. (1952). *The origins of intelligence in the child.* New York: International Universities Press.

Posner, M. I., & Keele, S. W. (1968). On the genesis of abstract ideas. *Journal of Experimental Psychology, 77,* 353–362.

Poulin-Dubois, D., Lepage, A., & Ferland, D. (1996). Infants' concept of animacy. *Cognitive Development, 11,* 19–36.

Pylyshyn, Z. (1999). Is vision continuous with cognition? The case for cognitive inpenetrability of visual perception. *Behavioral and Brain Sciences, 22,* 341–423.

Quine, W. V. (1977). Natural kinds. In S. P. Schwartz (Ed.), *Naming, necessity, and natural kinds.* Ithaca, NY: Cornell University Press.

Quinn, P. C., & Eimas, P. D. (1996). Perceptual cues that permit categorical differentiation of animal species by infants. *Journal of Experimental Child Psychology, 63,* 189–211.

Quinn, P. C., & Eimas, P. D. (1997). A reexamination of the perceptual-to-conceptual shift in mental representations. *Review of General Psychology, 1,* 271–287.

Quinn, P. C., & Eimas, P. D. (1998). Evidence for a global categorical representation of humans by young infants. *Journal of Experimental Child Psychology, 69,* 151–174.

Quinn, P. C., & Eimas, P. D. (2000). The emergence of category representations during infancy: Are separate perceptual and conceptual processes required? *Journal of Cognition and Development. 1,* 55–61.

Quinn, P. C., Eimas, P. D., & Rosenkrantz, S. L. (1993). Evidence for representations of perceptually similar natural categories by 3-month-old and 4-month-old infants. *Perception, 22,* 463–475.

Quinn, P. C., & Johnson, M. H. (2000). Global-before-basic object categorization in connectionist networks and 2-month-old infants. *Infancy, 1,* 31–46.

Rakison, D. H., & Butterworth, G. E. (1998a). Infant attention to object structure in early categorization. *Developmental Psychology, 34,* 1310–1325.

Rakison, D. H., & Butterworth, G. E. (1998b). Infants' use of object parts in early categorization. *Developmental Psychology, 34,* 49–62.

Rakison, D. H., & Cohen, L. B. (1999). Infants' use of functional parts in basic-like categorization. *Developmental Science, 2,* 423–431.

Rakison, D. J., & Poulin-Dubois, D. (2001). The developmental origin of the animate-inanimate distinction. *Psychological Bulletin, 127,* 209–228.

Rescorla, L. (1980). Overextension in early language development. *Journal of Child Language, 9,* 321–335.

Santos, L. R., & Caramazza, A. (2002). The domain-specific hypothesis: A developmental and comparative perspective on category-specific deficits. In E. Forde & G. Humphreys (Eds.), *Category-specificity in brain and mind.* Hove, UK: Psychology Press.

Saylor, M., Baird, J. A., & Baldwin, D. (2000, July). Infants' parsing of dynamic human behavior. Poster presented at the eleventh Biennial Conference on Infant Studies, Brighton, UK.

Shipley, E. F., Kuhn, I. F., & Madden, E. C. (1983). Mothers' use of superordinate category terms. *Journal of Child Language, 10,* 571–588.

Smith, E. E., Patalano, A. L, & Jonides, J. (1998) Alternative mechanisms of categorization. *Cognition, 65,* 167–196.

Warrington, E. K. (1975). The selective impairment of semantic memory. *Quarterly Journal of Experimental Psychology, 27*, 635–657.

Warrington, E. K., & McCarthy, R. A. (1987). Categories of knowledge: Further fractionations and an attempted integration. *Brain, 110*, 1273–1296.

Waxman, S. R., & Gelman, R. (1986). Preschoolers' use of superordinate relations in classification and language. *Cognitive Development, 1*, 139–156.

Waxman, S. R., & Markow, D. B. (1995). Words as invitations to form categories: Evidence from 12- to 13-month-old infants. *Cognitive Psychology, 29*, 257–302.

Waxman, S. R., & Shipley, E. F., & Shepperson, B. (1991). Establishing new subcategories: The role of category labels and existing knowledge. *Child Development, 62*, 127–138.

Woodward, A. L. (1998). Infants selectively encode the goal object of an actor's reach. *Cognition, 69*, 1–34.

Younger, B. A., & Fearing, D. D. (1999). Parsing items into separate categories: Developmental change in infant categorization. *Child Development, 70*, 291–303.

Zentall, T. R. (2000). Symbolic representation by pigeons. *Current Directions in Psychological Science, 9*, 118–123.

CHAPTER SIX

Principles of Developmental Change in Infants' Category Formation

Lisa M. Oakes and Kelly L. Madole

CATEGORIZATION IS ONE of the most fundamental of cognitive processes. The ability to categorize may be especially important in infancy, when an enormous amount of new information is encountered every day. By forming groups of similar objects, infants can effectively reduce the amount of information they must process, learn, and remember (for example, they can treat a new dog as a member of a familiar category), as well as make inferences from past experience to encounters with new objects (for example, categorizing an object as a dog allows infants to form expectations for what it will eat and whether it will bite if its tail is pulled).

Over the past 25 years, a great deal of research has focused on understanding the development of categorization abilities in infancy (see Hayne, 1996; Madole & Oakes, 1999; Quinn & Eimas, 1996, 1997, for recent reviews). Despite the growing body of literature in infants' categorization (or perhaps because of it), there is considerable controversy over basic issues in the study of categorization. For example, there has been much debate over the relative importance of conceptual features (features that cannot be seen) and perceptual features (what objects look like) in infants' formation of categories (e.g., Eimas, 1994; Jones & Smith, 1993; Madole & Oakes, 1999; Mandler, 1988, 1992; Rakison, chap. 7), an issue that has also has been discussed in the context of adult cognitive processes (e.g., Goldstone & Barsalou, 1998). In addition, theorists have argued about whether different tasks used to assess categorization tap the same processes or different ones (e.g., Mandler & Bauer, 1988; Oakes & Madole, 2000). We recently proposed a framework for making sense of the existing literature on the early development of categorization abilities (Madole & Oakes, 1999) and on the basis of this framework proposed directions for future research (Oakes & Madole, 2000). In our framework, we emphasized a process-oriented approach to the study of categorization in infancy. Specifically, we argued that a clear picture of categorization in infancy and how it is related to categorization at other points in development will emerge only if researchers focus on the processes that infants use to form categories.

Our framework departs from a recent emphasis on establishing the content of infants' categories. Much of the past research on infant categorization has been aimed at describing the particular categories to which infants at different ages respond. This descriptive or content-oriented approach is useful in at least two ways. First, when delimiting the parameters of any newly discovered developmental phenomenon, it may be necessary to first establish through basic demonstrations that the phenomenon does, in fact, exist. Thus, Cohen and Caputo's (1978) demonstration that infants responded to the category *stuffed animals* and Mandler and McDonough's (1993) demonstration that infants responded to a category of *birds* that excludes airplanes (and vice versa) served to highlight the fact that infants can indeed form categories that map onto adult conceptual understanding, although the infants' categorical representation may or may not be based on conceptual features. Second, establishing that infants are sensitive to particular categorical distinctions is important when those categorical distinctions serve as the foundation for further important developmental achievements. So, for example, demonstrations such as Leinbach and Fagot's (1993) that infants at 7 months of age attend to gender categories may be critical for understanding the early development of gender stereotyping.

However, a simple inventory of the categories to which infants attend tells us little about the processes by which those categories were formed (see Madole & Oakes, 1999). Thus, in the long run, this approach will provide only a limited understanding of categorization in infancy. For example, simply demonstrating that 3-month-old infants respond categorically to dogs versus cats in a visual familiarization task does not provide any direct insight into how the category was formed. Although such findings provide a good starting point for understanding the categorization abilities of 3-month-old infants, on their own they tell us little about what kinds of features are important in their differentiation of dogs from cats. In addition, from these findings alone we do not know whether infants of this age will respond to dogs versus cats in a different context. To fully understand the development of categorization, we must move beyond descriptions of the categories to which infants attend and ask questions about the processes underlying the ability to form these categories. Quinn and his colleagues, for example, have demonstrated that 3- to 4-month-old infants' formation of a category of dogs that does not include cats relies on their being familiarized with perceptually similar items (Quinn et al., 1993) and that they have access to information about the heads and faces of the animals (Quinn & Eimas, 1996a; Spencer, Quinn, Johnson, & Karmiloff-Smith, 1997). Ideally, an inventory of the categories to which infants might respond at any particular age, and in any particular task, would flow naturally from a full understanding of how these categories are formed.

We assume that the basic process by which categories are formed changes little, if at all, during development. However, the particular categories to which infants respond, the extension of those categories, and the inferences that can be drawn about category members do change. For example, a 4-month-old infant may differentiate animals from furniture (Behl-Chadha, 1996), but only much later would that infant infer that only animals drink (Mandler & McDonough, 1996). What, precisely, has changed? On the one hand, the infant may have qualitatively different categories that he or she uses at different times or in different contexts (Mandler, 1988, 1992, chap. 5). Alternatively, the infant may make use of a developmentally stable ability to integrate new information into existing categories, as that new information becomes available (Eimas, 1994; Madole & Oakes, 1999; Rakison, chap. 7). We believe this second account better explains the development of categorization in the first years of life. In particular, we argue that these developmental changes seem to be related to changes in the information infants use when forming categories.

In this chapter we will use the following metaphor to illustrate this point. Categorization can be understood as a process of building structures from available materials. The complexity of the structures varies as a function of the type of building materials (that is, object features) that are available. We believe that the basic process for building the structures changes little with development but that the availability of building materials (i.e., information about exemplars) does change considerably. As a result, the structures made from those materials will change. Specifically, through developmental changes in abilities such as memory, language, and motor skills, infants gain access to new sources of information that can be used to form categories. As a result, we see changes in the resulting structures (categories).

Note that this is a very dynamic view of categorization. That is, we do not assume that categories are fixed representational structures that must be acquired and, once acquired, are possessed by the infant. Rather, we assume that infants flexibly categorize the items they encounter using available information. As a result, infants may categorize the same item differently at different points in development, and they may categorize that item differently in different contexts at the same point in development.

On the basis of our framework and previously reported results, we propose three principles for how access to information changes with development and how the resulting categories differ (see table 6.1). We use these principles as a means of structuring our understanding of how infants' categories evolve as new information becomes available. Thus, these are principles that describe developmental changes in the kinds of information infants use in forming categories—not principles that infants use to form categories. Moreover, we do not suggest that this is an exhaustive list of the factors that influence infant categorization. Rather we propose these principles as a means of stimulating research and discussion on the processes shaping the development of categorization.

Our first principle is that the development of motor, cognitive, and linguistic abilities broadens the pool of features that enter into infants' category judgements. Thus, older infants, who have more sophisticated motor, cognitive, and linguistic abilities, have a wider range of information available to form categories than do younger infants. For example, older infants might use features such as *eats*, *runs*, and *barks* to categorize dogs, whereas younger infants fail to use such features because they do not have the information processing abilities to attend to and remember such features. Instead, younger infants might rely on features such as *has four legs* and *has a tail* to categorize these same exemplars. As a result, the extension of the category *dog* will change with development.

TABLE 6.1. Principles for How Access to Information Available for Categorization Changes with Development

Principle 1	The development of motor, cognitive, and linguistic abilities broadens the pool of features.
Principle 2	With development, infants become able to take advantage of the information available in different contexts.
Principle 3	Increased background knowledge constrains the pool of potential features.

The second principle is that as infants develop they become better able to take advantage of the information available to them in different contexts. There are large contextual differences that influence the information that infants can use to form categories. For example, sometimes infants encounter objects one at a time (for example, when pulling Tupperware bowls and lids out of a drawer), and other times they encounter several at once (for example, when the bowls and lids are scattered all over the floor). The presence of other objects introduces comparative information—information that is not as accessible when objects are encountered one at a time. Some contexts allow visual inspection only (for example, when objects are located on a high shelf or depicted in books), and other contexts allow other types of inspection (for example, when objects are within reach they can be touched and manipulated). Whether or not objects can be manipulated has implications for infants' access to information, such as weight, texture, and so on, that may be useful for forming categories. Thus, contextual variations determine, in part, what information is available for forming categories. However, contextual differences also correspond to differences in demands on infants' other cognitive systems. For example, when multiple objects are presented at one time, the infant must deploy attentional systems to effectively select some items to attend to and inhibit attending to other objects. Thus, younger infants may have more difficulty than older infants in taking advantage of the information available in different contexts.

The third principle is that infants' increasing background knowledge actually constrains the pool of potential features. At the same time that developmental changes in motor, cognitive, and linguistic abilities help to increase the amount of information available, infants develop the ability to inhibit or ignore distracting or irrelevant information (for example, weight when categorizing replicas of animals), and their background knowledge and expectations about objects increases. Older infants, therefore, are capable of selectively attending to only the most relevant information. As infants acquire knowledge about the typical functions of objects (e.g., objects with wheels can be rolled), typical correlations among features (e.g., objects with eyes have mouths), and how objects typically act (for example, objects with faces typically eat and drink), such knowledge may influence how they perceive, learn about, and remember the novel objects they encounter. Thus, although older infants have access to more types of information, they also have additional knowledge that helps them constrain their use of this information.

Note that these principles predict a three-step developmental trajectory. First, infants will use only a few features to form category groups because they have access to limited types of information. Later, the types of information will be expanded with the development of motor, cognitive, and linguistic abilities and as they experience category exemplars in a wider range of contexts. However, at this point infants may use features that are both relevant and irrelevant for category membership. Thus, the final step is using background knowledge to narrow the potential pool of features to only those that are most predictive of category membership.

We do not expect that there are specific ages at which each of these developmental achievements is attained. Rather, this is the general developmental trajectory proposed for infants' category formation, and the particular ages at which any change is observed will depend on how categorization is assessed and the kinds of objects that infants are asked to categorize.

In the following sections we will discuss each of these principles in detail. An important part of such a discussion is the implications of each principle for developmental changes in the kinds of categories to which infants respond. Although little data exist to directly address this issue, there are a few studies that illustrate each principle and how the principle impacts the development of categorization. An important goal of future research is to more closely evaluate each of these principles in determining developmental changes in infants' categorization.

Principle 1: The Development of Motor, Cognitive, and Linguistic Abilities Widens the Pool of Features Available for Category Formation

We have argued that one of the most important changes in infants' developing categorization abilities is a change in the features or attributes they use in forming categories (Madole & Oakes, 1999; Oakes & Madole, 2000). In particular, as infants develop, they gain access to a broader range of features they can use to form categories. If we view categorization as a process of building meaningful structures based on the construction materials on hand, then as more building materials (features) become available, we would expect to see increasingly sophisticated and complex structures (categories) emerge. We will first describe some of the factors that would account for a broadening of the range of features to which infants attend. We will then briefly review evidence suggesting that there are parallel changes in infants' categorical responding.

Increases in the Features to Which Infants Can Attend

Only if infants can detect features of objects will those features be available for categorization. Why do new features become available? There are a number of developmental changes that might be implicated in this process. For very young infants, differences at the sensory and basic perceptual level may be relevant. Basic visual perceptual abilities, such as the ability to perceive color, form, and depth, develop early in the first year, and some are present even at birth (Slater, 1998). As infants become able to detect these new features of the visual world, those features would be available for forming categories of objects.

Other types of changes may be responsible for the apparent change from perceptually based to conceptually based categorization. Specifically, changes in motor, information-processing, and linguistic abilities allow children increasing access to "nonobvious" or conceptual features—that is, features other than an object's appearance (Madole & Oakes, 1999). Examples of the kinds of features made available by these changes are outlined in table 6.2. In the following paragraphs, we consider the implications of some of these developmental changes for the kinds of information available to infants.

Developmental Changes in Motor Abilities   There are significant changes in infants' motor abilities in the first year of life, and these changes impact the kinds of information that infants notice and learn about the world. Developmental changes in independent locomotion, for example, have been related to changes in depth perception (Bertenthal, Campos, & Kermoian, 1995). In addition, changes in manipulatory behavior, such as bimanual manipulation, the emergence of fingering, and so on, lead to changes in the kinds of object properties that infants discover (Bushnell & Boudreau, 1993; Lockman & McHale, 1989). That is, changes in infants' abilities to manipulate objects may increase the salience of properties such as shape, texture, and rigidity.

Indeed, a broad range of motor achievements might influence infants' developing manipulatory behavior and, as a result, the kinds of information to which they have access. For example, Rochat and Goubet (1995) demonstrated that the emergence of self-sitting behavior in infancy frees the infants' arms for a greater range of manual exploratory behaviors. The emergence of these new exploratory behaviors may in turn make it possible for infants to notice object properties that they were previously unable to detect. For example, once infants no longer need their arms to support themselves while sitting, they can determine the weight of an object by picking it up. Thus, the use of these properties in categorizing objects also should emerge as a function of an infant's ability to maintain his or her posture in a sitting position.

It is clear that infants' rapidly increasing abilities to navigate and manipulate the world result in increasing access to new types of information about the objects they encounter. One consequence of such changes is that older infants will have access to a wider range of features to form categories of those objects than will younger infants.

TABLE 6.2. Examples of New Features That Become Available as a Function of Development in Different Domains

Domain	New ability	Features made available
Motor skills	Manual manipulation	Texture, rigidity
	Self-sitting frees arms for picking up objects	Object weight
Cognitive	Integrating spatiotemporal information	Function
	Recognition of correlational structure	Feature correlations
Linguistic	Associating labels with objects	Object labels

Developmental Changes in Information-Processing Abilities Developmental changes in basic information-processing abilities also probably contribute to the kinds of features infants can use in forming categories. For example, increases in infants' memory abilities (Diamond, 1985; Rovee-Collier & Hayne, 1987) should lead to changes in infants' ability to use features that require integrating information over space or time. Developmental changes in infants' ability to integrate information in form perception were demonstrated by Skouteris, McKenzie, and Day (1992). Eight-, 10-, and 12-month-old infants were familiarized with a point-light tracing of a two-dimensional form and tested with a familiar form and a novel form. Only the oldest infants showed a preference for the novel form. Thus the ability to integrate spatiotemporal information of simple shapes appears to develop late in the first year of life. Remarkably consistent results were obtained by Arterberry (1993), who showed that infants' ability to perceive the size of an object seen moving through the aperture of an occluder did not develop until 12 months of age. It is not clear whether the development of this ability is based primarily on changes in memory or on changes in a separate ability to integrate information presented over space and time. Nonetheless, it seems reasonable to conclude that if there are developmental changes in infants' ability to recognize object features that require such spatiotemporal integration, then there will be parallel developmental changes in infants' ability to use these features in categorizing objects.

The emerging ability to integrate spatiotemporal information also should allow infants to attend to object features such as function that are not readily apparent in a static depiction of an object (for example, a picture of an object or an object sitting on a shelf). Although there is no single definition of function, it has been argued that functional properties encompass dynamic rather than static information and that they require integration of information over time (Nelson, 1979). Therefore, information about an object's form (for example, shape, color, or presence of some part) can be determined from a static depiction of that object, but information about function (for example, what happens if the object is shaken or how it is typically used) cannot. If there are developmental changes in infants' ability to integrate dynamic information over time, then there should also be developmental changes in infants' ability to perceive the dynamic functions of objects. Madole, Oakes, and Cohen (1993) found evidence of just such a developmental change. In this study, 10- and 14-month-old infants were familiarized with a single object. The objects were constructed of Legos and had a characteristic form (e.g., red and rectangular or yellow and round) and a characteristic function (e.g., the wheels move when the object is rolled versus the object rattles when it is shaken). Infants received trials with two objects that differed in form, in function, or in both form and function. First, infants' preferences (measured by the duration of their focused visual attention on each trial) for one of the two objects was assessed. Then infants were familiarized with the other object. Finally, their preference for the now novel item was assessed again.

Infants' preferences for the "novel" object both before and after familiarization are presented in figure 6.1. It can be seen that the 10-month-old infants' preference for the novel object significantly increased when the two objects differed in terms of form or both form and function, but not when the objects differed only in terms

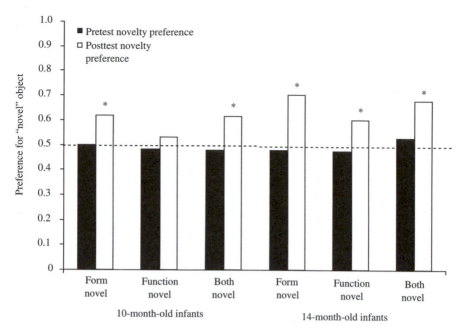

Figure 6.1. Novelty preference score before and after familiarization for 10- and 14-month-old infants in Madole, Oakes, and Cohen (1993) (no preference of .50 is indicated by the dashed line). The familiar and novel items differed either in terms of form, function, or both form and function. Conditions in which the preference for the novel item changed significantly from pre- to posttest are indicated by an asterisk (p < .05, two-tailed).

of function (the objects looked identical). These younger infants appeared only to attend to the form of these objects in this task. The 14-month-old infants' preference for the novel item, in contrast, significantly increased in all three conditions, suggesting that they attended to both object form and function in this task. Obviously, infants' attention to form and function will vary with the particular form and functions used, the context in which infants experience the objects, and other factors, but these results demonstrate that older infants have access to more object features than do younger infants to use in their categorization.

The emergence of an ability to integrate information over space and time is one aspect of developing information-processing skills. Other important developmental changes take place in infants' information-processing skills that influence their use of object features in categorization. For example, it has been suggested that attention to correlations among object features is a cornerstone of adult categorization (Rosch, Mervis, Gray, Johnson, & Boyes-Braem, 1976). That is, individual features may be less important to how objects are categorized than clusters of features that tend to cooccur. Younger and Cohen (1986; see also chap. 4) have demonstrated that infants' attention to such feature correlations shows important developmental changes. When infants were familiarized with objects in which two features always cooccurred, 7-month-old infants, but not 4-month-old infants, noticed when the features were combined in a novel way. Thus, we would expect that the use of these feature correlations to categorize objects would not be evident until the second half of the first year of life.

Developmental Changes in Linguistic Skills   Finally, changes in linguistic skills are likely to lead to an increase in the number of features that infants use in categorization. Clearly, developmental changes in children's productive and receptive linguistic skills will provide access to previously unavailable information. For example, when children can ask questions, and understand the answers to these questions, they can determine whether particular items have blood inside, whether particular toys require batteries to work, and where animals typically live. However, emerging language abilities may play an even more fundamental role in making features of objects available or salient.

For example, one feature of objects made available by infants' emerging language abilities is the objects' labels. Before children understand that objects have labels and before they have begun attaching labels to objects, a common label will not help infants to form categories. However, when children recognize that objects have labels and are capable of attaching labels to objects, they can use common labels to notice category membership. Werker and her colleagues (Werker, Cohen, Lloyd, Casasola, & Stager, 1998) recently observed that 14-month-old infants could learn the correlation between a particular word and a particular object. At this point, but not before, infants presumably could use such word–object correlations to learn category membership. It is not clear that infants do learn category membership only through a common label, but the presence of a common label may highlight similarities among objects that might not otherwise be salient.

Changes in language ability also may make salient different features of objects (see chaps. 4, 11). For example, Samuelson (2000) found that as infants learned the names for solid, shape-based items, they attended more to shape as a basis for labeling. In other words, children whose vocabularies included few names for solid, shape-based items were less likely than children whose vocabularies included more names for solid, shape-based items to assume that a new label referred to objects of similar shape. Thus, acquiring shape-based labels made shape a more salient feature in a labeling context. Developmental changes in language, therefore, made children attend more to one type of object feature.

Developmental Changes in the Use of Features in Categorization

The developmental changes described here should result in an increase in the set of features that can act as the input to the categorization process. As a result, there should be changes in the kinds of categories that infants form that parallel the changes in the features recognized by infants. Only a subset of the changes we described earlier have been studied in terms of their effect on infants' categorization abilities. However, the existing evidence supports the notion that developmental changes in information processing and linguistic abilities influence the kinds of features infants use when forming categories.

Two important avenues of research have demonstrated that developmental changes in information processing lead to changes in the kinds of categories that infants form. As described above, one consequence of infants' increasing ability to integrate spatiotemporal information is their emerging ability to attend to objects' functions. The emergence of this ability then impacts infants' category formation. For example, Madole, Cohen, and Bradley (1994) found that 14-month-old infants, but not 10-month-old infants, used functional information to form categories of objects (for example, objects that rolled) even when the objects differed widely in appearance. Note that learning that some types of objects roll requires integrating information over space and time, an ability that, as already described, does not emerge until approximately 12 months of age (e.g., Arterberry, 1993). Likewise Madole (1993) found that 14-month-old infants who were habituated to a category of objects sharing a number of parts attended more to functional object parts than nonfunctional parts. Thus it appears that by the beginning of the second year of life, infants' developing information-processing skills allow them to use object function as a feature in object categorization.

A second line of research has looked at how infants' ability to detect feature correlations is reflected in the way they categorize objects. Younger and Cohen (1986; chap. 4) found that not only does the ability to detect the correlational structure of objects change with development but also the ability to use that correlational structure in forming categories develops. As described earlier, Younger and Cohen (1986) observed that 7-month-old infants recognized that features of schematic animals were correlated. However, it was not until 10 months that infants could use these correlations to form categories of the animals. Thus, changes in infants' information-processing abilities do seem to influence the kinds of features they use in forming categories.

In addition, an increasing literature is demonstrating that the use of language in category contexts influences the kinds of features to which infants attend (chap. 11). For example, Waxman (1999, chap. 9) recently observed that 13-month-old infants' categorization based on a common property such as color versus taxonomic category membership depended on the language used during familiarization. In this investigation, infants were familiarized with a collection of objects that were identical in terms of some property such as color (e.g., four purple horses, or a purple cat, purple plate, purple spatula, and purple bottle), and then were tested with two novel objects—one that was the same in terms of that property (e.g., a new purple horse) and one that differed in terms of that property (e.g., a blue horse). Infants who were provided with an adjective during familiarization with the objects (regardless of whether those objects were all from the same category) responded to property-based commonalities. Thus, language highlighted the property that the items had in common, and infants flexibly grouped objects on the basis of such commonalities.

Finally, Samuelson and Smith (1999) recently observed that very young children's reliance on shape as a basis of category generalization depended on the children's developing noun vocabularies. Children in the early stages of language learning did not generalize the names for solid things on the basis of similarity of shape until they had already acquired many nouns. Thus, attention to shape as a basis for categorization (at least in a naming task) seems to be influenced by vocabulary development.

These examples show that as children gain access to new information about objects, their categorization of those objects changes. In other words, not only does the pool of features available to infants in forming categories widen but also the availability of those features shapes the kinds of categories infants form. Obviously, the findings described here are just a first step at understanding how the increased pool of features changes categorization. However, it is clear that, as stated in principle 1, categorization changes as infants gain access to new types of information.

Principle 2: With Development, Infants Become Able to Take Advantage of Information Available in Different Contexts

In real-world settings, infants encounter category exemplars in a wide variety of contexts, and those contexts may differ in how easily infants can use the available features to form categories of those exemplars. In our building metaphor, even though a set of materials might be used in the construction of structures, those materials will be used only if they are available. It is not enough to be capable of using a piece of information to form categories; that piece of information must be available and salient. Contexts differ in how easily information can be observed. Moreover, developmental changes in other cognitive abilities may make it more or less easy for infants to take advantage of information that is present in a given context.

There are at least two important differences in contexts that might facilitate or inhibit infants' use of information to form categories (see table 6.3). First, contexts differ in the kinds of other objects that are present. In some settings, infants encounter category members in the presence of other members of the same category, as well as members of contrasting categories. For example, a child may see several different cups in the kitchen cabinet along with other cups as well as other dishes. This context may make salient the similarities between different cups (e.g., general shape)

TABLE 6.3. How Features of the Context Influence the Availability of Different Types of Information

Feature of context	Information available	Skills required to take advantage of this aspect of the context
1. Presence of other objects		
From same category	Within-category similarities	Ability to divide attention among multiple objects
From different category	Between-category differences	Ability to divide attention among multiple objects
2. Accessibility of objects		
• Out of reach (e.g., on high shelf, in book)	Object shape, color, form	Ability to perceive visual features of objects
• Within reach (e.g., on low shelf)	Object texture, weight, taste	Ability to pick up and manipulate objects

and the differences between cups and other types of dishes. In other settings, infants may see only one item from a particular category in the context of items from other categories. For example, a child may see a cup next to his mother's computer. In this context, comparing the individual item to other items in the category requires that the infant remember other encounters with category members. Thus, similarities to other items within the category may be less salient. However, differences between items from different categories (cups and computers) may be highlighted. As a result, such contextual differences translate into differences in the availability of information about similarities and differences both within and between categories.

Second, contexts differ in how infants interact with objects. As a result, different features of objects may be made more or less salient. For example, an infant who encounters a dog barking behind a fence may notice different features of the dog than does an infant who pets a friendly dog. In the first case, features of the dog, such as *barks loudly* and *jumps*, may be salient. In the second case, features not available in the first context, such as *has a wet tongue* and *is furry*, are available, and those features may be the most salient. Thus, these contextual differences translate into actual differences in the particular information about category members that is available.

Obviously, contexts differ in a number of ways, and these are only two contextual factors that may influence category formation. However, these contextual differences have important implications for the development of categorization in infancy. The impact of both contextual features will depend on the development of the kinds of skills described here. Only if infants can effectively divide their attention among multiple objects will being presented with several exemplars at one time highlight similarities among those items. Likewise, only if infants have the perceptual and cognitive abilities to detect and remember barking, jumping, and so on, will they use those features in forming a category of the object. Thus, one consequence of the developmental changes described in the previous section is that older infants will be better able to take advantage of contextual differences to attend to and use the most relevant features for categorization.

The Presence of Multiple Objects

The presence or absence of same- and other-category exemplars provides infants with the opportunity to directly compare exemplars. Gentner and her colleagues (e.g., Gentner & Medina, 1998) have argued that the act of comparing items highlights similarities and differences among items. As a result, comparing items should facilitate categorization. Indeed, some recent research suggests that young children's category-related behavior is facilitated when they are encouraged to compare items. For example, Namy, Smith, and Gershkoff-Stowe (1997) found that 18-month-old infants who were encouraged to directly compare items exhibited stronger categorical responding in a sequential touching–type task than did infants who were not encouraged to compare the items. Infants in the compare condition were presented with the items to be categorized and a shape sorter in which only one type of item would fit. Successfully inserting only the correct items into the shape sorter forced infants to compare items from the two different groups. Infants in the no-compare group were given the same familiarization with the items in the absence of the shape sorter. In general, infants in the compare group exhibited more sophisticated categorical responding in a subsequent sequential-touching task.

In a recent investigation, Oakes, Kannass, Lyons, Thompson, and Laughlin (2000) similarly found that opportunities to compare items facilitated infants' performance on a sequential-touching task. Thirteen- and 16-month-old infants were presented with multiple exemplars from the *people* and *sea animals* categories, all at one time, and thus they could make both within-category comparisons and between-category comparisons. To explore the role of such comparisons on infants' categorization in this context, Oakes et al. evaluated infants' category-related touching in three different conditions. First, infants were presented with eight plastic replicas of people and sea animals in a standard sequential-touching task—four items from each category were randomly arranged on a tray and infants were allowed to manipulate them in any way they wished for 4 minutes. The mean run-lengths during the first and second 2-minute segments are presented in the left side of figure 6.2.[1] Importantly, the mean run-length is an indication not of whether or not infants' compared items but of whether or not they attended to one or both categories. The question being asked here was whether differences in the opportunities to compare items influenced infants' attention to the categorical distinction.

As has been found previously (Oakes, Plumert, Lansink, & Merryman, 1996), 13-month-old infants initially showed little systematic category-related touching in this context—their mean run-length in the first segment was not significantly greater than chance, and their mean run-length in the second segment approached significance ($p = .06$, one-tailed). Sixteen-month-old infants, in contrast, responded to the category in both segments—both mean run-lengths were significantly greater than chance, $p < .05$, one-tailed. Thus, this finding suggests that it is only relatively late in infancy that children can easily take advantage of the presence of other objects to determine within-category similarity and between-category differences.

Opportunities to compare items, however, are necessarily accompanied by greater demands on infants' other abilities. Because comparison of items can only occur when multiple objects are encountered at one time, contexts in which direct comparison of items is facilitated also require that infants be able to effectively manipulate and attend to multiple objects at one time. As a result, infants' ability to take advantage of these comparison opportunities may change with development. That is, older infants have better memories, are more proficient at dividing their attention among multiple objects, and so on. As infants develop such skills they will be better able to compare multiple objects when they are presented. In the experiment described earlier, effectively comparing items required manipulating and attending to eight objects at one time. Limitations on motor and attentional abilities make it more difficult for very young infants to take advantage of opportunities to compare items in such contexts. Indeed, attempts at using sequential touching with infants under 1 year of age have largely been unsuccessful (Oakes et al., 1996).

In a second experiment, Oakes et al. (2000) assessed infants' systematic category-related touching in a context in which comparisons were possible but the number of items to which infants needed to attend to at one time was reduced. Specifically, in this study the items were presented on a divided tray for the first segment, with four items on each side of a short divider that bisected the tray. Note that infants

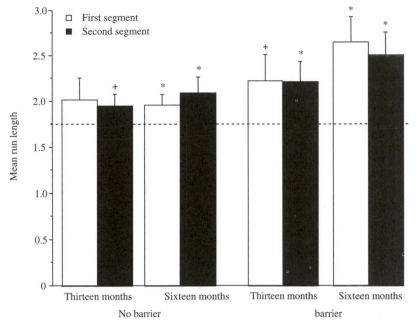

Figure 6.2. Mean run-lengths for 13- and 16-month-old infants in Oakes, Kannass, Lyons, Thompson, and Laughlin (2000). Separate mean run-lengths are given for the first and second 2-minute segments of the experimental session. The toys in the "no barrier" condition were randomly arranged on an undivided tray in the first 2 minutes, and the toys in the "barrier" condition were arranged on a divided tray in the first 2 minutes (see text for further explanation). The value of the mean run-length expected by chance (1.75) is indicated by a dashed line. Mean run-lengths that were significantly greater than chance (p < .05, one-tailed) are indicated by an asterisk. Mean run-lengths that were marginally greater than chance (p = .06, one-tailed) are indicated by a cross.

could easily compare all eight objects if they chose, but the presence of the divider may have helped them direct their attention to four (or fewer) of the objects at one time. Thus, this manipulation preserved infants' ability to compare items within and between categories, while compensating for one demanding feature of the task. During the second segment, the divider was removed, and infants were presented with the toys in a standard sequential-touching task.

The mean run-lengths are presented in the right side of figure 6.2, and it can be seen that both 13- and 16-month-old infants exhibited more sophisticated category-related touching in this experiment. At both ages, infants' level of systematic category-related touching was higher in both segments of this experiment than in the original experiment in which no divider was used. In this case, the mean run-length of the 13-month-old infants in the first segment (when the divider was in place) was marginally greater than chance ($p = .06$, one-tailed), and their mean run-length in the second segment (when the divider was removed) was significantly greater than chance, $p < .05$. The mean run-lengths of the 16-month-old infants were significantly greater than chance in both segments, $p < .05$. These results are consistent with the notion that even when infants are provided with opportunities to compare items, demands on other cognitive systems (in this case attending to multiple objects at one time) may interfere with their ability to use those opportunities to note similarities and differences among objects.

A third experiment confirmed that the opportunities to make both within- and between-category comparisons are essential for infants to engage in sophisticated category-related touching. In this experiment, 13- and 16-month-old infants initially were presented with only four items at one time—the four people followed by the four sea animals, or vice versa. The logic was that allowing infants to only attend to four items at once while making the categorical contrast more salient (i.e., all the items from one category were presented together) might facilitate their category-related touching even further. However, if the opportunity to make both within- and between-category comparisons is important for infants' category-related touching in this context, then this manipulation will not facilitate their category-related touching. Infants received two 1-minute trials with four toys; thus the amount of initial familiarization was the same as the first segment in the other studies. Then infants were presented with all eight toys in a standard sequential-touching task for 2 minutes. The mean run-lengths for this sequential-touching segment are presented in figure 6.3, and it can be seen that infants' responding was quite similar to when they were initially presented with the eight items on the undivided tray. The mean run-length for the 16-month-old infants, but not for the 13-month-old infants, was significantly greater than chance, $p < .05$. Thus, infants' category-related touching was facilitated only when demands on their cognitive systems were reduced while preserving opportunities to make both within- and between-category contrasts.

These results show that at 13 months the attentional demands of the task appear to determine, in part, infants' ability to categorize, but motor limitations, attentional limitations, or both may influence younger infants' ability to categorize in this task. In fact, opportunities to compare items do facilitate very young infants' categorization in tasks that place fewer demands on motor and information-processing resources. Oakes and Ribar (2001) found that young infants form a more exclusive category of stimuli when presented with items two at a time than when presented with the same items one at a time. Four-month-old infants were presented with a series of pictures of cats (or dogs). One group of infants saw the pictures one at a time, and a second group of infants saw the pictures in pairs. All infants were familiarized with exactly the same pictures of cats (or dogs). Following familiarization with one category, 4-month-old infants who saw the pictures one at a time formed an inclusive category—they failed to increase their attention to a novel dog or cat, but they did increase their attention to a truck. Four-month-old infants who saw the pictures two at a time, in contrast, formed an exclusive category—they preferred the novel out-of-category item (e.g., dog if familiarized with cats) to a novel within-category item (e.g., cat if familiarized with cats). Apparently being able to directly compare items from within the same category made the relevant features more salient.

Thus, contexts differ in ways that both facilitate and inhibit the comparison process. Comparing items seems to highlight similarities and differences among

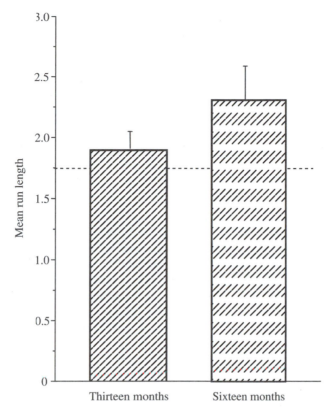

Figure 6.3. Mean run-lengths in the sequential-touching segment for 13- and 16-month-old infants in experiment 3 of Oakes et al. (2000). This segment followed an initial familiarization period in which infants received four toys on each of two 1-minute trials (see text for details). The value of the mean run-length expected by chance (1.75) is indicated by a dashed line, and mean run-lengths that were greater than chance (p < .05, one tailed) are indicated by an asterisk.

them. By comparing items, infants may more easily recognize the features relevant for forming particular category groupings. However, opportunities to compare items place different demands on infants' other cognitive abilities. For infants to benefit from comparison, opportunities to compare must match their other cognitive abilities. Therefore, one way the context shapes the kinds of features that infants may use in forming categories is by supporting or inhibiting their ability to compare items.

Variations in How Infants Experience Objects

A second contextual difference is the manner in which infants experience category exemplars. Specifically, in some contexts, such as looking at books or looking at objects placed out of reach, infants have access only to visual information about objects. Categories formed in these contexts are likely to be based on features such as overall shape and coloring. Such features will be useful in forming some categories, but reliance only on these features will be limiting—for example, access to only static visual representations will not allow one to form a category based on the function of the object. In other contexts, infants can actually manipulate objects (or see objects manipulated), and thus they have access to information other than what those objects look like. When infants can actually manipulate objects, they can taste them, feel how heavy they are, and determine what sound they make when thrown on the floor. Note that attention to such features may cause infants to form categories that are less similar to adult categories than would attention to other features. Certainly, infants may form a useful category of *heavy things* or *smooth objects*, but categories such as *lids*, *shirts*, and *cars* may be more useful in a wider variety of contexts (e.g., learning labels).

When experimental contexts vary in terms of the information that is available, infants do form correspondingly different categories. Specifically, infants formed broader categories when they were able to manipulate objects than when they could only visually inspect them. In one study, Oakes, Coppage, and Dingel (1997) found that 10-month-old infants tested in an object-examining task formed separate categories for land animals (e.g., cow, horse, rabbit) and sea animals (e.g., manatee, killer whale, walrus) when familiarized with a set of similar items (e.g., zebra, dog, cow) but a single global category that included both land and sea animals when familiarized with a more variable set of items (e.g., bear, rabbit, ram). Recently, Oakes and Lyons (2001), using exactly the same stimuli, found that 10-month-old infants tested in a visual familiarization task formed separate categories for land and sea animals regardless of which set of stimuli was used. The object-examining task used by Oakes et al. (1997) involved handing the infants the objects and allowing them to actually manipulate them. The visual familiarization task used by Oakes and Lyons (2001) involved showing infants pictures of the same objects on a computer screen. In both studies, infants were initially familiarized with a series of land or sea animals, presented one at a time. Half of the infants were presented with items that adults rated as similar to one another, and half of the infants were presented with items that adults rated as different from one another. Following familiarization with land or sea animals, infants were tested with a novel land animal, a novel sea animal, and a truck. Thus, the only difference between the two studies was in whether or not infants could handle the objects.

Infants' levels of visual attention to the last trial with a familiar item and the test trials with a novel within-category item and novel out-of-category item in each condition of the two studies are presented in figure 6.4. Clearly, in the Oakes et al. (1997) study infants only responded to exclusive categories of land *or* sea animals when presented with items that adults rated as similar. In that condition, infants increased their attention significantly to the novel item from the other category (i.e., the novel sea animal if familiarized with land animals) but not to the novel item from the familiar category. When familiarized with a variable set of items, in contrast, 10-month-old infants in the Oakes et al. (1997) study failed to increase their attention significantly even to the novel out-of-category item (although they did so to a truck). Infants apparently formed an inclusive category that included both land *and*

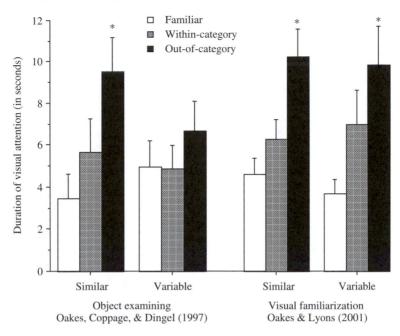

Figure 6.4. Duration of visual attention to a familiar item, a novel within-category item, and a novel out-of-category item (in Oakes, Coppage, and Dingel [1997] and Oakes and Lyons [2001] as a function of familiarization condition. Infants in the similar *condition were familiarized with items that were similar to one another, and infants in the* variable *condition were familiarized with items that were more varied (see text for additional details). Significant increases in attention to novel items (as compared to the familiar item) are indicated by an asterisk (p < .05, two-tailed).*

sea animals. In the Oakes and Lyons (2001) study, 10-month-old infants in both conditions exhibited the same pattern—they increased their looking significantly to the novel item from the contrasting category but not to the novel item from the familiar category. That is, in both conditions, infants formed an exclusive category of land *or* sea animals. Additional work needs to be done to understand the full extent of such contextual differences in infants' categorization, but results like these demonstrate that infants do use different features in different contexts.

Why do 10-month-old infants rely more heavily on perceptual similarity to divide animals into land animals and sea animals in an object-examining task than in a visual familiarization task? One possibility is that the availability of information irrelevant to the land animal–sea animal distinction (e.g., how heavy the objects are) in the object-examining task distracts infants from information more relevant to the distinction (e.g., legs versus fins). That is, developmental changes in the ability to process all of the information that is present more efficiently and ignore distracting or irrelevant information may be one factor that influences categorization. In other words, younger infants may be overwhelmed by the amount of information available when they are allowed to handle objects, and as a result they have more difficulty focusing on the most relevant features for forming categories of the objects.

Moreover, infants may not always be able to take advantage of these features when categorizing the object, even when those features are made salient by the context. As the abilities described in the first section of this chapter develop, infants will be better able to recognize all of the features available in a context. For infants to use all of the features available in a context, they must have the motor, perceptual, and cognitive abilities required to detect and remember those features. In the studies described here, 10-month-old infants may have been distracted by the weight of the land and sea animals in an object-examining task, but younger infants who would be less able to pick up the objects may be less distracted by those features. Thus, one consequence of the developmental changes described in the first section is that contextual differences should have a greater influence on infants' categorization of objects when there is a larger pool of features to which they can attend.

In summary, contextual variations contribute to the kinds of features infants use when forming categories. Infants form more exclusive categories when provided with opportunities to directly compare items. Infants form different categories in contexts in which they can actually touch and feel objects than in contexts in which they can only look at objects. However, whether or not infants use the information that is available about object features in a given context depends on the demands placed on their other cognitive abilities. Infants will be unable to compare items if they are presented with more items at once to which they can simultaneously attend. Similarly, infants will be able to use weight and texture as features if they are relevant and ignore those features if they are irrelevant only if they can efficiently deal with the amount of information present in the context. In general, however, the data are consistent with principle 2: With development infants become able to take advantage of the information available in different contexts.

Principle 3: Increases in Background Knowledge Constrain the Pool of Potential Features for Forming Categories

As described in the preceding sections, there are a number of developmental changes that lead to an increase in the number of features that infants can use when categorizing objects. Paradoxically, this pool of features also appears to *narrow* with development. In our building metaphor, we might argue that infants learn to be selective in the materials they use when forming structures. Although there may be an abundance of material available to construct categories, some of this material will provide a firmer foundation for complex structures than will others. With development infants come to realize which information provides the most useful foundation for forming and revising categories.

This reduction in the number of attributes for categorizing objects may be influenced by several developmental changes (see table 6.4). First, infants develop the ability to inhibit responding to or ignore distracting, irrelevant information (e.g., weight when categorizing replicas of animals). There are well-documented develop-

TABLE 6.4. Ways the Pool of Potential Attributes Is Reduced

Developmental change	Effect on reducing the pool of attributes
Resist attending to distracting features	Infants can ignore features, such as weight, that are not highly correlated with category membership
Inhibit responding to some features	Ability to selectively attend to features that are highly correlated with category membership
Increases in background knowledge	Allow infants to attend to "meaningful" features of objects and ignore "arbitrary" ones
Increased understanding of objects	Constrains the types of feature correlations to which infants will attend

mental changes in attentional processes (e.g., Ruff & Rothbart, 1996) that might be responsible for infants becoming better at inhibiting their attention to irrelevant features of objects. In addition, there are developmental changes in categorization that seem to indicate that infants are increasingly able to inhibit irrelevant or distracting information. As described earlier, Oakes et al. (1997) observed that 10-month-old infants relied on the level of perceptual variability when differentiating land from sea animals in an object-examining task. Thirteen-month-old infants, however, differentiated the categories regardless of the level of perceptual variability. This developmental change may reflect 13-month-old infants' ability to attend to the relevant features (e.g., legs versus fins) and ignore irrelevant distracting ones (e.g., weight).

Increases in infants' background knowledge about objects also may contribute to the narrowing of potential features. Indeed, research with adults shows that background knowledge can be used to restrict the pool of features they use in forming categories. Spalding and Murphy (1996, 1999), for example, have found that adults presented with objects characterized by the same set of feature more easily formed categories of those objects if the features cohere according to their existing background knowledge (e.g., *arctic vehicles*) than if the features do not cohere according to such knowledge.

At least two sets of studies suggest a similar process in the development of infants' attention to object features. Both of these studies suggest that as infants gain an understanding of how objects are typically constructed, they constrain the features they attend to and use in forming categories. In a study of infants' attention to structure–function correlations, Madole and Cohen (1995) reported that younger infants attended to both "arbitrary" and "meaningful" correlations and older infants attended only to the meaningful ones. Arbitrary correlations were those in which the form of one part of the object predicted the function of a different part—for example, the form of a protrusion at the top of the object predicted whether or not the wheels rolled. Meaningful correlations were those in which the form of one part was correlated with the function of that part—for example, the form of the wheels predicted whether or not they rolled. Fourteen- and 18-month-old infants were habituated to a set of objects embodying these correlations and were tested with objects that either maintained or violated the correlation. Fourteen-month-old infants dishabituated when either the meaningful or arbitrary correlations were violated, whereas 18-month-old infants dishabituated only when meaningful correlations were violated. Thus, 18-month-old infants restricted their attention only to feature correlations that were sensible, given their background knowledge and experience, and as a result they actually attended to fewer features correlations than did younger infants.

Rakison and his colleagues (Rakison & Butterworth, 1998; Rakison & Cohen, 1999) have observed a similar restricting of the features infants use when attending to categories of objects in a sequential-touching task. Rakison and Butterworth (1998), for example, evaluated infants' attention to the distinction between *animals* and *vehicles* as compared with attention to the distinction between *things with legs* and *things with wheels*. When presented with a collection of objects in which all of the animals had legs and all of the vehicles had wheels, infants as young as 14 months responded to the categorical distinction between animals and vehicles in a sequential-touching task. However, when presented with a collection of objects in which some of the animals had legs and some had wheels and some of the vehicles had legs and some had wheels, 14-month-old infants responded to the distinction between *things with legs* and *things with wheels*. Older infants did not categorize the objects on the basis of this single, salient feature. In a different investigation, Rakison and Cohen (1999) observed that 22-month-old infants would categorize objects as *cows* and *cars* even if none of the objects had wheels or legs, or if all of the objects had both wheels and legs. Note that by providing infants with a choice of how to categorize the objects— either taxonomically (animals versus vehicles or cows versus cars, presumably defined by features other than legs or wheels) or on the basis of the presence of a particular set of features (legs versus wheels)—and observing the conditions under which infants responded to one category versus the other, Rakison and his colleagues have uncovered developmental differences in the kinds of features that are important in infants' categorization. Younger infants categorize on the basis of salient features that can only be imperfectly mapped onto taxonomic categorical membership, and older infants can use more subtle features that more closely mapped onto adultlike categories.

Thus, consistent with principle 3, the pool of features that infants use in forming categories appears to narrow as they gain a more sophisticated understanding of the world. That is, as infants form expectations for how objects are constructed, those expectations shape the kinds of features they use in forming categories. As these examples illustrate, older infants are actually less flexible in using features to form categories than are younger infants.

Conclusions

We have described three principles for how infants' use of information in forming categories changes. In general, we have described category formation as a process of constructing increasingly complex structures using available materials. We argue that there is little developmental change in the basic process of building, but that there are changes in the materials available for construction. These changes occur in a principled and predictable way. First, there are basic developmental changes in infants' motor, cognitive, and linguistic abilities, and these changes broaden the pool of features available for categorization. Second, the contexts in which objects are encountered differ in the accessibility of different object features, and with development infants are better able to take advantage of the information available in different contexts. Finally, changes in background knowledge lead to a refining of the features that infants use in making category judgements.

There are at least two important ways that the principles we have presented can be used for understanding the development of categorization during infancy. First, they allow us to understand developmental changes in categorical responding that have been reported in the infant categorization literature but have not always been easily explained. For example, this framework provides an explanation for the apparent contradiction that infants form exclusive categories when tested at a young age in visual familiarization tasks (e.g., Quinn et al., 1993) and yet form inclusive categories when tested at an older age in object handling tasks (e.g., Mandler & McDonough, 1993). Specifically, such differences may reflect differences in the information infants can use when forming categories in those experimental contexts, rather than differences in the kind of categories tapped by different experimental tasks.

Second, these principles allow us to make a priori predictions that can be used to guide further research. Specifically, by evaluating the information available to infants (as a result of their developing skills, the nature of the context, and infants' background knowledge), we can predict the conditions under which they would respond to a more or less exclusive category. So we expect that the categories formed by younger infants will differ from those formed by older infants in systematic ways— they will be more context dependent and based on less reliable information than will the categories of older infants.

As an illustration, consider an example from the literature on infants' categorization of a different type of stimuli—human faces. If our framework can provide understanding in this domain, it is clearly general and is broadly applicable. Leinbach and Fagot (1993) observed that by around 7 months of age infants categorized pictures of human faces on the basis of sex when cues such as clothing style and hair length were present. However, when these cues were absent (and presumably, facial configuration was the only useful cue), infants failed to respond categorically until around 12 months of age. These conflicting results make it difficult to determine whether 7-month-old infants possess categories of human faces as male and female or whether this category does not truly emerge until much later in infancy. In other words, from these results we have difficulty drawing definitive conclusions about when infants have a concept of sex.

However, the principles we proposed here allow us to interpret findings such as these in a process-oriented framework that should have universal applicability. First, these results can be interpreted in terms of the kinds of features available to infants at different ages. There is a long history of research evaluating infants' attention to configural versus local features, particularly in their perception of faces. For example, Caron and his colleagues (Caron, Caron, Caldwell, & Weiss, 1973) argue that infants do not discriminate faces on the basis of full-face configurations until 5 months, and continued developmental changes in this ability contribute to infants' ability to categorize faces on the basis of emotional expression by 7 months (Caron, Caron, & Myers, 1982). Other evidence suggests that the presence and absence of teeth are particularly important for 7-month-old infants' differentiation of facial expressions (Phillips, Wagner, Fells, & Lynch, 1990). More recent evidence has shown hemispheric specialization in infants' processing of configural versus local facial features, as well as evidence of developmental changes in interhemispheric transfer of this information (e.g., de Schonen, Deruelle, Mancini, & Pascalis, 1993; de Schonen, Mancini, & Leigeios, 1998). On the basis of these findings, we would predict that developmental changes in infants' categorization of faces are related to developmental changes in attention to facial configuration cues. Thus, the differences observed by Leinbach and Fagot for 7- and 12-month-old infants' categorization of faces may reflect differences in infants' ability to attend to configural versus local features of those faces.

Second, the context in which the category exemplars were presented may have enhanced the accessibility of some cues over others. Infants were serially presented with static images of faces. Thus, they had no access to information about voice or body movement and had little opportunity to easily and directly compare male and female faces. As described earlier, contextual differences like these seem to have profound influences on whether young infants form relatively exclusive or relatively inclusive categories (Oakes & Ribar, 2001). Thus, the 7-month-old infants observed by Leinbach and Fagot may have had difficulty determining the relevant cues on which to base their categorization of these faces. Perhaps if the faces had been presented in pairs, or if they had been presented in a context in which additional information was available, then 7-month-old infants would have responded to the differences between male and female faces. Indeed, work by Fagan and Singer (1979) suggests that when faces are presented in pairs, even 5-month-old infants are sensitive to the differences between male faces and female faces.

Finally, differences in infants' background knowledge about what features are relevant when forming categories of faces may have contributed to the developmental difference observed by Leinbach and Fagot. Specifically, by 12 months infants might have learned that although clothing and hairstyle are strongly associated with sex, facial features are more highly associated with this category membership. Seven-month-old infants may have had more difficulty in these studies because they were less able to differentially attend to features that were relevant to the categorization over irrelevant features. This interpretation is clearly consistent with the results described earlier for developmental changes in infants' attention to particular features of objects.

It should be clear from this analysis that interpreting the results reported by Leinbach and Fagot (1993) in terms of the age at which infants do not have a concept of sex oversimplified infants' categorization of faces in this investigation. Instead, this analysis demonstrates that infants' tendency to respond categorically to faces on the basis of sex is an evolving ability that depends on both endogenous and exogenous factors.

The principles we have proposed also allow us to make a priori predictions about how infants' categorization should change. Therefore, we should be able to confirm the hypotheses raised by the analyses of the Leinbach and Fagot (1993) results and extend them to new kinds of category judgements. For example, we can make testable predictions about developmental changes in infants' use of static information and dynamic information and their use of the correlation between static and dynamic information in sex categorization. We can also extend these predictions to other kinds of categories.

In summary, we have proposed a principled, three-stage developmental trajectory in infants' categorization abilities. First, with emerging skills, infants are able to make use of an increasingly broad set of features when categorizing objects. Second, contextual factors influence the kinds of features that infants can make use of in categorization. Infants' developing cognitive skills interact with these contextual factors to determine the pool of features available for making category judgments. Finally, background knowledge about the relationship among features serves to narrow the set of features to those that are most predictive of category membership. We emphasize that infants' categorical awareness should never be viewed as an "all or none" phenomenon. Instead, one of the most important features of this approach is its focus on understanding the process by which infants' categories evolve over time. We believe that this approach can generate substantive research into the understanding of early categorization.

Acknowledgments

Preparation of this manuscript was supported, in part, by grant HD36060 awarded to Lisa Oakes by the National Institutes of Health. We would like to thank David Rakison and Ann Ellis for helpful comments on an earlier draft of this manuscript. Correspondences should be addressed to Lisa M. Oakes, Department of Psychology, University of Iowa, Iowa City, IA 52240 (lisa-oakes@uiowa.edu) or Kelly L. Madole, Department of Psychology, Western Kentucky University, 1 Big Red Way, Bowling Green, KY 42103 (Kelly.Madole@wku.edu).

Note

1. Infants' mean run-lengths were calculated by dividing the total number of touches by the number of individual runs of touches to items within a category (i.e., a series of touches to items within one category without touching items from the contrasting category). The value of the mean run-length expected by chance is 1.75 (Mandler, Fivush, & Reznick, 1987). Most previous studies using contrasts like the one used here involved only 2-minute sequential-touching segments. Thus, the mean run-lengths in the first segment are comparable to those obtained in most studies using sequential touching (e.g., Mandler et al., 1987, 1991; Rakison & Butterworth, 1998), and those in the second segment allow comparisons to one previous study using essentially the same contrast (Oakes et al., 1996) and comparisons of different studies within this investigation.

References

Arterberry, M. E. (1993). Development of spatiotemporal integration in infancy. *Infant Behavior and Development, 16*, 343–364.

Behl-Chadha, G. (1996). Basic-level and superordinate-like categorical representations early in infancy. *Cognition, 60*, 105–141.

Bertenthal, B. I., Campos, J. J., & Kermoian, R. (1995). An epigenetic perspective on the development of self-produced locomotion and its consequences. *Current Directions in Psychological Science, 3*, 140–145.

Bushnell, E. W., & Boudreau, J. P. (1993). Motor development and the mind: The potential role of motor abilities as a determinant of aspects of perceptual development. *Child Development, 64,* 1005–1021.

Caron, A. J., Caron, R. F., Caldwell, R. C., & Weiss, S. J. (1973). Infant perception of the structural properties of the face. *Developmental Psychology, 9,* 385–399.

Caron, A. J., Caron, R. F., & Myers, R. S. (1982). Abstraction of invariant face expressions in infancy. *Child Development, 53,* 1008–1015.

Cohen, L. B., & Caputo, N. F. (1978, May). *Instructing infants to respond to perceptual categories.* Presented at the Annual Meeting of the Midwestern Psychological Association, Chicago.

de Schonen, S., Deruelle, C., Mancini, J., & Pascalis, O. (1993). Hemispheric differences in face processing and brain maturation. In B. de Boysson-Bardies & S. de Schonen (Eds.), *Developmental neurocognition: Speech and face processing in the first year of life* (Vol. 69, pp. 149–163). Dordrecht: Kluwer.

de Schonen, S., Mancini, J., & Leigeios, F. (1998). About functional corital specialization: The development of face recognition. In F. Simion & G. Butterworth (Eds.), *The development of sensory, motor, and cognitive capacities in early infancy* (pp. 103–120). Hove, UK: Psychology Press.

Diamond, A. (1985). Development of the ability to use recall to guide action, as indicated by infants' performance on AB. *Child Development, 56,* 868–883.

Eimas, P. (1994). Categorization in early infancy and the continuity of development. *Cognition, 50,* 83–93.

Fagan, J. F., & Singer, L. T. (1979). The role of simple feature differences in infants' recognition of faces. *Infant Behavior and Development, 2,* 39–45.

Gentner, D., & Medina, J. (1998). Similarity and the development of rules. *Cognition, 6,* 263–297.

Goldstone, R. L., & Barsalou, L. W. (1998). Reuniting perception and conception. *Cognition, 65,* 231–262.

Hayne, H. (1996). Categorization in infancy. In C. Rovee-Collier & L. P. Lipsitt (Eds.), *Advances in infancy* (Vol. 10, pp. 79–120). Norwood, NJ: Ablex.

Jones, S. S., & Smith, L. B. (1993). The place of perception in children's concepts. *Cognitive Development, 8,* 113–139.

Leinbach, M. D., & Fagot, B. I. (1993). Categorical habituation to male and female faces: Gender schematic processing in infancy. *Infant Behavior and Development, 16,* 317–332.

Lockman, J. J., & McHale, J. P. (1989). Object manipulation in infancy: Developmental and contextual determinants. In J. J. Lockman & N. Hazen (Eds.), *Action in social context: Perspectives on early development* (pp. 129–167). New York: Plenum.

Madole, K. L. (1993, March). *The role of functional properties in infants' categorization of objects.* Paper presented at the Biennial Meeting of the Society for Research in Child Development, New Orleans, LA.

Madole, K. L., & Cohen, L. B. (1995). The role of object parts in infants' attention to form-function correlations. *Developmental Psychology, 31,* 317–332.

Madole, K. L., Cohen, L. B., & Bradley, K. (1994, June). *Ten-month-old infants categorize form but not function.* Paper presented at the Ninth Biennial Conference for Infant Studies, Paris.

Madole, K. L., & Oakes, L. M. (1999). Making sense of infant categorization: Stable processes and changing representations. *Developmental Review, 19,* 263–296.

Madole, K. L., Oakes, L. M., & Cohen, L. B. (1993). Developmental changes in infants' attention to function and form-function correlations. *Cognitive Development, 8,* 189–209.

Mandler, J. M. (1988). How to build a baby: On the development of an accessible representational system. *Cognitive Development, 3,* 113–136.

Mandler, J. M. (1992). How to build a baby: II. Conceptual primitives. *Psychological Review*, 99, 587–604.

Mandler, J. M., & Bauer, P. J. (1988). The cradle of categorization: Is the basic level basic? *Cognitive Development*, 3, 247–264.

Mandler, J. M., Bauer, P. J., & McDonough, L. (1991). Separating the sheep from the goats: Differentiating global categories. *Cognitive Psychology*, 23, 263–298.

Mandler, J. M., Fivush, R., & Reznick, J. S. (1987). The development of contextual categories. *Cognitive Development*, 2, 339–354.

Mandler, J. M., & McDonough, L. (1993). Concept formation in infancy. *Cognitive Development*, 8, 281–318.

Mandler, J. M., & McDonough, L. (1996). Drinking and driving don't mix: Inductive generalization in infancy. *Cognition*, 59, 307–335.

Namy, L. L., Smith, L. B., & Gershkoff-Stowe, L. (1997). Young children's discovery of spatial classification. *Cognitive Development*, 12, 163–184.

Nelson, K. (1979). Explorations in the development of a functional semantic system. In W. A. Collins (Ed.), *The Minnesota symposium on child psychology: Children's language and communication.* (Vol. 12, pp. 47–81). Hillsdale, NJ: Erlbaum.

Oakes, L. M., Coppage, D. J., & Dingel, A. (1997). By land or by sea: The role of perceptual similarity in infants' categorization of animals. *Developmental Psychology*, 33, 396–407.

Oakes, L. M., Kannass, K. N., Lyons, A. K., Thompson, P., & Laughlin, M. (2000). *The roles of attentional demands and comparison on infants' categorical responding: The development of behavior in the sequential-touching task.* Unpublished manuscript.

Oakes, L. M., & Lyons, A. K. (2001). *Perceptual variability and infants' categorization in visual familiarization.* Manuscript submitted for publication.

Oakes, L. M., & Madole, K. L. (2000). The future of infant categorization research: A process-oriented approach. *Child Development*, 71, 119–126.

Oakes, L. M., Plumert, J. M., Lansink, J. M., & Merryman, J. D. (1996). Evidence for task-dependent categorization in infancy. *Infant Behavior and Development*, 19, 425–440.

Oakes, L. M., Ribar, R. J. (2001). *The role of comparison in infant categorization.* Manuscript submitted for publication.

Phillips, R. D., Wagner, S. H., Fells, C. A., & Lynch, M. (1990). Do infants recognize emotion in facial expression? Categorical and "metaphorical" evidence. *Infant Behavior and Development*, 13, 71–84.

Quinn, P. C., & Eimas, P. D. (1996a). Perceptual cues that permit categorical differentiation of animal species by infants. *Journal of Experimental Child Psychology*, 63, 189–211.

Quinn, P. C., & Eimas, P. D. (1996b). Perceptual organization and categorization in young infants. In C. Rovee-Collier & L. P. Lipsitt (Eds.), *Advances in infancy research* (Vol. 10, pp. 1–36). Norwood, NJ: Ablex.

Quinn, P. C., & Eimas, P. D. (1997). A reexamination of the perceptual-to-conceptual shift in mental representations. *Review of General Psychology*, 1, 171–187.

Quinn, P. C., Eimas, P. D., & Rosenkrantz, S. L. (1993). Evidence for representation of perceptually similar categories by 3-month-old and 4-month-old infants. *Perception*, 22, 463–475.

Rakison, D. H., & Butterworth, G. E. (1998). Infants' use of object parts in early categorization. *Developmental Psychology*, 34, 49–62.

Rakison, D. H., & Cohen, L. B. (1999). Infants' use of functional parts in basic-like categorization. *Developmental Science*, 2, 423–431.

Rochat, P., & Goubet, N. (1995). Development of sitting and reaching in 5- to 6-month-old infants. *Infant Behavior and Development*, 18, 53–68.

Rosch, E., Mervis, C. B., Gray, W. D., Johnson, D. M., & Boyes-Braem, P. (1976). Basic objects in natural categories. *Cognitive Psychology, 8,* 382–439.

Rovee-Collier, C., & Hayne, H. (1987). Reactivation of infant memory: Implications for cognitive development. In H. W. Reese (Ed.), *Advances in child development and behavior* (Vol. 20, pp. 185–238). Orlando, FL: Academic Press.

Ruff, H. A., & Rothbart, M. K. (1996). *Attention in early development.* New York: Oxford University Press.

Samuelson, L. K. (2000). *Statistical regularities in vocabulary guide language acquisition in 15- 20-month-olds and connectionist models.* Unpublished doctoral dissertation, Indiana University, Bloomington.

Samuelson, L. K., & Smith, L. B. (1999). Early noun vocabularies: Do ontology, category structure and syntax correspond? *Cognition, 73,* 1–33.

Skouteris, H., McKenzie, B. E., & Day, R. H. (1992). Integration of sequential information for shape perception by infants: A developmental study. *Child Development, 63,* 1164–1176.

Slater, A. (1998). The competent infant: Innate organisation and early learning in infant visual perception. In A. Slater (Ed.), *Perceptual development: Visual, auditory, and speech perception in infancy* (pp. 105–130). Hove, UK: Psychology Press.

Spalding, T. L., & Murphy, G. L. (1996). Effects of background knowledge on category construction. *Journal of Experimental Psychology: Learning, Memory, and Cognition, 22,* 525–538.

Spalding, T. L., & Murphy, G. L. (1999). What is learned in knowledge-related categories? Evidence from typicality and feature frequency judgments. *Memory and Cognition, 27,* 856–867.

Spencer, J., Quinn, P. C., Johnson, M. H., Karmiloff-Smith, A. (1997). Heads you win, tails you lose: Evidence for young infants categorizing mammals by head and facial features. *Early Development & Parenting, 6,* 113–126.

Waxman, S. R. (1999). Specifying the scope of 13-month-olds' expectations for novel words. *Cognition, 70,* B35–B50.

Werker, J. F., Cohen, L. B., Lloyd, V. L., Casasola, M., & Stager, C. L. (1998). Acquisition of word-object associations by 14-month-old infants. *Developmental Psychology, 34,* 1289–1309.

Younger, B. A., & Cohen, L. B. (1986). Developmental changes in infants' perception of correlations among attributes. *Child Development, 57,* 803–815.

CHAPTER SEVEN

Parts, Motion, and the Development of the Animate-Inanimate Distinction in Infancy

David H. Rakison

Taste your legs, sir; put them to motion.
Shakespeare, Twelfth Night

Since things in motion sooner catch the eye than what not stirs.
Shakespeare, Troilus and Cressida

THERE IS NO QUESTION that as adults we are aware of the various properties, abilities, and characteristics of the things around us.[1] In addition to being able to recognize, for example, animals and people on the basis of their external perceptual appearance—that which "can be seen" (Keil, 1989)—we also know that they are biological entities capable of self-propelled motion, and that they possess mental states such as goals, beliefs, and desires. Likewise, we can recognize rocks, plants, toys, and vehicles by their perceptual properties, but we are also aware that the members of these categories engage in a more limited kind of movement—they are, for instance, generally caused to move by other objects—and they are incapable of possessing any kind of psychological states.

This kind of understanding about the physical, biological, and psychological properties of animate entities and inanimate objects is thought by many to be well developed by the time that children reach preschool age (e.g., Gelman & Markman, 1986, 1987; Keil, 1991; Mandler, 1992). For example, there is evidence that 3- and 4-year-olds know whether different ontological kinds—such as a statue, a man, and a marmoset—are able to go up and down a hill "all by itself" (Massey & Gelman, 1988). Likewise, children in this age range show an understanding of several aspects of growth and illness (e.g., Backscheider, Shatz, & Gelman, 1993; Springer & Keil, 1991), and they make inductions about category membership on the basis of nonobservable biological properties rather than perceptual appearances, when given a choice between the two (Gelman & Coley, 1990; Gelman & Markman, 1986, 1987). By comparison, very young infants seem oblivious to these deeper, *nonobservable* properties. Indeed, it is now well established that categorization in the first 6 months of life or so is based predominantly on attributes that are readily available in the perceptual array (see e.g., Behl-Chadha, 1996; Quinn & Eimas, 1996b, 1997). It has been shown, for example, that 3- to 4-month-olds in a visual familiarization procedure can form categorical representations of cats that exclude dogs (Quinn, Eimas, & Rosenkrantz, 1993) and of mammals that exclude furniture (Behl-Chadha, 1996; see also Younger & Fearing, 1999). Infants at this age show little understanding, however, of the nonobvious properties commonly associated with animates or inanimates (Rakison & Poulin-Dubois, 2001).

From Perception to Conception?

Although the available evidence points to the fact that young infants categorize objects on the basis of perceptual information—what is called perceptual categorization—and that preschoolers have acquired knowledge and make use of nonobvious information, what is often called conceptual categorization, the process underlying the acquisition of an understanding of the properties that differentiate animate entities from inanimates objects remains somewhat opaque. For many developmentalists, this issue is best portrayed as the "perceptual to conceptual shift" whereby early categories are formed on the basis of perceptual resemblance, whereas later categories, following a stagelike transformation in representational structure and content, are formed primarily on the basis of nonobvious properties (e.g., Gelman & Markman, 1986, 1987; Keil, 1981, 1991; Murphy & Medin, 1985; Piaget, 1952). This dichotomous characterization of early categorization has, however, recently been criticized not only as an oversimplification but also as a mischaracterization of representational change (e.g., Jones & L. Smith, 1993; Madole & Oakes, 1999; Quinn & Eimas, 1997; for a more general criticism of stage-based theories of development, see Siegler, 1996, 2000). For instance, one group of researchers has proposed that no transition or shift occurs because categorization continues to rely on perceptual information throughout the lifespan (Eimas, 1994; Jones & Smith, 1993; Quinn & Eimas, 1997; Rakison & Poulin-Dubois, 2001; Smith & Heise, 1992), whereas others have argued that there is no need for a shift because perceptual and conceptual categorization develop side by side (e.g., Mandler, 2000).

An additional problem that arises in consideration of the development of early knowledge about physical, biological, and psychological properties of objects concerns the ontological status of different attributes. In general, the term *perceptual* tends to refer to that which is readily available in the perceptual input—for example, shape, color, texture, external attributes, and so on—whereas the terms *nonobvious* or *conceptual* tend to refer to internal parts or structures or to specific physically, psychologically, or biologically functional properties; for example, possessing blood or a brain, possessing a motor engine, or the ability to fly. Unfortunately, however, the different properties of objects cannot be classified quite as neatly as these characterizations suggest. It is ambiguous, for example, whether properties such as "chases sticks" or "barks" should be thought of as perceptual or conceptual attributes of dogs (Mandler, 1997), and it is unclear where to draw the line between properties that are readily available in the perceptual input—color and shape, for example—and those that are only intermittently available to the perceptual system, such as "gives birth to puppies" or "engages in self-propelled motion."

Theses of the Chapter

It is evident from the discussion thus far that I believe that researchers who focus on early category and concept development for objects in the world need to focus not only on the nature of conceptual structure and its contents but also on the processes of conceptual change whereby various information is integrated into infants' emerging representations for people, animals, and things. In this chapter, I will attempt to examine both of these issues. In particular, I will argue that infants develop representations for objects in the world, and the properties associated with the member of each of those domains, through a process of continual, incremental learning. This view of representational enrichment, which is in many ways akin to that forwarded by Quinn and Eimas (1997, 2000; Eimas, 1994), has at its core the idea that the information that underlies the developing concepts of infants and children is fundamentally perceptual in nature. Thus, one theme of the chapter is that no "perceptual-to-conceptual" shift occurs in infants or young children. To be sure, infants begin to incorporate into their representations information about objects that is considered by many to be nonobvious; yet I will argue that the same associative learning process is applied both for "perceptual" and "nonobvious" information because there is in fact no qualitative difference—both in terms of the input and the representations that result—between them.

A second thesis of the chapter is that infants' representations, and indeed those of older children and adults, are grounded in clusters of correlated attributes. This idea is now over 20 years old (Rosch, Mervis, Gray, Johnson, & Boyes-Braem, 1976; Rosch, 1978) and has resurfaced a number of times in the intervening period as a potential organizing principle of categories and the concepts that characterize them. For instance, Smith and Heise (1992) suggested that through experience infants start to attend to the attributes that are part of correlations, and Madole and Oakes (1999) similarly argued that infants ignore arbitrary form–function correlations because their experience allows them to focus only on meaningful relationships, such as, for example, those in which form predicts function.

These preceding formulations, and those that rely on similarity as the foundation of representations' structure and content, have generally been undermined by an *insufficiency of constraints* argument (e.g., Keil, 1981; Murphy & Medin, 1985). The crux of this argument is that because there are so many correlations available in the world, it is impossible to know a priori which ones are significant for category membership and which ones are not. I will argue, however, that infants possess inherent attention biases that, coupled with an associative learning mechanism, direct them to attend to and to encode specific correlations among attributes. These correlations are often those that involve dynamic attributes and that could be considered causally or functionally relevant. In contrast to previous arguments that lay theories bind or structure concepts by making sense of such relationships (Murphy & Medin, 1985), I will argue that feature correlations are grounded in causal relations observed during infancy and early childhood and that theories about feature correlations emerge only when such information is required.

I will start by outlining the three attention biases that, among others, are crucial in directing the infant toward specific kinds of information; namely, those that involve causal relations between static and dynamic attributes. I will then outline in more detail how attention to these relations, in conjunction with an associative learning mechanism, leads to the development of representations that include both perceptual and nonobvious information. I will cite studies from my lab, and from other infancy researchers, to support this view. Finally, I will present data from the inductive generalization paradigm that suggest that infants in the second year of life are only starting to develop associations between different categories of objects and the motion characteristics of those objects.

Early Attention Biases

It has been well documented that, as far as infants are concerned, not all properties and characteristics of things in the world are equally salient. It would be impossible for any species to "carve nature at its joints" if those joints did not in some way stand out. Ontological kinds have properties in common that not only allow them to be seen as similar to one another but also as different from other classes of objects. In this section, I propose a number of inherent attention biases—though other terms such as *constraints* or *learning enablers* could just as easily describe them—that facilitate attention to these properties and in turn allow the development of knowledge about the various categories of things that exist in the world. These biases relate to infants' predilection to attend to parts, the attention-capturing role of movement, and the importance of relative size; however, here I will focus primarily on the effects of motion and object attributes in the development of representations of objects.

It is important to note that I do not hold that these are the only attentional biases that infants possess: It has been shown for example, that neonates orient to faces more than to nonfaces (Morton & Johnson, 1991) and that older infants look longer at complex stimuli than at simple stimuli (Fantz, 1961) and orient their heads to locate a sound (Clarkson, Clifton, & Morrongiello, 1985). Such biases are clearly also important in directing infants' attention toward significant stimuli. However, my claim here is that the learning enablers outlined in this section, presumably in conjunction with these other attention biases, allow infants quickly to learn about the various physically and psychologically causal properties of objects and their attributes.

Attention to Parts

A first bias relates to the way that infants, from early in the first year of life, are adept at dissecting objects into their component parts and subsequently recombining those parts into wholes (e.g., Biederman, 1987, 1990; Cohen & Younger, 1983, 1986; Slater, Mattock, Brown, Burnham, & Young, 1991; Triesman, 1985, 1986; Younger & Cohen, 1983, 1986). This capacity is crucial in the construal of a three-dimensional world from a two-dimensional retinal image, and it allows object recognition even if components of an object are occluded from view. For instance, in the context of adult visual perception, Triesman (1986) argued that "the analysis of properties and parts precedes their synthesis" (p. 117), and Salapatek (1975), in a more developmental view, claimed that "the very early perception of two-dimensional stimuli must be regarded as the perception of parts rather than wholes" (p. 226). Indeed, there is evidence that even newborns process simple stimuli such as red and green vertical and diagonal colored stripes in terms of their components (color and orientation) rather than in terms of separate properties (color or orientation) (Slater et al., 1991).

Over the past 20 years, a number of researchers have examined the role of parts and part structure on infant, children, and adult object recognition and categorization. With regard to adults, Palmer, Rosch, and Chase (1981) found that they agree on the viewpoints of common objects that are more *canonical* than others, and that these viewpoints tended to reveal the more important parts in contour. Hoffman and Richards (1984) presented a principle whereby local minima are used to decompose contours into parts, while Biederman (1985) provided evidence that recognition uses inflection points—that is, the point in a curve where a change occurs from concave to convex, or vice versa—to determine a number of component parts. Moreover, parts that are engendered through these kinds of principles have been shown to have consequences in other tasks; for example, they are quickly identified as belonging to a particular form (Palmer, 1977), and they are considered to play an important role in the structural descriptions of objects (Hoffman & Richards, 1984). Likewise, 5-year-old children group exemplars from one category more readily when they share parts, and they detect missing parts more quickly when they are external and affect structure (e.g., legs) than when they are internal and do not affect structure or shape (Tversky, 1989).

With regard to infants, Younger and Cohen (1983, 1986; Younger, 1993) used the habituation procedure to show that by 4 months of age infants can detect individual parts of an object—often a schematic animal—and by 7 months they can detect correlations among such parts. However, it is not until 10 months of age that infants can extract correlations of attributes that are embedded within a category (Younger & Cohen, 1986). More recently, Rakison and Butterworth (1998a, 1998b) used the object manipulation, or sequential touching, paradigm to test whether 14- to 22-month-olds' superordinate- and basic-like categorization is affected by object parts such as legs and wheels. In this paradigm, infants are presented with eight items—usually four each from two categories—and their sequential touching behavior is measured; systematic successive touches to exemplars of each of the categories is taken as evidence of classification. In one experiment, Rakison and Butterworth (1998b, exp. 1) presented infants with different-part contrasts—for example, animals versus vehicles or furniture versus vehicles—as well as same-part contrasts; for example, animals versus insects or insects versus furniture. Results revealed that infants categorized different-part contrasts approximately 8 months before they categorized same-part contrasts.

In a second experiment, Rakison and Butterworth (1998b, exp. 2) used the same procedure with 14-, 18-, and 22-month-olds but made modifications to the exemplars to examine more closely the basis for early categorization. Each infant was presented with four conditions with animals and vehicles, the specific exemplars being the same as those used in the earlier experiment. The four conditions are illustrated in table 7.1. In one condition, infants were presented with normal animals and normal vehicles (control task); in a second condition, infants were tested with a contrast of animals without legs and vehicles without wheels (no parts task); in a third condition, they were given a contrast of animals and vehicles, all of which had both legs and wheels (matched parts task); in a final condition, called the across-category confound task, infants were presented with two animals and two vehicles that possessed wheels but no legs, as well as two animals and two vehicles that possessed legs but no wheels. Examples of these stimuli are presented in figure 7.1.

The strength of the across-category confound task is that infants have a "choice" to categorize exemplars by superordinate category membership—by grouping, for example, all the animals together—or by part relations; for example, grouping together two unmodified vehicles with two animals with wheels. Infants' sequential touching behavior across the four contrasts supported the notion that until at least 1½ years of age, parts are sufficient and perhaps necessary for categorization of superordinate-like domains. Infants in all three age groups categorized the unmodified animals as different from the unmodified vehicles, suggesting that they indeed do have knowledge about these domains. However, all three age groups failed to categorize the animals as different from the vehicle when the exemplars possessed legs and wheels (matched parts task) as well as when the exemplars possessed no differentiating large parts (no parts task). The results from the final condition provided even stronger evidence for the role of parts in early categorization: infants at 14 and 18 months grouped objects on the basis of parts relations—that is, "things with legs" and "things with wheels"—rather than superordinate category membership, and infants at 22 months failed to categorize on either basis.

These experiments lend support to the idea that parts act as the basis for early categorization. The ability to form categories at the superordinate level is commonly viewed as evidence of an understanding of the conceptual, or nonobvious, relations that exist between members of those domains (Mandler & Bauer, 1988; Mandler, Bauer, & McDonough, 1991), yet infants' behavior in these experiments seemed to be driven very much by perceptual attributes. It may well be that infants, until at least 22 months of age, do not understand that relations exist within the members of a specific category—for instance, that cats have whiskers—as well as across the members of broader category; for instance, that cats, dogs, and zebras are mammals (Rakison & Butterworth, 1998b; Rakison, 2000a, b). Moreover, infants' behavior in the tasks suggests that they may have formed categories on-line; that is, the items used to form a category may be dependent on those that are available and the attri-

TABLE 7.1. Object Manipulation Tasks and Exemplars in Rakison and Butterworth (1998b, Exp. 2)

Task	Animals	Vehicles
Control task		
Animals	Cow	All-terrain vehicle (ATV)
versus	Dog	Train
Vehicles	Goose	Bus
	Walrus	Motorbike
Matched parts task		
Animals with wheels and legs	Cow with wheels and legs	ATV with wheels and legs
versus	Dog with wheels and legs	Train with wheels and legs
Vehicles with wheels and legs	Goose with wheels and legs	Bus with wheels and legs
	Walrus with wheels and legs	Motorbike with wheels and legs
No parts task		
Animals without legs	Cow without legs	ATV without wheels
versus	Dog without legs	Train without wheels
Vehicle without wheels	Goose without legs	Bus without wheels
	Walrus without legs	Motorbike without wheels
Across-category confound task		
Animals, two with legs and two with wheels	Cow with wheels and without legs	ATV with legs and without wheels
versus	Dogs with wheels and without legs	Train with legs and without wheels
Vehicles, two with legs and two with wheels	Goose	Bus
		Motorbike
or		
Object with wheels	ATV with legs and without wheels	Cow with wheels and without legs
versus		Dog with wheels and without legs
Object with legs	Train with legs and without wheels	Bus
	Goose	Motorbike
	Walrus	

butes possessed by those stimuli (see also Jones & L. Smith, 1993; Oakes, Coppage, & Dingel, 1997; Quinn, Eimas, & Rosenkrantz, 1993).

To investigate whether object parts are also important in early categorization at the basic level, Leslie B. Cohen and I (Rakison & Cohen, 1999) presented 14- to 22-month-old infants with the same four tasks used by Rakison and Butterworth (1998b, exp. 2) with contrasts of cows and cars. A basic-level contrast of this type differs from a superordinate contrast of animals and vehicles in that within-category similarity is relatively high—that is, cows look alike whereas animals do not—though the level of between-category contrast is equivalent in each case; that is, both contrasts are of animals and vehicles. As a further measure of infants' knowledge about

Figure 7.1. Examples of stimuli used by Rakison and Butterworth (1998b, exp. 2).

the motions of the objects represented by the stimuli, we also recorded the number of times that infants made "rolling" or "walking/jumping" actions.

Infants' sequential touching behavior across the four tasks revealed that parts are important in basic-like categorization but that their importance varies depending on the level of within- and between-category similarity. As expected from the experiments by Rakison and Butterworth (1998b), infants at 14, 18, and 22 months of age categorized unmodified cars as different from unmodified cows. Yet in the task in which the parts were removed from the cars and cows, the youngest age group failed to categorize the stimuli as different. Moreover, in the task in which parts were attached to the cars and cows—that is, when they all possessed legs and wheels—the

14- and the 18-month-olds failed to categorize the two stimulus sets as different. The 22-month-olds, in contrast, categorized the cars and the cows as different on all three tasks. Somewhat surprisingly, on the across-category confound task, infants in all three age groups categorized objects not by parts but instead as cows and cars. Overall, these results imply that infants attend to object parts in categorization, but that the level of within-category dissimilarity influences this bias and that perceptual features other than large, functional ones may play a significant role in class membership decisions. For example, infants at 18 months of age categorized cars and cows without legs and wheels as different but categorized cows and cars with both legs and wheels as equivalent. This suggests that in the absence of parts like legs and wheels, 18-month-old infants are able to attend to other feature similarities to form categories, but in a context when stimuli possess legs as well as wheels, the same infants attend to these parts in category formation.

The analyses of infants' functional responses provided an interesting insight into the reason for infants' attention to large parts. Although the overall number of functional behaviors by infants was low, the 14-month-olds as well as the 18-month-olds tended to "roll" and "walk" the toy stimuli with parts more than those without parts, and the 22-month-olds made a similar number of functional responses to those objects with and without parts. Of particular interest was that infants in the across-category confound task, who did not categorize on the basis of parts, tended to "roll" or "walk" the novel stimuli on the basis of their parts rather than their ontological status. That is, instead of making a car with legs "roll," infants made it "walk," and instead of making a cow with wheels "walk," infants made it "roll."

In a further series of experiments, George Butterworth and I (Rakison & Butterworth, 1998a) examined whether infants attend to parts per se or to the structure given by those parts. Infants may group together animals and furniture not because they both possess legs but rather because those parts give objects a similar overall structure; namely, a body with four vertically oriented attributes in a rectangular configuration. In one experiment, for example, we again used the object-manipulation paradigm with 14-, 18-, and 22-month-olds to examine categorization of animals, vehicles, and furniture when object structure was modified in orientation alone (e.g., four legs inverted and placed on top of the body of an object) or in orientation and configuration (e.g., four legs at tangential angles). Infants' sequential touching behavior was consistent with the idea that part structure is as important, if not more important, than the presence of parts themselves; animals were categorized as different from vehicles by 14- and 18-month-olds when parts maintained their configuration but were placed in a novel orientation, but they were not categorized as different when the common configuration of parts was violated.

To summarize, the research on 1- to 2-year-old infants' behavior in the sequential-touching paradigm suggests that parts and part structure play a primary role in category membership decisions. The evidence suggests that object parts such as legs and wheels are sufficient and, depending on the levels of within- and between-category similarity, necessary for categorization. The data also suggest that infants between 14 and 18 months are flexible in the categories they form; that is, they appear to create categories on-line that are dependent on the available stimuli and the attributes of those stimuli. Finally, the data suggest that infants around

14 months of age may have started to connect certain motion characteristics with objects, or more specifically, with the part that are causally related to those motion characteristics.

The Role of Movement

A wide range of evidence supports the idea that movement has an "attention-grabbing" effect on infants. From birth, infants are able visually to track a simple stimulus, and they are more likely to do so for facelike configurations than for random or blank stimuli (Morton & Johnson, 1991). Newborns also show a visual preference for moving stimuli over static ones (Slater, 1989), and infants between the ages of 7 and 21 weeks orient to a small moving object in a visual field of static objects (Dannemiller, 2000). By 2 to 3 months of age, infants' ability to perceive particular characteristics of objects is dependent on the presence of movement cues. For instance, 2-month-olds who are habituated to a moving rod that is partly occluded perceive it as a complete object (Johnson & Aslin, 1995), yet 3- to 4-month-olds do not perceive the rod as complete if the two parts fail to move (Kellman & Spelke, 1983).

Moreover, by 3 months of age infants prefer a moving point-light display of a human to an unstructured or random point-light display, and they show no preference between the same displays when they do not move (Bertenthal, 1993). Along the same lines, recent evidence from Arterberry and Bornstein (in press) suggests that 3-month-old infants can categorize point-light displays of animals as different from point-light displays of vehicles. According to Kellman (1993), this role of motion in specifying an object's characteristics is an innate or maturational *primitive process*, and to this end there is evidence that infants as well as adults more easily detect an object's properties when it moves than when it is still (Burnham & Day, 1979; Washburn, 1993; Werker, Cohen, Lloyd, Casasola, & Stager, 1998).

Why should motion have such a facilitating effect on infants' attention to object properties? I posit that infants, as with other species, find object motion particularly salient because of an evolved adaptive mechanism for predator and prey detection. Many species are known to have visual systems that are specifically designed for their particular environments and the tasks faced in those environments; for instance, the frog retina has a "bug" detector, and the rabbit retina is thought to have, among other things, a "hawk" detector (Marr, 1982). Perhaps more compelling, the seminal work of Seyfarth and Cheney (1986; see also Evans & Marler, 1995) suggests that young vervets use motion cues to identify and categorize potential predators, and they will often make mistaken "eagle" alarm calls for a variety of birds and even nonbirds such as swiftly falling leaves. If other species show such an innate sensitivity to motion, usually in the context of predator or prey identification, I see no reason why humans would not have evolved the same, or at least a similar, visual mechanism. Such a mechanism would be crucial in drawing infants' attention to specific, significant information, or, as Dannemiller (1998) put it, "selective attention mechanisms are necessary to resolve the problems of where to look next in a visual field that is populated with multiple objects (as it usually is)" (p. 269). For the time being, the important message here is that movement, presumably both at a global level (object moves from A to B) and at a local level (part X moves on object A), is highly salient to infants.

The Role of Size

A minor early attention bias concerns the fact that large parts and large objects are initially more salient than small parts and small objects. I use the terms *large* and *small* in relation to size to refer to relative rather than absolute terms. Thus, a large part can be defined as one that composes a relatively high proportion of the whole object of which it is a component, and a small part can be defined as one that composes a relatively low proportion of the whole object of which it is a component. It remains to be seen what the exact part-to-object ratio need be for a part to be considered large or small; nonetheless, it has been shown that, for adults at least, the salience of a part increases as the ratio of its observable area to the observable area of the whole silhouette increases. Research on the role of relative part size on infants' categorizing behavior has not yet been performed; however, there is evidence that newborns possess shape and size constancy (Slater & Morrison, 1985) and that when presented with two identical cubes, they look longest at the one that produces the larger retinal image (Slater, Mattock, & Brown, 1990).

Concept Formation and Associative Learning

Thus far I have argued that infants possess inherent mechanisms that bias them to attend to object parts, and the movement of large attributes and of objects. The section on the role of object parts outlined evidence that infants at the beginning of the second year categorize animate entities and inanimate objects on the basis of attributes such as legs and wheels. This behavior is clearly a case of what is known as perceptual categorization. But how does this early predilection to attend to object parts, as well as to movement, facilitate the development of what is known as "conceptual" categorization? That is, how can attention to the attributes of objects lead to the emergence of concepts that encapsulate motion properties such as self-propulsion and agency or psychological properties such as goal-directed action? This kind of knowledge is what, among other things, allows adults to make the distinction between animate entities and inanimate objects. It is important to note, however, that the categories "animate" and "inanimate" are not naturally occurring in the same way as, for example, "dogs" or "Rottweilers"; more probably, they are constructs of the adult mind that provide an additional, extremely broad grouping of things in the world.

The functional analysis provided by Rakison and Cohen (1999) is, in my opinion, a provocative clue to the nature of the development of infants' knowledge about different object kinds. Recall that the data suggest that infants at 14 and 18 months are starting to relate a movement pattern with the object part with which it is causally related, whereas infants at 22 months have associated movement patterns with specific parts as well as the body of objects. My claim is that the distinctive aspect of attributes such as legs and wheels is that they move, and, perhaps more important, this movement tends to cooccur with a function, motion, or psychologically related act. For example, the legs of an animate entity move predominantly when that entity engages in some kind of locomotion, the wheels of a vehicle move only when that vehicle itself is in motion, and the fingers of an empty hand move conjointly when about to engage in a goal-directed grasp. The salience of local motion and of global motion—that of the attribute and of the whole object, respectively—together are powerful attention-grabbing stimuli; however, it is that infants are able to associate these two dynamic cues that allows them ultimately to go beyond information given in the perceptual array.

My broader claim is that infants possess an inherent domain–general association learning mechanism that, following detection of dynamic as well as static attributes by one or more of the perceptual systems, encodes highly correlated relations among them. In the case of dynamic cues—those relating to motion, for example—these correlations connect a readily perceptually available attribute with a particular action. The result is a represented associative link that embodies what has come to be labeled "conceptual" knowledge or understanding. But I argue that there is no need to apply the kind of rich description to these representations that has been suggested in previous formulations of concept development (e.g., Leslie, 1995; Mandler, 1992; Spelke, Breinlinger, Macomber, & Jacobson, 1992). Instead, these associations should be considered in terms of an *expectation*, such that the perception of one constituent of the correlation elicits an anticipation about the presence of the other (for a more detailed and general discussion of infants' expectations see Haith, Wentworth, & Canfield, 1993; Roberts, 1998). For the kind of expectations outlined here, what is connected is a readily perceptually available attribute—wings, for instance—with an intermittently perceptually available motion characteristic; for example, flying, self-propulsion, and so on.

Initially, after having encountered only a few instances that exhibit a particular relation, the perception of one component of that relation will not necessarily trigger the other component; to depict the noncausal state of this preliminary connection, elsewhere I have labeled it an elementary association (Rakison & Poulin-Dubois, 2001, 2002). Following repeated exposures to the same correlation, the strength of the correlation becomes such that the perception of one part of the correlation can trigger the expectation that the other is present—what I have labeled a secondary association (for a similar view of gradual strengthening of representations, see Munakata, McClelland, Johnson, & Siegler, 1997). It is worth noting at this juncture that I use the term *association* to refer to the mental representation of correlations that exist between spatially or temporally co-occurring attributes objects, properties, or events in the world. I do not use the term to refer to any kind of a stimulus-response connection, because these invariably involve the self rather than external properties exclusively; in other words, I am discussing stimulus-stimulus relations.

I posit that the represented associations, once they have developed sufficiently to allow for expectations to be triggered, may be thought of as the preliminary development of a *meaning* about an object or its attributes. That is, objects that were initially grouped together because they share similar attributes would start to be categorized as equivalent because they engage in similar kinds of actions or functions. Over time, additional attributes and properties of an object become associated with the initial pairing—even if such attributes are not causally related to the action involved—and ultimately, with the onset of labeling, these associations are generalized to whole objects. Even at this point, however, the different kinds of information about objects embodied in representations need not be thought of as conceptual or nonobvious; rather, there is a connection between static and dynamic perceptual cues that allows for categorization that appears to go beyond the information given in the perceptual array.

Within this framework, I propose that any attributes or properties of objects, even those that are classically held to be nonobvious, can be thought of as perceptual because they are represented following input through one or more of the sensory systems. A good deal of this information, particularly that which is referred to as perceptual in the literature, is dealt with by the visual system, as when, for example, an infant observes that a dog has a tail and four legs (see also Eimas, 1994). As an infant becomes older and language becomes a viable input system, information about objects—particularly that referred to as nonobvious—will be acquired through labeling. The information that arrives through these distinct input systems need not be represented in fundamentally different ways. In a similar manner, it is assumed that perceptually readily available surface features—facial features, for example—are represented similarly to those surface features that are less perceptually accessible (e.g., the paws of a dog or a person's belly button). To put it plainly, there is no logical reason why "unobservable" properties should be representationally distinct, in a qualitative sense, from those that are more readily available in the perceptual input.

To make this process clear, consider the example of how infants might come to learn about the properties of dogs, and in particular the motion properties of dogs. This progression is illustrated in figure 7.2. Most probably, infants' first basis for categorization of dogs would be their larger parts such as legs, faces, or tails (e.g., Quinn & Eimas, 1996a; Rakison & Butterworth, 1998b). In line with the global-to-basic trend observed in a number of studies (e.g., Mandler et al., 1991; Mandler & Bauer, 1988; Younger & Fearing, 1999), attention to such parts would not allow for a division of, say, dogs from cats or other similar mammals, but it would allow for a division to be made between dogs and vehicles, plants, tools, and so on. At the same time, infants may start to discriminate the different motion patterns that are characteristic of different object kinds; for example, they might discriminate smooth from irregular motion or self-propelled from caused motion. They would not know, however, which object kinds perform which particular motion (Rakison & Poulin-Dubois, 2001). During the second year of life, following repeated observations of dogs engaging in particular motions (e.g., nonlinear movement, self-propulsion), I suggest that infants would start to associate legs with those motions; that is, "things with legs are self-propelled." Initially, after only a few observations, this association would be weak and would not trigger the kind of expectation discussed earlier; however, following a considerable number of encounters with instances that exhibit the same part-motion relation, the association would become strong enough to allow for prediction of one attribute based on the perception of the other. Again, infants at this point would not categorize dogs as different from cats, but they would treat

Discrimination of irregular from
smooth motion paths

Categorization of objects by parts

Association of causal feature (legs) with irregular motion path

Association of whole object and other features (e.g., tail, facial features) \
with irregular motion path

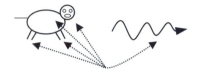

Association of category (e.g., dogs) with irregular motion path

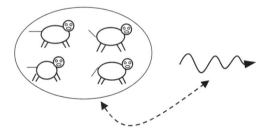

Time

Figure 7.2. Depiction of the development of association-based representations. Time is given on the vertical axis.

furniture, whose legs do not afford movement, as different from dogs. Over time infants would detect other attributes of dogs, and these would start to be incorporated into the initial association, such that the representation can be thought of in terms of "things with legs, eyes, fur, and a tail walk." This process, I suggest, would occur in parallel for a number of different properties connected with dogs; thus, dog mouths would become associated with barking, and tail-wagging would become associated with alert, happy behavior (on the part of the dog, that is).

With the onset of language, I speculate that the associations are drawn together under one label, so that the utterance "dog" triggers the attributes, both static and dynamic, that have come to be associated with dogs. Indeed, I suggest that language plays a singularly important role in this process because it not only allows for the acquisition of properties that are nonobservable but also speeds up the process of representational development by allowing rapid one- or two-shot learning—a form of fast-mapping—of such information, which is then applied across the category. In other words, in contrast to information about objects that is encountered through the visual, tactile, and auditory systems, input from language is assumed by infants to refer not to one particular exemplar but rather to all members of the basic and superordinate category to which the original referent is drawn. For example, if an infant is told that a cat possesses a brain, or cat DNA, following only one or two such labeling episodes, this fact will be extended to dogs, people, cows, and indeed all those exemplars that are considered alike to a cat. This notion, though currently lacking direct empirical support, is in line with infants' overextension errors on the basis of perceptual or featural similarity (see e.g., Nelson, 1974; Rescorla, 1980), preschoolers' attribution errors (Carey, 1985), connectionist simulations of match-to-sample studies (chap. 14), and a number of constraints that are thought to be particular to early word acquisition (see e.g., Markman, 1991; chap. 11).

This proposed view has at its core the idea that representational development is a process of enrichment rather than a stagelike shift in conceptual format and structure. Through a continual accumulation of associations that includes both static and dynamic readily perceptually available properties, as well as those that are less readily perceptually available, infants progressively develop concepts for animates and inanimates that incorporate the various characteristics that make the members of those categories distinct (for adults at least). In this sense, this proposal is very much in line with the view of Quinn and Eimas (1997, 2000; Eimas, 1994; chap. 3). My view differs, however, in a number of fundamental respects from previous proposals that are also grounded in perceptual information. Most notably, in my opinion the current proposal is not weakened by the *insufficiency of constraints* argument that has been levied against previous similarity-based formulations of concept formation (Keil, 1981, 1991; Murphy & Medin, 1985). Recall that the claim is that theories of conceptual structure and content that are based on similarity—as is a theory grounded in the ability to detect and encode clusters of correlated attributes—are doomed to fail because there are so many similarities (or correlations) to which, in principle, one could attend that it is impossible to know which ones are important for category membership. I argue that the position outlined in this chapter overcomes this problem by highlighting attention biases that help to guide infants, as well as children and adults, toward particular attributes and relations among attributes. And it is no accident that these relations tend to be those that are causally relevant and that are good predictors of category membership; the human mind has evolved to carve nature at its joints in a parsimonious, productive, and generally veridical manner.

This view also differs from previous perceptually based formulations in that it outlines how the continuous addition of associative links can operate as a mechanism for representational change. According to previous perceptually based theoretical proposals of concept development (e.g., Eimas, 1994; Jones & Smith, 1993; Quinn and Eimas, 1997), it is not clear how infants develop knowledge that goes beyond the information available in the perceptual input. Eimas (1994), for example, writes that "the common aspects of the features for animate things, for example, biological motion, that are found in the categorical representations for different species are presumed to be recognized and abstracted" (p. 87). According to Eimas, this process of "abstraction" is a form of categorization that leads to the formation of associations between, for example, facial features and legs with locomotion. This is a reasonable claim; yet the continual addition of associative links does not in and of itself explain how infants' concepts start to incorporate that which is held to be nonobvious knowledge. In other words, it does not explain how quantitative representational enrichment leads to qualitative representational change or, at least, the appearance of qualitative representational change. I too argue that infants' representational development is best characterized as a process of enrichment, with associative links added over time. But in addition, I posit that an ever increasingly sensitive perceptual system, along with the emergence of language and advances in motor skills that allow for greater exploration of the environment, causes the appearance of qualitative change. To be more specific, my claim is that infants' representations appear to undergo conceptual change as different kinds of information becomes available to the sensory systems, but the basic learning process is the same for the acquisition of perceptual and "conceptual" information (see also Madole & Oakes, 1999; chap. 6). An infant cannot understand that a dog has a heart because it simply does not have access to this kind of information; however, once language becomes a viable input system, such details can be incorporated into the already existing representation. There is no reason why this process should be thought of in terms of qualitative change, as is often the case in the developmental literature (e.g., Gelman & Markman, 1986; Carey, 1991, 1995). Rather, it is just another case of perceptually given information becoming associated with that which was earlier acquired through the various sensory input systems.

One of the key claims for the qualitative representational difference between perceptual and so-called nonobvious properties is that preschoolers tend to choose the latter to make category membership decision. For instance, when 4-year-olds are asked which of two objects belong with or are "like" a target object, they tend to choose nonobvious properties such as "warm-blooded" or "has a heart" over perceptual features, such as shape, when the two are pitted against each other (e.g., Gelman & Markman, 1986, 1987). However, I believe that such data fit comfortably with the kind of perceptually grounded proposal presented here. After all, this pattern of behavior is to be expected if, as hypothesized, toddlers and young children treat labeled properties such as "this has a brain" as applying broadly across the category of the original stimulus as well as those categories that are judged to be similar to that first category. If this is the case, then children's behavior in the sort of inductive inference tasks described earlier should not be surprising, in that when given a choice between a highly (if not perfectly) correlated property for category membership and a less highly correlated property for category membership, children choose the former over the latter. For instance, it is true to that all dogs possess a heart but not all dogs have tails, and so if the two properties are pitted against each other, the property "has a heart" is a superior bet on which to make an inductive inference. It is important to note, however, that I am not saying that perceptual, surface properties play no role in category membership decisions. On the contrary, I believe that such properties are primary in everyday judgments about "what something is." However, given a choice between two properties, infants, children, and adults will choose the one that is better correlated with category membership (for data supporting this view, see chap. 14).

The continuation of this idea is that in contrast to the widely accepted view that people employ causal explanations to make sense of correlations among features (e.g., Medin & Ortony, 1989; Murphy & Medin, 1985), I propose that it is the associations between properties and causal features formed during infancy that bind or structure concepts. Lay theories, I wish to argue, are later attached to these associations either during formal learning or as and when needed. In many cases, adults know that two features are correlated, but they may have no understanding of the causal relation between those two features, nor need they develop some kind of lay theory to explain it in order to possess a functional concept. For example, I know that the computer I am working on, as with all computers, has some kind of silicon chips inside it, but I have not attempted to develop an explanation for how the chips make the computer function, though I could develop such a theory on-line if one were needed for some reason. Similarly, Smith (2000; see also chap. 11) has argued that the model for all cognition is the dynamic creation of a moment of knowing out of previous moments of knowing; that is, perceiving and remembering are very much influenced by "the immediate input, the just preceding events, and the long-term experience of the perceiver" (Smith; 2000, p. 96). This does not mean, however, that the view presented here is completely at odds with the idea that theories help to provide categories coherence. For instance, Murphy and Medin (1985) argued that "concepts that have their features connected by structure-function relationships or by causal schemata of one sort or another will be more coherent than those that do not" (p. 313). My claim is that the causal link between attributes is inherent in the association between them that is formed early on in life, and when lay theories are developed to explain this causal link they will act to bind or cohere further the concept.

On the surface, at least, it is counterintuitive to consider that gradual associative learning can lead to qualitative changes in behavior. It is therefore worth briefly considering current work on connectionist models of cognition that attest to such a finding (see chap. 14). In particular, Schafer and Mareschal (2001) recently endeavored to model the behavior of 8- and 14-month-old infants in label-object associative learning tasks by Stager and Werker (1997). The results of the original study revealed that the younger age group discriminated two highly similar phonemes (bih-dih) whereas the older age group could only discriminate two relatively distinct ones (lif-neem). To explain these results, Stager and Werker (1997) posited that older and younger infants process the phonemes in qualitatively different ways, such that the 8-month-olds processed the labels phonetically and the 14-month-olds processed the labels phonemically. Furthermore, Stager and Werker (1997) suggested that stagelike transitions were responsible for these qualitatively distinct types of processing. Schaffer and Mareschal (in press) tested this interpretation by examining the ability of "younger" and "older" networks to learn specific label-object pairs within an artificial language. (The "younger" networks were exposed to fewer examples of the artificial language than the "older" networks.) Despite the fact that the connectionist models relied only on associative, continuous learning, the simulations matched closely the behavior of the two age groups in the study by Stager and Werker (1997); that is, the older networks discriminated only the dissimilar phonemes, and the younger network discriminated the similar phonemes.

Can Infants Form Associations?

What evidence is there that infants are capable of forming association-based representations? There is now a considerable database that reveals that well within the first year of life, infants develop the ability to detect and encode clusters of correlated attributes. For instance, by 7 months of age infants perceive correlations among the attributes of a schematic animal, and by 10 months they can extract the same correlations when embedded in a category (Younger & Cohen, 1986; for a review see chap. 4). During the same period, infants also start to attend to dynamic relations. By 4 months, they are capable of detecting nonarbitrary relations, such as the relationship between the shape of a mouth and a vowel sound (Kuhl & Meltzoff, 1982, 1988), and by 7 months they are sensitive to arbitrary intermodal relations, such as the relationship between temporally synchronous vocalizations and moving objects (Gogate & Bahrick, 1998). Notably, however, the ability to process dynamic relations in the first year of life appears to occur only for those that have been frequently encountered by the infant—as is the case for mouth opening and vowel sounds, or in the presence of a *facilitating cue*, such as, in the case of a sound and object relation, temporal synchrony, intensity shift, or common rhythm. This suggests that although infants' associative learning mechanism allows them to learn relations among static and dynamic stimuli in the first 12 months of life, it is not yet fully operational.

Between 12 and 14 months, infants become considerably more adept at detecting and encoding correlations among auditory and visual dynamic cues. An excellent demonstration of this developing ability can be found in a study by Werker et al. (1998) in which 10- and 14-month-old infants were tested with the *Switch* design in the habituation procedure. In the habituation phase of an experiment with this design, infants are shown attribute A^1 paired with attribute B^1 in one trial and attribute A^2 paired with attribute B^2 in another trial. Once habituated to these stimuli, infants are presented with a trial in which the attributes pairings are switched—for example, attribute A^1 is shown with attribute B^2—and a trial in which the attribute pairings remain unchanged from that shown during habituation. In the work by Werker et al. (1998), a label ("lif" or "neem") was one attribute in each habituation trial, and an object (a dog or a truck) was the other attribute. This design is especially ideal for examining infants' ability to learn correlations, because relatively long looking time to the "switch" test trial can only be caused by infants' detection of a novel attribute pairing and not by the introduction of a novel attribute (because no novel attributes are introduced). Indeed, Werker et al. (1998) found that 14-month-olds, but not younger infants, associate a label with an object and do so only when the object in question is moving during the habituation trials. Although infants younger than

14 months did not learn the relation between a label and a word, additional experiments by the same authors (Werker et al., 1998) revealed that they did process independently each of the attributes the events; that is, they processed the object and the label but did not associate them.

There is also evidence that infants between 14 and 18 months are starting to develop the ability to learn correlations that exist between two perceptual cues. Madole, Oakes, and Cohen (1993), for example, used the object-examination paradigm with 10-, 14-, and 18-month-olds to test whether infants could associate an object's form—that is, its shape—with its function. During the habituation phase of the task, infants were familiarized with two different objects that had the same form–function relation (e.g., objects with wheels that rolled). They were then tested with an object that maintained the familiar form-function relation, an object that violated the form-function relationship, and a completely novel object. Results revealed that the 18-month-olds, but not the two younger age groups, learned the correlation between form and function. These data were extended by Madole and Cohen (1995), who examined 14- and 18-month-old infants' ability to attend to form-function relations akin to those found in the real word. Infants were familiarized with objects in which a particular part (e.g., wheels) was correlated with a particular function (e.g., rolling). Infants at both 14 and 18 months learned the relationship between parts and their function, as suggested by their relatively long attention to a stimulus that violated the learned correlation. The authors also familiarized infants with part-function correlations unlike those found in the real world; that is, the form of one part predicted the function of another part. Under these conditions, the younger infants learned the form-function correlation, suggesting that they are unconstrained in the correlations to which they will attend, whereas the older infants responded as if they have not learned the correlation.

As the studies presented in this section suggest, there is considerable evidence that infants in the first 1½ years of life begin to attend to correlations not only among static attributes but also among dynamic ones. Although this evidence suggests that the mechanism for learning about animate entities and inanimate objects comes on-line early in life, it does not provide direct confirmation that infants are able to represent these things via the relation between moving parts and motion characteristics. To examine precisely this issue, I have recently examined infants' ability to attend to correlations among features in a motion event (Rakison & Poulin-Dubois, 2002). In particular, I used a variation of the switch design to test the idea that infants are biased to attend to dynamic attributes in an event and to correlate those attributes. In one series of studies, 10-, 14-, and 18-month-old infants were habituated to two events in which an object moved across a screen. Each object consisted of a combination of a unique moving part (yellow cigar shapes that moved horizontally or green diamond shapes that moved vertically), with a unique body (red oval or blue pot-shape) and a unique motion path (rectilinear or curvilinear). Infants might see during habituation a blue-bodied object with yellow horizontally moving parts traveling along a linear trajectory and a red-bodied object with green vertically moving parts traveling along a curvilinear trajectory (the combination of parts, body, and motion path were counterbalanced across the participants). Examples of the objects and the motion paths are shown in figure 7.3.

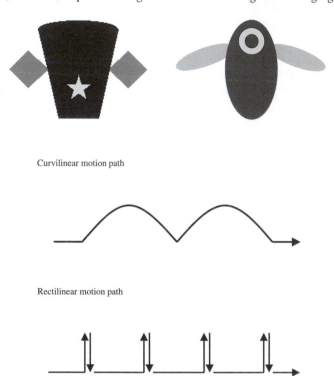

Figure 7.3. *Examples of objects (parts and body) and motion paths of stimuli used by Rakison and Poulin-Dubois (2002).*

During the test phase of the experiment, infants were shown one trial in which the parts were switched in relation to the pairing seen during habituation, one trial in which the body was switched in relation to the pairing seen during habituation, one trial in which the motion was switched compared to that seen earlier, and one trial that was the same as that seen during habituation. For example, given the two habituation stimuli described, in the *parts switch* infants might see the blue-bodied object traveling linearly but with green horizontally moving parts, in the *object switch* they might see the blue-bodied object with green vertically moving parts traveling along a curvilinear trajectory, and in the *motion switch* they might see blue-bodied object with green vertically moving parts traveling along a linear trajectory. It is important to note that during all the test trials, the object parts moved exactly as they had during habituation; in other words, the yellow parts always moved up and down, and the green parts always moved in and out. What is appealing about this design is that it presents infants with multiple correlations among the stimuli—namely, part-trajectory, object-trajectory, part-object, part-object-trajectory—and gives infants the "choice" to attend to one, none, or a number of them. If, during habituation, infants associated object parts with a motion path, they should look longer at the parts switch and the motion switch test trials than at the familiar test trial. If, on the other hand, infants associated the parts and body of the objects, they should look longer at the part switch and the body switch test trials than the familiar trial. If infants attended to the relation between object's bodies and motion trajectory, they should increase visual attention to the body switch and the motion switch test trials compared to the familiar test trial. Finally, if infants associated multiple attributes in the events, they should recover visual fixation to all three test trials relative to the familiar trial.

The results of the experiments not only were consistent with previous research on early attention to dynamic correlations (e.g., Madole & Cohen, 1995; Werker et al., 1998) but also supported the idea that correlations between dynamic cues are privileged in the infants' processing of events. Infants at 10 months of age failed to learn any of the correlations, and a subsequent experiment revealed that they could process independently the static bodies of the objects but not the dynamic parts or motion trajectory of the object. In contrast, infants at 14 months attended to the correlation between an object's parts and its motion trajectory. This is not to say, however, that 14-month-olds did not attend in some respect to part-body relations. As can be seen in figure 7.4, the 14-month-old infants did not recover visual attention to the motion switch, as might be expected. This finding was attributed to the fact that many infants (15 out of 24) looked away from the motion switch test trial early in the event because the part-body relation was not violated and therefore did not see the violation in the part-motion relation. As can also be seen in figure 7.4, the 18-month-olds attended to all of the correlations among the attributes in the event; that is, they had learned that objects with particular parts and a particular body moved in a certain way.

Recall that I earlier argued that the motion of functional parts is crucial in drawing infants' attention to causally relevant relations involving those parts. To test this idea, in a separate experiment 14- and 18-month-olds were presented with the same habituation and tests events as those described here, but in these events the parts of the objects did not move. As can be seen in figure 7.5, 14-month-old infants under these conditions no longer learned the correlation between object parts and a motion trajectory (or any other correlations in the events), and 18-month-olds attended only to the correlation between parts and motion trajectory. The behavior of the older group in this experiment suggested to me that by this age they had learned—that is, they expected—that the external parts of an object are often related to the motion characteristics of that object. Although admittedly speculative based on this limited evidence, this conclusion is consistent with the "hopping" and "rolling" behavior performed by infants on the stimuli without moving parts in the study by Rakison and Cohen (1999).

In line with the position presented earlier in the chapter, these data provide strong support for the idea that infants start to learn about the "nonobvious" characteristics of objects, at least those related to motion, by forming associations between functional, causally relevant object parts and those characteristics. In a short period of time, presumably following repeated exposures to exemplars that exhibit similar relations, infants generalize this association to encompass whole objects. Concurrently, the strength of the associations develop such that expectations about the presence of one component is triggered by observation of the other component; in this way, infants come to expect that "things with legs walk" and "things with wheels roll," and they do not need to see such a thing engaging in an action to know that it is capable of that action.

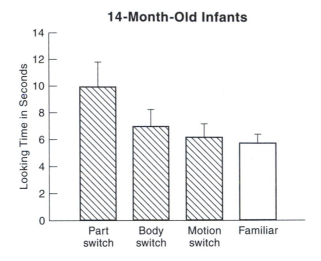

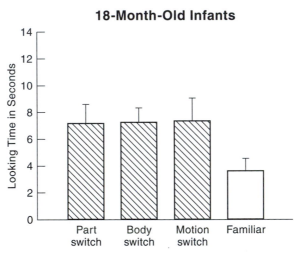

Figure 7.4. Infants' looking time (in seconds) to test stimuli with moving parts in Rakison and Poulin-Dubois (2002, exp. 1). The 14-month-olds looked significantly longer at the part switch test trial (in which the parts–motion correlation is violated) than at the familiar test trial (there were no other reliable effects). The 18-month-olds looked significantly longer at the part, body, and motion switch than at the familiar test trial.

Infants' Knowledge of the Properties
of Animates and Inanimates

It is hopefully evident at this point that the claim here is that the formation of associations leads to a coherent concept rather than the other way round. According to some researchers (e.g., Mandler, 1992, chap. 5), it is an early concept of animal that underlies the formation of associations between attributes of that category and the

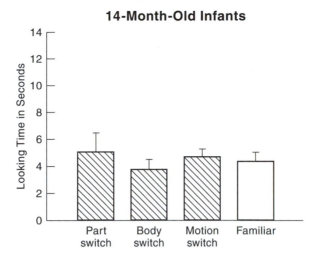

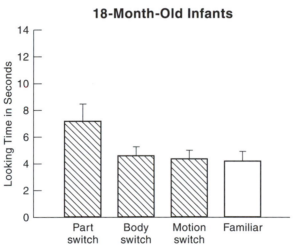

Figure 7.5. Infants' looking time (in seconds) to test stimuli with nonmoving parts in Rakison and Poulin-Dubois (2002, exp. 2). The 14-month-olds looked equally long at all four test trials. The 18-month-olds looked significantly longer at the part switch test trial (in which the parts–motion correlation is violated) than at the familiar test trial (there were no other reliable effects).

characteristics of those attributes (e.g., animals drink and sleep). In my view, this is a case of putting the cart before the horse. It seems the wrong way round to ascribe young infants with relatively advanced concepts that embody the properties of animates and the properties of inanimates and then to suggest that additional, presumably more concrete characteristics of objects are later added to these concepts. Is it not more parsimonious, and indeed fitting with the data, to presume that category and concept formation begins with rudimentary perceptually grounded concepts that are gradually augmented by the addition of information about static and dynamic properties as and when the sensory systems allow? Indeed, in a recent review of the literature on this issue, Rakison and Poulin-Dubois (2001) found very little evidence that infants under 16 months of age had associated motion- or psychological-related characteristics to animates or inanimates. The one exception to this rule was that in many cases infants had associated animate-appropriate properties to people (e.g., Poulin-Dubois, Lepage, & Ferland, 1996; Woodward, 1998, 1999).

If, as has been suggested (e.g., Mandler, 2000, chap. 5), infants have concepts for animates and inanimates—or perhaps more simply for animals and vehicles—one would expect them to display knowledge of the properties of the members of these categories. Accordingly, Mandler and McDonough (1996, 1998) have used the generalized imitation, or *inductive generalization*, procedure in a series of studies to test exactly this issue. Mandler (chap. 5) provides an excellent summary of these studies, and I highlight here only two aspects of the results that appear to provide support for a precocious infant concept former. First, when an experimenter models a dog drinking from a cup or a car being "started" with a key, 14-month-olds are more likely to generalize those behaviors to a novel appropriate exemplar (a cat for the drinking and a truck for the keying) than to a novel inappropriate exemplar (Mandler & McDonough, 1996). Second, when an experimenter models the same kind of events as those described earlier with both an appropriate and an inappropriate exemplar— for instance, a dog and a car are shown to drink from a cup—infants model the event with the correct novel category member. These results, in conjunction with those from a number of other experiments (e.g., Mandler & McDonough, 1998), were interpreted to mean that infants know that animals engage in certain actions and vehicles engage in different actions.

There are a number of reasons to doubt this rich explanation of the data, however. Elsewhere, I have argued that infants' behavior in inductive generalization studies can be explained by processes of perceptual matching and imitation (Rakison & Poulin-Dubois, 2000, 2001); that is, during the test phase of the task, infants do not demonstrate any kind of conceptual knowledge but rather they choose to imitate the observed events with the exemplar that is most perceptually similar to that used by the experimenter. Infants observe an action modeled by an experimenter with a certain exemplar—usually a prototypical animal or vehicle—and they then choose the most similar available stimulus to that exemplar during the test phase of the experiment. Indeed, in tasks in which the two test stimuli are perceptually similar— a cat and a dog, for example—infants tend to use both of them to repeat the observed action (Mandler & McDonough, 1998; chap. 5). There is no need for infants to make any kind of induction about the capabilities of either the exemplar used to model the events or the stimuli presented during the test phase. In all likelihood, adults would use the same kind of procedure if they were shown a completely novel task and offered the chance to repeat that task with one of two novel exemplars, one of which was similar to the original stimulus and one that was not similar.

I have recently used the inductive generalization technique to test 14- and 18-month-old infants' understanding of the motions of animals and vehicles (Rakison & Poulin-Dubois, 2000). Following a baseline phase, an experimenter modeled with a dog a motion event typical of an animal—jumping over a block or going upstairs—or modeled with a car a motion event typical of a vehicle: jumping from one ramp to another (what we called the Evel Knievil jump) or moving back and forth on a U-shaped ramp. To make the events salient to the infants, each one was accompanied by a neutral sound such as "wee" for the ramp-jumping event. These events are illustrated in figure 7.6. In the test phase, infants were presented with two stimuli, one from the vehicle domain (a motorbike, a truck, a bus, or a tractor) and one from the animal domain (a rabbit, a cat, a horse, or a cow). Infants' behavior in the task suggested that they have started to develop knowledge about the motion capabilities of animals and vehicles; that is, both age groups performed more actions with the appropriate exemplar in the generalization phase than in the baseline phase. However, the low level of responses in the task—both age groups repeated about one of the four events—and the fact that the 18-month-olds showed no improvement in performance over the 14-month-olds suggested that other factors may have been at work.

To test the robustness of these data and the hypothesis that perceptual matching and imitation drove infants' behavior, in a second experiment the same tasks were presented to infants except that an inappropriate exemplar was used to model the tasks; for example, the experimenter modeled the stairs event with a car rather than a dog. As can be seen in figure 7.7, a quite different pattern of results from that of the earlier experiment was found. Infants in both age groups chose to model the events with an inappropriate exemplar—using the "distractor" truck to go upstairs, for example—with the same regularity that they had used the appropriate exemplar—the "target"—in the first experiment. Note that although the performance of infants with the target stimulus appears to be high in the test phase,

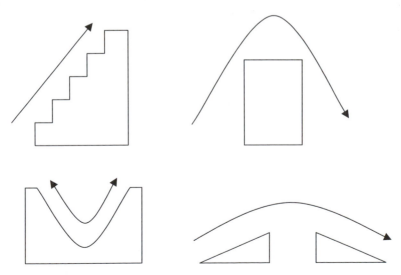

Figure 7.6. Schematics of motion events shown to 14- and 18-month-old infants in Rakison and Poulin-Dubois (2000).

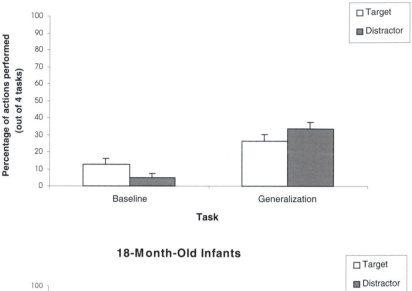

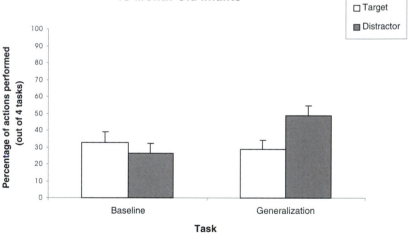

Figure 7.7. Percentage of 14- and 18-month-old infants in the inductive generalization paradigm using the target (appropriate) or distractor (inappropriate) exemplar across four tasks in which a distracter exemplar was used to model the action.

there was no significant increase between performance in that phase and that in the baseline condition.

It is possible that infants' tendency to model events with the distractor exemplar in the experiment just described resulted from the fact that they possessed little knowledge about the relatively specific events that were used. It could be argued, for example, that infants have had relatively little experience with events such as "going upstairs" or "a U-shaped ramp" and that in the absence of such knowledge, infants applied a matching and imitation procedure to complete the tasks. To address this issue, in a separate study (Rakison & Poulin-Dubois, 2000) infants were tested with general motion characteristics thought to be among the earliest learned (see e.g., Leslie & Keeble, 1987; Mandler, 1992), namely, the motion path of an object (smooth vs. irregular) and causal role (agent vs. recipient). To test early knowledge of path of motion, during the modeling phase for one condition infants observed a car rolling along a block, and for another condition they observed a dog "hopping" along a block. To test early knowledge of causal role, during the modeling phase for two conditions infants observed a dog move down a set of stairs and contact a car, which then proceeded to move. For one of these trials, infants were then asked to replace the agent with either a novel animal or novel vehicle, and in the other trial they were asked to replace the recipient with either a novel animal or novel vehicle. Note that although vehicles can appear to act as agents of an action and animals can be the recipients of an action, the prototypical roles played by agents and recipients tend to be animates and inanimates respectively.

Two separate sets of 14-month-olds were tested: One group observed the events modeled with the appropriate, or target, exemplar (as described earlier), and the other group observed the events modeled with the inappropriate, or distractor, exemplar; for example, a dog was observed hopping or a car was observed acting as an agent. Consistent with the results of the earlier experiments, infants repeated the events with the most similar exemplar to that observed during the modeling phase. Thus, infants would use, for example, a rabbit as an agent if the dog was observed in that role during the modeling phase. On other hand, and as can be seen in figure 7.8, infants would use a tractor as an agent if the car was observed as the agent during the modeling phase.

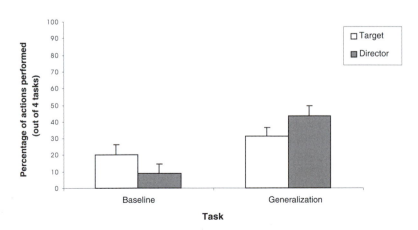

14-Month-Old Infants: Distractor Modeled Action

Figure 7.8. Percentage of 14-month-old infants in the inductive generalization paradigm using the target (appropriate) or distracter (inappropriate) exemplar across four tasks in which an inappropriate exemplar was used to model the action.

I believe that these experiments, which constitute the first systematic attempt to examine infants' knowledge about the various motions of animals and vehicles, provide strong evidence that responses in the inductive generalization tasks are only partially driven by knowledge about the objects and events tested (see Mandler, 2000, chap. 5; Mandler & McDonough, 1996, 1998). Does this mean that infants around 14 to 18 months of age have not yet associated any motion characteristics with specific object kinds or the parts of those kinds? The habituation-based experiments described earlier suggest that it is not until 14 months or so that infants become able to represent dynamic correlations, and the fact that this ability emerges between 10 and 14 months implies that it is not until some time later that dynamic correlations in the real world are encoded. This is not to say, however, that infants necessarily brought no previous understanding about the motions of animals and vehicles to the inductive generalization tasks. For example, Mandler and McDonough (1998) found that infants in the inductive generalization paradigm, irrespective of the exemplar used in the modeling phase, will use a vehicle and an animal to repeat domain-general properties such as going into a building. It is quite possible that this sort of behavior suggests that infants possess broad knowledge about the activities of objects—that is, they are aware that things go in and out of different places—although it is just as likely that infants had no knowledge about these actions and used the available stimuli randomly. Nevertheless, the data presented in this chapter suggest that infants' responses in the inductive generalization task might well be guided by a process of perceptual matching and imitation rather than by a process of categorical induction. It is difficult to envisage an alternative explanation for why infants tended to imitate motion events with the inappropriate category after having seen an experimenter model those events with a prototypical member of that inappropriate category.

Concluding Remarks

I have argued in this chapter that the basic process underlying concept formation is that of associative learning. This inherent learning mechanism comes on-line in the first year of life, but it is constrained at this point by the relative incompetence of the various sensory systems. As infants' visual system improves, for example, so they are able to detect more fine-grained detail among the static features of objects, as well as being able to locate various dynamic cues at the local and global level. Likewise, as language starts to develop more fully in the second year, infants can use it to obtain substantial information about the properties of objects, most notably those that are not directly available in the perceptual array.

Infants' first concepts of animate entities and inanimate objects, and the category membership judgments that follow from them, are presumably grounded in static perceptual cues such as legs, wheels, facial features, and so on (Quinn & Eimas, 1996a, 1997; Rakison & Butterworth, 1998b). As dynamic information becomes available to the visual and auditory systems around the beginning of the second year of life, it is associated to the initial concepts such that infants begin to expect that an object that possesses a particular attribute will be capable of exhibiting a particular behavior, or that an object that exhibits a particular behavior will possess a certain attribute. This process gives rise to the appearance of qualitative change—in the sense that categorization might at this point be based on cues that are not readily available in the perceptual input—but it is clearly a case of gradual enrichment, or quantitative development. With the onset of language, concepts again seem to undergo a radical change. Objects are categorized on the basis of labels and shape, and then later, around 3 or 4 years, on the basis of nonobservable attributes depending on the context. As I have argued in this chapter, a relatively simple process of associative learning can account for these putative changes without the need to invoke some kind of specialized process for the abstraction of different properties of objects or dual processes that deal with perceptual and conceptual information independently (see Mandler, 1992, 2000).

The idea that not all correlations are born equal is likely to raise a few eyebrows. It has been widely accepted that the "insufficiency of constraints" argument is a fatal one for perceptually based views of concept development, largely because no one has yet proposed any kind of organizing principle that would act to constrain perception in the process of category and concept formation (Keil, 1991; Murphy & Medin, 1985). There is no longer a reason for researchers to be limited by such a view. As I have attempted to demonstrate here, it is important to discover on what properties or attributes infants, children, and adults base their category membership decisions and to seek to understand why those bases are salient or important rather than any others. The data reviewed in this chapter suggest that young infants are predisposed to attend to static cues and that older infants attend to dynamic cues—both at the global level, in terms of objects, and at the local level, in terms of the parts of those objects—and that by 14 months or so, they are able to associate these kinds of cues. I believe that this chapter provides a first step in providing a truly perceptual account of concept development by highlighting attributes that are potential candidates for attracting infants' attention toward the information that is relevant for category membership. Undoubtedly, there are many more important salient attributes of objects, as well as other mechanisms for learning—such as, for example, the predilection to habituate to familiar stimuli—that are not discussed here. One task for researchers in the years to come is to identify what these salient attributes and learning mechanisms are and to discover their role in the early representational development of infants.

Acknowledgments

Thanks to Lisa Oakes for helpful comments on a previous version of this chapter and to Annika Fasnacht and Marta Biarnes for help in preparation. Correspondence should be addressed to David H. Rakison, Department of Psychology, Carnegie Mellon University, 5000 Forbes Avenue, Pittsburgh, PA 15213. (*rakison@andrew.cmu.edu.*).

Notes

1. Throughout the chapter I use the terms *property* and *characteristic* to refer to any predicate that can be asserted of some or all of the members of a category (Hampton & Dubois, 1993). I use the terms *attribute* and *feature* to refer to particular aspects of a property or charac-

teristic, whereby an attribute or feature is a property with a number of independent states or possibilities. For example, the property "is large" can be considered in terms of the attribute "size," and, likewise, the characteristic "self-propelled movement" can be considered in terms of the attribute "manner of initial motion."

2. I rely on Smith's (1995) definitions in my discussion of categories and concepts. To categorize something is to decide that it is a member of a category of objects, events, or properties that belong together. Mental representations of categories are used to decide which things belong together, and it is these mental representation that are referred to as concepts. Thus, in line with Margolis's (1994) view, the term *category* tends to refer to collections of things in the world, whereas the term *concept* refers to the representation of those collections.

References

Arterberry, M. E., & Bornstein M. H. (in press). Three-month-old infants' categorization of animals and vehicles based on static and dynamic attributes. *Journal of Experimental Child Psychology.*

Backscheider, A. G., Shatz, M., & Gelman, S. (1993). Preschoolers' ability to distinguish living kinds as a function of regrowth. *Child Development, 64,* 1242–1257.

Behl-Chadha, G. (1996). Basic-level and superordinate-like categorical representations in early infancy. *Cognition, 60,* 105–141.

Bertenthal, B. (1993). Infants' perception of biomechanical motions: Intrinsic image and knowledge based constraints. In C. Granrud (Ed.), *Visual perception and cognition in infancy: Carnegie-Mellon Symposia on Cognition* (Vol. 23), pp. 175–214). Hillsdale, NJ: Erlbaum.

Biederman, I. (1985). Human image understanding: Recent research and a theory. *Computer Vision, Graphics, and Image Processing, 32,* 29–73.

Biederman, I. (1987). Recognition-by-components: A theory of human image understanding. *Psychological Review, 94,* 115–147.

Biederman, I. (1990). Higher-level vision. In D. N. Osherman, S. M. Kosslyn, & J. M. Holerbach (Eds.), *Visual cognition and action: An invitation to cognitive science.* (pp. 41–72). Cambridge, MA: MIT Press.

Burnham, D. K., & Day, R. H. (1979). Detection of color in rotating objects by infants and its generalization over changes in velocity. *Journal of Experimental Child Psychology, 6,* 191–204.

Carey, S. (1985). *Conceptual change in childhood.* Cambridge, MA: MIT Press.

Carey, S. (1991). Knowledge acquisition: Enrichment or conceptual change? In S. Carey & R. Gelman (Eds.), *The epigenesis of mind: Essays in biology and cognition* (pp. 1257–1291). Hillsdale, NJ: Erlbaum.

Carey, S. (1995). Continuity and discontinuity in cognitive development. In E. E. Smith & D. N. Osherson (Eds.), *Thinking: An invitation to cognitive science* (pp. 101–129). Cambridge, MA: MIT Press.

Clarkson, M. G., Clifton, R.K., & Morrongiello, B. A. (1985). The effects of sound duration on newborn's head orientation. *Journal of Experimental Child Psychology, 39,* 20–36.

Cohen, L. B., & Younger, B. A. (1984). Infant perception of angular relations. *Human Behavior and Development, 7,* 37–47.

Dannemiller, J. L. (1998). A competition model of exogenous orienting in 3.5-month-old infants. *Journal of Experimental Child Psychology, 68,* 169–201.

Dannemiller, J. L. (2000). Competition in early exogenous orienting between 7 and 21 weeks. *Journal of Experimental Child Psychology, 76,* 253–274.

Eimas, P. D. (1994). Categorization in infancy and the continuity of development. *Cognition, 50,* 83–93.

Evans, C. S., & Marler, P. (1995). Language and animal communication: Parallels and contrasts. In H. L. Roitblat & J. Meyer (Eds.), *Comparative approaches to cognitive science* (pp. 341–382). Cambridge, MA: MIT Press.

Fantz, R. L. (1961). The origin of form perception. *Scientific American, 204,* 66–72.

Gelman, S. A., & Coley, J. D. (1990). The importance of knowing a dodo is a bird: Categories and inferences in 2-year-old children. *Developmental Psychology, 26,* 796–804.

Gelman, S. A., and Markman, E. M. (1986). Categories and induction in young children. *Cognition, 23,* 183–209.

Gelman, S. A., & Markman, E. M. (1987). Young children's inductions from natural kinds: The role of categories and appearances. *Child Development, 58,* 1532–1541.

Gogate, L. J., & Bahrick, L. E. (1998). Intersensory redundancy facilitates learning of arbitrary relations between vowel sounds and objects in seven-month-old infants. *Journal of Experimental Child Psychology, 69,* 133–149.

Haith, M., Wentworth, N., & Canfield, R. (1993). The formation of expectations in early infancy. In C. Rovee Collier & L. P. Lipsitt (Eds.), *Advances in infancy research* (Vol. 8, pp. 217–249). Norwood, NJ: Ablex.

Hampton, J., & Dubois, D. (1993). Psychological models of concepts. In I. V. Mechelen, J. Hampton, R. S. Michalski, & P. Theuns (Eds.), *Categories and concepts: Theoretical views and inductive data analysis.* London: Academic Press.

Hoffman, D. D., & Richards, W. A. (1984). Parts of recognition. *Cognition, 18,* 65–96.

Johnson, S. P., & Aslin, R. (1995). Perception of object unity in 2-month-old infants. *Developmental Psychology, 31,* 739–745.

Jones, S. S., & Smith, L. B. (1993). The place of perception in children's concepts. *Cognitive Development, 8,* 113–139.

Keil, F. C. (1981). Constraints on knowledge and cognitive development. *Psychological Review, 88,* 197–227.

Keil, F. C. (1989). *Concepts, kinds, and cognitive development.* Cambridge, MA: MIT Press.

Keil, F. C. (1991). The emergence of theoretical beliefs as constraints on concepts. In S. Carey & R. Gelman (Eds.), *The epigenesis of mind* (pp. 133–169). Hillsdale, NJ: Erlbaum.

Kellman, P. J. (1993). Kinematic foundations of infant visual perception. In C. Granrud (Ed.), *Visual perception and cognition in infancy* (pp. 121–173). Hillsdale, NJ: Erlbaum.

Kellman, P. J., & Spelke, E. S. (1983). Perception of partly occluded objects in infancy. *Cognitive Psychology, 15,* 483–524.

Kuhl, P. K., & Meltzoff, A. N. (1982). The bimodal perception of speech in infancy. *Science, 218,* 1138–1141.

Kuhl, P. K., & Meltzoff, A. N. (1988). Speech as an intermodal object of perception. In A. Yonas (Ed.), *Perceptual development in infancy: The Minnesota Symposia on Child Psychology* (Vol. 20, pp. 235–266). Hillsdale, NJ: Erlbaum.

Leslie, A. (1995). A theory of agency. In D. Sperber, D. Premack, & A. J. Premack (Eds.), *Causal cognition* (pp. 121–141). Oxford: Clarendon.

Leslie, A. M., & Keeble, S. (1987). Do six-month-old infants perceive causality? *Cognition, 25,* 265–288.

Madole, K. L., & Cohen, L. B. (1995). The role of object parts in infants' attention to form-function correlations. *Developmental Psychology, 31,* 637–648.

Madole, K. L., & Oakes, L. M. (1999). Making sense of infant categorization: Stable processes and changing representations. *Developmental Review, 19,* 263–296.

Madole, K. L., Oakes, L. M., & Cohen, L. B. (1993). Developmental changes in infants' attention to function and form-function correlations. *Cognitive Development, 8,* 189–209.

Mandler, J. M. (1988). How to build a baby: On the development of an accessible representational system. *Cognitive Development, 3,* 113–136.

Mandler, J. M. (1992). How to build a baby: II. Conceptual primitives. *Psychological Review*, 99, 587–604.

Mandler, J. M. (1997). Development of categorisation: Perceptual and conceptual categories. In G. Bremner, A. Slater, & G. Butterworth (Eds.), *Infant development: Recent advances* (pp. 163–189). Hillsdale, NJ: Erlbaum.

Mandler, J. M. (2000). Perceptual and conceptual processes in infancy. *Journal of Cognition and Development*, 1, 3–36.

Mandler, J. M., & Bauer, P. J. (1988). The cradle of categorization: Is the basic level basic? *Cognitive Development*, 3, 247–264.

Mandler, J. M., Bauer, P. J., & McDonough, L. (1991). Separating the sheep from the goats: Differentiating global categories. *Cognitive Psychology*, 23, 263–298.

Mandler, J. M., & McDonough, L. (1996). Drinking and driving don't mix: Inductive generalization in infancy. *Cognition*, 59, 307–335.

Mandler, J. M., & McDonough, L. (1998). Studies in inductive inference in infancy. *Cognitive Psychology*, 37, 60–96.

Margolis, E. (1994). A reassessment of the shift from classical theory of concepts to prototype theory. *Cognition*, 51, 73–89.

Markman, E. M. (1991). The whole-object, taxonomic and mutual exclusivity assumptions as initial constraints on word meanings. In S. A. Gelman & J. A Byrnes (Eds.), *Perspectives on language and thought* (pp. 72–106). Cambridge: Cambridge University Press.

Marr, D. (1982). *Vision*. San Francisco: Freedman.

Massey, C. M., & Gelman, R. (1988). Preschoolers' ability to decide whether a photographed unfamiliar object can move itself. *Developmental Psychology*, 24, 307–317.

Medin, D. L., & Ortony, A. (1989). Psychological essentialism. In S. Vosniadou & A. Artony (Eds.), *Similarity and Anological Reasoning*. New York: Cambridge University Press.

Morton, J., & Johnson, M. H. (1991). CONSPEC and CONLERN: A two-process theory of infant recognition. *Psychological Review*, 98, 164–181.

Munakata, Y., McClelland, J. L., Johnson, M. H., & Siegler, R. S. (1997). Rethinking infant knowledge: Toward an adaptive process account of successes and failures in object permanence tasks. *Psychological Review*, 104, 686–713.

Murphy, G. L., & Medin, D. L. (1985). The role of theories in conceptual coherence. *Psychological Review*, 92, 289–316.

Nelson, K. (1974). Concept, word and sentence: Interrelations in acquisition and development. *Psychological Review*, 81, 267–285.

Oakes, L. M., Coppage, D. J., & Dingel, A. (1997). By land or sea: The role of perceptual similarity in infants' categorization of animals. *Developmental Psychology*, 33, 396–407.

Palmer, S. E. (1977). Hierarchical structure in perceptual representation. *Cognitive Psychology*, 9, 441–474.

Palmer, S. E., Rosch, E., and Chase, P. (1981). Canonical perspective and the perception of objects. In J. B. Long and A. D. Baddeley (Eds.), *Attention and performance* (Vol. 9, pp. 135–151). Hillsdale, NJ: Erlbaum.

Piaget, J. (1952). *The origins of intelligence in the childhood*. New York: International Universities Press.

Poulin-Dubois, D., Lepage, A., & Ferland, D. (1996). Infants' concept of animacy. *Cognitive Development*, 11, 19–36.

Quinn, P. C., & Eimas, P. D. (1996b). Perceptual organization and categorization in young infants. In C. Rovee-Collier & L. P. Lipsitt (Eds.), *Advances in infancy research* (Vol. 11, pp. 1–36). Norwood, NJ: Ablex.

Quinn, P. C., & Eimas, P. D. (1996a). Perceptual cues that permit categorical differentiation of animal species by infants. *Journal of Experimental Child Psychology*, 63, 189–211.

Quinn, P. C., & Eimas, P. D. (1997). A reexamination of the perceptual-to-conceptual shift in mental representations. *Review of General Psychology, 1,* 271–287.

Quinn, P. C., & Eimas, P. D. (2000). The emergence of category representations during infancy: Are separate perceptual and conceptual processes required? *Journal of Cognition and Development, 1,* 55–61.

Quinn, P. C., Eimas, P. D., & Rosenkrantz, S. L. (1993). Evidence for representations of perceptually similar natural categories by 3-month-olds and 4-month-old infants. *Perception, 22,* 463–475.

Rakison, D. H., (2000b). When a rose is just a rose: The illusion of taxonomies in infant categorization. *Infancy, 1,* 77–90.

Rakison, D. H. (2000a). A correlation-based mechanism of representational development. Manuscript submitted for publication.

Rakison, D. H., & Butterworth, G. (1998b). Infants' use of parts in early categorization. *Developmental Psychology, 34,* 49–62.

Rakison, D. H., & Butterworth, G. (1998a). Infant attention to object structure in early categorization. *Developmental Psychology, 34,* 1310–1325.

Rakison, D. H., & Cohen, L. B. (1999). Infants' use of functional parts in basic-like categorization. *Developmental Science, 2,* 423–432.

Rakison, D. H., & Poulin-Dubois, D. (2000, July). Infants' understanding of animate and inanimate motion events. In D. H. Rakison (Chair), *Components of the animate-inanimate distinction in infancy.* Paper presented at the twelfth Biennial International Conference on Infant Studies, Brighton, UK.

Rakison, D. H., & Poulin-Dubois, D. (2001). The developmental origin of the animate-inanimate distinction. *Psychological Bulletin, 127,* 209–228.

Rakison, D. H., & Poulin-Dubois, D. (2002). You go this way and I'll go that way: Developmental changes in infants' attention to correlations among dynamic features in motion events. *Child Development, 73,* 682–699.

Rescorla, L. (1980). Overextension in early language development. *Journal of Child Language, 7,* 321–335.

Roberts, K. (1998). Linguistic and nonlinguistic factors influencing infant categorization: Studies of the relationship between cognition and language. In C. Rovee Collier & L. P. Lipsitt (Eds.), *Advances in infancy research* (Vol. 11, pp. 45–107). London: Ablex.

Rosch, E. (1978). Principles of categorization. In E. Rosch, & B. Lloyd (Eds.), *Cognition and categorization* (pp. 27–48). Hillsdale, NJ: Erlbaum.

Rosch, E., Mervis, C. B., Gray, W. D., Johnson, D. M., & Boyes-Braem, P. (1976). Basic objects in natural categories. *Cognitive Psychology, 8,* 382–439.

Salapatek, P. (1975). Pattern perception in infancy. In L. B. Cohen & P. Salapatek (Eds.), *Infant perception from sensation to cognition.* (Vol. 1, pp. 133–248). New York: Academic Press.

Schafer, G., & Mareschal, D. (2001). Modeling infant speech sound discrimination using simple associative networks. *Infancy, 2,* 7–28.

Seyfarth, R. M., & Cheney, D. L. (1986). Vocal development in vervet monkeys. *Animal Behavior, 34,* 1640–1658.

Siegler, R. S. (1996). *Emerging minds: The process of change in children's thinking.* New York: Oxford University Press.

Siegler, R. S. (2000). The rebirth of children's learning. *Child Development, 71,* 26–35.

Slater, A. M. (1989). Visual memory and perception in early infancy. In A. Slater & G. Bremner (Eds.), *Infant development* (pp. 43–72). Hove, UK: Erlbaum.

Slater, A. M., Mattock, A., & Brown, E. (1990). Size constancy at birth: Newborn infants' responses to retinal and real size. *Journal of Experimental Child Psychology, 49,* 314–322.

Slater, A. M., Mattock, A., Brown, E., & Bremner, J. G. (1991). Form perception at birth: Cohen and Younger (1984) revisited. *Journal of Experimental Child Psychology, 51*, 395–405.

Slater, A. M., Mattock, A., Brown, E., Burnham, D., & Young, A. W. (1991). Visual processing of stimulus compounds in newborn babies. *Perception, 20*, 29–33.

Slater, A. M., & Morrison, V. (1985). Shape constancy and slant perception at birth. *Perception, 14*, 337–344.

Smith, E. E. (1995). Concepts and categorization. In E. E. Smith & D. N. Osherson (Eds.), *Thinking: An invitation to cognitive science* (pp. 3–33). Cambridge, MA: MIT Press.

Smith, L. B. (2000). From knowledge to knowing: Real progress in the study of infant categorization. *Infancy, 1*(1), 91–97.

Smith, L. B., & Heise, D. (1992). Perceptual similarity and conceptual structure. In B. Burns (Ed.), *Percepts, concepts, and categories* (pp. 233–273). Amsterdam: Elsevier.

Springer, K., & Keil, F. C. (1991). Early differentiation of causal mechanisms appropriate to biological and nonbiological kinds. *Child Development, 62*, 767–781.

Spelke, E. S., Breinlinger, K., Macomber, J., & Jacobson, K. (1992). Origins of knowledge. *Psychological Review, 99*, 605–632.

Stager, C. L., & Werker, J. F. (1997). Infants listen for more phonetic detail in speech perception tasks than in word-learning tasks. *Nature 388*, 381–382.

Triesman, A. (1986). Properties, parts, and objects. In K. Boff, L. Kaufman, & J. Thomas (Eds.), *Handbook of Perception and Human Performance*, Vol. 2, (pp. 1–70). New York: Wiley.

Tversky, B. (1989). Parts, partonomies, and taxonomies. *Developmental Psychology, 25*, 983–995.

Washburn, D. A. (1993). The stimulus movement effect: Allocation of attention or artifact. *Journal of Experimental Psychology: Animal Behavior Process, 29*, 257–302.

Werker, J. F., Cohen, L. B., Lloyd, V. L., Casasola, M., & Stager, C. L. (1998). Acquisition of word-object associations by 14-month-old infants. *Developmental Psychology, 34*, 1289–1309.

Woodward, A. L. (1998). Infants selectively encode the goal object of an actor's reach. *Cognition, 69*, 1–34.

Woodward, A. L. (1999). Infants' ability to distinguish between purposeful and nonpurposeful behaviors. *Infant Behavior and Development, 22*.

Younger, B. A. (1993). Understanding category members as "the same sort of thing": Explicit categorization in ten-month infants. *Child Development, 64*, 309–320.

Younger, B. A., & Cohen, L. B. (1983). Infant perception of correlations among attributes. *Child Development, 54*, 858–867.

Younger, B. A., & Cohen, L. B. (1986). Developmental change in infants' perception of correlations among attributes. *Child Development, 57*, 803–815.

Younger, B. A., & Fearing, D. D. (1999). Parsing items into separate categories: Developmental change in infant categorization. *Child Development, 70*, 291–303.

CHAPTER EIGHT

Commentary on Part I
Unresolved Issues in Infant Categorization

Leslie B. Cohen

I T IS A PLEASURE to be able to contribute to this excellent book on early categorization and its development. I have had the good fortune to collaborate with some
of the authors in the infant section of the book and I am delighted by the way that
they, and others, have built on the early demonstration studies we and others reported in the 1970s. Today infant categorization is one of the foremost areas within
infant cognition, and rightly so.

The ability to categorize is so fundamental that even young infants must possess
it to some degree. It allows infants and adults alike to represent groups of objects
and events in the world and to act on the basis of those representations. Infants, as
well as adults, must be able to acquire at least some types of categories. Consider
what life would be like if they could not. Given that no two experiences are identical, learning from prior experience would be nonexistent and anticipating regularities in the world would be impossible. Oakes and Madole (chap. 6) make a similar
point, albeit more conservatively. According to them, "the ability to categorize may
be especially important in infancy, when an enormous amount of new information
is encountered every day. By forming groups of similar objects, infants can effectively reduce the amount of information they must process, learn, and remember"
(p. 132). But even if we can agree that from the outset young infants possess the ability to categorize, some of the most significant issues still remain. For example, what
exactly is the nature of these earliest categories and how do they change with development and experience?

In this chapter I shall raise a number of issues regarding infant categorization,
such as those just mentioned, that in my opinion have not yet been resolved. Many
of the issues I will address actually have been around for some time. Several were

raised as soon as evidence of infant categorization began to appear. Some, such as the difference between perceptual and conceptual categories, are currently being hotly debated (see chaps. 3, 5, 6, and 7). Other issues, however, such as whether there is a fundamental difference between very young infants' versus older infants' categories, are rarely emphasized. By identifying, or in some cases resurrecting, such issues my intent is to encourage us to consider early categorization in a slightly broader context, to stimulate some new ways of thinking about it, and possibly to generate additional researchable ideas.

Definition of Infant Categorization

I would like to begin with what must be one of the core issues in infant categorization: How does one know when infants have formed a category? Quinn (chap. 3) provides the usual operational definition of categorization. He writes: "categorization is assumed to occur when observers respond in an equivalent manner to discriminably different stimuli" (p. 52). Cohen and Younger (1983) proposed a similar definition, some years earlier, of categorization as "a recognized equivalence among stimuli, objects, or events that are discriminably different" (pp. 197–198). By employing this type of operational definition, both we and Quinn were emphasizing two essential conditions that must be satisfied before one can claim evidence for infant categorization: first, that infants respond equivalently to the various exemplars comprising the category, and second, that this responding occurs even when the exemplars are highly discriminable from one another.

The earliest report I know of on infant categorization satisfied both of these conditions. I find it interesting that this study is almost never mentioned in the infant categorization literature. Perhaps that is because the author, the late Harry McGurk, probably did not realize he was inventing a classic paradigm for studying infant categorization. He assumed, as the title of his article, "Infant Discrimination of Orientation," suggests, that he was examining the development of orientation perception. In fact the distinction, or lack thereof, between an infant responding in terms of an object property, like orientation, versus responding in terms of an actual category is an important issue to which I shall return shortly. But before I do, consider McGurk's (1972) design in more detail. It still serves as a model of demonstration studies on infant categorization.

McGurk's experiment is outlined in figure 8.1. Infants at 3, 6, 9, and 12 months of age were habituated to one of the three conditions shown in the figure. In condition A, infants were repeatedly shown the same stimulus, a line with a circle on top. In condition B, infants were shown that same stimulus but in changing orientations. Infants in condition C received different stimuli but in the same orientation. All three groups were tested with the two stimuli on the right side of figure 8.1.

What were the results and what do they mean? Very little was found for 3-month-olds. But at 6, 9, and 12 months, infants dishabituated to both test stimuli in condition A and only dishabituated to the Y-shaped stimulus in condition B. The results of condition A indicated that infants at 6, 9, and 12 months can make simple dis-

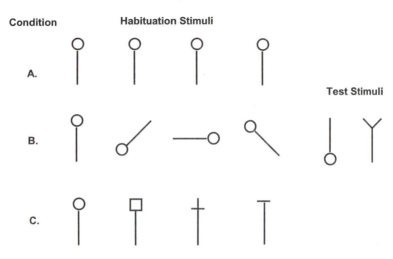

Figure 8.1. Design of McGurk (1972) experiment on infant perception of orientation.

criminations. They can discriminate the right-side-up circle stimulus from either the upside-down circle stimulus or a right-side-up Y. The results of condition B indicated that when the orientation of the circle stimulus varies during habituation, the infants generalize their habituation to the novel upside-down circle stimulus. This is an important finding with respect to categorization because is clear from the results of condition A that they can discriminate that test item, at least from the right-side-up one.

In condition C, after being habituated to different stimuli in the same orientation, there was a tendency for the 9- and 12-month-olds to dishabituate more to an old stimulus in a new orientation than to a new stimulus in the old orientation. Unfortunately, that difference did not reach significance. But the result provides a hint, at least, that 9- and 12-month olds may be able to respond to abstract orientation independent of the stimulus. And if they were responding to orientation, one knows from condition A that they were doing it despite the fact that they could discriminate the test stimulus in an old orientation from habituation stimuli in the same orientation.

Thus this study was the first to provide some evidence of infant categorization. It used a prototypic procedure for investigating one version of infant categorization, what some people call "infant perceptual categorization." In conditions B and C, infants were habituated to a set of changing exemplars and then tested with a new exemplar from the same category versus a member of a different category. The procedure comes close to following the operational definition given earlier. In condition B, infants responded equivalently to the right-side-up circle and the upside-down circle, even though condition A indicated that the stimuli could be discriminated from one another. In condition C, infants responded equivalently to the right-side-up circle and the right-side-up Y even though condition A indicated they could be discriminated from one another. So should one conclude that both condition B and condition C are instances of perceptual categorization? They both use the same procedure and fit the operational definition to the same degree. But most of us would probably agree that whereas the results of condition C, which tests for processing abstract orientation, should probably be considered a form of categorization, the results of condition B should not. Condition B more closely approximates something one would call perceptual constancy; that is, the perception of transformations of the same object (in this case transformations of orientation) as multiple examples of the same object. Perhaps our operational definition of categorization is inadequate. Perhaps "responding in an equivalent manner to discriminably different stimuli" may be a necessary condition for infant categorization but not a sufficient condition.

I shall return to this issue shortly, but first let us consider additional evidence. The McGurk (1972) study only provided the suggestion of true categorization, since the 9- and 12-month old infants in condition C did not look significantly longer at the nonexemplar than at the new exemplar from the old category. The study also provided a suggestion that perhaps perceptual constancy occurs earlier than categorization, because the 6-, 9-, and 12-month-olds provided clear evidence of orientation constancy, but only the 9- and 12-month olds provided any hint of categorization. Before one makes too much of this study, more definitive evidence is needed.

A few years after the McGurk (1972) study appeared, Cohen and Strauss (1977) used essentially the same procedure and a very similar design to investigate infant face perception. The design of their study is shown in table 8.1. Infants at 4, 6, and 8 months of age were given either condition A, B, or C. Infants in condition A were habituated to a single color photograph of an adult female face with a particular orientation and expression, for example, face 1A. The number (e.g., 1) refers to the particular person and the letter (e.g., A) refers to the combined orientation and expression, for example looking to the upper right with a smile on her face. Infants in condition B were habituated to different photographs, but they were always the same person with a variety of orientations and expressions. Infants in condition C were habituated to different females with a variety of orientations and expressions. On the test trials, infants in all three conditions were shown one of the females they had seen before, but for the first time looking straight ahead with a neutral expression, and a new female looking straight ahead with a neutral expression.

The results of Cohen and Strauss (1977) were similar to those found by McGurk (1972). At all three ages infants in condition A dishabituated to both test stimuli. Thus, they clearly discriminated the habituation face from both the same face with a new orientation and expression and from a novel face with a new orientation and expression. However, only the 6- and 8-month-olds provided evidence of generalization in conditions B, and only the 8-month-olds provided evidence of generalization in condition C. In condition B, infants were habituated to the same face in varying orientations and expressions. Both 6- and 8-month-olds generalized to that same face with a new orientation and expression but dishabituated to a novel face. In condition C, infants were habituated to different female faces in a variety of orientations and expressions. Now only the 8-month-olds generalized their habituated response to both test faces.

Thus, as in the McGurk study, the Cohen and Strauss study found evidence of both perceptual constancy and categorization. In condition B, the oldest infants general-

TABLE 8.1. Design from Cohen and Strauss (1977) Face Perception Experiment.

Condition	Habituation stimuli				Test stimuli	
A.	Face 1A	Face 1A	Face 1A	Face 1A		
B.	Face 1A	Face 1B	Face 1C	Face 1D	Face 1•	Face N•
C.	Face 1A	Face 2B	Face 3C	Face 4D		

ized to the same face but with a novel orientation and expression. One can consider that evidence for face or person constancy. In condition C, the oldest infants generalized to a new person's face. One can consider that evidence for face categorization.

Perceptual Constancy versus Perceptual Categorization

Are perceptual constancy and perceptual categorization the same or different phenomena? Are there any fundamental differences between the two, at least within the realm of infant perception and cognition? These are virtually unexplored questions, although Barbara Younger and I did raise the issue in a chapter several years ago (Younger & Cohen, 1985). Both infant perceptual constancy and infant perceptual categorization seem to fulfill the same operational definition. In both cases infants are responding equivalently to discriminably different stimuli. So when an infant responds in the same way to her mother when seen in a frontal pose, in profile, or even when only heard from the next room, is the infant demonstrating "mother constancy" or "mother categorization"? To complicate matters further, perceptual constancies seem to range from basic sensory phenomena, such as brightness constancy, to clearly cognitive phenomena, such as object constancy or mother constancy. Nevertheless, adults, at least, do not treat constancy and categorization as the same. Constancy is constrained by the types of permissible transformations an object can take under different conditions. Categories do not appear to have the same constraints. So, for example, if an object appears at a new location, distance, or in a new orientation, one would usually consider it to be the same object. However, if the object has a new objective size, color, or shape, one would usually consider it to be a different object, although it may well be a member of the same category. To my knowledge the presence or absence of this distinction between constancy and categorization has not been systematically investigated in infants.

Furthermore, there appears to be a developmental progression from the occurrence of perceptual constancy to the occurrence of perceptual categorization. Both McGurk (1972) and Cohen and Strauss (1977) found that perceptual constancy appeared at an earlier age than perceptual categorization. Recall that McGurk found evidence of perceptual constancy at 6 months of age and the possibility of perceptual categorization at 9 months; Cohen and Strauss found evidence of perceptual constancy at 6 months and perceptual categorization at 8 months. This developmental trend was present in both studies. In fact, an examination of the more recent literature reveals the same trend, although occasionally at considerably younger ages. Most studies report evidence of infant categorization by 7 or 10 months, but there are a few reports of categorization as early as 3 months of age (e.g., Eimas & Quinn, 1994; Quinn, Eimas, & Rosenkrantz, 1993). There also are several reports of perceptual constancy by 3 months (e.g., Bower, 1966; Caron, Caron, & Carlson, 1979; Day & McKenzie, 1981) and even some demonstrations of it in newborns (Granrud, 1987; Slater, Mattock, & Brown, 1990; Slater & Morison, 1985).

An interesting fact is that the most successful attempts at finding perceptual constancy by newborns use a procedure that mimics categorization studies. In the Granrud (1987) size constancy experiment, for example, infants were habituated to a ball at different distances and then were shown that ball at a new distance and a different size ball. Newborns in this study dishabituated to the different size ball as if they had formed a category of the ball to which they had been habituated. Slater and Morison (1985) also found evidence of shape constancy in newborns using a design that resembled a category study.

Finally, comparisons between infant perceptual constancy and perceptual categorization are usually confounded in the following sense. Constancy usually refers to equivalence despite variations in some single object property, such as brightness, color, size, or shape. Categorization usually refers to equivalence despite variations in multiple object properties (i.e., variations in the objects themselves). From a constructive, information-processing perspective, such as the one I have proposed (Cohen, 1991, 1998; Cohen & Cashon, 2001), categorization should be more complicated and difficult. According to this information-processing perspective, the development of infant perception and cognition is basically a bottom-up process. Infants first come to process features or properties of objects before they process the relations among those features that constitute specific objects. They then process the relationships among objects that define simple events, and finally the relationship among simple events that define more complex events or scenarios. Because object properties are the starting point, even if the same underlying representational process is involved in object constancy and the object categorization, I would expect object categorization to appear later than constancy. (By the same argument I would also expect event categorization to appear later than object categorization.) In any case the distinction, or lack thereof, between infant perceptual constancy and infant perceptual categorization is an issue that deserves further thought and investigation.

Categorical Perception versus Perceptual Categorization

In addition to perceptual constancy, infant categorical perception can also be contrasted with infant perceptual categorization. Infant categorical perception has most often been examined with respect to infants' organization of speech sounds, although it has also been reported with respect to infants' organization of color (Bornstein, Kessen, & Weiskopf, 1976). With respect to speech sounds, as Jusczyk (chap. 2) points out, the question is whether certain phonetic contrasts, such as /b/ versus /p/, which belong to different phonemic categories, are easily discriminated, whereas sounds belonging to the same phonemic category are more poorly discriminated. Research on infant categorical perception of speech also has a long history, beginning with the seminal study by Eimas, Siqueland, Jusczyk, and Vigorito (1971). In that study, infants as young as 1 month of age discriminated between /ba/ and /pa/ but were unable to discriminate between different instances of /ba/ or different instances of /pa/. In fact, one characteristic of categorical perception is that a sharp boundary exists between two phonemic categories (such as in /b/ versus /p/) and it is easier to discriminate sounds that go across that boundary than sounds that are on the same side of that boundary. My colleagues and I actually plotted out the discriminability function for 7-month-olds who were presented with the medial stop consonants /aba/ versus /apa/ (Cohen, Diehl, Oakes, & Loehlin, 1992). When the two speech stimuli were on different sides of the boundary, infants had little difficulty discriminating between them. However, when the stimuli were on the same side of the boundary (even though the physical difference between remained constant), infants had more difficulty discriminating between the sounds.

So is infant categorical perception an instance of perceptual categorization? The answer appears to be that it usually only meets one half of the definition. Infants' categorical perception, of speech, for example, certainly can be described as responding equivalently to groups of speech sounds. But it is not at all clear that the sounds comprising a group can be easily discriminated from one another.

In contrast, infants also appear to group together speech sounds from quite different speakers. Kuhl (1979, 1983) examined 6-month-old infants' discrimination of two vowel categories, for example /a/ as in "pop" versus /i/ as in "peep." The stimuli within each category varied in pitch contour (interrogative vs. declarative) and in talker identity (male, female, or child). She found that the infants discriminated between the vowel categories but generalized to instances within a single category, even though those instances were highly discriminable from one another. She concluded that the infants treated discriminably different members of the same vowel category as equivalent, and thus were categorizing speech sounds.

Another interesting case involves infants' reorganization of speech sounds at 10 to 12 months of age. Werker and her colleagues (Werker & Tees, 1984; Werker & LaLonde, 1988) have reported that infants can discriminate a wide variety of phonetic contrasts by 6 or 8 months of age. Some of these contrasts will be phonemic for a certain language (i.e., will produce a meaningful distinction) whereas others will not be phonemic. So, for example, the difference in the initial consonant in the syllables /ba/ and /da/ is phonemic for both English and Hindi. Just switching the initial consonant will change the meaning of a word. But the difference between the dental /da/ and the retroflex /Da/ is phonemic only for Hindi. Both English and Hindi infants can make both distinctions until about 10 months of age. Between 10 and 12 months, both groups continue to make the /ba/-/da/ distinction, but only the Hindi infants make the /da/-/Da/ distinction. Thus the language environment appears to make it more difficult for older infants to make a distinction that is not phonemic (or meaningful) in their native language. The question is why that should be the case. One possibility is that the infants actually lose sensitivity to nonnative contrasts; what once was discriminable now no longer is discriminable, or at least is less discriminable. The other possibility is that the infants are not losing sensitivity. Instead they are just responding similarly to equivalent but discriminable speech sounds. In other words, they are forming a true category, and what may begin as an instance of categorical perception becomes an instance of perceptual categorization.

One way to summarize the relationships between perceptual categorization, perceptual constancy, and categorical perception is shown in figure 8.2. Each of the three topics can be considered distinct, but each also overlaps to some extent with the other two. Perceptual categorization refers to grouping together multiple examples of different objects (or events) that are easily discriminable from one another. Perceptual constancy refers to grouping together multiple instances of a single object or event. The ease of discriminating among these instances plays a lesser role. Discriminability among exemplars is the crucial issue for categorical perception, and whether one considers the different instances (of speech sounds for example) as separate entities (e.g., allophones) or as different examples of the same entity (a phoneme) is of lesser concern. Needless to say, an important issue is whether these three topics can best be understood in terms of the same set of underlying processes or whether different sets of processes are responsible for each topic.

Perceptual Categorization versus Conceptual Categorization

No topic is more contentious in the infant categorization literature than the distinction between perceptual categorization and conceptual categorization. According to Mandler (1992, chap. 5) the two types of categorization are fundamentally different and independent. Perceptual categorization involves the formation of prototypes on the basis of perceptual features. It occurs effortlessly and automatically and does not involve abstract representation. Development of this type of category appears to go from the concrete to the abstract. Conceptual categorization, on the other hand, involves deliberation, meaning, and interpretation. Development often seems to go from the abstract to the more concrete. Both types of categories exist from an early age, with the only connection between them being a process of "perceptual analysis" by which perceptual information is abstracted into "image schemas," forms of conceptual primitives such as animacy, causality, and containment.

Others, including several authors in this book (e.g., see chaps. 3, 6, 7), argue that such a dual system for categorization is unnecessary. According to this perspective, abstract conceptual representation develops out of perceptual representation. This development occurs because of changes in infants' attentional, motor, cognitive, and linguistic abilities. These changes provide new types of information, such as nonperceptual, functional features and contextual constraints that mold and modify early perceptual categories.

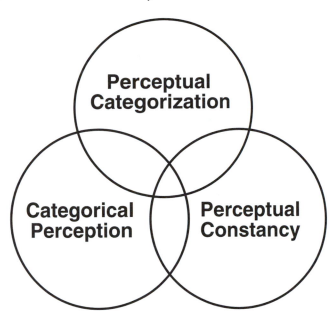

Figure 8.2. Possible relationships among perceptual categorization, categorical perception, and perceptual constancy.

Both sides of this debate are well represented in this book, and it is not my intention to restate all the arguments presented by each side. For what it is worth, however, I do tend to side more with the single categorization than the dual categorization approach. First, it seems highly unlikely, and rather unparsimonious, to have two separate categorization systems operating in parallel from early infancy. Second, as mentioned hereafter, considerable evidence now exists to show that these conceptual primitives, or "image schemas," from which the conceptual system is supposed to derive "meanings," develop slowly over the first 2 years of life. They themselves can best be described in simple perceptual terms at first and only later in more general and abstract terms. (See Cohen, Amsel, Redford, & Casasola [1998] for a description of the development of causality; chap. 7 for the development of animacy; and both chap. 3 and Casasola and Cohen (2002) for the development of spatial relations such as containment.)

However, the main point I would like to raise in the remainder of this chapter is that this core issue about infants having separate perceptual and conceptual systems versus a single unified system may be impossible to resolve because it is confounded with so many other difficult issues. Some of these related issues are themselves basic to our understanding of infant categorization. Some have been raised in the past and by authors herein. Others are rarely mentioned. Yet the issues must be recognized and resolved before one can achieve a real understanding of the processes underlying infants' acquisition of perceptual and conceptual categories.

Content versus Process

One confounding factor is the distinction between describing the content of infants' categories versus understanding the processes underlying acquisition of those categories. Barbara Younger and I made that distinction back in the early 1980s when we divided infant categorization research into "demonstration" studies versus "process" studies (Younger & Cohen, 1985). Oakes and Madole (chap. 6) make a similar point when they say that, "to fully understand the development of categorization, we must move beyond descriptions of the categories to which infants attend and ask questions about the processes underlying the ability to form these categories" (p. 133).

Demonstration studies merely provide evidence that infants have formed a category according to the operational definition stated earlier by showing that the infants respond equivalently to discriminably different stimuli. Studies on infants' categorization of stuffed animals versus flowers, dogs versus cats, land animals versus sea animals, or animals versus vehicles are all examples of demonstration studies. Even when these studies go further to show, for example, that infants attend to an animal's facial features more than its type of body (Quinn & Eimas, 1996) or an object's legs and wheels more than its overall shape (Rakison & Butterworth, 1998) the studies are not providing much information about the processes or mechanisms underlying category acquisition. (One exception would be the series of studies and connectionist simulations of dog versus cat categories reported in chap. 14.) Arguments about whether infants form basic-level categories earlier or later than global categories also are often not very informative, since they usually do not provide information about how those categories are formed or how the process of category formation changes with development.

The problem is exacerbated when one describes the task in terms of preexisting adult categories rather than infant categories. For example, infants may respond differently to sets of toys that an adult would represent as "animals" versus "vehicles." But that does not mean that infants have any representations that approximate these adult categories. As Rakison and Butterworth (1998) argued, infants may just be responding to "legs" versus "wheels." But even these terms can become confused with adult categories. Rakison and Butterworth found that infants fail to categorize as different animals with legs and tables with legs. However, it seems highly unlikely that a preverbal infant would form a single category that includes both items.

One of the principle reasons it is so difficult to discover underlying processes from these studies is that they use preexisting natural categories rather than specially constructed, highly controlled, artificial categories. Without being able to manipulate both the objects comprising a category and the features varying among those objects, it is difficult, if not impossible, to understand how infants form categories. Both the early research by Strauss (1979) on infant prototype formation and the extensive research by Younger (chap. 4) on infants' use of correlated attributes provide excellent examples of process studies. In both cases the investigators examined underlying processes by presenting artificially constructed exemplars to infants. Younger's work in particular has shown not only how important correlations among attributes are in forming categories but also how important they are for differentiating between categories (Younger, 1985). She also has spelled out in considerable detail age-related changes in the types of information that infants will tend to correlate (chap. 4). Recently Mareschal and French (2000) have taken process-oriented research to a new level. They have been able to simulate Younger's 1985 results on both category formation and category differentiation using a simple autoassociative connectionist model (see chap. 14).

One impressive aspect of this book is the number of authors who are moving past descriptions of infants' categories to propose a set of processes that they believe underlie infant categorization. I am glad to see that these authors recognize the importance of correlated information in category formation. They also make serious attempts to explain developmental changes in infant categorization and whether those changes represent modifications in the underlying processes or just the incorporation of new types of information into existing processes. For example, chapters 4, 6, and 7 present comprehensive new proposals regarding changes in these underlying processes. Even though the proposals differ, I believe all three are much more complementary than conflicting and all indicate important directions for future research on infant categorization.

Object Categories versus Event Categories

Most of the discussion on infant categorization relates to how infants categorize objects. Earlier I noted the similarity between the categorization of objects and the simpler, perhaps more basic categorization of an object property such as size, shape, or orientation. This type of categorization, usually called perceptual constancy, tends to appear earlier in infancy than object categorization. One can also look in the opposite direction and consider a more complex type of categorization—the categorization of events. Events involve dynamic change over time and usually include some type of interaction between or among different objects. As one might expect, infant event categorization tends to appear at a somewhat later age than object categorization. It also is more difficult to define than object categorization.

Consider a simple causal event such as a direct launching in which one object, A, moves across a stage and then hits a second object, B, causing B to move the remaining distance across the stage. One can ask what would constitute a category of that simple causal event. Several studies, during their habituation phases, varied the right-left orientation of the action in the launching event. On some trials infants saw object A enter from the left side of the stage and both objects move from left to right; on other trials they saw object A enter from the right side and the objects move from right to left. This variation in direction of movement did not seem to faze even young infants. They seemed to treat them both as instances of the same event (Oakes & Cohen, 1990). So does that mean the infants had formed an event category and would one call that category "causality?" It seems, at least to me, that the answer would be no. This grouping of two types of events that simply move in different directions is more analogous to perceptual constancy than to categorization, but at an event level rather than at an object level.

Other studies varied the objects comprising the event. The direction of action, contact, and timing remained the same, but a different pair of objects was shown on each trial (Cohen & Oakes, 1993). This manipulation seriously disrupted infant causal perception, and even infants as old as 10 months of age tended to fall back to a simpler, noncausal type of processing. But assuming that infants at some age can get beyond the individual objects and can perceive the type of underlying relationship, would they then have formed an event category? Perhaps, but the action has still remained constant. Perhaps the infants had just learned to disregard the particular objects involved in the event. Some might argue that in order for infants to form a true event category they must group together different instances of an event in which the specific action varies but the underlying meaning (e.g., a causal interaction) remains the same. So, for example, one might vary the angle at which object A hit object B and the subsequent direction of movement of object B. Only a subset of these events would actually represent a true causal event. Do infants group together as causal only this subset of events that conform to the laws of mechanics? Suppose they do. Can one then say the infants have acquired a category of causal events? Possibly. Of course, there are many causal events other than direct launchings. Perhaps in order for it to be considered a "real" causal category it must include qualitatively different examples of causal events.

It should be evident from this exercise that as one progresses in this sequence, the notion of causal category is becoming both more general and more abstract. In fact, the sequential order in which these types of categories have been described also probably follows the developmental order in which the categories would be acquired, that is, with perceptual constancy appearing first, followed by categorical perception, categorization of objects, and finally categorization of events. Such a developmental sequence has implications both for Mandler's notion of an image schema and her distinction between a category and a concept. First, it is clear that development of an image schema, such as one that represents the abstract meaning of causality, is a long, gradual process. Second, this developmental process proceeds from the concrete to the abstract just as in the case of the perceptual categorization of objects. A similar type of progression, based on the available evidence with infants, can be made for the development of other image schemas such as "animacy" (chap. 7) or "containment" (Casasola & Cohen, 2002). Thus it is difficult to understand how conceptual categorization can occur early in infancy when the abstract meanings (i.e., image schemas) required for this type of categorization are not yet available.

Prototypes versus Propositions

Another issue related to the distinction between perceptual and conceptual categorization is the supposed nature of the underlying representation. If one assumes that a category is essentially a summary representation of a set of exemplars, then a prototype view that includes multiple features, with or without the correlations among those features, would be an appropriate model. This type of model seems to be easiest to apply to object categories. Connectionist models of infant categorization (e.g., Mareschal & French, 2000; Quinn & Johnson, 1997, 2000) seem particularly well suited to constructing this type of representation.

On the other hand, certain other categories that at first seem to be abstract conceptual categories may actually be better described in terms of a set of propositions or rules. Categories that involve relationships between objects can be of this type. They include causal events such as "a direct launching" and spatial relationships such as "above," "below," "inside," "on top of," and "between" (Casasola & Cohen, 2002; chap. 3). In fact, these relationships between objects might even be better labeled as concepts rather than categories.

An important, unresolved theoretical question is whether both types of representation are needed or only one type is sufficient. Summary representations seem to work well in determining whether a new object is a member of an existing category. They also provide information about how the representations may be formed in the first place, but they may not be well suited for making inferences or in representing abstract concepts. (For a different view see chap. 14.) Propositional representations may work better in making inferences or in deciding how to classify a totally new object in terms of some abstract representation, but they do not provide much information about how the propositions are initially acquired.

In at least one area of infant categorization, the debate rages on. Marcus (1999) showed that 7-month-old infants could learn to categorize a sequence of syllables according to the order in which they appeared, for example, ABA. Once learned, they also could differentiate that sequence from another sequence, for example, AAB. Furthermore, the infants appeared to learn an abstract rule, given that they were able to generalize the originally learned sequence to an entirely new set of syllables. Marcus also claimed that, in principle, connectionist models can not learn such a rule. Of course Marcus's position has not gone unchallenged. Since Marcus's claim, at least nine different connectionist models have been reported that presumably can learn to approximate such a rule, using processes similar to prototype formation (see Shultz & Bale, 2001). Marcus, of course, has argued that these models are insufficient (Marcus, Vijayan, Bandi Rao, & Vishton, 1999). So the issue is still active and unresolved.

Other Issues

The issues raised in this chapter represent only a subset of those that could have been mentioned. For example, one could discuss the pros and cons of a presumed perceptual to conceptual shift, and how the distinction between perceptual and conceptual features is confounded by whether those features are apparent or are hidden and must be inferred. Both Rakison (chap. 7) and Oakes and Madole (chap. 6) raise this issue. A related issue is the apparent confounding between perceptual versus conceptual features on the one hand and structural versus functional features on the other.

Another issue, usually not raised in research on infant categorization, concerns the role of habituation (and possibly other procedures) in teaching infants categories. Are infants actually acquiring a category during the habituation phase of the experiment or does the experimental procedure simply indicate categories the infants had previously acquired? With process studies that train infants on artificial categories, the answer seems obvious. The infants are learning the category during the course of the experiment. But what about experiments that use so-called natural categories? It is usually unclear to what extent prior knowledge influences performance in the habituation task.

Connectionist models offer a promising way to investigate this issue as well. Recent models, for example, on infant word learning by Schafer and Mareschal (2001) and on infant causal perception by Chaput and Cohen (2001) explicitly incorporate the effects of prior knowledge in addition to on-line learning during the habituation phase of an actual experiment.

Yet another set of issues relates to the role of language in categorization. Several authors herein (see chaps. 5, 6, and 7) note that language can have an influence in categorization, but it is not that clear what the underlying mechanisms may be and how those mechanisms change with development. Some experimental findings suggest that the presence of a novel language label facilitates infants' abilities to form categories of objects even when the infants are 12 months of age or younger (e.g., Balaban & Waxman, 1997; Waxman & Markow, 1995). But how does the presence of language work? Does it increase the infants' attentiveness generally, increase it just to salient events, or possibly just to salient objects? (See also chap. 9.)

Choi, McDonough, Bowerman, and Mandler (1999) have reported that English- and Korean-speaking infants, 18 to 23 months of age, differ markedly in how they group spatial relationships into categories. But the authors differ in their interpretations about the role of language. Mandler (1996) believes infants map linguistic terms to preexisting spatial concepts. In contrast, Choi and Bowerman (1991) believe that language drives the acquisition of certain concepts. Our own empirical work (Casasola & Cohen, 2002) suggests that the answer is more complicated. First, we, like Quinn (chap. 3), found that categorization of spatial concepts proceeds from concrete instances to more general categories. Second, we found that certain categories, like containment, are learned prior to the onset of language, but others, like "support" or "tight fit," are not. Certainly much more research is needed to uncover the complex pattern of interactions that exist between category acquisition and language acquisition.

Concluding Comments

It should be evident from the excellent chapters in this book as well as from this commentary that infant categorization is an active, productive field and that real progress has been made in a relatively short period of time. We now know that the ability to categorize is present from birth, but the types of categories infants use increase dramatically over the first 2 years of life. Demonstration studies that sought to discover if infants have learned a particular category are being replaced by more analytic process studies that seek to understand how that category learning takes place. Even the investigation of single processes, such as the ability to correlate attributes, is being incorporated in more elaborate accounts of category acquisition that involve multiple processes. Furthermore, some of these accounts make a serious attempt to explain developmental changes in categorization and whether those changes include only the acquisition of new features or also qualitatively different ways of forming categories.

It is inevitable that unresolved issues will emerge in a field as active and significant as infant categorization. What is most exciting is that those issues are generating empirical questions both within and beyond the traditional realm of infant categorization research. In this commentary I have identified several of these issues. Some seem obvious and are currently being debated or researched. Others have not occurred to most investigators in the field.

The field of infant categorization is also being expanded. On the one hand it is being extended to include perceptual phenomena such as perceptual constancy and categorical perception. On the other hand it is being extended to more cognitive phenomena such as categorization of events, relational information, and even rule learning. New approaches, such as connectionist modeling, are beginning to have a significant impact on infant categorization research, and these connectionist models are producing predictions that can be tested empirically. Furthermore, the realization that categorization is not an isolated process is leading to a merging of two important areas, the study of early perceptual and cognitive development and the study of early language acquisition. As the chapters in this book indicate, our understanding of infant categorization is undergoing a major change. It is an exciting time to be in the field. Current research on infant categorization and the unresolved issues generated by that research are both contributing to that excitement.

Acknowledgments

Preparation of this chapter was supported in part by NICHD Grant R01-HD 23397. I thank Cara Cashon for her many helpful comments. Correspondence concerning this manuscript should be addressed to Leslie B. Cohen, Department of Psychology, University of Texas, Austin, TX 78712. Electronic mail can be sent to <cohen@psy.utexas.edu>.

References

Balaban, M. T., & Waxman, S. R. (1997). Do words facilitate object categorization in 9-month-old infants? *Journal of Experimental Child Psychology, 64,* 3–26.

Bornstein, M. H., Kessen, W., & Weiskopf, S. (1976). Color vision and hue categorization in young infants. *Journal of Experimental Psychology: Human Perception & Performance, 2,* 115–129.

Bower, T. G. R. (1966). Slant perception and shape constancy in infants. *Science, 151,* 832–834.

Caron, A. J., Caron, R. F., & Carlson, V. R. (1979). Infant perception of the invariant shape of objects in slant. *Child Development, 50,* 716–721.

Casasola, M., & Cohen, L. B. (2002). Infant categorization of containment, support and tight-fit spatial relationships. *Developmental Science, 5,* 247–264.

Chaput, H. H., & Cohen, L. B. (2001). A model of infant causal perception and its development. J. D. Moore and K. Stenning (Eds.), *Proceedings of the Twenty-Third Annual Conference of the Cognitive Science Society* (pp 182–187). Mahwah, NJ: Erlbaum.

Choi, S., & Bowerman, M. (1991). Learning to express motion events in English and Korean: The influence of language-specific lexicalization patterns. *Cognition, 41,* 83–121.

Choi, S., McDonough, L., Bowerman, M., & Mandler, J. M. (1999). Early sensitivity to language-specific spatial categories in English and Korean. *Cognitive Development, 14,* 241–268.

Cohen, L. B. (1991). Infant attention: An information processing approach. In M. J. Weiss & P. R. Zalazo (Eds.), *Newborn attention: Biological constraints and the influence of experience* (pp. 1–21).Norwood, NJ: Ablex.

Cohen, L. B. (1998). An information-processing approach to infant perception and cognition. In F. Simion & G. Butterworth (Eds.), *The development of sensory, motor, and cognitive capacities in early infancy* (pp. 277–300). Hove, UK: Psychology Press.

Cohen, L. B., Amsel, G., Redford, M. A., & Casasola, M. (1998). The development of infant causal perception. In A. Slater (ed.), *Perceptual development: Visual, auditory, and speech perception in infancy* (pp. 167–209). Hove, UK: Psychology Press.

Cohen, L. B., & Cashon, C. H. (2001). Infant object segregation implies information integration. *Journal of Experimental Child Psychology, 78,* 75–83.

Cohen, L. B., Diehl, R. L., Oakes, L. M., & Loehlin, J. C. (1992). Infant perception of /aba/ versus /apa/: Building a quantitative model of infant categorical discrimination. *Developmental Psychology, 28,* 261–272.

Cohen, L. B., & Oakes, L. M. (1993). How infants perceive a simple causal event. *Developmental Psychology, 29,* 421–433.

Cohen, L. B., & Strauss, M. S. (1977). Concept acquisition in the human infant. *Child Development, 50,* 419–424.

Cohen, L. B., & Younger, B. A. (1983). Perceptual categorization in the infant. In E. Scholnick (Ed.), *New trends in conceptual representation* (pp. 197–220). Hillsdale, NJ: Erlbaum.

Day, R. H., & McKenzie, B. E. (1981). Infant perception of the invariant size of approaching and receding objects. *Developmental Psychology, 17,* 181–309.

Eimas, P. D., & Quinn, P. C. (1994). Studies on the formation of perceptually based basic-level categories in young infants. *Child Development, 65,* 903–917.

Eimas, P. D., Siqueland, E. R., Jusczyk, P. W., & Vigorito, J. (1971). Speech perception in infants. *Science, 171,* 303–306.

Granrud, C. E. (1987). Size constancy in newborn human infants. *Supplement to Investigative Ophthalmology and Visual Science, 28,* 5.

Kuhl, P. K. (1979). Speech perception in early infancy: Perceptual constancy for spectrally dissimilar vowel categories. *Journal of the Acoustical Society of America, 66,* 1668–1679.

Kuhl, P. K. (1983). Perception of auditory equivalence classes for speech in early infancy. *Infant Behavior and Development, 6,* 263–285.

Mandler, J. M. (1992). How to build a baby: II. Conceptual primitives. *Psychological Review, 99,* 587–604.

Mandler, J. M. (1996). Preverbal representation and language. In P. Bloom, M. A. Peterson, L. Nadel, & M. F. Garrett (Eds.), *Language and space* (pp. 365–384). Cambridge, MA: MIT Press.

Marcus, G. F. (1999). Response: Rule learning by seven-month-old infants and neural networks. *Science, 284,* 875.

Marcus, G. F., Vijayan, S., Bandi Rao, S., & Vishton, P. M. (1999). Rule learning by seven-month-old infants. *Science, 283,* 77–80.

Mareschal, D., & French, R. (2000). Mechanisms of categorization in infancy. *Infancy, 1,* 59–76.

McGurk, H. (1972). Infant discrimination of orientation. *Journal of Experimental Child Psychology, 14,* 151–164.

Oakes, L. M., & Cohen, L. B. (1990). Infant perception of a causal event. *Cognitive Development, 5,* 193–207.

Quinn, P. C., & Eimas, P. D. (1996). Perceptual cues that permit categorical differentiation of animal species by infants. *Journal of Experimental Child Psychology, 63,* 189–211.

Quinn, P. C., Eimas, P. D., & Rosenkrantz, S. L (1993). Evidence for representations of perceptually similar natural categories by 3-month-old and 4-month-old infants. *Perception, 22,* 463–475.

Quinn, P. C., & Johnson, M. H. (1997). The emergence of perceptual category representations in young infants: A connectionist analysis. *Journal of Experimental Child Psychology, 66,* 236–263.

Quinn, P. C., & Johnson, M. H. (2000). Global before basic object categorization. *Infancy, 1,* 31–46.

Rakison, D. H., & Butterworth, G. E. (1998). Infants' use of object parts in early categorization. *Developmental Psychology, 34,* 49–62.

Schafer, G., & Mareschal, D. (2001). Modeling infant speech sound discrimination using simple associative networks. *Infancy, 2,* 7–28.

Shultz, T. R., & Bale, A. C. (2001). Neural network simulation of infant familiarization to artificial sentences: Rule-like behavior without explicit rules and variables. *Infancy, 2,* 501–536.

Slater, A., Mattock, A., & Brown, E. (1990). Size constancy at birth: Newborn infants' responses to retinal and real size. *Journal of Experimental Child Psychology, 49,* 314–322.

Slater, A., & Morison, V. (1985). Shape constancy and slant perception at birth. *Perception, 14,* 337–344.

Strauss, M. S. (1979). Abstraction of prototypical information in adults and 10-month-old infants. *Journal of Experimental Psychology: Human Learning and Memory, 5,* 618–632.

Waxman, S. R., & Markow, D. (1995). Words as invitations to form categories: Evidence from 12- to 13-month-old infants. *Cognitive Development, 29(3),* 257–302.

Werker, J. D., & Lalonde, C. E. (1988). The development of speech perception: Initial capabilities and the emergence of phonemic categories. *Developmental Psychology, 24,* 672–683.

Werker, J. D., & Tees, R. C. (1984). Cross-language speech perception: Evidence for perceptual reorganization during the first year of life. *Infant Behavior and Development, 7,* 49–63.

Younger, B. A. (1985). The segregation of items into categories by 10-month-old infants. *Child Development, 56,* 1574–1583.

Younger, B. A., & Cohen, L. B. (1985). How infants form categories. In G. Bower (Ed.), *The psychology of learning and motivation: Advances in research and theory,* (Vol. 19, pp. 211–247). New York: Academic Press.

PART TWO

Concepts and Categories during Early Language Development

Links between Object Categorization and Naming

Origins and Emergence in Human Infants

Sandra R. Waxman

Infants across the world's communities are raised in vastly different environments, surrounded by different objects, different customs, and different languages. Yet despite these differences, there are striking similarities in the most fundamental aspects of infant cognitive and language development. Within their first two years, infants develop two uniquely human capacities: they naturally establish rich and flexible repertoires of object categories, and they spontaneously acquire their native language. Each of these capacities, considered on its own, is a remarkable feat. But perhaps even more remarkable is the fact that even before they begin to produce words on their own, infants' conceptual and linguistic advances are powerfully and implicitly linked. These early links foster the acquisition of a stable set of object categories, guide the acquisition of the early lexicon, and serve as a foundation for the evolution of the finely tuned links between language and conceptual organization that characterize the mature system.

This chapter focuses on the origin and unfolding of these links between language and conceptual organization. I will argue that from the onset of acquisition, object naming and object categorization are linked. Infants across the world begin the task of word learning equipped with a broad, universal expectation that directs them to link novel words to commonalities among objects. This initial link supports the rapid acquisition of the increasingly sophisticated language and conceptual systems that are the hallmark of human development. And over the course of early acquisition, this initial link becomes fine-tuned, in accordance with the structure of the native language under acquisition.

This developmental proposal has several distinct advantages. First, it embraces the importance of considering both (1) any expectation(s) that the infant may bring to the task of acquisition and (2) any influence of the infant's environment in shaping those expectations. On this view, early acquisition is at once sufficiently *constrained* to permit infants to form rich categories of objects and to learn words to express them; it is also sufficiently *flexible* to accommodate systematic cultural and linguistic variation in categorization and naming patterns. Second, this developmental proposal is a dynamic one, in which any initial expectation(s) held by infants is not rigidly fixed throughout development but rather will evolve over the course of development, becoming fine-tuned in accordance with the regularities observed in the language under acquisition. Third, this developmental proposal assumes a bidirectional relation between language and conceptual organization. The conceptual system serves up several candidate concepts that may (or may not) be expressed in the native language under acquisition. The linguistic system also exerts an influence on conceptual structure, with words serving as invitations to form new categories and concepts and to discover the deep, often unobservable, relations among members of the same concept (Brown, 1956; Gelman & Coley, 1991; Waxman & Markow, 1995).

Early Milestones in Conceptual and Linguistic Organization

During their first year, infants form categories that capture both the similarities and differences among the objects they encounter, and they represent these categories in a stable fashion over time. Most of these early object categories will be at the basic level (i.e., *dog*) and the more inclusive global level (i.e., *animal*) (see chap. 3; Mandler, 1992). Infants use these early object categories as an inductive base to support inferences about novel members. They also begin to relate categories to one another on the basis of taxonomic (e.g., dogs are a kind of animal), thematic (e.g., dogs chase tennis balls), functional (e.g., dogs can pull babies on sleds), and other relations among them. In forming these early categories and relations among categories, infants attend flexibly to features of the objects, as well as to the (often transient) functions and actions in which these objects are engaged. Thus, early categories provide a core of conceptual continuity that endures from infancy through adulthood.

Concurrent with these conceptual advances, infants make remarkable strides in acquiring language. Well before they begin to comprehend or produce the words of their native language, infants show a special interest in speech sounds, as compared to other forms of auditory input. Later, by 6 months, infants become perceptually attuned to the distinct prosodic, morphologic, and phonologic elements of their native language (chap. 2; Jusczyk & Kemler Nelson, 1996; Kemler Nelson, Hirsh-Pasek, Jusczyk, & Cassidy, 1989; Morgan & Demuth, 1996; Shi, Werker, & Morgan, 1999; Werker, Lloyd, Pegg, & Polka, 1996). By their first birthdays, infants typically begin to produce their first words. These early words tend to refer to salient individuals (e.g., "Mama"), categories of objects (e.g., "cup," "doggie"), social routines (e.g., "bye-bye"), and actions (e.g., "up"). Infants in this period reveal a "noun advantage"; with words (e.g., nouns) that refer to salient (e.g., basic-level) object categories (e.g., cup, dog) being by far the predominant form (Au, Dapretto, & Song, 1994; for a different interpretation see Bloom, 1993; Choi & Gopnik, 1995; Gentner, 1982; Gentner & Boroditsky, 2001; Gleitman, 1990; Goldin-Meadow, Seligman, & Gelman, 1976; Huttenlocher & Smiley, 1987; Nelson, Hampson, & Shaw, 1993; Saah, Waxman, & Johnson, 1996; Tardif, 1996). By their second birthdays, most infants have mastered hundreds of words from various grammatical forms (e.g., nouns, verbs, adjectives) and have begun to combine these to form short phrases that conform broadly to the syntactic and semantic properties of their native language.

Thus, in addition to forming categories to capture commonalities and differences among the myriad objects and events that they encounter, infants rapidly and naturally learn words to express them. A review of the developmental literature reveals that during this early period of acquisition, there are powerful, implicit links between infants' conceptual and linguistic advances, and these links guide acquisition even before infants produce their first words.

Word Learning: At the Crossroad of Language and Conceptual Organization

Perhaps more than any other developmental achievement, word learning stands at the very crossroad of the conceptual and linguistic realms. What does it take to learn a word? At its most fundamental level, word learning depends on the learner's ability to establish a mapping between the linguistic entities that we call *words* and the actual entities to which they correspond in the *world*. What is the conceptual consequence of establishing this word-to-world mapping? And how do infants discover that the very same entity (e.g., the family dog) can be named flexibly, using different types of words, including proper nouns ("Magic"), count nouns ("dog," "pet," "puppy"), and adjectives ("frisky," "sleek," "fast"), and that these different types of words refer to different aspects (e.g., the individual object, a category of objects, or a property of the object)?

What Does It Take to Learn a Word?

The entrance into word learning is dramatic. "[M]y teacher placed my hand under the spout. As the cool stream gushed over one hand she spelled into the other the word *water*, first slowly, then rapidly. I stood still, my whole attention fixed upon the motions of her fingers. Suddenly I felt a misty consciousness as of something forgotten—a thrill of returning thought; and somehow the mystery of language was revealed to me. I knew then that 'w-a-t-e-r' meant the wonderful cool something that was flowing over my hand. That living word awakened my soul, gave it light, hope, joy, and set it free! . . . Everything had a name, and each name gave birth to a new thought" (Keller, 1904, pp. 22–23).

This passage conveys the conceptual power of establishing a word-to-world correspondence. To be sure, Keller's entrance into word learning differed in important ways from the more typical circumstances in which infants' first words are acquired. Normally developing infants begin producing their first words at approximately 1 year of age, but Keller acquired "w-a-t-e-r" when she was approximately 7 years of age.[1] Second, although in some cultures and some circumstances names are deliberately "taught," this practice is emphatically not universal. In some cultures (e.g., Western, well-educated communities), caretakers deliberately provide names for their infants, often even before the infants themselves can even speak. But in other communities, (e.g., Kahluli, see Ochs & Schieffelin, 1984), caretakers refrain from speaking directly to infants until the infants themselves begin to speak. Because infants from these communities acquire language on roughly the same timetable, it is clear that successful word learning does not depend on direct tutoring.

Third, in the typical course of events, words are seldom presented in isolation in the way that Annie Sullivan presented w-a-t-e-r. Instead, words tend to be embedded in a fluent stream of continuous speech. How do infants succeed in these cases? At a most general level, it helps that infants devote special attention to human speech; this serves them in good stead as they begin to single out the novel words (chap. 2; Jusczyk & Kemler Nelson, 1996). Another advantage is that caretakers tend to use infant-directed speech, or "motherese," when addressing infants and young children. The exaggerated pitch contours and phrase boundaries of this speech register facilitate the identification of distinct words and phrases in the continuous speech stream (Gleitman & Wanner, 1988). We also know that infants as young as 8 months of age are especially attentive to words that receive stress, particularly those at the end of a sentence or phrase boundary (e.g., "See the *water*?") (Fernald, 1992; Jusczyk & Aslin, 1995). In many languages (e.g., English, Spanish, French), nouns tend to occupy this privileged phrase-final position; in others (e.g., Mandarin Chinese [Tardif, 1996], Korean [Au et al., 1994; Choi & Gopnik, 1995; Kim, McGregor, & Thompson, 2000], and apparently Tzeltal and Itzaj Maya), this is less often the case. Despite these variations, infants across the world begin to produce their first words at roughly the same age, and the composition of their early lexicons are roughly comparable, with nouns (that is, words that are classified as nouns in the adult language) being the predominant early form (Au et al., 1994; Gentner, 1982; Gentner & Boroditsky, 2001; Gleitman, 1990; Goldin-Meadow et al., 1976; Huttenlocher & Smiley, 1987; Nelson et al., 1993; Saah et al., 1996; Tardif, 1996).

Fourth, although Annie Sullivan made sure that the referent of the word was available for Helen's inspection throughout the duration of the naming episode, this is not representative of the more typical word-learning scenario, in which infants must identify the referent (e.g., the family dog) amid an ever-changing current of events. In many cases, the referent is absent entirely (e.g., "Let's find the dog," uttered as the parent wakes the infant from a nap). In other cases, the referent may make only a fleeting appearance (e.g., "There goes the dog again!" uttered as Magic makes a fleeting appearance in the infant's room). Perhaps most perplexing, even if the referent is present throughout the naming episode, there is no guarantee that the infant will attend to it at the time that the novel word is introduced (e.g., "Go kiss Magic," uttered in an effort to pull the infants' attention away from a sleeping sibling).

The Puzzle of Word Learning

In the best of all scenarios, word learning takes place as one speaker (say, an adult) points toward an object or scene (say, an animal running across the yard) and utters a phrase ("Voilà, un chien" [in French], or "Look, a dog" [in English]). To successfully learn the word, the listener must (1) parse the relevant word (*chien* or *dog*) from the ongoing stream of speech, (2) identify the relevant entity (the dog) in the ongoing stream of activity in the world, and (3) establish a word-to-world correspondence. To put matters more formally, successful word learning rests on an ability to discover the relevant linguistic units, the relevant conceptual units, and the mappings between them.

Parsing the Relevant Word   By approximately 9 to 10 months, infants have become increasingly sensitive to the morphologic, phonetic, and prosodic cues that mark word and phrase boundaries (chap. 2; Jusczyk & Aslin, 1995; Kemler Nelson et al., 1989). Recent work reveals that infants' growing sensitivity to these cues permits them to distinguish between two very broad classes of words: *open class* words (or *content* words, including nouns, adjectives, verbs) and *closed class* words (or *function* words, including determiners and prepositions) (Shi et al., 1999). By 9 to 10 months, infants prefer to listen to open class, as compared to closed class, words.

This preference is likely related to perceptual salience: open class words typically receive greater stress and entail more interesting melodic contours than closed class words. Since this preference for open class words exists well before infants begin to map words systematically to meaning, it is reasonable to assume that it is not tied specifically to the domain of language, per se, or to the establishment of meaning. Nonetheless, this (presumably) perceptually based early preference represents an important first step on the road to word-learning, for it ensures that infants attend to just those words (the open class, content words) that are required if they are to anchor their first word-to-world mappings (Jusczyk & Kemler Nelson, 1996; Morgan & Demuth, 1996; Werker et al., 1996).

Identifying the Relevant Entity   Word learning also depends on the learner's ability to identify discrete objects in the environment, to notice relations among these objects, and to attend to the commonalities and distinctions among them that support categorization. Recent research has revealed that prelinguistic infants have considerable knowledge about objects (Baillargeon, 2000; Spelke, 2000) that serves to organize an impressive repertoire of concepts. Some of these prelinguistic concepts are focused around richly structured, conceptual relations (e.g., bottle; animal); others are focused around primarily perceptual relations (e.g., red; soft); most concepts incorporate both conceptual and perceptual factors (see chap. 3; Waxman & Markow, 1995). Since infants' ability to form concepts appears before the advent of word learning, it is reasonable to assume that at least some concepts are formed independently of language.

Establishing a Word-to-World Mapping   This is a monumental accomplishment. It is predicated on infants' ability to grasp the referential power of words and to infer the goals and intentions of others. By 10 months, infants appear to have made such connections (Baldwin & Baird, 1999; Guajardo & Woodward, 2000). Moreover, a successful mapping depends on the infants' ability to store in memory the sound of the new word and the mapping between that word and its intended referent. This aspect of word learning, sometimes known as "fast mapping," is evident when a child applies a word (*e.g.*, *dog*) to the same individual that was named by her caregiver (e.g., a pet dog named Magic).

This represents an important step, but successful word-learning requires more. It requires infants to go beyond this *word-to-object* mapping to establish a more abstract *word-to-category* mapping (Waxman & Booth, 2000b). For example, the acquisition of a count noun (e.g., dog) requires infants to extend a new word beyond the particular individual on which it was introduced, making an inferential leap, from an individual (Magic) to a category or kind (dog). Infants' spontaneous naming behavior reveals that they make such leaps. Rather than (merely) mapping words to the individuals on which they were introduced, infants extend these words systematically, and these extensions are guided by the grammatical form of the word itself.

Different Kinds of Words Highlight Different Aspects of the Same Scene   A fundamental feature of human language is that different kinds of words highlight different aspects of the same observed scene and support a unique pattern of extension. For example, in English, count nouns ("Look, it's a dog") typically refer to the named object itself and are extended to other members of the same object kind (other dogs); proper nouns ("Look, it's Magic") also refer to the named individual, but these are not extended further; although adjectives can also be applied correctly to that individual ("Look, it's furry"), they do not refer to the individual itself but to a property of the named individual, and they are extended to other objects sharing that property.

Recent research has documented that by 2½ to 3 years of age, children are sensitive to many of these links between kinds of words and kinds of relations among objects. Moreover, children recruit these links in the process of word learning (for a review, see Waxman, 1998). For example, they expect proper nouns to refer to individual objects (Hall, 1991, 1999; Jaswal & Markman, 2001), count nouns to refer to categories of objects (Waxman, 1999; Waxman & Markow, 1995), and adjectives to refer to properties of objects within basic level kinds (Waxman & Klibanoff, 2000; Waxman & Markow, 1998). Links like these could provide powerful support in word learning, particularly if presenting a novel word in its grammatical context permits the learner to narrow the range of possible interpretations.

How Do Infants Acquire These Word-to-World Links?

But which of these links, if any, are available to infants at the very onset of lexical acquisition? And how are these shaped over the course of development? There are three logically possible solutions to this question.

Possibility 1   First, consider the possibility that early lexical acquisition is guided by an a priori set of expectations, linking each distinct grammatical form (e.g., noun, adjective, verb) to a distinct type of meaning (e.g., object categories, object properties, actions). Implicit in this view is an assumption that a great deal of structure is built into the mind of the human infant, that this structure is specific to the domain of language, and that the expectations held by infants at the onset of word learning approximate those of adults, once the particular grammatical forms can be identified in the input.[2]

This possibility requires some further specification. For while it is certainly possible that links between *some* grammatical forms and their meaning may be available at the outset of lexical acquisition, it would be an oversimplification to posit that this is the case for all, or even most, such links. The cross-linguistic literature delineates some important boundary conditions on the range of potential "a priori" links. For example, the grammatical form *noun* enjoys considerable cross-linguistic stability. Across languages, this grammatical form is universally represented, and a core function of this grammatical form is to refer to individual objects (e.g., Agamemnon) and to categories of objects (e.g., tapir; mammal; animal). In contrast, other grammatical forms (particularly the predicates, including adjectives, prepositions, spatial terms) are much more variable in both the extent to which they are represented in various languages and the ways these forms are recruited to express meaning (Bowerman, 1996; Haryu & Imai, 1999; Imai & Gentner, 1997; Regier & Carlson, in press; Waxman, Senghas, & Benveniste, 1997).

This cross-linguistic variability is directly related to questions of early acquisition, for it reveals that infants' expectations linking these grammatical forms to their associated meanings cannot be fixed from the outset. Thus, although some links may indeed be universal and may be available at the very onset of word learning, other links (and in particular those involving the predicate system) must emerge later as infants *discover* (1) whether a particular grammatical form is realized in the language under acquisition and (2) how each form maps to meaning.

Possibility 2   A radically different possibility is that infants begin the task of word learning as tabulae rasae, equipped with no a priori expectations to guide the process of acquisition. Implicit in this view is a strong assumption that any expectations regarding word-to-world mappings must be learned, and that this process of learning is no different than any other kind of learning. The claim, sometimes described as a claim that word learning is the result of "dumb attentional mechanisms" (Smith, 1999) is that infants' first words, indeed first scores of words, are acquired without the guidance of any expectations. On this view, it is only once infants have established a sufficiently large lexicon that they will begin to notice correlations between types of words and their associated meanings. Thus, the claim is that any expectations linking lexical and conceptual organization become available only *after* the establishment of a sufficiently sizeable lexicon, and certainly after the onset of word learning. In recent work, Smith and her colleagues have proposed that the first evidence of any such expectations emerges only after infants have acquired 150 words in their productive lexicons. It follows, then, on this domain-general view, that the process of word learning at the very onset of lexical acquisition (when no links have yet been established) is qualitatively different in nature from later acquisition (when the lexicon has been established and can serve as a basis for creating these links). This position has been argued forcefully (Smith, 1999; chap. 11).

However, a review of the developmental literature casts serious doubt on this possibility. There is now ample evidence (reviewed hereafter) that infants do not approach the initial steps of word learning as tabulae rasae, but instead harbor powerful expectations linking words with concepts (Balaban & Waxman, 1997; Waxman & Markow, 1995; Xu, 1999). The fact that these nascent expectations are in place in advance of word learning constitutes strong evidence against the possibility that expectations linking lexical and conceptual organization (1) emerge after the onset of word learning or (2) must be induced bottom-up, from infants' existing lexicons.

Possibility 3   The shortcomings of these first two possibilities have led me to argue for a third possibility—that infants embark on the task of word learning equipped with a broad, universally shared expectation, linking words to commonalities among objects, and that this initially broad expectation is itself subsequently fine-tuned in accordance with the form-to-meaning mappings that are realized in the native language under acquisition.

The claim is that infants begin the process of lexical acquisition not as tabulae rasae but with an initial, broad expectation regarding word-to-world mappings already in place. This expectation serves to guide lexical acquisition from the start. There is growing evidence for this view. For example, novel words (independent of their grammatical form) highlight commonalities among named objects (Balaban & Waxman, 1997) in infants as young as 9 months of age. This early expectation linking words to commonalities among objects appears to be supported by several domain-general principles, including (1) a perceptual preference for listening to novel (open class) words over other auditory stimuli, and (2) a capacity to notice similarities and differences among objects. However, the expectation itself—linking words to commonalities—appears to be specific to word learning, for it applies to novel words but not to other auditory signals (e.g., tones, as described later).

This broad initial link serves (at least) three essential functions. First, because words direct attention to commonalities, this link facilitates the formation of an expanding repertoire of categories and concepts. In this way, words serve as invitations to form categories. Second, this initially broad expectation supports infants' first efforts to establish symbolic reference, to form a set of stable "word-to-world" mappings—in short, to establish a rudimentary lexicon. Finally, and perhaps most radically, this initially broad expectation sets the stage for the evolution of the more precise expectations linking particular grammatical forms (e.g., nouns, adjectives, verbs) to particular types of relations among objects (e.g., object categories, object properties, actions) in the native language under acquisition (Waxman, 1999).

How might this evolution come about? Infants' early expectation (that words refer broadly to commonalities) directs their attention to just the sorts of regularities (among objects and among grammatical forms) that will promote the rapid discovery of the distinct grammatical forms that are present in the input. As infants begin to identify the distinct grammatical forms in the input, they first tease apart the nouns (from among the other open class grammatical forms)[3] and map these specifically to object categories (from among the other types of commonalities, including property-based or action-based commonalities). Any subsequent linkages will build on this fundamental referential base and will be fine-tuned as a function of experience with the specific correlations between particular grammatical forms and their associated meanings in the native language.

Adjudicating among These Possibilities   To adjudicate among these possibilities, we must be able to ascertain, first, whether prelinguistic infants harbor any expectations regarding word-to-world mappings, and second, whether and how infants' expectations are shaped in the course of acquiring a native language. Both developmental and cross-linguistic evidence are relevant here. For example, developmental evidence documents that by 2½ to 3 years of age, children reveal very specific expectations linking particular grammatical forms to particular types of meaning. (For evidence regarding a link between proper nouns and individuals, see Hall, 1999; for evidence regarding a link for adjectives, see Klibanoff & Waxman, 2000; for evidence regarding a link between count nouns and object categories, see Waxman, 1998, for a review; Waxman et al., 1997.) Moreover, cross-linguistic evidence reveals that some of these expectations are more likely than others to be powerfully shaped by the structure of the native language that the child is in the process of acquiring (Waxman & Guasti, 2002; Waxman et al., 1997). For example, when it comes to mapping novel count nouns to meaning, children acquiring a range of languages (English, French, Spanish, Italian) share an expectation that novel nouns direct attention specifically to categories of objects (e.g., dog, animal) (Markman & Hutchinson, 1984; Waxman & Gelman, 1986). This outcome is consistent with cross-linguistic evidence regarding the stability of the grammatical form *noun* and with the possibility that a noun-to-category mapping may be a universal feature of human language (Dixon, 1982; Gentner, 1982; Waxman, Senghas, & Benveniste, 1997). In contrast, children's expectations for novel adjectives vary systematically as a function of the language they are acquiring. For children acquiring English and French, novel adjectives direct attention specifically to property-based commonalities among objects (e.g., color; texture). Adjectives do not direct attention to category-based commonalities. However, children acquiring Italian and Spanish show a very different pattern, mapping adjectives to both categories and properties of objects. This pattern is consistent with that observed in the adult grammar. This cross-linguistic and developmental variation in the adjective system suggests that the mappings for adjectives must be learned (Waxman & Guasti, 2002; Waxman et al., 1997), while leaving open the possibility that a broader initial expectation linking words to commonalities among objects may exist in advance of word learning.

These results, coupled with converging evidence from other paradigms (Bloom, 2000; Hall & Graham, 1999; Landau, 1994; Waxman & Hall, 1993) document clearly that preschool-aged children have the *linguistic* capacity to distinguish among the relevant grammatical forms (count noun vs. adjective), the *conceptual* or *perceptual* ability to appreciate different kinds of relations among objects (category- vs. property-based), and a tacit expectation that these linguistic and conceptual abilities are interwoven. These results also reveal that children's expectations for at least some grammatical forms (here, the adjectives) are shaped by the structure of the native language under acquisition. To discover which linkages (if any) guide acquisition from the outset, and how these are shaped by experience, we go on to consider infants on the very threshold of language acquisition.

An Initially General Link between Words and Concepts Exists in Advance of Lexical Acquisition

By the end of their first year, infants are well on their way to solving several key elements in the puzzle of word learning. They identify novel words in the input, detect likenesses and differences among objects, and take advantage of the rich social and pragmatic cues in which novel words are introduced. These accomplishments are impressive, but they do not, in themselves, provide evidence that naming has any consequences for prelinguistic infants' conceptual organization and categorization behavior. What remains to be seen is whether naming influences conceptual organization before the onset of productive language.

Cognitive Consequences of Naming in Prelinguistic Infants

Naming has important cognitive consequences, even in infants who have not yet begun to produce words on their own. First, by 10 months, infants devote more attention to objects that have been named than to objects that have been presented in silence (Baldwin & Markman, 1989). This effect appears to be specific to the domain of language. The evidence reveals that infants' increased attention stems specifically from the presentation of words and not from the attention-engaging functions of auditory stimulation more generally (Balaban & Waxman, 1997). Moreover, and perhaps more striking, the consequences of naming extend beyond the named individual. Balaban and Waxman (1997) documented these effects by comparing the effect of novel words versus tone sequences in 9-month-old infants. During a familiarization phase, infants saw a series of nine slides, each depicting a different member of a basic-level category (e.g., nine rabbits). Infants were randomly assigned to either a *Word* or a *Tone* condition. For infants in the *Word* condition, a naming phrase (e.g., "a rabbit!") accompanied the familiarization trials. For infants in the *Tone* condition, a sine-wave tone (matched to the naming phrase in amplitude, duration, and pause length) accompanied the familiarization trials. The familiarization phase was immediately followed by a test trial, in which infants in both conditions saw (1) a new member of the now-familiar category (e.g., another rabbit) and (2) an object from a novel category (e.g., a pig). Test trials were presented in silence.

If words focus attention on commonalities among objects, then infants hearing words during familiarization should notice the commonalities among the familiarization objects and should reveal a preference for the novel test object (e.g., the pig). If this effect is specific to words, and not to auditory stimulation more generally, then infants hearing tone sequences during familiarization should be less likely to notice the category-based commonalities and consequently less likely to reveal a novelty preference at test. The results echoed these predictions precisely. Only infants in the *Word* condition revealed a novelty preference at test. We therefore conclude that as early as 9 months of age, there is indeed something special about words, as opposed to a more general facilitative effect of auditory input. In addition, the cognitive consequence of naming extends beyond the named individual(s) to highlight commonalities among named individuals and to promote the formation of object categories.

Naming has other key consequences for cognition during this period as well. In particular, naming appears to support infants' ability to trace the identity of individual objects over time and place. Recent evidence suggests that 10-month-old infants often find it difficult to track the unique identity of two distinct objects (e.g., a ball and a duck) (Xu & Carey, 1996). However, this difficulty decreases dramatically if each of the objects is introduced in conjunction with a distinct name ("Look, a ball!)" (Xu, 1999).

Together, these results reveal that naming has powerful cognitive consequences, even in prelinguistic infants. Naming distinct objects with the *same* name highlights their commonalities and promotes the formation of object categories (Balaban & Waxman, 1997). Naming distinct objects with *distinct* names (e.g., *ball, duck*) highlights their differences and promotes the process of object individuation (Xu, 1999). Thus, even before infants themselves begin to name objects, naming supports the establishment of a stable repertoire of object categories and provides infants with a means of tracing the identity of individuals within these categories. These core conceptual abilities are facilitated by naming, and the links between naming and conceptual organization appear before the advent of productive language.

Cognitive Consequences of Naming in Infants Just Beginning to Establish a Lexicon

In this section, I begin to trace the evolution of infants' expectations regarding word-to-world mappings as they cross over an important developmental threshold and begin producing words on their own. Together with several of my colleagues, I have designed experiments to uncover the influence of naming on categorization in infants ranging from 11 to 24 months of age (Booth & Waxman, in press; Waxman, 1999; Waxman & Booth, 2000a; Waxman & Booth, in press; Waxman & Booth, 2001; Waxman & Markow, 1998).

Some Methodological and Design Issues

Each experiment in this section is essentially an object categorization task, which compares infants' categorization of objects in "neutral" conditions (involving no novel words) with their categorization in the context of hearing a novel word. If naming facilitates categorization, then infants hearing novel words should categorize more successfully than infants in *No Word* control conditions. Because our goal is to examine an abstract linkage between naming and conceptual organization, we introduce novel words (e.g., *fauna*) rather than familiar ones (e.g., *animal*) in an effort to ensure that words we introduce have no established associations for the infants. Because we are also interested in tracing infants' emerging sensitivity to distinct grammatical forms, we vary the syntactic frame in which the novel words are embedded. In all conditions, infants hear short, simple constructions that are characteristic of infant-directed speech and that provide unambiguous structural evidence of the word's grammatical form. To introduce a novel word as a noun, we say, for example, "This is a *blicket*." We can also present the same word as an adjective by presenting it within a different frame, saying, for example, "This is a *blick-ish* one." (See Gerken & McIntosh, 1993, and Waxman & Markow, 1995, 1998, for evidence that infants are sensitive to these distinct frames.) In the *No Word* control conditions, we introduce no novel words but offer the same strong social and pragmatic support as in the experimental conditions. We point out the objects, saying, for example, "Do you like this?" or "Look at this." Performance in this *No Word* control condition assesses how readily infants form the various categories presented in our tasks (e.g., dog, animal, purple things). Performance in the *Noun* and *Adjective* conditions assesses the role of naming in this important endeavor. Including these two conditions permits us to test the specificity of the relation between grammatical form and meaning.

Naming and Category-Based Commonalities

We began by adapting the standard novelty preference task to examine the influence of novel words on object categorization in 12- to 14-month-old infants (see Waxman & Markow, 1995, for a complete description). (See fig. 9.1 for a sample set of stimuli and introductory phrases.) During a familiarization phase, an experimenter offered an infant four different toys from a given category (e.g., four animals) one at a time, in random order. This was immediately followed by a *test phase*, in which the experimenter simultaneously presented both (1) a new member of the now-familiar category (e.g., another animal) and (2) an object from a novel category (e.g., a fruit). Each infant completed this task with four different sets of objects. Two involved basic-level categories (e.g., horses vs. cats); two involved more abstract superordinate-level categories (e.g., animals vs. fruit). Infants manipulated the toys freely, and their total accumulated manipulation time served as the dependent measure.

To identify any influence of novel words on categorization, we randomly assigned infants to one of three conditions. Infants in all conditions heard infant-directed speech. The conditions differed only in the experimenter's comments during familiarization. In the *No Word* condition (control), she said, "Look at this" as she introduced each object; in the *Noun* condition, she said, for example, "This one is a *blicket*." In the *Adjective* condition, she said, for example, "This one is *blick-ish*." In the test phase, infants in all conditions heard precisely the same phrase ("See what I have?").

If infants detect the presence of the novel word, and if novel words direct infants' attention to object categories, then infants who hear novel words in conjunction with the objects presented during familiarization should be more likely than those in the *No Word* condition to form object categories. Including both a *Noun* and *Adjective* condition permitted us to test the specificity of infants' initial expectation. If this expectation is initially general, as I have proposed, then infants in either the *Noun* and *Adjective* conditions should be more likely than those in the *No Word* condition to detect the category-based commonalities.

	Familiarization Phase				Test Phase	
	Trial 1	Trial 2	Trial 3	Trial 4		
Animal Set:						
	yellow duck	green raccoon	blue dog	orange lion	red cat	red apple
Noun	This one is. a(n) X	This one is a(n) X	See what I have?	This one is a(n) X	See what I have?	
Adjective	This one is X-ish	This one is X-ish	See what I have?	This one is X-ish	See what I have?	
No Word	Look at this.	Look at this.	See what I have?	Look at this.	See what I have?	

Figure 9.1. A schematic presentation of introductory phrases from Waxman & Markow (1995) and an example of a single stimulus set.

The results provided support for these predictions. First, infants reliably detected the novel words presented in fluent speech, and these novel words (both adjectives and nouns) promoted the formation of object categories. Second, in this experiment, and in several others in our laboratory, we find that the facilitative effect of novel words is most powerful on superordinate level sets. Infants in all three conditions noticed the category-based commonalities on the basic-level sets and therefore demonstrated reliable novelty-preferences. However on superordinate level sets, where the category-based commonalities were more difficult to detect,[4] infants in the *No Word* control condition failed to detect the commonalities among the familiarization objects and failed to reveal novelty preferences at test. Yet when the same superordinate-level familiarization objects were introduced in conjunction with novel words (either count nouns or adjectives), infants successfully detected the commonalities among them and revealed reliable novelty preferences at test. Thus, although infants had difficulty detecting the category-based commonalities on superordinate level sets in the absence of a novel word, there was a clear facilitative effect of novel words at this hierarchical level. We therefore conclude that novel words highlighted category-based commonalities and facilitated infants' formation of superordinate level categories.

Infants' successful formation of (superordinate-level) categories in the *Noun* and *Adjective* conditions, and their failure to do so in the *No Word* conditions, stands as clear evidence that a link between word learning and conceptual organization is in place. Following Roger Brown (1956), we interpret this as evidence that words serve as invitations to form categories. This invitation has several dramatic consequences. Novel words invited infants to assemble together objects that were otherwise perceived as disparate and supported the discovery of commonalities that otherwise went unnoticed (for related evidence, see Gentner & Namy, 1999; Gentner & Waxman, 1994). Naming may also have dramatic consequences in situations in which infants have already formed groupings and noticed (some of) the commonalities among objects. For example, although infants in this series successfully formed basic-level object categories (whether or not they were introduced to novel words), we know that their knowledge about these categories is not on a par with that of an older child or adult (Gelman, 1996; Keil, 1994). Despite this relative lack of information, children seem to expect that members of named object categories share deep, nonobvious commonalities. Indeed, children depend on these to support inference and induction. In our view, novel words serve as invitations, motivating infants and young children to discover the deeper commonalities that underlie our richly structured object categories (Barsalou, 1983; Gelman, 1996; Gelman, Coley, & Gottfried, 1994; Gelman & Medin, 1993; Kalish & Gelman, 1992; Keil, 1994; Landau, 1994; Landau, Smith, & Jones, 1988; Lassaline & Murphy, 1996; Macnamara, 1994; Markman, 1989; Medin & Heit, in press).

Naming and Property-Based Commonalities

In the next series of experiments, our goal was to capture more precisely the scope of this early expectation linking object naming and categorization. At issue is whether infants embark on the process of lexical acquisition with an expectation linking novel words specifically to category-based commonalities (e.g., *flamingos, animals*), or to a wider range of groupings, including, for example, property-based commonalities (e.g., color: *pink things*; texture: *soft things*) as well. To answer this question, we retained the logic and design of Waxman and Markow's (1995) original paradigm but shifted the focus from category-based commonalities (e.g., *flamingo, animal*) to property-based commonalities (e.g., *pink things, soft things*). This approach is predicated in the assumption that a principled psychological distinction can be made between object categories and object properties. Most current theorists distinguish object categories (also known as *kinds* or *sortals*) from other types of groupings (e.g., *pink things, things to pull from a burning house*) on at least three (related) grounds: Object categories (1) are richly structured, (2) capture many commonalities, including deep, nonobvious relations among properties (as opposed to isolated properties), and (3) serve as the basis for induction (Barsalou, 1983; Bhatt & Rovee-Collier, 1997; Gelman & Medin, 1993; Kalish & Gelman, 1992; Macnamara, 1994; Medin & Heit, in press; Murphy & Medin, 1985; Younger & Cohen, 1986). Although infants and children have less detailed knowledge about many object categories than do adults, they clearly expect named object categories to serve these functions (Gelman, 1996; Keil, 1994).

We focused on two properties—color and texture—because infants find these properties perceptually salient and because groupings based on these properties (e.g., *purple things*) readily cut across category boundaries (to include, e.g., a lollipop, a t-shirt, and a tricycle).[5] As in the previous experiment, infants were familiarized to four distinct objects. However, this time, the commonality among the familiarization objects was not category based; it was property based (either color, e.g., purple cat, purple plate, purple spatula, purple bottle, or texture, e.g., rough cup, rough ball, rough hat, rough boot). At test, all infants were presented with both (1) a new object embodying the now-familiar property (e.g., a purple horse) and (2) an object embodying a contrasting property (e.g., a blue horse). Infants were randomly assigned to either a *Noun, Adjective,* or *No Word* condition. As before, these conditions differed only in the instructions presented to the infants during familiarization (see fig. 9.2).

This design permitted us to ask whether infants link novel words (e.g., count nouns, adjectives) specifically to the commonalities underlying object categories from the start, or whether words might also direct infants' attention to the property-based commonalities presented in this task. The design also permitted us to ascertain whether infants distinguish between novel words presented as count nouns versus adjectives. Recall that in the previous series, infants treated these two grammatical forms identically with respect to object categorization (Waxman & Markow, 1995). Both nouns and adjectives directed infants' attention toward category-based commonalities (Waxman & Markow, 1995). However, whether infants distinguish between these grammatical forms in other contexts, and whether this distinction has consequences on the formation of groupings other than object categories, remains very much an open question.

We reasoned as follows. If infants attended to the property-based commonalities among the familiarization objects, then they should reveal a preference for the object with the novel property at test (e.g., the blue horse). If they attended to the category-based commonalities among the familiarization objects, then they should reveal no novelty preferences. The only commonality among familiarization objects was property based (e.g., color or texture; see fig. 9.2). Thus, infants attending to category-based commonalities should reveal no consistent preferences at test.

The results clarify the scope of infants' initial expectations regarding object naming and categorization. Infants in this series distinguished between novel words presented as count nouns versus adjectives. Infants hearing novel adjectives directed their attention primarily to the property-based commonalities among the familiarization objects, and revealed reliable preferences at test for the object with the new contrastive properties (e.g., the blue horse). In contrast, infants hearing novel nouns revealed

	Familiarization Phase				Test Phase	
	Trial 1	Trial 2	Trial 3	Trial 4		
Purple Set:						
	purple cat	purple plate	purple spatula	purple bottle	purple horse	blue horse
Noun	This one is a(n) X.	This one is a(n) X.	See what I have?	This one is a(n) X.	See what I have?	
	Do you like the X?	Do you like the X?		Do you like the X?		
Adjective	This one is X-ish.	This one is X-ish.		This one is X-ish.	See what I have?	
	Do you like	Do you like	See what I have?	Do you like		
	the X-ish one?	the X-ish one?		the X-ish one?		
No Word	Look here.	Look here.		Look here.	See what I have?	
	Look at this.	Look at this.	See what I have?	Look at this.		
	Do you like that?	Do you like that?		Do you like that?		

Figure 9.2. A schematic presentation of introductory phrases from Waxman (1999) and an example of a single stimulus set.

no consistent preferences at test. This, coupled with the infants' performance in the *No Word* control condition, suggests that nouns actually drew infants' attention away from the property-based commonalities.

Together, these two series of experiments offer some insight into infants' expectations regarding word-to-world mappings at the onset of lexical acquisition. By 13 months, infants appear to be sensitive to at least some grammatical form distinctions, and this sensitivity has consequences for their object categorization. Novel nouns directed infants' attention specifically to category-based commonalities (as in Waxman & Markow, 1995) but away from property-based commonalities (as in Waxman, 1999). Novel adjectives had a more general influence, highlighting both category-based commonalities (as in Waxman & Markow, 1995) and property-based commonalities (as in Waxman, 1999).

What are the implications of this outcome? First, these results call into question the possibility (possibility 1) that early lexical acquisition is guided by an a priori set of expectations, linking each distinct grammatical form (e.g., noun, adjective, verb) to a distinct type of meaning (e.g., object categories, object properties, actions), for infants do not make as fine a set of distinctions as do more mature speakers (as is evident from infants' apparently general expectation for adjectives). Second, these results challenge the claim (possibility 2) that infants begin the task of word learning equipped with no expectations to guide the process of acquisition, for even novel words have a clear effect on the categorization of objects.

These results favor the possibility (possibility 3) that infants begin the task of lexical acquisition equipped with a general expectation linking words (independent of grammatical form) to commonalities among objects. The results also suggest that by 13 months of age, infants have already begun to refine this initially general expectation. At this developmental moment, infants' expectation for novel words presented as count nouns appears to be more finely tuned than their expectations for adjectives. Clearly, the infants' grammatical form distinctions are not as well defined as those of more mature speakers. And clearly, their repertoire of knowledge about individual objects, categories of objects, and properties of objects is not as rich as those of their elders. Yet by 13 months, infants do appear to share with their elders a deep insight—that there are different types of words (here, count nouns and adjectives) and that these draw attention to different types of commonalities among objects (here, category- and property-based commonalities). If this is the case, then infants have begun to make the transition from an initially general expectation linking words (in general) to commonalities (in general), and have begun to develop a more specific set of expectations for the various grammatical forms. Because this is such a powerful claim, and because it has such powerful implications for theories of acquisition, we have gone on to submit this claim to rigorous empirical test.

Fine-tuning an Initially General Expectation

The primary goal of this series was to trace the proposed developmental trajectory from an initially general expectation linking novel open class words (either count nouns or adjectives) broadly to commonalities among objects (either category- or property-based) to a more specific set of expectations. We therefore examined the influence of novel nouns and adjectives on infants from 11 to 14 months of age. We expected that 11-month-olds would reveal a very general expectation and that the older infants would have begun to transition to a more specific set of expectations. At each age, we asked (1) whether infants could construe the very *same* set of objects (e.g., four purple animals) either as members of an *object category* (animals) or as embodying an *object property* (purple), and (2) whether their construal was influenced as a function of naming.

This is important because in previous work, the evidence that naming promotes attention to object categories was documented with one set of materials and the link between naming and attention to object properties with another. For example, in experiments documenting the contribution of naming to infants' attention to category-based commonalities (Balaban & Waxman, 1997; Fulkerson & Haaf, 1998; Waxman & Markow, 1995), the only consistent relation among the familiarization objects was category based (e.g., animals). In experiments demonstrating the effect of naming on infants' attention to object properties (Waxman, 1999), the only consistent relation shared by the familiarization and test objects was property based (e.g., purple things). By introducing infants to a set of objects (e.g., purple animals) that share both an *object category* (animals) and an *object property* (purple), we can discover whether their attention to category-based and property-based commonalities is affected by naming, and more specifically, whether it is systematically affected by the grammatical form of the name provided.

A third goal of this series is methodological. Virtually all of the evidence reviewed thus far regarding infants' expectations in word learning has been based entirely on one measure: the novelty-preference task. It remains to be seen whether infants' expectations are sufficiently strong to support performance beyond this task. Therefore, in the current series, we asked whether infants' expectations would influence performance in a word extension task. Our goal here was to bridge a longstanding methodological gap between research with infants and preschoolers. From the onset of word learning, infants advance from producing single-word utterances (at approximately 9 to 12 months) to creating rich multiword expressions (at approximately 24 months). We have proposed that in the intervening period, infants' initially general expectation (that words, in general, highlight commonalities among objects, in general) become fine-tuned as infants develop the more specific expectations characteristic of their native language (that nouns refer to category-based, but not property-based, commonalities and that adjectives refer to property-based, but not category-based, commonalities, etc.). But our view of this critical transition period has been clouded, at least in part, by the difficulties of accommodating the very different behavioral capacities of individuals at either end. Novelty-preference tasks have been successful with infants, but beyond 18 months of age, infants lose interest in such tasks. Word-extension tasks have been successful with toddlers and preschoolers but lack sensitivity with infants under 18 months, who have difficulty choosing systematically among objects in forced-choice tasks.

To bridge this methodological gap, we developed a new method that weds features of the novelty-preference procedure with those of the word-extension paradigms. The procedure involved three distinct phases (see fig. 9.3 for a schematic

	Familiarization		Contrast	Test	
	Trial 1	Trial 2		Category	Property
Purple Animal Set:	bear lion	elephant dog	red apple	purple horse vs. purple chair	purple horse vs. blue horse
Noun	These are blickets. This one is a blicket & This one is a blicket	These are blickets. This one is a blicket & This one is a blicket	Uh-oh, this one is not a blicket!	Can you give me the blicket?	Can you give me the blicket?
Adjective	These are blickish. This one is blickish & This one is a blickish	These are blickish. This one is blickish & This one is a blickish	Uh-oh, this one is not blickish!	Can you give me the blickish one?	Can you give me the blickish one?
No Word	Look at these. Look at this one & Look at this one	Look at these. Look at this one & Look at this one	Uh-oh, look at this one!	Can you give one?	Can you give me one?

Figure 9.3. A schematic presentation of introductory phrases from Waxman & Booth (1999) and an example of a single stimulus set.

description of the procedure and a summary of the instructions presented in each condition).

In the familiarization phase, the experimenter introduced infants in all conditions to four objects, all drawn from the same object category (e.g., four horses or four animals) and embodying the same object property (e.g., purple). These were presented in pairs, and infants manipulated them freely. During the *Contrast phase*, the experimenter presented a new object (e.g., a brown rolling-pin), drawn from a contrastive object category and embodying a contrastive object property. She shook her head solemnly, and said either, for example, "Uh oh! This one is not a *blicket*" (*Noun* condition), "Uh oh! This one is not *blickish*" (*Adjective* condition), or "Uh oh! Look at this one" (*No Word* condition). She then re-presented a target object drawn from the original set of familiarization objects (e.g., a purple horse) and happily exclaimed, for example, "Yay, this one is a *blicket*" (*Noun* condition), "Yay, this one is *blickish*," or "Yay, look at this one" (*No Word* condition). She placed this target object in front of the infant and outstretched her palm, asking, for example, "Can you give me the *blicket*?" (*Noun* condition), "Can you give me the *blickish* one?" (*Adjective* condition) or "Can you give me that one?"(*No Word* condition).

In the *Test phase*, half of the infants in each condition received *Category* test trials (e.g., a purple horse vs. a purple chair). The remaining infants received *Property* test trials (e.g., a purple horse vs. a blue horse). Each infant was permitted to play freely with the test pair for 20 seconds. We have found that when infants are permitted to play with both test objects briefly before testing, they are more likely to select between these two objects when presented with a forced-choice test. After the 20 seconds had elapsed, the experimenter retrieved the test pair.

To assess *word-extension*, she presented a target object, drawn from the set of familiarization objects (e.g., a purple horse), and drew attention to it by pointing. She then presented the two test objects, placing them easily within the infant's reach, and asked the infant to choose one. (See fig. 9.3 for the precise instruction used in each condition.) Each infant completed this entire procedure four times, with four different sets of objects, two representing basic level object categories and two representing superordinate level categories.

If infants begin the process of lexical acquisition with a general expectation linking words (in general) to commonalities among objects (in general), then at 11 months, both nouns and adjectives should highlight both category-based (e.g., animal) and property-based (e.g., purple things) commonalities among the familiarization objects. If this initial expectation is subsequently refined, as infants discover the more precise links between particular grammatical forms and their associated meaning, then for more advanced learners, a more specific pattern should emerge. If a specific expectation for nouns is first to emerge from the initially general expectation, then infants should extend count nouns specifically to category-based commonalities but should continue to extend adjectives broadly to both category- and property-based commonalities.

The results, which are depicted in table 9.1, provided strong support for these predictions. At 11 months, infants hearing novel words (both nouns and adjectives) performed differently from those in the *No Word* condition. Infants extended both novel nouns and adjectives consistently to the familiar test object (e.g., the purple horse) on both category and property trials. This confirms that at the very onset of building a lexicon, (1) novel words direct infants' attention broadly to both category- and property-based commonalities among named objects, and (2) this link is sufficiently strong to support the infants' extension of novel words. This constitutes evidence in support of the proposal that infants on the very threshold of word learning harbor a general expectation linking words (both nouns and adjectives) broadly to commonalities (both category- and property-based) among objects.

The results from the 14-month-old infants also support the prediction that once word learning is underway and infants have established a modest lexicon, a more specific pattern of expectations should emerge. Based on our previous work (Waxman, 1999; Waxman & Booth, 2000a), we expected that at 14 months, infants would

TABLE 9.1. Means and Standard Deviations of the Proportion of Word-Extension Test Trials on Which the Familiar Object Was Chosen

	14-month-olds (Waxman & Booth, in press-b)		11-month-olds (Waxman & Booth, in press-a)	
	M	*SD*	*M*	*SD*
Noun				
Category	.68*	.13	.57	.24
Property	.44	.15	.55	.14
Adjective				
Category	.50	.18	.59	.24
Property	.52	.17	.58	.15
No word				
Category	X	X	.46	.15
Property	X	X	.49	.09

*$p < .05$ versus chance of .50.

begin to distinguish count nouns (from among the other grammatical forms) and to map these specifically to category-based commonalities. We expected that 14-month-olds' expectations for adjectives would still be quite general and that words from this grammatical form would direct their attention broadly toward commonalities (be they category or property based). In support of this aspect of our proposal, we found that by 14 months, infants were more likely to extend novel nouns to the familiar object (e.g., purple horse) on category trials (e.g., purple horse vs. purple plate) than on property trials (e.g., purple horse vs. blue horse) (M = .68 vs. .44, respectively). This suggests that they expect nouns to refer to category-based, rather than to property-based, commonalities among objects. However, infants' expectations regarding the extension of novel adjectives were more general. Infants hearing adjectives were equally likely to select the familiar object on both types of test trials (M = .50 vs. .52, respectively). This result has now been replicated (Waxman, 1999; Waxman & Booth, 2000a), using various other properties (e.g., color, texture).

Clearly, by 14 months of age, infants are sensitive to (at least some of) the relevant cues that distinguish count nouns from adjectives, and they recruit these distinctions in the task of word learning. This is consistent with the view that as infants begin to refine their initially general expectation for word-to-world linkages, they first tease apart the nouns from among the other grammatical forms, and map them specifically to category-based commonalities. During this transition from general to more specific expectations, infants' expectation for adjectives remains more general, with adjectives highlighting both category- and property-based commonalities. The more specific expectations linking adjectives to their associated types of meaning is a subsequent developmental accomplishment, one that appears to depend on infants' prior establishment of the link between count nouns and object categories, and one that is shaped by the semantic and syntactic properties of adjectives in the language under acquisition. (See Waxman et al. [1997] for evidence that this expectation for adjectives is indeed sensitive to cross-linguistic variation.)

The Evidence in Review

Bolstered by the current evidence, I return to a question I posed earlier: what expectations, if any, do infants recruit in the process of mapping their first word-to-world mappings, and how do these evolve over development? I have argued (1) that infants begin the task of word learning with a broad initial expectation that links novel words (independent of their grammatical form) to commonalities among named objects, and (2) that this initial expectation is subsequently fine-tuned as infants gain experience with the specific correlations between particular grammatical forms and their associated meanings in the native language (Waxman, 1999; Waxman & Booth, 2001; Waxman & Markow, 1995).

Our results are entirely consistent with this proposal. Eleven-month-olds begin the task of lexical acquisition with a general expectation linking novel words (in general) to commonalities among objects (in general). More specific expectations linking particular kinds of words to particular types of meaning (e.g., linking nouns to object categories) begin to emerge later, once the process of word learning is well under way. These more specific expectations, which begin to appear in infants close to 14 months of age (Waxman, 1999; Waxman & Booth, in press-b; Waxman & Markow, 1995), do not emerge all of a piece. Instead, some expectations (e.g., linking nouns to object categories) appear earlier than others (e.g., linking adjectives to properties).

The Three Possibilities Revisited

In full view of these results, reconsider the three possibilities raised earlier. First, there is the possibility that early acquisition is guided by an a priori set of expectations, linking each type of word (e.g., noun, adjective, verb) to a particular type of meaning (e.g., object categories, object properties, actions). The evidence reported here does not support this possibility in its strongest form. As has been shown, infants appear to begin the task of word learning with a link that is considerably more general than that of the more mature language user. We therefore conclude that infants' specific expectations linking particular grammatical forms to their meaning are not fixed from the outset. Instead, infants seem to discover how the various grammatical forms (and in particular, the predicates) are mapped to meaning in the language under acquisition.

One caveat is in order here. Based on my review of the adult cross-linguistic literature, I suggested that *some* links between particular grammatical forms and meaning may indeed be universal. In particular, the noun-category link enjoys considerable cross-linguistic stability. This is also the link that is first to emerge from a more general expectation. For most other grammatical forms, there is considerable cross-linguistic variability in the mappings to meaning (Bowerman, 1996; Haryu & Imai, 1999; Imai & Gentner, 1997; Regier & Carlson, in press; Waxman et al., 1997). This link also appears to emerge later in acquisition, and may indeed be predicated on the prior establishment of the noun-category linkage. This caveat is relevant to my own proposal (possibility 3) and will therefore be discussed more fully later.

Second, there is the possibility that infants begin the task of word learning as tabulae rasae, equipped with no expectations to guide early acquisition (Smith, 1999). We find no support for this possibility, particularly because infants as young as 9 to 12 months of age reveal a powerful, albeit general, expectation linking words with concepts (Balaban & Waxman, 1997; Waxman & Markow, 1995; Xu, 1999). The fact that this nascent expectation is in place in advance of word learning undermines Smith's claim that infants' expectations (1) must emerge after the onset of word learning or (2) must be induced on the basis of an extensive existing lexicon.

Third, I offered a developmental proposal, suggesting that (1) infants embark on the task of word learning equipped with a broad, universally shared expectation that links novel words (independent of their grammatical form) broadly to a wide range of commonalities among named objects, and that (2) this initial expectation is subsequently fine-tuned as infants gain experience with the particular grammatical forms in their native language and their links to meaning. The results of our experiments fit well with this proposal.

I have suggested that the initially general expectation, which appears at 11 months before the advent of productive language, is universally available and provides the foundation for infants' early establishment of symbolic reference and lexical acquisition. It also sets the stage for the evolution of the more specific expectations, which are calibrated in accordance with the observed correlations between particular grammatical forms and their associated meanings in the language under acquisition (Waxman, 1999; Waxman & Booth, 2000a; Waxman & Markow, 1995). The evidence summarized in this chapter supports this aspect of the proposal. By 14 months, infants' expectations have indeed become more fine-tuned than those that emerged at 11 months. The evidence goes one step further to reveal that as infants develop this more specific set of expectations, they first distinguish the count nouns (as compared to other grammatical forms) and map them specifically to category-based, but not property-based, commonalities among objects.

Why Is the Noun-Category Link the First Specific Link to Emerge?

On the basis of the current evidence, we cannot be certain why this is the case. This new result fits well within the framework of several different theoretical alternatives. For example, it is consistent with the possibility that a link between count nouns and object categories, which is a universal feature in the design of human languages, is innate. Across languages, the grammatical form *noun* is always represented, and a core semantic function of this grammatical form is to pick out individual objects and categories of objects. In contrast, there is substantially more cross-linguistic variation in the extent to which the grammatical form *adjective* is represented, and there is considerably more variation in the types of meaning associated with this form (Dixon, 1982). It is therefore possible that although an expectation linking nouns to object categories might be "there from the start," it is clear that any specific expectation regarding adjectives instead would emerge later, as infants come to identify the adjectives in the input and to discover how these map to meaning in the particular language under acquisition.

On the other hand, this noun-category link, though universal, may itself be learned. Gleitman and her colleagues (Fisher, Hall, Rakowitz, & Gleitman, 1994; Gillette, Gleitman, Gleitman, & Lederer, 1999; Snedeker & Gleitman, 1999) have provided a demonstration proof that learners successfully map nouns to concrete objects and categories of objects (e.g., dog, animal) by observing the word-to-world pairings that are available in the input (ongoing scenes of events and maternal input). Other types of words require additional structural, linguistic information, and this information can only become available once infants have acquired a repertoire of concrete nouns. An examination of infants' early lexicons is also consistent with the experimental evidence that I have offered concerning the early emergence of the noun-to-category link, and with the possibility that this link is learned. Recall that nouns constitute the greatest proportion of words in infants' early lexicons. Because these words refer predominantly to individual objects and categories of objects, it is possible that a link between nouns and object categories happens to be the one that is most readily discovered by infants.

Whatever its origins—induced or innate—the early emergence of a noun-category linkage is probably universal. This interpretation accords well with most current theories of language acquisition, which assume that the learner must be able to identify the nouns in the input and map them to entities in the world if they are to discover the other grammatical forms and their links to meaning (Dixon, 1982; Gentner, 1982; Gleitman, 1990; Grimshaw, 1994; Huttenlocher & Smiley, 1987; Maratsos, 1998; Pinker, 1984; Talmy, 1985; Waxman, 1999; Wierzbicka, 1986). Indeed, the argument is that the acquisition of these other grammatical forms must be grounded in the prior acquisition of nouns.

Conclusions

The goal of this chapter has been to articulate a developmental account of the powerful relation between word learning and conceptual organization. I proposed that (1) infants begin the task of word learning equipped with a broad, initial, and universally available expectation linking novel words (independent of their grammatical form) to a wide range of commonalities among named objects; (2) this initially general expectation sets the stage for the evolution of more specific expectations, calibrated in accordance with the correlations between particular grammatical forms and their associated meanings in the language under acquisition; and (3) these expectations support the rapid acquisition of increasingly sophisticated language and conceptual systems that are the hallmark of human development (Waxman, 1999; Waxman & Booth, 2000a; Waxman & Markow, 1995).

This developmental account has several distinct strengths. First, it embraces both the importance of the expectations imposed by the learner and the shaping role of the environment. The power of adopting this integrative approach to questions of acquisition has been recognized across disciplines. It can be seen in the elegant work of Marler (1991) on the acquisition of birdsong, of Held and Hein (1963) on the acquisition of depth perception in kittens, of Baillargeon (1993) and Spelke (1993) on the acquisition of physical knowledge about objects in human infants, and of R. Gelman (1991) on the acquisition of number concepts. Although each of these research programs considers very different domains of knowledge, they are all committed to considering carefully the relative contributions of both (1) the amount and type of information present in the environment, and (2) the structure or constraints imposed by the learner when characterizing the rapid acquisition of complex, sophisticated systems. (See Gallistel, Brown, Carey, Gelman, & Keil, 1991, for an extended discussion of this topic.)

In the case of word learning, this interplay between factors inherent in the child and factors within the environment is essential. Infants across the world will encounter different objects, will acquire different languages, and will be provided with different types of language input and training (Cole, Gay, Glick, & Sharp, 1971; Laboratory of Comparative Human Cognition, 1983). I have offered a proposal in which early acquisition is sufficiently constrained to permit infants to form fundamental categories of objects and to learn the words to express them, and sufficiently flexible to accommodate the systematic variations in the word-to-world mappings that occur across languages. In my view, infants' initial general expectation, or constraint, is available from the start, and it serves to direct the infant's attention toward precisely the sorts of information and regularities that will support the rapid acquisition of complex systems of knowledge, including the acquisition of words and the flexible formation of rich object categories (Gelman & Williams, 1999).

I conclude by articulating the cognitive consequences of infants' initially broad expectation linking word learning and conceptual organization. First, it guides infants in building a lexicon and establishing reference. Second, words serve as invitations to form categories. Providing a common name to a diverse set of objects directs infants' attention to the commonalities (perceptual or conceptual) among them. In this way, word learning supports the early establishment of object categories that figure largely in conceptual tasks and reasoning from infancy through adulthood. Third, words promote inductive inference. Providing a common name initiates a search for deeper, perhaps nonobvious commonalities among named entities. This promotes induction and permits rapid learning about categories of objects. Third, words promote object individuation. Applying unique names to unique individuals highlights the distinctions (perceptual or conceptual) among them and provides infants with a means for tracing the identity of those individuals over time. Fourth, early word learning is the foundation for subsequent language acquisition. Infants' initial expectations support the establishment of a stable lexicon and a stable repertoire of object categories. This provides a foundation for identifying the more specific grammatical form categories and discovering how these map to meaning in the native language.

Notes

1. Note that this was, in fact, Keller's second language. She had begun to acquire English before becoming deaf and blind.

2. There have been two distinct formulations of this possibility, syntactic bootstrapping (Gleitman, 1990) and semantic bootstrapping (Pinker, 1987), as well as an in-principle resolution of these formulations (Grimshaw, 1994).

3. We suspect that infants' discovery of grammatical form is aided by cues that are perceptually available in the input. For instance, we suspect that infants will notice which words tend to be stressed or inflected, which tend to be preceded consistently by (unstressed) closed class words, which tend to occur in particular positions (initial, final) within phrases, and so on. These cues, which are perceptually available in the input, are also integral cues to grammatical form.

4. This pattern is consistent with evidence regarding the salience of basic-level categories in early development (Rosch, Mervis, Gray, Johnson, & Boyes-Braem, 1976) but is at odds with Mandler's claim for a developmental precedence of global over basic-level categories (chap. 5). For a full discussion of this issue, see Waxman (in press).

5. In contrast, an object's shape may be more centrally related to category membership, particularly for simple artifacts and for animate objects (Waxman & Braig, 1996).

References

Au, T. K., Dapretto, M., & Song, Y. K. (1994). Input vs. constraints: Early word acquisition in Korean and English. *Journal of Memory and Language, 33*(5), 567–582.

Baillargeon, R. (1993). The object concept revisited: New direction in the investigation of infants' physical knowledge. In C. Granrud (Ed.), *Visual perception and cognition in infancy: Carnegie-Mellon Symposia on Cognition* (pp. 265–315). Hillsdale, NJ: Erlbaum.

Baillargeon, R. (2000). How do infants learn about the physical world? In D. Muir & A. Slater (Eds.), *Infant development: The essential readings. Essential readings in development psychology* (pp. 195–212). Malden, MA: Blackwell.

Balaban, M. T., & Waxman, S. R. (1997). Do words facilitate object categorization in 9-month-old infants? *Journal of Experimental Child Psychology, 64*(1), 3–26.

Baldwin, D. A., & Baird, J. A. (1999). Action analysis: A gateway to intentional inference. In P. Rochat (Ed.), *Early social cognition: Understanding others in the first months of life* (pp. 215–240). Mahwah, NJ: Erlbaum.

Baldwin, D. A., & Markman, E. M. (1989). Establishing word-object relations: A first step. *Child Development, 60*(2), 381–398.

Barsalou, L. W. (1983). Ad hoc categories. *Memory & Cognition, 11*(3), 211–227.

Bhatt, R. S., & Rovee-Collier, C. (1997). Dissociation between features and feature relations in infant memory: Effects of memory load. *Journal of Experimental Child Psychology, 67*(1), 69–89.

Bloom, P. (1993). Overview: Controversies in language acquisition. In P. Bloom (Ed.), *Language acquisition: Core readings* (pp. 5–48). Cambridge, MA: MIT Press.

Bloom, P. (2000). *How children learn the meanings of words.* Cambridge, MA: MIT Press.

Booth, A. E., & Waxman, S. R. (in press). Object functions and object names: Effects on categorization in 14-month-old infants. *Developmental Psychology.*

Bowerman, M. (1996). The origins of children's spatial semantic categories: Cognitive versus linguistic determinants. In J. J. Gumperz & S. C. Levinson (Eds.), *Rethinking linguistic relativity* Studies in the social and cultural foundations of language, No. 17 (pp. 145–176). Cambridge: Cambridge University Press.

Brown, R. (1956). The original word game. In J. S. Bruner, J. J. Goodnow, & G. A. Austin (Eds.), *A study of thinking* (pp. 247–312). New York: Wiley.

Choi, S., & Gopnik, A. (1995). Early acquisition of verbs in Korean: A cross-linguistic study. *Journal of Child Language, 22*(3), 497–529.

Cole, M., Gay, J., Glick, J. A., & Sharp, D. W. (1971). *The cultural context of learning and thinking.* New York: Basic Books.

Dixon, R. M. W. (1982). *Where have all the adjectives gone?* Berlin: Mouton.

Fernald, A. (1992). Meaningful melodies in mothers' speech to infants. In H. Papousek, U. Jurgens, & M. Papousek (Eds.), *Nonverbal vocal communication: Comparative and developmental approaches: Studies in emotion and social interaction* (pp. 262–282). New York: Cambridge University Press.

Fisher, C., Hall, G., Rakowitz, S., & Gleitman, L. (1994). When it is better to receive than to give: Syntactic and conceptual constraints on vocabulary growth. *Lingua, 92,* 333–376.

Fulkerson, A. L., & Haaf, R. A. (1998, April). *New words for new things: The relationship between novel labels and twelve-month-olds' categorization of novel objects.* Paper presented at the International Conference on Infant Studies, Atlanta, GA.

Gallistel, C. R., Brown, A. L., Carey, S., Gelman, R., & Keil, F. C. (1991). Lessons from animal learning for the study of cognitive development. In S. Carey & R. Gelman (Eds.), *The epigenesis of mind: Essays on biology and cognition. The Jean Piaget Symposium series* (pp. 3–36). Hillsdale, NJ: Erlbaum.

Gelman, R. (1991). Epigenetic foundations of knowledge structures: Initial and transcendent constructions. In S. Carey & R. Gelman (Eds.), *The epigenesis of mind: Essays on biology and cognition* [*Jean Piaget Symposium series*] (pp. 293–322). Hillsdale, NJ: Erlbaum.

Gelman, R., & Williams, E. M. (1998). Enabling constraints for cognitive development and learning: domain-specificity and epigenesis. In W. Damon (Series Ed.) and D. Kuhn & R. S. Siegler (Vol. Eds.), *Handbook of child psychology: Vol. 2. Cognition, perception, and language,* (5th ed., pp. 575–630). New York: Wiley.

Gelman, S. A. (1996). Concepts and theories. In R. Gelman & T. Kit-Fong (Eds.), *Perceptual and cognitive development: Handbook of perception and cognition* (2nd ed., pp. 117–150). San Diego: Academic Press.

Gelman, S. A., & Coley, J. D. (1991). Language and categorization: The acquisition of natural kind terms. In S. A. Gelman & J. P. Byrnes (Eds.), *Perspectives on language and thought: Interrelations in development* (pp. 146–196). New York: Cambridge University Press.

Gelman, S. A., Coley, J. D., & Gottfried, G. M. (1994). Essentialist beliefs in children: The acquisition of concepts and theories. In L. A. Hirschfeld & S. A. Gelman (Eds.), *Mapping the mind: Domain specificity in cognition and culture* (pp. 341–365). New York: Cambridge University Press.

Gelman, S. A., & Medin, D. L. (1993). What's so essential about essentialism? A different perspective on the interaction of perception, language, and conceptual knowledge. *Cognitive Development, 8*(2), 157–167.

Gentner, D. (1982). Why nouns are learned before verbs: Linguistic relativity versus natural partitioning. In S. Kuczaj (Ed.), *Language development: Language, thought, and culture* (Vol. 2, pp. 301–334). Hillsdale, NJ: Erlbaum.

Gentner, D., & Boroditsky, L. (2001). Individuation, relativity, and early word learning. In M. Bowerman & S. Levinson (Eds.), *Language acquisition and conceptual development.* (pp. 215–256). Cambridge: Cambridge University Press.

Gentner, D., & Namy, L. (1999). Comparison in the development of categories. *Cognitive Development, 14,* 487–513.

Gentner, D., & Waxman, S. R. (1994, June). *Perceptual and conceptual bootstrapping in early word meaning.* Paper presented at the meeting of the International Conference on Infancy Studies, Paris.

Gerken, L., & McIntosh, B. J. (1993). Interplay of function morphemes and prosody in early language. *Developmental Psychology, 29*(3), 448–457.

Gillette, J., Gleitman, H., Gleitman, L., & Lederer, A. (1999). Human simulations of vocabulary learning. *Cognition, 73*(2), 135–176.

Gleitman, L. (1990). The structural sources of verb meanings. *Language Acquisition: A Journal of Developmental Linguistics, 1*(1), 3–55.

Gleitman, L. R., & Wanner, E. (1988). Current issues in language learning. In M. H. Bornstein & M. E. Lamb (Eds.), *Developmental psychology: An advanced textbook* (2nd ed. pp. 297–356). Hillsdale, NJ: Erlbaum.

Goldin-Meadow, S., Seligman, M. E., & Gelman, R. (1976). Language in the two-year-old. *Cognition, 4*(2), 189–202.

Grimshaw, J. (1994). Minimal projection and clause structure. In B. Lust & M. Suner (Eds.), *Syntactic theory and first language acquisition: Cross-linguistic perspectives* (Vol. 1, pp. 75-83). Hillsdale, NJ: Erlbaum.

Guajardo, J. J., & Woodward, A. L. (2000, July). *Using habituation to index infants' understanding of pointing.* Paper presented at the 12th biennial meeting of the International Society for Infant Studies, Brighton, UK.

Hall, D. G. (1991). Acquiring proper nouns for familiar and unfamiliar animate objects: Two-year-olds' word-learning biases. *Child Development, 62*(5), 1142–1154.

Hall, D. G. (1999). Semantics and the acquisition of proper names. In R. Jackendoff, P. Bloom, & K. Wynn (Eds.), *Language, logic, and concepts: Essays in memory of John Macnamara* (pp. 337–372). Cambridge, MA: MIT Press.

Hall, D. G., & Graham, S. A. (1999). Lexical form class information guides word-to-object mapping in preschoolers. *Child Development, 70*(1), 78–91.

Haryu, E., & Imai, M. (1999). Controlling the application of the mutual exclusivity assumption in the acquisition of lexical hierarchies. *Japanese Psychological Research, 41*(1), 21–34.

Held, R., & Hein, A. (1963). Movement-produced stimulation in the development of visually guided behavior. *Journal of Comparative and Physiological Psychology, 56*(5), 872–876.

Huttenlocher, J., & Smiley, P. (1987). Early word meanings: The case of object names. *Cognitive Psychology, 19*(1), 63–89.

Imai, M., & Gentner, D. (1997). A cross-linguistic study of early word meaning: Universal ontology and linguistic influence *cognition, 62,* 169–200.

Jaswal, V. K., & Markman, E. M. (2001). Learning proper and common names in inferential versus ostensive contexts. *Child Development, 72*(3), 768–786.

Jusczyk, P., & Aslin, R. N. (1995). Infants' detection of the sound patterns of words in fluent speech. *Cognitive Psychology, 29*(1), 1–23.

Jusczyk, P. W., & Kemler Nelson, D. G. (1996). Syntactic units, prosody, and psychological reality during infancy. In J. L. Morgan & K. Demuth (Eds.), *Signal to syntax: Bootstrapping from speech to grammar in early acquisition* (pp. 389–408). Mahwah, NJ: Erlbaum.

Kalish, C. W., & Gelman, S. A. (1992). On wooden pillows: Multiple classification and children's category-based inductions. *Child Development, 63*(6), 1536–1557.

Keil, F. C. (1994). The birth and nurturance of concepts by domains: The origins of concepts of living things. In L. A. Hirschfeld & S. A. Gelman (Eds.), *Mapping the mind: Domain specificity in cognition and culture* (pp. 234–254). New York: Cambridge University Press.

Keller, H. (1904). *The story of my life.* New York: Doubleday, Page.

Kemler Nelson, D. G., Hirsh-Pasek, K., Jusczyk, P. W., & Cassidy, K. W. (1989). How the prosodic cues in motherese might assist language learning. *Journal of Child Language, 16*(1), 55–68.

Kim, M., McGregor, K. K., & Thompson, C. K. (2000). Early lexical development in English- and Korean-speaking children: Language-general and language-specific patterns. *Journal of Child Language, 27*(2), 225–254.

Klibanoff, R. S., & Waxman, S. R. (2000). Basic level object categories support the acquisition of novel adjectives: Evidence from preschool-aged children. *Child Development, 71*(3), 649–659.

Laboratory of Comparative Human Cognition. (1983). Culture and cognitive development. In P. Mussen (Ed.), *Handbook of child psychology: History, theory, and methods* (Vol. 1, pp. 295–356). New York: Wiley.

Landau, B. (1994). Object shape, object name, and object kind: Representation and development. In D. L. Medin (Ed.), *The psychology of learning and motivation: Advances in research and theory* (Vol. 31, pp. 253–304). San Diego: Academic Press.

Landau, B., Smith, L. B., & Jones, S. S. (1988). The importance of shape in early lexical learning. *Cognitive Development, 3*(3), 299–321.

Lassaline, M. E., & Murphy, G. L. (1996). Induction and category coherence. *Psychonomic Bulletin & Review, 3*(1), 95–99.

Lyons, J. (1977). *Semantics.* New York: Cambridge University Press.

Macnamara, J. (1994). Logic and cognition. In J. Macnamara & G. E. Reyes (Eds.), *The logical foundations of cognition.* [Vancouver studies in cognitive science] (Vol. 4, pp. 11–34). New York: Oxford University Press.

Mandler, J. M. (1992). How to build a baby: II. Conceptual primitives. *Psychological Review, 99*(4), 587–604.

Maratsos, M. (1998). The acquisition of grammar. In W. Damon (Series Ed.) and D. Kuhn & R. S. Siegler (Vol. Eds.), *Handbook of child psychology:* Vol. 2. *Cognition, perception, and language* (5th ed., pp. 421–466). New York: Wiley.

Markman, E. M. (1989). *Categorization and naming in children: Problems of induction.* Cambridge, MA: MIT Press.

Markman, E. M., & Hutchinson, J. E. (1984). Children's sensitivity to constraints on word meaning: Taxonomic versus thematic relations. *Cognitive Psychology, 16*(1), 1–27.

Marler, P. (1991). The instinct to learn. In S. Carey & R. Gelman (Eds.), *The epigenesis of mind: Essays on biology and cognition.* Hillsdale, NJ: Erlbaum.

Medin, D. L., & Heit, E. (Eds.). (in press). *Categorization.* San Diego: Academic Press.

Morgan, J. L., & Demuth, K. (Eds.). (1996). *Signal to syntax: Bootstrapping from speech to grammar in early acquisition.* Mahwah, NJ: Erlbaum.

Murphy, G. L., & Medin, D. L. (1985). The role of theories in conceptual coherence. *Psychological Review, 92*(3), 289–316.

Nelson, K., Hampson, J., & Shaw, L. K. (1993). Nouns in early lexicons: Evidence, explanations and implications. *Journal of Child Language, 20*(1), 61–84.

Ochs, E., & Schieffelin, B. (1984). Language acquisition and socialization. In R. Shweder & R. LeVine (Eds.), *Culture theory.* Cambridge: Cambridge University Press.

Pinker, S. (1984). *Language learnability and language development.* Cambridge, MA: Harvard University Press.

Pinker, S. (1987). The bootstrapping problem in language acquisition. In B. MacWhinney (Ed.), *Mechanisms of language aquisition* (pp. 399–441). Hillsdale, NJ: Erlbaum.

Regier, T., & Carlson, L. (in press). Grounding spatial language in perception: An empirical and computational investigation. *Journal of Experimental Psychology: General.*

Rosch, E., Mervis, C. B., Gray, W. D., Johnson, D. M., & Boyes-Braem, P. (1976). Basic objects in natural categories. *Cognitive Psychology, 8*(3), 382–439.

Saah, M. I., Waxman, S. R., & Johnson, J. (1996, April). *The composition of children's early lexicons as a function of age and vocabulary size.* Paper presented at the International Conference on Infancy Studies Providence, RI.

Shi, R., Werker, J. F., & Morgan, J. L. (1999). Newborn infants' sensitivity to perceptual cues to lexical and grammatical words. *Cognition, 72*(2), B11–B21.

Smith, L. B. (1999). Children's noun learning: How general learning processes make specialized learning mechanisms. In B. MacWhinney (Ed.), *The emergence of language* (pp. 277–303). Mahwah, NJ: Erlbaum.

Snedeker, J., & Gleitman, L. (1999, November). *Knowing what you know: Metacognitive monitoring and the origin of the object category bias.* Paper presented at the 24th annual Boston University Conference on Language Development, Somerville, MA.

Spelke, E. S. (1993). Object perception. In A. I. Goldman (Ed.), *Readings in philosophy and cognitive science* (pp. 447–460). Cambridge: MIT Press.

Spelke, E. S. (2000). Nativism, empiricism, and the origins of knowledge. In D. Muir & A. Slater (Eds.), *Infant development: The essential readings. Essential readings in development psychology* (pp. 36–51). Malden, MA: Blackwell.

Talmy, L. (1985). Lexicalization patterns: Semantic structure in lexical forms. In T. Shopen (Ed.), *Language typology and syntactic description* (Vol. 3, pp. 249–291). San Diego: Academic Press.

Tardif, T. (1996). Nouns are not always learned before verbs: Evidence from Mandarin speakers' early vocabularies. *Developmental Psychology, 32*(3), 492–504.

Waxman, S. R. (1998). Linking object categorization and naming: Early expectations and the shaping role of language. In D. L. Medin (Ed.), *The psychology of learning and motivation* (Vol. 38, pp. 249–291). San Diego: Academic Press.

Waxman, S. R. (1999). Specifying the scope of 13-month-olds' expectations for novel words. *Cognition, 70*(3), B35–B50.

Waxman, S. R., & Booth, A. E. (2000a). Distinguishing count nouns from adjectives: Evidence from 14-month-olds' novelty preference and word extension. In S. C. Howell, S. A. Fish, & T. Keith-Lucas (Eds.) *Proceedings of the 24th Annual Boston University Conference on Language Development.* Somerville, MA: Cascadilla Press.

Waxman, S. R., & Booth, A. E. (2000b). Principles that are invoked in the acquisition of words, but not facts. *Cognition, 77*(2), Netherlands: Elsevier.

Waxman, S. R., & Booth, A. E. (2001). Seeing pink elephants: Fourteen-month-olds' interpretations of novel nouns and adjectives. *Cognitive Psychology, 43*(3), 217–242.

Waxman, S. R., & Booth, A. E. (in press). The origins and evolution of links between word learning and conceptual organization: New evidence from 11-month-olds. *Developmental Science.*

Waxman, S. R., & Braig, B. (1996, April). *Stars and starfish: How far can shape take us?* Paper presented at the International Conference on Infancy Studies, Providence, RI.

Waxman, S. R., & Gelman, R. (1986). Preschoolers' use of superordinate relations in classification and language. *Cognitive Development, 1*(2), 139–156.

Waxman, S. R., & Guasti, M. T. (2002). Cross-linguistic differences in children's extensions of novel count nouns and adjectives: Evidence from Italian. Unpublished manuscript.

Waxman, S. R., & Hall, D. G. (1993). The development of a linkage between count nouns and object categories: Evidence from fifteen- to twenty-one-month-old infants. *Child Development, 64*(4), 1224–1241.

Waxman, S. R., & Klibanoff, R. S. (2000). The role of comparison in the extension of novel adjectives. *Developmental Psychology, 36*(5), 571–581.

Waxman, S. R., & Markow, D. B. (1995). Words as invitations to form categories: Evidence from 12- to 13-month-old infants. *Cognitive Psychology, 29*(3), 257–302.

Waxman, S. R., & Markow, D. B. (1998). Object properties and object kind: Twenty-one-month-old infants' extension of novel adjectives. *Child Development, 69*(5), 1313–1329.

Waxman, S. R., Senghas, A., & Benveniste, S. (1997). A cross-linguistic examination of the noun-category bias: Its existence and specificity in French- and Spanish-speaking pre-school-aged children. *Cognitive Psychology, 32*(3), 183–218.

Werker, J. F., Lloyd, V. L., Pegg, J. E., & Polka, L. (1996). Putting the baby in the bootstraps: Toward a more complete understanding of the role of the input in infant speech processing. In J. L. Morgan & K. Demuth (Eds.), *Signal to syntax: Bootstrapping from speech to grammar in early acquisition* (pp. 427–447). Mahwah, NJ: Erlbaum.

Wierzbicka, A. (1986). Does language reflect culture? Evidence from Australian English. *Language in Society, 15*(3), 349–373.

Xu, F. (1999). Object individuation and object identity in infancy: The role of spatio-temporal information, object property information, and language. *Acta Psychologica, 102*(2–3), 113–136.

Xu, F., & Carey, S. (1996). Infants' metaphysics: The case of numerical identity. *Cognitive Psychology, 30*(2), 111–153.

Younger, B. A., & Cohen, L. B. (1986). Developmental change in infants' perception of correlations among attributes. *Child Development, 57*(3), 803–815.

CHAPTER TEN

Transaction of Child Cognitive-Linguistic Abilities and Adult Input in the Acquisition of Lexical Categories at the Basic and Subordinate Levels

Carolyn B. Mervis, John R. Pani, and Ariel M. Pani

STUDIES OF CATEGORY DEVELOPMENT typically are cross-sectional, use a group design, and focus on one or at most a few categories or category labels. Furthermore, designs usually are experimental rather than observational. This approach is highly practical and the chapters in this book provide ample evidence of its success in advancing our understanding of category and conceptual development and early lexical acquisition (for the latter, see also Golinkoff et al., 2000). Developmental timetables have been provided for changes in the types of information an infant or child uses in forming categories, as measured by habituation, preferential looking or handling, or sequential touching or sorting. Similarly, developmental timetables have been proposed for changes in the lexical principles governing the extension of toddlers' and preschoolers' object labels, as measured by comprehension or production of object names. Developmental timetables also have been offered for children's attention to particular aspects of the social/pragmatic context when acquiring new words. Given their practicality, particularly in terms of the (relative) speed at which the research can be carried out and results obtained, narrowly focused cross-sectional studies using experimental designs are likely to continue to be the dominant approach to category or lexical development.

This chapter is based on a very different, but complementary, approach: an intensive longitudinal case study, using a primarily observational design, of one child's lexical development beginning with the first object word that he comprehended.

Rather than considering only a few categories, we consider Ari's acquisition of the *bird* domain, focusing on the initial extension and evolution of the categories underlying the 38 labels for types of birds that Ari had acquired by age 24 months, with some consideration of acquisition through age 2½ years. Category development at both the basic and subordinate levels is considered within the framework of the evolving transaction of child background knowledge, child social, conceptual (including lexical principles) and linguistic (especially morphosyntactic) abilities, and adult input. We begin by outlining the theoretical framework within which we addressed Ari's acquisition of the *bird* domain.

Category Structure and the Initial Extension of Early Object Words

The onset of referential lexical comprehension depends on the confluence of three more basic abilities from the domains of categorization, speech perception, and social interaction. All of these abilities typically begin to be evidenced at age 9 or 10 months, providing crucial support for the onset of referential comprehension of object names at this time. Within the domain of categorization, 10-month-old infants (but not 7-month-olds) are able to form categories on the basis of correlated form attributes (Younger & Cohen, 1983, 1986). Furthermore, at this age, infants are able to explicitly categorize novel objects into two separate form-correlation–based categories from the same higher-level category (e.g., cats and horses) even when the researcher interleaves members of the two categories during the familiarization phase of the experiment, a form of recategorization that typically results in basic-level categories (Younger & Fearing, 1999). (For an excellent overview of changes in categorization abilities at this time, see chap. 4.) Within the domain of speech perception, 9-month-old infants (but not 6-month-olds) demonstrate statistical learning based on correlations between syllable sequences and suprasegmental rhythm information, allowing them to extract multisyllabic "words" from a continuous stream of speech (Morgan & Saffran, 1995). Within the domain of social interaction, 9- and 10-month-old infants begin to engage in episodes of joint attention in which the infant coordinates his or her attention to both another person and a topic (e.g., an interesting object). Joint attention may be initiated by an adult following the child's focus of attention. During the period from 9 to 12 months, however, infants also begin to be able to follow in on their communicative partner's focus of attention, either by tracking that person's gaze or by following a pointing gesture (Carpenter, Nagell, & Tomasello, 1998).

All of these new skills result from changes in the ability to integrate information within a domain. Fundamental changes in integrative abilities at age 9 or 10 months result in the formation of both complex visual categories and complex speech categories (chap. 4). In addition, fundamental changes in infants' integrative abilities in social interactions at this time result in the ability to engage in considerably more complex social episodes (such as triadic interactions). The onset of referential comprehension, also at this time, suggests that infants' new integrative abilities are not restricted to a single domain but rather can operate across domains. The result for the 10-month-old infant is the ability to segment a word (usually the appropriate one) from the speech stream produced by his or her communicative partner while sharing that person's focus of attention, to map that word to the focus of his or her attention, and to extend the word to other members of the same prelinguistic category to which the initial referent belongs. Because these are newly emerging abilities, their simultaneous application requires considerable effort, which is likely to be expended only in cases in which the infant is particularly interested in the referent. (The importance of child interest has been stressed by Bloom, 2000, p. 19, in her Relevance Principle: "Language learning is enhanced when the words a child hears bear upon and are pertinent to the objects of engagement, interest, and feelings that are the child's contents of mind.") Thus, infants' first words, whether measured by comprehension or production, will be labels for persons, objects, or actions that are particularly important to them.

Infants' first object words are labels for prelinguistic basic-level categories (Mervis, 1984). That first words would refer to categories at this level makes sense; as Rosch, Mervis, Gray, Johnson, and Boyes-Braem (1976) argued, categories at the basic level are more fundamental psychologically than categories at other hierarchical levels. Basic-level categories stand out as categories because they are based on large clusters of correlated attributes that show relatively little overlap across categories at this level. In our world, basic-level categories are the most general categories whose members share similar overall shapes (formed of correlated form attributes arranged in particular configurations; Tversky & Hemenway, 1984) and similar characteristic actions or functions. As Younger and Cohen have shown repeatedly (see chap. 4 for a review), 10-month-old infants are highly proficient at forming basic-level categories based on correlated form attributes. Behavioral data indicate that at this age, infants also are able to incorporate function or characteristic action behavior into the clusters of correlated form attributes (see Piaget, 1954). For example, 10-month-olds consider spherical objects to afford rolling and cup-shaped objects to afford drinking. The most basic category formation principle is the Form-Function Principle: *the form and function of objects are noticeably correlated; use this correlation as the basis for categorization* (Mervis, 1990; Mervis, Mervis, Johnson, & Bertrand, 1992). (Four additional categorization principles are discussed later in this chapter.) By the age of 10 months, infants have learned enough about their world to be able to apply the Form-Function Principle to construct categories.

Nevertheless, 10-month-olds' use of the same principle(s) used by adults does not necessarily yield identical categories. The actual categories formed on the basis of these principles will vary because different groups attend to different attributes of the same object, as a function of different experiences or different levels of expertise (Mervis, 1987). Because very young children may not share adults' knowledge of culturally appropriate functions of particular objects and the form attributes correlated with those functions, these children may deemphasize attributes that are important from an adult perspective. At the same time, very young children may notice a function (and its correlated form attributes) for that object that adults ignore, leading the children to emphasize features that are unimportant to adults. In these situations, child-basic categories will differ systematically from the corresponding adult-basic categories. For example, results of research with toddlers who are developing normally and toddlers who have Down syndrome or Williams syndrome indicate that the child-basic *ball* category typically includes not only baseballs, volleyballs, and tennis balls but also spherical candles, spherical coin banks, and spherical or multisided beads—objects that adults would not consider to be balls but that nevertheless are ball-shaped and can roll. At the same time, very young children may exclude footballs from their *ball* category because a football's overall shape is not spherical and footballs do not roll in the same manner as typical balls do (Mervis, 1984, 1987; Mervis & Bertrand, 1997).

Mervis (1987) has identified three reasons why very young children might initially attend to a different set of attributes for an object or assign a different weight to an attribute of an object than adults would, leading to the inclusion of additional objects in child-basic categories that would be excluded from the adult-basic category labeled by the same name. First, very young children are likely to be unaware of the cultural significance of certain objects. For example, children who are just beginning to acquire language are unlikely to realize that candles are for burning to make light. Therefore, a spherical candle's wick and wax are likely to be ignored, in favor of known attributes such as "spherical" and "rolls." Accordingly, spherical candles will be assigned to the child-basic *ball* category. Second, the child may be aware of the attributes that are important to the adult category assignment, but the salience of this set of attributes may be less than the salience of the set of attributes that supports the child-basic category. Thus, a young child who has learned about the cultural significance of candles may consider a spherical candle to be both a *ball* and a *candle*. Third, the child may include false attributes in making correlations. For example, the mistaken belief that a tiger says "meow" (as the child's mother may say Mervis & Mervis, 1982) may contribute to the child's decision to categorize it as a *kitty*.

In cases in which very young children form a child-basic category that excludes objects that adults would include in the adult-basic category labeled by the same name, the child typically has a more narrow definition of the acceptable range of values for one or more of the attributes included in the cluster of correlated attributes underlying the category. For example, both adults and children expect kitties to have fur. Infants and toddlers who are just beginning to acquire language, however, may require this fur to be plush and relatively plain. Thus, a toy housecat made of a flowered cotton fabric or a live sphinx (hairless) cat may be excluded from the child's *kitty* category, even though an adult would consider it a *kitty*. Infants and toddlers who are just beginning to acquire language may also exclude two-dimensional representations from their object categories (Mervis, 1987).

Which objects, then, may be expected to be included in an initial child-basic category? Predictions may be made based on the Form-Function Principle. Basic-level categories are the most general categories whose members share similar overall shapes (similar patterns of form attribute correlations) and correlated functions or characteristic actions. This prediction is moderated by at least two factors. First, as Kogan (1971) has shown, the breadth of a category may vary as a function of a child's cognitive style. Variability due to cognitive style should be limited to the inclusion or exclusion of borderline category members (e.g., for the *chair* category, items such as beanbag chairs, stools with backs, and sassy seats). Second, as Mervis and Pani

(1980) have demonstrated, the initial exemplar on which a child bases a category will have a strong impact on the early extension of that category. If the initial exemplar is a good example of the category, the person (whether child or adult) is likely to form the predicted basic-level category. In contrast, if the initial exemplar is a poor example of its category, the person is likely to severely undergeneralize the category. For example, the initial exemplar of Ari's *lion* category was highly atypical of lions. As a result, for several weeks, he used the word "lion" to refer only to this lion and photographs of it. More typical lions, meanwhile, were included in his *kitty* category (Mervis, 1987).

When children first begin to acquire object labels, children often do not assign objects to the categories corresponding to the labels provided by adults for those objects. Instead, labels are extended based on the child's prelinguistic categories. Mothers of children who are developing normally often label objects to correspond with the categories to which they expect their child to assign an object. Thus, these mothers are likely to label a spherical bank "ball" and a leopard "kitty." Mothers of children with developmental delay, however, typically label objects with their correct (from an adult perspective) name and may try to prevent the child from using an object in a child-basic manner (e.g., rolling a spherical candle). Despite these differences in input, however, both children who are developing normally and children with developmental delay form the same initial child-basic categories (as measured by lexical comprehension and production), including objects that the child considers to fit the form-function correlation underlying the category (e.g., including leopards and tigers in the *kitty* category) and excluding objects that the child considers not to fit this correlation (e.g., flat flowered cotton housecat-shaped sachets), regardless of how these are labeled by their communicative partners (Mervis, 1984, 1987).

Evolution of Child-Basic Categories

Child-basic object categories eventually evolve to correspond to the adult-basic categories labeled with the same name. This process, in the case of categories that were initially overextended (or the overextended portion of a category that initially overlaps the adult one), involves first learning new category assignments for the overgeneralized objects and then separating the initial category from the new category(s), such that any given object is included in only one basic-level category. For categories that were initially underextended (or the underextended portion of a category that initially overlaps the adult one), two situations may obtain. First, the undergeneralized objects may have been included in a different child-basic category. If so, the process of evolution is the same as that described for initially overextended categories. If the undergeneralized objects instead have not yet been assigned to any category, the process of evolution will involve expanding the range of attribute values that are acceptable for membership in the category.

The process of basic-level category evolution, like the process of initial acquisition of toddlers' first child-basic categories, is a cooperative effort between the child the child's communicative partners (see also Hirsh-Pasek, Golinkoff, & Hollich's [2000], emergent coalition model). Once again, the child's attention to attribute correlations will be critical, although, as described hereafter, this time the child will need to attend to or emphasize different attributes from those previously considered important. Oakes and Madole (chap. 6) have discussed broad developmental changes that result in the reduction of the pool of potential attributes to which an infant or toddler attends when categorizing objects. Two of these developmental changes—increases in background knowledge and increased understanding of objects—play a particularly important role in category evolution. The child's interest in the object and its attributes also is important in determining the timing of acquisition of the new category (Bloom's [2000] Relevance Principle). As the child's lexical and syntactic abilities increase, the child will be more likely to benefit from adult verbal input regarding category assignment. Furthermore, the child's willingness to engage adults in interactions that are likely to yield new information about attributes or categorization also plays a major role. All that said, the role of the communicative partner is important as well. In almost all cases, these people will be the source of labels for the new categories. The manner in which these labels are provided, in interaction with the child's developmental level, will have a major impact on whether or not the new labels are learned and category evolution begun.

The first step in category evolution involves focusing on a different set of attributes of a particular object (or object type), as expressed in the Form-Function/Additional Category Principle: Assign *a category member to an additional, newly formed category if you are given concrete evidence of a new attribute basis for that category* (Mervis, 1990; Mervis et al., 1992). Because this principle follows directly from the initial Form-Function Principle, toddlers should be able to use the Additional Category Principle from the time they can use the Form-Function Principle.

Given the Form-Function/Additional Category Principle, one would expect that the most successful methods of introducing the adult-basic label for an object currently included in a child-basic category labeled by a different name would involve a clear indication of the attribute basis for the new category. Strategies that involve making certain that the child is focused on the relevant attributes at the time the new name is provided should be most effective. In some cases, the child initiates this focus. For example, one toddler in the longitudinal study described in Mervis and Canada (1983) bit into a spherical candle and (as one would expect under the circumstances) ended up with wax on her teeth. She pulled the candle out of her mouth and said, "Yucky ball." At this point, her mother took advantage of the situation to tell the child that the object was a candle. When the girl was tested at the end of the play session, she demonstrated comprehension of the word "candle," although she continued to consider the spherical candle to be a *ball* as well. Unlike the Mutual Exclusivity Principle (Markman, 1989), the Form-Function/Additional Category Principle does not mandate deletion of objects included in the new category from the old category. Such deletion will not occur until the child realizes that only the attribute correlation that provides the foundation for the new category is relevant for categorization of the objects in question. The child may come to this realization on the basis of either further interactions with the relevant objects or, eventually, the Authority Principles, acquired later.

In most cases, new labels are introduced by communicative partners without an indication from the child that the child is already focused on the relevant attributes. Under these circumstances, the input strategy most likely to be effective in encouraging a child to learn a new label for an object for which the child already has a basic-level name is for the communicative partner to describe and point out the parts of the object that are important to the new category (i.e., form information), along with naming and demonstrating the functions that are correlated with those parts. Chapman, Leonard, and Mervis (1986) and Banigan and Mervis (1988) have shown that this type of strategy is effective in inducing comprehension of new labels for objects previously included in such child-basic categories as *ball, car,* and *kitty.* As the child becomes more linguistically advanced, provision of verbal descriptions of attribute information without physical indication of the attributes should become increasingly effective.

Of course, communicative partners can (and often do) simply provide the correct label without any accompanying attribute information and without a request (either implicit, as in the candle example earlier, or explicit) from the child. As would be expected, given the Form-Function/Additional Category Principle, this method has been shown repeatedly to be unsuccessful in inducing young toddlers either to comprehend the new label or to begin to form a new category (e.g., Banigan & Mervis, 1988; Chapman et al., 1986; Gruendel, 1977). Although this strategy will eventually be successful, success depends on the child's acquisition of the more advanced operating principles subsumed under the Authority Principle: *There exist people (authorities) who know more about forms, functions, and form-function correlations than you do. When these people label an object, they probably are referring to a valid category.*

The Authority Principle requires acceptance of another person's authority on labeling and categorization matters, even when the child does not immediately understand the basis for the authority's label or category assignment. This general principle may be divided into two components, which themselves may be acquired in a developmental order. The concept that an additional category should be formed if an authority labels an object with a different name than the one the child would have used is expressed in the Authority/Additional Category Principle: *If an authority labels an object with a name different from the one you would have used, and the category named by the authority's label is not yet part of your repertoire, form a new category and assign the object to that category.* Once this principle is in place, the child will be able to benefit from hearing a new label (assuming the child is focused on, or is able to switch focus to, the relevant object) without any further explanation.

As with the Form-Function/Additional Category Principle, the Authority/Additional Category Principle does not necessarily yield mutually exclusive categories. The development of mutually exclusive categories depends on another Authority Principle, the Authority/Coordinate Deletion Principle: *If an authority labels an object with a name different from the one you would have used, and you have reason to believe that the two categories are coordinate, delete the object from its previously assigned category.* This principle is similar to Markman's (1989) Mutual Exclusivity Principle. An important difference between the two, however, is the point at which the child begins to use the principles. Mutual Exclusivity is expected to be available from the beginning of word learning; it is considered a foundational principle that helps toddlers begin to acquire words. In contrast, the Authority/Coordinate Deletion Principle is acquired relatively late; the realization that coordinate categories do not overlap is based on experience and does not occur until the child has acquired a large number of coordinate categories.

Acquisition of Subordinate-Level Categories

A given object may be categorized at a variety of hierarchical levels. For example, a particular green apple is simultaneously a Granny Smith apple (subordinate level), an apple (basic level), and a fruit (superordinate level). The basic level is the default level for categorization (Brown, 1958; Mervis, Johnson, & Mervis, 1994; Rosch et al., 1976) for both adults and children. Accordingly, it is not surprising that the vast majority of toddlers' object words are labels for basic-level categories. For example, there are very few subordinate-level words on the vocabulary checklist included in the MacArthur Communicative Development Inventory: Words and Sentences (Fenson, Dale, Reznick, Bates, & Thal, 1994), a measure for assessing the language of children aged 16 to 30 months.

Mastery of subordinate categorization is necessary for a child to acquire expertise within a domain (e.g., dinosaurs, trucks). In order to acquire subordinate categories, children must first realize that a given object can have more than one name. The earliest realization occurs in reference to proper names; by 18 months, most children know that they are both [first name] and "baby" and that while other children their age are babies, they are not [first name]. Once children understand that objects can have more than one name, they may begin to acquire not only proper names for members of a particular basic-level category but also subordinate names for basic-level categories. Acquisition of subordinate-level names and categories is greatly facilitated by adult provision of inclusion statements. For example, the communicative partner could tell a child "That dog is a collie" or provide a more general statement, such as "That kind of dog is called a collie," or an even more general statement, such as "A collie is a kind of dog." Comprehension of the first type of statement requires that the child be comfortable in assigning objects to more than one category and that the child understand that the use of the indefinite article indicates that the following word refers to a category and is not a proper name. Comprehension of inclusion statements using the word "kind" further requires that the child have a concept of "kind."

Once children have either the linguistic concept of the indefinite article or the cognitive concept of "kind," they can use the same Form-Function Principles that they used to acquire basic level categories to form categories at the subordinate level. This time, however, they will need to notice much more specific attribute correlations. Whereas the correlated attribute clusters underlying basic-level categories typically rely on correlations among parts, those underlying subordinate-level categories typically rely on correlations among modifications of parts. Thus, subordinate-level categorization is likely to be dependent on the acquisition of concepts of quality (concepts often denoted by adjectives). For example, differentiation among songbirds requires attention not to wings and feathers, as was important for telling a bird from a mammal, but rather to the color patterns and size of creatures all of whom are feathered and winged. In the case of the *bird* domain, then, acquisition of most subordinate-level categories cannot occur until the child both has the concept of "color" and has acquired several color terms. Size concepts also are important.

Without the conceptual and linguistic knowledge that underlies subordinate-level categorization in general and in the relevant domain in particular, children are unlikely to acquire subordinate-level categories. (Even if they learn a label that is at the subordinate level for adults, it is likely to be treated as the name for a basic level category; see the schoolbus example in Johnson & Mervis, 1997a.) Once children have the necessary conceptual and linguistic knowledge, they will be more likely to form subordinate level categories if they either have noticed the relevant subordinate-level attributes themselves or an adult points them out explicitly in a manner the child can understand (Mervis et al., 1994). Acquisition of subordinate-level names (and the formation of the relevant category) simply on the basis of provision of an inclusion statement relies on the Authority Principles.

The progression we have outlined here could be investigated in a series of individual experiments each designed to address a small segment of the process of early lexical development. Alternatively, this progression could be examined in a broad sweep by studying the naturalistic acquisition of an entire domain, over a long period of time. Although such a study lacks experimental control, it has the advantage of allowing for observation of the natural transaction of child background knowledge, linguistic knowledge, memory ability, and interest in a domain with adult input as the child acquires an entire object domain. The intensive nature of such a study makes it likely that it will focus on a single child. In the remainder of this chapter, we describe the methods and major findings from such a case study, focusing on the acquisition of the *bird* domain.

Method

Case study methodology is designed to provide intensive investigation of domains that are rapidly changing (Dromi, 1987). This method is particularly valuable for studying psychological processes that are complex, may be context bound, and are highly dynamic—three characteristics intrinsic to early lexical and categorical development. The use of case study methods allows one to trace the impact, of particular kinds of lexical input, in interaction with particular levels of background knowledge, on acquisition of new words and changes in extension of old ones. Although causality cannot be inferred, one can identify likely causal relations, which may then be tested experimentally. The importance of continuous data collection to the understanding of the extremely complex process of early language development cannot be stressed enough. Longitudinal studies involving monthly (or even weekly) sessions often miss important but brief intermediate stages in language development (Mervis & Johnson, 1991) and dramatically underestimate the proportion of children's words that are overextended at some point in development (Mervis et al., 1992). Cross-sectional studies, by definition, are even more likely to miss brief but important aspects of early lexical development.

At the same time, the case study method as applied to lexical development has been criticized for both its literary (as opposed to scientific) style and reliance on anecdotal data. (e.g., Braunwald & Brislin, 1979; Gale & Gale, 1900). These criticisms may be addressed by using event-sampling methods, that is, choosing *a priori* to record a particular type of behavior(s) and particular types of contextual information and then recording the occurrence and context of these behaviors as they take place. This form of event sampling characterizes the systematic diary method—the method used in this study.

Participant

Ari (the third author) was the participant in this study. He was an only child throughout the course of the study.

Case Study Components

The diary study had four components: systematic entries of instances of naturally occurring spontaneous or elicited production or comprehension; quasi-experimental probes designed to establish the extension of Ari's early object names; videotaped and audiotaped play sessions, and notes concerning Ari's overall cognitive, language, social, and motor development. Each component is described separately here. More detailed information about these components is provided in Mervis et al. (1992).

Diary Entries   Recording of diary entries began at age 0;10.18 (0 years, 10 months, and 18 days). Entries were recorded by Ari's mother and father (the first two authors) and by Ari's maternal aunt. All three recorders had professional training in research methodology, and two had training in phonetics and phonology, which was very helpful in interpreting Ari's early speech. In addition, other individuals who interacted frequently with Ari reported instances of comprehension or production to one of the recorders; these instances were added to the records. During the period of the diary study, Ari spent relatively little time in childcare.

Virtually complete records of lexical production were kept until Ari was age 1;4.00, at which point his productive vocabulary included about 85 words. From then until Ari was 1;10.00, a predetermined set of rules was followed for which instances were entered into the diary. All new words and all instances of underextension and overextension were recorded, as were all instances of words that appeared to be in transition. To the extent possible, the first instance of appropriate production of each relatively new word in reference to a particular object was recorded each day; additional instances were recorded when possible. Records concerning color names were kept until all 11 basic color terms consistently were used correctly. From age 1;10.01 to age 2;00.01, all new words produced were recorded, along with instances of over- or underextension. Written notes on particular topics of interest (e.g., subordinate and superordinate labels), including the same contextual information as the diary entries, were kept for the next several months.

Quasi-experimental Probes   To establish the extension of Ari's early words, efforts were made to provide him with a wide range of potential exemplars and non-exemplars. Most often, adults simply placed objects in Ari's vicinity and then waited to see what he called them. Ari was also taken to places such as zoos or farms so that he would have an opportunity to label a variety of birds. In addition, both his parents and his grandparents had bird feeders that were frequented by a number of bird species. Systematic testing of comprehension and production of crucial potential referents was conducted, primarily during the first several weeks of the study (to help establish the extension of his earliest words).

Play Sessions   Ari participated in two types of monthly play sessions with his mother. In the first, Ari played with his own toys; the toys varied from month to month, depending on his current interests. In the second, a standard set of toys, based on the set used in a previous longitudinal study (Mervis, 1984; Mervis & Mervis, 1988), was used. This set included a blackbird, a mallard, and a swan. Play sessions were recorded from age 11 months to age 2 years 6 months.

Notes on Other Aspects of Ari's Development   To provide information about Ari's overall development, new cognitive, social, and motor accomplishments were recorded as they occurred.

Databases and Coding

The 38,925 diary entries were assigned to one of five databases, depending on whether the entry was an instance of comprehension or of production; and for production, whether or not the word was a proper noun, common noun, or some other part of speech and whether or not the referent was visible at the time Ari produced the word. The four databases used for the analyses in the present chapter are as follows.

Production of Common Nouns with Visible Referents   This database includes 19,937 entries, of which 2,822 involve production of either "bird" or the name of a type of bird. Entries include the context immediately preceding Ari's utterance, his utterance, the adult response to his utterance, and, if applicable, the remainder of that particular interaction (including any additional times that Ari labeled the referent).

The coding of the entries is described in detail in Mervis et al. (1992). Only codes relevant to the analyses described in this chapter are described here. A referent dictionary was created that provided a description of and assigned a code to each of the objects that Ari labeled. A code was assigned to each word/referent pair, indicating the relation between the label Ari used and the object to which he referred (e.g., correct, slight overextension, significant overextension, symbolic play). Responses were coded in detail, indicating: the general tone of the response (in terms of whether the adult agreed with or disagreed with Ari's label); whether the adult repeated Ari's label and, if so, if the repetition was qualified (e.g., looks like a [label]), whether the adult requested another label, and Ari's response to that request. If the adult provided a new label for the object, the hierarchical level of the new label was coded, as well as the relation between the new label and Ari's label in terms of mutual exclusivity and the strategies used to introduce the new label (including any attributes mentioned and whether or not the adult used a contrast referent). Ari's response, if any, to a label introduced by the adult was coded for agreement or disagreement with the adult label or attribute information. Ari's response to any adult disagreement with his label was also indicated.

Production of Common Nouns with Nonvisible Referents   This database includes 6,562 entries. These entries were coded for date, word, category, context, and response.

Production of Non-nouns   This database includes 8,677 entries. Entries were coded for word, date, context, and response. A code for part of speech (e.g., verb, adjective, adverb) was used as a preliminary basis for subdividing Ari's non-noun vocabulary.

Comprehension   This database includes 1,032 entries, covering both comprehension trials to which Ari did respond and those to which he did not. The latter are particularly relevant to understanding certain aspects of underextension. Entries were coded for date and divided into context, action, and response. The context contains all information up to and including the request for Ari to get something or do something. The action section describes Ari's response, including both nonverbal and verbal behavior. The response section contains the adult's response to Ari's action. One-part requests (those that asked Ari to do only one thing, e.g., "Where's the kitty?") were further coded for word used by the adult; category, level, and word/referent relation (for nouns); or part of speech (for non-nouns).

Findings

We divide our presentation of findings into four areas. First, we consider category extension and evolution as measured by lexical comprehension and production for *bird* (the name of the domain). Second, we consider the initial category extensions for the 38 names of types of birds that Ari acquired prior to age 24 months. Third, we consider the impact of several types of adult input that vary in the amount of scaffolding they provide for acquisition of the new word and the category underlying it, for basic-level categories within the *bird* domain. In particular, we describe changes in the effectiveness of particular input strategies, as a function of Ari's increasing cognitive sophistication, including his eventual realization that knowledgeable adults, rather than he, were the source of correct category names. To illustrate these processes, we consider the evolution of Ari's initial *duck* category. Fourth, we consider in detail the acquisition of subordinate categorization in the *bird* domain. Here we address the transaction of adult input, increases in Ari's syntactic knowledge, increases in Ari's knowledge of cognitive domains critical for differentiating subordinate bird categories (e.g., color, size), and the impact of "learning how to learn"—knowing which types of attributes are likely to be important for categorization at the subordinate level in the *bird* domain—on Ari's acquisition of subordinate bird names and categories.

Category Extension and Evolution: *Bird*

Ari first comprehended the word "bird" at age 1;1.6 and first produced "bird" 8 days later. "Bird" was the 12th word in his productive vocabulary. Animals, and particularly members of the *bird* domain, were prominently featured in his lexicon at that time; "bird" was Ari's sixth label for a type of animal and third label (after "duck" and "owl") for members of the *bird* domain. Thus, Ari's interest in animals in general and birds in particular was apparent in his first words, providing strong support for Bloom's (2000) Relevance Principle.

At the time that Ari first comprehended "bird," he had been exposed to a large number of exemplars of the *bird* domain, only some of which had been named for him. Objects that had been called "bird" in speech addressed to Ari included the following plush toys: cardinal, bluebird, goldfinch, blackbird, seagull, eagle, vulture; a wind-up chicken; pictures of a variety of songbirds; and several species of live songbirds. In addition, there were several porcelain songbirds and several engravings of songbirds that had not been named for Ari. Other bird names that had been used in speech addressed to Ari included "duck," "goose," "owl," "chicken," "penguin," "seagull," and "vulture."

The evolution of Ari's pattern of extension for "bird" is indicated in table 10.1. Ari's *bird* category was based, from the beginning, on the Form-Function Principle. Initially (periods 1 and 2), birds were small creatures with songbird-shaped torsos and small beaks that chirped (or said "tweet") and sat in trees and bushes. Ari's *bird* category contrasted with his already established *duck* category; *ducks* were somewhat larger creatures with duck-shaped torsos and long bills that said "quack" and swam. Thus, *bird* was initially underextended, but in line with the Form-Function Principle. The single overextension that was produced was to a small mouse sitting on the branch of a tree. The evolution of Ari's *bird* category during period 3 involved a gradual process of expanding the range of acceptable attribute values until medium-sized birds that were not waterfowl were accepted as *birds*. Overextensions based on salient attributes associated with the correlated attribute cluster underlying Ari's *bird* category continued to occur. During period 4, Ari's *bird* category further evolved to include waterfowl as well as very large land, shore, and waterbirds. Acceptance of these creatures as *birds* depended on Ari's ability to comprehend inclusion statements (e.g., "An X is a [kind of] bird."); comprehension of such statements allowed him to expand the range of attribute values to encompass the entire avian domain, while still abiding by the Form-Function Principle.

Initial Extensions of Categories Included in the *Bird* Domain

By age 24 months, Ari had acquired the names for 38 types of birds. The initial extensions for the categories underlying these names (as measured by lexical comprehension and production) are indicated in table 10.2.

Categories for Which the Initial Exemplar was Highly Atypical   For two of the 38 categories (*woodpecker*, *parrot*), the first exemplar that adults labeled for Ari was highly atypical. At the time Ari first produced "woodpecker" and "parrot," no typi-

TABLE 10.1. Pattern of Extension of the Category *Bird* during Four Developmental Periods, as Measured by Lexical Comprehension and Production

Period[a]	Onset marked by:	Correct extension[b]	Overextensions	Underextensions
1 (1;1.6)	First comprehension of "bird"	Bluebird Cardinal Chickadee	none	All nonsongbirds
2 (1;1.14)	First production of "bird"	Hummingbird Parakeet Bird-shaped button Cedar waxwing Meadowlark Bluejay Sparrow Robin	Mouse sitting in tree	All nonsongbirds except hummingbirds
3 (1;2.20)	First production of "bird" in relation to a bird larger than a songbird	Chicken Flock of birds flying overhead In response to hearing out-of-sight birds chirping Eagle Owl (in tree) Pigeon Seagull Crested crane Penguin (picture) Quail Woodpecker	Mouse sitting in tree Lowly worm Seal with flippers extended (picture)	Pelican Flamingo Stork Ostrich Duck Goose Swan
4 (1;6.14)	First indication of hierarchical understanding	Pelican Flamingo Stork Ostrich Duck[c] Goose Swan	Abstract flower in tree	None

[a] Age at onset of period is indicated in parentheses.

[b] Cumulative across periods. For period 1, all correct extensions are listed. For period 2, the total set of correct extensions is composed of the categories listed in periods 1 and 2. For periods 3 and 4, examples of new correct extensions are given.

[c] On three prior occasions, Ari had labeled ducks "birdie." The first (age 1;2.20) involved a picture of a rubber duck; other than this instance, Ari always labeled rubber ducks "duckie." The second (age 1;2.23) involved a flock of ducks flying high overhead; it is likely that Ari realized these were ducks. In the third (age 1;2.30), Ari started to label a toy mallard "birdie" but cut himself off midword and said "duckie."

TABLE 10.2. Relation of Ari's Initial Extension to Adult Extension, for *Bird* Categories Acquired by Age 24 Months

Bird name	Age at first production	Initial extension pattern
Duck	0;11.9	Overlap: underextended to all two-dimensional representations of ducks, plastic duck rattle, Donald Duck pop-up figure; over-extended to carved wooden grebe, wind-up chicken, porcelain goose, Big Bird, swan[a]
Owl	1;1.10	Overlap: Undergeneralized with regard to toy owl with fur, pink felt owl; overgeneralized to penguin, various similar-sized landbirds, chick, stylized songbirds, panda, eagle, raccoon (all seen face-on)
Rooster	1;2.23	Overgeneralized to chicken, muscovy duck, quail, toucan, kangaroo[b]
Turkey	1;4.23	Overlap: Undergeneralized to baby turkeys; overgeneralized to rooster, chicken, quail, partridge that had a face like a turkey, sand hill crane
Penguin	1;5.8	Overlap: Undergeneralized to embroidered penguin; overgeneralized to auklets
Chicken	1;5.12	Undergeneralized to wind-up chicken, otherwise correct
Chick	1;5.24	Correct
Eagle	1;5.27	Overlap: Undergeneralized to line drawing of eagle from the side with its wings spread; overgeneralized to hawk, caracara, parrot, vulture (all seen in typical "eagle" pose)
Seagull	1;6.5	Overgeneralized to pigeon, puffin, bluebird, drawings of flying merganser ducks and flying vulture
Goose	1;6.6	Overlap: Undergeneralized to white geese; overgeneralized to black swan and flamingo
Cardinal	1;6.7	Overgeneralized to pyrrhuloxia, bluejay, meadowlark
Swan	1;6.11	Overlap: Undergeneralized to baby swans, swan-shaped planter (labeled "duckie"), black swan (labeled "duckie" and then, when questioned, "goose"); overgeneralized to goose with very long neck, white duck, peacock, willow ptarmigan in winter plumage, baby flamingo (white)
Woodpecker	1;6;29	Initially used only in reference to drawings of a particular large stylized woodpecker. Undergeneralized to all typical woodpeckers initially, then overgeneralized to wall creeper that has its beak pressed against a stone wall and to rainbow lorikeet that has its beak pressed against a tree
Bluejay	1;7.7	Overgeneralized to bluebird, chickadee, nuthatch, black crested titmouse, crow with a profile like a bluejay
Robin	1;7.21	Overgeneralized to song sparrow, bluebird, red-breasted blackbird
Ostrich	1;7.23	Overlap; Undergeneralized to baby ostriches; overgeneralized to very large goose picture, emu, rhea
Chickadee	1;8.20	Basically correct (overgeneralized once, to grosbeak)
Pelican	1;8.21	Overgeneralized to stylized white bird with huge bill, ibis, and once to toucan, vulture, and tern
Peacock	1;8.29	Basically correct: (undergeneralized once to stylized drawing; overgeneralized once, to pheasant)
Pigeon	1;8.29	Overgeneralized to dove, starling that looks like a skinny pigeon
Mallard	1;9.5	Correct
Bluebird	1;9.2	Correct
Goldfinch	1;9.6	Correct
Blackbird	1;9.6	Correct

continued

TABLE 10.2. (*continued*)

Bird name	Age at first production	Initial extension pattern
Flamingo	1;9.9	Overlap: Undergeneralized to baby flamingos; overgeneralized to spoonbill, ibis
Parrot	1;9.11	Initially used only if reference to sulfur-crested cockatoo. Undergeneralized to typical parrots for a few days; a few days after that, overgeneralized to puffin, toucan
Canary	1;11.2	Correct
Pheasant	1;11.2	Correct
Sparrow	1;11.2	Correct
Crow	1;11.4	Correct
Tanager	1;11.7	Correct
Meadowlark	1;11.7	Basically correct (overgeneralized once, to robin w/spotted breast)
Finch	1;11.7	Correct
Junco	1;11.7	Correct
Puffin	1;11.12	Basically correct (overextended twice to toucans)
Wood duck	1;11.16	Correct
Toucan	1;11.24	Basically correct (overextended once, to hornbill)
Grosbeak	1;11.28	Correct

[a]Ari was not exposed to any large water or shore birds during the first month after he began to produce "duck." However, his inclusion of Big Bird in duck suggests that he would have considered these types of birds to be ducks, had he had the opportunity. "Duck" was overextended to include these birds, as measured by both comprehension and production, the first time that Ari saw them.

[b]Although Ari labeled the kangaroo "rooster" twice, this was probably a production error; when asked where the rooster was, Ari looked all around, including at the kangaroo, but did not point to anything. Ari's aunt, who was with him at the time, thought that perhaps the way the kangaroo's ears stood up motivated Ari to label it "rooster."

cal members of these categories had been labeled for him. The results of previous research (e.g., Mervis, 1987; Mervis & Pani, 1980) suggest that under these circumstances, Ari would initially severely underextend the names for these two categories. As predicted, the initial extensions of *woodpecker* and *parrot* were extremely narrow.

Ari first produced "woodpecker" when he was not quite 19 months old. At that time, his productive vocabulary included names for 12 other types of birds, all of which had been extended from the beginning to other typical members of the same category; most of these words were reliably extended beyond the limits of the adult category labeled by the same name. Thus, Ari's general pattern of experience with labels for birds would have led him to believe that the *woodpecker* category included multiple exemplars. However, his initial exemplar was a stylized drawing of a very large and unusually patterned woodpecker with a very large crest. Ari labeled both this initial picture and other pictures (in the same book) of what was clearly the same (or a very similar) bird "woodpecker." When shown photographs and accurate drawings of woodpeckers shortly after he first labeled the stylized drawings, however, he refused to label them "woodpecker." His parents then made an effort to expose Ari to typical referents and to label them "woodpecker." Subsequently, Ari began to extend "woodpecker" to include not only other woodpeckers but also wall creepers (which have the same body and bill shape as the initial woodpecker referent and other large types of woodpecker) and a rainbow lorikeet with its beak pressed against a tree (as woodpeckers often are depicted). Ari showed the same pattern of initial acquisition for "parrot."

Categories for Which the Initial Exemplar Was Typical   For 36 of the 38 types of birds, the initial exemplar(s) labeled for Ari were good examples of their category. Under this circumstance, initial extension was predicted to include not only the exemplars that had first been labeled for Ari but also, at a minimum, other typical exemplars of the category. As expected, Ari rapidly generalized these labels to (at least) other representative members of the category. Of the first 12 bird names that he learned, 10 were related to the adult category by overlap, that is, simultaneous overextension and underextension. This situation is well illustrated by the initial relation between Ari's *duck* category and the adult-basic *duck* category. "Duck" was the first object label that Ari comprehended and the first word that he produced. At the time, he did not realize that two-dimensional representations of ducks were in fact *ducks*. He also did not consider stylized three-dimensional representations of ducks to be *ducks*. At the same time, he included not only live ducks and realistic three-dimensional representations of ducks in his *duck* category but also other types of waterfowl and Big Bird. The attribute basis for Ari's *duck* category was described in the previous section and is clearly based on the Form-Function Principle.

By the time Ari acquired his second word for a type of bird, he understood that (realistic) pictures of objects represented their three-dimensional counterparts. Thus, he no longer routinely undergeneralized words to two-dimensional representations. Other types of underextension continued to occur, however. In many cases, these were in response to stylized (and therefore atypical) representations. The most consistent form of underextension, and one that continued well beyond Ari's first 12 names for birds, involved baby exemplars of categories in which the juveniles do not look like smaller versions of their parents. For example, most waterfowl and waterbird juveniles look more like ducks than like their parent species. At the time Ari first learned the names of these types of birds (e.g., goose, swan, flamingo), he typically considered the adults to be appropriately labeled by the new name but was confident that the juveniles were baby ducks. These overextensions continued for several months.

Even though they fit the Form-Function Principle, the initial extensions of 8 of Ari's first 12 bird names were relatively broad, generalizing well beyond the boundaries of the adult categories labeled by the same name. Beginning at age 19 months, however, this pattern changed. Initial categories still fit the Form-Function Principle, and Ari initially underextended the new labels to extremely stylized exemplars and/or babies that did not resemble their parents. In this manner, the initial extensions of categories acquired after age 19 months were consistent with those for categories acquired earlier. However, the extent of overgeneralization was greatly decreased. Most categories either were never overextended or were only slightly overextended. Possible reasons for Ari's shift to a more mature initial extension pattern are considered in the next two sections.

Impact of Adult Input

By age 24 months, Ari had acquired the names for 14 basic-level categories in the *bird* domain. The extension of each of these category names, as measured by production, was appropriate. In table 10.3, a summary is provided of the types of input that were given Ari for each of these category names, including the type of input that led him to acquire each of these words, along with age of acquisition. The types of input provided for Ari regarding names for kinds of birds varied substantially, as did their effectiveness both in inducing him to learn the new name and form a corresponding category (if one had not been formed already) and in encouraging him to separate the new categories from old categories that are coordinate rather than hierarchical in the mature categorization system for the *bird* domain. In this section, we consider the relative effectiveness of these strategies in transaction with Ari's increasing linguistic and cognitive capabilities, both in general and with regard to the *bird* domain.

Labels for Basic-Level Categories Whose Members Were Not Initially Included in Duck   At age 16 months, Ari had divided the *bird* domain into four categories: ducks (including all waterfowl, large landfowl, large waterbirds, and medium or large shorebirds); birds (including "songbirds," medium-sized birds such as seagulls, penguins, crested cranes, and birds of prey, except owls); owls; and roosters (including chickens and other medium-sized landfowl). Although adults had used "rooster" only to refer to roosters, Ari immediately generalized "rooster" to refer to both male and female chickens and similar domestic fowl. The four categories included in Ari's *bird* domain overlapped slightly. For example, eagles were occasionally considered to be owls, and quail sometimes were considered to be ducks. Each of the four categories was acquired in the same laborious way expected for early-acquired words (e.g., Hollich et al., 2000): multiple repetitions, often including the sounds made by these types of birds, provided at times that Ari clearly was interested in the referent.

In the next month, Ari acquired three additional names for basic-level categories in the *bird* domain: "chicken," "penquin," and "eagle." Ari treated "chicken" as a synonym for "rooster," using the two words interchangeably to refer to both hens and roosters, until he was almost 19 months old. Beginning when Ari was 16 months old, he acquired several books that had pictures of penguins in them. He was very interested in the penguins, so adults often labeled them for him. After he began to label penguins and related waterbirds "penguin," he still occasionally referred to them as "bird." (At this time, *bird* was coordinate with *penguin*, rather than superordinate.) The third label that Ari acquired was "eagle." Unlike "chicken" and "penguin," which were frequently used in speech addressed to Ari in the weeks before he acquired them, "eagle" was almost never used. One day, however, when Ari was playing with his stuffed animals, the adult who was taking care of him labeled the eagle "eagle" and showed Ari the characteristic swooping motion that eagles make. (This motion contrasts sharply with the smooth flight pattern that Ari and his parents used when making songbirds "fly.") This was the first time that Ari was told the name of a *bird* category accompanied by an illustration of an important attribute of category members. This type of input was clearly effective: Ari comprehended "eagle" immediately and produced it spontaneously for the first time later the same day.

TABLE 10.3. Input Regarding Labels for Basic-Level Categories[a] in the *Bird* Domain

Label	Age of acquisition	Type of input successful in inducing acquisition of new category[b]	Previously unsuccessful input	Referred to as "duck" after first production of new label?
Types of birds not initially included in duck				
Owl	1;1.10	L + D ("hoot")	L, L + D ("hoot")	No
Rooster[c]	1;2.23	L + D ("cock-a-doodle-doo")	L, L + D ("cock-a-doodle-doo")	No
Penguin	1;5.8	L	L	No
Chicken	1;5.12	No information available	L, L + D ("cluck")	only wind-up chicken[d]
Eagle	1;5.27	L + I (swooping motion)	L	No
Types of birds initially included in duck				
Duck	0;11.9	L + D ("quack")	L, L + D ("quack")	—
Turkey	1;4.23	L + D ("gobble")	L, L + D ("gobble), L (R)	Yes
Goose	1;6.6	L + D ("The goose says honk") + I (goose honking) + C (live duck, "duckie says quack")	L, L (R)	Yes
Swan	1;6.11	L (R) + D ("very long neck," "big") + I (points as indicates attributes) + C (duck: little)	L, L (R)	Yes
Ostrich	1;7.23	L (R) + D ("long long neck and long long legs and it's fluffy in the middle") + I (points as indicates attributes)	L	Yes
Pelican	1;8.21	L (S) + H ("That's a special kind of birdie. That's a pelican") + D ("BIG BEAK") + I (pelican has its beak up in the air, showing its throat)	L	No
Peacock	1;8.29	L + H ("We're going to see a birdie called a peacock")	L	No
Flamingo	1;9.9	L + D ("pink," "long neck")	L (R)	Only juveniles
Pheasant	1;11.2	A + L + D ("VERY long tail")	L	No
Puffin	1;11.12	L (R)	none	No

[a]In some cases, the decision regarding whether to consider a category basic level or subordinate was difficult. In such cases, categories were considered basic level if adults are likely to call exemplars "bird" when talking to young children. Unclear cases are included in table 10.5 under the heading "medium-sized land birds."
[b]A = label requested by Ari; L = label; D = verbal description of attributes; I = illustration of attributes (e.g., pointing to, making characteristic sound), C = contrast exemplar; H = explicit inclusion (hierarchical) statement; R = provided in rejection of Ari's incorrect label; S = provided in response to Ari labeling the referent "bird" (specification).
[c]Although "rooster" is a subordinate level category for adults, it is included in table 10.2 because Ari originally treated it as a basic-level category term for chicken-type birds.
[d]Ari never considered the wind-up chicken to be a "chicken." It is unclear what type of bird this object was intended to represent (see drawing in Mervis, 1987). Based on the comb and the tail structure, Ari's parents decided to call it "chicken." However, over the course of the diary study, Ari labeled this object only "duck" or "bird."

In summary, although Ari had acquired the names for 5 basic-level (and "non-*duck*") categories of *bird* prior to age 18 months, acquisition of all but one of these names occurred only after multiple adult uses of the label (often accompanied by the referent's characteristic sound) when Ari was focused on the relevant object. In contrast, the one label that adults provided in conjunction with an illustration of a characteristic action was acquired immediately.

Labels for Basic-Level Categories Whose Members Were Initially Included in Duck   Ari's child-basic *duck* category initially included a wide variety of waterfowl, large land fowl, and large long-legged shorebirds or waterbirds. By the time he was 24 months old, this initial child-basic category had evolved into 10 adult-basic level categories (see table 10.3). These categories can be divided into those whose names were acquired relatively early (prior to age 20 months, when Ari acquired the Authority Principle) and those acquired later. These two periods are distinguished both by the type of adult input needed in order for Ari to learn the category name and the relation between the new category and Ari's child-basic *duck* category once the new name had been acquired.

During the early period, Ari acquired labels for four types of birds that initially had been included in *duck*. The first, "turkey," was acquired in the same manner as most of Ari's other early basic-level categories: repeated use by adults, often accompanied by "gobble-gobble" (adults' rendition of a turkey sound) when Ari was focused on a picture of a turkey or a live turkey. The three remaining labels ("goose," "swan," "ostrich") were learned on the basis of a very different type of input: a combination of label, description of attributes important to the new category, and illustration of these attributes. In all three cases, this type of input was immediately successful in inducing Ari to learn the new label. The ease with which Ari learned these labels contrasted sharply with his unwillingness to learn the same names when presented with different input. Ari had often heard adults use all three correct names at times in which he was clearly focused on the referent. For example, in the case of "goose," his mother had tried an experiment about a month prior to Ari's acquisition of the word: during six consecutive readings of one of Ari's favorite books, she called the goose in the story "goose" and told him that the goose says "honk." Despite all this input, Ari did not comprehend or produce "goose." In contrast, when Ari heard a live goose honking and was clearly interested and surprised, his father took advantage of the situation to tell Ari that the creature was a goose and that geese say "honk." Even after Ari had acquired these four labels and their underlying categories, he still continued to occasionally call category members "duckie." Thus, his *turkey, goose, swan,* and *ostrich* categories continued to overlap with his *duck* category.

During the second period, Ari acquired five additional labels for birds that had been included in his child-basic *duck* category. During the first period, adults had used all these labels in reference to the appropriate bird species, but without any explanation. At the time, Ari did not learn any of the labels. In contrast, he learned all five labels on the basis of the first input that was provided about them during the second period. The first label, "pelican," was acquired on the basis of input similar to that used successfully during the first period, but accompanied by a hierarchical statement. The input provided for the remaining four labels was more limited, in one case including only the category label provided as a correction of Ari's incorrect label. In another case, the input was provided in the absence of any referent at all, consisting of a simple hierarchical statement made prior to leaving for a trip to the zoo, "We're going to see a birdie called a peacock." When Ari arrived at the zoo, the first type of bird that he saw was a turkey. He correctly labeled it "turkey." The next bird he saw was a peacock; as soon as he saw it, he labeled it, "peacock." During this period, once Ari produced a new label, adult members of that species were never referred to as "duck" again. Baby flamingos, however, continued to be labeled "duck."

Juveniles: A Special Case Ari's difficulty in correctly identifying juvenile flamingos occurred because their overall shape is considerably more similar to that of a duck (adult or juvenile) than that of an adult flamingo. Ari consistently labeled baby geese, swans, and ostriches, as well as baby flamingos, "duck" long after he reliably categorized adult members correctly. A similar problem obtained with baby land fowl, many of which do not look at all like adults of the same species. Ari typically called these babies "birdie." For example, at age 18 months (2 months after he first said "turkey") Ari labeled a picture of an adult turkey "turkey" and then labeled the baby turkey standing next to the adult "birdie." A few days later, Ari looked at a different picture of adult and baby turkeys and labeled the adults "turkey." His mother then pointed at the baby turkeys and said, "Those are turkeys, too, Ari." Ari's response was to look at his mother "quite incredulously."

Ari's progression in realizing that babies are of the same species as their parents, regardless of how similar they look, involved at least four steps. An example of each step is provided in table 10.4. Initially, babies were categorized by their overall shape, whether or not that matched their parents' classification and regardless of how adults labeled the babies. A transitional period followed, during which Ari's first reaction continued to be to classify babies as ducks, regardless of parental species. After adult-encouraged reflection, however, he was able to classify the babies by their parents' species. Ari's mother noted in the diary record accompanying the second entry in table 10.4 that she "had the definite impression at this point that Ari was trying to settle a conflict between two systems: that is, the perceptual input, which suggested that this was a duck, since baby flamingoes look like ducklings, and the conceptual system, which suggested that since the baby flamingo was with adult flamingoes, it probably was a baby flamingo rather than a baby duck. This is probably the first time I have seen evidence that Ari understands that there are two such systems and that they may be in conflict and one will have to decide which one to rely on." In the next period, Ari correctly classified baby birds by parental species. At the start of this period, such classification clearly took considerable cognitive effort and occasioned considerable pride. (See Bloom [2000] for the importance of emotion in language development.) In the final period, Ari clearly considered there to be no question what species babies belonged to, as evidenced by his use of the linguistic construction "baby ones," which entails the presupposition that the juveniles are of the same species as the adult that had just been labeled. Not quite 2 years later, when Ari was 3;7.29, he stated this principle explicitly, as part of a conversation he initiated spontaneously: "If I was a bottlenose dolphin, then I would know that you would be a bottlenose dolphin, too. Because your baby would *have* to be a bottlenose dolphin.

TABLE 10.4. Progression in Realizing That Baby Birds Who Don't Look Like Their Parents Are Still of the Same Species

---

1. Baby bird is what it looks like, regardless of what its parents are:

(age 1;6;19)
M and A looking at book of photographs of animals.
A (looking at adult swan): Swan.
M: A swan!
This sequence is repeated for four more pictures of adult swans.
M (touching baby swan that is next to the adult swan A has just labeled): What's that, Ari?
A: Duck.
M: You know what, Ari? That's a baby swan.

2. First instinct is that baby bird is what it looks like. With help, may realize that baby animal is what its parents are.

(age 1;9.13)
A and M are looking at a book with realistic color drawings of animals.
A (touching a picture of an adult flamingo): Pink flamingo.
M: That's a pink flamingo.
A (touching baby flamingo): Duckie.
M: Is that a duckie, Ari? (M sounds puzzled.)
A: Duckie.
M: Oh, that's a duckie.
A hesitates, staring at the picture.
A (looking up at M): Baby flamingo.

3. Babies are definitely the same species as their parents, even if they don't look like them.

(age 1;9.17)
M and A are looking at a book of photographs of farm animals.
A (touching mother swan): Swan.
M: That's a swan. And who's that? (as M touches the cygnets)
A: (looking at M with a proud smile): Baby swans.
M: Those are baby swans. Very good!

4. Baby animals must *be the same species as their parents, even if they look like something else.*

(age 1;11.17)
A and M are reading a story book that has realistic drawings of animals.
A (looking at adult ostrich): Ostrich.
M (touching a baby ostrich): Who's that?
A (referring to all the babies): Baby ones!
M: Those are the baby ones.

I would always have to be the same kind of animal as you." This realization leads to attention to a different type of perceptual attribute for classification of baby animals: rather than attending to particular physical characteristics of the baby, attending to a relational attribute, proximity to adult animals. (See Oakes & Madole's discussion (chap. 6) of developmental changes in the types of attributes to which attention is directed and Rakison's discussion (chap. 7) of how the use of perceptual attributes can lead to conceptual change.) At the same time, the knowledge that the baby must be of the same species as the accompanying adult encourages the child to search for less apparent physical characteristics of the baby that will permit it to be classified correctly even in the absence of an adult and to rely on these characteristics rather than the more immediately apparent similarities in overall shape. For example, cygnets have black feet, rather than the orange feet that ducklings typically have. (Johnson & Mervis [1994, 1997b] discuss the role of this type of change in attribute salience in the development of expertise.)

Acquisition of Subordinate-Level Categories in the *Bird* Domain

Ari acquired 21 subordinate-level bird names, along with their underlying categories, prior to age 24 months. These included 15 types of "songbirds," 2 kinds of ducks, and 4 kinds of medium-sized land birds. In this section, we consider the impact of the transaction of adult input, increases in Ari's syntactic knowledge and knowledge of cognitive domains critical for differentiating subordinate bird categories (e.g., color, size), and the impact of "learning how to learn"—knowing which types of attributes are likely to be important for categorization at the subordinate level in the *bird* domain—on Ari's acquisition of these subordinate-level categories and category names.

Acquisition of subordinate-level categories depends on understanding that a given object can be a member of more than one category. By the time Ari was 17½ months old, it was clear that he had acquired this concept. At this point, he referred to his pet cat as both "Nutmeg" and "kitty" and to several of the children he knew both by their first names and as "kid." Once he had this type of knowledge, he was in a position to begin to acquire subordinate categories and their names. However, an adult simply providing a subordinate name was not adequate for Ari to treat the label as subordinate. Without an explicit indication that the label referred to a subordinate category, it was likely to be interpreted as a basic-level term (as had happened earlier for Ari, when Ari interpreted "rooster" as referring to all chickenlike birds rather than just to roosters or just to male chickenlike birds). Prior to age 20 months, adults had used simple deictic utterances to introduce the names of seven subordinate bird names to Ari; many of these names were used by adults on multiple occasions. As indicated in table 10.5, Ari never comprehended or produced any of these subordinate labels based on deictic input alone.

The best way to provide an explicit indication that a label is at the subordinate level is through inclusion statements. Such statements often include the word "kind." Alternatively, inclusion statements may simply rely on the indefinite article to convey the notion of inclusion, as in "This bird is called a cardinal" or, more abstractly, "A cardinal is a bird." Ari first demonstrated appropriate productive use of the indefinite article a few days before he turned 18 months old. He first produced the word "kind" when he was 18½ months old. Thus, by the time Ari was 18 months old, he understood the concept of labeling an object at more than one hierarchical level and had the syntactic knowledge to understand inclusion statements that relied only on the indefinite article. Adult provision of a subordinate label as part of an inclusion statement but without either an explanation of

the basis for the subordinate category or an indication from him that he had noticed a basis for it would still have been unlikely to result in acquisition of the new
label and its underlying category, however. The success of inclusion statements
alone in inducing the acquisition of a new label and its underlying category is
dependent on the acquisition of the Authority Principles, which Ari did not evidence until age 20 months.

Within the *bird* domain, color is a primary basis for differentiating among types
of birds at the subordinate level. Thus, acquisition of subordinate bird categories
depends in part on both acquisition of the nonverbal concept of 'color' and acquisition of basic-level color terms and their underlying categories. Ari first demonstrated nonlinguistic knowledge of 'color' just before he turned 18 months old. He
produced his first referential color term at age 1;6.24 and by age 1;8.5 had produced
all 11 basic color names referentially (Mervis, Bertrand, & Pani, 1995).

Ari produced his first subordinate-level name for a type of bird ("cardinal") at
age 1;6.7, about 2 weeks before he began to produce color terms. The diary entries
relevant to acquisition of "cardinal" are provided in table 10.6. As is clear from the
table, Ari was extremely interested in this cardinal. At the same time, it was an extremely good exemplar of *cardinal*. This combination led his father not only to label
the cardinal "birdie" but eventually to tell Ari "That birdie's a cardinal," an inclusion statement. As soon as he was tested, Ari demonstrated referential comprehension of "cardinal" as the name of the appropriate subordinate-level category, rather
than as a synonym for "bird." At the same time, he also continued to consider cardinals to be birds, as evidenced by comprehension and production of "bird" in reference to cardinals. During the remainder of the early period, Ari acquired three other
subordinate bird names; explicit color input was provided for two of these (Mervis
et al., 1995).

During the later period, when Ari had acquired the Authority Principle, he would
have been expected to be able to learn new subordinate labels on the basis of input
that provided only an inclusion statement. This type of input was provided for three
types of birds, and, as expected, Ari succeeded in learning all three names and determining for himself the attribute basis for the subordinate category, such that all
three names were extended appropriately. Adults also continued to introduce
subordinate-level names using attribute and/or hierarchical information; these types
of input also were consistently effective. Finally, when Ari was 23 months old, one
subordinate label was introduced by itself, in a simple deictic utterance. This label
was successfully acquired as well; Ari already was able to use the Authority Principle
and had a solid concept of 'hierarchy.'

Ari's strong interest in categorizing birds at the subordinate level is especially well
demonstrated by his coinage of subordinate labels for the three types of birds corresponding to his plush birds for which adults had not provided subordinate-level
labels: bluebird, blackbird, and goldfinch. Ari appropriated color names for all three
of these subordinate labels. These clearly were intended as names for the kinds of
birds represented by these toys, rather than simple descriptive phrases. For example,
Ari used "yellowbird" only in reference to goldfinches; despite multiple opportunities to use this term in reference to canaries (which are entirely yellow) and meadow-
larks (which have yellow breasts), Ari never did so. He continued to refer to these

TABLE 10.5. Input Regarding Labels for Subordinate-Level Categories[a] in the *Bird* Domain

Label	Age of acquisition	Type of input successful in inducing acquisition of new category[b]	Previously unsuccessful input
"Songbirds"			
Cardinal	1;6.7	L + H ("Ari, that's a cardinal. That birdie's a cardinal." (After A shows great interest in this cardinal)	L
Woodpecker	1;6.29	L + D ("He goes peck peck peck against the tree) + I (pecking)	None
Bluejay	1;7.7	L BG (R) + D ("No that's not a cardinal, Ari. See the blue on the back and the white on the tummy? The white face and the blue everywhere else? That's a bluejay.")	L
Robin	1;7.21	L + H ("That birdie is called a robin.") + D ("red tummy," "brown back")	None
Chickadee	1;8.20	L BG (R) + D ("That's not a jay. You know what that is? That's a chickadee. The chickadee has a white bib and a black hat.")	L
Bluebird	1;9.2	Label coined by Ari	L
Goldfinch	1;9.2	Label coined by Ari	None
Blackbird	1;9.2	Label coined by Ari	None
Canary	1;11.2	L (A) + D ("all yellow," "likes to sing in its cage")	None
Sparrow	1;11.2	No information available	L
Tanager	1;11.7	L (S) + H ("That kind of birdie is called a tanager.")	None
Meadowlark	1;11.7	L (A) + D ("yellow tummy," "black necklace")	Same as successful; A initially comprehended "meadowlark" but forgot the name a month later
Finch	1;11.7	L + H ("That birdie's a finch. It's called a finch.") ("red chin," "red bib") + C ("What color bib does a chickadee have?" Ari: "Black." No chickadee present)	L
Junco	1;11.7	L + H ("That's a junco birdie.") + C (implied; finch had just been labeled and described for Ari)	L

266

Grosbeak	1;11.28	L	None
Subordinates of duck			
Mallard	1;9.5	No information available	No information available
Wood duck	1;11.16	L + H (implied by inclusion of "duck" in subordinate label) + D ("red on its tummy," "white stripes")	None
Medium-sized land birds			
Pigeon	1;8.29	L + H ("Do you know what kind of birdie that is? That's a pigeon.")	None
Parrot	1;9.11	L (to poor example; yielded severe underextension); a few days later, L + H (to typical examples; yielded appropriate extension)	None
Crow	1;11.4	L (R) + D ("all black")	None
Toucan	1;11.24	L (R) + D ("long beak with many colors")	None

[a] In some cases, the decision regarding whether to consider a category basic level or subordinate was difficult. Unclear cases are included in this table under the heading "medium-sized land birds."

[b] A = label requested by Ari; L = label; D = verbal description of attributes; I = illustration of attributes (e.g., pointing to, making characteristic sound); C = contrast exemplar; H = inclusion (inclusion) statement, R = input provided in rejection of Ari's incorrect label, S = input provided in response to Ari labeling the referent "bird" (specification).

TABLE 10.6. Example of Bloom's (2000) Relevance Principle: Ari's Acquisition of His First Subordinate *Bird* Category

---

(age 1;5.29)

Ari [A] is in the sandbox, and his father [F] is supervising him. The ensuing event is recorded as follows in the diary database:

At one point, F sees a male cardinal on the phone wire which reaches the neighbors' house, which is relatively close to A's backyard. It is a very red and vivid looking bird.

F: Ari. Look. A bird. (as F points up to the wire)

F picks A up and walks over near the bird.

F: Ari, look. See the birdie?

A looks at the bird and says: "Hi! Hi!" in a way that he reserves for very special animate objects.

F: Hi! Hi birdie.

A: Hi!

F: Ari, that's a cardinal. That birdie's a cardinal.

A attempts to imitate "cardinal," saying "carnal."

F: That's a cardinal.

A again attempts to imitate "cardinal."

A is holding his blue garden hoe and he holds the hoe up to the cardinal as if to offer it and says: Com'ere. Com'ere. (as if to say, "Com'ere" and "Here, you can have the hoe.")

F: Com'ere cardinal. Com'ere cardinal.

A repeats holding up the hoe and saying "Com'ere" several more times.

At various times while F and A are watching the cardinal, F says, "That's a cardinal, Ari," and A then attempted to imitate "cardinal."

A few hours later, Ari's mother [M] shows A a plush cardinal and says, "What's that?"

A: Birdie.

M: Birdie? What kind of birdie?

A: Kind.

M, F, and Aunt Cindy [C] laugh.

M to F and C: I don't even know how to ask the question so that he can understand it.

C: What's the name of the birdie, Ari?

A: Tweet-tweet.

M: Oh, the birdie's name is 'Tweet Tweet."

Later, M sets down the plush cardinal, bluejay, blackbird, and robin and says: Where's the cardinal, Ari?

A immediately hands M the cardinal.

M holds out her other hand, but A doesn't put anything in it.

Instead A points at the cardinal and says: Corda (cardinal).

M: Yes, that's the cardinal, Ari. Very good.

---

types of birds as "bird" until he acquired the correct subordinate names 2 months later. The same type of pattern obtained for "bluebird" and "blackbird." By age 23 months, Ari was convinced that every bird belonged to some subordinate category; as a result, he began to explicitly request subordinate-level names. At least by age 30 months, Ari also had "learned how to learn" subordinate bird categories, permitting him to know which characteristics of novel birds were likely to be relevant to determining their subordinate-level category. This knowledge provided him with a basis for providing sufficiently accurate descriptions of birds that he had seen but for which he did not have a subordinate-level name to enable adults to help him to identify the bird, as indicated in the example in table 10.7. These strategies served him well; by age 4 years, Ari knew and used appropriately 49 names for "songbirds" at the subordinate or subsubordinate level (Johnson & Mervis, 1994).

Summary and Conclusion

Ten-month-old infants are able to form categories based on correlated attributes spontaneously (e.g., chap. 4), to isolate words from the speech stream (e.g., Morgan & Saffran, 1995), and to engage in triadic interactions with adults (e.g., Akhtar & Tomasello, 2000). Each of these represents a major developmental advance. The integration of these three abilities, in situations in which the child is highly motivated by interest in the object of reference (see Bloom, 2000), allows the infant to begin to learn names for object categories. Conceptual abilities, linguistic abilities, and social interaction abilities continue to evolve across childhood and beyond. For example, children's background knowledge regarding the principles (implicit or explicit) on which object categories are based, related conceptual domains (e.g., color), and particular object domains (in Ari's case, especially the *bird* domain) changes dramatically during the toddler years. Memory ability also increases substantially. Similarly, children make great strides in acquiring both morphology and syntax, allowing them increasingly to benefit from adult linguistic input. Adult input also evolves during this period from relatively short utterances focused primarily on the here and now to considerably more complex utterances regarding not only the present but also the future and the past.

TABLE 10.7. Example of the Effect of "Learning How to Learn" on Acquisition of a New Subordinate *Bird* Category and Name

---

(age 2;5.28)

A is standing on a chair, looking out of the bedroom window.

A: I saw a birdie, Mommy, but I didn't know what it was, but it flew away. It had red on its head and a brown back and red on its tail. What was it, Mommy?

M: Was it little like a sparrow or big like a bluejay?

A: It was little like a sparrow.

M: I don't know what it was, but when we go downstairs, we'll look in the bird books and see if we can find a picture of it. Then Mommy will be able to tell you what kind of bird it was.

About 15 minutes later, M gets out the Peterson bird guide and the Audubon bird guide. M turns to the feeder picture in the Peterson guide.

A looks at the picture and then touches the redpoll, saying: It was that birdie, Mommy.

M turns to the page that describes the redpoll, and A again chooses the redpoll. (A purple finch and a house finch, which are similar to redpolls, were available both times and A consistently rejected them in favor of the redpoll.)

M: I think the birdie you saw was a redpoll.

A: Redpoll.

Later, M opens the Audubon guide to the relevant page, and A again chooses the redpoll as the bird that he had seen.

During the same period, children become more attuned to adult input and therefore more able to benefit from that input. The transaction of these evolving abilities continues to shape category and lexical development across childhood. These evolving transactions from the onset of lexical acquisition to "learning how to learn" about a particular domain may be summarized as follows.

First Object Words

Infants' first object words are names for categories of objects in which they are intrinsically interested. These categories are based on correlated attributes (Form-Function Principle) that the child either has discovered for him- or herself or that have been highlighted for the child nonverbally. The role of adult linguistic input is to provide labels for these nonlinguistic categories, in social situations in which the child and adult are focused on the same object. For the child who is just beginning to acquire language, paying attention to an object, a social partner, and linguistic input simultaneously is extremely challenging and likely to happen only when the child is especially interested in a particular object. Because of memory limitations, this convergence of object, word, focused attention, and interest on a particular object or type of object will have to occur repeatedly in order for the child to learn the label. For the same reason, input in which the object label is in utterance-final position is most likely to be effective (Slobin, 1985).

Children's extensions of category labels, as measured by comprehension and production, indicate that, at the onset of lexical acquisition, adult input is used primarily to obtain labels for objects and their categories, rather than to delimit these categories. Although child-basic categories are based on the same principle as adults' basic-level object categories (Form-Function Principle), children often notice different attributes of objects or weight attributes differently than adults. In these cases, children use their nonlinguistic categories, rather than adult input, to determine the extension of the new word. Thus, although adults are important in that they provide exposure to objects in which the child is particularly interested and provide labels for these objects (in our culture, often when the child already is focused on the object), child characteristics are particularly important in determining the onset of referential comprehension and production of object names, which labels are learned first, and the extension of these labels.

Evolution of Early Object Categories

Children's early object categories eventually evolve to correspond to the adult-basic categories labeled by the same names. An important step in this evolution is the acquisition of the correct names for objects that are included in the initial child-basic category but not in the adult-basic category labeled by the same name. In many cases, adults repeatedly provide the correct label when talking with the child. Despite the ready availability of the correct name, however, children who are just beginning to talk are unlikely to learn it (see also Markman's [1989] Mutual Exclusivity Principle) until they are able to identify a correlated attribute basis for the new label. That is, category evolution is based on changes in the attributes that a child attends to for the relevant objects, or on changes in the weight that the child assigns to particular attributes, leading to attention to a different correlated attribute cluster for the same object (Form-Function/Additional Category Principle). Although the child sometimes notices these attributes on his or her own, in most cases they are pointed out by the child's communicative partner. Comprehension of the new label is most likely if the adult provides the new label in the context of an explanation, including both a verbal description and physical demonstration of the attribute basis for a new category, and if the child is attending to and interested in the object. Comprehension of this label, however, does not lead to the immediate separation of the old and new categories. Instead, the child includes the object in both the old and the new categories simultaneously.

Once children acquire the Authority/Additional Category Principle, they are able to learn new category names for objects included in a child-basic category labeled by a different name, even when the only input provided is the correct label. Learning a new label leads to the child's search for a new correlated attribute cluster on which to base the category that will underlie the new label. Automatic separation of the old and new categories as soon as the new category name is learned depends on the Authority/Coordinate Deletion Principle. Acquisition of these principles permits the child to benefit from cryptic adult input that negates the child's category assignment for an object or type of object.

Acquisition of Subordinate Categories

Acquisition of subordinate categories also depends on a transaction between adult and child. Once again, certain types of foundational background knowledge (both cognitive and linguistic) are critical. First, the child must have at least an implicit understanding of the concept of hierarchy—that the same object can belong to two categories at different levels of generality. Second, the child must have the linguistic concepts necessary to differentiate between a proper noun and a common noun (in English, the indefinite article). Understanding of the concept of 'kind' is also helpful. Third, the child has to have sufficient conceptual knowledge (nonverbal and/or verbal) of the attribute domains that are important for differentiating among subordinate categories in the given object domain. This knowledge is important because subordinate categories are also based on correlated attribute clusters, although these clusters tend to involve qualifications of the form and function attributes included in the attribute cluster underlying the basic-level category, rather than different attributes. In general, as for basic-level categories, the child's communicative partners will be the source of subordinate-level category names.

Assuming that the child has sufficient background knowledge to acquire subordinate category names in a particular domain, the manner in which these names are provided will determine in large part whether or not the child actually learns them. Thus, the adult once again plays an important role. Subordinate names that are provided in simple deictic utterances are likely to be interpreted as synonyms for the basic-level category (e.g., Mervis et al., 1994) unless the name itself includes the basic-level label. Subordinate names that are provided as part of an inclusion statement should be easier to learn; names provided with both an inclusion statement and an explanation of the attribute basis for the category should be the easiest.

Similarly, subordinate names provided as part of an inclusion statement after the child has indicated that the child has noticed an unusual attribute of the object should be acquired relatively easily. As for early basic-level category names, acquisition of initial subordinate-level names is extremely challenging so is most likely to involve objects in which the child is especially interested.

After the child learns a critical mass of subordinate-level names and categories for members of a domain, the child should realize that all members of the domain belong to subordinate-level categories and have subordinate-level names. This realization should spur the child to request subordinate-level names for domain members for which the child does not yet have a subordinate name. (By now, the interest, or at least cooperation, of the child's communicative partners is also critical so that the child has access to a source of subordinate-level labels.) Some children may also coin subordinate-level names for domain members. Regardless of the source of the subordinate name, these labels should be extended on the basis of the attribute basis that has been provided for the child or that the child has inferred. At the same time, the child should have realized the types of attribute qualities that are likely to be important for subordinate categorization within the domain. At this point, the child has "learned how to learn" about the domain, a critical step in rapid acquisition of expertise in the domain.

Between the ages of 10 and 23 months, Ari progressed from referential comprehension of his first object word to understanding of the concept of category hierarchy to knowing how to learn not only about the *bird* domain but about object domains in general, following the path just summarized. This impressive achievement for a child not yet 2 years old was the result of an evolving transaction between Ari's increasing conceptual knowledge (including category and lexical principles) and linguistic knowledge, his increasing memory abilities, his extreme interest and motivation to learn about birds, and his communicative partners' (supportive) linguistic and nonlinguistic input regarding, first, basic-level *bird* categories and, later, subordinate-level *bird* categories, in conjunction with their encouragement of Ari's interest in the *bird* domain. Although experiments focusing on many of the individual steps in this transaction remain to be conducted, the use of a systematic case study approach provides a unique opportunity to fully appreciate the transaction between child and communicative partners during the early period of lexical category development.

Acknowledgments

The research reported in this chapter was supported by grants from the National Science Foundation (BNS84-19036) and the National Institute of Child Health and Human Development (HD27942). Preparation of the chapter was supported, in part, by a grant from the National Institute of Child Health and Human Development (HD29957). We are grateful to Cindy Mervis, Zella Mervis, and Stanley Mervis for their participation in the data collection phase of the diary study. Cindy Mervis, Kathy Johnson, and Jacquelyn Bertrand were involved in both data reduction and data analysis. Cindy Mervis designed and programmed the original diary study database and associated queries. Joanie Robertson converted the original database from dBase to Access and created a series of forms that greatly facilitated the process of reviewing selected diary entries. Kathy Johnson, Lisa Oakes, and David Rakison provided thoughtful comments on a previous version of this chapter. Correspondence should be addressed to Carolyn Mervis, Department of Psychological and Brain Sciences, University of Louisville, Louisville, KY 40292 (cbmervis@louisville.edu).

References

Akhtar, N., & Tomasello, M. (2000). The social nature of words and word learning. In R. M. Golinkoff, K. Hirsh-Pasek, L. Bloom, L. B. Smith, A. L. Woodward, N. Akhtar, M. Tomasello, & G. Hollich, *Becoming a word learner: A debate on lexical acquisition* (pp. 115–135). Oxford: Oxford University Press.

Banigan, R. L., & Mervis, C. B. (1988). Role of adult input in young children's category evolution: II. An experimental study. *Journal of Child Language, 15,* 493–504.

Bloom, L. (2000). The intentionality model of word learning: How to learn a word, any word. In R. M. Golinkoff, K. Hirsh-Pasek, L. Bloom, L. B. Smith, A. L. Woodward, N. Akhtar, M. Tomasello, & G. Hollich, *Becoming a word learner: A debate on lexical acquisition* (pp. 19–50). Oxford: Oxford University Press.

Braunwald, S. R., & Brislin, R. W. (1979). The diary method updated. In E. Ochs & B. B. Schieffelin (Eds.), *Developmental pragmatics* (pp. 21–42). New York: Academic Press.

Brown, R. (1958). How shall a thing be called? *Psychological Review, 65,* 14–21.

Carpenter, M., Nagell, K., & Tomasello, M. (1998). Social cognition, joint attention, and communicative competence from 9 to 15 months of age. *Monographs of the Society for Research in Child Development, 63*(176, Serial No. 255).

Chapman, K. L., Leonard, L. B., & Mervis, C. B. (1986). The effects of feedback on young children's inappropriate word usage. *Journal of Child Language, 13,* 101–117.

Dromi, E. (1987). *Early lexical development.* New York: Cambridge University Press.

Fenson, L., Dale, P. S., Reznick, J. S., Bates, E., & Thal, D. (1994). Variability in early communicative development. *Monographs of the Society for Research in Child Development, 59*(Serial No. 242).

Gale, M. C., & Gale, H. (1900). The vocabularies of three children of one family to two and a half years of age. In H. Gale (Ed.), *Psychological studies* ([No. 1] pp. 70–117). Minneapolis: Gale.

Golinkoff, R. M., Hirsh-Pasek, K., Bloom, L., Smith, L. B., Woodward, A. L., Akhtar, N., Tomasello, M., & Hollich, G. (2000). *Becoming a word learner: A debate on lexical acquisition.* Oxford: Oxford University Press.

Gruendel, J. M. (1977). Referential extension in early language development. *Child Development, 48,* 1567–1576.

Hirsh-Pasek, K., Golinkoff, R. M., & Hollich, G. (2000). An emergentist coalition model for word learning: Mapping words to objects in a product of the interaction of multiple cues. In R. M. Golinkoff, K. Hirsh-Pasek, L. Bloom, L. B. Smith, A. L. Woodward, N. Akhtar, M. Tomasello, & G. Hollich, *Becoming a word learner: A debate on lexical acquisition* (pp. 136–164). Oxford: Oxford University Press.

Hollich, G. J., Hirsh-Pasek, K., Golinkoff, R. M., Brand, R. J., Brown, E., Chung, H. L., Hennon, E., & Rocroi, C. (2000) Breaking the language barrier: An emergentist coalition model for the origins of word learning. *Monographs of the Society for Research in Child Development, 65*(3, Serial No. 262).

Kogan, J. (1971). Educational implications of cognitive style. In G. Lesser (Ed.), *Psychology and educational practice* (pp. 242–292). Glenview, IL: Scott Foresman.

Johnson, K. E., & Mervis, C. B. (1994). Microgenetic analysis of first steps in children's acquisition of expertise on shorebirds. *Developmental Psychology, 30,* 418–435.

Johnson, K. E., & Mervis, C. B. (1997a). Development of children's understanding of basic-subordinate inclusion relations. *Developmental Psychology, 33,* 745–763.

Johnson, K. E., & Mervis, C. B. (1997b). Effects of varying levels of expertise on the basic level of categorization. *Journal of Experimental Psychology: General, 126,* 248–277.

Markman, E. M. (1989). *Categorization and naming in children: Problems of induction.* Cambridge, MA: MIT Press.

Mervis, C. B. (1984). Early lexical development: The contributions of mother and child. In C. Sophian (Ed.), *Origins of cognitive skills* (pp. 339–370). Hillsdale, NJ: Erlbaum.

Mervis, C. B. (1987). Child-basic object categories and early lexical development. In U. Neisser (Ed.), *Concepts and conceptual development: Ecological and intellectual factors in categorization* (pp. 201–233). Cambridge: Cambridge University Press.

Mervis, C. B. (1990). Operating principles, input, and early lexical development. *Comunicazioni di Psicologia Generale, 4,* 7–25.

Mervis, C. B., & Bertrand, J. (1997). Developmental relations between cognition and language: Evidence from Williams syndrome. In L. B. Adamson & M. A. Romski (Eds.), *Communication and language acquisition: Discoveries from atypical development* (pp. 75–106). New York: Brookes.

Mervis, C. B., Bertrand, J., & Pani, J. R. (1995). Transaction of cognitive-linguistic abilities and adult input: A case study of the acquisition of colour terms and colour-based subordinate categories. *British Journal of Developmental Psychology, 13,* 285–304.

Mervis, C. B., & Canada, K. (1983). On the existence of competence errors in early comprehension: A reply to Fremgen & Fay and Chapman & Thomson. *Journal of Child Language, 10,* 431–440.

Mervis, C. B., & Johnson, K. E. (1991). Acquisition of the plural morpheme: A case study. *Developmental Psychology, 27,* 222–235.

Mervis, C. B., Johnson, K. E., & Mervis, C. A. (1994). Acquisition of subordinate categories by 3-year-olds: The roles of attribute salience, linguistic input, and child characteristics. *Cognitive Development, 9,* 211–234.

Mervis, C. B., & Mervis, C. A. (1982). Leopards are kitty-cats: Object labeling by mothers for their 13 month olds. *Child Development, 53,* 267–273.

Mervis, C. B., & Mervis, C. A. (1988). Role of adult input in young children's category evolution: I. An observational study. *Journal of Child Language, 15,* 257–272.

Mervis, C. B., Mervis, C. A., Johnson, K. E., & Bertrand, J. (1992). Studying early lexical development: The value of the systematic diary method. In C. Rovee-Collier & L. P. Lipsitt (Eds.), *Advances in infancy research* (Vol. 7, pp. 291–378). Norwood, NJ: Ablex.

Mervis, C. B., & Pani, J. R. (1980). The acquisition of basic object categories. *Cognitive Psychology, 12,* 496–522.

Morgan, J. L., & Saffran, J. R. (1995). Emerging integration of sequential and suprasegmental information in preverbal speech segmentation. *Child Development, 66,* 911–936.

Piaget, J. (1954). *The construction of reality in the child.* New York: Basic Books.

Rosch, E., Mervis, C. B., Gray, W. D., Johnson, D. M., & Boyes-Braem, P. (1976). Basic objects in natural categories. *Cognitive Psychology, 8,* 382–439.

Slobin, D. I. (1985). Cross-linguistic evidence for the language making capacity. In D. I. Slobin (Ed.), *The cross-linguistic study of language acquisition: Vol. 2. Theoretical issues* (pp. 1157–1256). Hillsdale, NJ: Erlbaum.

Tversky, B., & Hemenway, K. (1984). Objects, parts, and categories. *Journal of Experimental Psychology: General, 113,* 169–193.

Younger, B. A., & Cohen, L. B. (1983). Infant perception of correlations among attributes. *Child Development, 54,* 858–867.

Younger, B. A., & Cohen, L. B. (1986). Developmental change in infants' perception of correlations among attributes. *Child Development, 57,* 803–815.

Younger, B. A., & Fearing, D. (1999). Parsing items into separate categories: Developmental change in infant categorization. *Child Development, 70,* 291–303.

CHAPTER ELEVEN

Making an Ontology
Cross-linguistic Evidence

Linda B. Smith, Eliana Colunga, and Hanako Yoshida

And every language is a vast pattern-system, different from others, in which are culturally ordained the forms and categories, by which the personality not only communicates, but also analyzes, notices, or neglects types of relationship and phenomena.

Benjamin L. Whorf, Language, Thought, and Reality

For the vocabulary of the language, in and of its self, to be a molder of thought, lexical dissections and categorizations of nature would have to be almost accidently formed, rather as though some Johnny Appleseed had scattered named categories capriciously over the earth.

E. Rosch, "Linguistic Relativity"

HUMAN CULTURES AND LANGUAGES are diverse. To some, these differences imply incommensurate ways of being human. To others, these differences only serve to underscore our profound sameness. Most cross-linguistic studies of categorization offer up their evidence on one side or the other of this philosophical divide. In this chapter, we summarize recent results from our cross-linguistic studies of early noun learning by English-speaking and Japanese-speaking children. The findings are clearly relevant to issues of linguistic and conceptual diversity. However, these issues were not the proximal impetus for our studies. Instead, our questions were pitched at a different level, to a mechanistic understanding of the development of categories and early noun learning. Still, by pursuing mechanisms of developmental change, we arrive at a deeper understanding of the processes that create both universal and linguistically specific ways of knowing.

Universal Ontological Distinctions?

The things we encounter in our everyday lives seem to fall naturally into different kinds. There are animate things that react and intentionally move; there are discrete things with stable forms that we move; and there are substances, masses with less regular forms, that also do not move on their own. This partition of things into animals, objects, and substances is sometimes considered an ontological partition in two senses: in the Aristotelian sense, that these are three different kinds of existence, and in the psychological sense, that these are distinct psychological kinds that provide a foundation for human category learning. There is empirical support for the second idea from children's judgments in novel noun generalization tasks.

Kind-Specific Generalizations of Newly Learned Nouns

The novel noun generalization task measures children's expectations about the category organization of different kinds. In this task, the experimenter presents the child with a novel entity and names it with a novel name, saying, for example, "this is the mel." The experimenter then presents choice items and asks the child which of these can be called by the same name, saying, for example, "show me the mel." This is an interesting task because the naming event itself provides the child with few constraints on the class to which the name applies. Thus, children's generalizations from this minimal task input provide insights into children's expectations about how nouns map to categories. And the evidence indicates that children's generalizations honor an organization of kinds into animates, inanimate objects, and substances.

In particular, when 2½- to 3-year-old children are presented with novel solid and rigidly shaped things, they consistently generalize the name only to new instances that match the exemplar in shape but not to instances that match in other ways (Imai, Gentner, & Uchida, 1994; Landau, Smith, & Jones, 1988, 1992, 1998; Soja, Carey, & Spelke, 1991). However, when the named entity is a nonsolid substance such as hair gel or lotion molded into a shape, same-aged children are more likely to generalize the name by its material and color (Soja et al., 1991; Soja, 1992). Finally, when the named entity has properties typical of animate things—eyes or feet or limbs—children generalize the name narrowly to objects that match the named example in both shape and texture (Jones, Smith & Landau, 1991; Jones & Smith, 1998; Yoshida & Smith, in press; see also Gelman & Coley, 1991; Keil, 1994; Markman, 1989). Further, increasing evidence suggests that children learning a variety of languages such as Korean, Japanese, English, and Spanish make similar distinctions, naming rigidly shaped things by shape, nonsolid substances by material, and depictions of animate things by shape and texture (e.g., Gathercole & Min, 1997; Imai & Gentner, 1997; Lucy, 1996; Yoshida & Smith, in press).

Where Does This Knowledge Come From?

Evidence That Language Learning Plays a Role

Four facts suggest that language learning contributes to children's developing understanding of different kinds, as follows:

- Categorization taking place in naming and non-naming tasks
- Emergence of kind-specific name generalizations with vocabulary growth
- Modulation of kind-specific name generalizations
- Cross-linguistic differences

First, children's attention to the different properties of different kinds is evident most robustly in naming tasks. Many of the experiments showing that children systematically extend novel names in different ways for different kinds have included non-naming control tasks (e.g., Imai, et al., 1994; Jones et al., 1991, 1998; Landau et al., 1988, 1992, 1998; Soja et al., 1991). These control tasks are identical to the novel noun generalization task, except the object is not named. Instead, children are shown the exemplar and then are asked what other objects are "like" or "go with" the exemplar. In these non-naming tasks, children do not systematically attend to the different properties of different kinds. This fact suggests a mechanistic link between naming and knowledge about the category organizations of different kinds.

Second, kind-specific name generalizations emerge with vocabulary growth (Jones & Smith, 1997; Jones et al., 1991; Landau et al., 1988; Samuelson & Smith, 1999, 2000; Smith, 1999; Soja et al., 1991). The evidence indicates that the tendency to attend to shape in the context of naming emerges only after children already know some nouns. Moreover, this so-called shape bias in naming becomes stronger with development and more specific to solid and rigidly shaped objects. A bias to extend names for animates by similarity in shape and texture and a bias to extend names for substances by similarity in material emerge later (see, especially, Jones et al., 1991; Samuelson & Smith, 2000). Thus, biases to attend to different properties when extending names for different kinds codevelop with increasing vocabulary, a fact consistent with the idea that children's word learning helps create their category knowledge.

Third, kind-specific name generalizations are modulated by syntactic cues. One area of relevant research concerns the influence of count and mass syntactic frames on English-speaking children's interpretations of novel object and substance names. Count nouns are nouns that take the plural and can be preceded by words such as *a*, *another*, *several*, and *few*, as well as numerals. Count nouns thus label things we think of as discrete—chairs, trucks, shirts, studies, and hopes. Mass nouns, in contrast, cannot be pluralized but instead are preceded by words such as *some*, *much*, and *little*. Mass nouns thus label things that are conceptualized as unbounded continuous masses—water, sand, applesauce, research, and justice. Past research shows that count syntactic frames (e.g., *a mel, another mel*) push children's attention to the shape of the named thing, whereas mass syntactic frames (e.g., *some mel, more mel*) push attention to material (e.g., Gathercole, Cramer, Somerville, & Jansen, 1995; McPherson, 1991, Soja, 1992). In brief, language exerts an on-line influence on children's category formation.

Fourth, although there are clear universals in the name generalizations of children learning different languages—solid rigid things tend to be named by shape, nonsolid things by material, and things with features suggesting animacy by joint similarity in shape and texture—there are differences as well, differences that we believe provide a potentially rich window on the role of language in creating knowledge about kinds. In the next section we present background evidence on differences between English and Japanese.

Language Differences

Individuation

Lucy (1992) proposed an animacy continuum that is intimately related to how languages individuate kinds. As illustrated in figure 11.1, this continuum orders kinds by the degree to which instances are marked as individuals by devices such as the plural and indefinite articles. On one extreme of Lucy's proposed continuum are animate entities, the kinds most likely to be treated as discrete entities by a language. On the other extreme are substances, the kinds least likely to be individualized by languages. In the middle are objects, entities that are treated as individuals by some languages but not by others. The key point is this: different languages emphasize different boundary points along a continuum of kinds from animate to substance.

English, with its count/mass distinction, is said to partition the continuum between objects and substances. Both common animal and object names—*cow* and *cup*—are count nouns. Both are thus kinds that English treats as discrete entities. Common substance names such as *milk*, *sand*, and *wood*, in contrast, are mass nouns in English. These are treated by the language as unbounded continuous entities. Thus, through devices such as the indefinite article, pluralization, and quantification,

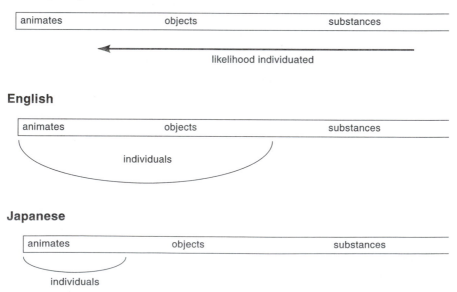

The animacy continuum

| animates | objects | substances |

likelihood individuated

English

| animates | objects | substances |

individuals

Japanese

| animates | objects | substances |

individuals

Figure 11.1. *The animacy continuum and individuation in English and Japanese.*

English treats animate and object names in the same way and differently from substance names.

The Japanese language, in contrast to English, appears to partition the continuum between animates and inanimates, treating only animates as discrete individuals. First, Japanese nouns that refer to multiple entities are not obligatorily pluralized. Thus *inu ga ita* could mean either "there was a dog" or "there were dogs." However, nouns referring to multiple humans or young animals are optionally pluralized with the suffix *tachi*. Thus, *koinu tachi ga ita* is "there were some puppies." The plural suffix appears not to be used on inanimate nouns. Second, when Japanese speakers do need to count discrete entities, they use a system of classifiers that often depend on the kind of thing being counted, much as English speakers count *loaves* of bread or *panes* of glass. The Japanese classifiers used for animates tend not to overlap with those used for inanimates. Finally, a distinction between animates and inanimates is also supported by other aspects of Japanese than plurals and quantification. Although not traditionally viewed as markers of individuation, there are additional aspects of Japanese that are closely linked to individuation and animacy (see Yoshida & Smith [in press], for further discussion). One of these is the distinction between *aru* and *iru*. For the very fundamental notion of existence ("there is") and spatial location ("be located"), Japanese has separate verbs for animates and inanimates: *aru* is "inanimate object exists/is located" and *iru* is "animate object exists/is located." Thus Japanese, through pluralization, its classifier system, and the *iru/aru* distinction in locative constructions, imposes a boundary between people and animals on the one hand and objects and substances on the other.

These are systematic language differences of the kind likely to matter in children's developing conceptualizations of kinds (Gumperz & Levinson, 1996; Lucy, 1996): noun categories in English are systematically partitioned into object names versus substance names, whereas noun categories in Japanese are systematically partitioned into names for animates versus names for inanimates. Both Quine (1969) and Lucy (1992) suggested that the partitions made by a language's system for marking individuals determines the ontological partitions made by speakers of that language.

Complete linguistic determination, however, seems unlikely, as there is relevant perceptual information about category structures that is available to speakers of all languages. Indeed, prelinguistic infants distinguish animate categories from objects that hold their shape and form, and also distinguish rigid forms from nonrigid ones (e.g., Spelke, Vishton, & Van-Hofsten, 1995).

Imai and Gentner's Results

Imai and Gentner's (1997) cross-linguistic study of the object–substance boundary provides clear evidence that both linguistic and perceptual information contribute to an object–substance distinction. In their study, they compared Japanese-speaking and English-speaking children's generalizations of names for novel solid and nonsolid forms. They used three kinds of stimulus sets: solid and complexly shaped things, solid but simply shaped things, and nonsolid and thus simply shaped substances. They did this because solids and nonsolids differ in the kinds of shapes they usually take. Solid things can be quite complex—with many angles and multiple parts.

Nonsolid substances, however, cannot take angular multipart shapes and over time relax toward rounded and accidental-appearing forms like splatters and drops.

In the experiment, Imai and Gentner presented children with an exemplar and named it with a novel noun. They used a syntactic frame in English that was neutral, consistent with either a count or mass noun. In this way, any language effects would be off-line effects, effects of a history of making distinctions between count and mass nouns in English and not making such a distinction in Japanese. After the exemplar was named, the child was shown two choice objects, one that matched the exemplar in shape and one that matched the exemplar in material. The child was asked to indicate the one called by the same name as the exemplar.

Imai and Gentner found that Japanese speakers and English speakers formed similar categories for solid complexly shaped things, generalizing a newly learned object name to new instances by shape. And speakers of both languages increased attention to material when the named entity was nonsolid. Imai and Gentner concluded from these similarities that the partition of objects from substances does not depend on linguistic individuation, since both English-speaking and Japanese-speaking participants treated solids and nonsolids differently, even though Japanese does not mark objects and substances differently.

However, Imai and Gentner also found differences between the novel noun generalizations of English and Japanese speakers. Most notably, English and Japanese speakers differed in their generalizations of names for simply shaped solids. Simply shaped solid things are like objects in the rigidity of their shapes but are like substances in the simplicity of their shapes. English speakers treated the simply shaped solid things as objects and generalized their names by shape, whereas Japanese speakers were more likely to generalize the name by material. The results suggest that as a consequence of different systems of individuation, Japanese and English speakers place the boundary between objects and substances in slightly different places. For speakers of English, solid things—both complexly and simply shaped—are categorized as objects, that is, by shape. For speakers of Japanese, simply shaped things—both solid and nonsolid—are more likely to be categorized as substances, that is, by material.

Ontologies as Statistical Regularities

Imai and Gentner's results show both universal and language-specific influences on children's "ontological" distinctions. We propose that both the universals and the differences are the product of the same statistical learning mechanism, arising from correlations among the perceptual properties of different kinds, lexical category structures, and linguistic devices concerned with individuation. This proposal is based on the following five core ideas.

1. *There are regularities that distinguish kinds of things in the world and our perceptual systems are sensitive to these regularities.* Solids, nonsolids, and animates present correlated bundles of perceptual properties.
2. *The nominal categories of languages honor these correlational bundles.* Languages evolved to fit the perceptual system and the world. Thus it

makes sense that lexical categories across-languages respect and make use of the same correlated perceptual properties that distinguish animates from solid objects and from nonsolid substances.

3. *Word learning enables higher-order generalizations.* Word learning may be mechanistically crucial to going beyond specific knowledge about specific kinds to developing the higher-order correlations that constitute kind-specific noun generalizations and ultimately abstract knowledge, knowledge we might rightly call an "ontology."

4. *The mechanism is associative learning.* The statistical regularities characteristic of early noun categories may be sufficient in and of themselves to create a partition of things into animals, objects, and substances. Ontologies in their psychological sense could be the generalizations that arise naturally from the statistical regularities across lexical categories.

5. *Linguistic regularities are part of the associative mix and thus bend knowledge in language-specific ways.* Linguistic forms that are regularly associated with correlated bundles of perceptual cues may reinforce the connections between those perceptual cues. In this way, systematic linguistic contrasts, such as those that compose a language's system of quantifying individuals, may differentially bolster and weaken perceptual correlations, changing how things are perceived and conceived.

We present preliminary support for these ideas in the remainder of this chapter. We do so by first concentrating on Imai and Gentner's finding of differences in the object-substance boundary for children learning English and Japanese. We then turn to a parallel phenomenon at the animal-object boundary. Finally, we propose how abstract ideas about even abstract kinds might emerge from these correlations across categories of concrete things.

Creating an Object-Substance Boundary

Early noun categories are highly structured. They present the kinds of regularities that could yield a partition of kinds into objects and substances. Specifically, early learned categories of solid things are well organized by shape, and early learned categories of nonsolids are typically well organized by material. This is so in both English and Japanese.

Regularities in the Early English Lexicon

Samuelson and Smith (1999) asked: What kinds of nouns do young children learning English know? Do they learn names for solid things in shape-based categories and names for nonsolid things in material-based categories? To answer these questions, Samuelson and Smith examined the structure of a set of nouns that are typically known by children at 30 months. More specifically, they examined the list of nouns that compose the MacArthur Communicative Developmental Inventory (MCDI). The MCDI is a parent checklist that is used by many researchers to measure the vocabulary of children from 16 to 30 months. The list of words on the MCDI was developed from extensive studies of parental diaries, in-laboratory testing of early vocabularies, and large normative studies (Fenson et al., 1993). The nouns contained on the MCDI are known by 50 percent of children at 30 months. Samuelson and Smith specifically examined the category structures of 312 nouns—all the nouns in the animals, vehicles, toys, food and drink, clothing, body parts, small household items, and furniture and rooms sections of the MCDI.

The method used to examine the category structure of these 312 early learned nouns was borrowed from the pioneering work of Rosch (1973). Adults were presented with each noun on the list of 312 and asked to think of the instances named by each noun. For example, they might be told: "Think of apples that you commonly experience." Then, while thinking about these instances, the adults were then asked a series of yes/no questions: "Are these similar in shape? Are these similar in color? Are these similar in material? Are these solid? Are these nonsolid?" A separate group of adults was presented with the criteria for distinguishing count and mass nouns and asked to judge whether each noun on the MCDI was a count or a mass noun or could be used both syntactic frames (e.g., *cake*). To classify a nominal category as possessing any of these properties, Samuelson and Smith required that 85 percent of the adults agreed with that characteristic. This conservative criterion was used to ensure that the regularities attributed to the early lexicon were likely to be ones that are manifest in the experiences of most young learners. In this way, each noun was categorized as shape-based, material-based, color-based, based on a combination (or all) of these properties, or based on none of these properties. Each noun was also classified as referring to solid or nonsolid things or ambiguous insolidity, and each noun was classified as a count noun, a mass noun, or as ambiguous in its syntactic category.

Figure 11.2 summarizes the key regularities in terms of Venn diagrams. In these diagrams, the relative size of each circle represents the relative numbers of nouns of that kind, and the size of the overlap between intersecting circles represents the relative number of nouns of both kinds. The circles on the left depict the relative number of count nouns, names for solid things, and names for categories organized by shape. The circles on the right represent the relative numbers of mass nouns, names for nonsolid substances, and names for things in categories organized by material. (Color is not shown because so few categories were judged to be similar in color independently of similarity in material.) What the figure shows is that many early nouns are count nouns, many refer to solid objects, and many name objects in shape-based categories. Moreover, count nouns, solid things, and shape similarity go together. The right side of figure 11.2 shows that there are many fewer nouns in this corpus that are mass nouns, name nonsolid things, and name categories organized by material. However, nonsolidity, mass-noun syntax, and material-based categories are correlated. Thus, the early English lexicon presents correlations among category structures, the perceptible properties of solid and nonsolid things, and count-mass syntactic cues. The regularities are clearly lopsided—much stronger on the solid, shape, count side than on the nonsolid, material, mass side.

One might ask: Why does the early noun corpus have the structure it does? Sandhofer, Smith, and Luo (2000) examined transcripts of parent speech to young

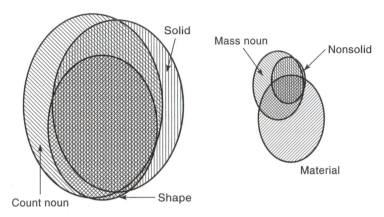

Figure 11.2. Venn diagrams illustrating the overlap among shape-based categories, solidity, and count syntax and material-based categories, nonsolidity, and mass syntax among the 312 early-learned English nouns.

children. They selected the most common 100 nouns and asked adults to judge the category structure, using the same method used by Samuelson and Smith. They found evidence for the same correlational structure as had Samuelson and Smith and the same emphasis on naming solid things in shape-based categories. We suspect that the structure of the common nouns children hear and use reflects deep truths about the perceptual regularities in the world and their functionality from a human perspective.

Children, however, must individually learn these deep truths. The evidence indicates that learning names for things is a crucial part of this. Children's kind-specific name generalizations become organized *as* they learn more and more names for different kinds (for review, see Smith, 1999). In line with previous results, Samuelson and Smith (1999) found that when children knew few nouns, they did not honor a distinction between solid and nonsolid things. Instead, they generalized novel names for solid things by shape only after they had already learned a substantial number of names for solid things, a fact that fits the idea that children's novel noun generalizations are themselves generalizations over the structure of already learned nouns. Further, children generalized names for solid things by shape long before they generalized names for nonsolid things by material—a fact that also aligns with the statistical regularities across early English noun categories.

Regularities in the Early Japanese Lexicon

What are early learned nouns in other languages like? Do they name the same kinds of categories as do the early English nouns? Colunga and Smith (2000) addressed this question by examining the nouns on the Japanese MCDI. The Japanese MCDI, like the English one, is a parent checklist of early-learned words and phrases. The Japanese MCDI was independently constructed and normalized across large samples of children learning Japanese as their first language (Ogura & Watamaki, 1997; Ogura,

Yamashita, Murase, & Dale, 1993). The Japanese MCDI, like its English counterpart, contains the words and phrases that 50 percent of children in the normalized samples know at 30 months. The list of nouns on the Japanese MCDI thus are a good measure of the first nouns learned by children learning Japanese.

When one compares the list of early English nouns and the list of early Japanese nouns, some differences are immediately apparent. For example, the Japanese checklist has more animal terms (52 vs. 43), more food terms (77 vs. 68), more people terms (34 vs. 26), and more body parts (33 vs. 27). In contrast, the English checklist has more names for artifacts. And the specific lexical categories differ. There is little overlap among early food categories, the dominant segment of names for nonsolid substances in both vocabularies. In addition, there are many differences in animal names. The Japanese list of animal terms includes *shrimp, crab, hippopotamus, kangaroo, koala, rhinoceros,* and *swallow*—none of which are on the English list of early known animal names. But, importantly, the early Japanese corpus, like the early English one, presents clear evidence of different category organizations for solid and nonsolid things.

In an effort to understand whether early English and Japanese nouns lexicalize categories of solid and nonsolid things similarly, Colunga & Smith (2000) examined the category structures of all food and concrete object terms on the Japanese and English lists. (That is, unlike Samuelson and Smith, they excluded animal terms and abstract terms such as "friend.") In total, 167 nouns on the Japanese MCDI are food or concrete object terms, and 150 nouns on the English MCDI are food or concrete object terms. Colunga and Smith asked native speakers to judge the category structure of each noun category using the same method as did Samuelson and Smith.

The results are presented in figure 11.3 as Venn diagrams. The larger outline area represents all the nouns that were judged in the language—including those that did not reach the strict agreement criteria. The smaller rectangles inside the larger area indicate by size the numbers of lexical items that did reach the strict agreement criteria. Black areas represent the numbers of nouns judged to refer to solid things, and white areas represent the numbers of nouns judged to refer to nonsolid things. Horizontal stripes indicate the numbers of nouns judged to refer to objects of similar shape, and vertical stripes the numbers of nouns judged to be similar in material and/or color.

As can be seen, in both languages about half of these early learned nouns refer to solid objects (42 percent in English, 48 percent in Japanese) and there are fewer (24 in English, 21 in Japanese) that name nonsolids. Further, in both languages more nouns were judged to refer to things similar in shape (38 percent in English, 49 percent in Japanese) than to things similar in material and/or color (31 percent in English, 20 percent in Japanese). And, crucially, solidity and category organization are correlated. Again, the correlation is very strong for solidity and within-category similarity in shape, with most of the words that were classified as referring to solid things also judged to refer to things that were similar in shape (79 percent in English, 93 percent in Japanese), and most of the words that were classified as referring to things similar in shape were also classified as referring to solid things (88 percent in English, 90 percent in Japanese). Again, the correlation was weaker for nonsolids and material-based category organizations. Whereas words that were classified as refer-

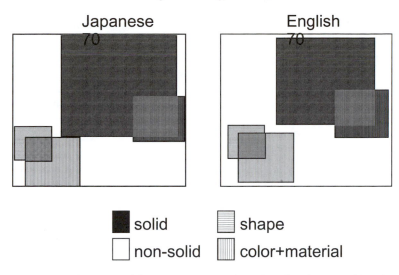

Figure 11.3. Venn diagrams of the overlap among shape-based and material based categories and the solidity and nonsolidity of instances for early learned food and object terms in English and Japanese.

ring to nonsolids were judged to refer to things that were similar in material (96 percent in English, 81 percent in Japanese), the correlation did not hold in the opposite direction (49 percent in English, 52 percent in Japanese).

The key result, then, is this: the same regularities characterize object and substance terms in the two languages.

Network Simulations

Are these regularities enough in and of themselves to create the universals in children's kind-specific generalizations? If children's knowledge about solid objects and nonsolid substances are the direct product of the statistical regularities among the nouns children know, then a simple learner of statistical regularities, a connectionist net, should develop similar knowledge if trained on a "vocabulary" similar to that of young children. Thus, we tested the idea of "ontology" as statistical regularities by feeding these regularities to a simple statistical learner.

Importantly, although connectionist networks are simple associative learners, the generalization the network needs to make to reproduce children's kind-specific noun generalizations is not simple. It requires going from simple associations to abstract, rule-like generalizations. For example, in the training phase of the simulations, we taught networks names for specific instances of specific categories—for example, the word "ball" associated with round things of variable color and material and the word "sand" associated with things of a particular material and range of colors. These kinds of associations are easy for networks to learn; and it is easy for networks to generalize from some specific instances of a category (e.g., from specific balls) to new instances of the same category (e.g., to never-before-encountered balls). The theoretical question, however, concerns not the learning and generalization of these specific categories but the emergence of the higher-level abstraction: that solidity signals the relevance of shape and that nonsolidity signals the relevance of material—for objects and substances never encountered before and shapes and materials never experienced before. Thus, prior to the simulations, it was an open question: Are the correlational structures manifest in early English and Japanese noun vocabularies enough to yield kind-specific category organizations when given novel things?

To address this question, Colunga and Smith (2000) taught the early English vocabulary to one set of networks and the early Japanese vocabulary to another. Two specific issues were at stake: (1) Would both sets of networks learn the same distinction, naming complexly shaped solid things by shape and nonsolid substances by material? and (2) Could the small differences in the statistical structures of the early noun lexicon in the two languages possibly be sufficient to create the differences in how English-speaking and Japanese-speaking children generalize names for simply shaped solids?

The Network   We used a Hopfield network, which is a simple recurrent network. The networks were trained using contrastive Hebbian learning, an algorithm that adjusts weights on the basis of the correlations between unit activations. Figure 11.4 shows the architecture of the network. It has a word layer, in which each unit corresponds to one word in the training vocabulary. Individual objects are represented on what we call the object layer. Activation patterns on this layer represent the shape and material of each individual object or substance presented to the network. More specifically, the shape and material of an object (say the roundness of a particular ball and its yellow rubbery material) are represented by an activation pattern along the whole layer, in a distributed fashion. In the solidity layer, one unit stands for solid and another for nonsolid. Finally, there is a hidden layer that is connected to all the other layers and recurrently with itself. Note that the word layer and the object layers are only connected through the hidden layer; there are no direct connections among them.

Training   We trained networks on the "English" or "Japanese" nouns. The goal was to mimic the vocabulary learning that a child brings into a novel noun generalization experiment. The statistical regularities characteristic of the early vocabularies were built into the network's training set in the following way. First, for each word that the network was to be taught, a pattern was generated to represent its value along the relevant dimension—the dimension that the English-speaking and Japanese-speaking adults said characterized the similarities of objects named by the noun. Second, at each presentation of the word, the value along the irrelevant dimension for that lexical category was varied randomly. For example, the word "ball" was judged by the English-speaking adults in the Samuelson and Smith (1999) study to refer to things that were similar in shape; thus, a particular pattern of activation was randomly chosen and then assigned to represent ball-shape. All balls presented to the network were defined as having this shape, although each ball presented to the network also consisted of a unique and randomly generated pattern defining the ma-

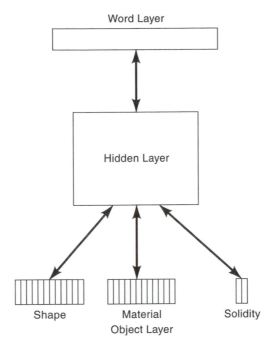

Figure 11.4. The architecture of the network used by Colunga and Smith. See text for further clarification.

terial and color. So whenever the network got the unit representing the word "ball," it also got the pattern representing ball-shape along the shape dimension and a different pattern along the material dimension.

We also built into the training the shape regularities that distinguish solid and nonsolid things. Specifically, in the simulations, although instances of most solid categories were the same shape (in proportion to the adult judgments), instances of different solid categories differed greatly in shape, instantiating the full range of possible shapes. In contrast, instances of the same nonsolid category typically differed in shape (in the same proportions as the adult judgments), but overall, nonsolid instances for all categories of nonsolid things were drawn from a relatively restricted range of possible shapes.

Noun Generalization Test   After teaching a network the "English" or "Japanese" vocabulary, we tested the network's expectations about how novel solid and nonsolid things should be named. Our approach to testing the networks is based on our conceptualization of the novel noun generalization task. In that task, the child sees an exemplar and hears its name and then is presented with two choice items—one matching the exemplar in shape and one in material. We propose that the child generalizes the name to the choice item that is *perceived* as most similar to the exemplar. If, for example, the child *attends* exclusively to the shape of the named exemplar, then a test object that matches the exemplar in shape (although different from the exemplar in material) should be perceived as highly similar to the exemplar, and the child should generalize the name to that item. Thus, to measure selective attention, we asked if the network's internal representations of a named exemplar and a test object were similar. More specifically, we asked if the patterns of activations on the hidden layer for the named exemplar and shape-matching test item were more or less similar than the patterns of activation on the hidden layer for the named exemplar and the material-matching choice item. Thus on each test trial, a novel exemplar object was generated by randomly creating an activation pattern along the shape and material dimensions. Then a novel shape-matching test object was generated by combining the exemplar's shape pattern with a novel randomly generated material pattern. A similarity measure of the exemplar and the shape match was computed in terms of the distance between the activation patterns in the hidden layer after the exemplar and its shape match were presented. Similarly, a novel material-matching test object was generated by combining the exemplar's material pattern with a new randomly generated shape pattern and the similarity between exemplar and material match was computed. Finally, we used these similarity measures between the emergent patterns of activation on the hidden layer to calculate the probability of choosing the shape and the material match using Luce's forced choice rule (Luce, 2000).

In this way, we trained 10 networks (with 10 different randomly generated initial connection weights) with categories structured like the object and substance terms young English-speaking children know. During training, we presented multiple instances of each trained noun until the network stably produced the right noun when presented an instance of each kind. We taught nouns with different category organizations in the same proportions that are found in young English-speaking children's lexicons. We then tested each of these English networks in the novel noun generalization task—with 30 novel exemplars. These 30 test trials were divided evenly into three kinds: the exemplars were defined by patterns of activation that represented (1) solid and complexly shaped things, (2) solid and simply shaped things, and (3) nonsolid and simply shaped things. In the same way, we trained 10 networks with all the words in the Japanese corpus and, at the end of this training, tested those 10 Japanese networks with the same 30 novel noun generalization trials. If the statistical regularities in the two vocabularies are sufficient to create a common solidity–nonsolidity distinction as well as the cross-language differences, then the performances of these networks should look like the performances of the children in the Imai and Gentner's study.

Results   In figure 11.5A, we compare the performances of the networks to the patterns reported by Imai and Gentner (1997) for 2-year-olds—the relevant age for the training corpus. The solid bars show the 2-year-old children's performances from the Imai and Gentner study—the proportion of times children extended the name of the object to the test object matching in shape. Since children always chose between a shape-matching and material-matching test object, chance is .50, and systematic extensions by material are indicated by below-chance performance in the figure. The striped bars in the figure show the mean of the networks' performances.

(A)

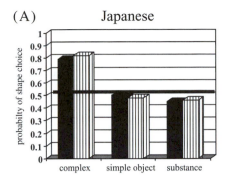

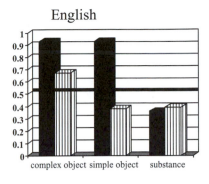

(B)

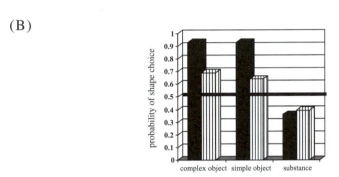

Figure 11.5. (A) The mean proportion of shape choices by English-speaking and Japanese-speaking 2-year-olds in Imai and Gentner (1997) experiment, as a function of the solidity of the exemplar and the mean proportion of shape choices predicted by the networks trained on early English or Japanese nouns. (B) The mean proportion of shape choices predicted by network trained on English nouns with correlated count-mass syntax, and for comparison, the mean proportion of shape choices by-2-year-old English-speaking children as a function of solidity, as reported by Imai & Gentner (1997).

Consider first the performances of the Japanese-speaking children and the networks trained on the Japanese noun categories. Names for complexly shaped objects are generalized by shape. Names for simple solids and for nonsolid substances are much less likely to be generalized by shape and often (more than half the time) are extended to new instances that match the named exemplar in material. The networks taught noun vocabularies with the same statistical structure as the noun vocabularies known by 2-year-old Japanese children generalize names for novel entities in the same way as the Japanese-speaking children. Complexly shaped things are named by shape, but simply shaped things—solid or nonsolid—are not. The fact that the networks mimic the performances of Japanese-speaking children tells us that the structure of the early noun lexicon is itself enough to create a distinction between objects and substances—with the boundary between object and substance being determined by the complexity of the shape.

Now consider the performances of the English-speaking children and the networks trained on the English noun categories. The children show a much stronger bias to extend names for solid things by shape than do the networks. This is particularly so for the solid simply shaped things. The children extend names for all solid things—simple or complex in shape—by shape; but they are more likely to extend names for nonsolid substances by material. Thus for English-speaking children, the partition between object categories organized by shape and substance categories organized by material is defined by solidity. The networks trained on the English nouns, in contrast, extend names for solid complexly shaped things by shape (reliably more often than expected by chance), but extend names for simply shaped things—solid or nonsolid—by material. The boundary between object and substance imposed by the English trained networks is based only on the statistical regularities in the early English noun categories and, like Japanese children but not English children, the boundary appears to be defined by complexity of shape rather than solidity. These results tell us that the structure of the early English noun lexicon is not enough in and of itself to explain English-speaking children's novel noun generalizations.

Adding Syntax

What is missing from the simulations of the English-speaking children? The obvious additional factor relevant to English-speaking children's learning is count–mass syntax. Therefore, in the next simulation, we added the count–mass syntax correlations to the English-trained networks.

For this simulation we added an additional input layer to those illustrated in figure 11.4: the syntax layer. The syntax layer had two units, one to represent count syntax and one for mass syntax. The networks were trained on the same English vocabulary, but now each noun was associated with count/mass syntax information, according to adults' judgments as collected by Samuelson and Smith (1999). Nouns that adults judged to be both count and mass nouns (e.g., "cake" and "muffin") were associated equally often with both the count and mass units "on."

The results of the network simulations are shown compared to children's performance in figure 11.5B. Although the connectionist networks trained on English with the correlated count–mass syntactic cues show a quantitatively weaker shape bias than do children, they were successful in simulating the qualitative pattern. The networks, like the children, now generalize names for solid things—simple and complex—by shape, and names for nonsolid things by material. Learning names for concrete objects and substances in both languages appears to create knowledge that objects and substances are named by different properties. But language-specific syntactic cues in English shift this "ontological" boundary relative to that of Japanese speakers.

Conclusion

The kinds of nouns known early by children learning English and by children learning Japanese present an organized structure. Most name solid things, and solid things with the same name tend to be similar in shape. A coherent subset of nouns name nonsolid substances, and substances with the same name tend to be similar in material. The simulations show that these regularities are sufficient to create the similarities in English-speaking and Japanese-speaking children's novel noun generalizations; that is, a shape bias when naming complexly shaped solids and (to a lesser degree) a material bias when naming nonsolids. Similarly structured lexical categories create similar knowledge about object and substance categories. The results also suggest that language-specific syntactic cues are part of the correlational mix, modulating the object–substance partition in language-specific ways.

The Animate-Object Boundary

If language-specific cues correlate with perceptible differences among kinds and influence ontological boundaries, then there should be cross-linguistic differences at the animate-object boundary for Japanese- and English-speaking children. This should be so because Japanese adds linguistic cues to the statistical mix that are correlated with an animal versus object-substance partition, just as English adds cues to the associative mix that are correlated with a animal-object versus substance partition.

Iru/Aru

Of all the distinctions in Japanese that focus on animacy, the *iru/aru* distinction seems a likely powerful force on the way Japanese children think about objects. This distinction involves fundamental notions of existence ("there is") and spatial location ("be located"). In English we use the same verb "be" for a dog, a cup, and water, saying: *there is a dog, there is a cup*, and *there is water*. However, the Japanese verb *iru* is used for a dog, and *aru* is used for a cup or water. *Iru* implies being in a place by one's own will. *Aru*, on the other hand, implies "having been left" at a place. Importantly, *iru* is used whenever one refers to entities that behave intentionally, for example, people and animals. Critically, *iru* is also used by adult speakers (and children) when inanimates are conceptualized as animates. For example, *iru* is used by adults when referring to dolls and toys as the animates they depict in play and conversations with children. Thus every time a Japanese-speaker refers to the location of an object, the speaker must decide if the object is to be conceptualized as animate or inanimate.

Yoshida and Smith (2001, in press) demonstrated that 2- to 3-year-old Japanese-speaking children understand the implications of *iru* and *aru* in a novel noun generalization task. The children in this study were monolingual and were tested in Japan. The children were presented with three-dimensional objects that were ambiguous and could be seen as depictions of animates or artifacts. As illustrated in figure 11.6, each object had four pipe-cleaner appendages. The objects could be conceptualized as animal depictions if the appendages were construed as limbs, but they also could be easily viewed (as least by our intuitions) as artifacts and not animal-like at all. The exemplar objects were named either using a sentence frame with *aru* (suggesting an artifact) or with *iru* (suggesting an animate entity). In a yes/no version of the novel name generalization task, the child was shown the exemplar and told its name—"This

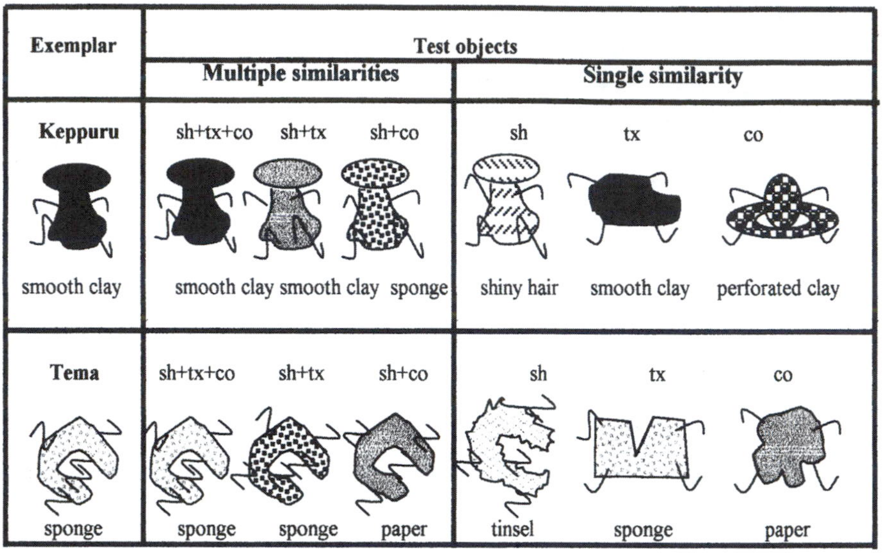

Exemplar	Test objects					
	Multiple similarities			**Single similarity**		
Keppuru	sh+tx+co	sh+tx	sh+co	sh	tx	co
smooth clay	smooth clay	smooth clay	sponge	shiny hair	smooth clay	perforated clay
Tema	sh+tx+co	sh+tx	sh+co	sh	tx	co
sponge	sponge	sponge	paper	tinsel	sponge	paper

Figure 11.6. The ambiguous objects used by Yoshida and Smith.

is a mobit"—and then each test object was presented individually. The child was asked about each test object "Is this a mobit?" The results are shown in figure 11.7. When the novel name was presented in a sentence frame containing *aru*, the Japanese-speaking children generalized the name to all test objects matching the exemplar in shape, regardless of whether these test objects matched or mismatched the exemplar on the other properties. In contrast, when the exemplar's name was presented in the context of *iru*, children generalized the name conservatively, only to objects that matched the exemplar on multiple properties, and particularly in shape and texture. The pattern in the *iru* condition fits past findings on children's extensions of names for animal-like things; for animals, shape alone is not enough, and multiple similarities are required to extend the name (e.g., Jones et al., 1991; Jones & Smith, 1997).

These results provide three important pieces of information. First, the linguistic cues of *iru/aru* alter the way Japanese-speaking children categorize novel objects. This tells us that young Japanese-speaking children do have knowledge of at least one linguistic device that privileges animate kinds. Second, young Japanese-speaking children generalize names for implied artifacts to new instances more broadly than they generalize names for implied animals. Third, the results tell us that linguistic cues, at least explicitly present ones, can alter how the same perceptual entity is conceptualized—as a depiction of an animate or artifact kind.

Variation at the Animate-Object Boundary

In the world, animate and inanimate things differ in many ways. They have different properties, such as eyes and limbs versus angular parts. They move differently. And people talk about them differently. In brief, the world presents the learner with

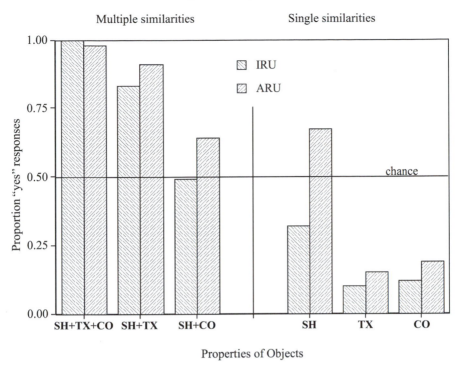

Multiple similarities   Single similarities

Figure 11.7. Mean "yes" responses—the name of the exemplar extends to the test object—by Japanese-speaking children, when the name was presented in locative contructions using iru *or* aru, *as a function of the properties of the test object that match those of the named exemplar: shape (SH), texture (TX), color (CO).*

a richly structured set of associations. *Iru* and *aru* and a host of other linguistic distinctions centered on animacy are part of this associative mix for children learning Japanese. Does this alter the way Japanese children perceive animate and inanimate things? We hypothesized that Japanese children, relative to their English counterparts, might be hypersensitive as to whether some object should be construed as an animate versus an artifact. That is, given ambiguous objects with features merely suggestive of limbs, Japanese-speaking children should be more likely than English-speaking children to see the appendages as limblike and to construe the objects as depictions of animate things, even when the linguistic context is neutral and offers no suggestion as to how the object should be construed. This should be so if the linguistic distinction in the language heightens attention to cues relevant to making perceptual distinctions (see Lucy, 1996).

Yoshida and Smith (in press) tested this prediction by comparing 2- to 3-year old Japanese- and English-speaking children's name generalizations using the same stimuli as in figure 11.6. The sentence frames used in Japanese were nonlocative constructions that did not require *iru/aru*, rather, the same sentence frame could be used with both animates and inanimates.

Figure 11.8 shows the mean proportion of "yes" responses as a function of language and individual test objects. As is apparent, when presented with ambiguous objects named with novel names in a neutral sentence frame, Japanese-speaking children generalized the names in the same way they did when the name was presented in the context of *iru*, a context that unambiguously implies animacy. That is, Japanese-speaking children generalized the exemplar's name only to items that matched the exemplar in both shape and texture and rejected all other test objects as instances of the lexical category. In contrast, the English-speaking children generalized the novel names in the same way that Japanese-speaking children had when the name had been presented in the context of *aru*, a context that unambiguously implies an inanimate thing. English-speaking children, like Japanese-speaking children in the *aru* condition, generalized the name to all objects that matched the exemplar in shape—both when that object matched in other properties and when it did not.

Here, again, we see the effect of the language one is learning on the ontological boundary. *Iru* and *aru* are correlated with things that present different perceptible properties—those that distinguish a real and unambiguous animate, like a living dog, from an inanimate thing, like a cup. *Iru* and *aru* are also correlated with lexical category structure—categories organized by joint similarity in shape and texture versus

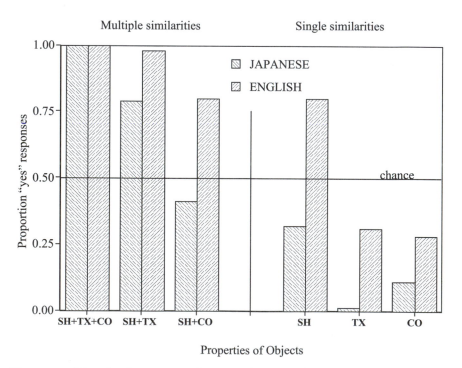

Figure 11.8. Mean "yes" responses—the name of the exemplar extends to the test object—by Japanese-speaking and English-speaking children, when the name was presented in a neutral syntactic frame, as a function of the properties of the test object that match those of the named exemplar: shape (SH), texture (TX), color (CO).

categories organized by shape alone. The result of these added linguistic cues to the correlational structure is that Japanese-speaking children are more likely than English-speaking children to see the appendages as limbs and the objects as depictions of an animate kind.

Cross-language Differences Only at the Boundary

Yoshida and Smith (in press, 2001) also compared Japanese- and English-speaking children's generalizations of names for unambiguous depictions of animates (rounded bodylike forms with eyes) and unambiguous depictions of artifacts (angular, complex, multipart shapes). With unambiguous exemplars, Japanese- and English-speaking children extended the exemplars' names in the same way. Names for unambiguous depictions of animates were extended to new instances narrowly, by shape and texture. Names for unambiguous artifacts were extended broadly by shape. Thus, the cross-linguistic effects at the animate-object boundary, like those at the object-substance boundary, appear evident only for ambiguous entities that lie near the boundary.

These findings make sense if linguistic cues are *one* influence in a correlational soup that also includes perceptual cues and learned lexical category structures. If perceptual cues strongly predict (and perhaps determine) lexical category structure, as seems to be the case in the early noun lexicon, linguistic cues may push conceptualizations one way or the other only in perceptually ambiguous cases. This is an important idea for thinking about how language-specific structures might influence the formation of even more abstract ideas.

Summary

Children learning all languages are presented with three sources of information relevant to forming "ontological" distinctions. These are illustrated in figure 11.9. First, there are the different kinds of things in world—from formless liquids to deformable substances to simple wood to complex artifacts and natural kinds to animate things. These different kinds present—*statistically and in a graded way*—different perceptible properties. Second, there are also the lexical categories that children are learning. The similarity structure of these categories is statistically correlated with the perceptible properties of different kinds. Liquids that have no shape of their own may tend to be named by material (and color), artifacts with rigid and stable shapes may tend to be named by shape, and animates with their rich correlational structures may be named by multiple properties that include texture and shape. Third, there are linguistic devices specific to specific languages that correlate with these regularities in perceptual properties and category organizations. If children are associative learners, and if all these sources of information are blended together in a learned ontology, then one would predict both universals and a coherent bending of those universals in language and culturally specific ways. This is what the pattern of results here suggests. Children learning English and children learning Japanese learn to carve up the world in the same way because of deep regularities in that world and because the two languages organize lexical categories of concrete kinds in pretty much the same way.

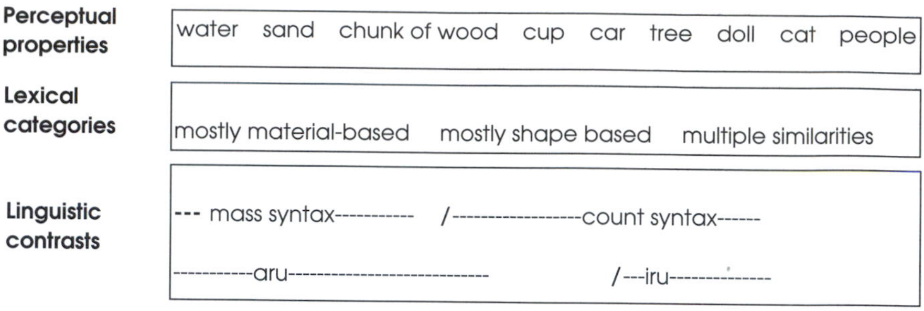

Perceptual properties	water sand chunk of wood cup car tree doll cat people

Lexical categories	mostly material-based mostly shape based multiple similarities

Linguistic contrasts	--- mass syntax---------- /------------------count syntax------ ----------aru------------------------ /---iru--------------

Figure 11.9. *Three sources of information about animates, objects, and substances.*

How These Correlations May Build Abstract Ideas

The early lexicon is small and is not representative of the full range of nouns that children ultimately learn. For the most part, the early noun lexicon is filled with names for the concrete, palpable things that dominate domestic life. The adult lexicon includes, in addition, names for abstract ideas, ideas that sometimes also seem to be divided into abstract categories of animate, object, and substance. For example, speakers of English pluralize and count "hopes" as if hopes were bounded and discrete kinds. Speakers of English, however, do not pluralize "justice" but speak of meting it out in portions, as if justice were a continuous and unbounded substance. These abstract ideas may be built on or be metaphoric extensions of the perceptual structures of concrete objects and substances (see Lakoff & Johnson, 1980; Levinson, 1996).

Figure 11.10 illustrates hypothesized correlations among perceptual properties and from perceptual properties to lexical category structure. Although not illustrated, it seems likely that these various connections vary in strength, depending on the strength of relations in the world. For example, objects with angles and multiple parts are highly likely to be solid (since complex angular shapes cannot be readily formed from nonsolid substances). Thus angularity strongly predicts solidity and multiple parts, and each of these cues and the whole cluster predicts categorization by shape. Analogously, nonsolid objects tend to be rounded and simply shaped, although many simply shaped things can also be solid. Thus, simple shape and roundedness weakly predict nonsolidity and categorization by material, but simple shape, roundedness, and nonsolidity would jointly predict more strongly categorization by material. Finally, a strong cluster of interrelated cues would seem to characterize animate things, and all these cues predict categorization by multiple similarities. The correlations in figure 11.10 derive from the perceptual regularities in the world, regularities that appear to be honored in the category structures of the common concrete nouns of both English and Japanese.

What do the differences between English and Japanese languages add to these perceptual correlations? As illustrated in figure 11.11, perceptual properties and category structures characteristic of animates are also associated with particular linguistic forms in Japanese and perceptual properties and category structures characteristic of inanimates are associated with contrasting forms. Figure 11.12 illustrates how perceptual properties and category structures characteristic of animates and objects are

PERCEPTUAL CUES   CATEGORY STRUCTURE

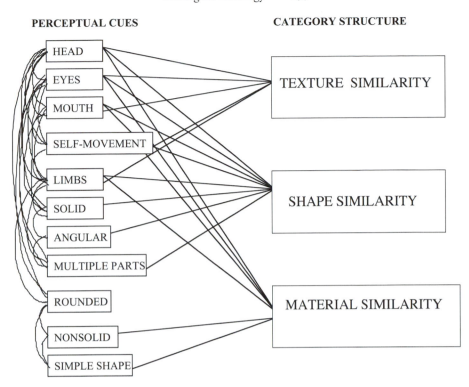

Figure 11.10. Correlations between perceptual properties and lexical category structure.

also associated with particular linguistic forms in English and how perceptual properties and category structures characteristic of nonsolids are associated with contrasting forms. One can also see in these illustrations how the addition of linguistic
cues to a name generalization task can influence children's name generalizations;
how in Soja's (1992) study, saying *a mel* increased English-speaking children's generalizations by shape, whereas saying *some mel* increased their generalizations by
material, and how in Yoshida and Smith's (2000) study, saying *iru* increased Japanese-speaking children's generalizations by shape and texture, whereas saying *aru*
increased their generalization by shape alone.

Importantly, however, systematic linguistic contrasts do more than just shift attention on-line. The evidence suggests that they also differentially bolster and weaken
perceptual correlations, changing, in a sense, how things are perceived. Figures 11.11
and 11.12 illustrate how this may be so in an associative learner. The interconnections among perceptible cues associated with animacy—head, eyes, limbs, self-
movement—may be strengthened by their joint association with linguistic forms in
Japanese. Because of their connections to the same cluster of linguistic cues, the feature "limblike appendages" may be more strongly linked to self-movement and to
eyes for Japanese speakers than for English speakers. The implication is that for Japanese speakers, vaguely suggestive limbs—because of reinforcing connections pro-

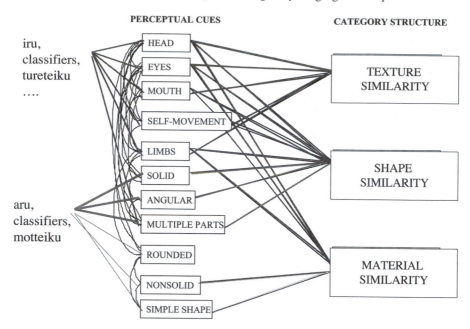

Figure 11.11. *Correlations among Japanese linguistic cues, perceptual properties, and lexical category structure.*

vided by the Japanese language—may be more likely to bring forth ideas associated with animate things, including categorization by multiple properties. Thus, vaguely limblike appendages may be a stronger cue suggestive of animacy for Japanese than English speakers. Analogously, the linguistic forms in English that signal discrete countable things may reinforce the connections between cues that are characteristic of objects and between those cues and categorization by shape. Thus, even in tasks in which those linguistic cues are not present, solidity—even in the context of a simple shape—may robustly lead to categorization by shape. Although speculative, these ideas fit the general workings of interactive-activation models of associative learning (Billman & Heit 1989; Colunga & Gasser 1998; Kersten & Billman 1997; McClelland & Rumelhart 1981): overlapping connections reinforce each other such that one cue alone can bring forth activation of a whole correlated cluster.

Intriguingly, the strengthened connections that are the consequences of these so-called gang effects in associative learning may play an important formative role in abstract ideas. Ideas of animacy or objectness that do not depend on perceptual cues may emerge through links from linguistic cues to category structures. If the relations illustrated in figures 11.11 and 11.12 capture the regularities that actually exist, then the most basic assumptions of associative learning predict that linguistic cues like the indefinite article should give rise to ideas of boundedness and that *iru* should give rise to ideas of self-movement. In this way, hopes may be abstract objects and spirits may have intention.

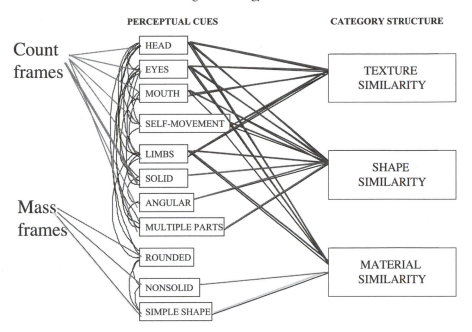

PERCEPTUAL CUES   CATEGORY STRUCTURE

Count frames

Mass frames

HEAD
EYES
MOUTH
SELF-MOVEMENT
LIMBS
SOLID
ANGULAR
MULTIPLE PARTS
ROUNDED
NONSOLID
SIMPLE SHAPE

TEXTURE SIMILARITY

SHAPE SIMILARITY

MATERIAL SIMILARITY

Figure 11.12. Correlations among English linguistic cues, perceptual properties, and lexical category structure.

Conclusions

The evidence presented in this chapter provides empirical support for five core ideas, as follows:

1. *There are regularities that distinguish kinds of categories.* Solid things can be complexly shaped, nonsolid things cannot, and animate things are characterized by bundles of correlated properties.
2. *The nominal categories of languages honor these correlational bundles.* Concrete nouns in both English and Japanese—the nouns learned early—name complexly shaped solid things by shape, nonsolid things by material, and animate things by multiple similarities, including similarities in shape and texture.
3. *Learning names for things enables higher-order generalizations.* Simple associative devices, when taught pairings between names and individual object categories, learn more than just how those trained names map to categories. They also learn the correlations that characterize different kinds, for example, how object categories are structured differently from substance categories.
4. *The mechanism is associative learning.* The simulation studies clearly demonstrate how ontologies in the psychological sense could arise

naturally from the correlational bundles in the world and the regularities across lexical categories that are mapped to those bundles.

5. *Linguistic regularities are part of the correlational mix that creates ontologies, and thus language-specific properties will bend psychological ontologies in language-specific ways.*

These ideas of ontologies as statistical regularities suggest a profound sameness in all human knowledge. They also suggest the genuine possibility that there are culturally distinct ways of knowing. Universality will be found amid the correlations and statistical regularities that are grounded in perception, the structure of the world, and in concrete lexical categories. Diversity, unique ways of knowing specific to specific cultures, will arise from variations in how the systematic contrasts in a language correlate with early-learned statistical regularities and will show itself most dramatically in ideas about abstract kinds. Both universality and diversity are the natural products of the statistical regularities among properties of concrete things, their category structures, and the exquisite variations in how languages reflect and extend deep truths about concrete kinds.

Acknowledgments

The empirical and simulation studies of early noun learning by English-speaking and Japanese-speaking children were supported by a grant from the National Institutes of Mental Health, R01 MH60200. We thank Michael Gasser and Larissa Samuelson for their many contributions to the ideas and experiments summarized here.

References

Billman, D., & Heit, E. (1989). Observational learning from internal feedback: A simulation of an adaptive learning method. *Cognitive Science, 12,* 587–625.

Colunga, E., & Gasser, M. (1998). Linguistic relativity and word acquisition: A computational approach. *Annual Conference of the Cognitive Science Society, 20,* 244–249.

Colunga, E., & Smith, L. B. (2000) Learning to learn words: a cross-linguistic study of the shape and material biases. *Boston University Child Language Development Proceedings, 24,* 197–207.

Fenson, L., Dale, P., Reznick, J. S., Bates, E., Hartung, J., Pethick, S., & Reilly, J. (1993). *MacArthur Communicative Development Inventories.* San Diego: Singular.

Gathercole, V., & Min, H. (1997). Word meaning biases or language-specific effects? Evidence from English, Spanish and Korean. *First Language, 17,* 31–56.

Gathercole, V., Cramer, L., Somerville, S., & Jansen, M. (1995). Ontological categories and function: Acquisition of new names. *Cognitive Development, 10,* 225–251.

Gelman, S. A., & Coley, J. D. (1991). Language and categorization: The acquisition of natural kind terms. In S. A. Gelman & J. P. Byrnes (Eds.), *Perspectives on language and thought: Interrelations in development* (pp. 146–196). Cambridge: Cambridge University Press.

Gentner, D. & Boroditsky, L. (in press). Individuation, relativity, and early word learning. In M. Bowerman & S. Levinson (Eds.), *Language acquisition and conceptual development.* England: Cambridge University Press.

Gumperz, J. C., & Levinson, S. C. (1996). Introduction to part 1. In J. C. Gumperz & S. C. Levinson (Eds.), *Rethinking linguistic relativity* (pp. 21–36). Cambridge: Cambridge University Press.

Imai, M., & Gentner, D. (1997). A cross-linguistic study of early word meaning: Universal ontology and linguistic influence. *Cognition, 62,* 169–200.

Imai, M., Gentner, D., & Uchida, N. (1994). Children's theories of word meaning: The role of shape similarity in early acquisition. *Cognitive Development, 9,* 45–76.

Jones, S., & Smith, L. B. (1998). How children name objects with shoes. *Cognitive Development, 13,* 323–334.

Jones, S. S., Smith, L. B., & Landau, B. (1991). Object properties and knowledge in early lexical learning. *Child Development, 62,* 499–516.

Keil, F. (1994). Explanation, association, and the acquisition of word meaning. In L. R. Gleitman & B. Landau (Eds.), *Lexical acquisition* (pp. 169–197). Cambridge, MA: MIT Press.

Kersten, A., & Billman, D. (1997). Event category learning. *Journal of Experimental Psychology: Learning, Memory, and Cognition, 23,* 638–658.

Lakoff, G., & Johnson, M. (1980). *Metaphors we live by.* Chicago: University of Chicago Press, 1980.

Landau, B., Smith, L. B., & Jones, S. S. (1988). The importance of shape in early lexical learning. *Cognitive Development, 3,* 299–321.

Landau, B., Smith, L. B., & Jones, S. S. (1992). Syntactic context and the shape bias in children's and adult's lexical learning. *Journal of Memory and Language, 31,* 807–825.

Landau, B., Smith, L. B., & Jones, S. (1998) Object shape, object function, and object name. *Journal of Memory and Language, 38,* 1–27.

Levinson, S. C. (1996). Relativity in spatial conception and description. In J. J. Gumperz & S. C. Levinson (Eds.), *Rethinking linguistic relativity* (pp. 177–202). Cambridge: Cambridge University Press.

Luce, R. D. (2000). *Utility of gains and losses: Measurement-theoretical and experimental approaches.* Mahwah, NJ: Erlbaum.

Lucy, J. A. (1992). *Language diversity and thought: A reformulation of the linguistic relativity hypothesis.* Cambridge: Cambridge University Press.

Lucy, J. A. (1996). The scope of linguistic relativity: An analysis and review of empirical research. In J. C. Gumperz & S. C. Levinson (Eds.), *Rethinking linguistic relativity* (pp. 37–69). Cambridge: Cambridge University Press.

McClelland, J., & Rumelhart, D. E. (1981). An interactive-activation model of context effects in letter perception: An account of basic findings. *Psychological Review, 88,* 373–407.

McPherson, L. (1991). A little goes a long way: Evidence for a perceptual basis of learning for the noun categories COUNT and MASS. *Journal of Child Language, 18,* 315–338.

Markman, E. M. (1989). *Categorization and naming in children: Problems of induction.* Cambridge, MA: MIT Press.

Ogura, T., Yamashita, Y., Murase, T., & Dale, P. (1993, April). *Some preliminary findings from the Japanese Early Communicative Inventory.* Paper presented at the Sixth International Conference for Child Language, Toronto.

Ogura, T., & Watamaki, T. (1997). *Japanese communicative developmental inventories: User's guide and technical manual.* San Diego: Singular.

Quine, W. V. (1969). *Ontological relativity and other essays.* New York: Columbia University Press.

Rosch, E. (1973). On the internal structure of perceptual and semantic categories. In T. E. Moore (Ed.), *Cognitive development and the acquisition of language* (pp. 111–144). San Diego: Academic Press.

Sandhofer, C. M., Smith, L. B., & Luo, J. (2000). Counting nouns and verbs in the input: Differential frequencies, different kinds of learning? *Journal of Child Language, 27,* 561–585.

Samuelson, L., & Smith, L. B. (1999). Early noun vocabularies: Do ontology, category structure, and syntax correspond? *Cognition, 73*, 1–33.

Samuelson, L., & Smith, L. B. (in press). Attention to rigid and deformable shape in naming and non-naming tasks. *Child Development.*

Smith, L. B. (1999). Children's noun learning: How general learning processes make specialized learning mechanisms. In B. MacWhinney (Ed.), *The emergence of language* (pp. 277–303). Hillsdale, NJ: LEA.

Soja, N. (1992). Inferences about the meanings of nouns: The relationship between perception and syntax. *Cognitive Development, 7*, 29–46.

Soja, N., Carey, S., & Spelke, E. (1991). Ontological categories guide young children's inductions of word meanings: Object terms and substance terms. *Cognition, 38*, 179–211.

Spelke, E. S., Vishton, P., & Von-Hofsten, C. (1995). Object perception, object-directed action, and physical knowledge in infancy. In M. S. Gazzaniga (Eds.), *The cognitive neurosciences* (pp. 165–179). Cambridge, MA: MIT Press.

Yoshida, H., & Smith, L. B. (in press). Shifting ontological boundaries: How Japanese- and English-speaking children generalize names for animals and artifacts. *Developmental Science.*

Yoshida, H., & Smith, L. B. (2001). Early noun learning depends on the language being learned, *Cognition, 82*(2), B63–B74.

CHAPTER TWELVE

Words, Kinds, and Causal Powers

A Theory Theory Perspective on Early Naming and Categorization

Alison Gopnik and Thierry Nazzi

Fᴏʀ sᴏᴍᴇ 25 ʏᴇᴀʀs, the prevailing theories of categorization in philosophy have invoked the idea of "kinds" (Kripke, 1972; Putnam, 1975). When we look at how adults use words to refer to categories of things, we find that they only rarely categorize objects on the basis of their common properties. Instead, adults seem to categorize objects together when they believe that they belong to the same "kind," that is, that they share some common, abstract "essence." Psychological investigations of adults have largely confirmed these philosophical intuitions; adults do seem to group objects together based on "kinds" rather than properties (Murphy & Medin, 1985; Rips, 1989).

Several investigators, particularly Gelman and her colleagues (Gelman & Coley, 1990; Gelman & Markman, 1986), have argued that children as young as 2 years old also categorize and name objects based on kinds (see also Mandler & McDonough, 1993; Mervis & Bertrand, 1994; Soja, Carey, & Spelke, 1991). Other investigators, in contrast, have suggested that young children categorize and name objects on the basis of perceptual properties such as shape (Imai, Gentner, & Uchida, 1994; Landau, Smith, & Jones, 1988). However, the question of whether children use names to refer to kinds has been bedeviled by the problem that the philosophical notion is not easily translatable into empirical predictions. In the philosophical literature, the concept of kinds refers to the idea that members of a category share an "essence," a common, abstract, ontological property, and that names refer to this essence (Putnam, 1975). Obviously, it is difficult to ask 3-year-olds if they conceive of objects or use names in this way.

This methodological problem also raises a deeper question: Why would adults or children organize the world in term of kinds? Why invoke mysterious, invisible, underlying essences when perceptual properties would do? What functional or evolutionary basis could there be for such a cognitive practice?

We will argue that, at least on many occasions, categorizing objects into "kinds" should be seen as making a claim about the common causal powers of those objects (see also Ahn, Gelman, Amsterlaw, Hohenstein, & Kalish, 2000; Rehder, 1999; Strevens, 2000). On the causal powers view, we assume that something about an object causes the object's characteristic properties. This common underlying cause is responsible for the correlation among the properties of the object. This common underlying cause is also shared by other objects of the same kind and is responsible for the patterns of correlation of properties among all of those objects. We can think of the "essence" of a category as a sort of causal placeholder. To say that members of a kind share an "essence" is to say that their characteristic properties are due to a common cause, even if we may not be able to exactly identify that cause.

Different types of causal relations may be involved in different types of "kinds." For biological natural kinds, such as tigers and lemons, the causal relations are likely to involve the detailed internal structure of the object, as well as biological causal processes such as growth and inheritance (Gelman & Wellman, 1991). For physical or material natural kinds, they involve the material composition of the object (Soja et al., 1991). For artifacts, these relations involve intentional causal processes, in particular the intentions of the designer of the object and the goals the object is intended to serve (Gelman & Bloom, 2000; Kemler Nelson, 1995; Kemler Nelson, Frankenfield, Morris, & Blair, 2000; Kemler Nelson, Russell, Duke, & Jones, 2000).

One characteristic of kinds is that they support induction. An object that is a member of a kind will prove to have the same novel properties as other members of the kind (see, e.g., Gelman & Markman, 1986). However, the justification for these inductive inferences has been rather mysterious. *Why* would we assume that an object that has the same name as another object would also prove to have the same novel properties? Assuming that the common properties of kind members are due to an underlying common cause licenses such inductions. If we now discover that members of the kind consistently have some other property in common, we can assume that that property is also caused by the object's "essence." This causal inference allows us to predict that the new property will also be present in new members of the kind.

The causal powers view predicts that prior knowledge about causal relations will influence categorization. For example, several studies suggest that for older children and adults, who already know about causal relations, common causes are more likely to be important in defining a kind category than common effects (Ahn et al., 2000; Rehder, 1999). Common DNA or common internal structure is more likely to define category membership than common color, just because DNA or internal structure is more likely to be a cause of other properties of the object than color.

But, on our view, we may also work backward from the correlational patterns among properties to inferences about causal structure—even if we don't know exactly which causal mechanisms are involved. So, for example, if we notice a characteristic pattern of correlations among properties of objects, say that long-haired animals have slower metabolisms and are more likely to be prey, we may infer that there is a common cause of all these properties, even if initially we aren't sure what that cause actually is. Similarly, when several members of an existing kind, like cats, turn out to have a particular new property, say immunity to foot-and-mouth disease, we may infer that the common essence that caused this property in one cat will also be the cause of the property in the other cats, even if we cannot specify that causal relation in detail.

Another consequence of the causal view is that the effects of an object's "essence" will not be limited to properties of the objects themselves. The causal powers of the object may be responsible for the intrinsic properties of the object, but they will also be responsible, more widely, for causal effects on other objects or events. On our view, then, children and adults should pay special attention to the broader causal effects of objects when they categorize them. Notice that this view contrasts with the view that children or adults are simply registering patterns of correlation among the object properties (see, e.g., Jones & Smith, 1993; chap. 4, 7). On our view, children and adults do pay attention to correlations among properties, but their categorization is more than just a summary of those correlations. Instead, they use those correlations to infer causal powers. Those powers may have effects that extend well beyond the object itself.

In fact, inductions about causal effects on other objects play a particularly important role in the philosophical arguments in favor of natural kinds. For example, consider Putnam's classic "Twin Earth" arguments (Putnam, 1975). The stuff that runs in waters and streams on Earth and on the faraway planet Twin Earth is perceptually indistinguishable, and so my twin on Twin Earth and I will have associated the same perceptual experiences with "water." Nevertheless, unbeknownst to us, Twin Earth water really has a very different chemical composition than water; it is made of XYZ rather than H_2O. Our intuition in this case, according to Putnam, is that the words refer to different kinds of things, in spite of the fact that they are associated with the same perceptual features. How does this intuition translate into an empirical prediction? The prediction is that some causal effects of XYZ will turn out to be different from the causal effects of H_2O. This is how the scientists will eventually discriminate between them. In fact, in the scientific case, these new predictions will often turn out to involve causal relations among objects rather than intrinsic properties. H_2O and XYZ may register differently on a spectrometer, for example, or react differently with other chemicals.

We argue, then, that in their kind understanding people assume that perceptual features are important only insofar as they are an indicator of underlying causal powers. Hence objects that look similar but appear to have different causal powers will be considered to belong to different kinds and will receive different names. Conversely, the fact that perceptually similar objects receive different names will be a cue to the fact that they belong to different kinds and have different causal powers.

This interpretation of kind reasoning as a species of causal reasoning makes a great deal of functional and evolutionary sense. Often—in fact, usually—the causal structure of the world and the causal powers of objects are not immediately apparent. Television remotes make the set turn on, magnets make filings move toward them, water makes a plant grow, the sun makes you get sunburned, a snake makes you scared, but none of these causal relations are perceptually obvious. We can't simply predict how an object will affect other objects by seeing what it looks like. In fact, similar-looking objects may have different causal effects on other objects, the stereo remote doesn't turn on the television, ordinary metal doesn't attract filings, vodka kills plants, indoor lights don't burn you, garden hoses aren't scary. Somehow we must learn about these causal powers of objects, determine which objects do or do not have those powers, and name them accordingly.

Moreover, understanding hidden causal powers, and categorizing objects in terms of them, is extremely useful. It allows us to make important predictions about what will happen in the future, through the process of causal induction. It also allows us to intervene in the world effectively to make things happen ourselves. We can make televisions turn on or plants grow or scare our relatives. By putting objects in the same group or giving them the same name, we are making a powerful prediction about their current and future causal powers.

Even more important, assuming that names refer to kinds allows us to quickly and efficiently learn about the causal powers of objects from others and to communicate our own knowledge about causal powers to them. A child (or an adult) who hears that two objects have the same name knows much more than just that the objects look the same (which is obvious in any case). She also knows that the objects' properties have a common cause and that this will lead to common effects in the future.

The Theory Theory and Causal Maps

The idea that kinds involve common causal powers is one part of our broader conception of the nature of cognition and cognitive development—and in particular our interpretation of "the theory theory." The theory theory is the idea that much adult knowledge, particularly our knowledge of the physical, biological, and psychological world, consists of "intuitive" or "naïve" or "folk" theories (Murphy & Medin, 1985; Rips, 1989). Similarly, cognitive developmentalists argue that children formulate and revise a succession of such intuitive theories (Carey, 1985; Gopnik, 1988; Gopnik & Meltzoff, 1997; Keil, 1989; Wellman, 1990; Wellman & Gelman, 1997). This idea rests on an analogy between everyday knowledge and scientific theories. Advocates of the theory theory have drawn up lists of features that are shared by these two kinds of knowledge (see e.g., Gopnik & Wellman, 1994). The assumption behind this work has been that there are common cognitive structures and processes, common representations and rules that underlie both everyday knowledge and scientific knowledge.

Formulating the analogy between the history of science and development has been an important first step, but it is time to try to describe in some detail the representations and rules that could underpin both these types of knowledge. In order to specify both the idea of theories and of kinds more precisely, it is necessary to flesh out the nature of those cognitive structures and processes in more detail. Ideally, such an account should include ideas about the computational character of these representations and rules.

We have recently begun to outline a more developed cognitive and computational account of the theory theory. In particular, we argue that many everyday theories and everyday theory changes involve a type of representation we call a "causal map" (Gopnik, 2000; Gopnik & Glymour, 2002). A causal map is an abstract, coherent, learned representation of the causal relationships among kinds of objects and events in the world. These maps are analogous to the spatial cognitive maps used by many animals (O'Keefe & Nadel, 1978; Tolman, 1932).

These representations are different from some more familiar kinds of causal knowledge. For example, there is some evidence that certain kinds of specific causal inferences, such as inferences about the interactions of moving objects, are in place very early and may even be hardwired (Leslie, 1982; Michotte, 1962). For example, there is evidence that adults and children assume that when one object collides with another object it will cause the second object to move. Michotte (1962) showed that adults who see such abstract movement patterns of objects in an animated film automatically interpret them as causal interactions. He interpreted this as evidence for the "perception" of causality. Following Michotte, developmentalists have shown that infants who witness such movement patterns show distinctive looking-time patterns, which suggest that they understand something about physical causality (Leslie, 1982; Oakes & Cohen, 1995).

In addition, familiar types of learning such as classical and operant conditioning may also be seen as involving implicit causal inferences. Many modern investigators of animal cognition suggest that these types of learning are effective because they capture the causal character of events (Gallistel, 1990; Shanks & Dickinson, 1987).

Causal maps, however, go beyond either of these types of causal knowledge. Unlike the perceptual Michottean principles, these maps do not simply involve a few basic notions of folk physics but may involve a wide variety of novel causal relations. And unlike the Michottean principles, causal maps may be learned. Unlike classical conditioning, these relationships do not just involve a few ecologically significant events such as food or pain. Unlike operant conditioning, they do not just involve the organism's own actions but rather involve judgments of the causal relations among objects and events in the world that are independent of our actions upon them.

"Everyday" or "folk" theories seem to have much of the character of causal maps. Such everyday theories represent causal relations among a wide range of objects and events in the world independently of the relation of the observer to those actions. They postulate coherent relations among such objects and events that support a wide range of predictions, interpretations, and interventions. Moreover, theories, like causal maps, are learned through our experience of and interaction with the world around us.

The idea of causal maps also seems to capture the scope of "theory theories" very well. The theory theory has been very successfully applied to our everyday knowledge of the physical, biological, and psychological worlds. However, the theory theory does not seem to be as naturally applicable to other types of knowledge, for example, purely spatial knowledge, syntactic or phonological knowledge, musical knowledge, or mathematical knowledge. Nor does it apply to the much more loosely organized knowledge involved in empirical generalizations, scripts, or associations (Gopnik &

Meltzoff, 1997). But these types of knowledge also do not appear to involve causal claims in the same way as do folk physics, biology, and psychology. Conversely, some kinds of knowledge that do involve causal information, like the kinds of knowledge involved in operant or classical conditioning, do not seem to have the abstract, coherent, nonegocentric character of causal maps, and we would not want to say that this sort of knowledge was theoretical.

On this view, kinds, in everyday understanding, would be the sort of entities that appear in causal maps. In fact, the standard view in philosophy of science is that kinds in scientific theories are defined by the causal relations they enter into—what is sometimes called their "causal role." Gold, from a scientific point of view, is not gold because it glitters but because it has a particular, regular set of causal interactions with other elements, regularities that are explained by atomic theory. If the analogy between science and everyday understanding is correct, everyday kinds also should be defined by their causal role.

Bayes Nets

We have proposed, then, that children and adults construct causal maps: nonegocentric, abstract, coherent representations of causal relations among objects and events. There has recently been a great deal of computational work investigating similar representations. The representations commonly called "Bayes nets" can model complex causal structures and generate appropriate predictions and interventions. A wide range of normatively accurate causal inferences can be made, and, in many circumstances, they can be made in a computationally tractable way. The Bayes net representation and inference algorithms allow one sometimes to uncover hidden unobserved causes, to disentangle complex interactions among causes, to make inferences about probabilistic causal relations, and to generate counterfactuals (see: Glymour, 2001; Glymour & Cooper, 1999; Jordan, 1998; Pearl, 1988, 2000; Spirtes, Glymour, & Scheines, 1993, 2000).

This work has largely taken place in computer science, statistics, and philosophy of science. But these computational theories might also provide important suggestions about how human beings, and particularly young children, represent causal information. Causal maps might be a kind of Bayes net.

The details of the Bayes net formalism are complex, but the basic logic is quite simple and familiar. Causal relationships between events are systematically related to patterns of conditional probability among those events. This fact allows us to use causal knowledge to make predictions about probabilities, and it also allows us to use probabilities to make inferences about causal relations. Take the very simplest case, where x and y are the only events. If we know that x causes y, and we observe that x occurs, then we can predict that y will be more likely to occur. Similarly, if we know that x causes y, and we want y to occur, we can intervene to make x occur and assume that y is likely to follow. Finally, if we know that when x occurs y is likely to occur, that is, we know that x and y are correlated, we can work backward and infer that there is a causal relation between them.

For example, suppose x is drinking wine, and y is insomnia. If I already know that drinking wine causes insomnia, I can predict that if I drink wine I'll be more likely to stay awake. If I want to stay awake I should drink wine, and if I want to avoid insomnia I should avoid wine. On the other hand, if I simply observe that when I drink wine I am more likely to stay awake, I may work backward to infer that drinking wine causes my insomnia.

The trouble, of course, is that this simple case is too simple. Introducing just one more type of event makes the story a lot more complex. For example, suppose we introduce z, going to parties. X, y, and z could be related in a number of different ways. For example, z could be a common cause of x and y. Going to parties could make me more likely to drink wine, and it could also, independently, make me more likely to stay awake from sheer excitement. On the other hand, z could cause x, which in turn could cause y, in a causal chain. Going to parties could make me more likely to drink wine, which could make me more likely to stay awake (see fig. 12.1).

These two different causal structures will lead to very different predictions about the conditional probabilities of the events, and to different interventions. If I know that the right causal structure is A, the common cause, for example, I would predict that I will stay awake after a party, even if I don't drink. If I know that it is B, the causal chain, I would predict that I will only stay awake after a party if I do drink. Similarly, my techniques for avoiding insomnia will be quite different in the two cases.

Conversely, different patterns of conditional probabilities among the three events will allow me to infer different causal structures. Simply seeing that x and y are correlated won't tell me which of these two causal structures is correct—hence, of course, the mantra that correlation doesn't imply causation. However, I can make the right inference if I consider whether x is correlated with y *conditional on z*. For example, if I observe that wine and insomnia are not correlated in the cases in which I go to a

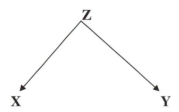

A. Parties are a common cause of wine-drinking and insomnia

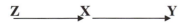

B. Parties cause wine-drinking which causes insomnia

Figure 12.1. Two alternate causal structures for three variables.

party, and are also not correlated in the cases in which I do not go to a party, I may conclude that A is right. If I observe that wine and insomnia are correlated whether or not I go to a party (even though I am less likely to drink if I do not go to a party), I may conclude that B is right.

Bayes nets generalize and formalize this kind of reasoning about the relations between conditional probabilities and causal structure. Bayes nets are directed graphs, like the ones in figure 12.1 or the more complex graph in figure 12.2. The nodes of the graph represent variables whose values are properties of the system to which the net applies. "Color," for example, might be a variable with many possible values; "weight" might be a variable with two values, heavy and light, or with a continuum of values. When Bayes nets are given a causal interpretation, a directed edge from one variable to another, X to Y, for example, says that an intervention that varies the value of X but otherwise does not alter the causal relations among the variables will change the value of Y. In short, changing X will cause Y to change.

In a causal Bayes net we assign a probability to each value of each variable, subject to a fundamental rule: the causal Markov assumption. The Markov assumption says that if the edges of the graphs represent causal relations, then there will only be some patterns of conditional probabilities of the variables, and not others. It is a generalization of the sort of reasoning used in the wine/insomnia example. The Markov assumption constrains the probabilities that can be associated with a network. In particular, it says that the various possible values of any variable, X, are independent of the values of any set of variables in the network that does not contain an effect (a descendant of X), conditional on the values of the parents of X. So, for example; applied to the directed graph in figure 12.2, the Markov assumption says that the value of X is independent of $\{R, Z\}$ conditional on any values of variables in the set $\{S, Y\}$.

Bayes nets allow us to make causal predictions from observations. Information that a system has some property or properties often changes the probabilities of other features of the system. In the preceding example, if I know that wine causes insomnia and I know that you have been drinking, that makes it more likely to be true that you

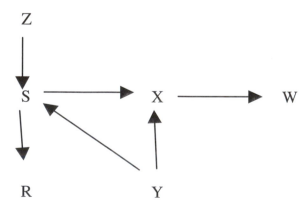

Figure 12.2. A causal graph.

will have insomnia. Conversely, if I know that you have insomnia, that makes it more likely that you had been drinking earlier. Such changes are represented in Bayes nets by the conditional probability of values of a variable, given values for another variable or variables. Bayes net representations simplify such calculations in many cases. In the network just described, the probability of a value of X conditional on a value of R may be calculated from the values of $p(R \mid S)$, $p(S)$ and $p(X \mid S)$ (see Pearl, 1988). This allows us to predict the value of X if we know the value of R. Bayes nets also provide a natural way of assessing and representing counter-factual claims (Pearl, 2000).

When we intervene in the world we specifically predict the outcome of an action. The probabilities for various outcomes of an action that directly alters a feature are not necessarily the same as the probabilities of those outcomes conditional on that altered feature. Simply observing is not the same as intervening. In our example, for instance, if I observe that you are awake now, that will make it more likely that you drank wine last night, but if I intervene to keep you awake now, that won't make it more likely that you drank wine last night. Suppose R in the graph (fig. 12.2) has two values, red and pink. Because the value of S influences R, the conditional probabilities of values of S given that R = red will be different from the conditional probabilities of values of S given that R = pink. Because S influences X, the probabilities of values of X will also be different on the two values of R. *Observing* the value of R gives information about the value of X. But R has no influence on S or X, either direct or indirect, so if the causal relations are as depicted, acting from outside the causal relations represented in the diagram to change the value of R will do nothing to change the value of S or X. Over any Bayes network, it is possible to compute which variables will be indirectly altered by an action or intervention that directly changes the value of another variable (see Glymour & Cooper, 1999; Spirtes et al., 1993, 2000).

Bayes nets thus have two of the features that are needed for applying causal maps: they permit prediction from observations, and they permit prediction of the effects of interventions. With an accurate causal map, that is, the correct Bayes net representation, we can accurately predict that y will happen when x happens, or that a particular change in x will lead to a particular change in y, even when the causal relations we are considering are quite complex. Similarly, we can accurately predict that if we intervene to change x then we will bring about a change in y.

This formalism thus provides a natural way of representing causal relations, and it allows for their use in prediction and intervention. The formalism also allows us to work backward from patterns of conditional probability to causal structure—it allows learning. Given a particular set of conditional probabilities among variables, the formalism can tell us which causal structures are compatible with those probabilities. Moreover, a variety of algorithms have been designed that do this in a computationally efficient way (Glymour & Cooper, 1999; Jordan, 1998). In fact, some algorithms will correctly infer hidden unobserved causal variables on the basis of the patterns of correlation of observed variables. In recent work in artificial intelligence, systems using Bayes nets can infer accurate, if often incomplete, accounts of causal structure from suitable correlational data in fields ranging from epidemiology to mineralogy to genetics.

The Bayes net formalism, then, provides a way of representing and computing normatively accurate causal predictions and interventions and also provides algorithms for learning causal structure from data. The last 30 years of research in developmental psychology have taught us that even very young children know a great deal about the causal structure of the world and can generate causal predictions and interventions in a wide range of domains. Some of this knowledge may be innate, but children also seem to learn an almost incredible amount about the causal structure of the world in a relatively short time. In fact, this has been one of the major contributions of work in the theory theory. We have proposed that children may use more heuristic implicit versions of the Bayes net computational tools to accomplish these feats (Gopnik & Glymour, 2002; Gopnik, Sobel, Schulz, & Glymour, 2001).

How could we represent the idea of kinds in this sort of formalism? We may think of kinds as a certain subset of variables in a causal graphical model. This subset has two characteristics. First, a kind variable is the common cause of a set of other variables. Second, those other variables are all properties common to a group of objects. So to say that an object is a member of the kind "tiger" is to say that there is a variable called "tiger" that is a common cause of other values of other properties of the same object (e.g., having stripes, being a predator, growling) and is also a common cause of those properties of other objects of the same category/kind. To say that an object is a member of a kind is to say that its features, and similar features of other members of the kind, have a common cause in a relevant causal graph. Reasoning about kinds, on this view, is a particular type of causal reasoning.

Notice, again, that this sort of representation of kinds would allow for two types of reasoning. First, we could use our existing causal knowledge to make kind inferences. We could consult our causal graph and see if there is a common cause for a set of object properties, and if so, what that cause is likely to be. But we could also draw conclusions about kind membership by simply looking at the pattern of correlations among object properties. If those patterns are consistent with a "common cause" structure, we might posit a common "essence" that caused the properties, even if we had no prior knowledge of that causal relation.

Naming, Sorting, and Causal Induction in 2- to 4-Year-Olds: The Blicket Detector

How do these theoretical ideas translate into an empirical research program? The Bayes net formalism gives us a natural way of representing causal categories, and of relating causal structure to patterns of dependent and independent probability. The computational work in causal inference means that we can investigate whether adults and children make causal inferences when correct inferences are possible and avoid making such inferences when they are not and, ideally, can investigate the detailed procedures by which such inferences are, in fact, made in adults and children. Of course, these procedures may or may not be similar to the procedures used in computer science. The first step in this research program is to determine if very young children, do, in fact, make causal judgments, learn new causal relations, and, most significantly for the present purposes, produce causal categorizations. If children do categorize causally, then we can import the full power of the Bayes net formalism to make predictions about what those categorizations should be like and how they should be related to other kinds of knowledge and behavior (see e.g., Gopnik et al., 2001). However, if children instead simply categorize on the basis of perceptual features, then this entire project would fail to get off the ground.

We predict that children will categorize objects together, and give them the same name, when they believe that the objects have common causal powers. Similarly, when children see others categorize objects together or give them the same name, they will assume that those objects have common causal powers. In fact, there is some evidence that adults and even older children categorize kinds in terms of causal powers in just this way (Ahn et al., 2000; Rehder, 1999). Rheder (1999) has demonstrated empirically that they do so in a way that is predicted by the Bayes net formalism. But, of course, adults have extensive experience and often explicit training in causal inference. We predict that this will also be true of much younger children.

In a series of recent experiments, we "invented" a brand-new causal power of objects: whether or not they made a particular machine work. We constructed a new machine, the "blicket detector": a box that lights up and plays music when certain objects, but not others, are placed on it. This apparatus presents children with a new, never-encountered causal relation, of which they are given direct experience with real objects. Since we had complete control over this property, we could also directly pit it against perceptual features of objects. We could arrange to have perceptually identical objects that did or did not display the causal power. We then explored whether children would use the causal power as a basis for naming the objects and whether children would use names to guide their inductions about this causal power. We also explored how these behaviors were related to perceptual similarities and differences among the objects.

In these experiments, children are presented with a box measuring 5 by 7 by 3 inches, made of wood with a red Lucite top. Two wires emerge from the detector's side. One is plugged into an electrical outlet. The other runs to a switchbox. If the switchbox is in the "on" position, the detector will light up and play music when an object is placed on it. If the switchbox is in the "off" position, the detector does nothing when an object is placed on it. During the experiment, this wire runs to a confederate who surreptitiously flips the switch on to allow an object to set the machine off or flips it off to ensure that an object will not set the machine off. The wire and switchbox are hidden from the children's view, and they have no suspicion of the role of the confederate, whom they never see. The apparatus is designed so that when the switch is on, the box "turns on" as soon as the object makes contact with it and continues to light up and play music as long as the object continues to make contact with it. It "turns off" as soon as the object ceases to make contact with it. This provides a strong impression that something about the object itself caused the effect. The "objects" can vary according to the experiment and include wooden blocks, as well as more "natural" objects like small rocks and hardware parts. We will report the results with blocks, but in fact we obtained identical results with both types of objects (see fig. 12.3).

In one experiment (Gopnik & Sobel, 2000, exp. 1), 2-, 3-, and 4-year-olds were shown four wooden blocks. The experimenter placed each block on the machine in succession and then carefully returned it to its original location. Two blocks set the machine off, and two did not. After this was demonstrated twice, children were told

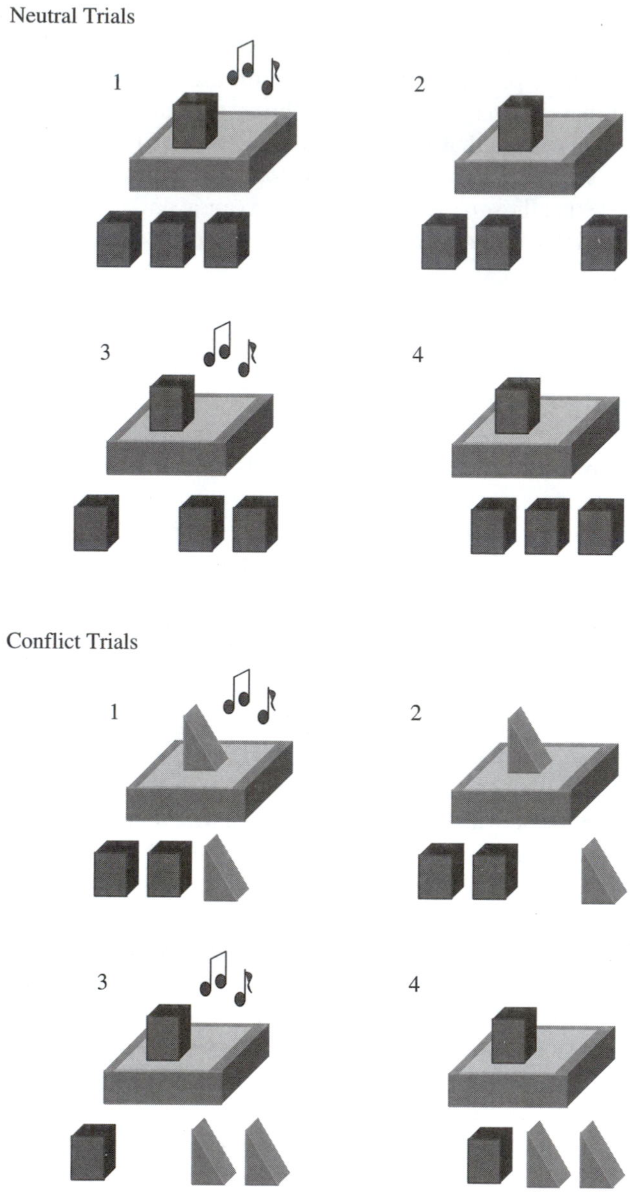

Neutral Trials

Conflict Trials

Figure 12.3. The blicket detector—neutral and conflict trials.

that one of the objects that had set the machine off was a "blicket." Then the experimenter asked the child to give him the other "blicket." Importantly, children were
not told that the machine was a blicket detector and had no prior exposure to this
novel causal property.

Children were given two types of sets of blocks, neutral sets and conflict sets. In
the neutral sets, the blocks were either all identical or all different. In the conflict
sets, there were two pairs of perceptually identical objects, one member of each pair
would set the machine off and the other would not. Here the perceptual features of
the object actually conflicted with the objects' causal powers (see fig. 12.3).

In the neutral tasks, even the 2-year-olds categorized the object on the basis of its
causal power. In the conflict tasks, 2-year-olds chose as the other "blicket" the perceptually similar object more often than the causally similar object, but still chose
the causal object more frequently than a distracter object. The 3- and 4-year-old
children were equally likely to choose the causally or perceptually similar object as
the "blicket" (see fig. 12.4).

In a control condition (Gopnik & Sobel, 2000, exp. 2), the same machine and
objects were presented to other children of the same ages with the same procedure.
However, in this condition the object did not appear to be causally related to the
machine. Instead of placing each object on the machine, the experimenter would
hold each object over the machine. For two of the objects, he would simultaneously
press the top of the detector with his hand, which activated it. For the other two, he
simply held his hand near the top of the detector but did not press it, and nothing
happened. Children were then told that one of the blocks that had been associated
with the machine's activity was a "blicket" and were asked to show the experimenter
the other "blicket." In contrast to the first experiment, children of all ages chose at
chance in the neutral tasks and used the perceptual properties of the object as a basis
for categorization in the conflict tasks. Children would not categorize an object as a
"blicket" on the basis of a mere association between that object and the machine's
activation by the experimenter (see fig. 12.4). They would only categorize when there
appeared to be a causal relation between the block and the machine.

In a second condition, we showed that children would not only use causal powers
as a guide to names but also use names as a guide to causal powers. In this experiment, we told children that two of the objects were called "blickets" and two were
not. The experimenter then picked up one of the "blickets" and showed that it activated the machine. The children were asked to choose "another one that will make
the machine go." Thus this experiment was analogous to the induction studies of
Gelman and Coley, 1990 and Gelman and Markman, 1986, but with real objects dis-
playing real novel causal powers. Again 2-, 3-, and 4-year-olds predicted that the
objects with the same name would have the same causal powers in the neutral condition. The 3- and 4-year-olds clearly did this even in the conflict condition when
this prediction conflicted with a perceptual categorization (e.g., when one "blicket"
was a green square and the other was a red cylinder, while the two non-"blickets"
were also a green square and a red cylinder). This effect was less strong for the
2-year-olds (see fig. 12.5).

It is important to say that children, particularly 2-year-olds, did sometimes use
perceptual features as a basis for categorization or induction in the conflict condi-

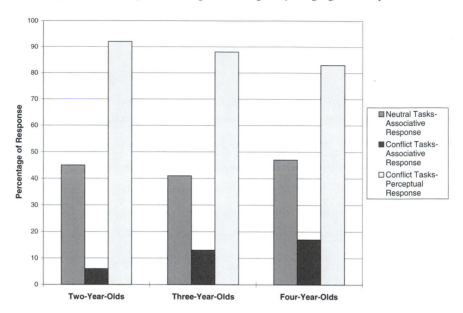

Figure 12.4. Performance of children on control condition.

tions. However, it turned out that these children also tended to misremember the causal information or the object's name. Many of the 3- and 4-year-olds, and most of the 2-year-olds, who said that the perceptually identical object was the "blicket" also said, incorrectly, that that the object had set off the detector. Similarly, when they predicted that the perceptually identical object would activate the detector, they also tended to say, incorrectly, that that object had been called a "blicket." That is, if they said that the two green squares were both "blickets," they were also likely to say, incorrectly, that both green squares had set off the machine. Conversely, if they said that the two green squares would both activate the machine, they were also likely to say, incorrectly, that they had both been labeled "blickets."

This suggests that names and causal powers may have been linked even for children who made a perceptual response. These memory errors may suggest that children, and particularly the younger children, assume that perceptual, causal, and linguistic properties are correlated. In fact, of course, this is usually true, and the inference from common features to common causal powers is correct. Most of the time, when objects have the identical shape, color, and size, they also have the same causal powers. For these children, this fact guides not only their categorizations and inductions but also their memory. They seem to assume that the identical objects *must* have the same causal powers and simply ignore the data to the contrary. In contrast, if children were simply using a purely perceptual strategy to categorize, name, and make inductions about objects, these errors are puzzling.

In a second study, we set out to test this hypothesis about memory errors more systematically (Nazzi & Gopnik, 2000). In earlier studies, investigators in the shape versus kind debate had shown that either perceptual or nonperceptual cues may be

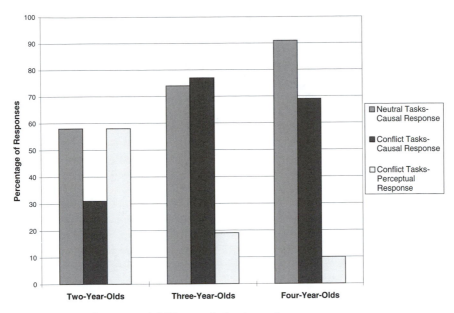

Figure 12.5. Performance of children on induction task.

used in categorization, but no one had systematically pitted these cues against one another. The Gopnik and Sobel (2000) study suggested that younger children might rely more heavily on perceptual cues than older children, but there were no significant age effects, only a trend. Moreover, it was possible that the memory errors occurred simply because children were confused about the task. In this study, we followed exactly the same procedure as in Gopnik and Sobel but added a memory control task at the start of each session: children were simply asked to report which object had set off the machine, without also categorizing the objects. All the children did well on this task. We also used a smaller range of children at each age, comparing 3½- and 4½-year-old children born within a 2-3 months range. This allowed us to reveal an age effect, with younger children making more perceptual responses than older children.

The memory errors showed that almost all of the age effect was due to the fact that younger children were more likely to assume a correlation between perception and causation than older children. Children in each age group said that the perceptual object was a "blicket" but correctly remembered that it had not set off the machine on about 20 percent of the trials. However, the younger children falsely reported a correlation between the perceptual and causal features of the objects (e.g., they said that the perceptually similar object both was a "blicket" and had set off the machine before) in 46 percent of the trials. The older children only made this error on 12 percent of the trials.

This suggests that the developmental effect is not simply due to a shift from perceptual to causal responding. Rather the younger children appeared to treat perceptual cues as a guide to causal ones, to the point of misremembering cases where those cues are not correlated. This may also help to explain the debate in the literature. In real life, perceptual cues, and particularly shape, are highly correlated with causal powers. Other things being equal, objects with the same shape are also likely to have similar causal powers. Children may, in fact, use shape to categorize and name objects. However, they may do so almost entirely because for them shape is a good predictor of causal powers. When the data shows them that shape and causal powers conflict, they either reinterpret the data (at age 3) or prefer causal powers (at age 4).

Sorting, Naming, and Causal Powers

So far we have talked about two indices of categorization, naming and causal induction, and we have shown that these two phenomena are closely related in children as young as 30 months old. When children know that objects have the same causal powers, they predict that they will have the same name, and vice versa. Another— nonlinguistic—index of categorization is manual sorting, whereby children will put similar objects in the same location. How are these three indices of categorization— sorting, naming, and causal induction—related to one another?

We designed a simplified "blicket detector" paradigm to ask this question for 30-month-olds (Nazzi, 2001; Nazzi & Gopnik, 2002). In this paradigm children saw the experimenter place three perceptually different objects on the detector, twice in a row. Two of the objects consistently activated the detector, and one did not. The experimenter then picked up one of the active objects and presented the child with the other two objects. In the sorting condition, he visibly placed one of the active objects in one hand and asked, "Can you give me the one that goes with this one?" Thus, in this condition, children had to put the causally similar objects in the same location, rather than give them the same name. In the action condition, he asked the child to actually make the machine work ("Can you make it work?"), testing whether children really had inferred the causal power of the objects correctly. We also included a control condition, just like the control in the Gopnik and Sobel (2000) study already described. In this condition, the experimenter held the objects up over the detector and then either pressed the top of the detector to activate it, or held his hand near the machine but did not activate it.

Thirty-month-olds consistently used the causal powers of an object to sort the objects, just as they did to name the objects: 78 percent of the time they placed together objects that had made the detector work, and 79 percent of the time they correctly predicted that the object would make it work again. This suggests that there is a link not only between causal induction and naming but also between causal induction and categorization more generally. Moreover, as in Gopnik and Sobel (2000), 30-month-old children did not physically sort objects together or use them to activate the machine when the objects were simply associated with the machine in a noncausal way. They were at chance in both tasks. This again suggests that children are reacting to causal powers and not mere associations.

These experiments, then, demonstrate that children's understanding of the structure of kinds develops between 30 months and 4½ years of age, by which time they have reached something similar to the adult conception. In particular, we have converging evidence that children as young as 30 months old will give perceptually different objects the same name, and sort them together, when they have the same causal powers. Similarly, they will use naming as a guide to causal induction even without perceptual cues. Even in cases where perceptual categorization conflicts with causal categorization, the younger children will sometimes, and the older children usually, rely on causal cues. And even when, in conditions of conflict, perceptual cues are used, those cues seem to be correlated with causal powers. Moreover, and importantly, children will not just categorize on the basis of any type of similarity. When objects are merely associated with effects but do not actually cause them, children will not use those associations as a basis for naming or sorting the objects.

In fact, the crucial developmental change in this period appears to be a loosening of initially tight correlations between perception and causation. The younger children seem more inclined to believe that perceptual, linguistic, and causal similarities will be correlated, while the older children seem more willing to imagine that perceptual cues could conflict with linguistic or causal cues.

Naming and Sorting in 18-Month-Olds

What about even younger children? In a further experiment with "the blicket detector," we did not find similar effects with 24-month-olds (Nazzi, 2001; Nazzi & Gopnik, 2002). This seems to go against the idea that younger children have a similar understanding of kinds and causal powers. However, this conclusion might be too strong. First, it cannot be totally excluded at this point that the failure of the 24-month-olds is due to the attention and memory demands of this task. Second, in other studies, we have explored two abilities that do emerge in younger children and that may be indicators of, or at least prerequisites for, "kind" understanding. These are the ability to sort all the objects in a group into multiple categories and the ability to sort perceptually dissimilar objects together when they receive the same name.

A number of studies dating back to the 1970s demonstrate some important changes in children's sorting behavior at about 18 months. From about a year of age, children will categorize objects by placing similar objects in the same location (Gopnik & Meltzoff, 1987, 1992; Nelson, 1973; Ricciuti, 1965; Starkey, 1981; Sugarman, 1983) In these studies, children are given a mixed group of objects (e.g., four identical yellow rectangles and four identical clear pillboxes) and are allowed to spontaneously manipulate those objects. Children as young as 9 months of age will place the similar objects in one group in the same location. However, while this behavior might be indicative of categorization, it might also just reflect a preference for one type of object over another. It is only at about 18 months that children will systematically and exhaustively sort all the objects in a group into separate locations. We demonstrated that children will also do this when the objects in each group are not identical but belong to the same "basic-level" category, using for example a set of four different rings and four different pencils. We also suggested that this ability might be related to an understanding of "kinds" (Gopnik & Meltzoff, 1992).

We also demonstrated that there was a close empirical connection between this sort of exhaustive sorting and naming. In longitudinal studies, children began to systematically and exhaustively sort objects into multiple categories (Gopnik & Meltzoff, 1987) a week or so before they had a "naming spurt"—a sudden sharp increase in their naming vocabulary. In cross-sectional studies, similarly, the ability to exhaustively sort objects into multiple categories was highly correlated with the number of names children used, and with their mothers' report of a naming spurt (Gopnik & Meltzoff, 1987, 1992). Moreover, this relationship was quite specific, it remained strong even when age was held constant, and there was no parallel relation between the naming spurt and other cognitive developments that take place at about the same time, such as means-ends and object permanence achievements (Gopnik & Meltzoff, 1992). Mervis and Bertrand (1994, 1995, 1997) replicated this finding both with typically developing children and children with Down syndrome. It is interesting that, they did not find this relation in children with Williams syndrome, who appear to approach language development in a way that is very different from these other groups. Mervis and Bertrand (1994) also showed that exhaustive sorting was related to the achievement of "fast mapping": Children who produced exhaustive sorting were also more likely to quickly learn to attribute new words to unnamed objects.

The fact that the naming spurt and the new categorization abilities occurred so closely together suggested an intriguing possibility—perhaps the emergence of the new linguistic ability to learn names itself facilitates a cognitive change in children's sorting abilities. In fact, this relation between naming and sorting parallels two other independent relations between language and cognition in this period. In even earlier work, we demonstrated parallel relations between the acquisition of words for disappearance, such as "all gone," and object-permanence abilities, and of words relating to action, such as "uh-oh," and means-ends abilities (Gopnik, 1982, 1984, Gopnik & Meltzoff, 1984). We have argued that in all these cases the linguistic and cognitive abilities may emerge in tandem and be mutually facilitating—the cognitive developments spark the linguistic acquisitions, and the linguistic developments also strengthen the cognitive changes (Gopnik & Meltzoff, 1997).

Particularly dramatic evidence for this sort of "neo-Whorfian" link between naming and sorting comes from cross-linguistic studies. Korean relies much more heavily on verb morphology than English and often omits nouns. In a series of studies, we found that Korean-speaking mothers used significantly fewer nouns in their speech to children than English-speaking mothers (Choi & Gopnik, 1995; Gopnik & Choi, 1990, 1995; Gopnik, Choi, & Baumberger, 1996). In turn, Korean-speaking children used significantly fewer nouns and more verbs in their own early language than English-speakers, a result replicated by Tardif, Gelman, and Xu (1999) for Mandarin speakers. In fact, the Korean speakers, as well as Mandarin speakers, often used verbs at the same time or before they used nouns, a definitive refutation of the widespread idea that nouns precede verbs in development.

More significant for the current argument, however, the cognitive development of the two groups of children also differed (Gopnik & Choi, 1990; Gopnik et al., 1996). The Korean speakers began to produce exhaustive sorting significantly later than the English speakers. Just as important, however, this effect was not due to some across-the-board cognitive delay. The Korean-speaking children were actually advanced in means-ends understanding compared to the English speakers. Means-ends abilities, which involve an understanding of skilled goal-directed action, are conceptually more closely related to the verbs that play a prominent role in early Korean vocabularies. This cross-linguistic result suggested a quite specific link between the experience of hearing many new names and the tendency to sort objects into groups. The most plausible explanation for this finding was that the linguistic differences in the input to the children actually caused the cognitive differences. Hearing new names might lead children to categorize and sort objects in a new way.

In a more recent experiment (Nazzi & Gopnik, 2001), we tested this idea further by exploring whether hearing that objects were given the same name would actually lead children to sort those objects together. Could we demonstrate an effect of naming on sorting more directly? Sixteen- and 20-month-olds were given triads of objects that were completely different perceptually. In one condition, two of the objects were given the same name by the experimenter and a third object was given a different name. Then, just as in our earlier sorting experiment, the experimenter put one of the two similarly named objects in his hand and asked, "Can you give me the one that goes with this one?" Twenty-month-olds, but not 16-month-olds, physically sorted the objects with the same name together.

Moreover, this ability was related to vocabulary size. Not only did the 20-month-olds have significantly larger vocabularies than the younger children but also, among the 20-month-olds, vocabulary size was highly correlated with performance on the sorting task. This suggests that the capacity to sort objects into entirely new non-obvious categories based on names may itself be related to the naming spurt. In a control condition, children received a visual categorization task, in which two of the objects were perceptually similar, and no names were used. As one might expect, 16-month-olds and 20-month-olds performed equally well on this task, and there was no correlation to vocabulary size.

In summary, then, both the capacity to sort objects exhaustively into multiple categories and to sort perceptually dissimilar objects together on the basis of a common name seem to emerge at around 18 months. Both these abilities seem to be related to children's own productive naming vocabulary. Moreover, there is evidence, from the cross-linguistic studies, that the experience of hearing names may actually contribute to these sorting abilities.

Both these abilities also seem to be related to kind understanding. In multiple-category sorting, children seem to go beyond simple perceptual generalizations. Instead, children seem to assume that all objects belong in some category or another. The capacity to sort completely dissimilar objects into a common category is even more obviously related to kind understanding. Indeed, the very nature of kind understanding involves this ability to go beyond perceptual similarities and dissimilarities and to categorize objects together in a more abstract way.

We do not know how these early sorting abilities are related to an understanding of causal powers. In Gopnik and Sobel (2000) and Nazzi (2001), we did not find the first signs of causal categorization until 30 months. It may be that the earlier types of understanding are prerequisites for a causal powers view of kinds, or it may be that such a view emerges in tandem with these abilities and we have not yet designed a way to test it. Some support for the first alternative comes from the Gopnik and Sobel (2000) finding that it was easier to predict causal powers from the names given to objects than to give the same name to objects having similar causal powers. It is possible that children's experiences with language, particularly the experience of hearing the same name applied to perceptually dissimilar objects, itself leads them to look beyond perceptual similarities and that this, in turn, leads them to the idea of categorizing objects in terms of causal powers.

Kind Understanding before 18 Months

Thus we see development between 30 months and 4½ years leading to something very much like full-blown kind/causal power understanding, and we see some of the first signs of an understanding of kinds emerging at 18 months in tandem with the emergence of a naming spurt. What about even younger, preverbal infants? Here the picture seems to us much murkier. It is clear that, from birth, infants can individuate and identify objects. Like other organisms, infants can also discriminate among objects perceptually and can make perceptual generalizations.

It is also clear that, at least from very early in development, and quite possibly from birth, infants can make certain kinds of causal predictions and interventions and can learn about new causal relations. This capacity seems clear from the extensive literature on young infants' understanding of principles of folk physics (see, e.g., Bower, 1974; Baillargeon, Kotovsky, & Needham, 1995; Leslie, 1982; Oakes & Cohen, 1995; Spelke, Breinlinger, Macomber, & Jacobson, 1992), as well as from the earlier literature on infants' understanding of contingency (Watson, & Ramey, 1987) and the emerging literature on infants' understanding of the actions of others (Gergely, Nádasdy, Csibra, & Bíró, 1995; Meltzoff, 1995; Woodward, 1998). It seems that very young infants know that certain objects will have consistent causal effects on others in regular ways, and they also know that their own actions and the actions of others will have certain regular causal effects (see also chaps. 4 and 7).

We do not know, however, when children begin to combine their perceptual categorizations of objects and their causal knowledge. When do children first conceive of categories of spatially individuated, distinct, objects that nevertheless have common underlying causal powers, and that will have similar causal powers in the future? Many of the early types of causal understanding do not seem to have this character. Rather than seeing object categories as the sorts of things that define causal powers, infants initially appear to focus on movement paths and trajectories, for objects, or patterns of intentional action, for people. Certainly, to our minds there is no clear evidence in early infancy that children go beyond perceptual similarities and differences in their object categorizations, though those similarities and differences may sometimes be quite general or abstract (as in the types of categorization reported by Mandler & McDonough [1993]). On the other hand, this question has yet to be tested in an appropriate and systematic way.

There is some evidence that toward the end of the first year, children do begin to link their perceptual categorizations and their causal inductions. This evidence comes from a study of children's exploratory behavior (Baldwin, Markman, & Melartin, 1993). In this study, 9- to 26-month-old infants saw an unexpected novel causal property of an object (e.g., a can that made a cow noise when it was turned over). Then they were presented with perceptually similar objects that did not exhibit this property. Children explored those objects in a way that suggested that they were surprised by this fact. They seemed to expect the original causal property to generalize to the new objects.

This kind of linkage between perceptual and causal similarity might be the first emergence of the sort of conception of kinds that we see quite clearly in 30-month-olds. Recall that these older children seemed to think that perceptual similarities and causal powers are tightly correlated. However, this linkage must, paradoxically, be loosened in order to develop a full conception of kinds.

Learning

We might propose then a three-stage understanding of the link between perceptual and causal categorization, producing a kind of U-shaped curve. The youngest infants might simply see no relation at all between perceptual object categorization and causal prediction. The older infants and young toddlers might begin to link these cues. They begin to believe that perceptual similarity will predict causal similarity. Only the older 3- and 4-year-olds, however, begin to believe that while this linkage usually holds, it can be broken, and that this is due to deeper facts about the essences of objects.

An interesting possibility is that language itself is a major factor in these changes in children's developing understanding of kinds and causal powers. There is evidence that toward the end of the first year, linguistic cues may focus infants' attention on perceptual similarities among objects (see, e.g., Waxman & Markow, 1995; Woodward, Markman, & Fitzsimmons, 1994). In these early cases, however, the language cues seem simply to be facilitating types of perceptual generalization that children can make independently. Nevertheless, this sort of linguistic effect might be the first step in a process of leading children to place objects together in a more abstract and profound way. We see this in our 20-month-old's ability to use names to categorize objects even in the absence of any perceptual similarities at all (Nazzi & Gopnik, 2001). Similarly, in unpublished work, Baldwin has found that linguistic cues facilitate the exploratory causal inductions of children at least at 20 months of age (Baldwin, personal communication). Twenty-month-old children who heard that two partially similar objects were given the same name were more likely to predict that they would have the same novel nonobvious causal property.

In fact, children might realize that the link between perception and causal inference can be loosened precisely because of the fact that there is also a link between the names of objects and their causal powers. Learning names sets up a kind of three-term relationship between perceptual similarities, causal powers, and names. Names give children a way to state a causal power similarity that is decoupled from a perceptual similarity. We see the first step in this process in our 20-month-old's ability to use names to establish categories in a way that goes beyond perceptual similarity. By age 3 or 4, these children are also able to relate those name-based categories to causal powers in a way that completely bypasses perceptual similarity.

Similarly, the insight of the naming spurt, namely the realization that all things have names, may be related to the insight that all objects belong in categories, an insight that seems to underlie exhaustive sorting. Empirically, these two developments are closely related. Moreover, in the cross-linguistic work, we have demonstrated a direct effect of language input on exhaustive sorting.

If we are correct that there are these developmental changes in children's understanding of kinds and causal powers, where do those changes come from? Is a causal powers view of categorization innate? If not, what learning mechanisms propel children to develop a conception of kinds and causal powers?

The last question, the question of mechanisms of learning, seems to us to be *the* crucial question we should be addressing in cognitive development in general. Fortunately, in the case of causal categorization, reasoning, inference, and induction, there are parallel developments in philosophy and computer science that may be particularly helpful. The formalism of graphical causal models, as discussed earlier, provides powerful, formal techniques for making accurate causal inferences. In particular, within the Bayes net framework, it is possible to construct algorithms that infer causal structure from patterns of correlation among events. These algorithms are provably accurate and, at least in many cases, computationally efficient. The formalism provides powerful tools for reliably inferring causal structures from patterns of evidence.

We are just beginning to explore whether very young children actually use implicit versions of these computational learning procedures. In a recent set of experiments, we have discovered that children can determine the correct causal categorization of objects—that is, can determine which objects are "blickets"—by employing some of the same basic axioms as these computational systems (Gopnik et al., 2001). Two-, 3-, and 4-year-old children could accurately infer the causal powers of an object by considering the patterns of variation and covariation between that object, other objects, and the "blicket detector"'s behavior.

This sort of learning might also be responsible for some of the broader developmental changes in children's categorizations that we described. One way of thinking of the learning process is that children are driven to look for ever deeper and more powerful causal analyses of the world around them. There will be significant and informative patterns of correlation among the perceptual features of objects, the names they are given, and their causal effects. Children may be detecting and using these patterns of correlation to make causal predictions and inductions. In particular, children may reason backward from the patterns of correlation among perceptual and linguistic features of objects and their effects on other objects to infer underlying causal powers of those objects.

Note that the claim is not that children are simply covariation detectors or that they match patterns of correlation in the input in their own behavior (as proposed by Jones & Smith, 1993, Smith et al., 1996). Rather, we would argue that children use covariation information in combination with other kinds of knowledge, in order to uncover underlying causal structure.

Conclusion

We have argued that "kinds" can be usefully understood as groups of objects with common current and future causal powers. This stems from our general conception of intuitive theories as "causal maps": abstract representations of the causal structure of the world. In a series of empirical studies, we have shown that children do categorize and name objects on the basis of their causal powers, from at least 30 months of age. Even younger children, around 18 months old, already show the ability to sort objects into multiple, exhaustive categories and to sort entirely perceptually dissimilar objects together when they are given a common name. These abilities do not appear to be present in younger infants. They also seem to be highly correlated with the acquisition of names and particularly with a naming spurt.

There also seem to be important changes in children's kind understanding. We suggest that the youngest infants may not relate perceptual similarities among objects and causal powers at all. At a later stage, from about 1 year until about 3 or 4, children do seem to predict strong correlations between perceptual similarities and causal powers. However, with the acquisition of language, children may have the further realization that names are correlated with causal powers in a way that may bypass perceptual similarities. Eventually, this may be what leads them to a deeper conception of underlying essences.

Causal inference, induction, and learning seem to us particularly promising avenues of investigation for several reasons. Empirically, we have discovered that causal understanding plays an important and deep role in a great deal of children's early knowledge, including their knowledge of categories. From a functional and evolutionary perspective, causal understanding is profoundly adaptive. And methodologically, the problem of causal inference is an area where powerful formal and computational tools and techniques are available. Such tools may help us make real progress toward a developmental science that is both genuinely developmental and genuinely scientific.

Acknowledgments

Clark Glymour and Michael Strevens made extremely helpful comments on and contributions to this chapter. We are also grateful to Tamar Kushnir, Laura Schulz, and David Sobel, as well as all of the participants in our studies. Address for correspondence: Alison Gopnik, Department of Psychology, University of California at Berkeley, Berkeley, CA 94720 (gopnik@socrates.berkeley.edu).

References

Ahn, W. K., Gelman, S. A., Amsterlaw, J. A., Hohenstein, J., & Kalish, C. W. (2000). Causal status effect in children's categorization. *Cognition, 76*, 35–44.

Baillargeon, R., Kotovsky, L., & Needham, A. (1995). The acquisition of physical knowledge in infancy. In D. Sperber and D. Premack (Eds.), *Causal cognition: A multidisciplinary debate* (pp. 79–116). New York: Oxford University Press.

Baldwin, D. A., Markman, E. M., & Melartin, R. L. (1993). Infants' ability to draw inferences about nonobvious properties: Evidence from exploratory play. *Child Development, 64,* 711–728.

Bower, T. G. (1974). *Development in infancy.* San Francisco: Freeman.

Carey, S. (1985). *Conceptual change in childhood.* Cambridge, MA: MIT Press.

Choi, S., & Gopnik, A. (1995). Early acquisition of verbs in Korean: A cross-linguistic study. *Journal of Child Language, 22,* 497–530

Gallistel, C. R. (1990). *The organization of learning.* Cambridge, MA: MIT Press.

Gelman, S. A., & Bloom, P. (2000). Children are sensitive to how an object was created when deciding what to name it. *Cognition, 76,* 91–103.

Gelman, S. A., & Coley, J. (1990). The importance of knowing a dodo is a bird: Categories and inferences in 2-year-old children. *Developmental Psychology, 26,* 796–804.

Gelman, S. A., & Markman, E. (1986). Categories and induction in young children. *Cognition, 23,* 213–244.

Gelman, S. A., & Wellman, H. M. (1991). Insides and essence: Early understandings of the non-obvious. *Cognition, 38,* 213–244.

Gergely, G., Nádasdy, Z., Csibra, G., & Biro, S. (1995). Taking the intentional stance at 12 months of age. *Cognition, 56,* 165–193.

Glymour, C. (2001). *The mind's arrows: Bayes nets and graphical causal models in psychology.* Cambridge, MA: MIT Press.

Glymour, C., & Cooper, G. (1999). *Computation, causation, and discovery.* Menlo Park, CA: MIT Press.

Gopnik, A. (1982). Words and plans: Early language and the development of intelligent action. *Journal of Child Language, 9,* 303–318.

Gopnik, A. (1984). The acquisition of gone and the development of the object concept. *Journal of Child Language, 11,* 273–292.

Gopnik, A. (1988). Conceptual and semantic development as theory change: The case of object permanence. *Mind and Language, 3,* 197–216.

Gopnik, A. (2000). Explanation as orgasm and the drive for causal understanding: The evolution, function and phenomenology of the theory-formation system. In F. Keil & R. Wilson (Eds.), *Cognition and explanation* (pp. 299–323). Cambridge, MA: MIT Press.

Gopnik, A., & Choi, S. (1990). Do linguistic differences lead to cognitive differences? A cross-linguistic study of semantic and cognitive development. *First Language, 10,* 199–215.

Gopnik, A., & Choi, S. (1995). Names, relational words, and cognitive development in English and Korean speakers: Nouns not always learned before verbs. In M. Tomasello and W. E. Merriman (Eds.), *Beyond names for things: Young children's acquisition of verbs* (pp. 63–80). Hillsdale, NJ: Erlbaum.

Gopnik, A., Choi, S., & Baumberger, T. (1996). Cross-linguistic differences in early semantic and cognitive development. *Cognitive Development, 11,* 197–227.

Gopnik, A., & Glymour, C. (2002). Causal maps and Bayes nets: A cognitive and computational account of theory-formation. In P. Carruthers, S. Stich, and M. Siegal (Eds.), *The cognitive basis of science.* Cambridge: Cambridge University Press.

Gopnik, A., & Meltzoff, A. N. (1984). Semantic and cognitive development in 15- to 21-month-old children. *Journal of Child Language, 11,* 495–513.

Gopnik, A., & Meltzoff, A. N. (1987). The development of categorization in the second year and its relation to other cognitive and linguistic developments. *Child Development, 58,* 1523–1531.

Gopnik, A., & Meltzoff, A. N. (1992). Categorization and naming: Basic-level sorting in eighteen-month-olds and its relationship to language. *Child Development, 63*, 1091–1103.

Gopnik, A., & Meltzoff, A. (1997). *Words, thoughts and theories.* Cambridge, MA: MIT Press.

Gopnik, A., & Sobel, D. (2000). Detecting blickets: How young children use information about novel causal powers in categorization and induction. *Child Development, 71*, 1205–1222.

Gopnik, A., Sobel, D. M., Schulz, L., & Glymour, C. (2001). Causal learning mechanisms in very young children: Two, three, and four-year-olds infer causal relations from patterns of variation and covariation probability. *Developmental Psychology, 37*, 620–629.

Gopnik, A., & Wellman, H. M. (1994). The theory theory. In L. A. Hirschfeld and S. A. Gelman (Eds.), *Mapping the mind: domain specificity in cognition and culture* (pp. 257–293). New York: Cambridge University Press.

Imai, M., Gentner, D., & Uchida, N. (1994) Children's theories of word meaning: The role of shape similarity in early acquisition. *Cognitive Development, 9*, 45–75.

Jones, S. S., & Smith, L. B. (1993). The place of perception in children's concepts. *Cognitive Development, 8*, 113–139.

Jordan, M. (Ed.). (1998). *Learning in graphical models.* Cambridge, MA: MIT Press.

Keil, F. C. (1989). *Concepts, kinds, and cognitive development.* Cambridge, MA: MIT Press.

Kemler Nelson, D. G. (1995). Principle-based inferences in young children's categorization: Revisiting the impact of function on the naming of artifacts. *Cognitive Development, 10*, 347–380.

Kemler Nelson, D. G., Frankenfield, A., Morris, C., & Blair, E. (2000). Young children's use of functional information to categorize artifacts: Three factors that matter. *Cognition, 77*, 133–168.

Kemler Nelson, D. G., Russell, R., Duke, N., & Jones, K. (2000). When young children name artifacts by their functions. *Child Development, 71*, 1271–1288.

Kripke, S. (1972). *Naming and necessity.* Cambridge, MA: Harvard University Press.

Landau, B., Smith, L. B., & Jones, S. S. (1988). The importance of shape in early lexical learning. *Cognitive Development, 3*, 299–321.

Leslie, A. M. (1982). The perception of causality in infants. *Perception, 11*, 173–186.

Mandler, J. M., & McDonough, L. (1993). Concept formation in infancy. *Cognitive Development, 8*, 291–318.

Meltzoff, A. N. (1995). Understanding the intentions of others: Re-enactment of intended acts by 18-month-old children. *Developmental Psychology, 31*, 838–850.

Mervis, C. B., & Bertrand, J. (1994). Acquisition of the novel name-nameless category (N3C) principle. *Child Development, 65*, 1646–1662.

Mervis, C. B., & Bertrand, J. (1995). Acquisition of the novel name-nameless category (N3C) principle by young children who have Down syndrome. *American Journal on Mental Retardation, 100*, 231–243.

Mervis, C. B., & Bertrand, J. (1997). Developmental relations between cognition and language: Evidence from Williams syndrome. In L. B. Adamson & M. A. Romski (Eds.), *Research on communication and language disorders: Contributions to theories of language development.* New York: Brookes.

Michotte, A. (1962). *Causalité, permanence, et réalité phénoménales.* Louvain: Publications Universitaires.

Murphy, G. L., & Medin, D. L. (1985). The role of theories in conceptual coherence. *Psychological Review, 92*, 289–316.

Nazzi, T. (2001, April). *When do children start using causal properties to categorize objects?*

Poster presented at the Biennial meeting of the Society for Research on Child Development, Minneapolis, MN.

Nazzi, T., & Gopnik, A. (2000). A shift in children's use of perceptual and causal cues to categorization. *Developmental Science, 4,* 389–396.

Nazzi, T., & Gopnik, A. (2001). Linguistic and cognitive abilities in infancy: When does language become a tool for categorization? *Cognition, 80,* 11–20.

Nazzi, T., & Gopnik, A. (2002). *The emergence of the use of causal cues to object categorization.* Manuscript submitted for publication.

Nelson, K. (1973). Structure and strategy in learning to talk. *Monographs of the Society for Research in Child Development, 38* (1–2, Serial No. 149).

Oakes, L. M., & Cohen, L. B. (1995). Infant causal perception. In C. Rovee-Collier and L. P. Lipsitt (Eds.), *Advances in infancy research* (Vol. 9, pp. 1–54). Norwood, NJ: Ablex.

O'Keefe, J., & Nadel, L. (1978). *The hippocampus as a cognitive map.* New York: Oxford University Press.

Pearl, J. (1988). *Probabilistic reasoning in intelligent systems.* San Mateo, CA: Morgan Kaufman Press.

Pearl, J. (2000). *Causality.* New York: Oxford University Press.

Putnam, H. (1975). *Mind, language, and reality.* New York: Cambridge University Press.

Rehder, B. (1999). A causal model theory of categorization. In *Proceedings of the 21st Annual Conference of the Cognitive Science Society* (pp. 595–600). Vancouver, British Columbia: Cognitive Science Society.

Ricciuti, H. N. (1965). Object grouping and selective ordering behaviors in infants 12 to 24 months old. *Merrill-Palmer Quarterly, 11,* 129–148.

Rips, L. (1989). Similarity, typicality, and categorization. In S. Vosniadou and A. Ortony (Eds.), *Similarity and analogical reasoning.* New York: Cambridge University Press.

Shanks, D. R., & Dickinson, A. (1987). Associative accounts of causality judgment. In G. H. Bower (Ed.), *The psychology of learning and motivation: Advances in research and theory* (Vol. 21, pp. 229–261). San Diego, CA: Academic Press.

Smith, L. B., Jones, S. S., & Landau, B. (1996). Naming in young children: A dumb attentional mechanism? *Cognition, 60,* 143–171.

Soja, N., Carey, S., & Spelke, E. S. (1991). Ontological categories guide young children's inductions of word meaning: object terms and substance terms. *Cognition, 38,* 179–211.

Spelke, E. S., Breinlinger, K., Macomber, J., & Jacobson, K. (1992). Origins of knowledge. *Psychological Review, 99,* 605–632.

Spirtes, P., Glymour, C., & Scheines, R. (1993, 2000). *Causation, prediction, and search.* Cambridge, MA: MIT Press.

Starkey, D. (1981). The origins of concept formation: Object sorting and object preference in early infancy. *Child Development, 52,* 489–497.

Strevens, M. (2000). The essentialist aspect of naive theories. *Cognition, 74,* 149–175.

Sugarman, S. (1983). *Children's early thought: Developments in classification.* New York: Cambridge University Press.

Tardif, T., Gelman, S. A., & Xu, F. (1999). Putting the "noun bias" in context: A comparison of English and Mandarin. *Child Development, 70,* 620–635.

Tolman, E. C. (1932). *Purposive behavior in animals and men.* New York: Century Co.

Watson, J. S., & Ramey, C. T. (1987). Reactions to response-contingent stimulation in early infancy. In J. Oates and S. Sheldon (Eds.), *Cognitive development in infancy.* New Jersey: Erlbaum.

Waxman, S. R., & Markow, D. B. (1995). Words as invitations to form categories: Evidence from 12- to 13-month-old infants. *Cognitive Psychology, 29,* 257–302.

Wellman, H. M. (1990). *The child's theory of mind.* Cambridge, MA: MIT Press.

Wellman, H. M., & Gelman, S. A. (1997). Cognitive development: Foundational theories of core domains. *Annual Review of Psychology, 43,* 337–375.

Woodward, A. L. (1998). Infants selectively encode the goal object of an actor's reach. *Cognition, 69,* 1–34.

Woodward, A. L., Markman, E. M., & Fitzsimmons, C. M. (1994). Rapid word learning in 13- and 18-month-olds. *Developmental Psychology, 30,* 553–566.

CHAPTER THIRTEEN

Theory-Based Categorization in Early Childhood

Susan A. Gelman and Melissa A. Koenig

I N THIS CHAPTER, we argue that children's categories as expressed in language are "theory based." By this we mean that the categories of young children include information about ontology, causation, function, intentions, and other properties that are not directly observable. Moreover, children use their categories to form important inferences and explanations that go beyond the available evidence. In staking these claims, we explicitly build on recent proposals by Carey, Gopnik, and others suggesting that children's thought is organized into intuitive framework theories that, like scientific theories, help children organize experience, make predictions, and causally interpret their world (Carey, 1985; Gopnik & Wellman, 1994; Gopnik & Meltzoff, 1997) (what Robert Siegler [personal communication] recently termed "core knowledge theories"). The crucial additional claim here is that such theories are reflected in the individual categories that children form (see also Gelman, 1996).

This is a controversial position. It is controversial in light of traditional theories that propose that children form concepts that are concrete, perceptually based, and qualitatively distinct from the more sophisticated, conceptually advanced categories that adults form (e.g., Inhelder & Piaget, 1964; Tversky, 1985). It also appears to conflict with recent theoretical approaches that highlight the power of domain-general processes to build up deceptively "complex" concepts from simple building blocks ("dumb attentional mechanisms"; Smith, Jones, & Landau, 1996). Thus, after reviewing evidence for children's theory-based concepts in the bulk of the chapter, we discuss the controversy and our take on it.

In the first part of this chapter we review evidence for theory-based concepts; in the second, we discuss what sort of explanatory model best accounts for these concepts. We compare two sorts of models, "dumb attentional mechanisms" versus "concepts-in-theories," and argue that the former is incomplete in ways that the latter complement and address. In this second discussion, we also briefly touch on the difficult and largely unresolved issue of how prelinguistic categorization differs from categories once children have language.

Evidence for Theory-Based Concepts

Fifteen years ago, Murphy and Medin (1985) argued that adult concepts are best construed as inhering in intuitive "theories." One major thrust to the argument was the limitations of similarity as an explanatory mechanism. There are epistemological problems with defining similarity in a theory-neutral way, as Goodman (1972) points out. Depending on what counts as a feature, any two objects could be as similar as any other two. A Jeep and a blade of grass have innumerable features in common, because both weigh less than 2 tons, are green, are found on Earth, are visible to the naked eye, and so on. Similarity-based accounts do not explain conceptual coherence, nor do they account for conceptual combination (e.g., how we determine a category such as "pet fish," which is not simply the conjunction of the most typical features of "pet" and "fish").

Moreover, much of categorization requires appeal to more knowledge-rich, explanatory models. An intuitive example, supplied by Murphy and Medin (1985), concerns the hypothetical example of a man at a party who jumps into a swimming pool fully clothed. One might classify him as "drunk," not because of his physical resemblance to other intoxicated individuals but rather because the category supplies a plausible explanation of his actions. Especially within certain domains (e.g., the domain of living kinds), categorization shows evidence of inductive potential, use of nonobvious information, and openness to revision—properties associated with theory-based accounts.

The theory view does not *replace* approaches that argue that people attend to on-line, at-hand statistical information: collation of features, salience, similarity, prototypes, exemplars, and the like; instead, it argues for their insufficiency. For example, prototypes are accurate descriptions of the information people use to identify category instances on many tasks. Importantly, however, such accounts do not provide the full story. Thus, we agree with those who argue that a hybrid approach, incorporating both theory and similarity, is needed (Keil, Smith, Simons, & Levin, 1998; Murphy, 2000).

There is now growing evidence that for adults, concepts are influenced by theoretical belief systems and cannot be characterized by statistical information alone (Heit & Rubenstein, 1994; Keil, 1989; Murphy & Allopenna, 1994; Murphy & Medin, 1985; Pazzani, 1991; Quine, 1977; Rips, 1989; Rips & Collins, 1993; Spalding & Murphy, 1999; see Murphy, 1993, for review). How subjects incorporate different features into their category judgments varies, depending on their theories about the domain (Wisniewski & Medin, 1994). The probability of accepting novel instances as category members is also dependent on theoretical beliefs rather than statistical correlations (Medin & Shoben, 1988). Thus, in some cases a property equally true of two different concepts is more central to one than the other (e.g., the property "curved" is more central to boomerangs than to bananas, even though in all our prior experience, "curved" applies equally often to both concepts). The extent to which features are weighted in classification judgments is influenced by causal understandings: properties that are causes are viewed as more central to a concept than properties that are effects (Ahn & Lassaline, 1996), again demonstrating that correlations alone cannot account for the centrality and significance of features in a concept (see also Ahn, Kalish, Medin, & Gelman, 1995; White, 1995; Keil, 1989).

There is also evidence that people's ability to categorize successfully is intimately tied to the kinds of explanations they can generate. Explanatory structures, known by their power to relate items in a causal framework, appear to guide and shape common cognitive activities, even when explanations have not been explicitly provided by investigators (Murphy, 2000). For example, Murphy and his colleagues have designed experiments in which subjects form their own concepts of unfamiliar items (such as underwater dwelling or floating house) and have varied only whether or not the features of the items could be potentially linked by an explanatory scheme. In their results, categories that included features that were related and linked to a theme were learned much faster than those with unrelated features (Murphy & Allopenna, 1994). Lassaline and Murphy (1996) also found that subjects who were asked questions about feature relations (e.g., "If a building has a brick extension, what kind of heating does it have?") discovered the correct category more often that those who were only asked about feature frequencies (e.g., "How many items have brick exteriors?"). In addition, Spalding and Murphy (1999) found that knowledge aids even in acquiring featural details, such that subjects in knowledge conditions estimated frequency more accurately than control subjects. In general, people appear to benefit by their ability to form concepts in which features are linked in sensible causal frameworks.

The theory-based model of concepts is argued to be a *contributor to* concept development rather than the *outcome of* concept development (see Wellman & Gelman, 1992). Murphy (1993) argues that, without theoretical commitments of some sort, it may be difficult for children to acquire concepts at all. He posits that theories help concept learners in three respects: (1) theories help identify those features that are relevant to a concept; (2) theories constrain how (e.g., along which dimensions) similarity should be computed; and (3) theories can influence how concepts are stored in memory. The implication here is that concept acquisition may proceed more smoothly with the help of theories, even though the theories themselves are changing developmentally.

What is the evidence for theory-based concepts in children? Most directly, children's concepts incorporate information about ontology, causation, and nonobvious properties, including function and intention (Carey, 1985; Gopnik & Sobel, 2000; Wellman & Gelman, 1998). In addition, they are open-ended, in the sense of fostering inductive inferences about novel properties. For ease of exposition, we have organized the literature review that follows into distinct sections that address each of these kinds of evidence separately. However, as will become clear, the different sections are related and overlapping. For example, children's use of the animate–inanimate distinction is relevant to discussions of ontology, causation, and nonobvious properties.

Ontology

Keil (1979, p. 1) defines ontological knowledge as "one's conception of the basic categories of existence, of what sorts of things there are." Ontologies form the foundation of intuitive framework theories. For example, physics deals with masses, velocities, energy. Psychology deals with thoughts, desires, beliefs. Biology deals with species, genes, reproduction. The same entity can be construed in different theories: thus, a person is at once a physical mass and is possessing psychological states and undergoing biological processes. The difference between an ontological distinction and other categorical distinctions is that, with ontologies, predicates assigned to the wrong ontological category are not false—they are nonsensical. For example, "The cow is green" is false but sensible; in contrast, "The cow is one hour long" is an ontological category error and nonsensical (Sommers, 1963; Keil, 1979).

When do children begin to honor ontological distinctions, in their categories and in their language? There is a rich literature demonstrating that children honor at least two ontological distinctions quite early in life, that of mental versus physical (Wellman, 1990), and that of animate versus inanimate (Rakison & Poulin-Dubois, 2001; Gelman & Opfer, in press). We focus primarily on the latter, as its relevance for categorization is especially clear.

Many studies show that even infants distinguish animate from inanimate on a variety of measures. One immediate question is whether this is correctly construed as a conceptual distinction or instead can be reduced to other features that correlate with the ontological distinction. For example, a child may distinguish mammals and vehicles in a manner that appears to reflect an ontological distinction between animate and animate. However, it is possible that lower-level perceptual analyses yield the categorical distinction. One way to examine whether animacy is wholly a perceptually based distinction or one with ontological significance is to determine what meaning it has for the child. Legerstee (1992) suggests that the animate–inanimate distinction extends beyond a perceptual discrimination ability and has conceptual implications even for young infants:

> when very young infants face people and things, they respond differently to the two classes. Rather than a perceptual differentiation, this ability appears to be conceptual and driven by different underlying mechanisms that are specific to the social and nonsocial domain. These structures allow the infants to act on the basis of abstract representations of events in the world. (p. 65)

Some of the earliest evidence that infants distinguish people from inanimate objects comes from infants' socioemotional reactions: for example, gazing, smiling, and cooing (Legerstee, Pomerlau, Malcuit, and Feider, 1987). Furthermore, several researchers have proposed that infants imbue animates (particularly people) with important psychological characteristics, and that infants distinguish "surface" behaviors from "deeper" psychological interpretations of those behaviors (Baron-Cohen, 1995; Legerstee, Barna, & DiAdamo, 2000; Meltzoff, 1995; Premack & Premack, 1997; Woodward, 1998).

What is the evidence that ontological distinctions—especially the animate–inanimate distinction—are honored in children's categories? Evidence includes both explicit category judgments tasks and implicit ways that ontology influences other aspects of language.

Explicit: Animacy as Basis of Category Judgments   There is ample evidence that, in children's classifications, ontology can trump other salient information, such as object shape. By 9 months of age, infants group together different basic-level animal categories (e.g., dogs and fish) and separate birds-with-outspread-wings from airplanes (Mandler & McDonough, 1993). Ten-month-olds classify together containers differing in shape and distinguish between same-shaped objects that differ in their capacity to contain (Kolstad & Baillargeon, 1996). By age 2 years, children weight substance more heavily than shape on a match-to-sample task on which the items are nonsolid masses (Soja, Carey, & Spelke, 1991). Even children's overextension errors (e.g., referring to a cow as "a dog") are not based primarily on shape alone but rather typically require similarity on both shape and taxonomic relatedness (Gelman, Croft, Fu, Clausner, and Gottfried, 1996).

By 3 and 4 years of age, children treat plants and animals as belonging to a single category (living things), despite the extreme differences in shape between, say, a cow and a tree (Backscheider, Shatz, & Gelman, 1993; Hickling & Gelman, 1995). Conversely, children treat humans and apes as belonging to distinctly different categories, despite their greater similarity. Thus, when given triads consisting of a human, a nonhuman primate, and a nonprimate animal, elementary school children are more likely than adults to group together the primate and the animal, isolating the human (Johnson, Mervis, & Boster, 1992). This pattern is also found among preschoolers, even when the primate and animal differ radically in shape (e.g., chimpanzee and centipede) (Coley, 1993). By age 7, children can sort objects into superordinate categories in ways that require overlooking shape (e.g., classifying a snake with other animals or a sailboat with wheeled vehicles) (Sigel, 1953, 1983).

A classic and insightful example of how children's categories reflect animacy is found in a study by Massey and Gelman (1988). Children 3 and 4 years of age were asked to say which of a series of unfamiliar entities could go up a hill by itself. Children were remarkably accurate, especially considering that the items were unfamiliar and that superficial cues were potentially misleading. For example, one of the inanimate entities was a statue with a face and legs, yet children appropriately judged that it could not go up a hill by itself. Conversely, one of the animate entities was an echidna, without a clearly identifiable animal shape, yet children appropriately judged that it could go up a hill by itself. Clearly, perceptual information was key here—children had only perceptual information to guide their choices. Nonetheless, what they found relevant was not "similarity" in some overall sense but rather those subtle perceptual cues that revealed the animacy of the object.

Despite studies such as these, the notion that words capture theory-based categories is called into question by studies suggesting that shape is a crucial component of children's semantic representations, even overriding ontological distinctions. On this view, children have a general shape bias in their interpretations of novel count nouns, such that a new word (e.g., "a dax") is assumed to refer to a set of objects that share a common shape (Imai, Gentner, & Uchida, 1994; Landau, Smith, & Jones, 1988; Landau, Jones, & Smith, 1992; Baldwin, 1989, 1992; see Woodward & Markman,

1998, for discussion). One interpretation of the bias is that ontological status is irrelevant, at least in naming and perhaps in conceptualization (e.g., toy bears and real bears are both "bears" because they have a common shape; Jones & Smith, 1993). In favor of this position, many studies indicate that shape is an important and salient feature for children, particularly in word-learning contexts (Baldwin, 1989, 1992). Certainly, on tasks that provide information only about perceptual dimensions (e.g., sorting of simple, novel artifacts that vary only in shape, texture, and color), shape is an especially salient dimension.

However, we suggest that shape is not the sole or even primary factor in children's naming and classification. Instead, its salience derives largely from its value as an index or predictor of other information (Gelman & Ebeling, 1998; Medin, 1989; Soja, Carey, & Spelke, 1992; Waxman & Braig, 1996). When ontological knowledge and theoretical beliefs are available, and when they conflict with shape, children can and do sort and name on the basis of these other factors (see Gelman & Diesendruck, 1999, for review).

If this interpretation is correct, then when children receive information about theoretical kind directly, this should influence which features are deemed relevant and used in children's judgments. Preliminary support for the conceptual reading comes from Keil's (1994, 1995) studies demonstrating that verbal cues alone and domain cues alone can shift the weighting of subjects' features. When the same object is described as a "frog" versus a "rock," subjects make use of different perceptual features to extend the word (shape and surface markings, in the case of the frog; color and surface markings in the case of the rock).

Implicit: Animacy Revealed in Linguistic Judgments   By the time children can talk, animacy is expressed in language. Cross-linguistically, animacy is marked via pronouns (as in English: he/she vs. it), classifiers, selectional restrictions on which verbs can appear with which nouns (e.g., Silverstein, 1986; Croft, 1990), and so on. Although there is no single respect in which animacy influences syntactic development across the world's languages (e.g., Martinez, 2000), animacy is clearly a pervasive theme that informs and structures the way speakers communicate.

For children learning English, subject nouns are typically animate and object nouns tend to be inanimate (Bloom, 1993; Slobin, 1985), and children are aware of these regularities by preschool age if not earlier (Golinkoff, Harding, Carlson, & Sexton, 1984). For children learning English, animacy is an important factor in learning the passive construction (Dewart, 1979; Koff, Kramer, & Fowles, 1980; Lempert, 1989, 1990) and in the types of implicit causal attributions children make when interpreting verbs (Corrigan & Stevenson, 1994).

We have recently completed a pair of experiments examining the implicit role of animacy in children's verb interpretation. Specifically, these studies find that semantic interpretations of the verb "move" depend on whether the subject noun is animate versus inanimate (Gelman & Koenig, 2001). In English, it is grammatically permissible for any subject noun—either animate or inanimate—to be either an agent or a patient of the verb "move." However, if children link animacy and agency, then they may assume that animate subjects are *restricted* to being agents. To make this concrete, consider transporting a caged, sleeping mouse from one side of a room to the other. We predicted that people would say that the *cage* moved but that the *mouse* didn't. In other words, the semantics of the verb "move" should differ, depending on whether the subject noun is animate or inanimate.

To test this idea, we showed participants videotapes of items being carried in a person's hand. Half the items were animate (e.g., a mouse); half the items were inanimate (e.g., a block). Subjects were simply asked, for each, "Did the X move?" (e.g., "Did the mouse move?" "Did the block move?"). Results indicated a sizable and consistent animacy effect, for both 5-year-olds and adults: inanimate objects elicited more than double the number of "yes" responses than did animates. We interpret this result as indicating that animate subjects are typically assumed to be agents, so that "Did the mouse move?" means "Did the mouse move by itself?" whereas "Did the block move?" need not imply that the block moved by itself. Thus the word "move" appears to mean different things, depending on whether the subject noun is animate or inanimate. We take this as evidence of the implicit use of an ontological distinction, animacy, in children's categories.

Three aspects of the design of the studies illustrate the power of the animacy-agency link for these participants. First, we fully crossed animacy and agency (for example, including animals that were patients as well as artifacts that were agents). Second, we equated the spatiotemporal features of the display, across the two domains, but still found domain differences. Third, in the real world animals can be agents or patients, but children and adults nonetheless tended to reject the possibility of animate subjects being patients of intransitive verbs, in their language.

Summary   Ontological information appears to be central to children's early classifications and implicit language judgments. We are agnostic as to the question of how and when ontological distinctions emerge. Nonetheless, they have privileged status by age 3, and can even override salient perceptual information. Moreover, ontology continues to exert powerful effects on concepts and reasoning, into adulthood (with college students holding stubbornly persistent misconceptions about scientific processes that can be traced to ontological errors; for example, misconstruing evolutionary theory because evolution is treated as part of an "event ontology" rather than an "equilibration ontology"; Slotta, Chi, & Joram, 1995).

Causation

Gelman and Kalish (1993) proposed that if children's categories are theory-based, then causes should be crucial to their category representations. What this means is that, when comparing causal features to other, noncausal features, causal features should be more central to the category—even for children. For example, if there is an illness for which a particular virus causes a particular rash, then children should categorize the illness based on presence or absence of the virus, not presence or absence of the rash. Relatedly, Keil et al. (1998) argue against the commonly held assumption that children's earliest concepts are merely lists of features (see Clark, 1973, for review), and suggest instead that even young children attend to causal relations *among* features in constructing concepts. (See Sperber, Premack, & Premack, 1995, for fuller discussion of causal reasoning.)

Similarly, Barrett, Abdi, Murphy, and Gallagher (1993) note that "concept learn-ing involves more than simply keeping a running tally of which features are asso-ciated with which concept" (p. 1612) and present data suggesting that children's intuitive theories help determine which properties and which feature correlations children attend to in their classifications. For example, when asked to categorize novel birds into one of two categories, children of elementary-school age noticed correla-tions that were supported by causal links and used such correlations to categorize new members (e.g., correlation between brain size and memory). The children did not make use of features that correlated equally well but were unsupported by a theory (e.g., the correlation between structure of heart and shape of beak). Krascum and Andrew (1998) likewise found beneficial effects of causal information on category learning in children as young as 4 and 5 years of age. As the authors note, "the mean-ingfulness of individual features is not a significant factor in children's category learn-ing, and instead, what is important is that attributes within a category can be linked in a theory-coherent manner" (p. 343).

Recent evidence from Gopnik and Sobel (2000) extends the effect to even younger children. In their studies, 2-, 3-, and 4-year-olds learned that a novel object with a novel name (e.g., "a blicket") had a certain causal power (i.e., placing the object on a machine would (apparently) cause the machine to light up and play music). Re-sults indicate that even 2-year-olds use causal information to guide both naming and induction. Importantly, they do so more than in a control condition, in which the blicket is *associated* with the machine setting off but appears *not* to cause it. Thus, correlational information alone did not determine children's naming.

Ahn (1998) formulated a specific version of the causal hypothesis that she termed the "causal status hypothesis," in which causal features are more central than effect features. Thus, even given equal frequency, cause and effect features will be weighted differently. This is a particularly intriguing claim, in that both cause and effect fea-tures participate in causal relations. Intuitive examples of adult categorization sup-port such a claim. For example, illnesses are often categorized by the virus that causes the symptoms of that illness rather than by the symptoms alone. When the causal status of features is manipulated experimentally, adults weighted the identical fea-ture more heavily when it served as a cause than when it served as an effect (Ahn & Lassaline, 1996). Of particular interest to this context, Ahn, Gelman, Amsterlaw, Hohenstein, and Kalish (2000) found evidence for the causal status effect in children 7–9 years of age. Children learned descriptions of novel animals, in which one fea-ture caused two other features. When asked to determine which test item was more likely to be an example of the animal they had learned, children preferred an animal with a cause feature and an effect feature rather than an animal with two effect features.

Summary   Causation is privileged in children's categorizations, in several respects. Properties that enter into causally meaningful links are better remembered and are treated as more central to the category than properties that are not causally mean-ingful. Even 2-year-olds use cause features—on both naming and induction tasks—to categorize, even when such features conflict with salient perceptual information. Finally, causes are treated as more diagnostic of category membership than effects (Ahn's "causal status hypothesis").

Function

Kemler Nelson, Russell, Duke, and Jones (2000) explain the importance of function to a theory-based approach as follows:

> attention to functional information can be understood as evidence for conceptual categories when it supplements or overrides the pull of superficial, functionally irrelevant aspects of appearance as the basis for using artifact names. The use of functional information implicates interpretive mechanisms beyond those of immediate perception and indicates a mode of categorization that is at least partly knowledge based, rather than strictly perceptually driven. (p. 1271)

However, the extent to which children are capable of using function for their classifications, particularly in word learning, is highly controversial. Smith, Jones, and Landau (1996) argued that 3-year-old children selectively ignore functional information when extending new labels. The basis of their argument is that word learning is guided by "dumb" (i.e., nonreflective, involuntary, automatic) attentional mechanisms. They conclude, on the basis of a series of experiments, that "children's naming was immune to influence from information about function" (p. 143). Their evidence included a series of four experiments in which 3-year-olds—unlike adults—failed to use function when extending novel labels to novel objects.

Landau, Smith, and Jones (1998) extended this line of work using a greater range of both novel and familiar objects. Across three studies of similar design, 2-, 3-, and 5-year-olds and adults were asked to extend labels (naming task) or to infer novel functions (function task; e.g., "Could you carry water with this one?"). In general, children selected on the basis of function on the function task, and on the basis of shape on the naming task, regardless of whether or not they were presented with explicit demonstrations of function.

If these provocative results are interpreted as the authors suggest, this would be damaging to the "concepts in theories" position that we are arguing for in this chapter. Nonetheless, the theory position could be saved in either of two ways. One possibility is that (1) function is indeed used by children to categorize, but at a later point in development, compared to the subjects in the Landau experiments (Smith et al., 1996; Gentner & Rattermann, 1991). This possibility, if true, would weaken the theory position, particularly the suggestion made earlier that theories contribute to concept development, rather than being the outcome of concept development (Murphy, 1993). It would argue for a developmental shift, from perceptually based to theory-based categorization. In contrast, the argument that we favor is that (2) children can and do use functional information while naming but that certain items and tasks have limited children's capacity in prior studies. When care is taken to design tasks and items that reflect functions that are salient, sensible, and nonarbitrary, then young children incorporate function into their naming from as early as 2 years of age. The latter argument has been pursued vigorously in the past few years; the evidence that supports it is as follows.

Kemler Nelson, Russell, et al. (2000) point out that children cannot be expected to appreciate just any type of function they encounter, any more than would an adult.

They suggest that, for a fair test, it is critical to examine function/structure relations that are "compelling and nonarbitrary in a way that young children can make sense of (and may expect)" (p. 1272). Specifically, Kemler Nelson posits that the functionally relevant aspects of an object's design should be easily perceptible, that structure/function relations should be based on principles of causality that are familiar to young children, and that function/structure relations should be "convincing." For example, Kemler Nelson et al. (1995) introduced 3-, 4-, and 5-year-old children to a novel artifact that could function in two distinct and novel ways, for example, with brushes to paint four parallel lines and with wires that could be plucked to make music. Thus, certain features were contingent on one function, whereas other features were contingent on the other. Each child encountered only one of these functions, in either a painter or instrument condition, when the target artifact was named "a stennet." When asked to extend the novel name to test objects that varied from the target in similarity and function, children tended to extend the name in accord with the function that they saw demonstrated (though similarity relations were also taken into account).

Similarly, Diesendruck and Markson (1999) argue that young children can appreciate function when it is a permanent, exclusive property of an object (as opposed to just something that the object "does," as in Smith et al., 1996) that is made readily available (e.g., through explicit demonstration and explanation, e.g., "This was made for X"). When these conditions are met, even 3-year-olds appreciate function and use it as the basis of classification. Thus 3-year-olds participated in a sorting task with triads of novel objects. Each target object was paired with an object that was similar in shape but which could not perform the function, and an object different in shape but that could perform the function. When the function was explicitly stated, demonstrated, and shown to be exclusive to one of the test choices, children typically sorted on the basis of function.

Kemler Nelson (1999) also examined the effect that direct experience with object function has on toddlers' novel label extensions. Some children were given direct prior experience manipulating test objects before a naming session, whereas other children were not given this opportunity. Toddlers successfully generalized novel names on the basis of function, but only if they had had previous direct experience with the objects. These results demonstrate that there are conditions under which function guides naming decisions in children as young as 2 years of age. However, the results also suggest that toddlers' understanding of function may be less robust than that of older children.

In other cases, however, minimal direct experience with test objects is sufficient to allow toddlers to use functional properties in their naming decisions (Kemler Nelson, Russell, et al., 2000). In experiment 2 in Kemler Nelson, Russell, et al. (2000), 2-year-olds' naming decisions reflected object functions, despite the fact that the functions were never demonstrated by an experimenter but instead were discovered by the children during the course of the experiment.

What is it that makes a function more compelling to children? Kemler Nelson, Frankenfield, Morris, and Blair (2000) found that 4-year-old children were more likely to generalize novel names for artifacts when functions "made sense" and were more reasonably related to structure and, as such, were the functions intended by a designer. For example, a "sensible" (plausible) function for an object with a horizontal and vertical tube might be "when you put balls in here, it drops them one at a time," whereas an implausible function for the same object might be "a toy snake can wriggle in it." That is, although the object could readily carry out either of these functions, only the first is likely to be a function designed by the creator of the object.

Similarly, Bloom (2000) proposed that function is used to the extent that it is perceived as intentional—specifically, as intended by the designer of the object under consideration. For example, children relied on function when it was highly specific and unlikely to be an accidental function (e.g., an object with a hinged part shaped to fit into its base like a puzzle piece; Kemler Nelson, Russell, et al., 2000) but did not rely on function when it was a simple and general function that depended only on the substance that the object was made of and so was potentially accidental (e.g., a square, U-shaped object that "a toy dog sits in"; Smith et al., 1996). Indeed, when children view two objects of *identical* shape that have clearly different intended functions (e.g., an object and its same-shaped container), they do not sort the same-shaped objects together (Bloom, Markson, & Diesendruck, 1998).

A consideration of form–function relations makes clear that perceptual and conceptual information often interrelate. Even infants can attend selectively to the relationship between form and function, as opposed to either property independently (Madole, Oakes & Cohen, 1993). Furthermore, 18-month-olds, but not 14-month-olds, attend to certain form–function correlations more than others. When form and function were correlated within parts (e.g., wheels of a certain type correlated with wheels rolling), as opposed to across parts (e.g., top of a certain type correlated with wheels rolling), 18-month-olds dishabituated to correlation violations. As the authors note, the failure to dishabituate to violations of correlations across two different object parts (i.e., the top and the wheels) could suggest that, by 18 months, infants have certain expectations regarding the kinds of part–function correlations that should exist in objects (Madole & Cohen, 1995).

Thus, form–function correspondences are important for guiding children's attention to particular perceptual features. In other words, form–function relations offer a more structured motivation for why certain features, and not others, are salient to young children. For example, in a study with 2- to 4-year-olds, McCarrell and Callanan (1995) found that children make use of functional information when drawing inferences about object behavior. Children were more likely to make use of perceptual similarity as a basis for novel inferences, when similarity was supported by correspondences between form and function. For example, after looking at pictures of two creatures that differed only in eye size and leg length, children were invited to make an inference concerning sight ("Which one sees really well in the dark?") or movement ("Which one can jump really high?"). Children attended selectively to certain perceptual features when a particular function was described (eyes, when the question concerned sight; legs, when the question concerned movement).

Summary   As mentioned earlier, the theory view does not aim to *replace* an appeal to similarity in accounts of categorization; instead, it argues for the insufficiency of accounts that rely only on similarity to explain categorization decision in development. Evidence from research on children's understanding of function suggests that although perceptual similarity is readily available and used by early categorizers and labelers, it is does not provide a satisfactory account for why children attend to functional information when forming categories in linguistic and nonlinguistic contexts. Moreover, function plays an important role in guiding children's attentions to certain perceptual features more than others.

Intentions

Human intentions represent a special case of nonobservable property to which infants appear to have access and interest from an early age. For example, Johnson, Slaughter, and Carey (1998) found that 12-month-olds selectively follow the gaze of an object when certain cues of intentionality are provided. Specifically, infants were significantly more likely to follow the "gaze" of an artificial object when it possessed animatelike facial characteristics (i.e., eyes, ears, nose on head) and/or provided contingent motion (i.e., bleeps and blinking lights). The authors take such results to suggest that "an early concept of intentional being" may play a role in conceptual development (p. 237).

Moreover, infants' classification of events, as measured by habituation studies, are mediated by attention to an actor's goals. In a series of studies, Woodward (1998) habituated 6- and 9-month-old infants to an event in which a hand and arm reached over the course of a directed path to grasp one of two toys. In the test events, the position of the two toys was reversed and infants witnessed the arm reach either along a different path for the same toy or along the same path for a different toy. During test, both age groups looked longer at the change-in-goal events than at the change-in-path events—thus (implicitly) categorizing as similar those two events for which the "actor" (i.e., the hand) had the same underlying goal, despite the fact that such events were physically dissimilar. Further support for this interpretation is that 6-month-olds responded differently when the appendage involved was not an animate hand and arm but instead a mechanical claw. With regard to the mechanical limbs, infants looked longer at the events that depicted a path change than a goal change. In sum, infants selectively encode human action in line with more mature understandings of intentional or goal-directed action, and categorize events on this basis.

Further evidence of children's attention to the goals of an agent comes from Tomasello and Barton (1994) who found that 2-year-olds use behavioral cues to an actor's intentions when making sense of a new verb. In this study, an experimenter introduced a novel verb (e.g., "Let's dax Mickey Mouse") before producing two novel actions, one accidental and one purposeful. Each of the two actions used was purposeful for half of the participants, so that any effects could not be due to idiosyncracies of the designed actions. Regardless of which action was purposeful and which was accidental, 2-year-olds interpreted the verb as the name for the purposeful, not the accidental, action. Children inferred the intentions of the speaker and took them to apply to the act done on purpose and extended verb meaning accordingly.

Intentionality is also used in children's extensions of nouns. Bloom and Markson (1998) tested directly the role of intentionality in children's naming of representational drawings. For example, on a drawing task, children were asked to draw a lollipop and a balloon and were asked later to name (with 3-year-olds) or describe (with 4-year-olds) the pictures. The actual pictures that resulted were by shape (e.g., children reliably labeled the stick with a circle on top as a "lollipop" or as a "balloon" depending on their original intentions). Thus, intentionality—not outward appearance—determined how the drawing was named.

Gelman and Ebeling (1998) employed a different sort of task but found comparable results: intentionality influenced how 3- and 4-year-olds name representations. Children viewed simple shapes that were described as having been created either intentionally (e.g., by using paint in art class) or accidentally (e.g., by spilling paint on the floor). When they were asked "What is this?" only the children who heard about intentional acts of creation showed a strong tendency to name the representation (e.g., "a bear"). Those who heard accidental origins were much more likely to describe the materials of which the item was created (e.g., "paint").

To examine the generalizabilty of such findings beyond the world of artwork, Gelman and Bloom (2000) found converging results in a similar design in which pictures were replaced by actual artifacts that were described as either intentionally or accidentally created. Thus, for example, a jagged piece of Plexiglas was much more likely to be categorized as "a knife" if it was created through intentional means than if it was created through accidental means. Importantly, these results demonstrate that children make critical use of intent when naming and classifying both artifacts and representational drawings.

Summary   Human intentions are an integral part of children's word meanings by at least 3 years of age. Children attend to whether an event is accidental or intentional when determining how to name events, objects, and representations. Thus, a given display is named differently, depending on the child's construal of the intentional status of the display. Altogether, these results indicate that a particular nonobvious property—that of intentions—plays a critical role in early categorization.

Nonobvious Properties

The importance of nonobvious properties can be seen in several respects. It can be seen in the centrality of function and intentions in children's categories, as already summarized. It also can be seen in children's formulation of specific theories (often biological) that posit nonvisible constructs, such as germs (Au, Sidle, & Rollins, 1993; Kalish, 1996; Siegal, 1988), elements of reproduction (Springer, 1996), or cooties (Hirschfeld, 1999; Martinez, Hirschfeld, & Heyman, 1999). That children appear to learn and accept such constructs readily would argue against the notion that their concepts depend on concrete, perceptually apparent properties.

Furthermore, studies that focus specifically on nonobvious properties, such as internal parts or substance, find that children rely on such properties for categorizing (see also R. Gelman & Williams, 1998). (Precisely when in development children do so is a matter of some dispute, however.) In a classic series of studies, Keil (1989) asked children to consider animals and objects that had undergone transformations leading them to appear to be something else—for example, a raccoon that underwent an operation so that it looked and acted like a skunk. Second-graders realized that animal identity was unaffected by superficial transformations (e.g., the animal was judged to be a raccoon despite its skunklike properties).

Even younger children demonstrated a similar understanding when considering items that were transformed to resemble something from a different ontological category (e.g., preschoolers reported that a porcupine that was transformed to look like a cactus was still a porcupine) or that were transformed by means of a costume. Gelman and Wellman (1991) similarly found that preschool children appreciated that for some objects, insides are more important than outsides for judgments of identity and functioning (e.g., a dog without its insides cannot bark and is not a dog, whereas a dog without its outsides can bark and is a dog). Moreover, when asked what differentiates pairs of identical-looking animals that differ in kind (e.g., dog vs. wolf; butterfly vs. moth), both 5-year-olds and adults are more likely to invoke internal parts/substance than the irrelevant property of age (Lizotte, 2001).

Interestingly, children appreciate *that* insides are important at an age when they do not yet know much about *what* insides objects have. For example, although 4-year-olds recognize that insides are crucial to object identity (Gelman & Wellman, 1991) and expect that animal insides differ in consistent ways from machine insides (Simons & Keil, 1995), they cannot accurately identify which photo corresponds to the insides of an animal, or which photo corresponds to the insides of a machine (Simons & Keil, 1995). This result led Simons and Keil to suggest that children's grasp of insides is an abstract appreciation that precedes a concrete, detailed understanding. This is a surprising reversal of the usual developmental story (that concrete understandings precede abstractions), and implies that children may be predisposed to consider nonobvious properties important, even in the absence of direct evidence.

Internal properties can be crucial to children's word learning. Diesendruck, Gelman, and Lebowitz (1998) conducted a study that capitalized on a well-known word-learning error studied by Markman and others (Markman, 1989; Merriman & Bowman, 1989). Children have a powerful tendency to assume that each object has only one label, the "mutual exclusivity" assumption. For example, if a child knows that a poodle is a "dog," she will typically deny that it is a "poodle" or an "animal." Diesendruck et al. predicted that children would overcome this mutual exclusivity tendency if they learned that dogs and poodles (for instance) share nonobvious properties. Three- to 5-year-olds learned new words for a series of animals, and then were tested on their interpretations of the new words. For example, children saw two distinct kinds of squirrels (a standard squirrel and a flying squirrel) and heard: "This one [the flying squirrel] is a squirrel; it's a mef. This one [the standard squirrel] is a squirrel; it's not a mef." Before teaching the new word, the experimenter described how the two instances were alike. In the "insides" condition, internal, hidden properties were described (e.g., "has the same stuff inside . . . the same kind of bones, blood, muscles, and brain"). In the control condition, superficial similarities were described (e.g., "is the same size . . . it lives in the same zoo in the same kind of cage").

The labeling phase alone provided all the information children needed to construct the hierarchy accurately. However, we know from past work (e.g., Gelman, Wilcox, & Clark, 1989; Markman, 1989) that children tend to collapse such a hierarchy into two mutually exclusive sets. The question, then, is whether the brief description of internal similarities is sufficient to alter subjects' patterns of word learning. Indeed, the results demonstrated a clearcut condition effect. When the similarities were superficial, children showed their usual pattern of treating the two labels (e.g., "squirrel" and "mef") as mutually exclusive. In contrast, describing internal similarities helped children overcome the error. Diesendruck (in press) has recently replicated this finding in Brazil, with Portuguese-speaking children of widely varying socioeconomic backgrounds. Again, there was the same weakening of mutual exclusivity in the "insides" condition.

Summary   In contrast to the view that children rely on concrete, perceptually obvious features for categorizing their world, nonobvious properties are surprisingly salient in young children's categories. In part this can be seen in the preceding sections on function and intentionality; in part it can be seen in children's early emerging conceptions of "germs" and "cooties"; and in part it can be seen in children's understanding of the centrality of internal parts to object identity. Interestingly, children's attention to internal parts may reflect a general expectation that internal parts will be relevant, an expectation that even precedes children's particular knowledge about specific insides.

Inferences about Novel Properties

Gopnik and Wellman (1994) point out that one of the crucial functions of theories is to enable predictions (p. 261). Thus, if children's categories are theory based, such categories should guide the sorts of inferences children make. Indeed, there is evidence that 14-month-old infants' inductive inferences are guided by the theoretically significant distinction between animate and inanimate, so that an action such as placing a key on an entity is restricted to inanimates, whereas giving an entity something to drink is restricted to animates (Mandler & McDonough, 1996, 1998; see chaps. 5 and 7 for extended discussion of this and related work). It will be of interest in future research to explore the sorts of properties for which ontological categories are deemed relevant, and how such inferences develop over infancy and toddlerhood.

In addition to the inductive potential of ontological categories, basic-level categories encoded in language also have enormous inductive potential. In a sense, we might wish to say that each basic-level kind functions as a minitheory, or Kuhnian paradigm: "object[s] for further articulation and specification under new or more stringent conditions" (Kuhn, 1970, p. 23). Years ago, Gelman and Markman (1986, 1987) demonstrated that categories have an *inductive* function even for preschool children, that is, they have the potential to generate novel inferences. For example, children are more likely to generalize a newly learned property from a brontosaurus to a triceratops (both "dinosaurs," though radically different in appearance) than from a rhinoceros to a triceratops (highly similar in appearance, though different kinds). These findings have been replicated and extended in intriguing ways to categories of different hierarchical levels (e.g., Waxman, Lynch, Casey, & Baer, 1997) and to categories in the social domain (Heyman & Gelman, 1998, 1999).

Thus, children do not assume that labels are mere conveniences—ways of efficiently referring to perceptually encountered information in a shorthand way. Instead, children expect certain labels—and the categories to which they refer—to capture properties well beyond those they have already encountered. A variety of control studies showed that these effects were not simply a response bias due to hearing the same word for the two category members. For example, children do not base inferences consistently on novel labels (Davidson & Gelman, 1990), nor do they generalize accidental properties, such as an animal's age, on the basis of category membership (Gelman & Markman, 1986).

Moreover, inductions about kinds are related in a hierarchical fashion—what Elizabeth Shipley terms "overhypotheses" (Shipley, 1993). For example, children have a general expectation that, for animals, members of a kind tend to be alike with respect to habitat, diet, and movement. More plainly put, this means that when children encounter a novel kind (e.g., wallabees), they assume that members of this kind will all tend to live in the same kind of habitat, eat the same kinds of food, and move in the same manner—even before they learn the habitat, diet, or movement of a single instance. In this respect, we might say that children's category-based inferences partly reflect a specifically *biological* theory of animal kinds.

Category-based inferences appear to be pervasive, too, in the language of both adults and children, in the form of *generic noun phrases* (e.g., "*Cats* are furry"). Generics highlight the generality of properties and downplay exceptions (such as hairless cats; Carlson & Pelletier, 1995; Prasada, 2000). Importantly, they are frequent in the talk that even 2-year-olds hear (Gelman, Coley, et al., 1998; Pappas & Gelman, 1998) and tend to be domain-specific in their application, appearing more frequently for animals than artifacts (Gelman, Coley, et al., 1998; Gelman & Tardif, 1998). Moreover, the available evidence suggests that even young children understand the implications of generics. When 4-year-olds hear novel properties in generic form (e.g., "Bears like to eat ants"), they generalize such properties to other members of the category at above-chance levels, and significantly more frequently than when hearing novel properties ascribed to "some" members of the category (e.g., "Some bears like to eat ants"; Gelman, Star, & Flukes, 2000). That speakers of many different languages distinguish between generic and nongeneric properties (Carlson & Pelletier, 1995; Gelman & Tardif, 1998) suggests that the underlying cognitive distinction is fundamental. More speculatively, that generics are the *unmarked* plural form (at least in English) suggests that generic statements are the typical, normative sorts of plural statement that speakers will make.

Summary   Children's categories, from at least 2½ years of age, have a fundamental property of inductive potential: they are structured in a way that presumes that novel inferences can be made that conform to category boundaries. Moreover, a common property of many of the world's languages is a capacity to refer to generic categories, thereby once again implicitly conveying categorywide generalizations. In an important sense, then, children's categories are open-ended, enabling change and growth as knowledge changes and grows. This, too, is a feature of theories.

In Summary, What Is a Theory-Based Concept?

Many of children's concepts are theory based. We have reviewed four types of evidence to support this claim: the centrality of ontology, of causal features, and of nonobvious constructs (including function, intentionality, and internal parts), and the open-ended and corrigible nature of children's categories (thus allowing for and even fostering inductive inferences). In some cases, concepts are embedded in an identifiable, articulable theory (e.g., "beliefs" and "desires" in a theory of mind). In other cases, such a theory has not yet been identified, but the components of a theory (ontology, causation, nonobvious features) are present from an early age.

How to Explain What Categorizers Know: Theories versus Competing Claims

We began by saying that the theory view of young children's categories is controversial. There appear to be roughly four sorts of disputes: debates about what the data show and hence what are the relevant phenomena; a concern that a simpler explanation can be found that does not require an appeal to theories; a desire for explicit formulations; and a desire for a developmental account that can explain reorganizations with age. We will briefly discuss each of these issues.

Debates about the Phenomena

There is genuine disagreement among researchers concerning the nature of the phenomena, in other words, what children's early concepts are like. One clear case in point is the debate concerning the so-called shape bias (e.g., Gelman & Medin, 1993; Smith et al., 1996): Do children privilege shape or do they privilege ontological information? Another clear case involves disagreements concerning the use of function early in development (e.g., Kemler Nelson, 1999; Smith et al., 1996). Can young children make use of function to guide their categorization judgments or not?

The empirical issue is a difficult one, in part because often these "competing" accounts converge in the real world (e.g., as noted earlier, shape is typically an excellent predictor of ontological status). Thus, evidence favoring one position may also (unwittingly) be evidence favoring another position. For example, early accounts of children's overextension errors were treated as evidence that children have a shape bias; only later was it apparent that words extended on the basis of shape most typically are simultaneously extended on the basis of ontological kind (e.g., "apple" applied to oranges and pears; "dog" applied to cows and hippos; Gelman, Croft, et al., 1998). However, with clever experimental manipulations (and real-world natural examples, thanks to the cleverness of natural selection), we can tease apart these typically converging factors. And even under such tightly controlled conditions, different experiments do yield genuinely different kinds of results.

How to reconcile the conflicting results? The first step is to acknowledge that children exhibit great flexibility in what information they use when classifying (Deak & Bauer, 1995, 1996). By at least 3 years of age, children's categories sensitively reflect factors that include task, category type, and how theory-relevant information is instantiated.[1] We have focused in our review on the many ways that children's categories reflect theory-based information. In addition, there are indeed conditions in which shape is used most readily and function is ignored. We propose that the salience of factors such as shape derives largely from their value as predictors of other information (see also Medin, 1989; Soja et al., 1992; Ward, Becker, Hass, and Vila, 1991; Waxman & Braig, 1996). Conversely, the salience of function, intentionality, and nonobvious properties derives largely from children's capacity to attend to and process them. Thus, to predict children's categorization performance, we can at minimum ask: What is the category? What is the task? And how is theory-relevant information instantiated?

What Is the Category?   Concepts are highly varied, even for young children. They range from simple labels of immediate perceptual experience (e.g., red, cold) to internal emotional states (e.g., sad) to natural-kind terms (e.g., animal, bear, oak tree). Researchers often choose to focus on a select subset, for simplicity's sake— but do so at a cost, as different concepts appear to be best understood in terms of different models (e.g., Mervis & Rosch, 1981). Thus, a category of simple geometric shapes that vary only on the dimensions of size, shape, and texture, orthogonally varied, is going to yield attention to perceptual features. By definition, such stimuli *cannot* reveal attention to function, intentions, or nonobvious properties. Conversely, the studies we have reviewed have primarily included real-world categories (or close analogues; e.g., invented animal kinds), often biological kinds, that include proper- ties that go "beyond the information given" (in Bruner's terminology) and seem to reveal a theory-constructing mind.

What Is the Task?   People use categories for many different purposes; different tasks reflect these purposes to greater or lesser degrees; and task differences can thus yield use of different kinds of information. For example, contrast the big-game hunter with the biologist in her lab. The hunter's goal is rapid identification of an animal when time and visibility are limited and thus is likely to encourage use of the most salient of surface properties (e.g., identifying a deer on the basis of a flash of white, which at times has tragic consequences, as when a hunter shoots a person wearing white mittens). In contrast, the biologist's goal is often to construct the most accu- rate and elaborated knowledge of a species possible and thus is likely to encourage the use of multiple, nonobvious cues (e.g., identifying relatedness among frog sub- species based on DNA sequencing).

Task differences appear to have sizable influences on children's category judg- ments. Some contrasts that have been studied include: classification versus word extension (Markman, 1989); classification versus inference (Yamauchi & Markman, 1998); considering a single instance versus comparing across instances (Gentner & Namy, 1999); inferring a category versus inferring a property (Gelman, Collman, & Maccoby, 1986; Gopnik & Sobel, 2000); quick processing versus slow processing (Kemler Nelson, Frankenfield, et al., 2000); and dishabituation versus sequential touching of objects (Mandler & McDonough, 1993). In each of these cases, children's judgments differ considerably as a function of the task.

How Is the Theory-Relevant Information Instantiated?   As noted earlier, an experi- ment testing whether children make use of functional information is influenced by the degree to which that function is salient and compelling to young children (Kemler

Nelson, Frankenfield, et al., 2000). Likewise, a test of whether children use onto-logical information in their classifications will depend on whether children have acquired the relevant ontological distinction (Keil, 1989). The more general point is that children have the capacity to make use of theories but will fall back on other information when the theory-based information is inaccessible, for whatever reason.

Why Consider These to Be Theories? Can't a Simpler Explanation be Found?

As noted in several places throughout the chapter, theory-based categorization does not *supplant* perceptual information; indeed, perceptual information is typically intertwined with information about functions, ontologies, nonobvious properties, and so on (see discussion by Gelman & Medin, 1993; Jones & Smith, 1993). For ex-ample, function is cued by form–function correspondences. Likewise, determining an entity's ontological status—even with tricky cases such as statues, which in many respects are more similar to entities of a contrasting ontological type—typically re-quires perceptual information of some sort (e.g., Massey & Gelman, 1988). Even for basic-level kinds, which we argue are "essentialized" and predictive of nonobvious features, perception is an important (though fallible) source of information for iden-tifying instances. Thus, an appeal to theories should not be misinterpreted as stand-ing in opposition to a perceptual account (see also Gelman & Medin, 1993). In this sense, we construe the theory position as more moderate and less controversial than it is at times portrayed.

Moreover, the search for perceptual cues that correlate with ontology, causation, and so on is an important and productive enterprise, one that reveals interesting and surprising discoveries. For example, Michotte's classic work on the perception of causality (1963) is an excellent example of how dynamic perceptual cues invoke a causal interpretation in the viewer; likewise, Johannsen's work on the paths of move-ment reveal important cues by which people distinguish animate from inanimate (1973; Bertenthal, 1996). Another intriguing example is that of Eimas and Quinn (1994, Quinn & Eimas, 1996), who have discovered robust perceptual cues that children use to categorize at multiple levels, as well as the work of Rakison and Butterworth (1998), who have documented the importance of object parts to categorization in infancy.

The intermingling of perception and theory, and the success with which some researchers have found perceptual bases to judgments that we have termed "theory based," together raise the challenging question of whether all this talk of theories is superfluous. Can we recast the developmental findings reviewed above, as showing evidence that children attend to perceptual information, albeit highly sophisticated perceptual information? This is a position that is favored by some who argue that early categories are based primarily on non-strategic attentional processes (Smith et al., 1996).

For example, instead of saying that children attend to ontological information, why not say that they attend to particular perceptual features, such as eyes (Landau et al., 1988) or legs (Rakison & Butterworth, 1998)? In support of such an approach, researchers have found that 18-month-olds distinguish toy animals (with legs) from toy vehicles (with wheels; Mandler, Bauer, & McDonough, 1991), and by 14 months of age will even violate the animal–vehicle distinction when toy animals are portrayed as having wheels rather than legs and toy vehicles are portrayed as having legs rather than wheels (Rakison & Butterworth, 1998). However, a problem with this strategy is that identifying the perceptual features can be a circular exercise. For example, consider the argument that animates can be identified by the perceptual feature of legs. This argument runs into trouble when we consider that only some legs are animate. Legs of a table or chair are inanimate, yet infants do not treat animals and furniture as a single group. One could say that table legs aren't *really* legs—that language is misleading in this respect. Table legs don't have feet and toes, for example. But this argument runs into problems, too, as some inanimate legs do have feet and toes (e.g., the legs on a bathtub or statue).

Alternatively, perhaps the perceptually relevant features exist but are subtler—features such as texture, contour, or material kind (e.g., see Smith & Heise [1992] for an intriguing study that contour differentiates animates from inanimates). On this view, legs per se may not be definitive, but perhaps texture is. Yet even this retreat is problematic, as the available evidence suggests that, although a cluster of features are relevant for identifying entities as animate, none are decisive. For example, Johnson et al. (1998) found that even by 12 months of age, children use *either* the static perceptual cues of facial features *or* the dynamic perceptual cues of contingency (an object moving and making sounds, in response to the child's own movements) to identify a novel entity as animate (our interpretation; evidenced by the child following the "gaze" of the entity). This sort of finding suggests that the perceptual cues are interpreted in the service of identifying ontological kind, rather than vice versa.

The difficulty of "reducing" ontology to perception is further emphasized when one considers how subtle, context sensitive, and flexible are the perceptual features that correspond to the distinction between intentional versus nonintentional being (i.e., the ontological category of psychological kind). The same movement can be interpreted as either intentional or accidental, depending on the background knowledge of the observer (Bargh, 1990). Moreover, psychological "readings" of an event are culturally sensitive. For example, how people interpret the movement of cartoon fish in a dynamic display varies notably as a function of the cultural background of the research participants (Morris, Nisbett, & Peng, 1995). More generally, we doubt that any straightforward algorithm can be devised to allow a reading of intentionality to emerge from perceptual considerations alone. Indeed, we would argue, any attempt to do so would necessarily entail "sneaking in" concepts such as "knowledge," "causal understanding," or "belief" in order to make the perceptual redescription work. In so doing, the notion of "perceptual" would be extended so broadly as to lose much of its power and meaning (Gelman & Medin, 1993).

In brief, our argument is that any alternative (nontheory) account of children's concepts still needs to incorporate domain-specific knowledge, ontological distinctions, causal understanding, and so on. Therefore, it seems crucial to invoke theories in an explanatory account of children's concepts.

Lack of Explicitness

The word "theory" is a potentially vague term with many different interpretations. Indeed, some of the debates concerning the value of the theory approach emerge because of (implicit) disagreements concerning what constitutes a theory (e.g., see Wellman's [1990] contrast between a scientific theory and a naïve theory). Future work in this area should be aimed at adding precision and tests of falsifiability (for some excellent starts, see Carey, 1985; Gopnik & Wellman, 1994).

Nonetheless, despite whatever lack of explicitness remains concerning the theory theory broadly construed, specific components of this approach are admirably precise. For example, Ahn's "causal status" hypothesis is a testable theory with clear-cut predictions. Likewise, arguments concerning the relative importance of ontology versus shape, though in some sense misguided (since ontology and shape tend to correlate in the real world), remain altogether unambiguous in their predictions.

Moreover, we are led to ask whether the theoretical constructs in the alternative view are any more explicit. The apparent gain in precision that comes by invoking similarity, attention, salience, and feature distinctiveness may be only illusory. Recall that problems with the construct of "similarity" were at the heart of the Murphy and Medin (1985) critique of standard approaches to concepts. The tools proposed by the "dumb-attentional account" do not solve the problems discussed in this chapter. Simple induction, abstraction, and salience no doubt guide human reasoning. But they fail to explain why children employ the unobservable causal constructs documented throughout the chapter, and they seem to propose underspecified mechanisms of conceptual change. (See Keil et al., 1998 for further explication.)

A final point in this section is that the apparent bedrocks of information processing (e.g., memory, attention) are themselves influenced by theories. Memory is notorious for conforming to theory (rather than memory being a neutral source of information). For example, Keil (1989) noted that children at times had difficulty learning about animals for which origins and featural information conflicted (e.g., an animal that looked like a horse but had cow parents), erroneously remembering one piece of information as conforming to the other (e.g., that the parents were horses). Similarly, Gopnik and Sobel (2000) documented that children's memory for causal information was more often misremembered when it conflicted with perceptual similarity than when it matched perceptual similarity. (See also Flavell, Flavell, Green, and Moses, 1990, Heyman and Gelman, 1999, and Signorella, 1987 for other examples of this phenomenon.) Likewise, attention is certainly guided by prior knowledge, interests, and expectations (Gopnik & Wellman, 1994). More generally, top-down influences on cognitive processes have been recognized and studied for many years (Barsalou, 1992), thus arguing for the influence of theories at multiple levels.

Developmental Issues

A final concern is that the theory theory may pay too little attention to the important developmental changes that take place in categorization during the childhood years. This concern is undoubtedly rooted in the fact that the theory view proposes greater developmental continuity than traditional views, such as Piaget's (e.g., Inhelder & Piaget, 1964). In contrast to a perceptual to conceptual shift, the theory view argues that more sophisticated concepts are present from very early on (Gelman, 1996). However, nearly all the work reviewed in this chapter (and cited as evidence for theory-based categorization) examines children who are at least 3 or 4 years old. Certainly a large gap in present knowledge concerns how these understandings develop, and what are the developmental precursors to the accomplishments of preschool-aged children. We therefore stress that it will be crucial to examine these issues in younger children, including infants.

The developmental question is theoretically significant for at least two reasons. First, it raises the possibility that there may indeed be a "perceptual to conceptual shift"—but one that occurs at an earlier point in development than previously believed. For example, perhaps the shift from "perceptual" to "conceptual" categories occurs when comparing 1-year-olds to 2-year-olds, rather than when comparing 5-year-olds to 7-year-olds. This possibility can be posed in slightly different terms: Is there ever a point in development when children's concepts are "pretheoretic"? And if so, how do theories "switch on"? Ongoing research (e.g., by Mandler, 1988, 1992; Quinn & Eimas, 1996; Rakison & Cohen, 1999; Rakison & Poulin-Dubois, 2001) provides exciting forays into these difficult issues. We remain agnostic on this point, though we lean toward the assumption that children's concepts are never entirely pretheoretic. (See Keil et al., 1998, for fuller discussion of these issues.)

A second reason that a comparison with prelinguistic infants is important is the possibility that language may have an important role in children's concepts. Prelinguistically, infants use categories to make inductive inferences, even concerning nonobvious properties (Baldwin, Markman, & Melartin, 1993). A key question that remains is how the acquisition of language modifies this inductive capacity, if at all. Language may be crucial for anchoring kinds and for conveying culturally sanctioned categories (Gelman & Heyman, 1999; Gelman, Hollander, Star, & Heyman, 2000). For example, language readily conveys that a whale is a not a fish, but such information may be difficult if not impossible to convey in the absence of language. Language labels are thus one of the most efficient ways of passing down to future generations the hard-won knowledge of those who came before.

Thus, we agree that developmental issues have not been sufficiently explored in research to date. However, it is misleading to characterize the theory view as nondevelopmental. Theories are assumed to change over time, perhaps entailing fundamental reorganizations, and such changes yield important parallels to standard developmental theories (e.g., Carey, 1985; Gopnik & Wellman, 1994; Wellman & Gelman, 1998). Moreover, we suggest that a theory view has greater power to explain *causes* of conceptual change, by articulating the relation between theories and evidence. Whether or not a single piece of evidence suffices to verify or falsify a hypothesis may depend on how "valued" and powerful the hypothesis is. If it explains and predicts a lot (e.g., people act according to goals), then we are likely to retain it even in light of much falsifying data (e.g., irrational behavior).

Summary and Conclusions

We have argued that, by preschool age, children's categories are "theory based" in at least two separate senses: they incorporate information beyond the obvious, including ontology, causality, intentions, and functions, and they foster novel inferences. Evidence from numerous laboratories investigating children ages 2–5 years and beyond provide a wealth of converging evidence for this position. However, the position remains controversial, because of at least four considerations: debates concerning the phenomena; a desire for a simpler explanation that does not appeal to theories; a desire for explicit formulations; and a desire for a developmental account that can explain reorganizations with age. In briefly reviewing each of these issues, we have argued that a domain-general, similarity-based account is insufficient to account for the wealth of evidence and that a theory-based approach provides theoretical parsimony. Among the many fruitful questions that remain for future research, it will be important to discover what sorts of developmental precursors are found in infancy and early toddlerhood, the extent to which there is developmental continuity versus discontinuity, and the role that language plays in fostering theory-based categorizaiton.

Acknowledgments

Support for writing this chapter was provided by NICHD Grant R01–HD36043 to the first author. We thank David Rakison and Lisa Oakes for their helpful comments on this chapter.

Note

1. An unresolved question of great theoretical significance is when such flexibility emerges: Is it built into the cognitive system, or is it itself a developmental outcome?

References

Ahn, W. (1998). Why are different features central for natural kinds and artifacts? The role of causal status in determining feature centrality. *Cognition, 69,* 135–178.
Ahn, W., Gelman, S. A., Amsterlaw, J. A., Hohenstein, J., & Kalish, C. W. (2000). Causal status effect in children's categorization. *Cognition, 76,* B35–B43.
Ahn, W., Kalish, C. W., Medin, D. L., & Gelman, S. A. (1995). The role of covariation versus mechanism information in causal attribution. *Cognition, 54,* 299–352.
Ahn, W., Kim, N. S., Lassaline, M. E., & Dennis, M. (in press). Causal status as a determinant of feature centrality. *Cognitive Psychology.*
Ahn, W., & Lassaline, M. E. (1996). *Causal structure in categorization.* Unpublished manuscript.
Au, T. K., Sidle, A. L., & Rollins, K. B. (1993). Developing an intuitive understanding of conservation and contamination: Invisible particles as a plausible mechanism. *Developmental Psychology, 29,* 286–299.
Backscheider, A. G., Shatz, M., & Gelman, S. A. (1993). Preschoolers' ability to distinguish living kinds as a function of regrowth. *Child Development, 64,* 1242–1257.
Baldwin, D. (1989). Priorities in children's expectations about object label reference: Form over color. *Child Development, 60,* 1291–1306.

Baldwin, D. (1992). Clarifying the role of shape in children's taxonomic assumption. *Journal of Experimental Child Psychology, 54*, 392–416.

Baldwin, D. A., Markman, E. M., & Melartin, R. L. (1993). Infants' ability to draw inferences about nonobvious object properties: Evidence from exploratory play. *Child Development, 64*, 711–728.

Bargh, J. A. (1990). Goal ≠ intent: Goal-directed thought and behavior are often unintentional. *Psychological Inquiry, 1*, 248–277.

Baron-Cohen, S. (1995). *Mindblindness: An essay on autism and theory of mind.* Cambridge, MA: MIT Press.

Barrett, S. E., Abdi, H., Murphy, G. L., & Gallagher, J. M. (1993). Theory-based correlations and their role in children's concepts. *Child Development, 64*, 1595–1616.

Barsalou, L. W. (1992). *Cognitive psychology: An overview for cognitive scientists.* Hillsdale, NJ: Erlbaum.

Bertenthal, B. I. (1996). Origins and early development of perception, action, and representation. *Annual Review of Psychology, 47*, 431–459.

Bloom, L. (1993). *The transition from infancy to language: Acquiring the power of expression.* Cambridge: Cambridge University Press.

Bloom, P. (2000). *How children learn the meanings of words.* Cambridge, MA: MIT Press.

Bloom, P., & Markson, L. (1998). Intention and analogy in children's naming of pictorial representations. *Psychological Science, 9*, 200–204.

Bloom, P., Markson, L., & Diesendruck, G. (1998). *Origins of the shape bias.* Unpublished ms., University of Arizona, Tucson.

Carey, S. (1985). *Conceptual change in childhood.* Cambridge, MA: MIT Press.

Carlson, G., & Pelletier, F. J. (1995). *The generic book.* Chicago: Chicago University Press.

Clark, E. V. (1973). What's in a word? On the child's acquisition of semantics in his first language. In T. E. Moore (Ed.), *Cognitive development and the acquisition of language.* New York: Academic Press.

Coley, J. (1993). *Emerging differentiation of folkbiology and folkpsychology: Similarity judgments and property attributions.* Unpublished doctoral dissertation, University of Michigan, Ann Arbor.

Corrigan, R., & Stevenson, C. (1994). Children's causal attributions to states and events described by different classes of verbs. *Cognitive Development, 9*, 235–256.

Croft, W. (1990). *Typology and universals.* New York: Cambridge University Press.

Davidson, N., & Gelman, S. A. (1990). Inductions from novel categories: The role of language and conceptual structure. *Cognitive Development, 5*, 151–176.

Deak, G. O., & Bauer, P. J. (1995). The effects of task comprehension on preschoolers' and adults' categorization choices. *Journal of Experimental Child Psychology, 60*, 393–427.

Deak, G. O., & Bauer, P. J. (1996). The dynamics of preschoolers' categorization choices. *Child Development, 67*, 740–767.

Dewart, M. H. (1979). The role of animate and inanimate nouns in determining sentence voice. *British Journal of Psychology, 70*, 135–141.

Diesendruck, G. (in press). Children's use of conceptual knowledge in the acquisition of object labels. *Developmental Psychology.*

Diesendruck, G., Gelman, S. A., & Lebowitz, K. (1998). Conceptual and linguistic biases in children's word learning. *Developmental Psychology, 34*, 823–839.

Diesendruck, G., & Markson, L. (1999, April). *Function as a criterion in children's object naming.* Poster presented at the biennial meeting of the Society for Research in Child Development, Albuquerque, NM.

Eimas, P. D., & Quinn, P. C. (1994). Studies on the formation of perceptually based basic-level categories in young infants. *Child Development, 65*, 903–917.

Flavell, J. H., Flavell, E. R., Green, F. L., & Moses, L. J. (1990). Young children's understanding of fact beliefs versus value beliefs. *Child Development, 61,* 915–928.

Gelman, R., & Williams, E. M. (1998). Enabling constraints for cognitive development and learning: Domain specificity and epigenesis. In D. Kuhn & R. Siegler (Eds.), *Handbook of child psychology: Vol. 2. Cognitive development* (5th ed., pp. 575–630). New York: Wiley.

Gelman, S. A. (1996). Concepts and theories. In R. Gelman & T. Kit-Fong (Eds.), *Perceptual and cognitive development. Handbook of perception and cognition* (2nd ed., pp. 117–150). San Diego: Academic Press.

Gelman, S. A., & Bloom, P. (2000). Young children are sensitive to how an object was created when deciding what to name it. *Cognition, 76,* 91–103.

Gelman, S. A., Coley, J. D., Rosengren, K. S., Hartman, E., & Pappas, A. (1998). Beyond labeling: The role of maternal input in the acquisition of richly structured categories. *Monographs of the Society for Research in Child Development, 63*(1), Serial No. 253.

Gelman, S. A., Collman, P., & Maccoby, E. E. (1986). Inferring properties from categories versus inferring categories from properties: The case of gender. *Child Development, 57,* 396–404.

Gelman, S. A., Croft, W., Fu, P., Clausner, T., & Gottfried, G. (1998). Why is a pomegranate an apple? The role of shape, taxonomic relatedness, and prior lexical knowledge in children's overextensions of apple and dog. *Journal of Child Language, 25,* 267–291.

Gelman, S. A., & Diesendruck, G. (1999). What's in a concept? Context, variability and psychological essentialism. In I. E. Sigel (Ed.), *Development of mental representation: Theories and applications* (pp. 87–111). Mahwah, NJ: Erlbaum.

Gelman, S. A., & Ebeling, K. S. (1998). Shape and representational status in children's early naming. *Cognition, 66,* B35–B47.

Gelman, S. A., & Heyman, G. D. (1999). Carrot-eaters and creature-believers: The effects of lexicalization on children's inferences about social categories. *Psychological Science, 10,* 489–493.

Gelman, S. A., Hollander, M., Star, J., & Heyman, G. D. (2000). The role of language in the construction of kinds. In D. Medin (Ed.), *Psychology of learning and motivation* (Vol. 39, pp. 201–263). New York: Academic Press.

Gelman, S. A., & Kalish, C. W. (1993). Categories and causality. In R. Pasnak & M. L. Howe (Eds.), *Emerging themes in cognitive development* (pp. 3–32). New York: Springer-Verlag.

Gelman, S. A., & Koenig, M. A. (2001). The role of animacy in children's understanding of *move. Journal of Child Language, 28,* 683–701.

Gelman, S. A., & Markman, E. M. (1986). Categories and induction in young children. *Cognition, 23,* 183–209.

Gelman, S. A., & Markman, E. M. (1987). Young children's inductions from natural kinds: The role of categories and appearances. *Child Development, 58,* 1532–1541.

Gelman, S. A., & Medin, D. L. (1993). What's so essential about essentialism? A different perspective on the interaction of perception, language, and conceptual knowledge. *Cognitive Development, 8,* 157–167.

Gelman, S. A., & Opfer, J. (in press). The development of the animate-inanimate distinction. In U. Goswami (Ed.), *Handbook of childhood cognitive development.* London: Blackwell.

Gelman, S. A., Star, J. R., & Flukes, J. E. (2000). *Children's use of generics in inductive inferences.* Unpublished manuscript, University of Michigan at Ann Arbor.

Gelman, S. A., & Tardif, T. (1998). Acquisition of nouns and verbs in Mandarin and English. In E. V. Clark (Ed.), *The Proceedings of the Twenty-ninth Annual Child Language Research Forum* (pp. 27–36). Stanford, CA: Center for the Study of Language and Information.

Gelman, S. A., & Wellman, H. M. (1991). Insides and essences: Early understandings of the non-obvious. *Cognition, 38*, 213–244.

Gelman, S. A., Wilcox, S. A., & Clark, E. V. (1989). Conceptual and lexical heirarchies in young children. *Cognitive Development, 4*, 309–326.

Gentner, D., & Namy, L. (1999). Comparison in the development of categories. *Cognitive Development, 14*, 487–513.

Gentner, D., & Rattermann, M. J. (1991). Language and the career of similarity. In S. A. Gelman & J. P. Byrnes (Eds.), *Perspectives on language and thought: Interrelations in development* (pp. 225–277). New York: Cambridge University Press.

Golinkoff, R. M., Harding, C. G., Carlson, V., & Sexton, M. W. (1984). The infant's perception of causal events: The distinction between animate and inanimate objects. In L. P. Lipsitt & C. Rovee-Collier (Eds.), *Advances in infancy research.* Norwood, NJ: Ablex.

Goodman, N. (1972). Seven strictures on similarity. In N. Goodman (Ed.), *Problems and projects* (pp. 437–447). Indianapolis: Bobbs-Merrill.

Gopnik, A., & Meltzoff, A. N. (1997). *Words, thoughts and theories.* Cambridge, MA: MIT Press.

Gopnik, A., & Sobel, D. (2000). Detecting blickets: How young children use information about novel causal powers in categorization and induction. *Child Development, 71*, 1205–1222.

Gopnik, A., & Wellman, H. M. (1994). The theory theory. In L. A. Hirschfeld and S. A. Gelman (Eds.), *Mapping the mind: Domain specificity in cognition and culture* (pp. 257–293). New York: Cambridge University Press.

Heit, E., & Rubenstein, J. (1994). Similarity and property effects in inductive reasoning. *Journal of Experimental Psychology: Learning, Memory, & Cognition, 20*, 411–422.

Heyman, G. D., & Gelman, S. A. (1998). Young children use motive information to make trait inferences. *Developmental Psychology, 34*, 310–321.

Heyman, G. D., & Gelman, S. A. (1999). The use of trait labels in making psychological inferences. *Child Development, 70*, 604–619.

Hickling, A. K., & Gelman, S. A. (1995). How does your garden grow? Early conceptualization of seeds and their place in plant growth cycle. *Child Development, 66*, 856–876.

Hirschfeld, L. A. (1996). *Race in the making: Cognition, culture, and the child's construction of human kinds.* Cambridge, MA: MIT Press.

Hirschfeld, L. A. (1999). *L'enfant terrible:* Anthropology and its aversion to children. *Etnofoor, 12*, 5–26.

Imai, M., Gentner, D., & Uchida, N. (1994). Children's theories of word meaning: The role of shape similarity in early acquisition. *Cognitive Development, 9*, 45–75.

Inhelder, B., & Piaget J. (1964). *The early growth of logic in the child.* London: Routledge and Kegan Paul.

Johannsen, G. (1973). Visual perception of biological motion and a model for its analysis. *Perception and Psychophysics, 14*, 201–211.

Johnson, K. E., Mervis, C. B., & Boster, J. S. (1992). Developmental changes within the structure of the mammal domain. *Developmental Psychology, 28*, 74–83.

Johnson, S. C., Slaughter, V., & Carey, S. (1998). Whose gaze will infants follow? The elicitation of gaze following in 12-month-olds. *Developmental Science, 1*, 233–238.

Jones, S. S., & Smith, L. B. (1993). The place of perception in children's concepts. *Cognitive Development, 8*, 113–139.

Kalish, C. W. (1996). Preschoolers' understanding of germs as invisible mechanisms. *Cognitive Development, 11*, 83–106.

Keil, F. C. (1979). *Semantic and conceptual development: An ontological perspective.* Cambridge, MA: MIT Press.

Keil, F. C. (1989). *Concepts, kinds and cognitive development.* Cambridge, MA: MIT Press.

Keil, F. C. (1994). The birth and nurturance of concepts by domains: The origins of concepts of living things. In L. A. Hirschfeld & S. A. Gelman (Eds.), *Mapping the mind: Domain specificity in cognition and culture.* New York: Cambridge University Press.

Keil, F. C. (1995). The growth of causal undersandings of natural kinds. In D. Sperber & D. Premack (Eds.), *Causal Cognition: A multidisciplinary debate.* New York: Oxford University Press.

Keil, F. C., Smith, W. C., Simons, D. J., & Levin, D. T. (1998). Two dogmas of conceptual empiricism: Implications for hybrid models of the structure of knowledge. *Cognition, 65,* 103–135.

Kemler Nelson, D. G. (1999). Attention to functional properties in toddlers' naming and poblem-solving. *Cognitive Development, 14,* 77–100.

Kemler Nelson, D. G., & Eleven Swarthmore College Students. (1995). Principle-based inferences in young children's categorization: Revisiting the impact of function on the naming of artifacts. *Cognitive Development, 10,* 347–380.

Kemler Nelson, D. G., Frankenfield, A., Morris, C., & Blair, E. (2000). Young children's use of functional information to categorize artifacts: Three factors that matter. *Cognition, 77,* 133–168.

Kemler Nelson, D. G., Russell, R., Duke, N., & Jones, K. (2000). Two-year-olds will name artifacts by their functions. *Child Development, 71,* 1271–1288.

Koff, E., Kramer, P. E., & Fowles, B. (1980). Effects of event probability and animateness on children's comprehension of active and passive sentences. *Journal of Psychology, 104,* 157–163.

Kolstad, V., & Baillargeon, R. (1996). *Appearance- and knowledge-based responses of 10.5-month-old infants to containers.* Unpublished manuscript, University of Illinois at Champaign-Urbana.

Kuhn, T. S. (1970). *The structure of scientific revolutions,* 2nd ed. Chicago: University of Chicago Press.

Krascum, R. M., & Andrew, S. (1998). The effects of theories on children's acquisition of family-resemblance categories. *Child Development, 69,* 333–346.

Landau, B., Jones, S. S., & Smith, L. B. (1992). Perception, ontology, and naming in young children: Commentary on Soja, Carey and Spelke. *Cognition, 43,* 85–91.

Landau, B., Smith, L. B., & Jones, S. S. (1988). The importance of shape in early lexical learning. *Cognitive Development, 3,* 299–321.

Landau, B., Smith, L. B., & Jones, S. S. (1998). Object shape, object function, and object name. *Journal of Memory and Language, 38,* 1–27.

Lassaline, M. E., & Murphy, G. L. (1996). Induction and category coherence. *Psychonomic Bulletin and Review, 3,* 95–99.

Legerstee, M. (1992). A review of the animate-inanimate distinction in infancy: Implications for models of social and cognitive knowing. *Early Development and Parenting, 1,* 59–67.

Legerstee, M., Barna, J., & Diadamo, C. (2000). Precursors to the development of intention at 6 months: Understanding people and their actions. *Developmental Psychology, 36,* 627–634.

Legerstee, M., Pomerlau, A., Malcuit, G., & Feider, H. (1987). The development of infants' responses to people and a doll: Implications for research in communication. *Infant Behavior and Development, 10,* 81–95.

Lempert, H. (1989). Animacy constraints on preschool children's acquisition of syntax. *Child Development, 60,* 237–245.

Lempert, H. (1990). Acquisition of passives: The role of patient animacy, salience, and lexical accessibility. *Journal of Child Language, 17,* 677–696.

Lizotte, D. J. (2001, April). *Children's conception of the essential aspects of animal kinds.* Poster presented at the biennial meeting of the Society for Research in Child Development, Minneapolis, MN.

Madole, K., & Cohen, L. B. (1995). The role of object parts in infants' attention to form-function correlations. *Developmental Psychology, 31,* 637–648.

Madole, K., Cohen, L. B., & Bradley, K. (1994, June). *Ten-month-old infants categorize form but not function.* Poster presented at the Ninth Biennial International Conference for Infant Studies, Paris.

Madole, K., Oakes, L. M., & Cohen, L. B. (1993). Developmental changes in infants' attention to function and form-function correlations. *Cognitive Development, 8,* 189–209.

Mandler, J. M. (1988). How to build a baby: I. On the development of an accessible representational system. *Cognitive Development, 3,* 113–136.

Mandler, J. M. (1992). How to build a baby: II. Conceptual primitives. *Psychological Review, 99,* 587–604.

Mandler, J. M., Bauer, P. J., & McDonough, L. (1991). Separating the sheep from the goats: Differentiating global categories. *Cognitive Psychology, 23,* 263–298.

Mandler, J. M., & McDonough, L. (1993). Concept formation in infancy. *Cognitive Development, 8,* 291–318.

Mandler, J. M., & McDonough, L. (1996). Drinking and driving don't mix: Inductive generalization in infancy. *Cognition, 59,* 307–335.

Mandler, J. M., & McDonough, L. (1998). On developing a knowledge base in infancy. *Developmental Psychology, 34,* 1274–1288.

Markman, E. M. (1989). *Categorization and naming in children: Problems of induction.* Cambridge, MA: MIT Press.

Martinez, I. M. (2000). *The effects of language on children's understanding of agency and causation.* Unpublished doctoral dissertation, University of Michigan, Ann Arbor.

Martinez, I., Hirschfeld, L. A., & Heyman, G. (1999, March). *Children's conceptions of the transmission of properties across social categories.* Paper presented at the 11th Annual meeting of the American Psychological Society, Denver.

Massey, C. M., & Gelman, R. (1988). Preschooler's ability to decide whether a photographed unfamiliar object can move itself. *Developmental Psychology, 24,* 307–317.

McCarrell, N. S., & Callanan, M. A. (1995). Form-function correspondence in children's inference. *Child Development, 66,* 532–546.

Medin, D. L. (1989). Concepts and conceptual structure. *American Psychologist, 44,* 1469–1481.

Medin, D. L., & Shoben, E. J. (1988). Context and structure in conceptual combination. *Cogntive Psychology, 20,* 158–190.

Meltzoff, A. N. (1995). Understanding the intentions of others: Re-enactment of intended acts by 18-month-old children. *Developmental Psychology, 31,* 838–850.

Merriman, W. E., & Bowman, L. L. (1989). The mutual exclusivity bias in children's word learning. *Monographs of the Society for Research in Child Development, 54*(3–4). Serial No. 220.

Mervis, C. B., & Rosch, E. (1981). Categorization of natural objects. *Annual Review of Psychology, 32,* 89–115.

Michotte, A. (1963). *The perception of causality.* London: Methuen.

Morris, M. W., Nisbett, R. E., & Peng, K. (1995). Causal attribution across domains and cultures. In D. Sperber, D. Premack, & A. J. Premack (Eds.), *Causal cognition* (pp. 577–614). New York: Oxford University Press.

Murphy, G. L. (1993). Theories and concept formation. In I. Van Mechelen & J. Hampton (Eds.), *Categories and concepts: Theoretical views and inductive data analysis. Cognitive science series* (pp. 172–200). London: Academic Press.

Murphy, G. L. (2000). Explanatory concepts. In F. C. Keil & R. A. Wilson (Eds.) *Explanation and cognition* (pp. 361–392). Cambridge, MA: MIT Press.

Murphy, G. L., & Allopenna, P. D. (1994). The locus of knowledge effects in concept learning. *Journal of Experimental Psychology: Learning, Memory, and Cognition, 20,* 904–919.

Murphy, G. L., & Medin, D. L. (1985). The role of theories in conceptual coherence. *Psychological Review, 92,* 289–316.

Pappas, A., & Gelman, S. A. (1998). Generic noun phrases in mother-child conversations. *Journal of Child Language, 25,* 19–33.

Pazzani, M. J. (1991). Influence of prior knowledge on concept acquisition: Experimental and computational results. *Journal of Experimental Psychology: Learning, Memory, and Cognition, 17,* 416–432.

Prasada, S. (2000). Acquiring generic knowledge. *Trends in Cognitive Sciences, 4,* 66–72.

Premack, D., & Premack, A. J. (1997). Motor competence as integral to attribution of goal. *Cognition, 63,* 235–242.

Quine, W. V. O. (1977). Natural kinds. In S. P. Schwartz (Ed.), *Naming, necessity and natural kinds.* Ithaca, NY: Cornell University Press.

Quinn, P. C., & Eimas, P. D. (1996). Perceptual organization and categorization in young infants. In C. Rovee-Collier & L. P. Lipsitt (Eds.), *Advances in infancy research* (pp. 1–36). Norwood, NJ: Ablex.

Rakison, D. H., & Butterworth, G. E. (1998). Infants' use of object parts in early categorization. *Developmental Psychology, 34,* 49–62.

Rakison, D. H., & Cohen, L. B. (1999). Infants' use of functional parts in basic-like categorization. *Developmental Science, 2,* 423–431.

Rakison, D. H., & Poulin-Dubois, D. (2001). The developmental origin of the animate-inanimate distinction. *Psychological Bulletin, 127,* 209–228.

Rips, L. J. (1989). Similarity, typicality, and categorization. In S. Vosniadou & A. Ortony (Eds.), *Similarity and analogical reasoning* (pp. 21–59). New York: Cambridge University Press.

Rips, L. J., & Collins, A. (1993). Categories and resemblance. *Journal of Experimental Psychology: General, 30,* 468–486.

Rosch, E. (1978). Principles of categorization. In E. Rosch & B. B. Lloyd (Eds.), *Cognition and Categorization* (pp. 27–48). Hillsdale, NJ: Erlbaum.

Shipley, E. F. (1993). Categories, hierarchies, and induction. In D. Medin (Ed.), *The psychology of learning and motivation. Advances in research and theory* (pp. 265–301). San Diego: Academic Press.

Siegal, M. (1988). Children's knowledge of contagion and contamination as causes of illness. *Child Development, 59,* 1353–1359.

Sigel, I. E. (1953). Developmental trends in the abstraction ability of children. *Child Development, 24,* 131–144.

Sigel, I. E. (1983). Is the concept of the concept still elusive or what do we know about concept development? In E. K. Scholnick (Ed.), *New trends in conceptual representation: Challenges to Piaget's theory?* (pp. 239–273). Hillsdale, NJ: Erlbaum.

Signorella, M. L. (1987). Gender schemata: Individual differences and context effects. In L. S. Liben & M. L. Signorella (Eds.), *Children's gender schemata* (pp. 23–37). San Francisco: Jossey-Bass.

Silverstein, M. (1986). Cognitive implications of a referential hierarchy. In M. Hickmann (Ed.), *Social and functional approaches to language and thought* (pp. 125–164). New York: Academic Press.

Simons, D. J., & Keil, F. C. (1995). An abstract to concrete shift in the development of biological thought: The insides story. *Cognition, 56,* 129–163.

Slobin, D. I. (1985). *The cross-linguistic study of language acquisition: Vol. 1*. Hillsdale, NJ: Erlbaum.

Slotta, J. D., Chi, M. T., & Joram, E. (1995). Assessing students' misclassifications of physics concepts: An ontological basis for conceptual change. *Cognition and Instruction, 13*, 373–400.

Smith, L. B., & Heise, D. (1992). Perceptual similarity and conceptual structure. In B. Burns (Ed.), *Percepts, concepts, and categories* (pp. 233–271). Amsterdam: North-Holland.

Smith, L. B., Jones, S. S., & Landau, B. (1996). Naming in young children: a dumb attentional mechanism? *Cognition, 60*, 143–171.

Soja, N. N., Carey, S., & Spelke, E. S. (1991). Ontological categories guide young children's inductions of word meaning: Object terms and substance terms. *Cognition, 38*, 179–211.

Soja, N. N., Carey, S., & Spelke, E. S. (1992). Perception, ontology, and word meaning. *Cognition, 45*, 101–107.

Sommers, F. (1963). Types and ontology. *Philosophical Review, 72*, 327–363.

Spalding, T. L., & Murphy, G. L. (1999). What is learned in knowledge-related categories? Evidence from typicality and feature frequency judgments. *Memory and Cognition, 27*, 856–867.

Sperber, D., Premack, D., & Premack, A. J. (Eds.) (1995). *Causal cognition: A multidisciplinary debate*. New York: Oxford University Press.

Springer, K. (1996). Young children's understanding of a biological basis for parent-offspring relations. *Child Development, 67*, 2841–2856.

Tomasello, M., & Barton, M. E. (1994). Learning words in nonostensive contexts. *Developmental Psychology, 30*, 639–650.

Tversky, B. (1985). Development of taxonomic organization of named and pictured categories. *Developmental Psychology, 21*, 1111–1119.

Ward, T. B., Becker, A. H., Hass, S. D., & Vela, E. (1991). Attribute availability and the shape bias in children's category generalization. *Cognitive Development, 6*, 143–167.

Waxman, S. R., & Braig, B. (1996). *Stars and starfish: How far can shape take us?* Paper presented at the 10th Biennial Conference on Infant Studies, Providence, RI.

Waxman, S. R., Lynch, E. B., Casey, K. L., & Baer, L. (1997). Setters and samoyeds: The emergence of subordinate level categories as a basis for inductive inference in preschool-age children. *Developmental Psychology, 33*, 1074–1090.

Wellman, H. M. (1990). *The child's theory of mind*. Cambridge, MA: MIT Press.

Wellman, H. M., & Gelman, S. A. (1992). Cognitive development: foundational theories of core domains. *Annual Review of Psychology, 43*, 337–375.

Wellman, H. M., & Gelman, S. A. (1998). Knowledge acquisition. In D. Kuhn & R. Siegler (Eds.), *Handbook of child psychology: Vol. 2. Cognitive development* (5th ed., pp. 523–573). New York: Wiley.

White, P. A. (1995). *The understanding of causation and the production of action: From infancy to adulthood*. Hove UK: Erlbaum.

Wisniewski, E. J., & Medin, D. L. (1994). On the interaction of theory and data in concept learning. *Cognitive Science, 18*, 221–281.

Woodward, A. L. (1998). Infants selectively encode the goal object of an actor's reach. *Cognition, 69*, 1–34.

Woodward, A. L., & Markman, E. M. (1998). Early word learning. In D. Kuhn & R. Siegler (Eds.), *Handbook of child psychology: Vol. 2. Cognitive development* (5th ed., pp. 371–420). New York: Wiley.

Yamauchi, T., & Markman, A. B. (1998). Category learning by inference and classification. *Journal of Memory and Language, 39*, 124–148.

CHAPTER FOURTEEN

The Acquisition and Use of Implicit Categories in Early Development

Denis Mareschal

T HE CURRENT CONSENSUS in the adult literature is that human category learning relies on multiple systems (Ashby, Alfonso-Reese, Turken, & Waldron, 1998; Ashby, & Waldron, 1999; Erikson & Kruchke, 1998; Smith, Patalano, & Jonides, 1998). This conclusion is based on two strands of evidence (see Ashby & Ells, 2001, for a recent review of this evidence). First, there are dissociable memory systems in the brain with different characteristics, and each of these systems can, in principle, store category information. Second, different kinds of categorization tasks seem to load differently on these different memory systems.

The exact number of categorization systems remains an open question. However, it is generally agreed that one system is rule or theory based and is closely linked to the participants' verbal abilities. It is also agreed that the other system (or systems) involves implicit learning. However, there is little consensus about the nature of the implicit category learning system or whether the system itself can be subdivided into multiple subsystems (Ashby & Ells, 2001; Ashby & Waldron, 1999). Nevertheless, the key features of the implicit system are: (1) that learning appears to be procedural, and (2) that the product of learning is not available for explicit access by the cognitive system. Much of the current debate is centered on identifying the characteristics of these systems, discovering how they interact, and mapping these systems onto functional neural systems.

Thus, according to the adult literature, early infant categorization behaviors should reflect the functioning of the implicit system because infants are by definition prelinguistic and, therefore, do not have access to linguistic, theory-based modes of category formation. In this chapter, I will explore how far an implicit account of categorization can explain the categorization performance of infants and young children. To this end, I will discuss a combination of connectionist neural network modeling and experimental work with infants and young children.

Computational models provide an explicit formulation of the information-processing mechanisms that underlie performance on a task. Connectionist models are cognitive models loosely based on neural information processing (Elman, Bates, Johnson, Karmiloff-Smith, Parisi, & Plunkett, 1997; Mareschal, 2002; Mareschal & Shultz, 1996). They are not meant to be neural models. Instead, they are intended as cognitive models that embody some of the principles of neural information processing (e.g., associative correlation-based learning, distributed representations). Categorization in connectionist networks arises as a by-product of information storage in a dynamic associative memory (Knapp & Anderson, 1984). As the associative learning mechanism attempts to encode individual stimuli, features with predictive value that are repeatedly presented are reinforced, while features that are unique to individual exemplars are overwritten by the successive presentation of different exemplars. As a result, such networks develop an implicit, prototype-based category representation that reflects the distribution of features in the environment. It is implicit in the sense that: (1) there are no explicit representations of a category marked by the equivalent of a linguistic symbol, and (2) the categories are not usually explicitly retrievable by the system performing the categorization.

In assessing the role of implicit categorization, I will limit my discussion to two distinct research domains. The first is perceptual categorization in early infancy. Here, infants are shown a sequence of images that can be construed as forming a category. Because infants cannot speak, categorization is inferred from their subsequent preference for looking at novel members of the same category or novel members of a novel category. The second domain I will discuss is category-based inductive inference. In this domain, young children are presented with an exemplar that is labeled as being a member of one category but is more similar in appearance to a second category. The children are then required to infer a hidden property of the target object. Because label (verbal category information) and similarity (perceptual information) conflict, this paradigm allows one to assess how much young children rely on implicit similarity-based categories as opposed to verbal theory-based categories. In fact, my colleagues and I have found that much of children's inductive inference behavior can be explained by appealing to the same mechanisms that account for implicit categorization in infancy.

Infant Perceptual Categorization

Infant visual categorization tasks rely on preferential looking techniques, based on the finding that infants direct more attention to unfamiliar or unexpected stimuli. The standard interpretation of this behavior is that the infants are comparing an input stimulus to an internal representation of the same stimulus (e.g., Charlesworth, 1969; Cohen, 1973; Sokolov, 1963). As long as there is a discrepancy between the information stored in the internal representation and the visual input, the infant continues to attend to the stimulus. While attending to the stimulus, the infant updates its internal representation. When the information in the internal representation is no longer discrepant with respect to the visual input, attention is switched elsewhere. When a familiar object is presented, there is little or no attending, because the infant already has a reliable internal representation of that object. In contrast, when an unfamiliar or unexpected object is presented, there is much attending because an internal representation has to be constructed or adjusted. The degree to which the novel object differs from existing internal representations determines the amount of adjusting that has to be done, hence the duration of attention. We used a connectionist autoencoder to model the relation between attention and representation construction (Mareschal & French, 1997, 2000, Mareschal, French, & Quinn, 2000; Schafer & Mareschal, in press).

Connectionist models are computer models loosely based on the principles of neural information processing (Elman, Bates, Johnson, Karmiloff-Smith, Parisi, & Plunkett, 1996; McLeod, Plunkett, & Rolls, 1998; Rumelhart & McClelland, 1986) They are made up of simple processing units (idealized neurons) interconnected via weighted communication lines (idealized synapses). Units are often represented as circles, and the weighted communication lines as lines between these circles. Activation flows from unit to unit via these connection weights. However, most applications of connectionist networks impose constraints on the way activation can flow. Activation (information) is constrained to move in one direction only. Some units (those units through which information enters the network) are called *input units.* Other units (those units through which information leaves the network) are called *output units.* All other units are called *hidden units.* In a feed-forward network, information is first encoded as a pattern of activation across the bank of input units. That activation then filters up through a first layer of weights until it produces a pattern of activation across the band of hidden units. The pattern of activation produced across the hidden units is an *internal rerepresentation* of the information originally presented to the network. The activation at the hidden units continues to flow through the network until it reaches the output unit. The pattern of activation produced at the output units is taken as the network's response to the initial input.

The network's global behavior is determined by the connection weights. As activation flows through the network, it is transformed by the set of connection weights between successive layers in network. Learning (i.e., adapting one's behavior) is accomplished by tuning the connection weights until some stable behavior is obtained. Backpropagation (Rumelhart, Hinton, & William, 1986) is a popular training algorithm for connectionist networks that attempts to adjust the connection weights in the network such that the network's output gets progressively closer and closer to some desired target. The target can be set by some external agent (as is the case in supervised learning) or it can be obtained directly by the network when observing the environment (unsupervised learning). A more detailed discussion of connectionist methods and their application to modeling infant learning and development can be found elsewhere (e.g., Mareschal, 2000, 2002)

An autoencoder is a feedforward connectionist network with a single layer of hidden units (Ackley, Hinton, & Sejnowski, 1985; Rumelhart & McClelland, 1986; see fig. 14.1B). The network learns to reproduce on the output units the pattern of activation across the input units. Learning in such networks is unsupervised because the (perceptual) input signal also serves as the training signal for the output. The number of hidden units must be smaller than the number of input or output units. This architectural constraint produces a bottleneck in the flow of information through the network. Learning in an autoencoder consists of developing a more compact internal representation of the input (at the hidden-unit level) that is sufficiently reliable to reproduce all the information in the original input. Information is first compressed into an internal representation and then expanded to reproduce the original input. The successive cycles of training in the autoencoder are an iterative process by which a reliable internal representation of the input is developed. The reliability of the internal representation is tested by expanding it and comparing the resulting output predictions to the actual stimulus being encoded.

A direct implication of the iterative process of weight adjustment in connectionist networks is that, in general, networks with more error at the outputs will have to engage in more cycle of weight adjustments to reach some acceptable threshold of acceptable error than the number of cycles required by a network with an initially lower level of output error.

We suggest that during the period of captured attention, infants are actively involved in an iterative process of encoding visual input into an internal representation and then assessing that representation against continuing perceptual input. This is accomplished by using the internal representation to predict what the properties of the stimulus are. As long as the representation fails to predict the stimulus properties, the infant continues to fixate the stimulus and to update the internal representation.

This modeling approach has several implications. It suggests that infant looking times are positively correlated with network error. The greater the error, the longer the looking time. Stimuli presented for a very short time will be encoded less well than those presented for a longer period. However, prolonged exposure after error

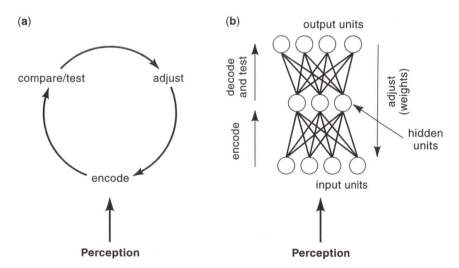

Figure 14.1. Habituation as representation construction in (A) infants and (B) autoencoder networks (adapted from Mareschal & French, 2000).

(attention) has fallen off will not improve memory of the stimulus. The degree to which error (looking time) increases on presentation of a novel object depends on the similarity between the novel object and the familiar object. Presenting a series of similar objects leads to a progressive error drop on future similar objects. A prototype of the set of objects leads to lower error than individual objects. All of this is true of both autoencoders (where output error is the measurable quantity) and infants (where looking time is the measurable quantity).

Asymmetric Exclusivity

At first glance, the perceptual categories acquired by infants appear to be similar to those developed by adults. However, occasionally, the infant categories differ dramatically from those of adults. Quinn, Eimas, and Rosenkrantz (1993) report one striking example. These authors found that when 3.5-month-olds were shown a series of cat photographs, the infants would develop a category of *Cat* that included novel cats and excluded novel dogs (in accordance with the adult category of *Cat*). However, when 3.5-month-olds were shown a series of dog photographs, they would develop a category of *Dog* that included novel dogs but also included novel cats (in contrast to the adult category of *Dog*). There is an asymmetry in the exclusivity of the Cat and Dog categories developed by 3.5-month-olds.

My colleagues and I explored whether the preferential looking model described earlier exhibited the same asymmetries (Mareschal, French, & Quinn, 2000). The actual stimuli used to familiarize and test the infants in the Quinn et al. (1993) studies were measured along 10 visible dimensions (i.e., head length, head width, eye separation, ear separation, ear length, nose length, nose width, leg length, vertical extent, and horizontal extent). We then presented these data to the autoencoder models. In doing so, we tried to steer as closely as possible to the original procedure used to familiarize infants. That is, networks were exposed to six pairs of stimuli for fixed period during the familiarization phase. Not only did the networks develop categorical representations of the cat and dog stimuli, but they developed the same exclusivity asymmetries as the infants had (i.e., the category of Cat excluded novel dogs, whereas the category of Dog did not exclude novel cats).

Because neural networks internalize the distribution statistics of features in their environment, we turned to the data for an explanation of this asymmetry. For almost all features, the distribution of Cat values was subsumed within the distribution of Dog values in the familiarization set used in these studies (fig. 14.2). That is, for these stimuli, most cats were plausible dogs, whereas most dogs were not plausible cats. This implied that infants' performance on these tasks is largely bottom-up. Behavior was determined by the feature distribution in the stimuli and not by an emerging taxonomic conceptual system.

The distribution account derived from the model predicts that the same asymmetry will persist even if infants and networks are familiarized with a mixed set of cat and dog exemplars. Indeed, changing the order of familiarization does not change the distribution of features in those exemplars. This prediction was first verified with the model, then tested with infants. Figure 14.3 show's the model's output error (looking time) when tested with a novel cat or a novel dog, for networks trained on eight

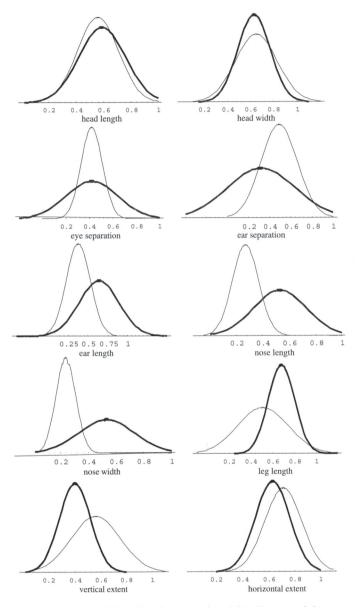

Figure 14.2. Probability distributions of cat (thin lines) and dog (thick lines) feature values (after Mareschal et al., 2000).

cats and four dogs (the mainly cat conditions) and for networks trained on eight dogs and four cats (the mainly dog condition). Networks in the mainly cat condition showed greater error to a novel dog than a novel cat, thereby predicting a strong preference for looking at a novel dog over a novel cat. In contrast, the networks in the mainly dog condition showed no difference in error to a novel dog or a novel cat, thereby predicting no preference for a novel cat or a novel dog.

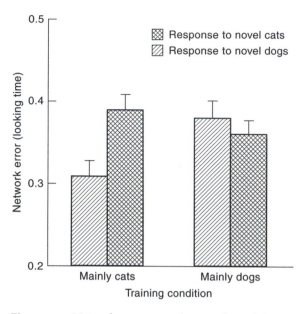

Figure 14.3. Network error to novel cats and novel dogs after training with eight cats and four dogs (mainly cats) or eight dogs and four cats (mainly dogs) (after Mareschal, French, & Quinn et al. 2000).

We found that 3- to 4-months-olds familiarized with 75 percent cats and 25 percent dogs formed a category of Cat that excluded dogs, whereas those familiarized with 75 percent dogs and 25 percent cats form a category of Dog that did not exclude cats (Mareschal, French, & Quinn, 2000). Thus, the asymmetric exclusivity of Cat and Dog perceptual categories was found to persist even with mixed familiarization, thereby corroborating the model's prediction.

Asymmetric Interference

Connectionist networks are very susceptible to a form of retroactive interference called catastrophic interference, in which subsequently acquired material overwrites previously acquired material (French, 1999; McCloskey & Cohen, 1989; Ratcliff, 1990). Because connectionist networks have been used to model a category-based memory system, one might expect to find evidence of catastrophic interference in young infants' sequential category learning.

Here again, my colleagues and I (Mareschal & French, 1997; Mareschal, Quinn, & French, 2002) used the autoencoder model described earlier to explore the effect of sequential category learning in infants and connectionist networks. The prior learning of one category may facilitate the subsequent learning of a second category by providing a contrasting reference that helps define the extension of the category. Alternatively, the prior learning of one category may inhibit the subsequent learning of a second category in a manner analogous to proactive interference. Equally, the subsequent learning of a second category may enhance the memory of the first category, or it may interfere with the memory of the first category.

The distribution account of Cat and Dog category learning predicts the presence of asymmetric interference in the sequential learning of these two categories. Learning Dog after having previously learned Cat should result in the eradication of the Cat category. This is because the majority of new dog exemplars encountered will lie outside the Cat category boundary. In contrast, learning Cat after previously having learned Dog should not interfere with the category of Dog. This is because most of the Cat exemplars encountered will be consistent with the previously acquired Dog category boundary. This prediction was confirmed with the model and was constituted a strong test of the model's category learning mechanisms.

The prediction of asymmetric retroactive interference was found to hold true for 3- to 4-month-olds required to learn the Cat and Dog categories sequentially using the same stimulus set as just described (Mareschal et al., 2002). That is, infants familiarized with cats first showed an initial preference for a novel dog when tested with a novel dog and a novel cat. However, following a second familiarization phase with dogs, the same infants subsequently failed to show a preference for a novel cat over a novel dog. This was interpreted as evidence that the initial Cat category representation had been interfered with by the intervening familiarization with dogs. In contrast, infants familiarized with dogs first showed no initial preference for a novel cat when tested with a novel dog and a novel cat. Moreover, following a second familiarization phase with cats, the same infants subsequently still failed to show a preference for a novel dog over a novel cat. This was interpreted as evidence that the initial Dog category representation had not been interfered with by the intervening familiarization with cats.

Both the asymmetries in category exclusivity and the interference can be traced to an inclusion relation in the distribution of feature values for cat and dog exemplars used to familiarize infants in the experimental procedure, and the fact that the hidden-unit representation in the network reflects this distribution. An analysis of the data explains *why* asymmetric categorization is observed in infant behavior, while the connectionist model explains *how* those data get translated into behavior. Knowing that there is an inclusion relation in the data is not enough to predict an asymmetry in the behavior. Many computational systems could process the same data and not produce an asymmetry in categorization. It is because the connectionist network develops internal representations that reflect the distribution of features in the data that this behavior is observed.

Developing Separate Categories

The previous sections describe how connectionist autoencoder networks can develop categories that have overlap structure similar to that of those developed by young infants. However, the goal of categorization is to separate items into distinct categories, not just to conjoin them. In this section I explore the basis on which distinct categories are developed by infants and connectionist autoencoder networks.

Younger (1985, 1990; chap. 4) examined 10-month-olds' abilities to use the correlation between the variation of attributes to segregate items into categories. In the real world certain ranges of attribute values tend to co-occur (Rosch, Mervis, Gray, Johnson, & Boyes-Braem, 1976). Thus, animals with long necks might tend to have long legs, whereas animals with short necks might tend to have short legs. Younger examined whether infants could use such covariation cues to segment artificial animal line drawings into separate categories.

In one experiment (Younger, 1985), infants were familiarized with either (1) a set of exemplars in which any feature value could occur with any other feature value, and (2) a set of exemplars in which sets of features were constrained to covary. They were then tested with either: (1) an exemplar whose attribute values were the average of all the previously experienced values along each dimension, or (2) an exemplar containing the modal attribute values (i.e., the most frequently experienced values) along each dimension. Preference for a modal versus the average stimulus was interpreted as evidence that the infants had formed a single category from all the exemplars (as evidenced by the greater familiarity of the average stimulus). Preference for the average stimulus was interpreted as evidence that the infants had formed two categories (as indicated by the lesser familiarity of the average stimulus) since the boundary between correlated clusters lay on the average values. Younger found that 10-month-olds looked more at the modal stimuli when the familiarization set was unconstrained (i.e., all attribute values occurred with every other attribute value), suggesting that they had formed a single representation of the complete set of exemplars. However, the 10-month-olds looked more at the average stimuli when the familiarization set was constrained such that ranges of feature values were correlated, suggesting that they had formed two distinct categories.

To model infant performance in this study, the same artificial animal stimuli used by Younger were measured for presentation to connectionist autoencoder networks (Mareschal & French, 2000). Twenty-four networks were presented with eight stimuli in which the full range of values in one dimension occurred with the full range of values in the other dimension (the broad condition). Another 24 networks were presented with the eight stimuli in which restricted ranges of values were correlated (the narrow condition). The networks in both conditions were then tested with stimuli made up of the average feature values or the modal feature values. As with the 10-month-olds, networks familiarized in the narrow condition showed more error (preferred to look) when presented with the average test stimulus than the modal test stimuli. Similarly, as with the 10-month-olds, networks familiarized in the broad condition showed more error (preferred to look) when presented with the modal test stimuli than the average test stimuli. Thus autoencoder networks use the same feature covariation information to separate out categories as infants do.

Internal Representations

One advantage of computer models is that they can be dissected to help understand what produces the observed behaviors. This section describes the internal representations developed by the networks and discusses how they lead to the observed categorization behaviors described here.

When an exemplar is presented to the network, activation flows from the input units to the hidden units. The pattern of activation across the hidden units is an internal representation of that input. It is the internal representation that drives the response at the output. Every exemplar will produce a different activation pattern across the hidden units. One way to explore these representations is to plot them as points in a three-dimensional space. For any given input, each of the three hidden units will have some activation value. These three values can be interpreted as co-ordinates within that three-dimensional space. Each internal representation (arising from each separate exemplar) corresponds to a point in that space.

Figure 14.4 shows the distribution of exemplars within the hidden-unit space for networks trained in the narrow and broad conditions in the preceding example. In the narrow condition (fig. 14.4A), exemplars are grouped together in two distinct clusters. One cluster corresponds to those exemplars forming one category, and the other cluster corresponds to those exemplars forming the second category. The test exemplars are also plotted. Note that the two modal exemplars each fall within (or very close to) one of the category clusters, whereas the average exemplar falls between the two clusters. This explains why there is more error (longer looking) to the average exemplar than to either of the modal exemplars. The modal patterns fall within areas that are well covered by the category representations, for which the network has already learned to make accurate responses. In contrast, the average pattern falls in an area that is not well covered, and hence, for which the network has no experience of making accurate responses.

Figure 14.4B shows the exemplars within hidden unit space for networks trained in the broad condition. The internal representations are spread throughout the hidden-unit space, reflecting the fact that the exemplars are maximally spread out. Remember that in this condition any feature value can occur with any other feature value. All three of the test stimuli (the average and modal stimuli) project to a similar location at the center of the space. This is because all three have comparable similarities (in terms of feature values) to all of the familiarization exemplars considered individually.

Finally, because the internal representations are located close to each other in hidden-unit space, the network will tend to respond to them in a similar fashion. Since they are in sparsely populated region of the space, the network has little experience with decoding these types of internal representations. As a result, it will output an average of all the outputs it is familiar with. This is fine for the average stimulus, since the correct response is precisely the average of all responses (remember that the autoencoder task requires the network to reproduce the original input values on the output units). It is completely inappropriate for the modal stimuli whose feature values lie at the ends of the possible ranges. Hence there is more error for the modal stimuli than the average stimulus.

It is important to note that there are no explicit representations of categories in these networks. Items from the same category are mapped onto similar internal representations (and are responded to in a similar fashion), whereas items from different categories are mapped onto very different internal representations (and are responded to in a dissimilar fashion). However, the clustering structure observed in fig. 14.4 (which captures the expected category partitioning) is a description of the network's internal states that is not directly available for processing by the network.

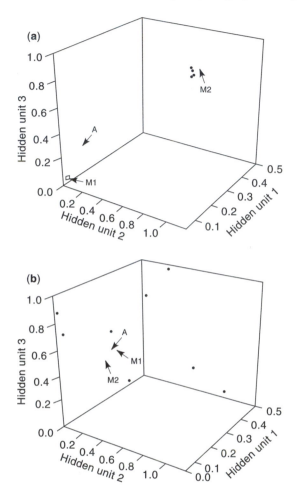

Figure 14.4. *Category representation in hidden-unit space (after Mareschal & French, 2000).*

Summary and Discussion

These simulations and associated empirical studies show that connectionist auto-encoder networks develop distinct perceptual categories in the same way that infants do when presented with the same stimuli as the infants. The basis for the emergence of distinct categories is the fact that connectionist networks develop internal representations that reflect the statistical distribution of features in the environment they encounter. As with infants, autoencoder networks can use feature correlation information to partition the world into distinct categories. The classification is implicit in the sense that it does not build on explicit verbal theories. Nor are the categories explicitly represented in the system. Instead, evidence of categorization is obtained through the observation of the system's behavior when required to classify a new exemplar.

An implication of this work is that perceptual categorization in early infancy is tantamount to implicit categorization in adults (Posner, 1969; Posner & Keele, 1970; Reed, 1972). Through exposure to exemplars, participants acquire some discriminant decision function that allows them to differentiate between exemplars that are part of the familiar set and those that are not part of this set. This decision function is implemented in the connection weights of the network.

In the next section I explore how important implicit categorization remains once language has appeared. There is clear evidence of links between the language and categorization systems. Indeed, early word learning is closely yoked to categorization (Meinst, Plunkett, & Harris, 1999), and categorization is itself effected by labeling (Waxman & Hall, 1993). Given the power of language as a representational system, we might expect the implicit categorization system to wane in importance with the emergence of language. However, as I shall show, although language and theory-based systems play an undeniable role, implicit categorization continues to play an important role in young children's—and even adults'—use of category information.

Implicit Category Use in Children's Reasoning

Early studies of categorization and induction in young children suggested that judgments regarding an object's category membership, or the likelihood of its sharing a property with another object, are made on a different basis depending on the child's age. Younger children apply a new fact to perceptually similar objects, while older children or adults utilize more profound conceptual information. This account of the perceptual/conceptual shift can be found throughout Piaget's work. The younger child is perceptually bound, and only after entering a subsequent stage of development can the child utilize abstract, and possibly theory-based, categorical information (Inhelder & Piaget, 1964).

Since Piaget, this view of the perceptual/conceptual shift has been undermined as younger and younger children have been shown to behave in ways that Piaget would not have expected. One set of counterexamples to Piaget are the induction studies discussed later (Carey, 1985; Gelman & Markman, 1986; Keil, 1989). These studies have shown that children as young as 3½ years old are able to make inferences that Piaget would have considered to be characteristic of much older children. The fact that children's induction behavior changes earlier than Piaget expected has been used as support for the view that conceptual development is fundamentally a formal process of the growth of theorylike structures.

In a seminal series of studies, Gelman and Markman (1986) presented 4-year-olds and adults with pairs of pictures of natural kind objects. Underneath each picture was written a fact about the object. For example, they might present a flamingo and a bat. Written under the picture of the flamingo are the words "This bird's heart has a right aortic arch," while under the bat is written "this bat's heart has a left aortic arch." Having thus labeled the objects and provided a fact about them, a third picture is presented. The third picture is of an object that is perceptually similar to one of the two previous objects but shares its label with the other. Thus, in the flamingo/bat example, the final picture is of a blackbird, labeled "bird." Perceptual and label information are in conflict as predictors of the fact. The child must tell the experimenter which fact is true of the final object (blackbird) and in so doing reveal whether the child is relying on perceptual similarity (mediated by the implicit categorization system) or shared identity (mediated by the verbal, theory-based categorization system) in making such inferences.

Although Gelman and Markman (1986) found that 4-year-olds rely on object labels as opposed to perceptual information when making inductions about natural kinds, studies with children younger than their participants are more equivocal. For example, McCarrell and Callanan's (1995) 2-year-old participants found perceptual information to be a more robust basis for induction than object labels. Other induction studies using different (though still natural kind) stimuli have also found a shift in the basis of induction across development, but that the onset of this shift depends on the concepts under investigation (Keil, 1989).

To make sense of these diverse findings, we must try to understand why younger children are sometimes observed as being more perceptually reliant and at other times more verbally reliant. Perhaps they have difficulty comprehending label information. Or perhaps they simply value perceptual information more than verbal information in certain contexts and with certain concepts (Freeman & Sera, 1996). Unfortunately, while plausible, these accounts do not answer the question of how and why a child's bias might change. As a first step in answering this question, we again developed a connectionist model.

A Model of Category-Based Inductive Inferences

Loose and Mareschal (1997) developed a connectionist autoencoder model of category-based inductive inferences in order to explore the cause of the shift from perceptual- to label-based inferences. A successful model should begin by demonstrating a reliance on perceptual information early in development, then, later in development, it should demonstrate a reliance on label information in drawing inferences.

The model begins with an ability to form perceptual categories prior to its ability to use label information. It is now clear that even very young prelinguistic children (infants) have impressive perceptual categorization abilities (Quinn & Eimas, 1996). The inductive inference model described here begins where the categorization models described earlier left off and is thus an extension of those models.

Figure 14.5 shows a schematic outline of the inference model. It consists of a fully connected autoencoder network. However, the input and output layers have been split into three separate banks encoding perceptual information, label information, and fact information, respectively. Each channel can be seen as processing information from different sources or modalities. The common hidden-unit layer implies that a single homogenous internal representation will be developed that incorporates information from these three channels. A similar approach has been used elsewhere to model early word learning (Chauvin, 1989; Plunkett, Sinha, Moller, & Stransby, 1992; Schafer & Mareschal, 2001).

In the interest of clarity, I will discuss only a very simple version of the model in which there are only two possible categories of objects (called A or B here). This allows identification of the mechanism by which a percept-to-label shift occurs. The mecha-

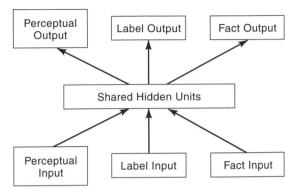

*Figure 14.5. Schema of inductive inference network.
Boxes represent banks of units, and arrows represent
full connectivity between different banks of units.
A shared internal representation emerges across the
hidden units.*

nism has subsequently been extended to multiple category contexts (Loose, 2000). In this model, the perceptual inputs for exemplars from each of the two categories were generated by adding noise drawn from a Gaussian distribution to each component of one of two perceptual prototypes (i.e., each exemplar was a noisy distortion of the prototype). The perceptual prototypes were defined as binary vectors, constrained to be greater than a certain fixed distance apart (i.e., minimum hamming distance = 36), with 50 percent of all values set to "1" and the other 50 percent set to "0."

Three different phases of training were used to capture the experience and testing of children of different ages. In phase 1, the network is trained only on perceptual autoassociation. This training is meant to capture the fact that all children tested in the category-based inductive inference studies arrive with prior perceptual categories. Note that during this phase, there is no training on either the label or fact pathways. By the end of this phase, networks have a categorization competence equivalent to that of young, prelinguistic infants.

In phase 2, the network is trained on paired percept-label autoassociation. This phase of training is meant to capture the fact that older children have had more opportunity to learn which labels go with which percepts (i.e., they have a better established vocabulary) than younger children. Models of the younger children (with less experience of naming) were provided with 1,000 training events (epochs) in this phase, whereas models of older children (with greater experience of naming) were provided with 30,000 training events (epochs) in this phase. There is no training on the fact pathway during phase 2.

The first two phases of training are intended to capture the differences in background knowledge/experience that children approach the inference task with at different ages. The third phase captures any learning that happens within the inference task itself. Networks are trained on the percept-fact associations but *not* the label-fact association. This is meant to capture the experiment itself, in which the child, coming to the task with the ability to categorize, coupled with varying degrees of experience with label information, is taught to associate a fact with a particular object. The amount of training for this is significantly less (typically around 100 epochs) than that used to model the development of percept-label associations.

Networks are *never* trained on the label-to-fact association. If there is such an association, then it will emerge by virtue of learning about percepts-plus-labels and percepts-plus-facts *separately*. The network's inductive ability (i.e., its ability to produce a fact when presented with perceptual and label information) is probed by presenting both percept and label inputs and observing the fact response at the output. Since the networks have always experienced the fact in association with the percept, and never in association with the label, one might expect the fact "inductive inference" always to be driven by the percept input. It turns out that this is not the case.

Figure 14.6 shows an example of network performance in the crucial conflicting percept and label condition. Each panel shows the input and output patterns observed on the input and output units when a particular configuration of perceptual and label information is clamped onto the input. Dark squares represent values of 1.0 and light squares represent values of 0.0. In this simple world, there are only two classes of objects. Every exemplar is generated from a perceptual prototype (A or B), has an associated category label (a or b), and inherits a fact (α or β). The different perceptual prototypes, labels, and facts will correspond to different patterns of activation (patterns of black and white squares) on the input and output unit banks. Fact information is never presented to the networks during testing. The lack of fact information is encoded by clamping all fact input units to the value 0.5 (an intermediate value between 0 and 1 that carries no information).

The top two panels of figure 14.6 show how the network responds when percept (A) is presented alongside label (b). The bottom two panels show how the network responds when percept (B) is presented alongside label (a). Note that in both cases the network is receiving conflicting perceptual and label information and must therefore "decide" on which source of information to base its response. A developmental dimension is also represented in the figure. The two panels on the left show the performance of a "young network" early in development, while the two panels on the right show the performance of an "old network" later in development. In particular, the fact output response is consistent with the perceptual input and not the conflicting label input.

Figure 14.6 shows that principle guiding the network's induction in the conflict condition shifts over the course of development from a reliance on perceptual information to a reliance on label information. Early in development, presentation of perceptual prototype (A) and label (b) to the network's inputs results in the production of prototype (A), label (a), and fact (α) as an output response (top left panel). The presentation of perceptual prototype (B) and label (a) to the network's inputs results in the production of prototype (B), label (b), and fact (β) as an output response (bottom left panel). In both cases, the network's output response (i.e., the object category, label, and fact) is driven by the *perceptual* input information only. In particular, the fact output is consistent with the perceptual input and not the conflicting label input.

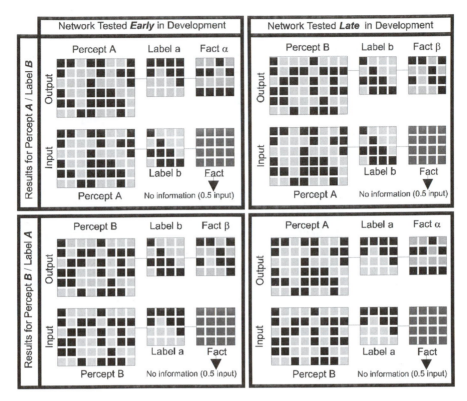

Figure 14.6. Schematic representation of a network's response to conflicting perceptual and label inputs, both early and late in development (after Loose & Mareschal, 1997).

A very different thing happens later in development. The basis on which the network retrieves a fact has shifted. When presented with perceptual prototype (A) and label (b), the network now produces prototype (B), label (b), and fact (β) (top right panel). Similarly, when presented with perceptual prototype (B) and label (a), the network produces prototype (A), label (a), and fact (α) (bottom right panel). Thus, later in development the network's output is driven by the *label* input information only, *not* the perceptual input information, as was the case earlier.

This shift in behavior can be explained as a combination of two factors. The first factor is that these networks develop a single internal representation that combines the information arriving from the different cue modalities. This single internal representation then triggers all three output responses for either object A or object B. Thus, the problem of inductive inference boils down to identifying which input cue is the best trigger of an internal representation that will in turn trigger the appropriate output. The second factor is that the perceptual inputs are more variable than the label inputs. As the network seeks to reduce error, it will discover that the most reliable trigger of the appropriate internal representation is the label input. In the networks, this is reflected by a gradual reduction in the weights between the perceptual inputs and the hidden representation, accompanied by a gradual increase in the weights between label input and the hidden representation.

An implication of this model is that the shift in reliance from perceptual to label information observed when children draw inductive inferences does not necessarily imply an emerging reliance on a verbal theory-based conceptual system. Indeed, these networks do not have such a system and still show this shift. The shift can be accounted for be appealing to the relative informativeness of the conflicting perceptual and label cues and reflects the operation of the same implicit categorization mechanisms discussed earlier.

Effects of Perceptual Variability on Children's and Adults' Inductive Inferences

This model makes a number of specific predictions about how children will respond when required to draw inferences from conflicting label and perceptual information. In particular, it predicts that children will be more likely to rely on label information when reasoning about a category with high perceptual variability than when reasoning with a category of low perceptual variability (Loose & Mareschal, 1997). This is because the relative benefit of shifting to label use is lower for a category that is perceptually homogeneous than for one that is perceptually heterogeneous. In contrast, perceptual variability plays no natural role in theory-based accounts of inductive reasoning.

In Loose and Mareschal (1999), we report on two studies that were designed to test these model predictions. In one study, we replicated the Gelman and Markman (1986) experimental procedure but used computer-generated novel kind categories that allowed us to control the variability of the categories underlying children's inferences. In this study, 8-year-olds began by playing a board game in which they learned to identify three classes of butterflies. These butterflies were computer generated, so the class variability could be controlled. Once the children had learned to classify a novel butterfly correctly into each of the three classes, they were taught a mutually exclusive fact about two of the three classes. They were then presented with a test butterfly that resembled members of one class but was labeled as a member of the other class. We found that the number of label-based inferences (as opposed to perceptually based inferences) was significantly greater when the test exemplar was taken from a high-variability class than when it was taken from a low-variability class. Thus, even with 8-year-olds, category variability is a significant predictor of whether children will rely on label information to draw inferences.

In a second study involving 4- to 5-year-olds, we explored the conditions under which label information would be used in inductive inferences. This study used a forced-choice procedure developed by Florian (1994). Two factors were manipulated: the variability of the training set (high or low) and the presence or absence of a label in the test phase.

In all conditions, children were first exposed to a set of artificial animal pictures similar to those used by Younger (1985) and printed on a single large sheet of paper. The child's attention was drawn to each individual exemplar to ensure that the child had formed a representation of the familiarization set as a whole. During the subsequent test phase, children in the label condition were told that the animals in the familiarization set were "wugs" and that there were other animals call "leeches." In the no-label condition, the experimenter used pronouns or the generic term "animals" when referring to any exemplars. Children were then told that all the [wugs/ animals] on the familiarization sheet shared a hidden property. To test inferences, the children were presented with a novel animal and asked whether this [wug/animal] shared that the same hidden property. In general, the children were more likely to make a correct response when reasoning about a low-variability category than a high-variability category. However, we also found a strong interaction. The presence or absence of label information had no impact on the children's inferences in the low-variability condition, but in the high-variability condition the children were far more likely to draw an inference consistent with label information. In other words, these 4- to 5-year-olds were more inclined to use label information, if available, when faced with a high-variability category than when faced with a low-variability category.

Finally, in a third related study, we (Loose & Mareschal, 1998) explored whether perceptual variability (hence implicit category formation) still played a role in adult inferences within a structured natural kind domain. Both the traditional and modern views of inference development imply that adults should use labels as a basis for inferences in a taxonomically structured domain, so category variability should not influence their performance. In this study, participants were trained to categorize different sets of artificial tropical seeds. Once they had learned the six target categories, they were taught a fact about each category. They were then tested with conflicting label and perceptual information and asked to infer the property of the test item. Even in this domain, the adults based the majority of their responses on perceptual similarity rather than shared label. A final labeling test verified that the participants had not forgotten the category labels and were not simply relying on perceptual similarity as a default response strategy.

Discussion of Inductive Reasoning Studies

We presented a connectionist model of the development of a reliance on label information as opposed to perceptual information when making inductive inferences. This model shows a percept-to-label shift without any ability to manipulate formal systems, as is the suggestion of the "concepts as theories" view. Evidence that younger children rely on labels is often taken as support for this view. However, we suggest that the development of label reliance may be seen as an emerging strategy for improving categorization accuracy in a noisy perceptual environment.

Our model predicts that differently labeled objects that are nevertheless perceptually confusable will promote induction on the basis of labels earlier than objects that are easier to distinguish perceptually. This prediction may shed some light on the contrasting results of different induction paradigms. The original studies by Gelman and Markman (1986, 1987) did not find significant evidence of a percept-to-label shift in subjects as young as 3.5 years old. Given their stimuli, this result is not surprising. Their studies rely on perceptually confusable natural kind stimuli (for example, blackbirds and bats). Our model predicts that these are the very cases that are most likely to promote reasoning on the basis of labels early on.

Some studies do not rely on perceptually confusable examples. Keil (1989) asked children older than the participants in Gelman and Markman's (1986, 1987) study to say whether a skunk that had been surgically transformed to look exactly like a racoon was in fact a racoon or not. In these studies, Keil found that young children were still reliant on perceptual information in making inductions, and only later did they realize that the truly salient characteristic for induction was the animal's label. Again, this is consistent with what our model would predict—the basis of induction will take longer to shift when perceptual categorization is more clear-cut.

However, studies involving other stimuli do not report the same findings (Keil, 1989). Even young children rely on object kind (label), as opposed to perceptual similarity, when presented with a toy dog and a real dog. Note, however, that while in our study all stimuli were presented equally often to the network, this is not true of children's learning. We might propose that toy dogs are precisely the kinds of objects that young children would have had a great deal of experience of—and thus the basis of induction with such objects would be more likely to have shifted. Our modeling work with multiple prototypes demonstrates that the basis of induction for different objects will shift at different times (Loose & Mareschal, 1997; Loose, 2000). An alternative, simple account of this is to say that the stuffed dogs and real dogs are perceptually similar and, therefore, will be differentiated by label use early in development. Again, this is compatible with the behavior of our model.

General Discussion

The adult categorization literature suggests that there are multiple systems of category learning (Ashby & Ells, 2001; Ashby, Alfonso-Reese, Turken, & Waldron, 1998; Ashby & Waldron, 1999; Erikson & Kruchke, 1998; Smith, Patalano, & Jonides, 1998). One system is language and theory based, whereas the other system is implicit and procedurally based. In this chapter I have surveyed evidence that implicit categorization plays an important role in explaining categorization throughout development.

In support of this claim, I have described connectionist models of perceptual categorization and category-based inductive inferences. The categorization process in these networks is inherently implicit. Moreover, the models do an excellent job of explaining early infant perceptual categorization. They also present a simple parsimonious account of the apparent percept-to-label shift in young children's category-based inductive inference. All of these models make predictions about how the distribution statistics of the exemplars used to familiarize children and infants will determine their subsequent behavior.

The models provide a theoretical framework for thinking about the emergence and use of categories. They provide a mechanistic causal account of development. The role of developmental psychologists is to elucidate the causal mechanism by which behaviors emerge and develop. A full causal explanation of these behaviors requires both an analysis of the information-processing mechanisms and the input environment. Connectionist models are a subset of computational models that stress neurally plausible sets of mechanisms. The correlation-based associative learning mechanisms embodied by these models explain *how* information is processed to produce an output behavior. An analysis of the distribution properties of the inputs—within the context of the information-processing mechanisms embodied by the networks—provides an explanation for *why* the behaviors emerge.

Although connectionist models are associationist, they have inherited the Hebbian tradition of associative learning rather than the Hullian tradition. In other words, *how* information is internally represented is just as important for understanding behavior as the statistics of the environment. This is well illustrated by the inductive inference model, in which the presence of a shared internal representation plays a crucial role in explaining the shift from perceptual- to label-based inductive inference.

So what might be a developmental account of the acquisition and use of implicit categories? The inductive inference work best illustrates how such categories could be acquired and develop over the lifespan. Early in development, categories are based on perceptual information alone. The structure of the categories acquired is determined by the distribution characteristics of the features of objects encountered in the environment. The categories are formed because the learning system (i.e., the brain) is engaged in developing a reliable, compressed internal representation of the objects in its environment. This internal code stores information that is relevant for the tasks the agent has previously been engaged in and thus will probably be engaged in again.

Efficiency is also what drives the system to rely on label information when that information becomes available. Labeling (word learning) begins when the infant already has a substantial number of perceptual categories encoded. However, because there is less variability in label use than in the perceptual appearance of a class of objects, the system learns that the label is better predictor of the internal representation that encodes all information relevant to that category.

This process may even underlie category learning at all ages (i.e., in childhood and adulthood alike). When acquiring a new category, the child or adult gathers perceptual information in order to form a perceptual prototype of the category that will allow it to recognize exemplars of this category in the future. At this stage, label information is just another feature. Once a reliable internal representation of the category has been acquired, the system discovers that the most reliable predictor of category membership is the label, when such label information is available. Labels then become the primary trigger for activating the category internal representation, and all information related to the category (i.e., both visible and invisible facts associated with this representation). The ease with which the system will identify a label as the primary predictor of the category will depend on the variability of perceptual features. If there is little feature variability, then the system will take longer to identify a label as a key predictor.

One could think of this process as analogous to a novice-to-expert shift. The novice who is unfamiliar with a category initially begins by learning the perceptual boundaries of a category in order to establish which objects are members of the new category. Only once they have acquired some kind of internal representation of the category will they seek to optimize their ability to recognize membership to this category by identifying a reduced optimal set of features that allow for rapid and proper categorization. Evidence corroborating this account can be found in Loose and

Mareschal (1998), where we taught adults a novel perceptual category (seeds) within a familiar domain (plant). Even after training, the adults remained novices at identifying the seeds and had weak implicit representations of the categories involved. They relied heavily on perceptual information, even though they were aware of which label went with which perceptual category. On the basis of the preceding discussion, I would predict that when these adult participants have acquired a much more robust perceptual representation of the seed categories, they will shift to using label information as a predictor of category membership in the same way that young children do as they acquire more experience of the perceptual world.

The developmental account proposed throughout this chapter has a number of advantages with regards to parsimony. It argues for the continuity of the mechanisms that underlie infants', children's, and adults' categorization behaviors. Indeed, the same correlation-based associationist mechanisms were found to account for early infant perceptual categorization and children's and adults' category formation and use in inductive inference tasks. These mechanisms can be linked to the implicit categorization system identified in the adult literature.

This last point begs the question of why one system (e.g., the implicit system) is used over another system (e.g., the verbal system) in a particular task. One possible answer to this is the degree of perceptual poverty of the exemplars presented to an individual. I have already mentioned that children are more likely to use label information if required to reason about a heterogeneous perceptual category. One could take this argument further and suggest that impoverished stimuli that require active interpretation by individuals are more likely to elicit the use of a theory-based categorization system than the procedural implicit system. The line drawing stimuli originally used by Gelman and Markman (1986) are a good example of such impoverished stimuli. I am not denying the presence of verbal, theory-based categories (there is clear evidence of these both in the developmental and adult literature), but I am suggesting that the importance of this mode of categorization in everyday life, during which we encounter richly defined perceptual objects, may have been overstated.

Acknowledgments

Support for the research reported in this chapter, as well as the writing of the chapter, was provided in part by the Royal Society, the British Academy (grant SG-29819), European Commission RTN grant CT-2000-00065, and the Economic and Social Research Council UK (grant R000239112). Much of the work on inductive inference was carried out as part of Jon Loose's doctoral dissertation at Exeter University.

References

Ackley, D. H., Hinton, G. E., & Sejnowski, T. J. (1985). A learning algorithm for Boltzman machines. *Cognitive Science*, 9, 147–169.

Ashby, F. G., & Ells, I. (2001). The neurobiology of human category learning. *Trends in Cognitive Science*, 5, 204–210.

Ashby, F. G., & Waldron, E. M. (1999). On the nature of implicit categorization. *Psychonomic Bulletin & Review*, 6, 363–378.

Ashby, F. G., Alfonso-Reese, L. A., Turken, A. U., & Waldron, E. M. (1998). A neuropsychological theory of multiple systems in category learning. *Psychological Review, 105*, 442–481.

Behl-Chadha, G. (1996). Basic-level and superordinate-like categorical representations in early infancy. *Cognition, 60*, 105–141.

Carey, S. (1985). *Conceptual change in childhood*. Cambridge, MA: MIT Press.

Charlesworth, W. R. (1969). The role of surprise in cognitive development. In D. Elkind & J. Flavell (Eds.), *Studies in cognitive development. Essays in honor of Jean Piaget* (pp. 257–314). Oxford: Oxford University Press.

Chauvin, Y. (1989). Toward a connectionist model of symbolic emergence. In *Proceedings of the 11th Conference of the Cognitive Science Society* (pp. 580–587). Hillsdale, NJ: Erlbaum.

Cohen, L. B. (1973). A two-process model of infant visual attention. *Merrill-Palmer Quarterly, 19*, 157–180.

Cottrell, G. W., Munro, P., & Zipser, D. (1988). Image compression by backpropagation: an example of extensional programming. In N. E. Sharkey (Ed.), *Advances in cognitive science* (Vol. 3, pp. 208–240). Norwood, NJ: Ablex.

Elman, J. L., Bates, E. A., Johnson, M. H., Karmiloff-Smith, A., Parisi, D., & Plunkett, K. (1996). *Rethinking innateness: A connectionist perspective on development*. Cambridge, MA: MIT Press.

Erikson, M. A., & Kruschke, J. K. (1998). Rules and examplars in category learning. *Journal of Experimental Psychology: General, 127*, 107–140.

Florian, J. (1994). Stripes do not a zebra make, or do they? Conceptual and perceptual information in inductive inference. *Developmental Psychology, 30*, 88–101.

Freeman, K., & Sera, M. (1996). Reliance on visual and verbal information across ontological kinds: What do children know about animals and machines? *Cognitive Development, 11*, 315–341.

French, R. M. (1999). Catastrophic forgetting in connectionist networks. *Trends in Cognitive Science, 3*, 128–135.

Gelman, S., & Markman, E. (1987). Young children's inductions from natural kinds: The role of categories and appearances. *Child Development, 57*, 1532–1541.

Gelman, S., & Markman, E. (1986). Categories and induction in young children. *Cognition, 23*, 183–209.

Inhelder, B., & Piaget, J. (1964). *The early growth of logic in the child*. New York: Norton.

Keil, F. (1989). *Concepts, kinds and cognitive development*. Cambridge, MA: MIT Press.

Knapp, A. G., & Anderson, J. A. (1984). Theory of categorization based on distributed memory storage. *Journal of Experimental Psychology: Learning, Memory, and Cognition, 10*, 616–637.

Loose, J. (2000). *A connectionist investigation of category-based inductive reasoning in young children*. Unpublished doctoral dissertation, Exeter University, Exeter, UK.

Loose, J. J., & Mareschal, D. (1997).When a word is worth a thousand pictures: A connectionist account of the percept to label shift in children's inductive reasoning. In M. G. Shafto & P. Langley (Eds.), *Proceedings of the 19th Annual Conference of the Cognitive Science Society* (pp. 454–459). London: Erlbaum.

Loose, J., & Mareschal, D. (1998). Inductive reasoning tasks revisited: Object labels aren't always the basis of inference within taxonomic domains. In M. A. Gernsbacher & S. J. Derry (Eds.), *Proceedings of the 20th Annual Conference of the Cognitive Science Society* (pp. 627–632). London: Erlbaum.

Loose, J., & Mareschal, D. (1999). Inductive reasoning revisited: Children's reliance on category labels and appearance. In M. Hahn & S. C. Stone (Eds.), *Proceedings of the 21st Annual Conference of the Cognitive Science Society* (pp. 320–325). London: Erlbaum.

Mandler, J. M. (2000a). Perceptual and conceptual processes in infancy. *Journal of Cognition and Development, 1,* 3–36.

Mandler, J. M. (2000b). What global-before-basic trend? Commentary on perceptually based approaches to early categorization. *Infancy, 1,* 99–110.

Mandler, J. M., Bauer, P. J., & McDonough, L. (1991). Separating the sheep from the goats: Differentiating global categories. *Cognitive Psychology, 23,* 263–298.

Mandler, J. M., & McDonough, L. (1998). On developing a knowledge base in infancy. *Developmental Psychology, 34,* 1274–1288.

Mareschal, D. (2000). Connectionist modelling and infant development. In D. Muir and A. M. Slater (Eds.), *Essential readings in psychology: Infant development* (pp. 55–65). Oxford: Blackwell.

Mareschal, D. (2002). Connectionist methods in infancy research. In J. Fagen & H. Hayne (Eds.), *Progress in infancy research* (Vol. 2, pp. 71–119). Mahwah, NJ.

Mareschal, D., & French, R. M. (1997). A connectionist account of interference effects in early infant memory and categorization. In M. G. Shafto & P. Langley (Eds.), *Proceedings of the 19th Annual Conference of the Cognitive Science Society* (pp. 484–489). Mahwah, NJ: Erlbaum.

Mareschal, D., & French, R. M. (2000). Mechanisms of categorization in infancy. *Infancy, 1,* 59–76.

Mareschal, D., French, R. M., & Quinn, P. C. (2000). A connectionist account of asymmetric category learning in early infancy. *Developmental Psychology, 36,* 635–645.

Mareschal, D., Quinn, P. C., & French, R. M. (2002). Asymmetric interference in 3- to 4-month-olds' sequential category learning. *Cognitive Science, 26,* 377–389.

Mareschal, D., & Shultz, T. R. (1996). Generative connectionist networks and constructivist cognitive development. *Cognitive Development, 11,* 571–603.

McCarrell, N., & Callanan, M. (1995). Form-function correspondences in children's inference. *Child Development, 66,* 532–546.

McCloskey, M., & Cohen, N. J. (1989). Catastrophic interference in connectionist networks: The sequential learning problem. In G. H. Bower (Ed.), *The psychology of learning and motivation* (Vol. 23, pp. 109–164). New York: Academic Press.

McLeod, P., Plunkett, K., & Rolls, E. T. (1998). Introduction to connectionist modeling of cognitive processes. Oxford: Oxford University Press.

Meints, K., Plunkett, K., & Harris, P. L. (1999). When does an ostrich become a bird? The role of typicality in early word comprehension. *Developmental Psychology, 35,* 1072–1078.

Mervis, C. B., & Rosch, E. (1981). Categorization of natural objects. *Annual Review of Psychology, 32,* 89–115.

Murphy, G., & Medin, D. (1985). The role of theories in conceptual coherence. *Psychological Review, 92,* 289–316.

Plunkett, K., Sinha, C., Møller, M. F., & Strandsby, O. (1992). Symbol grounding or the emergence of symbols? Vocabulary growth in children and a connectionist net. *Connection Science, 4,* 293–312.

Posner, M. I. (1969). Abstraction and the process of recognition. In G. H. Bower & J. T. Spence (Eds.), *The psychology of learning and motivation* (Vol. 3, pp. 53–87). New York: Academic Press.

Posner, M. I. I., & Keele, S. W. (1970). Retention of abstract ideas. *Journal of Experimental Psychology, 83,* 304–308.

Quinn, P. C., & Eimas, P. D. (1996). Perceptual organization and categorization in young infants. *Advances in Infancy Research, 10,* 1–36.

Quinn, P. C., Eimas, P. D., & Rosenkrantz, S. L. (1993). Evidence for representations of perceptually similar natural categories by 3-month-old and 4-month-old infants. *Perception, 22,* 463–475.

Quinn, P. C., Johnson, M. H., Mareschal, D., Rakison, D. H., & Younger, B. A. (2000). Understanding early categorization: One process or two: A response to Mandler and Smith. *Infancy, 1,* 111–122.

Ratcliff, R. (1990). Connectionist models of recognition memory: Constraints imposed by learning and forgetting functions. *Psychological Review, 97,* 285–308

Reed, S. K. (1972). Pattern recognition and categorization. *Cognitive Psychology, 3,* 382–407.

Rosch, E., Mervis, C. B., Gray, W. D., Johnson, D. M., & Boyes-Braem, P. (1976). Basic objects in natural categories. *Cognitive Psychology, 8,* 382–439.

Rumelhart, D. E., Hinton, G. E., & Williams, R. J. (1986). Learning representations by back-propagating errors. *Nature* 323, 533–536.

Rumelhart, D., & McClelland, J. (1986). *Parallel distributed processing: Vol. 1.* Cambridge, MA: MIT Press.

Schafer, G., & Mareschal, D. (2001). Modeling infant speech sound discrimination using simple associative networks. *Infancy, 2,* 7–28.

Smith, E. E., Patalano, A. L., & Jonides, J. (1998). Alternative strategies for categorization. *Cognition, 65,* 167–196.

Sokolov, E. N. (1963). *Perception and the conditioned reflex.* Hillsdale, NJ: Erlbaum.

Waxman, S. R., & Hall, D. G. (1993). The development of linkage between count nouns and object categories: Evidence from fifteen- to twenty-one-month-old infants. *Child Development, 64,* 1224–1241.

Younger, B. A. (1985). The segregation of items into categories by ten-month-old infants. *Child Development, 56,* 1574–1583.

Younger, B. A. (1990). Infants' detection of correlations among feature categories. *Child Development, 61,* 614–620.

CHAPTER FIFTEEN

Commentary on Part II
Abilities and Assumptions Underlying Conceptual Development

Ellen M. Markman and Vikram K. Jaswal

SOME OF THE MOST fundamental questions one can ask about cognitive development are related to the nativist-empiricist debate: How do we best characterize
the initial state of the infant, and how do we explain the transition from the initial
state to the mature cognition of adults? Carey and Markman (1999) argued that, at
heart, this is a debate about whether there are domain-specific learning mechanisms.
The empiricist position is that the initial state can be characterized in terms of perception and that general, all-purpose learning mechanisms, which can form associations and detect correlations, are sufficient to account for the acquisition of
knowledge. Many of the outstanding issues in cognitive development center on
questions of the domain specificity of learning and of the need to postulate core
concepts or constraints on learning. Also central to the field are questions of whether
cognition, especially the cognition of infants and young children, should be characterized as perceptual or conceptual, and whether attributing "theories" to infants
and young children is necessary to account for their understanding of the world or
whether it is an anthropomorphic overinterpretation of the evidence. These six chapters on the nature of children's categories raise many of these most basic questions
about human cognition and its development and provide thoughtful discussions,
pertinent evidence, and elegant models for how best to characterize children's classifications. We will emphasize two of these questions in our comments: (1) Are children's classifications theory based or derived solely from computing correlations
over perceptual features? (2) What role does language, in terms of naming categories, play?

Although we acknowledge that many of the questions remain open, we believe that the evidence favors a theory-based view of category development and suggests that language plays a critical role in the acquisition of a conceptual system, one that is not accounted for in an associationist model. There are two important qualifications to this conclusion, however. First, regardless of which position one takes, there is clear agreement that computing correlations over perceptual features plays an important role in children's developing categorizations, and that perceptual features are routinely used to identify category members. The debate is about whether such features and correlations are the whole story, not about whether they exist or are useful. Second, "theory-based" is not always an apt description. "Knowledge-based" may sometimes be closer, as might Mandler's (chap. 5) ideas about "interpretation," but even these notions often fail to capture the basis of children's classifications. We will argue that children often may rely on a vague, sometimes poorly specified and poorly understood notion that there is more than meets the eye, that there must be something that explains why things have the properties they do, but children may not know what it is.

This vague belief differs from children's naïve theories in domains such as physics, psychology, number, or space. In each of these domains, a theory is attributed to children because each of these conceptual frameworks has ontological concepts at its core, and some causal principles that operate in the domain to explain phenomena and generate predictions. For other classifications, however, it is not always clear what these core concepts and causal principles would be. In many cases, the ontology and causality may be derived from the foundational domain in which the classification is embedded; in fact, we argue that this is an important function of these domains. Once a lay biology has been set up, for example, then for any animal, one might expect that it has internal parts that perform some vital functions; that it will need nourishment to grow; and so on. So one fully legitimate way to think of categories as theory driven is that specific categories import the causal principles from the larger domain of which they are a part. In addition, as Gelman and Koenig and Gopnik and Nazzi mention in their chapters, children sometimes seem to hold essentialist views with minimal understanding of what the "essence" might be. Gopnik and Nazzi suggest that essentialism functions as a placeholder for some as-yet-unspecified causal mechanism. It is as if the child reasons, for example, "I know there is something that makes this a bird. Something must have caused it to have a beak, claws, and feathers, but I really don't know what." We propose that such "theory-based" categorization derives from children's faith that everything has a cause. Admittedly, the evidence for children's belief in determinism is not overwhelming, but see Bullock, Gelman, and Baillargeon (1982) for an argument that preschoolers hold such a belief.

Suppose children's essentialist "theory-based" beliefs are often little more than articles of faith—a belief that there must be a cause for the properties an object manifests, but not much understanding of what that cause might be. Would this shallow understanding trivialize the notion of theory-based categorization? We think not. In fact, this belief may serve as scaffolding for seeking out and representing relevant information. It could serve as a mechanism for motivating children to look beyond the obvious and as a way of reconciling disparities between superficial appearances and classifications when they arise.   ·

This shallow understanding also helps explain an inconsistency in the literature—why children sometimes reveal a shape bias in studies of classification (e.g., Baldwin, 1992; Imai, Gentner, & Uchida, 1994) yet show clear abilities to treat nonsimilar objects as members of the same kind and to base their inductions on kind membership rather than perceptual similarity (e.g., Gelman & Markman, 1986). The inconsistency hinges on whether children are asked to determine the appropriate categorization on their own versus whether they are asked to learn and use a classification provided for them. On their own, with only a vague notion of the causal mechanism, they may not spontaneously construct a nonobvious classification. But—and this is a critical point—children are not limited to categories they can construct on their own: When category membership is stipulated for them through a label, they willingly form nonobvious categories. Thus, children make two basic assumptions that work synergistically to enable them to move well beyond the classifications they could construct on their own: (1) they believe in a deeper, nonperceptual basis for categorization, and (2) they are willing to accept labels for things that to them may not seem to be the same kind of thing.

With this framework in mind, we turn now to a brief commentary on each of the preceding six chapters.

Associationist Approaches

The chapters by Mareschal (chap. 14) and by Smith, Colunga, and Yoshida (chap. 11) provide explicit, detailed models to tackle important and controversial issues in category development. Both propose that low-level, atheoretical, associative mechanisms, capable of extracting statistical regularities from the input and environment, are sufficient to explain the development of children's early categories (see also Younger, chap. 4). Links between features that frequently co-occur in the input are strengthened, while those between relatively infrequent, variable features are not. With time and training, certain expectations develop, so that on presentation of one feature (or more), a network (or child) will expect that other features that have been correlated with that one in the past will also be present.

Mareschal's (chap. 14) approach is impressive for its ability to model interesting aspects of behavior, to generate novel predictions, and to then verify these predictions through clever experimental research. For example, using an habituation paradigm, Quinn, Eimas, and Rosenkrantz (1993) found that 3.5-month-old infants exposed to exemplars of cats formed a category of Cat that excluded novel dogs, but those exposed to exemplars of dogs formed a category of Dog that did not exclude novel cats. Mareschal and his colleagues developed a connectionist autoencoder that succeeded in simulating the same asymmetry by exploiting the fact that the perceptual variability in the Cat category was smaller than that in the Dog category (Mareschal, French, & Quinn, 2000). For children and the network alike, this difference in perceptual variability made novel dogs unlikely cats but novel cats plausible dogs. In fact, on the basis of the distribution of perceptual features in the categories, even when the network was familiarized with a mixed set exemplars containing more dogs than cats, Mareschal and colleagues predicted that the same asymmetry would emerge. Indeed, it did, both in their model and when they conducted a new study with 3- and 4-month-olds.

Mareschal also developed a network to model what he calls the "percept-to-label" shift, or a shift from reliance on perceptual information to reliance on a category label when making inductive inferences. The model starts out more attuned to perceptual information than label information because it is assumed that younger children have less experience with labels. Thus, when the young network is shown an image that yields one representation but is then informed that it has a label that provides a different representation, it weighs the representation provided by the percept more heavily than the one provided by the label. As the network is trained that certain labels go with certain percepts, however, it learns that the label input is a more reliable guide to an accurate representation than the percept alone, because there is more variability in the perceptual input.

The performance of the network on this task does simulate a perceptual-to-conceptual shift, a developmental phenomenon that Piaget (Inhelder & Piaget, 1964) and others have suggested. However, along with a number of authors in this book (Gelman & Koenig; Mandler; Oakes & Madole; Rakison), we are not convinced that there is such a shift in development. On our view, whether perceptual or conceptual information is used to make an inference depends on the inference to be made and the theories possessed by the child. For example, Mareschal suggests that 4-year-olds rely on category labels more than perceptual information when making inductions about natural kinds (Gelman & Markman, 1986) and argues that results with younger children have been more equivocal. In particular, he writes that 2-year-olds in a study by McCarrell and Callanan (1995) found "*perceptual* information to be a more robust basis for induction than object labels" (p. 372). It is true that 2-year-olds found the perceptual information more compelling than the object labels in McCarrell and Callanan's study, but so did 4-year-olds. Indeed, even adults would probably find the perceptual information more compelling than the object labels using the materials from that study. For example, an animal with an accordion-like neck and called a *wug* was said to "stretch tall to eat cherries." When shown another animal that shared the accordion-like neck but that was called by a different name, preschoolers were quite likely to agree that it "stretches tall to eat cherries," and so would adults, we imagine. These results differ from those of Gelman and Markman because the stimuli were designed in radically different ways: McCarrell and Callanan's stimuli were designed explicitly to provide obvious correspondences between an object's form and function; Gelman and Markman's stimuli were designed explicitly to avoid any such cues.

Mareschal (chap. 14) seems to argue that a theory-based account of category development rests on a total reliance on category labels in inductive inference tasks. In fact, however, an ability to use perceptual and label information flexibly seems to be the norm, and seems very much in line with theory-based approaches: people use a label on induction tasks when it is relevant to the inference, and not otherwise, and they decide what is relevant by drawing on theory-based knowledge. For example, it would be inappropriate to use a category label to make an inference about whether a baseball *bat* could fly like a vampire *bat*, or whether a computer *mouse* would like cheese like a field *mouse* (see also P. Bloom, 2000). These items, though they share the same label, cross the animate-inanimate ontological boundary, and something true about one may not necessarily be true of the other. Massey and R. Gelman (1988) have shown that preschoolers are quite aware of the fact that, for example, a statue of an animal could not locomote on its own, while an unfamiliar echidna could, demonstrating an awareness that animate and inanimate things promote different kinds of inferences.

Another reason the flexibility in the information children use in induction tasks provides support for a theory-based account is that the weight given to the same perceptual feature can vary, depending on context. For example, in McCarrell and Callanan (1995), when the premise about the animal with the accordion-like neck was that it "stretched tall to eat cherries," the accordion-like neck was relevant, but when it was that it "gives its babies a ride," it was not. Even though children had presumably never seen an animal with an accordion-like neck, and it certainly had never been associated with stretching tall to eat cherries, they were able to create, on the fly, a causal theory connecting the two: "It can stretch tall to eat cherries because it has an accordion-like neck." Indeed, they may have drawn upon theories of physics (an accordion-like neck would be able to stretch), psychology (it wants to reach the cherries, so it will try to), and biology (it is an animate object and so therefore eats). (Children should not agree that it stretched tall to eat cherries if it was inanimate, because inanimate things do not eat; see Goodman, McDonough, & Brown, 1998.)

The "percept-to-label" network described by Mareschal can shift from reliance on perceptual information to reliance on category labels, depending on the amount of experience it has or the variability within a category. Indeed, the model makes the interesting prediction that label information will be more important when dealing with categories that are highly perceptually variable than those with low perceptual variability, a prediction borne out in experimental studies with children (Loose & Mareschal, 1999). However, at least the model detailed in this chapter does not seem to provide for the kind of flexibility just described, where context influences the inferences children (and adults) make. Furthermore, without some instantiated knowledge (possibly theory-based) about whether and how a particular perceptual feature can yield a particular property, we doubt it could account for the fact that the most accurate basis for induction depends on the induction to be made.

Smith et al. (chap. 11) use atheoretical associative mechanisms to explain how ontologies develop. Their approach is very ambitious in scope, attempting to provide a single theoretical framework to model crosscultural and cross-linguistic differences in categorization and labeling. One notable feature of the studies described in chapter 11 is the effort the authors took to provide their models with input that is both transparent and representative of the information in a child's environment. For example, they had English- and Japanese-speaking adult subjects provide ratings about the nouns on that language's version of the MacArthur CDI for toddlers in order to determine whether each noun was shape based, color based, material based, whether each referred to solid or nonsolids, and whether each was a count or mass noun.

Using these data as input to a network, they succeeded in modeling interesting patterns in the way that children of the two languages extend new nouns. Imai and Gentner (1997) found that both English-speaking and Japanese-speaking children extend a new word given to a novel complex solid object on the basis of its shape, and a new word given to a novel simple nonsolid on the basis of its material. However, whereas English-speaking children are also quite likely to extend a new word for a simple solid object on the basis of shape, Japanese-speaking children are more equivocal—some extend it on the basis of shape and others on the basis of material. Imai and Gentner argue that their results provide evidence for both prelinguistic, universal ontological knowledge about individuation (the similar results for complex objects and for nonsolids) as well as for more language-specific influences: English speakers group both simple and complex objects together as encoded by count nouns and as different from nonsolid objects, which are encoded as mass nouns; Japanese makes no grammatical distinctions between count and mass nouns, and so Japanese-speaking children can interpret a label applied to a simple object as a substance/material term or as an object term. In ambiguous cases then, the language being learned can influence children's interpretations of new words (Gentner & Boroditsky, 2000).

Smith et al. (chap. 11) suggest that, in fact, both the "universals and the differences are the product of the same statistical learning mechanism" (p. 280). On their model, even the ontological knowledge about individuation common in English and Japanese is the result of correlations in the input. As their rating studies indicate, toddlers exposed to either language learn the same kinds of words, and those words encode the same kinds of correlated perceptual features (e.g., solid objects encoded by words are consistent in shape but not material; nonsolids encoded by words are consistent in material but not shape). This seems plausible for determining the mapping rules between ontologies and lexical categories, but there seems to be some confusion about whether we are considering ontologies only as evidenced in words or ontologies more generally. As Imai and Gentner (1997) have argued, their results do not bear on children's understanding of the "essential properties and behavior of objects" (p. 193). Indeed, they argue that Japanese children in their study may have recognized that even simple objects had objectlike properties that would be different from the nonsolid stimuli (e.g., solidity, cohesiveness, etc.). What Imai and Gentner's results (and Smith et al.'s model) bear on is the interesting and important question of how children learn to extend new words. It is an open question about how or even whether these results relate to how children think or reason about the thing to which the word applies.

Moreover, there is a fundamental difference between establishing an ontology in the first place versus simply mapping existing ontological categories onto grammatical form classes. There is good evidence that even very young infants who have no words in their productive vocabularies can distinguish between solids and nonsolids. For example, in one study by Huntley-Fenner, Carey, and Solimando (2001), 8-month-old infants watched as one solid object was placed behind a screen and then a second solid object was added. If the screen was removed to reveal a single object, infants looked longer than if the screen was removed to reveal two objects (see Wynn, 1992). On the other hand, when infants of the same age watched as one cupful of sand was placed behind the screen and then a second cupful was added, they looked equally long at displays consisting of a single small pile of sand or two small piles. In other words, they could track solid objects but not nonsolid ones. The basic ontological classes of solids and nonsolids, then, predate the *lexical* ontological classes described in Imai and Gentner (1997) and modeled by Smith et al. (chap. 11).

Both Mareschal and Smith et al. attempt to model the impact of language on children's categorization. In Mareschal's work, when the label becomes a more reliable guide to category membership, it is weighted more heavily than an object's perceptual appearance. In Smith et al.'s work, when syntax is added, networks learning English become more like English-speaking children. In both models and in two other chapters in this book (chaps. 6, 7), language is treated as just another feature of an object, which happens to become more heavily weighted with age. But words are not features of objects; they *refer* to objects. For example, words are routinely used to refer to absent objects, as in "I wonder what is keeping Daddy." The word *Daddy* clearly refers to the person even in his absence. It isn't as if one feature of the man, his name, is present. No features are present, but the word continues to refer. Another way in which labels are not mere associates of objects is that when learning words, even very young children rely on a speaker's intent to refer to an object and not simply on an association between the word and object. For example, a word can be learned for an object that is not visible, so long as the speaker demonstrates an intent to refer to it (Akhtar & Tomasello, 1996). Conversely, children resist mistakenly learning a label for an object that is visible unless the speaker demonstrates an intent to refer to it (Baldwin, 1991). In short, a word is not just another feature of an object, and models need to account for the fact that even very young children treat words differently from mere associations.

Theory-Based Classification

As we have just shown, arguing for one end of the continuum are Smith et al. who believe that low-level attentional and perceptual mechanisms can account for children's lexical categorization without reference to deeper conceptual knowledge. Intermediate is Mareschal, who suggests that children undergo a perceptual to conceptual shift. The other end of the continuum is represented by Gelman and Koenig, who argue forcefully that young children's categories are theory based from the start, and that the kind of statistical mechanisms that Smith et al. and Mareschal propose are not sufficient to account for children's classifications. They believe, moreover, that the theories children hold are instrumental in their acquisition of categories rather than being merely a consequence of category learning. Some of the evidence for perceptually based categories, such as children's reliance on shape (Smith, Jones, & Landau, 1996), may be evidence that children sensibly use perceptual cues as good predictors of category membership rather than as definitive criteria per se. To make the case that children's categories are theory based, Gelman and Koenig (chap. 13) provide an extensive review and a unifying framework to interpret several lines of research that they argue distinguish theory-based categories from more perceptually based ones. On their view, theory-based categories incorporate information about properties that are not observable, such as ontology, causation, function, and intention. Theory-based categories also enable children to go beyond the information given to generate inferences, predictions, and explanations.

The ontological distinction that Gelman and Koenig emphasize, and with good reason (e.g., see discussion by Mandler, chap. 5), is the animate-inanimate distinction. Perceptual features such as shape, texture, and eyes contribute to infants' ability to distinguish animate from inanimate objects, but Gelman and Koenig cite evidence that babies and young children classify objects on the basis of animacy even when it is not based on such perceptual cues. The centrality of animacy is evident in the kinds of distinctions that languages make, and young children master a number of linguistic conventions that explicitly or implicitly code animacy. Gelman and Koenig remain uncertain about the age at which this ontological distinction emerges but argue that it has a clear privileged status by age 3.

Another implication of theory-based categorization is that causality should play a critical role in the representation of categories. Implicit causal knowledge guides attention to relevant features and their correlations in classification. Even in the face of salient noncausal perceptual features, very young children rely on features involved in causal relations to categorize objects and draw inductive inferences. We will return to the importance of causality when we discuss Gopnik and Nazzi's chapter.

A theory-based representation of artifacts implies attention to functionally relevant over functionally irrelevant perceptual features. Gelman and Koenig summarize the controversy surrounding whether young children are capable of relying on function in classifying objects. In particular, Smith et al. (1996) claim that 3-year-olds are not influenced by function in naming objects while Kemler Nelson (Kemler Nelson, Russell, Duke, & Jones, 2000) and others find that young children do use function as a basis for extending object labels. Gelman and Koenig argue that differences in task demands explain the differences in findings, and that when function is made salient and comprehensible to young children, even 2-year-olds attend to and rely on functional cues in naming objects. Because form and function are often related, an understanding of function leads young children to attend to relevant perceptual features.

For animate objects, intention is a nonperceptual property that affects how very young children classify objects, the inferences they draw, and their behavior toward the objects. Woodward (1998) has provided striking evidence that even 6-month-olds construe actions performed by animate but not inanimate objects as goal directed. Thus, some of the conceptual ramifications of the ontological distinction between animate and inanimate things may be available even in young infants. Perceptual features, such as eyes, are doubtless important for this distinction and for attributing intentionality to objects. But, as Gelman and Koenig note, neither animacy nor intention can be reduced to perceptual features. For example, Johnson, Slaughter, and Carey (1998) found that 12-month-olds will follow the "gaze" of a creature without eyes if the object had earlier responded contingently to the baby.

Intention also plays a role in children's reasoning about artifacts: children are sensitive to the function that the creator of an artifact had in mind when creating it and use that intended function in naming and reasoning tasks. For example, Bloom and Markson (1998) found that whether children considered a picture to be a lollipop or a balloon depended on their intent in drawing it, not on perceptual features that were the same in both cases. Similarly, Gelman and Bloom (2000) found that objects were considered to be artifacts if created intentionally rather than accidentally. For example, children will judge a jagged piece of Plexiglas to be a knife if it was created through intentional rather than accidental means.

Many of the criteria already mentioned, such as the importance of function in classifying artifacts, of intention in distinguishing animate from inanimate objects, and of the intention of the creator in classifying drawings and artifacts, are evidence that children rely on nonobvious properties in constructing their classifications of objects. Gelman and Koenig cite a range of other studies that document children's weighing internal parts or substance in categorizing objects. Moreover, such reliance on internal parts occurs before children have detailed knowledge or understanding of the parts or their functions.

Another way in which children's categorizations are more than a record of correlated perceptual features is that children use categories to make predictions and draw inferences about novel properties of objects. By age 2½, children assume that categories provide inductive potential. As Gelman and Koenig argue, "children do not assume that labels are mere conveniences—ways of efficiently referring to perceptually encountered information in a shorthand way. Instead, children expect certain labels—and the categories to which they refer—to capture properties well beyond those they have already encountered" (pp. 344–345). Labels are a form of cultural transmission of knowledge—allowing one individual to efficiently pass on nonobvious information to other individuals and later generations—and may be critical in helping children form theory-based categories.

One major strength of the theory-based approach as outlined by Gelman and Koenig is the number of different sources of converging evidence that support their framework. One should ask, however, whether all of this evidence is equally strong and resistant to low-level explanations. That is, to what extent could an associationist mechanism account for the various pieces of evidence that Gelman and her colleagues have assembled? For example, could a pattern of correlations that includes both the perceptual and behavioral cues of an object be sufficient for detecting animacy? If lower-level, domain-general mechanisms could explain some of the evidence they cite, does this diminish the strength of their overall argument for theory-based categorization? Another issue we alluded to earlier concerns the extent to which children's categories really are theory based per se, instead of reflecting isolated facts, sketchy knowledge, or even simply a faith that there must be an underlying cause even though it is unspecified or poorly understood. In other words, there are different kinds of support or instantiations of "nonobvious" properties, ranging from vague beliefs to well-articulated theories. It would be useful to specify more precisely whether each of these is equally strong evidence against associationist views of conceptual development.

Like Gelman and Koenig, Gopnik and Nazzi (chap. 12) argue that perceptually based accounts of categorization are insufficient. While Gelman and Koenig point to ontology, function, intention, and other nonobvious properties as evidence for young children's theory-based categories, Gopnik and Nazzi focus mainly on causality, arguing that essentialism reflects a belief that there is some common cause for the characteristic properties of objects (see Strevens, 2000, for an argument that children (and adults) may hold nonessentialist causal beliefs). On their view, all of the theory-based evidence reflects a belief in some causal mechanism. In the case of biological natural kinds, for example, internal structure will be postulated as the causal mechanism; in the case of artifacts, the purpose for which an object is designed will be the cause. Causal mechanisms predict and explain correlations among features, and provide a reason for believing in the inductive potential of categories. Gopnik and Nazzi propose not only that an object's underlying cause predicts the correlations among its properties but that children can reason from patterns of correlations to cause. Rather than simply attending to patterns of correlations of features as a summary of object characteristics, these patterns can actually be used to infer causal relations. In marked contrast to Smith et al. (chap. 11), for Gopnik and Nazzi "perceptual features are important only insofar as they are an indicator of underlying causal powers" (p. 305). In this analysis, Gopnik and Nazzi provide an original theoretical framework and powerful models of children's reasoning about cause-and-effect relations.

Based on this analysis, one might expect their research to focus on ways that children's essentialist theories account for the correlated features of objects, but Gopnik and Nazzi instead provide an analysis of casual relations between one object and others. It is important to note that there are likely to be major differences between explanations of why intrinsic properties cohere and explanations of how one object exerts an effect on others. As Abelev (2001) has argued, there are significant differences in children's ability to reason about intrinsic versus extrinsic properties of objects. Gopnik and Nazzi provide a compelling model of extrinsic cause-and-effect relations, but they have yet to apply it to the problem of why an object has the features it does. That said, we turn to summarize the detailed and subtle argument they make.

A good analog for the kind of problem Gopnik and Nazzi consider is magnetism. Two similar objects, say two spoons, can differ in terms of which is attracted to a magnet, while two dissimilar objects can both be attracted. Gopnik and Nazzi argue that children set up "causal maps" of the world that go beyond whatever fundamental causal notions or perception may be hardwired. These learned causal maps consist of "abstract, coherent, representation[s] of the causal relationships among kinds of objects and events" (p. 307), where causal relationships between events are systematically related to patterns of conditional probabilities among those events. The model also takes into account whether an outcome was produced by some intervention apart from the causal relations being analyzed.

To test these ideas, Gopnik and colleagues have predicted that children categorize and name objects on the basis of perceived common causal powers. They describe a number of studies designed to test these ideas with children ranging in age from 18 months to 4 years. Many of the studies used a procedure involving a "blicket detector": An object the experimenter called a *blicket* was placed on a machine and made the machine light up and play music. The key question was what other objects children would consider to be blickets—objects that were perceptually similar but failed to set the machine off or less similar objects that made the machine react. Three- and 4-year-olds were equally likely to choose causally or perceptually similar objects. Two-year-olds selected perceptually similar objects more often but still chose causally similar ones more often than a distractor object. In a control experiment, the contingencies were the same, but the experimenter held the object he called a *blicket* over the machine while he obviously pressed the machine with his other hand, apparently activating its lights and music. Now children routinely selected other blickets based on perceptual similarity. By analyzing the hand as an intervention that activated the machine, the same statistical association between the objects and the machine's activity was reinterpreted by the children. These initial studies established the basic findings that children name objects on the basis of their causal powers and that the causal maps they use go beyond simple statistical regularities.

As with any seminal work, these studies raise a number of questions. First, it is important to clarify the difference between the kind of analyses required to establish causal maps and the kind of statistical analyses assumed in the models of Smith et al. (chap. 11) and Mareschal (chap. 14): What is it about the Bayes nets, which work by establishing relations between conditional probabilities, that defies the assumptions of the associationist models? Where would the simpler statistics fail in terms of learning patterns of relations among conditional probabilities?

A second question concerns the domain specificity of the mechanism: What leads children to establish causal maps? Does a child need to suspect a causal relation in order to notice, represent, and analyze the relevant relations? If so, what would cause a child to initiate this analysis? To return to the point we made earlier about intrinsic versus extrinsic relations, seeing that something appears to make a machine light up might cause children to wonder what is happening or how it works. But simply observing a property of an object, for example, that a shirt is red or that a tiger has stripes, might not readily elicit the same desire for an explanation. In other words, seeing what appears to be an effect of one object on another might be an impetus to construct a causal analysis, while simply observing an object with its intrinsic properties might not. If a trigger is needed, then unless something draws their attention to a causal question, children might not routinely set up causal maps to explain why objects have the properties they do. If a trigger is not necessary, then is this propensity to set up causal maps totally unconstrained? Does a causal analysis run indiscriminately, continuously setting up relations between conditional probabilities for a huge number of coincidental events, with only a small percentage of them paying off? It seems more likely that some prescreening sets this analysis in motion—some sense that a causal question is of interest.

A third question, related to domain specificity, concerns the substantive content, such as core concepts and causal principles, of the theories. It is worth taking lay physics as a model of a theory and contrasting it with the causal theory Gopnik and Nazzi argue children create to explain the blicket detector. In lay physics, the theory has content with substantive concepts and causal principles at issue, not just an abstract map of patterns of conditional probabilities: objects move about in space and time, two objects cannot occupy the same space at the same time, and so on. It is unlikely that children have any such principles to distinguish blickets from non-blickets. Another question this research raises then is how causal maps might provide the scaffolding for the more substantive concepts that a causal theory will ultimately have.

Naming and the Scope of Lexical Categories

We turn now to directly address questions about the role of language in category development. Waxman (chap. 9) tackles a fundamental question at the heart of word learning. Her chapter is an attempt to reconcile two competing theories of how children learn words: one posits a priori expectations that link each type of word with a particular type of meaning, and the other suggests that these expectations are not a priori but develop during the course of word learning. Waxman's thoughtful solution to this debate is to suggest a combination of the two. She argues that children begin the process of word learning with an expectation, namely that words highlight commonalities between objects or, as she puts it, words serve as "invitations to form categories." Experience, however, provides children with the necessary input to learn that certain grammatical form classes highlight certain categories. For example, nouns highlight object-based categories, and adjectives highlight property-based ones. Because languages mark grammatical form classes in different ways, children must learn the relevant linguistic conventions in their language before they will have expectations about specific word-category links.

Using a procedure that combines elements of a novelty-preference task with elements of a word-extension task, Waxman and her colleagues have demonstrated just such a progression from a general expectation about words to more refined expectations about particular grammatical form classes. They have shown that 11-month-olds have a general expectation that words highlight categories but do not yet distinguish between nouns and adjectives. Fourteen-month-olds, on the other hand, are a bit more advanced: they are beginning to work out the word-category links, expecting nouns to extend to object categories, but they are not yet sure about adjectives, extending them to either object-based or property-based categories. Presumably, older infants would also expect nouns to highlight object-based categories, but they would expect adjectives to extend only to property-based ones. Even very young children, then, most of whom have barely begun producing their first words, do seem to have an expectation that words highlight commonalities between objects (see also discussions in Markman, 1992; Markman & Hutchinson, 1984; Hollich, Hirsh-Pasek, & Golinkoff, 2000). It remains an open question how these expectations are formed.

Mervis, Pani, and Pani (chap. 10) also argue that words highlight commonalities between objects. Like Waxman, they argue that a child's expectation about which features of a category are relevant to that category may differ from an adult's. However, whereas Waxman focused on how inexperience with grammatical form class can lead a child to make errors in extension, Mervis et al. focus on how inexperience with adult-relevant features of an object can lead to extension errors. On their argument, a child may think that certain features of an object are critical to its identity, when in fact these features may be irrelevant from an adult perspective. For example, a child may overextend *ball* to a ball-shaped candle because, from the child's point of view, its shape or rollability is its most important feature. Similarly, a child may fail to extend *ball* to a football because it lacks the shape associated with balls. This is not to say that children do not notice certain similarities between, for example, the football and more typically shaped balls; they merely emphasize certain features they believe to be more relevant (in the sense of L. Bloom, 1993).

Mervis et al. offer a unique approach to studying this issue, with exceptionally detailed diary data from one child's acquisition of words in the bird domain. Concentrating on a single child's acquisition of words in a single hierarchical category has the advantage of allowing for the careful study of how input affects uptake and how new words change a category's structure. Not many children younger than 2 years old have the elaborated hierarchies of birds that Ari had, and they may, in fact, lack any equally elaborated hierarchy. Nonetheless, the principles by which he learned new words and incorporated them into his existing lexicon have implications for theories about how children learn words and the power that labels come to have.

Given that children's categories as embodied in their lexical categories may not overlap perfectly with those of adults, the question taken up in Mervis et al.'s chapter is how they come to coincide. Mervis et al. argue that this process is the result of a cooperative effort between the child and his or her communicative partners. On Mervis et al.'s view, the input strategy used can influence the extent to which a child incorporates new information into an existing lexical entry. A strategy that highlights the distinguishing adult feature seems to be more effective at changing early lexical categories than a strategy where an adult simply provides a new label for a miscategorized object: highlighting the adult-relevant feature can make it clear why a new category assignment is appropriate for that object, thereby providing a hook for the child to begin forming a new category distinct from the known one. Later, children may learn a new label for a miscategorized object without any supporting information, but this requires that the child have what Mervis et al. call the authority principle, or the understanding/belief that "there exist people (authorities) who know more about forms, functions, and form-function correlations than you do" (p. 248). Note that an "authority principle" could be invoked to explain children's acceptance of adult input in domains other than language. Such an assumption might facilitate the acquisition of knowledge much more generally. In terms of category learning, the authority principle allows children to accept a category assignment even when they do not understand the basis for it.

On our view, a willingness to accept a category label for objects that children would not have classified together on their own is crucial to conceptual development. No longer is the child bound by perceptual categories, or even by functional (Kemler Nelson et al., 2000) or causal (Gopnik & Sobel, 2000) categories formed on the basis of the child's own experience. Instead, children can form categories on the basis of language, with a simple category label serving as a placeholder for some possibly as-yet-unspecified similarity or cluster of similarities that makes members of that category cohere.

Putnam (1975) has suggested that a key element of adult communication is that we frequently refer to things without necessarily knowing the criteria for use of the terms we use. He writes that "every linguistic community . . . possesses at least some terms whose associated 'criteria' are known only to a subset of the speakers who acquire the terms, and whose use by the other speakers depends upon a structured cooperation between them and the speakers in the relevant subsets" (p. 126). In his words, language use requires a "division of linguistic labor." For example, although most adult speakers of English could identify most instances of the term *tiger*, few would be able to provide a compelling explanation or test for what makes something a *tiger*; for that, we rely on experts (although, in fact, there may be no scientifically valid essentialist explanation; Gelman & Medin, 1993). By analogy, children who accept that two things they would not have spontaneously categorized together are members of the same kind will expect those things to have unobservable properties in common—properties relating to ontology, causation, function, essentialism, and so on that are the fundamental determinants of what something is, what it does, what you can expect from it, and so on. Note that, as our earlier discussion of McCarrell and Callanan (1995) showed, children do not blindly make the decision to treat two things called by the same name as the same kind of thing. They use all of the available information in making their decision, and which information is most relevant will depend on the type of theories children have.

Mervis et al. argue that Ari did not accept new category labels for miscategorized objects until about 20 months, which could be interpreted as meaning that prior to 20 months, he did not expect categories to have nonobvious similarities or did not yet possess the authority principle. We think this is a conservative estimate. In a recent study by Graham, Kilbreath, and Welder (2001), for example, 13-month-olds were quite likely to use a novel object to imitate an action that produced an interesting sound if that object looked highly similar to a demonstration object that had earlier been shown to produce the sound (see also Baldwin, Markman, & Melartin, 1993). They were unlikely to attempt to perform the action if the object was low in perceptual similarity. However, when 13-month-olds heard the object low in perceptual similarity called by the same name as the demonstration object, they were just as likely to attempt to perform the target action. In other words, these very young infants—just beginning to produce their first words—already expect category members to share unforeseen similarities, and they can use language to categorize objects in nonobvious ways. Similarly, Waxman and Markow (1995) have shown that a novel label applied to members of the same superordinate category can facilitate the formation of a superordinate category in 12-month-olds.

The child's version of the division of linguistic labor seems more appropriately characterized as a continuum rather than an all-or-none ability, with Waxman's "invitation to form categories" toward one end and Mervis et al.'s authority principle toward the other. That is, very young infants may be able to form a new category on the basis of familiar objects sharing the same novel label, as in Waxman and Markow (1995), or novel objects sharing the same novel label, as in Graham et al. (2001). But they may not be able to form a new category for an initially miscategorized object on the basis of linguistic information alone, as in the examples in Mervis et al. (chap. 10). Recategorizing an initially miscategorized object into a known category on the basis of linguistic information may be an even more advanced ability, requiring the child not only to accept that nonobvious features bind two dissimilar things together but also to discount the perceptual features of one of the objects entirely.

We have recently begun a series of studies that may shed light on this issue (Jaswal & Markman, 2002). Briefly, infants are shown, for example, that a dog plays with a stick and that a cat plays with a ball of yarn. They are then shown a computer-generated animal that adults and preschoolers have indicated looks very much like a dog (but that has some features of a cat), and infants are asked to show what it plays with. Some children hear this chimera called *this cat*, and some hear it referred to as *this one*. Twenty-four-month-olds who hear it referred to as *this cat* are quite likely to infer that it plays with yarn, while those who hear it referred to as *this one* are more likely to infer that it plays with a stick. For a category label to have this effect, children must be willing to set aside their own compelling, perceptually based classification in favor of a classification they do not understand. That is, they must accept "on faith" that there is a reason why an animal that looks very much like a dog is being called a *cat*. Whether children younger than 24 months can also use linguistic information in this way is the focus of ongoing work.

Of course, under most circumstances, using an object's appearance to determine its category membership is reliable (Landau, Smith, & Jones, 1988). A related objection is that in the real world, there are many more cues to an object's identity than the single, often purposely degraded or ambiguous image provided in many studies of category induction—cues like the way it moves, its smell, views from multiple vantage points, and so on (Jones & Smith, 1993). All of this is obviously true: there are very strong correspondences between appearance and identity; as adults, we may even think that there is a nonarbitrary relationship between the two (Medin & Ortony, 1989). Indeed, in a typical 2-year-old's productive vocabulary, most category labels represent categories whose members cohere perceptually (Samuelson & Smith, 1999). Ironically, we find that these objections actually bolster our case: despite the fact that appearances usually are a good clue as to category membership, and despite the fact that most count nouns encode perceptually similar objects, even very young children expect category members to share deeper similarities (though they may not know what those are), and they can use language to categorize objects in these nonobvious (and often underspecified) ways.

Conclusions: Prerequisites of a Theory of Conceptual Development

These six chapters, along with other recent advances in the field, point toward a set of principles, abilities, and phenomena that a complete theory of conceptual development must address. Extrapolating from this and other work, we propose that a coherent theory of children's categorization requires an integration of the following abilities of infants and young children.

Associative and Statistical Mechanisms

There are now several striking demonstrations of the power of associative mechanisms to pull out the correlational structure of objects in the environment (chaps. 4, 7, 11, 14), and even some work documenting infants' abilities to compute conditional probabilities over some kinds of events (Saffran, Aslin, & Newport, 1996). At a minimum, these computations of the relations between features provide useful partitions of the world. Are children ever limited to carving up the world into only those categories that cohere perceptually in this way? In our view, this remains an open question, but if there is such a limitation, it is only in early infancy. Moreover, there is even evidence that 10-month-olds don't or can't use such featural information for tracking numerical identify of objects and that they rely instead on spatial-temporal information (Xu & Carey, 1996). If infants rely solely on perceptual features to identify objects, why, then, would they resort to principles of lay physics for tracking object identity?

We agree that, throughout life, associative mechanisms supply crucial input into a system that constructs categories and that they provide information that is routinely used for identifying category members. What something looks like, sounds like, and feels like is important information about what it is. Important, but not definitive. We also agree that some of the mapping of categories to a given lexical item or to a given grammatical form class is accomplished in part by associative mechanisms. But existing models have a serious shortcoming: they treat words as features that enter into a correlational matrix. In fact, words are not features of objects; words are symbols that refer.

Causal/Theory Based Reasoning

Even infants encode at least some events in terms of causal relations, and there are several ways in which causality or theory-based reasoning play important roles in children's construction of categories and reasoning about kinds. We emphasize three points here.

1. *Relevant ontological/theoretical/causal knowledge is recruited where possible and where needed, even by infants.* A given category can be theory based without requiring new causal principles to be developed for each category or categorization decision. Instead, relevant principles that have already been established can be recruited as appropriate for a given category (see chap. 7). Even young infants honor onto-logical distinctions such as animate/inanimate or object/substance. These core ontological principles influence their categorization and can even cause them to categorize in ways that contradict an analysis based solely on perceptual features.

2. *Children believe in determinism.* Even very young children probably have at least a vague sense that all things must have a cause. This is reflected in children's essentialist beliefs about categories. This belief can serve as a motivation to seek a deeper, nonperceptual explanation for why things have the obvious and non-obvious properties they do. It also makes it plausible for children that two things that don't seem much alike could still be members of the same category. That is, children are willing to defy the output of the associative analysis on perceptual features because they take it on faith that there are deeper causes for things to be the way they are.

3. *There are some potentially domain specific learning mechanisms for constructing theory-based knowledge.* One form that these mechanisms take might be tied to specific foundational theories, such as lay physics or lay psychology, that infants may hold. A second form is the one that Gopnik and Nazzi advocate—a computational ability that enables the construction of causal relations.

The Division of Linguistic Labor

Even adults accept and use terms without being able to provide the scientific criteria for their use (e.g., Could you perform a test to distinguish between *gold* and *fool's gold*?), accepting what Putnam (1975) has called the division of linguistic labor. We all benefit from the accumulated knowledge of our culture, handed down to us, in part, through the categories that have proved useful to others in the past. The labels that objects are given can inform us about those categories even when we may not understand their basis. Thus, as many have argued, language serves as a mechanism for the cultural transmission of knowledge (Gelman, Hollander, Star, & Heyman, 2000; Gentner & Boroditsky, 2000; Tomasello, 1999).

Children with very little linguistic experience can use language to carve the world up differently from how they would do so spontaneously, suggesting that they also adhere to something like a division of linguistic labor. On our view, the division of linguistic labor and essentialism go hand in hand, complementing each other and allowing for the formation of categories that are not perceptually or even experientially based. That is, essentialist beliefs lead children to expect that category members share deeper, nonobvious similarities. A simple category label can serve as a placeholder for a theory about why two things are members of the same kind and can be used to make inferences when kind is relevant to the inference. But for language to have this power, children must sometimes be willing to accept counterintuitive and baffling labels that defy the output generated by lower-level associative mechanisms (e.g., Why is an eel a *fish*? Why are both tables and lamps *furniture*?). That children regularly do so suggests that they accept a division of linguistic labor and can use labels to learn categories that fly in the face of perceptual similarity.

In sum, the ability to compute statistics that partition the world into objects with correlated features is an important source of input into any system that must identify objects. But the ability of those domain-general learning mechanisms to account for apparently uniquely human assumptions about essentialism, causality, and nonobvious features—assumptions that enable deeper thinking and reasoning about objects—is questionable. It is these assumptions, in combination with the division of linguistic labor, that allow children to form categories they could not form on their own and to benefit from the accumulated knowledge of their culture.

Acknowledgments

We thank Susan Johnson and Josh Tenenbaum for helpful discussions about issues raised in this chapter.

References

Abelev, M. (2001). Multiple object identity comprehension in 3-year-olds: Appearance, pretense, function. Unpublished manuscript, Stanford University, Stanford, CA.
Akhtar, N., & Tomasello, M. (1996). Two-year-olds learn words for absent objects and actions. *British Journal of Developmental Psychology, 14,* 79–93.
Baldwin, D. A. (1991). Infants' contribution to the achievement of joint reference. *Child Development, 62,* 875–890.

Baldwin, D. A. (1992). Clarifying the role of shape in children's taxonomic assumption. *Journal of Experimental Child Psychology, 54*, 392–416.

Baldwin, D. A., Markman, E. M., & Melartin, R. L. (1993). Infants' ability to draw inferences about nonobvious object properties: Evidence from exploratory play. *Child Development, 64*, 711–728.

Bloom, L. (1993). *The transition from infancy to language: Acquiring the power of expression.* Cambridge: Cambridge University Press.

Bloom, P. (2000). *How children learn the meanings of words.* Cambridge, MA: MIT Press.

Bloom, P., & Markson, L. (1998). Intention and analogy in children's naming of pictorial representations. *Psychological Science, 9*, 200–204.

Bullock, M., Gelman, R., & Baillargeon, R. (1982). The development of causal reasoning. In W. E. Friedman (Ed.), *The developmental psychology of time* (pp. 209–254). New York: Academic Press.

Carey, S., & Markman, E. M. (1999). Cognitive development. In B. M. Bly & D. E. Rumelhart (Eds.), *Cognitive science* (pp. 201–254). San Diego: Academic Press.

Gelman, S. A., & Bloom, P. (2000). Young children are sensitive to how an object was created when deciding what to name it. *Cognition, 76*, 91–103.

Gelman, S. A., Hollander, M., Star, J., & Heyman, G. D. (2000). The role of language in the construction of kinds. *Psychology of Learning and Motivation, 39*, 201–263.

Gelman, S. A., & Markman, E. M. (1986). Categories and induction in young children. *Cognition, 23*, 183–208.

Gelman, S. A., & Medin, D. L. (1993). What's so essential about essentialism? A different perspective on the interaction of perception, language, and conceptual knowledge. *Cognitive Development, 8*, 157–167.

Gentner, D., & Boroditsky, L. (2000). Individuation, relativity and early word learning. In M. Bowerman & S. Levinson (Eds.), *Language acquisition and conceptual development* (pp. 215–256). Cambridge: Cambridge University Press.

Goodman, J. C., McDonough, L., & Brown, N. B. (1998). The role of semantic context and memory in the acquisition of novel nouns. *Child Development, 69*, 1330–1344.

Gopnik, A., & Sobel, D. M. (2000). Detecting blickets: How young children use information about novel causal powers in categorization and induction. *Child Development, 71*, 1205–1222.

Graham, S. A., Kilbreath, C. S., & Welder, A. N. (2001). Words and shape similarity guide 13-month-olds' inferences about nonobvious object properties. In J. D. Moore & K. Stenning (Eds.), *Proceedings of the 23rd Annual Conference of the Cognitive Science Society* (pp. 352–357). Hillsdale, NJ: Erlbaum.

Hollich, G. J., Hirsh-Pasek, K., Golinkoff, R. M. (2000). Breaking the language barrier: An emergentist coalition model for the origins of word learning. *Monographs of the Society for Research in Child Development, 65*(3, Serial No. 262).

Huntley-Fenner, G., Carey, S., & Solimando, A. (2001). Objects are individuals but stuff doesn't count: Perceived rigidity and cohesiveness influence infants' representations of small groups of discrete entities. Unpublished manuscript, Harvard University, Cambridge, MA.

Imai, M., & Gentner, D. (1997). A cross-linguistic study of early word meaning: Universal ontology and linguistic influence. *Cognition, 62*, 169–200.

Imai, M., Gentner, D., & Uchida, N. (1994). Children's theories of word meaning: The role of shape similarity in early acquisition. *Cognitive Development, 9*, 45–75.

Inhelder, B., & Piaget, J. (1964). *The early growth of logic in the child.* New York: Norton.

Jaswal, V. K., & Markman, E. M. (2002, April). *The effects of non-intuitive labels on toddlers' inferences.* Paper presented at the biennial meeting of the International Society on Infant Studies. Toronto, Canada.

Johnson, S., Slaughter, V., & Carey, S. (1998). Whose gaze will infants follow? The elicitation of gaze-following in 12-month-olds. *Developmental Science, 1,* 233–238.

Jones, S. S., & Smith, L. B. (1993). The place of perception in children's concepts. *Cognitive Development, 8,* 113–139.

Kemler Nelson, D. G., Russell, R., Duke, N., & Jones, K. (2000). Two-year-olds will name artifacts by their functions. *Child Development, 71,* 1271–1288.

Landau, B., Smith, L. B., & Jones, S. S. (1988). The importance of shape in early lexical learning. *Cognitive Development, 3,* 299–321.

Loose, J., & Mareschal, D. (1999). Inductive reasoning revisited: Children's reliance on category labels and appearance. In M. Hahn & S. C. Stone (Eds.), *Proceedings of the 21st Annual Conference of the Cognitive Science Society* (pp. 320–325). London: Erlbaum.

Mareschal, D., French, R. M., & Quinn, P. C. (2000). A connectionist account of asymmetric category learning in early infancy. *Developmental Psychology, 36,* 635–645.

Markman, E. M. (1992). Constraints on word learning: Speculations about their nature, origins, and domain specificity. In M. R. Gunnar & M. Maratsos (Eds.), *Modularity and constraints in language and cognition* (pp. 59–101). Hillsdale, NJ: Erlbaum.

Markman, E. M., and Hutchinson, J. E. (1984). Children's sensitivity to constraints on word meaning: Taxonomic versus thematic relations. *Cognitive Psychology, 16,* 1–27.

Massey, C. M., & Gelman, R. (1988). Preschoolers' ability to decide whether a photographed unfamiliar object can move itself. *Developmental Psychology, 24,* 307–317.

McCarrell, N., & Callanan, M. (1995). Form-function correspondences in children's inference. *Child Development, 66,* 532–546.

Medin, D. L., & Ortony, A. (1989). Psychological essentialism. In S. Vosniadou & A. Ortony (Eds.), *Similarity and analogical reasoning* (pp. 179–195). Cambridge: Cambridge University Press.

Putnam, H. (1975). The meaning of "meaning." In K. Gunderson (Ed.), *Language, mind, and knowledge* (Vol. 7, pp. 131–193). Minneapolis: University of Minnesota Press.

Quinn, P. C., Eimas, P. D., & Rosenkrantz, S. L. (1993). Evidence for representations of perceptually similar natural categories by 3-month-old and 4-month-old infants. *Perception, 22,* 463–475.

Saffran, J. R., Aslin, R. N., & Newport, E. L. (1996). Statistical learning by 8-month-old infants. *Science, 274,* 1926–1928.

Samuelson, L. K., & Smith, L. B. (1999). Early noun vocabularies: Do ontology, category structure and syntax correspond? *Cognition, 73,* 1–33.

Smith, L. B., Jones, S. S., & Landau, B. (1996). Naming in young children: a dumb attentional mechanism? *Cognition, 60,* 143–171.

Strevens, M. (2000). The essentialist aspect of naive theories. *Cognition, 74,* 149–175.

Tomasello, M. (1999). *The cultural origins of human cognition.* Cambridge, MA: Harvard University Press.

Waxman, S. R., & Markow, D. B. (1995). Words as invitations to form categories: Evidence from 12- to 13-month-old infants. *Cognitive Psychology, 29,* 257–302.

Woodward, A. L. (1998). Infants selectively encode the goal object of an actor's reach. *Cognition, 69,* 1–34.

Wynn, K. (1992). Addition and subtraction by human infants. *Nature, 358,* 749–750.

Xu, F., & Carey, S. (1996). Infants' metaphysics: The case of numerical identity. *Cognitive Psychology, 30,* 111–153.

CHAPTER SIXTEEN

Final Commentary
Conceptual Development from Origins to Asymptotes

Robert L. Goldstone and Mark K. Johansen

SCIENTISTS STUDYING ADULT CONCEPT LEARNING are typically careful to analyze the entire pattern of responses given across all of the trials of an experiment. Oftentimes the early trials are the most diagnostic because categorization accuracy quickly reaches an asymptote. We take some pride in tackling the hard problem of accounting for adaptive processes that account for category learning, unlike many psychophysicists, who simply throw out the first 1,000 trials because steady-state performance has not yet been reached. However, lest we grow too smug, the chapters of this book provide a great service by reminding us that even though we analyze the very first trial of our experiment, we are still studying conceptual change that occurs almost imperceptibly close to the asymptote. By the time that our 20-year-old subjects come to our laboratories, they have learned the majority of the concepts that they will ever learn and virtually all of their truly foundational concepts. Relatively brief laboratory training suffices to teach students the rule "circle above square" (Bruner, Goodnow, & Austin, 1956), a particular configuration of nine dots (Posner & Keele, 1968), or a new fact such as that grebes are birds, but this rapid learning is only possible because it builds upon a longer and more profound process by which concepts such as *Above* (chap. 3), *bird* (chap. 10), *animal* (chaps. 5, 14), and *animacy* (chaps. 7, 13) are learned.

Those of us who want to develop theories of the learning and representation of adult concepts cannot afford to remain blind to the conceptual development that makes possible adult concept use. This lifelong learning provides us with the fundamental representations that we subsequently combine and tweak. In assessing the contribution of developmental research on concepts and categories to our general understanding of human concepts, we will ask four questions. What are concepts? What is the relation between perception and concepts? What are the constraints on concept learning? What are promising future directions for research on concepts?

What Are Concepts?

A good starting place is Edward Smith's (1989) characterization of a concept as "a mental representation of a class or individual and deals with *what* is being represented and *how* that information is typically used during the categorization" (p. 502). It is common to distinguish between a concept and a category (e.g., Hampton & Dubois, 1993). A concept refers to a mentally possessed idea or notion, whereas a category refers to a set of entities that are grouped together. The concept *dog* is whatever psychological state signifies thoughts of dogs. The category *dog* consists of all the entities in the external world that are appropriately categorized as dogs. In short, concepts are in minds while categories are sets in the external world.

The question of whether concepts determine categories or vice versa is an important, foundational controversy and an extension of the longstanding debate in philosophy over whether concepts correspond to something in the world or are convenient habits of mind. If one assumes the primacy of external categories of entities (the realist and empiricist positions in philosophy), then one will tend to view concept learning as the enterprise of inductively creating mental structures that predict these categories. One extreme version of this view is the exemplar model of concept learning (Estes, 1994; Medin & Schaffer, 1978; Nosofsky, 1984), in which one's internal representation for a concept is nothing more than the set of all of the externally supplied examples of the concept to which one has been exposed. If one assumes the primacy of internal mental concepts (the nominalist and rationalist positions in philosophy), then one tends to view external categories as the end product of applying these internal concepts to observed entities. An extreme version of this approach is to argue that the external world does not inherently consist of rocks, dogs, and tables; these are mental concepts that organize an otherwise unstructured external world.

The authors of this book's chapters generally acknowledge the bidirectional influences between external categories and internal concepts. Some of the important differences of opinion can be expressed in terms of relative focus on one of these influences. Gelman and Koenig (chap. 13), Gopnik and Nazzi (chap. 12), and Mandler (chap. 5) stress the insufficiency of pure inductive learning from perceptually available information for establishing concepts. Mareschal (chap. 4), Rakison (chap. 7), Smith, Colunga, and Yoshida (chap. 11), and Younger (chap. 4) stress the unexpected power of the environmentally available cues that can be used to ground concepts. Still, there appears to be a convergence from all sides on the ideas that tabula rasae cannot form rich and properly constrained concepts and that our abstract concepts are tuned by feedback from perceptual sources. True conceptual learning is not contrary to internal structural constraint. Rather, it is only by having a properly constrained architecture that profound conceptual reorganization becomes possible. This lesson is learned anew every time a first-year graduate student in computer science sets out to hook a camera up to a computer, expose it to years of television input, and have the computer spontaneously organize itself. Flexible concept learning requires sophisticated processes and structures to get off the ground. The search space of possible concepts is incredibly large compared to the set of concepts that humans have found to be functional, and it is easy to forget about all the nonfunctional concepts that humans do not have precisely because we do not have them. Both metaknowledge and domain knowledge, either developmentally or evolutionarily learned, can provide structural constraints. These constraints serve to bias the search in concept space for functional concepts, that is, concepts that neither over nor undergeneralize and are thus maximally useful.

The Functions of Concepts

In assessing which concepts children have, it is useful to bear in mind some important functions of concepts. First, concepts are equivalence classes. In the classical notion of an equivalence class, distinguishable stimuli come to be treated as the same thing once they have been placed in the same category (Sidman, 1994). This kind of equivalence is too strong when it comes to human concepts because even when we place two objects into the same category, we do not treat them as the same thing for all purposes. Still, it is impressive the extent to which perceptually dissimilar things can be treated equivalently, given the appropriate conceptualization. To the biologist armed with a strong *mammal* concept, even whales and dogs may be treated as equivalent in terms of predictions about anatomy and physiology, infant feeding and rearing, and thermoregulation. Once one has formed a concept that treats all skunks as equivalent for some purposes, such as when a child hears several distinct animals labeled with the noun *skunk*, irrelevant variations among skunks can be greatly deemphasized and commonalities emphasized (Keil, 1989; chaps. 9, 13). Several of the chapters make recourse to this notion of stimulus equivalence, arguing that evidence for categorization by young children exists when perceptually discriminable stimuli are nonetheless treated similarly (chaps. 3, 5).

Second, concepts function as building blocks for complex thought. Just as an endless variety of architectural structures can be constructed out of a finite set of building blocks, so concepts act as building blocks for new concepts and an endless variety of complex thoughts. Once a concept has been formed, it can enter into compositions with other concepts. Studying how novel combinations of concepts are produced and comprehended is an active area in adult cognition (Murphy, 1988; Wisniewski, 1997). Similarly, once a concept has been established in childhood, it is subsequently used to build more sophisticated concepts (chaps. 7, 10, 13).

Third, concepts facilitate communication, which among other things allows people to acquire knowledge that enables them to make functional predictions in situations that they have not personally experienced. Communication between people is enormously facilitated if they can count on a set of common concepts (consider "Hey, there's a bear by the beehive"). People's concepts become more consistent and systematic over time in order to unambiguously establish reference for another individual with whom they need to communicate (Garrod & Doherty, 1994; Markman & Makin, 1998). Given the use of concepts for communication, it is not surprising that there are strong ties between concept learning and word learning (chaps. 2, 9–13). Waxman (chap. 9) argues that children learn not only word-to-object mappings but word-to-category mappings, making explicit the important role that concepts play in mediating between objects and words. Gelman and Koenig (chap. 13), Gopnik and Nazzi (chap. 12), and Waxman (chap. 9) show specific ways in which developing concepts not only provide a basis for language but are themselves transformed by language. Concepts provide a foundation for communication, but they do this not by remaining rigid and fixed (like the foundation of a house) but by adapting to the needs of communication (like the foundation supplied by a good pair of sandals) (see also Goldstone & Steyvers, 2001; chap. 11).

Fourth, and most important, concepts facilitate predictive inference by allowing people to generalize experience with some objects to other objects from the same category. Experience with one slobbering dog may lead one to suspect that an unfamiliar dog may have the same proclivity. Oakes and Madole (chap. 6) and Gelman and Koenig (chap. 13) take this inductive generalization function of concepts to be particularly important. Consistent with their focus on this function, the concepts that are most salient and probably most used by humans are exactly those that allow many properties to be inductively predicted.

Categories can be arranged roughly in order of their grounding by perceptual similarity: natural kinds (*dog* and *oak tree*), manmade artifacts (*hammer, airplane,* and *chair*), ad hoc categories (*things to take out of a burning house,* and *things that could be stood on to reach a light bulb*), and abstract schemas or metaphors (e.g., *events in which a kind action is repaid with cruelty, metaphorical prisons,* and *problems that are solved by breaking a large force into parts that converge on a target*). For the latter categories, members need not have very much in common at all. An unrewarding job and a relationship that cannot be ended may both be metaphorical prisons, but the situations may share little other than this. In contrast to these categories, most natural kinds and many artifacts are characterized by members that share many features (Rosch & Mervis, 1975), and as such they permit many inductive inferences. If we know something belongs to the category *dog*, then we know that it probably has four legs and two eyes, wags its tail as a sign of friendliness, is somebody's pet, pants, barks, is bigger than a breadbox, and so on.

Conversely, the features "has four legs," "tail wags," "barks," and "chases cats" tend to co-occur. So instead of saying "A four-legged, tail-wagging, bark-capable cat chaser crossed the road," little information and corresponding predictive inference potential is likely to be lost by saying "A dog crossed the road." In the same way that MP3 and zip files compress music and data by exploiting repetitions/redundancies in the files, concepts are a way of compressing reality's phenomenal stream by exploiting some of the repetitions that make reality predictable (Bar-Yam, 1999). Interestingly, in the adult category learning literature, Feldman (2000) has recently found a relationship between the difficulty of learning a set of arbitrary categories and the complexity or minimal descriptive length of the shortest rule specifying the two categories. He found that the more compressible the categories, that is, the shorter the description of the rule specifying them, the easier they are to learn. Predictability, learnability and compressibility are closely interrelated. Reality, unlike history, is destined to repeat itself only for those who know the right concepts.

Evidence for Concepts

Research on adult concept learning is dominated by a relatively small number of techniques to uncover conceptual representation. By far the most typical technique is to tell a subject "There are two categories to learn. When you see an item, make a guess as to its categorization. You will receive feedback indicating whether your categorization was correct." Another popular technique is to have subjects list features associated with a verbally presented concept. A third popular technique is to tell subjects that a thing has a certain property and ask them to indicate what is the likelihood that another thing has the property. This final technique has been successfully used with children less than 5 years of age (chaps. 12, 13), but oftentimes developmental psychologists have been forced by the limited attention spans, linguistic capacities, and meta-analytic abilities of their subjects to develop novel techniques for measuring conceptual knowledge. As Oakes and Madole (chap. 6) argue, the requirements of a categorization task influence conceptual representation, and the method of measuring a concept influences what concept a child is inferred to have. From this perspective, it is important to analyze the nature of the methods used to reveal concepts in children.

Developmental techniques, particularly those used with infants below the age of 2, are often indirect measures of concept learning that are related to generalization. Quinn (chap. 3) uses the preferential looking and generalization paradigm. Exemplars of one category (such as "triangle above line") are shown to infants, and the experimenter measures dishabituation to novel exemplars, with increased looking time suggesting that the exemplar is in a different category for the child. While Quinn (chap. 3) finds increased attention for novel rather than familiarized objects, Jusczyk (chap. 2) reports a considerable corpus of evidence from auditory speech processing that requires the assumption that familiarized objects attract a children's attention more than novel objects. These patterns of results are not irreconcilably inconsistent because of many differences in their paradigms. However, the discrepancy does highlight the importance of developing mechanistic process models underlying children's habituation, such as the type developed by Mareschal (chap. 14). Mandler (chap. 5) and Rakison (chap. 7) describe a technique that assumes that objects that are sequentially touched or sorted together are placed in a common category. Mandler and colleagues have used generalized imitation, where the infant is shown an object interacting with another object and encouraged to imitate the interaction with new objects. Waxman (chap. 9) explores generalization by labeling one object and observing what other objects a child selects when the label is repeated. Applying learned label-object associations in the reciprocal direction, Gopnik and Nazzi (chap. 12) use children's likelihood of applying the same label to two objects as a measure that they have been categorized together.

A noteworthy feature of several of these measures is that they do not require that the child has any established categories or concepts at all! Showing that a response generalizes from object A to B but not C does not show that A and B are in the same category, either in the sense that A and B are treated as equivalent, or that children have a preestablished cluster, definition, or characterization that includes both A and B but not C. Generalization is a truly universal phenomenon (Shepard, 1987) that only requires that objects be linked by similarity relations, not by categories. This is particularly true for "single-category" experiments in which a number of objects are familiarized and response generalization to other objects is observed. Such response generalization can occur on the basis of similarity between the familiarized and test objects even if none of the objects are categorized at all. This possibility is consistent with Mareschal's neural network modeling (chap. 14), in which concepts are not explicitly tokened in the network but rather are emergent and implicit results of stimulus processing. It is also consistent with Rakison's notion (chap. 7) that concepts are constructed on-line during categorization rather than having fixed and singular characterizations.

If simple response generalization does not indicate use of concepts or categories, and transfer of a learned label from a known to novel object can be viewed as simply another example of response generalization, then why is it ever necessary to talk about children possessing concepts? One answer is that once words are used to encompass a set of objects, the set seems to have more cohesion for the child. The child becomes interested in knowing what attributes characterize, if not define, the object brought together by a label and may be disposed to look for hidden, abstract, or theory-driven organization principles (Murphy & Medin, 1985; chaps. 5, 12, 13). Originally graded generalization responses give way to more discrete, categorical responses as a child gets more information about the members and attributes associated with a category, reflects on the commonalities possessed by the category members, and works to develop an economical and efficient representation to capture these commonalities.

What Is the Relation between Percepts and Concepts?

One of the primary tensions among this book's chapters, noted by Rakison (chap. 7) is in reconciling the roles of perceptual and nonperceptual information in forming concepts. Several of the chapters react against the intuitively compelling notion that there is a development trend from perceptually based concepts to abstraction-based ones. Several authors argue that even young children's concepts are based on causal, abstract, functional, theory-driven principles (chaps. 5, 7, 12, 13). Taking perhaps the most radical stance along these lines, Mandler (chap. 5) argues against a perceptual-to-conceptual trend because "if anything, development proceeds from the abstract to the concrete, rather than the other way around" (p. 104). Rakison (chap. 7) argues against the trend because he sees a common association-learning process that continues throughout childhood and is responsible for what appears to be increasingly abstract concepts. Likewise, Oakes and Madole (chap. 6) argue that children start off attending to few perceptual dimensions but gradually attend to more as they develop new ways of interacting with their world and then finish the U-shaped trajectory by attending to fewer perceptual dimensions because they use inductively acquired domain knowledge to constrain their attention.

Like these authors, we advocate a revision of the standard perceptual-to-conceptual trend. Our perspective is that perception and abstraction are better viewed as being related by a cycle rather than by a linear continuum. Reminiscent of proposals by several authors, including Rakison (chap. 7), Smith et al. (chap. 11), and Waxman (chap. 9), we will argue that *abstract* construals do not typically supplant perceptual ones but rather that abstract and perceptual construals mutually inform one another.

One of our main reasons for rejecting a simple perceptual-to-conceptual trend is that our developing categories not only are influenced by perception but also influence perception. Intentions, strategies, concepts, and knowledge all affect the perception of similarities among objects. Researchers have found that similarity assessments for a set of objects are affected by learned categorizations of those objects (Goldstone, Lippa, & Shiffrin, 2001; Lassaline, 1996; Livingston, Andrews, & Harnad, 1998). Although similarity ratings are strategic and sophisticated judgments themselves (Goldstone, 1994b), effects of categorization have also been found on tasks that tap more elementary perceptual processes like physical same/different judgments (Goldstone, 1994a) and part detection (Lin & Murphy, 1997). Electrical brain signals that occur as early as 170 milliseconds after the onset of a stimulus are affected by extended training (Fahle & Morgan, 1996) and lifelong expertise (Tanaka & Curran, 2001). Data such as these suggest that perception is adapted to promote the categories or responses required for performing a task, and these adaptations often occur at an early stage of processing (for a review, see Goldstone, 1998).

Our claim is that the development of categories, knowledge, and expertise frequently affects perceptual processing, particularly when these higher-level aspects are frequently important over an extended period of time, as is true of time scales that interest developmental psychologists. This may sound like a controversial claim for top-down processing, given the apparent self-enclosed modularity of perceptual systems (Fodor, 1983; Pylyshyn, 1999), but it is important to distinguish between two kinds of top-down processing. By one account, higher-level processes dynamically, and in a moment-to-moment fashion, affect the processing of lower-level processes. McClelland and Rumelhart's (1981) Interactive Activation Model of word perception is a classic example of this architecture, in which word-level and letter-level processing proceed simultaneously and mutually influence one another *as a word is presented*. There are strong limits on the impact that this kind of top-down influence can have, set by the temporal course of processing. Electrical signals require about 10 milliseconds to propagate across one cortical neuron. Given that visual processing as little as 170 milliseconds after stimulus onset is modulated by knowledge (e.g. Tanaka & Curran, 2001), there are not many cycles of dynamic activation passing possible.

However, in situations where dynamic modulation of a bottom-up signal by a top-down source is implausible, a second kind of top-down effect is possible that does not require a gradually activated knowledge source to excite lower levels. A lower-level perceptual process can simply change its processing in response to consistently occurring, higher-level considerations. Such top-down effects can be accommodated by a strictly feed-forward neural architecture without bidirectional activation passing during the course of stimulus processing. Well-documented cases of this kind of change are apparent in the topographical representations of the primary sensory cortex. For example, monkeys trained to make discriminations between slightly different sound frequencies develop larger cortical representations for the presented frequencies than control monkeys (Recanzone, Schreiner, & Merzenich, 1993). Similarly, monkeys learning to make a tactile discrimination with one hand develop a larger cortical representation for that hand than for the other hand (Recanzone, Merzenich, & Jenkins, 1992). Elbert et al. (1995) measured brain activity in the somatosensory cortex of violinists as their fingers are lightly touched. There was greater activity in the sensory cortex for the left hand than the right hand, consistent with the observation that violinists use their left-hand fingers considerably more than their right-hand fingers. All that is required for these kinds of neural plasticity is that habitually important discriminations become sensitized. Although this is a commonplace form of perceptual learning, it also provides a mechanism by which the perceptual system is tuned to what is functionally important for an organism.

The argument that perceptual similarity is powerful because it can be tuned to an organism's needs is a two-edged sword. Turned around, a critic can argue that the flexibility of perception only exposes its inadequacy as a solid ground for explaining cognitive processes. Certainly, perceptual similarity's explanatory value is attenuated if it is based on exactly those processes that it attempts to explain (similar arguments are presented by Goodman, 1972). However, perceptual processing is slower to change than higher-level conceptual processing, and usually people cannot strategically change their own low-level perceptual processing. Perceptual processing changes, but principally because of the statistical regularities found in the environment (chaps. 2, 4). Transitory conceptions or task-specific needs will not typically modify perceptual systems permanently. However, if a task-dependent categorization is frequently made, or is particularly promising for its organizing power, then it may eventually change the perceptual similarities that are noticed.

The preceding argument for conceptually motivated perceptual change is a species of a more general argument that perception can ground our concepts because it is more sophisticated than it appears at first (neonatal) glance (Jones & Smith, 1993; chaps. 3, 7, 11, 14). Gelman and Koenig's rejoinder (chap. 13) to this argument is that perceptually available features, no matter how sophisticated, are not sufficient to explain how children see beyond costumes, stress the importance of internal structure (even if they have never seen these structures), respect ontological distinctions, and emphasize causal and theoretically motivated features. For example, Gelman and Koenig argue (chap. 13) that the concept *dog* is not characterizable as possessing the perceptually defined feature *leg* because other objects (such as tables) also possess legs, and retorting that it must be the "right kind" of leg is empty in that it drains the perceptual account of its explanatory power. We do not wish to argue against Gelman and Koenig's claim that knowledge and theories influence our categories, but we do suspect that children go through a process of figuring out how to refine and tune their perceptual features. A child might perhaps leave out critical information about movement, texture, and detail in their initial characterization of a dog's leg, making discrimination between a dog's leg and a stuffed dog's leg difficult. However, given the importance of distinguishing real dogs from stuffed dogs and animacy from inanimacy (chap. 7), the originally overgeneral description of leg will tend to be refined until it is a useful perceptual cue.

If perception is frequently motivated by and tuned to its function for higher-level cognition, then perception should not be replaced by abstract reasoning as suggested by a perceptual-to-conceptual developmental trend. Instead, the developmental trend is better described as one from default perception to tuned perception. One phenomenon that illustrates the cooperation between perception and cognition is *interpreted perception*, the process of seeing a thing *as* something (Wittgenstein, 1953). As a guppy is seen as a fish, as a pet, as a vertebrate, or as an interior decoration, the perceptual experience of the guppy changes, and it does so in ways systematically related to the observer's perspective and knowledge. For example, Lin and Murphy (1997) showed that adults in a feature detection task were particularly likely to detect features of a category example that were important as determined by their background knowledge. Hence the primary effect of increased knowledge may not be to reduce the cognitive impact of perception. Rather, it may be to enrich perceptual experience and consequently increase its impact.

What Constrains Concept Formation?

Young children are awash in a sea of features that can be used to form concepts, and this sea of features becomes even richer as their perceptual, motor, and linguistic abilities develop (chap. 6). The need for constraints on concept formation is one of the few theoretical points in the relatively young field of developmental categorization that virtually every chapter in this book assumes and bolsters. Unconstrained feature covariance calculations based on similarity do not provide a reasonable basis for concept formation because there are too many possible feature correlations in an infant's environment (Murphy & Medin, 1985), but there is little consensus in the field on what the dominant constraints are and where they come from. Opinions run from learned selective attention to perceptual features to innate domain knowledge. Nevertheless, there are several dominant themes—selective attention, language, and domain knowledge.

Selective Attention and Bootstrapping

Many of the constraints on concept formation discussed in this book can be construed as selective attention. Younger (chap. 4) argues for selective attention to correlated features, and Jusczyk (chap 2) for selective attention to certain sounds involved with speech. Rakison (chap. 7) emphasizes selective attention to motion and object parts. These last cues are noteworthy because they can potentially be selected early in the course of perceptual processing, yet they have consequences for deeper conceptual analysis, such as the determination of animacy, natural kinds, and object identity. The correlation between a simple perceptual property related to motion and the conceptual distinction between living things and manmade objects means that processes that selectively attend to the former can eventually inform the latter. Hence the original inspiration for the conceptual distinction may be perceptual in nature. The generalization of this phenomenon is "perceptual bootstrapping," according to which relatively sophisticated features and concepts emerge from originally crude and superficial processing.

Perceptual bootstrapping plays a major role in the chapters by Jusczyk, Mareschal, Oakes and Madole, Quinn, Rakison, Smith et al., and Waxman. Jusczyk (chap. 2) describes bootstrapping from phonemic categories to grammatical categories, and

Waxman (chap. 9; see also chap. 11), in turn, describes bootstrapping from grammatical categories to semantic distinctions. Rakison (chap. 7) describes bootstrapping from the appearance of bodily appendages to their function. Mareschal (chap. 14) describes bootstrapping from relatively raw image properties to animal categories. The essential requirement for bootstrapping to occur is that there exists a correlation between properties at different levels of sophistication. Psychologists may eschew confounded variables, but they are indispensable to systems that need to learn to increase their sophistication. For example, Younger (chap. 4) demonstrates infants' sensitivity to conjunctions of features, but conjunctions of features will frequently be correlated with overall similarity. If a simple object possesses the same conjunction of features as another object, the two objects will typically be overall similar to each other. Overall similarity, a property that young children seem to be particularly adept at processing (Smith & Kemler, 1978), can be used as an inroad for developing sensitivity to specific conjunctions of features. Despite psychologists' strivings for hygienic experiments, function, appearance, and meaning are tightly related to each other. Learning often proceeds by first responding intelligently for the wrong, superficial reasons and then gradually dispensing with the scaffolding provided by the superficial cues.

Linguistic Constraints

While Mandler (chap. 5) points out the very real dangers of assuming a one-to-one correspondence between words and concepts, the influence of language is so strong that it can override the influence of perceptual similarity for categorization in young children (chap. 12). From the point of view of researchers such as Waxman (chap. 9) and Oakes and Madole (chap. 6), entities with the same label are in the same category or at least have some properties in common. Labels impact selective attention and maybe even perception by emphasizing commonalities among objects that share them. In addition, a novel label is a sign that a member of a new category is present if a set of features can be found to form the basis for a new category (as discussed in chap. 10).

Instead of having to detect the clusters of covarying properties that are widely believed to form the basis for categories (e.g., Rosch & Mervis, 1975; chaps. 4, 7, 11, 14) through raw computation, language is a way of culturally transmitting previous clusters detected by authorities with linguistic ability (chaps. 10, 13). A label is a sign that useful covariance information is present and should be used to form a concept that other people have found to be functional. The label can be used as a core around which the concept is built (chaps. 7, 12), which can considerably reduce the amount of computation needed to find useful concepts: instead of calculating the correlations between each feature and every one of the other N features in the set of all experienced features, resulting in the need for computing and maintaining N^2 correlations (considering only pairwise correlations), only the correlations between each of the N features and the label need to be computed and maintained. Clearly infants can detect correlated features, as shown by, for example, Younger (chap. 4), and many researchers emphasize correlated features as a basis for concepts (Rosch & Mervis, 1975; chaps. 7, 14). In addition, Mareschal's modeling (chap. 14) shows that concepts have the potential to arise when labels are not explicitly provided. Still, the search for correlations needs to be constrained, and cultural domain knowledge embodied in language can provide powerful constraints.

Domain Knowledge and Metaknowledge: Innate and Learned

Domain knowledge constrains concept formation (chaps. 4, 13) and allows a child to generate concepts that are not solely based on perceptual similarity. Sensitivity to some domain-specific information is arguably innate, as with the categorical perception of certain speech sounds discussed by Jusczyk (chap. 2). Other information is learned, such as the relationship between form and function, as discussed by Oakes and Madole (chap. 6) and Mervis et al. (chap. 10). In a similar vein are the findings reported by Gopnik & Nazzi (chap. 12) on grouping objects based on functional rather than perceptual similarity as the child learns about object functions.

Knowledge can be in the form of broad metaknowledge about concept formation. For example, a child needs to at least implicitly realize that objects can be classified into a hierarchy of categories (chap. 10) and unlearn the mutual exclusivity assumption proposed by Markman (1989) and discussed by Gelman and Koenig (chap. 13). Another such principle might be: generalize widely until feedback indicates overgeneralization and then narrow the concept, possibly by splitting it into several new concepts.

Evolutionary learning and cultural learning significantly bolster individual learning. It is tempting to place the responsibility for certain types of domain knowledge in the magical hands of evolution by natural selection over long spans of time. The strong similarity between individual learning and behavioral evolution has been widely noted and is well summarized by Skinner (1966). This similarity suggests that evolutionary learning still needs to be supplemented with constraints that work for individual concept learning. The set of possible concepts is very large, even on an evolutionary time scale. A comparison of lifelong and evolutionary adaptation also suggests circumstances that foster each type of learning. At a first pass, humans seem to live in the same, reasonably fixed world, suggesting that adaptation across generations would be most effective. Indeed, many general environmental factors, such as color characteristics of sunlight, the position of the horizon, and the change in appearance that an approaching object undergoes, have all been mostly stable over the time that the human visual system has developed.

However, if we look more closely, there is an important sense in which different people face different environments. Namely, to a large extent, a person's environment consists of animals, people, and things made by people. Animals and people show considerable variability, and artifacts vary widely across cultures. Evolutionary pressures may have been able to build a perceptual system that is generally adept at processing faces (Bruce, 1998), but they could not have hardwired a neural system that was adept at processing a particular face such as John Kennedy's, for the simple reason that there is too much generational variability among faces. Individual faces show variability from generation to generation, and variability is apparent over only slightly longer intervals for artifacts, words, ecological environments, and animal appearances. Thus, we can be virtually positive that hand tools show too much variability over time for there to be a hardwired detector for hammers. Words and languages vary too much for there to be a hardwired detector for the written letter *A*. Biological organisms are too geographically diverse for people to have formed a hardwired "cow" detector. When environmental variability is high, the best strategy for an organism is to develop a general perceptual system that can adapt to its local conditions.

There is an even deeper sense in which people face different environments. People find themselves in different worlds because they choose to specialize. At least in part, individuals decide for themselves what objects they will be exposed to. The kinds of concept learning that the majority of the authors of this book discuss cannot be simply relegated to evolutionary adaptation, because considerable flexibility and tailoring of concepts is required. The constraints on lifelong learning described throughout this book thus assume critical importance. These constraints allow, rather than prevent (as might be thought), flexible concept learning that can be achieved in a single lifetime.

Learning Overhypotheses

The argument thus far has been that a learning system must have constraints on hypothesis formation in order to learn concepts in a practical amount of time but that a considerable amount of flexibility is still needed because different people face different worlds and tasks. One exciting possibility raised by several of the chapters is that some of the constraints may themselves be learnable. One way to think about this possibility is in terms of Nelson Goodman's (1954) notion of an overhypothesis, a hypothesis of the form "All As are B" where A and B are generalizations of terms used in any other hypothesis we're interested in (see Shipley, 1993, for a psychological treatment). One might have hypotheses that all dogs have four legs, all storks have two legs, and all worms have no legs. Generalizing over both animals and leg number, one could construct an overhypothesis that "all animals of a particular type have a characteristic number of legs." The power of such a hypothesis is that upon seeing only a single six-legged beetle, one can infer that all beetles have six legs. Research indicates that adults use probabilistic versions of overhypotheses such as these (Heit & Rubenstein, 1994).

Gelman and Koenig (chap. 13) explicitly argue for children's use of overhypotheses and consider such overhypotheses to be evidence for the theory-driven nature of concepts. Overhypotheses are also consistent with Mandler's evidence (chap. 5) that young children typically reason with concepts at a more abstract, superordinate level than basic-level categories. These authors do not argue for overhypotheses that are learned, but this is precisely the direction that Smith et al. (chap. 11), Oakes and Madole (chap. 6), Rakison (chap. 7), and Jusczyk (chap. 2) pursue. Smith et al. (chap. 11) argue for the critical role of word learning in developing higher-order hypotheses that go from token-to-token associations to type-to-type associations. For example, learning "that solidity signals the relevance of shape and that nonsolidity signals the relevance of material—for objects and substances never encountered before and shapes and materials never experienced before" (p. 286) involves forming an overhypothesis. Madole and Cohen (1995, discussed in chap. 7) describe how

14-month-old, but not 18-month-old, children learn part-function correlations that violate real-world events, suggesting that older children *acquire* constraints on the types of correlations that they will learn. Jusczyk (chap. 2) describes the role of early language experience in establishing general hypotheses about how stress patterns inform word boundaries. Children are flexible enough to acquire either the constraints imposed by a stress-timed language like English or a syllable-timed language like Italian, but once they imprint on the systematicities within a language, they are biased to segment speech streams into words according to these acquired biases.

Overhypotheses can greatly increase the power of inductive learning and generalization. One reason why inductive learning seems so hopelessly inefficient is that researchers ignore learning of associations between properties at multiple levels of abstraction. A child seeing a penguin is not just learning that penguins are black and white but is also learning about the relations between coloration, shape, behavior, climate, diet, and so on for birds, animals, and natural kinds. Overhypotheses do not release us from our dependency on constraints. In fact, given the unlimited number of abstract descriptions applicable to an observed event, constraints become particularly important in directing us toward useful levels of abstraction. We need constraints to bias our search for associations between birds and coloration When looking at penguins, rather than associations between objects located within 5 miles of us and the number of vowels in their labels. Still, the possibility that overhypotheses can be learned goes a long way toward severing the traditional connection between constraints and innateness. Not only do constraints permit (rather than limit) learning but inductive learning can also foster the construction of strong but flexible constraints.

Future Directions

With an eye toward the future, we describe what we think are some important avenues for future progress in the field of concept learning throughout development. First, assuming that children's concepts are just underdeveloped, less-functional concepts on their way to becoming more-functional adult concepts ignores the possibility that children's concepts may need to address different functional needs than adult concepts. We anticipate future work on the question "What functionality do children's concepts have that help the child survive into later childhood?"

Second, much recent work in the adult categorization field has focused on how adults represent categories. Partly because it is so much harder to determine what concepts a child has, compared to an adult, a lot of child categorization research has focused on what concepts a child has, rather than how those concepts are represented. Nevertheless, nothing so firmly establishes what concepts a mind has as determining how those concepts are represented.

Third, there has been a trend in the adult categorization literature toward computational-process models of category representation and learning. Such process models have many advantages, including that they force a theory to be specific and help to clarify hidden assumptions. For example, Mareschal (chap. 14) and Smith et al. (chap. 11) have used connectionist models to bolster their arguments. Consideration of a formal process model in the context of almost any theory and set of data is fruitful, if for no other reason than making clear that the relationship between the data and the theory is much looser than was originally apparent. This argument for process models is closely akin to the emphasis by Oakes and Madole (chap. 6) on the importance of studying the process of concept acquisition in young children.

Fourth, as discussed earlier in this chapter, the method used to ask the question "What concepts does a child have?" is likely to strongly affect the answer. For example, the various methodologies differ in the emphasis placed on perceptual similarity, partly as a consequence of how interactive the task is for the child. The methodologies used for children of different ages have been strongly guided by pragmatic constraints such as functional and linguistic ability. Nevertheless, it would be informative to see more systematic comparisons of these methodologies for the same children at the same time, presumably at an age when both methods are pragmatically useful. It is possible that some of the evidence for a perceptual-to-conceptual shift can be clarified in the light of comparing changing expedient methodologies.

Fifth, we believe that much of the progress of research on concepts will be to connect concepts to other concepts, to the perceptual world, and to language. One dissatisfaction with the currently popular concept representation methods—including rules, prototype, sets of examples, and category boundaries—is that one can easily be misled into imagining that one concept is independent of others. For example, one can list the exemplars that are included in the concept *bird*, or describe its central tendency, without making recourse to any other concepts. However, it is likely that all of our concepts are embedded in a network where each concept's meaning depends on other concepts, as well as perceptual processes and linguistic labels. The proper level of analysis may not be individual concepts as many researchers have assumed but systems of concepts. The connections between concepts and perception on the one hand and between concepts and language on the other hand reveal an important dual nature of concepts. Concepts are used both to recognize objects and to ground word meanings. Working out the details of this dual nature will go a long way toward understanding of how human thought can be both perceptual and symbolic.

In this chapter, we have described ways in which the power of inductive concept learning can be increased: by adapting perceptual processing to accommodate concept learning, by taking advantage of perceptual/conceptual correlations to bootstrap abstract properties, by embracing constraints, and by adapting these constraints over time. These principles will be only part of the story for how children and adults learn their concepts. Other important mechanisms were described by the previous chapters, but still more work is needed on novel mechanisms for acquiring rich, interconnected, perceptually grounded, and linguistically meaningful concepts. The field of conceptual development may still be in its infancy, but as the chapters in this book testify, this is the period where the most fundamental progress in conceptual organization can be found.

Acknowledgments

Many useful comments and suggestions were provided by Lisa Oakes and David Rakison. This research was supported by National Institute of Health Grant R01 MH56871 and National Science Foundation Grant 0125287. The first author can be reached by electronic mail at rgoldsto@indiana.edu, and further information about the laboratory can be found at http://cognitrn.psych.indiana.edu/.

References

Bar-Yam, Y. (1999). *Patterns of meaning*. Boston: New England Complex Systems Institute.

Bruce, V. (1998). *In the eye of the beholder: The science of face perception*. New York: Oxford University Press.

Bruner, J. S., Goodnow, J. J., & Austin, G. A. (1956). *A study of thinking*. New York: Wiley.

Elbert, T., Pantev, C., Wienbruch, C., Rockstroh, B., & Taub, E. (1995). Increased cortical representation of the fingers of the left hand in string players. *Science, 270*, 307–307.

Estes, W. K. (1994). *Classification and cognition*. New York: Oxford University Press.

Fahle, M., & Morgan, M. (1996). No transfer of perceptual learning between similar stimuli in the same retinal position. *Current Biology, 6*, 292–297.

Feldman, J. (2000). Minimization of Boolean complexity in human concept learning. *Nature, 407*, 630–633.

Fodor, J. A. (1983). *The modularity of mind*. Cambridge, MA: MIT Press. Bradford Books.

Garrod, S., & Doherty, G. (1994). Conversation, co-ordination and convention: An empirical investigation of how groups establish linguistic conventions. *Cognition, 53*, 181–215.

Goldstone, R. L. (1994a). Influences of categorization on perceptual discrimination. *Journal of Experimental Psychology: General, 123*, 178–200.

Goldstone, R. L. (1994b). The role of similarity in categorization: Providing a groundwork. *Cognition, 52*, 125–157.

Goldstone, R. L. (1998). Perceptual learning. *Annual Review of Psychology, 49*, 585–612.

Goldstone, R. L., Lippa, Y., & Shiffrin, R. M. (2001). Altering object representations through category learning. *Cognition, 78*, 27–43.

Goldstone, R. L., & Stevyers, M. (2001). The sensitization and differentiation of dimensions during category learning. *Journal of Experimental Psychology: General, 130*, 116–139.

Goodman, N. (1954). *Fact, fiction, and forecast*. London: Athlone Press.

Goodman, N. (1972). Seven strictures on similarity. In N. Goodman (Ed.), *Problems and projects* (pp. 341–352). New York: Bobbs-Merrill.

Hampton, J., & Dubois, D. (1993). Psychological models of concepts: Introduction. In I. V. Mechelin, J. Hampton, R. S. Michalski, & P. Theuns (Eds.), *Categories and concepts: Theoretical views and inductive data analysis* (pp. 11–33). London: Academic Press.

Heit, E., & Rubenstein, J. (1994). Similarity and property effects in inductive reasoning. *Journal of Experimental Psychology: Learning, Memory, and Cognition, 20*, 411–422.

Jones, S. S., & Smith, L. B. (1993). The place of perception in children's concepts. *Cognitive Development, 8*, 113–139.

Keil, F. C. (1989). *Concepts, kinds and development*. Cambridge, MA: MIT Press.

Lassaline, M. E. (1996). Structural alignment in induction and similarity. *Journal of Experimental Psychology: Learning, Memory, and Cognition, 22*, 754–770.

Lin, E. L., & Murphy, G. L. (1997). Effects of background knowledge on object categorization and part detection. *Journal of Experimental Psychology: Human Perception and Performance, 23*, 1153–1169.

Livingston, K. R., Andrews, J. K., & Harnad, S. (1998). Categorical perception effects induced by category learning. *Journal of Experimental Psychology: Learning, Memory, and Cognition, 24*, 732–753.

Madole, K. L., & Cohen, L. B. (1995). The role of parts in infants' attention to from-function correlations. *Developmental Psychology, 31*, 637–648.

Markman, A. B., & Makin, V. S. (1998). Referential communication and category acquisition. *Journal of Experimental Psychology: General, 127,* 331–354.

Markman, E. (1989). *Categorization and naming in children.* Cambridge, MA: MIT Press.

McClelland, J. L., & Rumelhart, D. E. (1981). An interactive activation model of context effects in letter perception: I. An account of basic findings. *Psychological Review, 88,* 375–407.

Medin, D. L., & Schaffer, M. M. (1978). Context theory of classification learning. *Psychological Review, 85,* 207–238.

Murphy, G. L. (1988). Comprehending complex concepts. *Cognitive Science, 12,* 529–562.

Murphy, G. L., & Medin, D. L. (1985). The role of theories in conceptual coherence. *Psychological Review, 92,* 289–316.

Nosofsky, R. M. (1984). Choice, similarity, and the context theory of classification. *Journal of Experimental Psychology: Learning, Memory, and Cognition, 10,* 104–114.

Posner, M. I., & Keele, S. W. (1968). On the genesis of abstract ideas. *Journal of Experimental Psychology, 77,* 353–363.

Pylyshyn, Z. (1999). Is vision continuous with cognition? The case of impenetrability of visual perception. *Behavioral and Brain Sciences, 22,* 341–423.

Recanzone, G. H., Merzenich, M. M., & Jenkins, W. M. (1992). Frequency discrimination training engaging a restricted skin surface results in an emergence of a cutaneous response zone in cortical area 3a. *Journal of Neurophysiology, 67,* 1057–1070.

Recanzone, G. H., Schreiner, C. E., & Merzenich, M. M. (1993). Plasticity in the frequency representation of primary auditory cortex following discrimination training in adult owl monkeys. *Journal of Neuroscience, 13,* 87–103.

Rosch, E., & Mervis, C. B. (1975). Family resemblance: Studies in the internal structure of categories. *Cognitive Psychology, 7,* 573–605.

Shepard, R. N. (1987). Toward a universal law of generalization for psychological science. *Science, 237,* 1317–1323.

Shipley, E. F. (1993). Categories, hierarchies, and induction. In D. L. Medin (Ed.), *The psychology of learning and motivation* (Vol. 30), pp. 265–301. Academic Press.

Sidman, M. (1994). *Equivalence relations and behavior: A research story.* Boston: Authors Cooperative.

Skinner, B. F. (1966). The phylogeny and ontogeny of behavior. *Science, 153,* 1205–1214.

Smith, E. E. (1989). Concepts and induction. In M. I. Posner (Ed.), *Foundations of cognitive science* (pp. 501–526). Cambridge, MA: MIT Press.

Smith, L. B., & Kemler, D. G. (1978). Levels of experienced dimensionality in children and adults. *Cognitive Psychology, 10,* 502–532.

Tanaka, J., & Curran, T. (2001). A neural basis for expert object recognition. *Psychological Science, 12,* 43–47.

Wisniewski, E. J. (1997). When concepts combine. *Psychonomic Bulletin and Review, 4,* 167–183.

Wittgenstein, L. (1953). *Philosophical investigations.* G. E. M. Anscombe (Ed.) New York: Macmillan.

Author Index

Italic page numbers indicate pages in reference lists where the citations occur.

Abdi, H., 77, 99, *100*, 337, *353*
Abelev, M., 393, *400*
Abramson, A. S., 28, 30, *43*, *44*, *46*
Ackley, D. H., 362, *380*
Aguiar, A., 114, *127*
Ahn, W. K., 304, 313, 325, 332, 337, *352*
Ahroon, W. A., 29, *47*
Akhtar, N., 242, 269, 273, 390, *400*
Alfonso-Reese, L. A., 360, 378, *381*
Allopenna, P. D., 331, 332, *358*
Altom, M., 77, 99, *101*
Amiel-Tison, C., 32, 33, *47*
Amsel, G., 201, *208*
Amsterlaw, J. A., 304, 313, 325, 337, *352*
Anderson, D. I., 54, *72*
Anderson, J. A., 361, *381*
Anderson, K., 62, *73*
Andrew, S., 337, *356*
Andrews, J. K., 409, *417*
Andruski, J. E., 31, *46*
Anglin, J. M., 7, 8, *20*
Arterberry, M. E., 138, 141, *155*, *188*
Ashby, F. G., 360, 378, *380*, *381*
Aslin, R. N., 14, *21*, 30, 36, 37, *43*, *45*, *48*, *49*, 77, *101*, 168, *189*, 216, 217, 239, 398, *402*
Atanassova, M., 59, *75*
Au, T. K., 215, 216, 236, 342, *352*
Austin, G. A., 3, *20*, 51, *72*, 403, *417*

Backscheider, A. G., 160, *188*, 334, *352*
Baer, L., 344, *359*
Bahrick, L. E., 33, *43*, 176, *189*
Baillargeon, R., 54, *72*, 114, *127*, 217, 235, *237*, 322, *325*, 334, *356*, *401*
Baird, J. A., 107, *130*, 218, *237*
Balaban, M. T., 52, *72*, 206, *207*, 220, 223, 229, 233, *237*
Baldwin, D. A., 107, *130*, 218, 222, *237*, 323, *326*, 334, 335, 351, *352*, *353*, 386, 390, 397, *400*, *401*
Bale, A. C., 205, *209*
Bandi Rao, S., 205, *208*
Banigan, R. L., 248, *273*
Barbu-Roth, M. A., 54, *72*
Bargh, J. A., 349, *353*
Barna, J., 106, 107, *128*, 333, *356*
Baron-Cohen, S., 333, *353*
Barrett, S. E., 77, 99, *100*, 337, *353*
Barsalou, L. W., 7, *21*, 53, *72*, 103, *127*, 132, *156*, 226, *237*, 350, *353*
Barton, M. E., 341, *359*
Bar-Yam, Y., 406, *417*
Bates, E. A., 87, *100*, 249, *273*, 300, 361, 362, *381*
Bauer, P. J., 8, 9, 15, 17, *20*, 22, 93, *100*, 115, 126, *127*, 129, 132, 157, 164, 171, *190*, 346, 349, *353*, *357*, *382*
Bauman, A., 32, 39, *45*
Baumberger, T., 320, *326*
Beach, C. M., 41, *44*

Becker, A. H., 347, *359*
Behl-Chadha, G., 6, *20*, 51, 71, 72, 93, *100*, 117, *127*, 133, *155*, 160, *188*, *381*
Benveniste, S., 219, 221, 232, 233, *241*
Bernstein Ratner, N., 40, *44*
Bertenthal, B. I., 54, *72*, 107, *127*, 137, *155*, 168, *188*, 348, *353*
Bertoncini, J., 28, 32, 33, 34, *45*, *47*, 117, *127*
Bertrand, J., 244, 245, 247, 250, 251, 252, 265, 274, 303, 320, *327*
Best, C. T., 30, *44*, *48*
Bhatt, R. S., 79, 89, 90, 91, 99, *100*, *102*, 226, *237*
Biederman, I., 54, *72*, 163, *188*
Bijeljac-Babic, R., 117, *127*
Billman, D., 88, *100*, 298, *300*, *301*
Bíró, S., 106, *127*, 322, *326*
Blair, E., 304, *327*, 339, 347, 348, *356*
Bloom, L., 242, 244, 247, 262, 269, 273, 335, *353*, 396, *401*
Bloom, P., 215, 221, *237*, 304, *326*, 340, 341, 342, *353*, *354*, 387, 391, *401*
Bohn, O.-S., 31, *48*
Booth, A. E., 223, 230, 231, 232, 233, 234, 235, *237*, *241*
Bornstein, M. H., *188*, 199, *207*
Boroditsky, L., 215, 216, 238, *300*, 389, *400*, *401*
Bosch, L., 35, *44*
Boster, J. S., 334, *355*

Boudreau, J. P., 137, *156*
Bower, T. G. R., 198, *207*, 322, *326*
Bowerman, M., 9, *20*, 54, 59, 72, 206, *208*, 219, 233, *237*
Bowman, L. L., 343, *357*
Boyes-Braem, P., 7, 8, *23*, 77, 101, 139, *158*, 161, *191*, 236, 240, 244, 249, *274*, 368, *383*
Bradley, K., *141*, *156*, 335, 347, *357*
Braig, B., 236, *241*, 347, *359*
Brand, R. J., 259, *273*
Braunwald, S. R., 251, *273*
Breinlinger, K., 170, *192*, 322, *328*
Bremner, J. G., 163, *192*
Brislin, R. W., 251, *273*
Brockbank, M., 106, *127*
Brown, A. L., 235, *237*
Brown, E., 51, *75*, 163, 169, *191*, *192*, 198, *209*, 259, *273*
Brown, N. B., 388, *401*
Brown, R., 42, *44*, 214, 225, *237*, 249, *273*
Bruce, V., 413, *417*
Bruner, J. S., 3, *20*, 51, *72*, 403, *417*
Buffuto, K. A., 29, *47*
Bukatko, D., 126, *128*
Bullock, M., *401*
Burnham, D. K., 31, *44*, 163, 168, *188*
Bushnell, E. W., 137, *156*
Butterworth, G. E., 12, 15, 18, *23*, 52, *75*, 119, *130*, 152, 155, *157*, 163, 164, 165, 166, 167, 171, 186, *191*, 202, *209*, 348, 349, *358*

Caldwell, R. C., 153, *156*
Callanan, M. A., 124, 125, *127*, 340, *357*, 372, *382*, 387, 388, 397, *402*
Campos, J. J., 54, *72*, 137, *155*
Canada, K., 247, *274*
Canfield, R., 170, *189*
Caputo, N. F., 133, *156*
Caramazza, A., 54, *72*, 122, *130*
Carey, S., 5, *20*, 52, 53, *72*, *75*, 118, *127*, 173, 174, *188*, 223, 235, *237*, *241*, 276, 277, 302, 303, 304, 306, *326*, *328*, 330, 332, 334, 335, 341, 347, 349, 350, 351, *353*, *355*, *359*, 371, *381*, 384, 389, 391, 399, *401*, *402*
Carlson, G., 335, 345, *353*
Carlson, L., 219, 233, *240*
Carlson, V. R., 198, *207*, 335, *355*
Caron, A. J., 153, 154, *156*, 198, *207*
Caron, R. F., 153, 154, *156*, 198, *207*

Carpenter, M., 243, *273*
Carter, D. M., 38, *44*
Casasola, M., 70, *72*, 91, *102*, 140, *158*, 168, 176, 177, 179, *192*, 201, 204, 205, 206, *207*, *208*
Casey, K. L., 344, *359*
Cashon, C. H., 198, *208*
Cassidy, K. W., 40, *45*, 214, 217, *239*
Chapman, K. L., 248, *273*
Chaput, H. H., 206, *207*
Charles Luce, J., 30, *45*
Charlesworth, W. R., 361, *381*
Chase, P., 163, *190*
Chauvin, Y., 372, *381*
Cheney, D. L., *191*
Chi, M. T., 336, *359*
Chistovich, L. A., 31, *46*
Choi, S., 9, *20*, 54, 59, *72*, 206, *207*, *208*, 215, *237*, 320, *326*
Christophe, A., 33, 34, 35, *44*, 47
Chung, H. L., 259, *273*
Clark, E. V., 7, 8, *20*, 343, *353*, *355*
Clark, J. E., 31, *44*
Clarkson, M. G., 162, *188*
Clausner, T., 334, 346, *354*
Clifton, R. K., 162, *188*
Cohen, L. B., 6, 12, 14, 15, *20*, 21, 22, 23, 62, 70, *72*, 79, 80, 81, 83, 84, 88, 90, 91, 92, 93, 97, 99, *100*, 101, *102*, 119, *130*, 133, 138, 139, 140, 141, 151, 152, *156*, *157*, *158*, 163, 165, 168, 169, 176, 177, 179, *188*, 189, *191*, *192*, 196, 197, 198, 199, 201, 202, 203, 204, 205, 206, *207*, *208*, *209*, 226, *241*, 243, *274*, 307, 322, *328*, 340, 351, *357*, *358*, 361, *381*, 414, *417*
Cohen, N. J., 366, *382*
Cole, M., 235, *237*
Coley, J. D., 114, *128*, 160, *189*, 214, 226, *238*, 276, *300*, 303, 315, *326*, 334, 345, *353*, *354*
Collins, A., 331, *358*
Collman, P., 17, *21*, 347, *354*
Colunga, E., 283, 284, 286, 298, *300*
Cooper, F. S., 28, *46*, *48*
Cooper, G., 308, 311, *326*
Cooper, R. P., 33, *47*
Coppage, D. J., 120, 125, *129*, 148, 149, 151, *157*, *165*, *190*
Corrigan, R., 335, *353*
Cottrell, G. W., *381*
Cowan, P., 51, *73*
Cramer, L., 277, *300*
Crisafi, M. A., 8, *22*

Croft, W., 334, 335, 346, *353*, *354*
Csibra, G., 106, *127*, 322, *326*
Cummins, M., 58, 59, 62, 63, 64, 65, 67, *74*
Curran, T., 409, *418*
Curtis, L. E., 62, *75*
Cutler, A., 30, 38, 41, *44*, *45*, *48*

Daehler, M. W., 126, *128*
Dale, P. S., 87, *100*, 249, *273*, 284, *300*, *301*
Dannemiller, J. L., 168, *188*
Dapretto, M., 215, 216, *236*
Davidson, N., 345, *353*
Day, R. H., 138, *158*, 168, *188*, 198, *208*
Deak, G. O., 17, *20*, 346, *353*
Dehaene-Lambertz, G., 33, *44*
Deloache, J. S., 62, *73*, *75*
Demuth, K., 214, 217, *240*
Dennis, M., *352*
Deruelle, C., 154, *156*
de Schonen, S., 154, *156*
Dewart, M. H., 335, *353*
DiAdamo, C., 106, 107, *128*, 333, *356*
Diamond, A., 92, *100*, 138, *156*
Dickinson, A., 307, *328*
Diehl, R. L., 199, *208*
Diesendruck, G., 335, 339, 340, 343, 344, *353*, *354*
Dingel, A., 120, 125, *129*, 148, 149, 151, *157*, *165*, *190*
Dixon, R. M. W., 221, 234, 235, *237*
Dobson, V., 63, 66, 67, 68, 69, *73*, *75*
Dodd, B., 31, *48*
Doherty, G., 405, *417*
Dooling, R. J., 29, *47*
Dromi, E., 250, *273*
Druss, B., 40, *45*
Dubois, D., 187, *189*, 404, *417*
Duke, N., 18, *21*, 304, *327*, 338, 339, 340, *356*, 391, 396, *402*
Dukes, K., 40, *47*

Earnshaw, L. J., 31, *44*
Ebeling, K. S., 335, 342, *354*
Edelman, G. M., 51, *73*
Edelson, S., 77, 99, *101*
Edwards, T. J., 28, *44*
Eimas, P. D., 6, 12, 14, *20*, 22, 23, 28, 29, 31, *44*, *47*, 50, 51, 52, 53, *71*, *72*, *73*, 74, 89, 93, 101, 104, 105, 116, 117, 121, *127*, *128*, *130*, 132, 133, 134, 153, *156*, *157*, 160, 161, 165, 171, 173, 174, 186, *188*, *190*, *191*, 198, 199, 202, *208*, *209*, 348, 351, *353*, *358*, 364, 372, *382*, 386, *402*

Elbert, T., 410, *417*
Ells, I., 360, 378, *380*
Elman, J. L., 118, *128*, 361, 362, *381*
Erikson, M. A., 360, 378, *381*
Estes, W. K., 404, *417*
Evans, C. S., 168, *189*

Fagan, J. F., 55, *73*, 117, *128*, 154, *156*
Fagot, B. I., 133, 153, 154, *156*
Fahle, M., 409, *417*
Fantz, R. L., 55, *73*, 162, *189*
Farah, M. J., 66, *75*
Fariello, G. R., 54, *73*
Fearing, D. D., 51, *76*, 79, 81, 95, 96, 97, 102, 117, *131*, 160, 171, 192, 243, *274*
Feider, H., 333, *356*
Feldman, J., 406, *417*
Fells, C. A., 154, *157*
Fenson, L., 87, *100*, 249, 273, *300*
Ferland, D., 52, *74*, 106, *130*, 182, *190*
Fernald, A., 29, *45*, 216, *237*
Fifer, W. P., 33, *47*
Fink, E. A., 29, *47*
Fisher, C. L., 40, 41, *44*, 234, *237*
Fitzsimmons, C. M., 323, *329*
Fivush, R., 121, *129*, 155, *157*
Flavell, E. R., 350, *354*
Flavell, J. H., 350, *354*
Florian, J. E., 17, *20*, 376, *381*
Flukes, J. E., 345, *354*
Fodor, J. A., 53, *73*, 409, *417*
Fong, C., 40, 41, *48*
Fowles, B., 335, *356*
Frankenfield, A., 304, *327*, 339, 347, 348, *356*
Freeman, K., 372, *381*
Freko, D., 77, 99, *101*
French, R. M., 19, *22*, 205, *208*, 362, 363, 364, 365, 366, 367, 368, 370, *381*, *382*, 386, *402*
Friederici, A. D., 30, *44*, *45*
Friedman, C. J., 29, *47*
Fry, D. B., 28, *44*
Frye, D., 106, 108, *128*
Fu, P., 334, 346, *354*
Fulkerson, A. L., 229, *237*
Furer, M. J., 66, 67, 68, 69, *75*

Gale, H., 251, *273*
Gale, M. C., 251, *273*
Gallagher, J. M., 77, 99, *100*, 337, *353*
Gallistel, C. R., 235, *237*, 307, *326*
Garrod, S., 405, *417*

Gasser, M., 298, *300*
Gathercole, V., 276, 277, *300*
Gay, J., 235, *237*
Gelman, R., 17, 22, 62, *75*, 126, *131*, 159, *190*, 215, 221, 235, 236, *237*, *238*, 241, 334, 342, 348, *354*, *357*, 388, 397, *401*, *402*
Gelman, S. A., 11, 16, 17, *21*, 23, 114, *128*, 159, 160, 174, *188*, *189*, 214, 226, *238*, 239, 276, *300*, 303, 304, 306, 313, 315, 320, *325*, 326, 328, 329, 332, 333, 334, 335, 336, 337, 342, 343, 344, 345, 346, 347, 348, 349, 350, 351, *352*, *353*, *354*, *355*, *358*, *359*, 371, 372, 376, 377, 378, 380, *381*, 386, 387, 391, 400, *401*
Gentner, D., 18, *21*, 143, *156*, 215, 216, 219, 221, 225, 233, 235, *238*, 239, 276, 277, 279, 288, 289, *300*, *301*, 303, *327*, 334, 338, 347, *355*, 386, 388, 389, 390, 400, *401*
Gergely, G., 106, *127*, 322, *326*
Gerken, L. A., 30, 41, 42, *44*, *47*, *48*, 224, *238*
Gershkoff-Stowe, L., 143, *157*
Gibson, E. J., 117, *128*
Gillette, J., 234, *238*
Gleitman, H., 234, *238*
Gleitman, L. R., 40, *44*, 215, 216, 234, 235, 236, *237*, *238*, 240
Glick, J. A., 235, *237*
Glymour, C., 307, 308, 311, 312, 313, 315, 324, *326*, *327*, 328
Goffman, L., 86, *102*
Gogate, L. J., 176, *189*
Goldin-Meadow, W., 215, 216, *238*
Goldstone, R. L., 7, *21*, 132, *156*, 406, 409, *417*
Golinkoff, R. M., 242, 246, 259, *273*, 335, *355*, *401*
Goodman, J. C., 388, *401*
Goodman, N., 331, *355*, 410, 414, *417*
Goodnow, J. J., 3, *20*, 51, 72, 403, *417*
Goodsitt, J., 92, *100*
Gopnik, A., 15, *21*, 78, 93, *100*, 215, *237*, 306, 307, 312, 313, 315, 316, 318, 319, 320, 321, 322, 323, 324, *326*, *327*, 328, 330, 332, 337, 344, 347, 350, 351, *355*, 396, *401*
Goshen-Gottstein, Y., 116, *129*
Gotlieb, S., 89, *102*
Gottfried, G. M., 226, *238*, 334, 346, *354*

Goubet, N., 137, *157*
Gould, J. L., 28, *44*
Graham, N., 122, *128*
Graham, S. A., 221, *239*, 397, *401*
Granrud, C. E., 198, *208*
Gray, W. D., 7, 8, *23*, 77, *101*, 139, *158*, 161, *191*, 236, 240, 244, 249, 274, 368, *383*
Green, F. L., 350, *354*
Grieser, D., 31, *44*
Grimshaw, J., 235, 236, *238*
Gruendel, J. M., 248, *273*
Guajardo, J. J., 218, *238*
Guasti, M. T., 221, *241*
Gumperz, J. C., 279, *300*

Haaf, R. A., 229, *237*
Haith, M. M., 56, *73*, 170, *189*
Hall, D. G., 218, 221, 234, *237*, *238*, 239, *241*, 371, *383*
Halsted, N., 32, 33, *47*
Hampson, J., 215, 216, 240
Hampton, J., 187, *189*, 404, *417*
Harding, C. G., 335, *355*
Hardy, J. K., 54, *73*
Harnad, S., 29, *44*, 409, *417*
Harris, K. S., 28, *46*, *48*
Harris, P. L., 371, *382*
Hartman, E., 345, *354*
Hartung, J., 87, *100*, *300*
Haryu, E, 219, 233, *239*
Hass, S. D., 78, *102*, 347, *359*
Haxby, J. V., 66, 68, *75*
Hayes, R. A., 51, *75*
Hayne, H., 15, *21*, 132, 138, *156*, *158*
Hein, A., 235, *239*
Heise, D., 88, *101*, 160, 161, *192*, 349, *359*
Heise, G. A., 28, *47*
Heit, E., 88, *100*, 226, 240, 298, *300*, 331, *355*, 414, *417*
Held, R., 235, *239*
Hemenway, K., 8, *23*, 244, *274*
Hennon, E., 259, *273*
Hertenstein, M. J., 54, *72*
Heyman, G. D., 342, 344, 350, 351, *354*, *355*, *357*, 400, *401*
Hickling, A. K., 334, *355*
Hickson, L., 31, *48*
Hillenbrand, J. M., 28, *44*
Hillis, A. E., 54, *72*
Hinton, G. E., 362, *380*, *383*
Hirschfeld, L. A., 342, *355*, *357*
Hirsh-Pasek, K., 40, 41, *45*, 214, 217, 239, 242, 246, 259, *273*, *401*
Hirtle, S. C., 54, *73*
Hodges, J. R., 122, *128*, 130

Hoffman, D. D., 163, *189*
Hohenstein, J., 304, 313, *325,*
337, 352
Höhle, B., 42, *45*
Hohne, E. A., 30, 32, 39, *45*
Hollander, M., 351, *354,* 400,
401
Hollich, G. J., 242, 246, 259,
273, 401
Houston, D. M., 33, *44, 45*
Hubbard, E. M., 54, *72*
Huntley-Fenner, G., 389, *401*
Hutchinson, J. E., 221, *240, 402*
Huttenlocher, J., 54, 58, 60, 62,
71, *73, 75,* 215, 216, 235, *239*

Imai, M., 18, *21,* 219, 233, *239,*
276, 277, 279, 288, 289, *301,*
303, *327,* 334, *355,* 386, 388,
389, 390, *401*
Inhelder, B., 330, 351, *355,* 371,
381, 387, *401*
Iverson, P., *31, 45*

Jacobson, K., 170, *192,* 322, *328*
Jansen, M., 277, *300*
Jaswal, V. K., 218, *239,* 397, *401*
Jenkins, W. M., 410, *418*
Johannsen, G., *355*
Johnson, D. M., 7, 8, *23,* 77, 90,
101, 139, *158,* 161, *191,* 236,
240, 244, *249,* 274, 368, *383*
Johnson, E. K., 35, *47*
Johnson, J., 215, 216, *240*
Johnson, K. E., 244, 247, 249,
250, 251, 252, 264, 269, 271,
273, 274, 334, *355*
Johnson, M. H., 19, *23,* 51, 52,
74, 75, 117, *130, 133, 158,* 162,
168, 170, *190,* 205, *209,* 296,
301, 361, 362, *381, 383*
Johnson, N. S., *100*
Johnson, S. C., 106, 109, *128,*
341, 349, *355,* 391, *402*
Johnson, S. P., 168, *189*
Johnston, J. R., 59, *73*
Jones, K., 18, *21,* 304, *327,* 338,
339, 340, *356,* 391, 396, *402*
Jones, S. S., 6, 12, 17, 18, *21,* 53,
73, 124, *128, 132, 156,* 160,
165, 173, *189,* 226, *239,* 276,
277, 292, *301,* 303, 305, 324,
327, 328, 330, 334, *335,* 338,
339, 340, 346, 348, *355, 356,*
359, 390, 391, 398, *402,* 410,
417
Jonides, J., 54, *73,* 103, *130,* 360,
378, *383*
Joram, E., 336, *359*
Jordan, M., *327,* 311308
Jusczyk, A. M., 30, 40, *45, 47*

Jusczyk, P. W., 12, 14, *20, 21,* 28,
29, 30, 31, 32, 33, 35, 37, 38,
39, 40, 41, 42, 43, *44, 45, 46,*
47, 48, 117, *127,* 199, *208,* 214,
216, 217, *239*

Kalish, C. W., 226, *239,* 304,
313, *325,* 332, 336, 337, 342,
352, 354, 355
Kannass, K. N., 144, 145, 147,
157
Karmiloff-Smith, A., 52, *75,*
133, 158, 361, 362, *381*
Kase, J., 58, 59, 62, 63, 64, 65,
67, *74*
Keeble, S., 185, *189*
Keele, S. W., 116, 118, *130,* 371,
382, 403, *418*
Keil, F. C., 5, 6, 11, 17, *21,* 52, *73,*
99, *100,* 108, *128,* 159, 160, 161,
173, 187, *189, 192,* 226, 235,
237, *239,* 276, *301,* 306, *327,*
331, 332, 333, 335, 336, 342,
343, 348, 350, 351, *355, 356,*
358, 371, 372, 378, *381,*405, *417*
Keller, H., 215, *239*
Kellman, P. J., 168, *189*
Kelly, W. J., 29, *47*
Kemler Nelson, D. G., 18, *21,*
40, 41, 45, 46, 47, 48, 77, 83,
86, *100, 101,* 114, 216, 217, *239,*
304, *327,* 338, 339, 340, 346,
347, *356,* 391, 396, *402,* 412,
418
Kennedy, L. J., 29, 30, 40, 41,
45, 117, *127*
Kermoian, R., 137, *155*
Kersten, A., 298, *301*
Kessen, W., 199, *207*
Kilbreath, C. S., 397, *401*
Kim, M., 216, *239*
Kim, N. S., *352*
Kinney, J. A., 28, *46*
Klein, R. E., 30, *46*
Klibanoff, R. S., 218, 221, *239,*
241
Knapp, A. G., 361, *381*
Koenig, M. A., 335, *354*
Koenig, N., 30, *45*
Koff, E., 335, *356*
Kogan, J., 245, *273*
Kohno, M., 30, *48*
Kolstad, V., 62, *73,* 334, *356*
Koós, O., 106, *127*
Kosslyn, S. M., 54, *73*
Kotovsky, L., 322, *325*
Kozhevnikova, E. V., 31, *46*
Kramer, P. E., 335, *356*
Krascum, R. M., 337, *356*
Kripke, S., 303, *327*
Kruschke, J. K., 360, 378, *381*

Kuhl, P. K., 12, *21,* 29, 31, *44, 45,*
46, 92, *100,* 176, *189,* 199, *208*
Kuhn, I. F., 124, *130*
Kuhn, T. S., 344, *356*
Kyratzis, A, 125, *128*

Laboratory of Comparative
Human Cognition, 235, *239*
Lacerda, F., 31, *46*
Lafleur, R., 30, *44*
Lakoff, G., 296, *301*
Lalonde, C. E., 12, *21,* 30, 49, 78,
79, 92, 93, *100,* 199, *209*
Lambertz, G., 32, 33, *47*
Landau, B., 18, *21,* 54, *73,* 221,
226, *239,* 276, 277, 292, *301,*
303, 324, *327, 328,* 330, 334,
338, 339, 340, 346, 348, *356,*
359, 390, 391, 398, *402*
Lane, H. L., 28, *46*
Lansink, J. M., 15, 22, 89, 93,
101, 144, 155, *157*
Lasky, R. E., 30, *46*
Lassaline, M. E., 226, *239,* 332,
337, *352, 356,* 409, *417*
Lauckner-Morano V. J., 31, *48*
Laughlin, M., 144, 145, 147, *157*
Leavitt, L. A., 28, *48*
Lebowitz, K., 343, *353*
Lederer, A., 234, *238*
Legerstee,M., 106, 107, *128,* 333,
356
Lehiste, I., 40, *46*
Leigeios, F., 154, *156*
Leinbach, M. D., *133,* 153, 154,
156
Lempert, H., 335, *356*
Leonard, L. B., 248, *273*
Lepage, A., 52, *74,* 106, *130,* 182,
190
Leslie, A. M., 106, *128,* 170, 185,
189, 307, 322, *327*
Levin, D. T., 331, 336, 350, 351,
356
Levinson, S. C., 279, 296, *300,*
301
Liben, L. S., 54, *74*
Liberman, A. M., 28, 29, *44, 46,*
48
Lichten, W., 28, *47*
Lieberman, P., 43, *46*
Lin, E. L., 409, 411, *417*
Lindblom, B., 31, *46*
Lippa, Y., 409, *417*
Lisker, L., 28, 30, 43, *46*
Lively, S. E., 31, *46*
Livingston, K. R., 409, *417*
Lizotte, D. J., 343, *357*
Lloyd, V. L., 91, *102,* 140, *158,*
168, 176, 177, 179, *192,* 214, 217,
241

Lockman, J. J., 137, *156*
Loehlin, J. C., 199, *208*
Lonardo, R., 126, *128*
Loose, J., *372*, 375, 376, 377, 378, 379, *381*, 388, *402*
Lucariello, J., 125, *128*
Luce, P. A., 30, 39, *45*, *46*
Luce, R. D., 288, *301*
Lucy, J. A., 276, 278, 279, 293, *301*
Luo, J., 282, *301*
Lynch, E. B., 344, *359*
Lynch, M., 154, *157*
Lyons, A. K., 144, 145, 147, 148, 149, *157*
Lyons, J., *239*
Lyytinen, P., 59, *75*

Maccoby, E. E., 17, *21*, 347, *354*
Macko, K. A., 66, 68, *74*
Macnamara, J., 226, *239*
Macomber, J., 170, *192*, 322, *328*
Madden, E. C., 124, *130*
Madole, K. L., 6, 12, 13, 14, 16, 17, *21*, 22, 51, 53, *73*, 81, 89, 91, *100*, 120, *128*, 132, 133, 134, 136, 137, 138, 139, 141, 151, *156*, *157*, 160, 161, 174, 177, *189*, 340, *357*, 414, *417*
Makin, V. S., 405, *418*
Malcuit, G., 333, *356*
Malt, B. C., 51, 53, *73*
Mancini, J., 154, *156*
Mandel, D. R., 40, 41, *44*, *46*
Mandler, J. M., 5, 6, 8, 9, 13, 14, 15, 16, 19, *21*, 22, 52, 53, *73*, 93, *100*, 104, 105, 106, 108, 109, 110, 112, 113, 115, 116, 117, 120, 121, 122, 124, 125, 126, 127, *127*, *128*, *129*, 132, 133, 134, 153, 155, *156*, *157*, 159, 160, 161, 164, 170, 171, 180, 182, 185, 186, 187, *189*, *190*, 200, 206, *208*, 214, *239*, 303, 322, *327*, 334, 344, 347, 349, 351, *357*, *382*
Maratsos, M., 235, *240*
Marcus, G. F., 205, *208*
Mareschal, D., 19, *22*, 51, *75*, 175, *191*, 205, 206, *208*, *209*, 361, 362, 363, 364, 365, 366, 367, 368, 370, 372, 375, 376, 377, 378, 380, *381*, *383*, 386, 388, *402*
Margolis, E., 4, *22*, *190*
Markman, A. B., 347, *359*, 405, *418*
Markman, E. M., 8, 16, 17, *21*, *22*, 53, *73*, 118, *127*, 159, 160, 173, 174, *189*, *190*, 218, 221,

222, 226, *237*, *239*, *240*, 247, 248, 270, *273*, 276, *301*, 303, 304, 315, 323, *326*, *329*, 334, 343, 344, 345, 347, 351, *353*, *354*, *357*, *359*, 371, 372, 376, 377, 378, 380, *381*, 384, 386, 387, 397, *401*, *402*, 413, *418*
Markow, D. B., 52, *75*, 114, 125, *131*, 206, *209*, 214, 217, 218, 220, 223, 224, 225, 226, 227, 228, 229, 232, 233, 234, 235, *241*, 323, *328*, 397, *402*
Markson, L., 339, 340, 341, *353*, 391, *401*
Marler, P., 28, *44*, *46*, *48*, 168, *189*, 235, *240*
Marr, D., 168, *190*
Marsh, R., 111, *129*
Martin, E., 58, 59, 62, 63, 64, 65, 67, *74*
Martinez, I. M., 342, *357*
Mash, C., 60, 61, 64, 68, *73*, *75*
Massey, C. M., 17, *22*, 159, *190*, 334, 348, *357*, 388, *402*
Mattock, A., 163, 169, *191*, *192*, 198, *209*
Mattys, S. L., 39, *46*
Maye, J., 30, *47*
McCarrell, N. S., 340, *357*, 372, *382*, 387, 388, 397, *402*
McCarthy, R. A., 121, *131*
McClelland, J. L., 116, *129*, 170, *190*, 298, *301*, 362, *383*, 409, *418*
McCloskey, M., 366, *382*
McDonough, L., 9, 14, 15, *22*, 52, 53, *73*, 109, 110, 111, 112, 113, 115, 117, 120, 121, 122, 123, 124, 125, 126, 127, *129*, 133, 134, 153, *157*, 164, 171, 182, 186, *190*, 206, *208*, 303, 322, *327*, 334, 344, 347, 349, *357*, *382*, 388, *401*
McGregor, K. K., 216, *239*
McGurk, H., 195, 196, 197, *208*
McHale, J. P., 137, *156*
McIntosh, B. J., 224, *238*
McKee, R. D., 117, *129*
McKenzie, B. E., 138, *158*, 198, *208*
McLeod, P., 362
McNamara, T. P., 54, *73*
McNeill, D., 43, *47*
McPherson, L., 277, *301*
McRoberts, G. W., 30, *44*
Medin, D. L., 6, 11, *22*, 77, 86, 98, 99, *101*, 118, *129*, 160, 161, 162, 173, 175, 187, *190*, 226, *238*, *240*, 303, 306, *327*, 331, 332, 335, 346, 347, 348, 349,

350, *352*, 354, *357*, *358*, *359*, *382*, 397, 398, *401*, *402*, 404, 408, 411, *418*
Medina, J., 143, *156*
Mehler, J., 32, 33, 34, *47*, 117, *127*
Meier, R. P., 41, *47*
Meints, K., 371, *382*
Mekos, D., 78, 83, 84, 87, *102*
Melartin, R. L., 323, *326*, 351, *353*, 397, *401*
Meltzoff, A. N., 15, *21*, 78, 93, *100*, 117, *129*, 176, *189*, 306, 308, 319, 320, 322, *326*, *327*, 330, 333, *355*, *357*
Menyuk, P., 30, *48*
Merriman, W. E., 343, *357*
Merryman, J. D., 15, *22*, 89, 93, *101*, 144, 155, *157*
Mervis, C. A., 244, 245, 247, 249, 250, 251, 252, 271, *274*
Mervis, C. B., 7, 8, 10, *22*, 23, 51, *74*, 77, *101*, 139, *158*, 161, *191*, 236, *240*, 244, 245, 246, 247, 248, 249, 250, 251, 252, 257, 260, 264, 265, 269, 271, *273*, *274*, 303, 320, *327*, 334, 347, *355*, *357*, 368, *382*, *383*, 406, 412, *418*
Merzenich, M. M., 409, 410, *418*
Michalski, R. S., 118, *129*
Michotte, A., 307, *327*, 348, *357*
Miller, G. A., 28, *47*
Miller, J. D., 29, *46*, *47*
Miller, J. L., 29, 31, *44*, *47*
Millikan, R. G., 53, *74*
Min, H., 276, *300*
Minifie, F. D., 28, *44*
Mishkin, M., 66, 68, *74*
Moller, M. F., 372, *382*
Moon, C., 33, *47*
Moore, C., 106, 108, *128*
Morgan, J. L., 39, 40, 41, 42, *46*, *47*, *48*, 79, 92, 93, 97, *100*, *101*, 214, 217, *240*, 243, 269, *274*
Morgan, M., 409, *417*
Morison, V., 198, *209*
Morris, C., 304, *327*, 339, 347, 348, *356*
Morris, M. W., 349, *357*
Morrison, V., 169, *192*
Morrongiello, B. A., 162, *188*
Morse, P. A., 28, *47*, *48*
Morton, J., 34, 35, *44*, 162, 168, *190*
Moscovitch, M., 116, *129*
Moses, L. J., 350, *354*
Mullennix, J., 30, 31, *45*
Munakata, Y., 170, *190*
Munro, P., *381*
Murase, T., 284, *301*

Murphy, G. L., 6, 11, 12, 22, 23, 77, 98, 99, *100, 101*, 151, *158*, 160, 161, 162, 173, 175, 187, *190*, 226, 239, 240, 303, 306, *327*, 331, 332, 337, 338, 350, *353, 356, 357, 358, 359*, 382, 405, 408, 409, 411, *417, 418*
Murray, J., 29, *45*
Myers, I., 106, 108, *128*
Myers, M., 29, *45*
Myers, R. S., 154, *156*

Nádasdy, Z., 322, *326*
Nadel, L., 307, *328*
Nagell, K., 243, *273*
Nakatani, L., 40, *47*
Namy, L. L., 143, *157*, 225, 238, 347, *355*
Narter, D. B., 63, 66, 67, 68, 69, *73, 75*
Nazzi, T., 34, 35, 40, *47*, 316, 318, 319, 321, 323, *327, 328*
Needham, A., 322, *325*
Neisser, U., 3, *22*
Nelson, K., 116, 124, 125, *128, 129, 138, 157*, 173, *190*, 215, 216, *240*, 319, *328*
Newcombe, N., 54, 58, 60, 62, *71, 73, 74, 75*
Newport, E. L., 30, 41, *47, 48*, 77, 99, *101*, 118, *129*, 398, *402*
Newsome, M., *45*
Nisbett, R. E., 349, *357*
Nishi, K., 30, *48*
Norris, C. M., 60, 61, 64, *75*
Norris, D. G., 38, *44*
Nosofsky, R. M., 404, *418*

Oakes, L. M., 6, 13, 14, 15, 16, 17, *21, 22*, 51, 53, 62, *72, 73*, 81, 89, 91, 93, 99, *100, 101*, 120, 125, *128, 129*, 132, 133, 134, 136, 137, 138, 139, 144, 145, 146, 147, 148, 149, 151, 154, 155, *156, 157*, 160, 161, 165, 174, 177, *189, 190*, 199, 203, 204, *208*, 307, 322, *328*, 340, *357*
Ochs, E., 216, *240*
Ogura, T., 283, *301*
O'Keefe, J., 307, *328*
Opfer, J., 333, *354*
O'Reilley, A. W., 114, *128*
Ortony, A., 6, *22*, 175, *190*, 398, *402*
Ostendorf, M., 40, 41, *48*

Palmer, S. E., 163, *190*
Pani, J. R., 245, 257, 265, *274*
Pantev, C, 410, *417*
Pappas, A., 345, *354, 358*
Parisi, D., 361, 362, *381*

Pascalis, O., 154, *156*
Pasko, R. N., 60, 61, 64, *75*
Pastore, L., 29, *47*
Pastore, R. E., 29, *47*
Patalano, A. L., 103, *130*, 360, 378, *383*
Patterson, K., 122, *128, 130*
Pauen, S., 122, *130*
Pazzani, M. J., 331, *358*
Pearl, J., 308, *328*
Pegg, J. E., 31, *47*, 214, 217, *241*
Pelletier, F. J., 345, *353*
Peng, K., 349, *357*
Peters, A., 40, *47*
Pethick, S., 87, *100, 300*
Phillips, R. D., 154, *157*
Piaget, J., 53, *74*, 105, *130*, 160, *190*, 244, *274*, 330, 351, *355*, 371, *381*, 387, *401*
Pick, H. L., 54, *73*
Pickens, J. N., 33, *43*
Pinker, S., 235, 236, *240*
Pisoni, D. B., 29, 30, 31, *45, 46, 48*
Piwoz, J., 41, *45*
Plumert, J. M., 15, *22*, 89, 93, *101*, 144, 155, *157*
Plunkett, K., 361, 362, 371, 372, *381, 382*
Polka, L., *31, 48*, 214, 217, *241*
Polly, J. L., 63, 66, 67, 68, 69, *75*
Pomerlau, A., 333, *356*
Posner, M. I., 116, 118, *130*, 371, 382, *403, 418*
Poulin-Dubois, D., 6, 7, 12, 23, 52, *74*, 105, 106, 111, *130*, 160, 170, 171, 177, 178, 180, 181, 182, 183, 184, 185, *190, 191*, 333, 351, *358*
Prasada, S., 345, *358*
Premack, A. J., 333, 336, *358, 359*
Premack, D., 333, 336, *358, 359*
Price, P. J., 40, 41, *48*
Puleo, J. S., 29, *47*
Putnam, H., 303, 305, *328*, 396, 400, *402*
Pylyshyn, Z., 116, *130*, 409, *418*

Quine, W. V. O., 108, *130*, 279, *301*, 331, *358*
Quinn, P. C., 6, 12, 14, 19, 20, *22, 23*, 50, 51, 52, 53, 55, 56, 57, 58, 59, 60, 61, 62, 63, 64, 65, 66, 67, 68, 69, *72, 73, 74, 75*, 89, 93, *101*, 104, 105, 116, 117, 121, 127, *128, 130*, 132, 133, 153, *157, 158*, 160, 161, 165, 171, 173, 186, *190, 191*, 198, 202, 205, *208, 209*, 348, 351, *353, 358*, 362, 364, 365, 366, 367, 372, *382, 383*, 386, *402*

Rakison, D. H., 6, 7, 12, 15, 18, *23*, 51, 52, *75*, 105, 111, 119, *130*, 132, 152, 155, *157*, 160, 163, 164, 165, 166, 167, 169, 170, 171, 177, 178, 179, 180, 181, 182, 183, 184, 185, 186, *191*, 202, *209*, 333, 348, 349, 351, *358*, 368, *383*
Rakowitz, S., 234, *237*
Ramey, C. T., 322, *328*
Ratcliff, R., 366, *383*
Rattermann, M. J., 338, *355*
Rauschecker, J. P., 28, *48*
Rawling, P., 106, 108, *128*
Recanzone, G. H., 409, 410, *418*
Redanz, N., 30, 38, *45*
Redford, M. A., 201, *208*
Reed, M., 29, *45*
Reed, S. K., 371, *383*
Regier, T., 219, 233, *240*
Rehder, B., 304, 313, *328*
Reilly, J., 87, *100, 300*
Rescorla, L., 123, *130*, 173, *191*
Reznick, J. S., 121, *129*, 155, *157*, 249, *273, 300*
Reznick, S., 87, *100*
Ribar, R. J., 146, 154, *157*
Ricciuti, H. N., 6, 15, *23*, 319, *328*
Richards, W. A., 163, *189*
Rips, L. J., 303, 306, *328*, 331, *358*
Roberts, K., 170, *191*
Rochat, P., 137, *157*
Rockstroh, B., 410, *417*
Rocroi, C., 259, *273*
Rollins, K. B., 342, *352*
Rolls, E. T., 362, *382*
Rosch, E., 7, 8, *22, 23*, 51, *75*, 77, 99, *101*, 139, *158*, 161, 163, *190, 191*, 236, *240*, 244, 249, *274*, 282, *301*, 347, *357, 358*, 368, 382, *383*, 406, 412, *418*
Rosengren, K. S., 345, *354*
Rosenkrantz, S. L., 14, *23*, 51, *74*, 89, 93, *101*, 116, *130*, 133, 153, *157*, 160, 165, *191*, 198, *209*, 364, *382*, 386, *402*
Rosner, B. S., 29, *45*
Rothbart, M. K., 151, *158*
Rovee, D., 89, *101*
Rovee-Collier, C., 79, 89, 90, 91, 99, *100, 101, 102*, 138, *158*, 226, *237*
Rubenstein, J., 331, *355*, 414, *417*
Ruff, H. A., 151, *158*
Rumelhart, D. E., 116, *129*, 298, *301*, 362, *383*, 409, *418*
Russell, R., 18, *21*, 304, *327*, 338, 339, 340, *356*, 391, 396, *402*
Ryskina, V. L., 31, *46*

Saah, M. I., 215, 216, *240*
Saffran, J. R., 30, *48*, 77, 79, 92, 93, 97, *101*, 243, 269, *274*, 398, *402*
Salapatek, P., 163, *191*
Samuelson, L. K., 16, *23*, 140, 141, *158*, 175, 277, 281, 283, 286, 290, *302*, 398, *402*
Sandberg, E. H., 54, 58, *73*, *75*
Sandhofer, C. M., 282, *301*
Santos, L. R., *122*, *130*
Sasaki, M., 30, *48*
Saylor, M., 107, *130*
Schafer, G., 175, *191*, 206, *209*, 362, 372, *383*
Schaffer, M. M., 86, 99, *101*, 404, *418*
Scheines, R., 308, 311, *328*
Schieffelin, B., 216, *240*
Schmader, T. M., 60, 61, 64, *75*
Schomberg, T., 30, *45*
Schreiber, J. C., 62, *75*
Schreiner, C. E., 409, *418*
Schroeder, K. E., 90, *100*
Schultz, T. R., 205, *209*, 361, *382*
Schulz, L., 312, 313, 315, 324, *327*
Scott, D. R., 41, *48*
Scott, J., 77, *101*
Sebastián-Gallés, N., 35, *44*
Sejnowski, T. J., 362, *380*
Seligman, M. E., 215, *238*
Senghas, A., 219, 221, 232, 233, *241*
Sera, M., 372, *381*
Sexton, M. W., 335, *355*
Seyfarth, R. M., *191*
Shady, M., 42, *48*
Shafer, V. L., 42, *48*
Shanks, D. R., 307, *328*
Shankweiler, D. P., 28, *46*
Sharp, D. W., 235, *237*
Shattuck-Hufnagel, S., 40, 41, *48*
Shatz, M., 160, *188*, 334, *352*
Shaw, L. K., 215, 216, *240*
Shepard, R. N., 407, *418*
Shepperson, B., 124, *131*
Shi, R., 42, *48*, 214, 217, *240*
Shiffrin, R. M., 409, *417*
Shipley, E. F., 124, *130*, *131*, 345, *358*, 414, *418*
Shoben, E. J., 331, *357*
Shucard, D. W., 42, *48*
Shucard, J. L., 42, *48*
Sidle, A. L., 342, *352*
Sidman, M., 405, *418*
Siegal, M., 342, *358*
Siegler, R. S., 160, 170, *190*, *191*
Sigel, I. E., 334, *358*
Signorella, M. L., 350, *358*
Silverstein, M., 335, *358*

Simons, D. J., 331, 336, 343, 350, 351, *356*, *358*
Singer, L. T., 117, *128*, 154, *156*
Sinha, C., 372, *382*
Siqueland, E. R., 12, *20*, 28, *44*, 199, *208*
Siraki, S., 30, *48*
Skinner, B. F., 413, *418*
Skouteris, H., 138, *158*
Slater, A. M., 51, 55, *75*, 136, *158*, 163, 168, 169, *191*, *192*, 198, *209*
Slaughter, V., 341, 349, *355*, 391, *402*
Slobin, D. I., 270, *274*, 335, *359*
Slotta, J. D., 336, *359*
Smiley, P., 215, 216, 235, *239*
Smith, E. E., *23*, 103, *130*, 188, *192*, 360, 378, *383*, 404, *418*
Smith, L. B., 6, 12, 16, 17, 18, *21*, *23*, 51, 53, *73*, *75*, 77, 88, 89, *101*, 124, *128*, 132, 141, 143, *156*, *157*, *158*, 160, 161, 165, 173, 175, 189, *192*, 219, 220, 226, 233, *239*, *240*, 242, 273, 276, 277, 281, 282, 283, 284, 286, 290, 291, 292, 295, 297, *300*, *301*, 302, 303, 305, 324, *327*, *328*, 330, 334, 335, 338, 339, 340, 346, 348, 349, *355*, *356*, *359*, 390, 391, 398, *402*, 410, 412, *417*, *418*
Smith, W. C., 331, 336, 350, 351, *356*
Snedeker, J., 234, *240*
Sobel, D. M., 312, 313, 315, 318, 321, 322, 324, *327*, 332, 337, 347, 350, *355*, 396, *401*
Sockaci, E., 106, 109, *128*
Soderstrom, M., 41, *48*
Soja, N. N., 276, 277, 297, *302*, 303, 304, *328*, 334, 335, 347, *359*
Sokolov, E. N., 361, *383*
Solimando, A., 389, *401*
Somerville, S., 277, *300*
Sommers, F., 333, *359*
Song, Y. K., 215, 216, *236*
Sorrentino, C. M., 53, *75*
Spalding, T. L., 12, *23*, 99, *101*, 151, *158*, 331, 332, *359*
Spelke, E. S., 62, *75*, 168, 170, 189, *192*, 217, 235, *240*, 276, 277, 279, *302*, 303, 304, 322, *328*, 334, 335, 347, *359*
Spencer, J., 52, *75*, 133, *158*
Sperber, D., 336, *359*
Spirtes, P., 308, 311, *328*
Springer, K., 160, *192*, 342, *359*
Squire, L., 117, *129*

Stager, C. L., 91, *102*, 140, *158*, 168, 175, 176, 177, 179, *192*
Star, J. R., 345, *354*, 351, *354*, 400, *401*
Starkey, D., 93, *101*, 319, *328*
Starkey, P., 62, *75*
Stevens, K. N., 31, *46*
Stevenson, C., 335, *353*
Stevyers, M., 406, *417*
Stolyarova, E. I., 31, *46*
Strandsby, O., 372, *382*
Strauss, M. S., 6, *20*, 62, *75*, 81, *101*, 196, 197, 202, *208*, *209*
Streeter, L. A., 30, *48*
Strevens, M., 304, *328*, 392, *402*
Studdert-Kennedy, M. G., 28, *46*, *48*
Sugarman, S., 78, 93, *101*, 319, *328*
Sundberg, U., 31, *46*
Sussman, J. E., 31, *48*
Svenkerud, V. Y., 30, *45*
Swoboda, P., 28, *48*
Syrdal-Lasky, A., 30, *46*

Takizawa, O., 30, *48*
Talmy, L., 235, *240*
Tanaka, J., 409, *418*
Tardif, T., 215, 216, *240*, 320, *328*, 345, *354*
Tarr, M. J., 52, *74*
Taub, E., 410, *417*
Tees, R. C., 30, *49*, 199, *209*
Tenenbaum, J. B., 53, *75*
Thal, D., 87, *100*, 249, *273*
Thelen, E., 51, *75*, 89, *101*
Thompson, C. K., 216, *239*
Thompson, P., 144, 145, 147, *157*
Thyer, N., 31, *48*
Tokura, H., 40, 41, *44*
Tolman, E. C., 307, *328*
Tomasello, M., 242, 243, 269, *273*, 341, *359*, 390, 400, *400*, *402*
Trask, R. L., 37, *48*
Triesman, A., 163, *192*
Tsushima, T., 30, *48*
Turken, A. U., 360, 378, *381*
Tversky, B., 8, *23*, 163, *192*, 244, *274*, 330, *359*

Uchida, N., 18, *21*, 276, 277, *301*, 303, *327*, 334, *355*, 386, *401*
Ungerleider, L. G., 66, 68, *74*, *75*
Uttal, D. H., 62, *75*
Uzunov, K., 58, *75*

van de Weijer, J., 36, *48*
Vecera, S. P., 66, *75*

Vela, E., 78, *102*, 347, *359*
Vigorito, J., 12, *20*, 28, *44*, 199, *208*
Vijayan, S., 205, *208*
Vishton, P. M., 205, *208*, 279, *302*
Von-Hofsten, C., 279, *302*
Vriezen, E., 116, *129*

Wagner, S. H., 154, *157*
Waldron, E. M., 360, 378, *380*, *381*
Walley, A. C., 29, *45*
Wanner, E., 40 *44*, 216, *238*
Ward, T. B., 77, *101*, *102*, 347, *359*
Warrington, E. K., 121, 122, *131*
Washburn, D. A., 168, *192*
Watamaki, T, 283, *301*
Watson J. S., 322, *328*
Wattenmaker, W. D., 118, *129*
Waxman, J. S., 323, *328*
Waxman, S. R., 52, *72*, *75*, 114, 124, 125, 126, *131*, 141, *158*, 206, *207*, 209, 214, 215, 216, 217, 218, 219, 220, 221, 222, 223, 224, 225, 226, 227, 228, 229, 230, 231, 232, 233, 234, 235, 236, *237*, *238*, *239*, 240, *241*, 335, 344, 347, *359*, 371, *383*, 397, *402*

Weir, C. C., 29, *47*
Weiskopf, S., 199, *207*
Weiss, S. J., 153, *156*
Weissenborn, J., 42, *45*
Weissman, S., 58, 59, 62, 63, 64, 65, 67, *74*
Weist, R. M., 58, 59, *75*
Welder, A. N., 397, *401*
Wellman, H. M., 11, *23*, 52, *75*, 304, 306, *326*, *327*, *329*, 330, 332, *333*, 343, 344, 350, 351, *355*, *359*
Wentworth, N., 170, *189*
Werker, J. D., 199, *209*
Werker, J. F., 12, *21*, 30, 31, 42, *47*, *48*, *49*, 78, 79, 91, 92, 93, 100, *102*, 140, *158*, 168, 175, 176, *177*, *179*, *192*, 214, 217, 240, *241*
Wessels, J. M. I., 30, *44*, *45*
Whalen, D. H., 29, *46*
White, P. A., 332, *359*
Whorf, B. L., 9, *23*
Wienbruch, C., 410, *417*
Wierzbicka, A, 235, *241*
Wilcox, S. A., 343, *355*
Wilk, A. C., 79, 90, 99, *102*
Williams, E. M., 236, *238*, 342, *354*
Williams, K. A., 31, *46*
Williams, R. J., 362, *383*

Wisniewski, E. J., 331, *359*, 405, *418*
Witherington, D., 54, *72*
Wittgenstein, L., 411, *418*
Woodward, A. L., 41, *45*, 106, *131*, 182, *192*, 218, *238*, 242, *273*, 322, 323, *329*, 333, 334, 341, *359*, 391, *402*
Woodward, J. Z., 36, *49*
Wynn, K., 389, *402*
Wysocka, J., 59, *75*

Xu, F., 52, 53, *75*, 220, 223, 233, *241*, 320, *328*, 399, *402*

Yamashita, Y., 284, *301*
Yamauchi, T., 347, *359*
Yoshida, H., 276, 291, 295, 297, *302*
Young, A. W., 163, *192*
Younger, B. A., 14, *23*, 51, *75*, 76, 78, 79, 80, 81, 82, 83, 84, 86, 87, 88, 89, 90, 91, 92, 93, 94, 95, 96, 97, 99, *102*, 117, *131*, 139, 141, *158*, 160, 163, 171, 176, *188*, *192*, 197, 202, 203, *208*, *209*, 226, *241*, 243, 274, 368, 376, *383*

Zentall, T. R., 107, *131*
Zipser, D., *381*

Subject Index

a priori expectations, in lexical concepts, 218–219, 228, 233
"above versus below"
  object-variation version of, 63–64
  as spatial relation, 53–58
abstract representations
  causal maps and, 308–312
  concepts and, 408–409
  from ontology correlations, 281, 296–299
  of similarity, 108, 115
  for spatial relations, 62–65, 68, 70
accessibility, of objects, impact on categorization, 135, 142, 147–150, 154
acoustics, in language development, 30
across-category confound task, 164, 167
ad hoc categories, 103
additional category principle, of basic-level categories, 247–248, 271
adjectives, learning of, 10, 221, 224–225
  evidence of, 234–235
  fine-tuning, 228–232
  as grounded in noun-category links, 234–235
adult-basic categories, children's evolution to, 246–249, 396
adult input, in lexical acquisition
  child-basic category evolution with, 246–249, 396
  early category structure and word extension, 216, 242–246
  of subordinate-level categories, 249–250; case study of bird domain, 259–264; on labeling, 264–267
  theory-based, 395–398, 400

adults
  associative learning by, 169, 173
  attribute correlation by, 98–99
  categorization by, 8, 10, 12
  conceptual system of, 118–122
  inductive reasoning by, 376–378
age-related categorization, 4, 133, 136
algorithms, causality correlation in, 311
allomorphs, 36
allophones
  categorization by infants, 31–32
  word segmentation and, 37–39
ambiguous objects, animate-object boundary of, 292
analytic processing
  by children, 77–78
  holistic vs., 83–86
animacy
  content vs. process of, 202
  as continuum, individuation and, 278–279
  explicit judgments about, 334–335, 350
  implicit judgments about, 335–336
  perceptual to conceptual shift of, 160–161, 201; in theory-based classification, 390–394; theory-based contrast to, 350–351
animate-object boundary, 291–296
  cross-language differences only at, 295
  iru/aru distinction in, 291–292; abstract ideas with, 297–299
  variation at, 292–295
animates
  categorization of: by infants, 105–108; by preschoolers, 18

animates (*continued*)
distinction from inanimates: attention biases with, 162–169, 171; based on property knowledge, 180–186; by infants, 119, 121–122, 159–162, 169–170, 180–187; by Japanese children, 292–295; perceptual cues for, 348–349; theory-based, 333–336, 348; through association, 169–180
individuation of through language, 278–281
information sources about, 295–296
arbitrary correlations, vs. meaningful correlations, 151–152, 161, 176
articulation, discrimination of by infants, 28
artifacts
children's understanding of, 17, 335, 393
infants' differentiation of, 119, 121–122
infants' encoding of shape of, 113–114
artificial categories, 8, 368
artificial intelligence, causality correlation in, 311
aru, in animate-object boundary, 291–292
abstract ideas with, 297–299
association-based representations
depiction of, 172–174
evidence in infants, 176–180
form-function relations in, 165–168, 177–180
trials of, 176–181, 187
associations and associationism
concept formation and, 162, 169–176
in connectionist models, 379–380
expectations with, 170, 186–187
by infants, 106–108, 115–116, 170; evidence of, 176–180; representations based on, 173–174
ontological, 281, 285, 293, 297–300
static vs. dynamic cues for, 162, 170–173, 177–179
theory-based approaches to, 386–390, 398–399
associative learning
by adults, 169, 173
animate vs. inanimate distinction with, 169–180
attribute correlation in, 169–176; evidence in infants, 176–180; perception of causality impact on, 323–325
concepts and, 162, 169–176; of language, 172–173; of motion, 169–176; of object parts, 169–176; of objects by infants, 176–186
developmental applications of, 378–380
as enrichment, 173–174
expectations in, 170, 186–187
meanings in, 170–171

perception and, 169–176, 281
phoneme categorization with, 175–176
through utterances, 172–173
asymmetric exclusivity, in implicit categorization, 364–367
asymmetric interference, in implicit categorization, 366–367
attention
to attribute correlation, 88–89
early biases of, 162–169, 171, 341; object shape as, 277, 346–347
goal-directed, 106–107, 118–119
impact on categorization: child-basic, 244–247; developmental decreases in, 150–152, 320; developmental increases in, 136–142, 144, 146; infant perceptual, 361–362; subordinate-level, 265, 269–272
to movement, 168–169
naming and, 229–232
in noun generalization test, 287–288
to object parts, 163–168
to object size, 169
selective, 85, 168, 411
word-extension and, 243–244
word learning and, 219–220, 228
attribute correlation
age impact on, 89, 98–99, 325
analytic vs. holistic processing of, 77–78, 83–86
arbitrary vs. meaningful, 151–152, 161, 176
in associative learning, 169–176; causality and, 323–325; evidence in infants, 176–180
attention to, 88–89; with child-basic categories, 244–247; decreases in infants', 150–152; increases in infants', 138–140; use in categorization, 140–150
categorization of, 8, 12, 77–78; explicit, 93–96, 350; process of, 81–83
as children's learning process, 323–325
infants' sensitivity to, 78–81, 88; in animate vs. inanimate distinction, 180–186; color-form, 90–91; in developing separate categories, 367–368; developmental changes in, 138–142, 147–150
insufficiency of constraints argument, 161–162
of movement (*see* motion)
perceptual processing of, 86–88
recategorization of, 78–79, 91–93, 97
redrawing boundaries on basis of, 97, 126
representations as grounded in, 161
static vs. dynamic cues for, 162, 170–173, 177–179
stimulus and: assessment of, 81–84; task dependencies, 89–91

theory-based approaches to, 386–390, 398–
399
attribute relations, 7–8
in spatial categorization, 69–70
authority principle, in categorization, 396–
397
basic-level, 247–249
subordinate-level, 261, 265, 271
autoencoder, in connectionist network
models, 362–364, 367–368, 370
of category-based inductive inferences,
372–376

background knowledge. *See* ontological
knowledge
barriers, impact on categorization, 137, 144–
145
basic-level categories, 7–9
attention to parts with, 163, 165–166
form-function principle of, 244–246
in infants' imitation behavior, 110–114
labeling in: case study of bird domain, 259–
264; with category member variance,
262–264; evolution of, 246–249, 396;
when members are initially included,
260–261; when members are not initially
included, 259–261
language acquisition and, 124–126; word-
extension in, 243–246
Bayes nets
definition of, 308, 310
of relations among objects and events, 310–
311; application to causal maps, 311–312,
324, 394
behavioral process, of internal
representations, by infants, 368–370,
378–380
belief systems, concepts based on, 331, 349, 399
"between," as spatial relation, 58–62, 64
between-category similarities
attention to parts and, 165–166
of multiple objects, 142–147
bias
in attention, 162–169, 171, 341
in attribute correlation, 99
in categorization by children, 12, 86
goal-directedness as, 106–107, 321, 347
in perceptual processing, 86–88
shape as, in naming, 277, 346–347
biology
causal maps application to, 307–308
children's theory of, 159–161, 345
equivalence concept of, 405
bird domain, as subordinate-level
categorization case study, 250–272

acquisition details in, 264–269
adult input impact on, 259–264, 266–267
baby vs. juvenile vs. adult members, 262–
264
category extension and evolution findings,
254
coding for, 252–253
components of, 251–252
comprehension trials in, 253
conclusive summary of, 269–272
databases for, 252–253
developmental notes in, 252
diary entries in, 251
findings of, 253–269
initial category extensions included in,
254–258
methodology for, 250–251
non-noun production, 253
noun production with referents, 252–253
noun production without referents, 253
participant of, 251
play sessions in, 252
quasi-experimental probes in, 252
blicket detector experiment
on 2- to 4-year-olds: for causal induction,
312–318, 393; for causal power, 318–319,
325
on 18-month-olds, for naming and sorting,
224, 319–322
bootstrapping, 40, 411–412
boundaries. *See* category boundaries
brain damage, knowledge loss of with, 122,
125

case study, of subordinate-level
categorization, 250–272. *See also* bird
domain
categorical perception, perceptual
categorization vs., 198–200
categories and categorization
abilities needed for learning, 12–13
abstract for spatial relations, 62–65
ad hoc, 103
by adults, 8, 10, 12
arbitrary vs. richly structured, 151–152, 161,
176
artificial, 8, 368
assessment of, 13–14; in infancy, 14–16;
modeling as, 4, 12, 18–19; with
preschoolers, 16–18
broadly applied, 12–13
causal theory of reference of, 4–5, 7
by children, 5–9, 11–12, 77
classical, 307–308
conceptual (*see* concepts)

categories and categorization (*continued*)
   constancy vs., in perception, 197–198
   content vs. process factor, 202–203
   correlation-based (*see* attribute
     correlation)
   definition of, 3–4; infants', 194–197
   developmental implications of acquisition
     of, 4, 98–99
   dynamic view of, 134, 138, 155
   explicit, 93–96, 334–335, 350
   general issues in, 4–5, 13–14
   hierarchies of, 7–9
   importance of, 193–194
   indices of, 318
   inductive inferences supported by, 4, 114–115
   by infants, 3, 5–7, 9, 11; assessment of, 14–
     16; definition of, 194–197; developmental,
     77–79, 92
   internal structure of (*see* internal
     representations)
   intuition about, 330–331, 337
   kinds of, 303–304, 351
   labeling of, 8, 10
   language and, 4, 9–13
   link between naming, 213–214, 235–236
   mutual exclusivity principle and, 7–9, 247,
     270
   natural, 206, 313, 371–372
   object vs. event, 203–204
   parsing objects into, 77–99
   perceptual (*see* perception)
   of spatial relation information, 13, 50–71
   of speech sounds, 28–32
   taxonomic, 7–9, 152
   theory-based (*see* theory-based categories)
   unresolved issues in, 193–207
category boundaries
   impact on naming, 226–227
   by infants, 115
   redrawing based on attribute correlation,
     97, 126
category extension, with subordinate-level
   categorization
   evolution of, 254
   with highly atypical exemplar, 254, 257–258
   initial, 254, 256–258
   patterns of, 254–255
   with typical exemplar, 258
causal induction. *See* causality
causal maps
   as abstract representation of interactions,
     308–312
   theory theory of, 307–308, 393–394
causal power, in distinction of kinds, 317–318,
   393–394

   correlation factor, 304–306
   by young children, 318–319, 324
causal status hypothesis, 337, 350
causality
   blicket detector experiment on, 312–319,
     322, 325, 393
   children's understanding of, 11–12, 304,
     312–319
   conditional probability in, 308–311, 394
   as essence of kinds, 6, 304; correlation of
     power of, 304–306, 398
   folk theories comparison to, 307–308, 322
   infants' appreciation of, 5, 7, 11, 322–323
   learning relationship to, 323–325
   memory errors in, 317–318, 320, 350
   naming, and sorting, 312–318
   in object distinction, 308–312; animate vs.
     inanimate, 162, 175, 179, 185; memory
     impact on, 317–318; vs. events, 203–204
   perceptual cues conflict and, 317–319, 323
   psychological, 6, 307–308
   spatial contiguity as necessary to, 12–13, 62
   in subordinate-level categories, 250–251
   theories' appeal to, 5, 11, 99, 336–337, 391, 393
   theory-based categories and, 344–345, 399
child-basic categories, 10, 244
   evolution of, 246–249, 396
children's theory of mind, 11–12
chunking, of language input, 27–49
   finding the right rhythm, 32–35
   grammatical organization, 39–42
   research review, 27–29, 42–43
   sound categorization, 27–32
   word segmentation problem, 36–39
classical conditioning, 307–308
classification. *See also* categories and
   categorization
   by children, 3, 5–6
   dimensions relevant to, 12–13, 347
   on nonperceptual basis, 11–12
   theory-based, 390–394
clauses, 40
clusters, spatial relations of, 54
co-occurrence, of attributes. *See* attribute
   correlation
cognitive development, 408–411. *See also*
   information processing
   assessment methods for, 13–14
   categorization as fundamental to, 3–8, 132–
     136
   connectionist models of, 175–176
   developmental implications of, 360–361,
     378–380
   impact on categorization, 134, 138–141, 152–
     155

with naming: in infants establishing a
  lexicon, 223; in prelinguistic infants,
  222–223
perceptual to conceptual, 408–411
profound effect of language on, 126
sorting abilities relationship to, 320–322, 324
spatial relation categorization and, 53–54
color, as naming factor, 226–228, 250
color-form correlations, infants' sensitivity
  to, 90–91, 163
commonalities. See similarity
communication, concepts as basis for, 405–406
communicative partners. See also adult input
  in child-basic category evolution, 246–249
  in subordinate-level categorization, 249–
  250, 272
complex thought, concepts as basis for, 330,
  405–406
comprehension, referential, 243–244
computational model
  of categorization, 4, 18–19; implicit, 361,
  367, 378–379
  of perceptual and causal categorization,
  312, 324–325
concentration, theory of infants', 105
concepts and conceptual categorization, 103–
  131
  age-related changes in development of, 4,
  133, 136
  associative learning and, 162, 169–176
  based on statistical information, 331, 398–
  399
  basic-level (see basic-level categories)
  bootstrapping and, 411–412
  brain damage impact on, 122, 125
  categories vs., 404
  complex, from simple, 330, 405–406
  constraints on, 411–415
  current issues in, 4–5, 13–14
  debates about children's, 346–348
  definition of, 3–4, 404–405
  developmental studies of, 403–404
  differentiation as development of, 118–122
  as dynamic process, 161–162
  with early language organization, 214–215
  essences and, 6, 348, 389, 393
  evidence for, 407–408
  external vs. internal, 404–405
  functions of, 4, 103–104, 405–406
  future directions for, 415–416
  and generalization, 108–116, 407–408
  as generative devices, 108–116
  infants' as foundation of adults', 118–122
  intuitive theory of, 330–331, 337
  language acquisition and, 4, 9–11, 122–126

and meanings, 5, 104, 115
origins of earliest, 104–108
perceptual categorization vs., 5–7, 116–118,
  200–201
perceptual shift to, 160–161, 205, 281, 371;
  dynamics of, 408–411; theory-based, 350–
  351, 390–394
and properties, 160–161, 205, 281
selective attention and, 411
in spatial categorization, 67–68
subordinate (see subordinate-level
  categories)
superordinate (see superordinate
  categories)
theory-based (see theory-based categories)
theory-theory of, 6, 306
"concepts-in-theories," 331, 377
concrete representations, for spatial relations,
  63–65, 68
conditional probability, in causality, 308–311,
  394
conditions, in orientation perception, 194–197
conflict trials, of causal induction, 304–315
connection weights, in neural information
  networks, 362–363, 371
connectionist models, of categorization, 12,
  18–19
  autoencoder dynamics in, 362–364, 367–
  368, 370
  cognition and, 175–176
  developmental implications of, 378–380,
  415–416
  for inductive inference, 372–376
  by infants, 51–52, 173, 204–205; asymmetric
  exclusivity in, 364–367; asymmetric
  interference in, 366–367; in implicit
  cognitive models, 361–364, 370–371
  in ontology simulation, 206, 285–291
conscious thought, by infants, 117
consonants, categorization by infants, 28–29
constancy, vs. categorization, in perception,
  197–198
constraints
  on concept formation, 411–415
  of developmental change, 135, 150–152
  insufficiency of, 161–162
  on word meanings, 234–235, 277, 346–347,
  364–357
content approach, to age-related
  categorization, 133, 202–203
context, impact on categorization, 4, 135, 142–
  143
  based on experience with object, 147–150
  conclusions about, 152–155
  with multiple objects, 143–147

contingency, infants' understanding of, 323, 349
coordinate deletion principle, of basic-level
    category evolution, 248–249
core knowledge. *See* ontological knowledge
correlation, of attributes. *See* attribute
    correlation
count-mass syntax, in ontology simulation,
    289–290, 297–298
covariance information, in concept
    formation, 413–414
cross-linguistic studies
    of animate-object boundaries, 291–296, 335
    of naming and sorting abilities, 321–322
    of object-substance boundaries, 278–281
    relevance of, 4, 33–35, 275
    universal ontological distinction in, 276,
        295–296, 300
    of word learning, 215–216, 221, 233
cues
    accessibility of, category formation and,
        135, 142, 147–150, 154
    in association-based representations, 176–
        180
    conceptual vs. perceptual, 6–7, 16
    facilitating, 176
    language-specific, 280–281, 291; abstract
        ideas from, 296–299
    moving (*see* motion)
    in preschooler categorization assessment,
        16–17
    static vs. dynamic, 162, 170–173, 177–179
    word segmentation and, 36–39
culture, word learning and, 215–216, 221, 233,
    242, 244, 351

descriptive approach, to age-related
    categorization, 133
determinism, children's belief in, 399
developmental change, 132–158
    with acquisition of hierarchies, 3–6, 8
    attribute correlations and, 4, 98–99
    background knowledge constraint on, 135,
        150–152
    causality impact on, 323–325
    conclusions about, 152–155
    contextual advantage of, 135, 142–150
    examples of, 77–79, 92
    with implicit cognitive processes, 360–361,
        378–380
    motor, cognitive, and linguistic abilities
        broadening of, 134, 136–142
    noun and adjective distinctions and, 10–11
    overview of principles of, 132–136
    research methodologies for, 13–18
    in spatial categorization, 68–70

theory-based limitations with, 350–351
    word-extension and, 242–246
differentiation
    as concept development process, 118–122
    definition of, 3–4
    in subordinate-level categorization, 249–
        250, 270
    as word learning basis, 220–221
dimensional objects, preschoolers'
    categorization of, 17–18
discrimination
    definition of, 3–4
    in orientation perception, 194–197
dishabituation, developmental changes
    impact on, 340, 347
dissimilarity, hierarchical maximization of,
    7–8
distraction
    in animate vs. inanimate distinction, 183–186
    impact on categorization, 150–152
doctrine of sim, 108–109
domain-general processes, 330
domain specificity
    child's conceptual understanding of, 10
    in infants' imitation behaviors, 112, 115
    knowledge of as concept constraint, 413–414
    of learning mechanisms, 385–386, 394, 399
    of subordinate-level categories, 249–250
"dumb attentional mechanisms," 219, 330, 350
duplex perception, 29–30
dynamic cues, for associations, 162, 170–173,
    177–179

early language
    acquisition of, 7–8, 10, 99, 122–126
    cognitive skills assessment and, 13–14
    fine-grained features of, 32–35
    speech sounds in, 12–13, 28–32
emotional expression, impact on
    categorization, 153–154
encoding
    of motion cues, 170
    of object locations, 50, 54, 68
    of object parts, 113–114, 119
    of object relations, 92, 399
    of perceptual categories, 360–361, 363–364,
        379
    of speech sounds, 30, 41
English vocabulary, regularity of
    in abstract idea correlations, 296–299
    associationism and, 388–389
    from MacArthur Communicative
        Development Inventory, 249, 281–283
    in simulation of object-substance
        boundaries, 285–291

enrichment
    associative learning as, 173–174
    of representations, 4, 7
equivalence class, 3, 405
essentialism
    shared by kinds of objects, 5, 303–304
    theory-based categories and, 6, 348, 389, 393
event categories, object categories vs., 203–204
events, as causal relations with objects, 308–312
evolution
    associative learning as, 173–174
    of child to adult-basic categories, 246–249, 396
    of early object categories, 4, 7, 270–271
exclusivity. *See* mutual exclusivity principle
exemplars. *See* models and modeling
exhaustive sorting, 320–322
expectations
    in associative learning, 170, 186–187
    lexical development and, 220–221; evidence of, 232–234; fine-tuning, 228–232; a priori, 218–219, 228, 233
experience, with objects
    function as factor, 338–341
    impact on categorization, 135, 142, 147–150
explanations, as categorization basis, 331–332
explicit categories
    of animacy, 334–335
    attribute correlation and, 93–96, 350
exploratory behavior, in infants, 323
extensions
    of categories: by infants, 123, 133–134; subordinate-level, 254–258
    of language, in preschooler categorization, 16–17
    of words (*see* word-extension)

face and facial expression
    impact on categorization, 153–154, 174
    infants' perception of, 196–197, 202, 341
facilitating cue, 176
facts, in category-based inductive inference model, 372–376
familiar test trial, for association-based representations, 176–181, 187
familiarization/novelty-preference, 14
    in attribute correlation, 94–96; developmental change impact on, 138–140, 146, 148–149
    in lexical acquisition, 222–225, 227, 229–230, 397
    in spatial relations, 52, 55, 63, 66
"fast mapping," 218, 320
features, of objects. *See* attribute *entries*

focused sampling, as learning mechanism, 88
folk theories, causality comparison to, 307–308, 322
forced-choice tasks, in naming, 229
form-function principle
    in association-based representations, 165–168, 177–180
    as basic category principle, 244–246; evolution of, 247–248, 254; theory-based, 340, 391, 396
    in subordinate-level categories, 254, 258, 270–271
formalism, of graphical causal models, 311–312, 324
function, theory-based categories and, 338–341, 391–392, 396
function words, 42, 338

gaze following, 14, 361–362
gender categories, 133, 153
generalization(s)
    concepts as basis for, 108–116, 407–408
    higher-order through word learning, 281, 299
    by infants, 15, 69
    kind-specific name: language learning role in, 276–279, 283; of novel objects, 283, 286–291
    in orientation perception, 194–197
    overhypothesis impact on, 415
    in subordinate-level categorization, 258
generalized imitation task
    in animate vs. inanimate distinction, 182–186
    components of, 15–16, 109–110
    models of infants', 109–113, 120, 407
global-level categories, 8–9
goal-directedness, as bias, 106–107, 321, 347
grammatical forms. *See specific form, e.g.,* nouns
grammatical organization. *See* parsing

habituation
    association-based representations and, 176–180, 187
    attention biases of, 163, 168–169, 171, 176
    in attribute correlation, 80–81, 83, 95–96
    definition of, 11
    developmental changes impact on, 151–152, 176
    in orientation perception, 194–197
    prior knowledge impact on, 205–206
    as representation construction in infants, 362–363
    theory-based categories and, 340, 347

head-turn preference procedure, 14
heuristics, causality correlation in, 312
hidden units, in connectionist network
  models, 362–363, 369–370
hierarchies
  basic, superordinate, and subordinate
    levels in, 7–9
  in subordinate-level categorization, 244,
    264–265, 271–272
  taxonomic, 7–9, 152
  theory-based categories and, 343, 345
higher-order generalizations, in word
  learning, 281, 299
holistic processing
  analytic vs., 83–86
  by children, 77–78
Hopfield network, for making an ontology,
  285–287
hypotheses, in concept formation, 414–415

ignoring abilities, impact on categorization,
  150–152
imitation, generalized, 15–16, 109–110
  in animate vs. inanimate distinction, 182–
    186
  models of infants', 109–113, 120, 407
implicit categories, 360–380
  of animacy, 335–336
  children's use of, 324–325; inductive
    inference domain, 371–378
  prelinguistic infants' use of: as inherent,
    360–361; perceptual categorization
    domain, 361–371
  theoretical framework for, 360, 378–380
inanimates/inanimacy. See animate entries
individual differences, in word learning, 7–8,
  10
individuation
  of objects (see object individuation)
  of substances, through language, 278–281
inductive generalization, by infants, 182–186
inductive inference model, category-based,
  372–376
  perceptual variability impact on, 376–377
inductive reasoning
  about related properties of kinds, 308–312
  associationist approaches to, 387–388, 398–
    399
  causal (see causality)
  classification approaches to, 390–394
  implicit category use in children's, 371–378;
    developmental implications of, 378–380;
    model of, 372–376; perception impact
    on, 376–377; research discussion, 377–
    378; research diversity, 371–372

overhypothesis impact on, 415
perceptual variability impact on, 376–377
problems of, 108–109
research directions for, 415–416
theory-based, 11–12
through categorizing, 4, 114–115
inferences
  about objects, 11; correlation of properties
    of kinds of, 308–312; novel, 16–17, 332,
    344–346
  category-based, 4; implicit, 360–361;
    inductive, 372–377; by infants, 105, 108,
    316; theory-based, 344–346, 392; by
    young children, 312–318
  causality and, 312–318
  classification vs., 347
  concepts as basis for, 406
  inductive model of, 372–376; perceptual
    variability impact on, 376–377
inflection points, 163
information processing. See also cognitive
  development
  conceptual implications of, 6–7
  increases in abilities for: conclusions
    about, 152–155; impact on categorization,
    134, 138–141
  of nonobservable properties, 11–12
innate structures, of implicit categories, 360–
  361
input units, in connectionist network
  models, 362–363, 369
insides, as object property, 71, 343
instructions, verbal, impact on
  categorization, 126
insufficiency of constraints, 161–162
integration skills, for subordinate-level
  categorization, 243
intentions, theory-based categories and, 341–
  342
  function as factor, 340, 391–392
interaction
  among objects and events, abstractions of,
    308–312
  with objects, impact on categorization, 135,
    143
interest. See attention
interference, in implicit categorization
  asymmetric, 366–367
  retroactive, 367
internal representations, by infants
  behavioral process of, 368–370, 378–380
  connectionist network models of, 362–363,
    368–370
  with perceptual categorization, 361–362
  through inductive reasoning, 371–378

interpretation, by infants, 104–108
  absence of, 116–117
intervention
  as Bayes nets feature, 311
  infants' abilities for, 322–323
intuitive theory, of concepts, 330–331, 337
irrelevant information, impact on
    categorization, 150–152
iru, in animate-object boundary, 291–292
  abstract ideas with, 297–299

Japanese vocabulary, regularity of
  in abstract idea correlations, 296–299
  in animate-object boundaries, 285–291
  associationism and, 388–389
  from MacArthur Communicative
    Development Inventory, 283–285
  in simulation of object-substance
    boundaries, 291–295

kind(s)
  Bayes nets representations of, 308–312
  as category basis, 303–304, 351
  causal powers of, 304–306, 318–319; theory
    theory of, 306–308
  children's understanding of, 276–277, 304;
    in 2- to 4-year-olds, 312–319; in 18–
    month-olds, 319–322; in preverbal
    infants, 322–323
  natural, 206, 313, 371–372
  statistical regularities of, 280–281, 299–300;
    network simulations of, 285–291
  in subordinate-level categorization, 249
kind-specific name generalizations
  language learning role in, 276–279, 283
  of novel objects, 283, 286–291
knowledge
  of animate vs. inanimate properties, 180–
    186
  causal maps relationship to, 307–308, 323
  core background (see ontological
    knowledge)
  loss of with brain damage, 122, 125
  sensorimotor, 105
  theory-relevant, instantiation of, 347–348

labels and labeling
  by adults vs. children, 8, 10, 12
  in category-based inductive inference
    model, 372–376; perceptual variability
    impact on, 376–377, 379
  developmental attention to, 137, 140, 379
  evolution of child-basic, 246–249, 396;
    adult input on, 264–267; case study of
    bird domain, 259–264

task assessment in, 14–15
theory-based categories and, 343–344, 387–
    388
landmark, in spatial relations, 58–61, 66, 70
language
  categorization role, 134, 140–141, 351;
    conclusions, 152–155; lexical perspectives,
    395–398, 400; in preschoolers, 16–17;
    research issues, 206
  chunking to find patterns, 27–49; finding
    the right rhythm, 32–35; grammatical
    organization, 39–42; research review,
    27–29, 42–43; sound categorization,
    27–32; word segmentation problem,
    36–39
  in concept formation, 4, 9, 11–12, 122–126;
    in associative learning, 172–173; as
    constraint, 412–413
  different proposals about, 9–10, 12–13
  labor divisions of, 397, 400
  native (see native language)
  in ontological distinctions, 295–296; causal
    powers impact on, 317–319
language development
  as children's learning factor, 323–324
  cognitive consequences of, 223–232, 324
  conceptual organization in, 214–215
  early stages of (see early language)
  in kind-specific name generalizations, 276–
    279, 283
  social interaction and, 4, 242–244
  sorting abilities relationship to, 320–322
  superordinate categories in, 124–126, 225
  word learning in, 215–222
learning
  associative (see associative learning)
  computational model of, 312, 324–325
  concept formation and, 162, 169–176;
    overhypothesis impact on, 414–415
  continual and incremental, 161–162
  domain-specific mechanisms of, 385–386,
    394, 399; constraints on, 413–414
  perceptual and causal categorization
    relationship to, 323–325
"learning how to learn," in subordinate-level
    categorization, 264, 269–270
"left versus right," 71
lexical categories
  naming and the scope of, 395–398
  in ontological distinctions, 295–296;
    abstract ideas from, 296–299
  principles of, 220, 242, 244
lexical development
  adult input in, 246–249; on labeling, 264–
    267; word extension and, 242–246

lexical development (*continued*)
  at basic category level, 242–243; evolution
    of, 246–249, 396; structure of, 243–246
  expectations as basis of, 220–221; evidence
    of, 232–234; fine-tuning, 228–232; a
    priori, 218–219, 228, 233
  foundation for, 213, 216, 281
  novel objects and, 222–223; attention
    impact, 229–232; category-based
    commonalities of, 224–226; property-
    based commonalities of, 226–228;
    research issues, 223–224
  review of evidence for, 232–235
  at subordinate category level, 249–269
  from a tabulae rasae, 219–220, 233
  timetables for, 242
  word and concept links prior to, 222–232
  word-extension with: of early object words,
    243–246; of novel vs. familiar objects,
    229–232
lexical principles, 220, 242, 244
linguistics. *See* language *entries*
locomotion, impact on categorization, 137

MacArthur Communicative Development
    Inventory (MCDI)
  English lexicon from, 249, 281–282
  Japanese lexicon from, 283–285
manipulatory manual behavior
  attention to parts with, 163–165, 167
  impact on categorization, 137, 144–145, 148,
    153
  task-oriented, 14–15
mapping. *See also* word-to-world links
  in word learning, 217–218; evidence of, 232–
    234
Markov assumption, in causality, 310
match-to-sample task, 126, 173
material, in perceptual cues and lexical
    category correlations, 296–297
  among English linguistic cues, 297–299
  among Japanese linguistic cues, 297–298
material-matching test object, in ontology
    simulation, 288–290
meaningful correlations, vs. arbitrary
    correlations, 151–152, 161, 176
meanings
  in associative learning, 170–171
  concept-related, 5, 104, 115
  shared, 5, 303–304
means-ends abilities, 321
memory
  of attribute correlations, 89–92, 399
  in implicit categorization tasks, 360–361,
    363–364, 379

of spatial relations, 50, 54–55, 62, 68, 138
of speech sounds instances, 30, 41
in subordinate-level categorization, 269, 272
memory errors, in causal induction, 317–318,
    320, 350
memory recall, by infants, 117
metaknowledge, as concept constraint, 413–414
models and modeling
  for categorization assessment, 4, 12, 17–19
  contextual nature of, 142–150
  in correlation-based categorization, 83–87
  with infant imitation behaviors, 109–113
  as prototype vs. proposition, 204–205
  in spatial relation categorization, 55–57, 59,
    67, 69
mora-timed linguistic rhythms, 34
morphemes, 37, 41
"motherese," 216
motion
  associative learning and concepts of, 169–
    176
  distinction by infants, 119, 121–122, 169–170;
    attention to as bias, 166–169, 171; from
    inanimacy, 159–162, 180–187; parts and,
    163–168, 171; size and, 169; through
    association, 169–176; through knowledge,
    180–186
  local vs. global, 170
  perceptual to conceptual shift of, 160–161
motion events, in animate vs. inanimate
    distinction, 183
motion path, in animate vs. inanimate
    distinction, 185–186
motor abilities, developmental increases in,
    impact on categorization, 134, 136–137, 144
  conclusions about, 152–155
movement. *See* motion
multilingual environments, 33
multiple objects, impact on categorization,
    135, 142–147
music, causal maps application to, 307–308
mutual exclusivity principle
  of categorization, 7–9, 247, 270
  in implicit categorization, asymmetric,
    364–367

naïve theories, domain-specific, 385, 394, 399
name generalization test
  linguistic cues in, 296–299 ·
  yes/no version of, 291–294
names and naming
  animate-object boundaries of, 291–296
  cognitive consequences of: in infants
    establishing a lexicon, 223; in
    prelinguistic infants, 222–223

commonalities and: category-based, 224–226; property-based, 226–228
early conceptual organization for, 214–215
higher-order generalizations with, 281, 299
kind-specific generalizations with, 276–279; of novel objects, 283, 286–291
learning relationship to, 323–325
lexical categories and, 395–398
links between object categorization, 213–214, 235–236
object-subject boundaries of, 281–291
in sorting: causal induction and, 312–318; causal powers and, 318–319
and sorting in 2- to 4-year-olds, 312–319
and sorting in 18-month olds, 319–322
subordinate-level categories in, 7–9
word learning as, 215–218
word-to-world links as, 216–222
native language
    acquiring, 27, 30–31; conceptual organization with, 214–215
    categorization association with, 206, 213, 220–221
    rhythmic properties of, 32–35
nativist-empiricist debate, 384–386
natural kinds, 206, 313, 371–372
navigation behavior, impact on categorization, 137
network simulations, of ontologies, 285–291
    Hopfield model, 286–287
    noun generalization test, 287–288
    overview of, 285–286
    results of, 288–290
    syntax layer in, 289–290
    training on, 286–287
neural information processing
    asymmetric exclusivity in, 364–367
    asymmetric interference in, 366–367
    connection weights in, 362–363, 371
    in implicit categorization, 361–362, 370–371
    models of (see connectionist models)
neutral trials, of causal induction, 304–315
nonobvious properties
    children's understanding of, 159–160, 174, 179
    theory-based categories and, 342–344, 348, 392, 398
nonsolid substances
    creating object boundaries for, 281–291
    ontological naming of, 280, 299; English lexicon for, 281–283; Japanese lexicon for, 283–285; network simulations for, 285–291
noun-category link, as first to emerge, 234–235
noun generalization test, in ontology simulation, 287–288, 291

noun phrases, generic, 345
nouns
    in early concept formation, 10, 18, 123–124, 141, 335
    intentional extension of, 341–342
    kind-specific generalizations of newly learned, 276, 283
    learning of, 221 216, 224–225; fine-tuning, 228–232; as first specific category, 234–235, 270; mapping evidence with, 232–234
    object-subject boundaries and, 282–283
novel category preference, in spatial relations, 55, 63, 66–67
novel noun generalization test, 227–228
novel objects
    acceptance of based on beliefs, 331
    correlation of attributes of, 89–90, 94
    impact on kind-specific name generalizations, 283, 286–291
    infants' spatial categorization of, 52, 55, 63, 66
    inferences about properties of: implicit, 379–380; theory-based categories and, 344–346
    in lexical acquisition, 222–223; category-based commonalities of, 224–226; property-based commonalities of, 226–228; research issues, 223–224
    preschoolers' categorization of, 16–17; function as factor, 338–341
    within-category vs. out-of-category, 148–149
novelty-preference task
    developmental change impact on, 138–140, 148–149
    in spatial relations, 52, 55
    in word learning, 229–232

object actions
    infants' categorization of, 105–108
    infants' differentiation of, 119, 121–122
    verbs as reference for, 10
object categories
    event categories vs., 203–204
    evolution of early, 270–271
    infants' perception of, 51–53
    links between naming, 213–214, 235–236; commonalities and, 224–226; fine-tuning, 228–232; property-based, 226–228
    nouns as reference for, 10, 12, 270
object context, impact on categorization, 135, 143–150
object-examination task, 120, 177
object features. See attribute entries

object individuation
  animacy continuum and, 278–279
  as concept development, 118–122
  labeling as, 8, 10, 137
  ontological knowledge about, 385, 389
  taxonomic, 7–9, 152
  through language, 278–281
object labels. *See* labels and labeling
object manipulation task, 14–15
  attention to parts with, 163–165, 167
  impact on categorization, 137, 144–145, 148, 153
object parts
  adult viewpoints of, 163
  associative learning and concepts of, 169–176; by infants, 176–186
  distinction by infants: animate-inaminate, 159–162, 180–187; attention to as bias, 163–168, 171; encoding of, 113–114, 119; movement and, 168–169; size and, 169; through association, 176–180; through knowledge, 180–186
  perceptual to conceptual shift of, 160–161
object properties
  adjectives as reference for, 10, 221, 224–225
  common: fine-tuning, 228–232; naming and, 226–228, 395–396
  developmental increases in infants' attention to, 136–142, 147–150
  infants' knowledge of animate vs. inanimate, 180–186
  perceptual to conceptual shift of, 205, 281, 371; ontological, 160–161, 389; theory-based contrast to, 350–351, 392–393
object shape. *See* shape
object size, infants' attention to as bias, 169, 171
object-sorting tasks, 95–96
object-substance boundary
  creating, 281–291
  early English lexicon regularities in, 281–283
  early Japanese lexicon regularities in, 283–285
  network simulations of, 285–291
object weight, developmental ability to detect, 137
object words. *See* nouns
objects
  content vs. process of, 202–203
  differentiation of (*see* object individuation)
  in infants' generalization behaviors, 108–116
  information sources about, 295–296
  parsing into categories, 77–99

representations of causal relations with events, 308–312
  spatial relations of (*see* spatial relation information)
  variations of, impact on spatial categorization, 63–64
ontological knowledge
  abstract ideas from correlation of, 281, 296–299
  animate-object boundaries based on, 291–296
  in children's categorization process, 12, 18, 119, 399; theory-relevant information and, 347–348, 385, 389
  core ideas of, 4–5, 11–12, 18, 280–281, 299–300
  definitional sources of, 276–278, 333
  impact on categorization, 135, 150–152, 154, 385
  impact on habituation, 205–206
  impact on kind-specific name generalizations, 276–277
  language differences and, 278–280
  object-substance boundaries based on, 281–291
  perceptual to conceptual shift of, 160–161, 281, 349; dynamics of, 408–411
  as statistical regularity, 280–281, 299; network simulations of, 285–291
  in subordinate-level categorization, 269, 271
  theory-based categories and, 333–336, 348–349, 385
operant conditioning, 15, 307–308
orientation, infants' perception of, 194–197
out-of-category similarities, of novel objects, 148–149
output units, in connectionist network models, 362–363
outside, as object property, 71, 343
overextensions, of language, 123
  in preschooler categorization, 16–17, 346
overgeneralizations, 115, 258
overhypotheses, as concept constraint, 414–415

parental speech. *See* adult input
parsing
  analytic vs. holistic, 77–78, 83–86
  of conceptual world, 11
  discovering through speech sounds, 39–42
  lexical acquisition and, 218–219
  of relevant word with word learning, 217
  in spatial relation categorization, 52–54
  through speech sounds, 39–42
  use of correlated attributes, 77–99

part-whole relations, infants' attention to, 113–114, 119
parts. *See* object parts
pattern recognition
  perceptual vs. conceptual, 117–118
  with speech sounds (*see* chunking)
"percept-to-label" network, 387–388
perception and perceptual categorization
  associative learning and, 169–176, 281
  categorical perception vs., 198–200
  child's theory of, 11–12
  cognition vs., 4–5, 117
  conceptual categorization vs., 5–7, 116–118, 200–201
  conceptual shift from, 160–161, 205, 281, 371; dynamics of, 408–411; theory-based, 350–351, 390–394
  constancy vs. categorization in, 197–198
  future directions for, 415–416
  by infants, 361–371; asymmetry and, 364–367; connectionist models, 361–364, 370–371; developmental implications, 378–380; inductive inference model, 372–376; internal representations and, 368–370; preferential looking as basis of, 14, 361–362; separate, 367–368; variability impact on inferences from, 376–377
  as object distinction cue, 295–296; abstract ideas from, 296–299; causal power impact on, 317–319, 323; in infants, 51–53, 323
  of orientation, 194–197
  perceptual constancy vs., 197–198
  of speech sounds, 27–28
  stylistic variation in, 86–88
  theory-based categories and, 348–349
perceptual constancy
  categorization vs., 197–198
  relational definition of, 200–201
perceptual reductionism, 105
performance, in prelinguistic cognition assessment, 13–14
phonemes, categorization of
  by adults, 30
  by infants, 28–29, 31–32
  perception influence on, 198–200
  through associative learning, 175–176
phonotactics, 37–39
phrases, 41–42, 216
physical properties, children's understanding of, 159–160
point-light displays, infants' attention to, 168
postures, impact on categorization, 137
predictions
  as Bayes nets feature, 311
  concepts as basis for, 406

infants' abilities for, 118, 322–323
  theory-based, 330–331, 392
preferential looking, 14, 361–362
preschoolers, categorization by
  assessment of, 16–18
  function as factor of, 338–341
prior knowledge. *See* ontological knowledge
probability, conditional, in causality, 308–311, 394
problem solving, by infants, 117
process, as infants' category factor, 202–203
pronouns, 335
property-based commonalities. *See* object properties
propositions, prototypes vs., 204–205
prosodic word patterns, 37–39
  grammatical organization and, 40–42
prototypes
  limitations of, 331
  of perceptual categorization, 378–379
  propositions vs., 204–205
psychology
  basic-level categories based on, 244
  causal maps application to, 6, 307–308
  children's understanding of, 159–161
  of ontologies, 299–300

reading, spatial relation features of, 54
reasoning. *See* inductive reasoning
recategorization, of attribute correlations, by infants, 78–79, 91–93, 97
referent, in word learning, 216, 244
  rudimentary, 220–221
regions, spatial relations of, 54
reinforcement, impact on categorization, 126
relevance, as lexical principle, 217, 244, 265, 268
representations
  abstract (*see* abstract representations)
  associative (*see* association-based representations)
  of causal relations among objects and events: abstract, 308–312; natural, 312–318
  conceptual vs. perceptual, 5–7, 116–118
  as grounded in correlations, 161
  internal (*see* internal representations)
  as prototype vs. proposition, 204–205
  specific, for spatial relations, 63–65, 68–69
research
  advancements in, 4–5, 29
  future directions for, 415–416
  key issues of, 4–5, 13–14
  unresolved issues for, 193–207

research methodology
    for infants, 14–16
    issues of, 13–14
    modeling as, 4, 12, 18–19
    with preschoolers, 16–18
rhythmic organization, of languages, 32–35
"right versus left," 71
rudimentary lexicon, in word learning, 220–221
rules, for classification, 3
    hierarchical, 7–9, 152

schema, conceptual vs. perceptual, 6, 89
    of infants, 104, 106
science, causal maps application to, 307–308, 330
selective attention, 85, 168, 411
self-sitting behavior, impact on
    categorization, 137
semantic development, 334–336
sensorimotor knowledge, 105
sentences, 40
sequential-touching task, 15, 93–95, 120
    attention to parts with, 163–167
    in multiple objects assessment, 143–147, 152
sex categories/stereotyping, 133, 153
shape
    of artifacts, infants' encoding of, 113–114, 119
    developmental ability to look beyond, 334–335
    of objects, as bias in naming, 277, 346–347
    in perceptual cues and lexical category
        correlations, 296–297; among English
        linguistic cues, 297–299; among Japanese
        linguistic cues, 297–298
shape-matching test object, in ontology
    simulation, 288–290
shared meanings, 5, 303–304
sim, doctrine of, 108–109
similarity
    children's perception of, 319; as learning
        factor, 323–325
    cognitive consequences of, 222–223
    conceptual vs. perceptual, 4, 408
    doctrine of, 108–109
    hierarchical maximization of, 7–8
    limitations of, 331, 350
    of multiple objects, within-category vs.
        between-category, 142–147
    naming and: category-based, 224–226;
        property-based, 226–228
    of novel objects, within-category vs. out-
        of-category, 148–150

in perceptual cues and lexical category
    correlations, 296–297, 397; among
    English linguistic cues, 297–299; among
    Japanese linguistic cues, 297–298
    words as reference for, 10, 126, 220–221;
        category- vs. property-based, 224–228
size, of objects, infants' attention to as bias,
    169, 171
social interaction, lexical development and,
    242–244
solid substances
    creating object boundaries for, 281–291
    ontological naming of, 279–280, 299;
        English lexicon for, 281–283; Japanese
        lexicon for, 283–285; network
        simulations for, 285–291
sorting
    by 2- to 4-year-olds, 8, 312–319
    by 18-month-olds, 319–322
    exhaustive, 320–322
    learning relationship to, 323–325
    naming: and causal induction, 312–318; and
        causal powers, 318–319
    task assessment in, 14–15
spatial relation information
    "above versus below" representations of,
        53–58
    abstract vs. concrete representations of,
        62–65, 68
    "between" representations of, 58–62
    categorization principles of, 13, 50–51,
        70
    causal maps application to, 307, 323
    developmental categorization of, 68–70
    natural stimuli as, 71
    object-variations impact on categorization,
        63–68
    perception by infants, 51–53, 138, 323
spatiotemporal information processing,
    impact on categories, 138, 141, 336
speech sounds
    categorization by infants, 12–13; chunking
        and, 27–32; interest factor, 214–215;
        perception influence on, 198–200
    in discovering grammatical organization,
        39–42
    fine-grained features of, 32–35
    pattern recognition with (see chunking)
    storing information about, 12–13, 30
static cues, for associations, 162, 170–173, 177–179
statistical information, concepts based on,
    331, 398–400
stereotyping, based on gender, 133, 153

stimulus
  assessment: in correlation-based
    categorization, 81–84, 87, 95; in
    orientation perception, 194–197; for
    prelinguistic cognition, 13; for
    preschoolers' categorization, 17–18
  in connectionist network models, 362–364,
    367–368
stress patterns
  in grammatical organization, 42
  of word segmentation, 37–39
stress-timed linguistic rhythms, 34
subordinate-level categories
  acquisition of, 249–250, 271–272
  bird domain case study, 250–272;
    acquisition details, 264–269; adult input
    impact, 259–264, 266–267; baby vs.
    juvenile vs. adult members, 262–264;
    category extension and evolution
    findings, 254; coding, 252–253;
    components, 251–252; comprehension
    trials, 253; conclusive summary, 269–
    272; databases, 252–253; developmental
    notes, 252; diary entries, 251; findings,
    253–269; initial category extensions
    included, 254–258; methodology, 250–
    251; non-noun production, 253; noun
    production with referents, 252–253;
    noun production without referents,
    253; participant, 251; play sessions, 252;
    quasi-experimental probes, 252
  domain-specificity of, 249–250
  form-function principle of, 254, 258, 270–
    271
  names and, 7–9
substances
  individuation of through language, 278–
    281
  information sources about, 295–296
  and their names, 216, 277, 279
substantive content, of theory-based
  categories, 394
superordinate categories
  attention to parts with, 163–164
  children's abilities to form, 334
  in language acquisition, 124–126, 225
  names and, 7–9
switch test trial, for association-based
  representations, 176–181
syllable-timed linguistic rhythms, 34–35
syllables
  infant categorization of, 205; structure for,
    243
  word segmentation and, 36–37

syntax
  causal maps application to, 307
  in ontological distinctions, 390; of
    animates-objects, 293–296; count-mass,
    289–290, 297–298
  of phrases, 41–42

tabulae rasae, lexical development and, 219–
    220, 233
target object
  in animate vs. inanimate distinction, 183–
    186
  in spatial relations, 58–61, 66, 70
task assessment
  in infancy, 14–16
  memory systems and, 360
  in prelinguistic cognition, 13–14
  with preschoolers, 16–18
  in theory-based categories, 347
task dependencies, in correlation-based
  categorization, 89–91, 93
taxonomic organization
  of categories, 7–9
  by infants, 152
  principle of, 7
texture
  as naming factor, 226–228
  in perceptual cues and lexical category
    correlations, 296–297; among English
    linguistic cues, 297–299; among Japanese
    linguistic cues, 297–298
theory-based categories
  associationist approaches to, 386–390, 398–
    399
  assumptions underlying, 384–386
  basic overview, 11–12, 330–332, 345–346,
    352
  causation and, 336–337
  classification approaches to, 390–394
  competing claims vs., 346–351
  concepts evidence of, 6, 331–346; debates
    about, 346–348
  essentialism and, 348, 389, 393
  function and, 338–341
  inferences about novel properties and,
    344–346
  intentions and, 341–342
  nonobvious properties and, 342–344, 348,
    392, 398
  ontology and, 333–336
  perceptual information and, 348–349
  prerequisites of, 398–400
  substantive content of, 394
theory of mind, children's, 11–12

theory theory
  of causal maps, 307–308
  premise of, 6, 306
tones, categorization by infants, 29
touching, category-related, 143–147
trajectory, in association-based motion
    representations, 178–179
triadic interactions, for subordinate-level
    categorization, 243
Twin Earth, 305

understanding(s), theory-based, 11–12
uniqueness, class membership vs., 3
"up and down," as spatial relation, 57, 59
utterances
  associative learning with, 172–173
  in grammatical organization, 39, 42
  infants' abilities to distinguish, 32–35, 37

verbal system, impact on categorization,
    126
  implicit systems vs., 360–361, 380
verbs, 10, 291, 321, 341
visual categorization, 148, 322
visual familiarization task, 148
vocabulary. See also English vocabulary;
    Japanese vocabulary
  acquisition of (see word learning)
  checklist assessment of, 249, 281–282
  cognitive consequences of: in infants
      establishing a lexicon, 223; in
      prelinguistic infants, 222–223
  cross-linguistic studies of, 215–216, 221, 233,
      275–300
  impact on categorization, 123–124, 141
  kind-specific name generalizations and,
      276–279, 283
  sorting abilities relationship to, 320–322
  word-to-world links and: acquisition of,
      218–222; correspondence with, 216–217;
      establishing a mapping, 217–218
voicing, categorization of
  by adults, 30
  by infants, 28–29, 31
vowels, categorization by infants, 28, 31

whole objects
  animate-object boundary of, 292
  infants' perception of, 224–232
  parts relations to, infants' attention to, 113–
      114, 119
within-category similarities
  attention to parts and, 167
  of multiple objects, 142–147
  of novel objects, 148–149
word-extension
  classification vs., 347
  intentional, 341–342
  in lexical development, 395; of early object
      words, 243–246; of novel vs. familiar
      objects, 229–232
  overextensions, 16–17, 123, 346
word learning. See also names and naming
  cognitive consequences of: in infants
      establishing a lexicon, 223; in
      prelinguistic infants, 222–223
  cultural aspects of, 215–216, 221, 233, 242,
      244, 351
  differences of scenes highlighted with, 218
  internal properties as crucial to, 343–344
  links to world and, 216–222
  process of, 7–8, 10, 99
  puzzle of, 217–218
  relevant entity identification in, 217
  relevant word parsing in, 217
  sorting abilities relationship to, 320–322
word meaning, constraints on
  bias as, 277, 346–347
  mutual exclusivity as, 364–367
  noun-category link as, 234–235
word recognition, spatial relation features of, 54
word segmentation, as chunking problem, 36–39
word-to-category mapping, 218
word-to-object mapping, 218
word-to-world links
  acquisition of, 218–222
  as correspondence, 216–217
  establishing a mapping with, 217–218
  evidence of, 232–234
  fine-tuning of, 228–232
  noun-category as first to emerge, 234–235

Studying for your
Midwifery Degree

Transforming Midwifery Practice series

You can find more information on each of these titles and our other learning resources at **www.sagepub.co.uk**. Many of these titles are also available in various e-book formats, please visit our website for more information.